REGULATING THE VISIBLE HAND?

Regulating the Visible Hand?

THE INSTITUTIONAL IMPLICATIONS OF CHINESE STATE CAPITALISM

Edited by Benjamin L. Liebman
and Curtis J. Milhaupt

OXFORD
UNIVERSITY PRESS

OXFORD
UNIVERSITY PRESS

Oxford University Press is a department of the University of Oxford. It furthers the University's objective of excellence in research, scholarship, and education by publishing worldwide.

Oxford New York
Auckland Cape Town Dar es Salaam Hong Kong Karachi Kuala Lumpur Madrid
Melbourne Mexico City Nairobi New Delhi Shanghai Taipei Toronto

With offices in
Argentina Austria Brazil Chile Czech Republic France Greece Guatemala Hungary
Italy Japan Poland Portugal Singapore South Korea Switzerland Thailand
Turkey Ukraine Vietnam

Published in the United States of America by
Oxford University Press
198 Madison Avenue, New York, NY 10016

Library of Congress Cataloging-in-Publication Data

Regulating the visible hand? : the institutional implications of Chinese state capitalism / edited by Benjamin L. Liebman and Curtis J. Milhaupt.
pages cm
Includes bibliographical references and index.
ISBN 978-0-19-025025-6 ((hardback) : alk. paper)
1. Government business enterprises—Law and legislation—China. 2. Corporate governance—Law and legislation—China. 3. Corporation law—China. 4. Public-private sector cooperation—China. 5. Finance—China. 6. Capitalism—China. 7. China—Economic policy. I. Liebman, Benjamin L., 1969- editor. II. Milhaupt, Curtis J., 1962- editor.
KNQ3217.R44 2016
346.51'06—dc23

2015013622

---

9 8 7 6 5 4 3 2 1

Printed in the United States of America on acid-free paper

Note to Readers

This publication is designed to provide accurate and authoritative information in regard to the subject matter covered. It is based upon sources believed to be accurate and reliable and is intended to be current as of the time it was written. It is sold with the understanding that the publisher is not engaged in rendering legal, accounting, or other professional services. If legal advice or other expert assistance is required, the services of a competent professional person should be sought. Also, to confirm that the information has not been affected or changed by recent developments, traditional legal research techniques should be used, including checking primary sources where appropriate.

(Based on the Declaration of Principles jointly adopted by a Committee of the American Bar Association and a Committee of Publishers and Associations.)

Contents

List of Contributors

Note: Chinese contributors are listed last name first, unless the author typically uses Western name order in his or her English-language publications.

Ruoying CHEN is an Associate Professor and Assistant Dean at Peking University Law School, with degrees from Peking University (LLB), Oxford University (MJuris) and the University of Chicago Law School (JSD). Her teaching and research focus on law and economics and government regulation of capital markets, environment, and land. She worked for Freshfields Bruckhaus Deringer on M&A and securities transactions, and taught at the University of Chicago Law School.

Donald Clarke is a Professor of Law at the George Washington University Law School. He specializes in modern Chinese law and writes the Chinese Law Prof blog. He is a member of the New York Bar and the Council on Foreign Relations.

Wei CUI is an Associate Professor at the Allard School of Law, University of British Columbia. He previously taught at China University of Political Science and Law, and has also held visiting appointments at Michigan, Columbia, and Melbourne Law Schools. During 2009–2010, he served as Senior Tax Counsel for the China Investment Corporation. He has also served as a consultant to the United Nations, the Budgetary Affairs Commission of China's National People's Congress, China's Ministry of Finance and State Administration of Taxation on a wide variety of tax policy matters.

DENG Feng is a Professor of Law at Peking University Law School and Co-director of Peking University Institute for Law & Economics. BA (1995), MPhil (1998) and PhD at Law (2001) from Renmin University of China Law School. Deng's research interests lie in corporation law, contract law, regulation, antitrust, and law and economics.

Mary E. Gallagher is an Associate Professor of political science at the University of Michigan where she is also the director of the Kenneth G. Lieberthal and Richard H. Rogel Center for Chinese Studies. She is also a faculty associate at the Center for Comparative Political Studies at the Institute for Social Research. From 2012 to 2013, she was a visiting scholar at the Koguan Law School at Shanghai Jiaotong University.

GUO Li is a Professor of Law at Peking University Law School, and the chief editor of *PKU Journal of Legal Studies*. He has also taught and researched at Cornell, Duke, Freiburg, Vanderbilt, and Case Western Reserve, and is the recipient of the Humboldt Foundation Fellowship. His scholarly interests cover financial laws, social development and comparative studies. He is a graduate of PKU, Southern Methodist, and Harvard Law School.

Nicholas Calcina Howson is a Professor of Law at the University of Michigan Law School. He has also taught at the University of California, Berkeley, Columbia, Cornell, and Harvard Law Schools. A former partner of Paul, Weiss, Rifkind, Wharton & Garrison LLP, he worked out of that firm's New York, Paris, London and Beijing Offices, finally as a managing partner of the firm's Asia Practice based in the Chinese capital.

Sergio G. Lazzarini (PhD, 2002, Washington University in St. Louis) is a Professor of Organization and Strategy at Insper Institute of Education and Research, Brazil. He does research on how institutional conditions affect business strategy, the organization of public-private interactions, and how private investors address social impact.

LIAO Fan is a Professor of Law at the Institute of International Law, Chinese Academy of Social Sciences. LLB (China Youth College of Political Studies, 1999), LLM (Southern Methodist University, 2002), PhD (Peking University, 2005). He has published three books (in Chinese) and over thirty articles (in Chinese and English). His major areas of research include corporate law, banking law, securities law, and international law.

Benjamin L. Liebman is the Robert L. Lieff Professor of Law and Director of the Center for Chinese Legal Studies at Columbia Law School. His current research focuses on Chinese tort law, on Chinese criminal procedure, on the impact of popular opinion and populism on the Chinese legal system, and on the evolution of China's courts and legal profession. Prior to joining the Columbia faculty in 2002, Professor Liebman was an associate in the London and Beijing offices of Sullivan & Cromwell. He also previously served as a law clerk to Justice David Souter and to Judge Sandra Lynch of the First Circuit. He is a graduate of Yale, Oxford, and Harvard Law School.

Li-Wen LIN is an Assistant Professor at the University of British Columbia Peter A. Allard School of Law. She holds a PhD degree in sociology from Columbia University and a JSD degree from the University of Illinois.

Curtis J. Milhaupt is the Parker Professor of Comparative Corporate Law, Director of the Parker School of Foreign and Comparative Law, Fuyo Professor of Japanese Law, and Director of the Center for Japanese Legal Studies, all at Columbia Law School. He is also a Research Associate of the European Corporate Governance Institute and a member of the American Law Institute.

Aldo Musacchio is an Associate Professor of Business at Brandeis University and a Faculty Research Fellow at the NBER. He has numerous journal articles and a book, *Reinventing State Capitalism*, examining the corporate governance arrangements of state-owned enterprises.

Michael D. Nolan is a partner in the Washington, DC office of Milbank, Tweed, Hadley & McCloy LLP. He has served as counsel or arbitrator in cases under AAA, ICC, ICSID, HKIAC, SIAC, UNCITRAL and other rules. He is an Adjunct Professor of Law at Georgetown University, General Counsel of the Intellectual Property Owners Association, and a member of the Board of Directors of the American Arbitration Association.

Mariana Pargendler is Professor of Law at Fundação Getulio Vargas School of Law in São Paulo (FGV Direito SP), where she serves as a director for the Center of Law, Economics, and Governance, and Global Associate Professor of Law at New York University School of Law. She holds LLM and JSD degrees from Yale Law School, and LLB and PhD degrees from the Federal University of Rio Grande do Sul.

Katharina Pistor is Walter E. Meyer Research Professor in Law & Social Problems and Michael I. Sovern Professor of Law at Columbia Law School and the director of Columbia Law School's Center on Global Legal Transformation. She is a member of the Berlin-Brandenburg Academy of Science, serves as Research Associate of the Center for Economic Policy Research and the Curatorium of Bucerius Law School.

Karl P. Sauvant is Resident Senior Fellow at the Columbia Center on Sustainable Investment, a joint center of Columbia Law School and the Earth Institute at Columbia University and Lecturer-in-Law and Senior Research Scholar at Columbia Law School. He is a Fellow of the Academy of International Business and an Honorary Fellow of the European International Business Academy.

Alex L. Wang is an Assistant Professor of Law at the UCLA School of Law. He was previously a senior attorney for the Natural Resources Defense Council (NRDC) based in Beijing and the founding director of NRDC's China Environmental Law & Governance Project for nearly six years. His primary research and teaching interests are in environmental law, Chinese law, and comparative law. He has also taught at UC Berkeley School of Law.

Mark Wu is an Assistant Professor of Law at Harvard Law School. He previously served as the Director for Intellectual Property in the Office of the U.S. Trade Representative and as an Economist and Operations Officer for the World Bank in China. He is a Faculty Director of the Berkman Center for Internet and Society and serves on a number of expert groups organized by the World Economic Forum and the International Centre for Trade and Sustainable Development on trade governance.

Angela Huyue ZHANG is a lecturer in competition law and trade at King's College London. Prior to joining King's, she practiced law for six years at offices of international law firms in Asia, the United States and Europe. She received her LLB degree from Peking University in 2004 and her JSD (2011), JD (2008), and LLM (2006) degrees all from the University of Chicago Law School.

ZHENG Lei is an Assistant Professor of Law at Zhengzhou University School of Law. His research interests include administrative Law, constitutional law and land use law. He received his PhD (2014) from Peking University Law School and his MA (2010) and BA (2006) from Zhengzhou University.

Wentong ZHENG is an Assistant Professor of Law at Levin College of Law, University of Florida. He received his BA and MA at Renmin University of China, his PhD in economics at Stanford University, and his JD at Stanford Law School. Professor Zheng's research interests include international trade, international business transactions, antitrust and competition policy, Chinese law, commercial law, and law and economics.

ZHOU Chun is an Assistant Professor at Zhejiang University Guanghua Law School. Her academic interests lie in comparative corporate law, commercial law and law and finance. She received her BA and PhD degrees from Peking University, and her LLM from Columbia Law School.

Acknowledgments

THIS PROJECT BEGAN with a workshop held at Columbia Law School in June 2014, at which the authors intensively discussed preliminary drafts of their chapters. We thank the Parker School of Foreign and Comparative Law and the Center for Chinese Legal Studies at Columbia Law School for generous financial support for the workshop. We are grateful to Terry Liu and Paulette Roberts for their help in organizing the workshop, and, together with Sara Kuperminc, their assistance in finalizing the manuscript for submission to the publisher. Alison Borochoff-Porte, Emma Kaplan, and Stephanie Persson, Columbia Law School JD Class of 2015, ably assisted us in editing the chapters.

Introduction

THE INSTITUTIONAL IMPLICATIONS OF CHINA'S ECONOMIC DEVELOPMENT

Benjamin L. Liebman and Curtis J. Milhaupt

IT IS COMMON knowledge that the Chinese economy has grown spectacularly—perhaps even to a historically unprecedented degree—over the past three decades. The path of reform leading to this high and sustained rate of growth featured the gradual, and at times halting, introduction of markets and private economic activity into a landscape of wide-ranging state intervention. Although the precise scale and continuing importance of the state sector in the Chinese economy today may be debated, in broad terms China's approach has clearly involved the combination of capitalist institutions and state power, a strategy now widely referred to as "state capitalism."[1] Although China is by no means the world's sole practitioner of state capitalism, it is arguably the most successful, and certainly the largest.

The economic and geopolitical implications of China's rise have been the subject of vast commentary. However, the *institutional* implications of China's transformative development under state capitalism have not been examined in a comprehensive, in-depth study. This volume addresses this gap in the literature by exploring the domestic

[1] IAN BREMMER, THE END OF THE FREE MARKET: WHO WINS THE WAR BETWEEN STATES AND CORPORATIONS? (2010); *The Visible Hand*, THE ECONOMIST (Jan. 21, 2012), http://www.economist.com/node/21542931.

and global institutional implications of Chinese state capitalism, and by placing China's variety of state capitalism in comparative perspective.

This mission statement may raise some questions in readers' minds. First, what exactly do we mean by Chinese state capitalism? We readily acknowledge that the concept of state capitalism is contestable and lacks a universally accepted definition. Indeed, the contributors to this volume likely would struggle to reach definitive agreement on this point, as well as the question whether there is a "Chinese model" of economic development. Mark Wu, for example, stresses the unique features of the contemporary Chinese economy, while Sergio Lazzarini and Aldo Mussachio argue that Chinese state capitalism shares significant structural traits with the Brazilian and Gulf states varieties. For purposes of our project, "Chinese state capitalism" connotes an economic approach involving (1) a comparatively high degree of direct state participation in the economy, particularly but not exclusively through state-owned enterprises (SOEs); and (2) the use of capitalist forms of economic organization—markets, corporations, and other investment vehicles—in combination with nondemocratic forms of public governance.

Some readers might take issue with the claim that China's contemporary economy is properly classified as state capitalism. A recent book by the prominent China specialist Nicholas Lardy,[2] for example, argues that private firms have been the principal driver of China's economic transformation and will be the main source of its future growth. He also disputes the contention, discussed by some contributors to this volume, that the state sector gained strength at the expense of the private sector during the Hu Jintao era (2002–2012). In short, he claims that the Chinese economy today is in important respects market oriented, not state oriented. We do not disagree with the thrust of this assessment, particularly the claim that the private sector is more dynamic and laden with potential than the state sector. But the emergence of markets and private firms does not, of itself, negate the continuing high degree of state intervention in the Chinese economy or the pervasive influence of the Communist Party on the workings of Chinese corporate capitalism.

Improving definitional clarity of the term "state capitalism" and measuring the respective contributions of the market and the state sector to China's economic growth are important undertakings. But these are not the aims of our project. We are interested in China's *institutional* trajectory—specifically, the design, implementation, and reform of laws and regulatory structures governing economic activity in China over the past three decades. The volume examines China's economic regulatory regimes across a wide range of fields, including antitrust, the environment, labor relations, taxation, and corporate governance. Examining the institutional underpinnings of the Chinese economy offers the potential to deepen understanding of what "Chinese state

[2] *See, e.g.*, Nicholas R. Lardy, Markets over Mao: The Rise of Private Business in China (2014).

capitalism" means well beyond attempts to frame a categorical definition. Our focus also allows us to examine how the major actors that have emerged in the first three decades of Chinese economic reform—many of them SOEs—shape lawmaking and enforcement in China, and how these same actors are disrupting settled assumptions in international regulatory regimes for trade, investment, and finance. Our approach provides fresh perspective on the question whether China represents a distinctive and sustainable approach to development.

By focusing on institutions, this volume also grapples with some major global implications of the emergence of China as an economic heavyweight. As Mark Wu's contribution to this volume shows, the contemporary Chinese political economy was not contemplated when the global trade regime was constructed. Similarly, as Karl P. Sauvant and Michael Nolan show, the overseas investment activity of Chinese firms raises concerns that constituencies in some host countries feel are not adequately addressed by the current foreign investment regime. These tensions will have to be resolved in some way, either through changes to Chinese regulatory structures and firms or to the global trade and investment regimes.

As noted, one of the principal mechanisms of Chinese state capitalism is the SOE.[3] As the name implies, an SOE is an economic enterprise, typically taking the form of a corporation, whose shares are wholly or significantly owned by a state agency or organ. The SOE thus places the state in dual and often conflicting roles: as institution designer and enforcer (the state's exclusive role in an ideal-type "market economy") on the one hand, and as a direct, commercial participant in the economy, on the other. The history of Chinese economic reform over the past three decades cannot be separated from the history of the SOE, and SOE reform is at the heart of the current economic reform proposals of President Xi Jinping. Moreover, Chinese SOEs are increasingly active players in the global economy, proliferating rapidly in the Global Fortune 500 rankings.[4] The role of SOEs is also intertwined with China's emergence as an economic power and the ambivalence this rise has engendered abroad. Rising outbound foreign direct investment by Chinese SOEs has been both welcomed and feared by host countries around the world.

From a comparative perspective, it is important to recognize that state capitalism, with an extensive role for SOEs, is one of several species of corporate capitalism alive in the global economy today. The corporate form is the basic building block of all economies, in

---

[3] Curtis J. Milhaupt and Wentong Zheng in Chapter 9 of this volume argue that the SOE is by no means the only mechanism of Chinese state capitalism, and caution against relying on ownership-based distinctions to understand the impact of the state on business enterprises.

[4] China now has the second largest number of Global Fortune 500 companies after the United States. About two-thirds of these companies are SOEs. FORTUNE 500 2014, http://fortune.com/fortune500/; *89 Chinese Firms Make It to Fortune Global 500 List*, ECON. TIMES INT'L (July 9, 2013), http://articles.economictimes.indiatimes.com/2013-07-09/news/40469474_1_chinese-companies-list-firms.

China as elsewhere. As several contributors to this volume explain, a crucial early move in China's reform process was "corporatization" of the economy. This entailed transformation of the production arms of state agencies into joint stock corporations.[5] Through this process, production functions were formally separated from public regulatory functions and cloaked in an organizational form that is prevalent and readily understood around the world—the corporation. Shares were issued to the corporation's governmental owners (in theory, on behalf of the ultimate owners, the Chinese people). Ostensibly, at least, the newly formed corporations were imbued with the standard corporate governance organs of boards of directors and shareholders meetings.

As Donald Clarke describes in his chapter, China enacted a Corporate Law with SOEs in mind to provide the norms of governance for and allocation of rights among the corporate stakeholders. Some of the best state assets were packaged into corporations that issued shares to minority public investors on Chinese and global capital markets. These listings, which would not have been possible without the transformation of state assets into an organizational form recognizable to international investors, provided capital, managerial expertise, and global visibility to the firms. Local governments in China were also integrally involved in the corporatization process. As one commentator has noted, "local legislative experiments [with incorporation rules, public offerings and capital requirements] significantly contributed to institutionalizing corporations and other business organizations in transitional China," greatly reducing the costs of developing the national corporate economy.[6]

Chinese SOEs, particularly at the national level, are organized into business groups comprised of numerous separate corporations arranged in hierarchical order. The decision to organize the firms into groups relatively early in the reform era was a strategy based on observations of economic development elsewhere, particularly the high growth economies of East Asia. Governmental encouragement of business group formation to foster the growth of national champions has been a common strategy around the developing world, followed by a wide range of governments pursuing diverse macroeconomic policies. Such countries include late nineteenth-century Japan under the Meiji oligarchs, South Korea under military strongman Park Chung Hee in the early 1970s, and Chile under Pinochet in the late 1970s and 1980s. The Chinese leadership's decision to organize its corporatized SOEs into groups probably reflected the same motivations for business group formation found in these and other developing countries, including

[5] In Chapter 2 in this volume, Donald Clarke persuasively argues that the corporatization project was driven by several misconceptions about what ailed China's state sector, and consequently about the potential for corporatization to remedy those ills. Nonetheless, there can be little doubt that corporatization was a necessary, if not sufficient, step in China's economic reform process.

[6] Jinhua Cheng, Dual Intergovernmental Transformation for Economic Growth: The States and the Rise of Domestic Corporate Markets in the Nineteenth-Century United States and Contemporary China 185 (2011) (unpublished JSD dissertation, Yale Law School) (on file with authors).

filling institutional voids in weak rule-of-law environments, internalizing capital markets, marshaling scarce resources (including both monetary capital and entrepreneurial human capital), and reducing the transaction costs of administering economic policy. Yet in China, organization of corporatized SOEs into groups has also been viewed as a mechanism for maintaining political control over key sectors of the economy.

Viewing state capitalism as a species of corporate capitalism illuminates key ways in which Chinese SOEs differ from corporations in economies where state ownership and state involvement in the economy is less extensive. Some of the differences are internal to the corporate form; others are external. The internal differences pertain to the way in which standard corporate structures and operations, such as the working of the board of directors, have been supplemented or altered by Chinese Communist Party organs, which parallel and permeate Chinese SOE structures. The external differences pertain to how Chinese corporations are treated as actors in the political economy, including the comparatively limited degree of autonomy they enjoy from the state (whether state-owned or privately owned, as Curtis J. Milhaupt and Wentong Zheng discuss in this volume), and the comparatively broad scope of objectives that state-owned corporations pursue, extending beyond the corporation's shareholders and employees—to include executing state policies and advancing the soft power of the state itself. Put differently, in Chinese state capitalism, the corporation is treated by the state, or political actors closely identified with the state, as an integral part of Party-state governance and not simply as an object of regulation as in other species of corporate capitalism. As the chapters in this volume demonstrate, this has profound implications for China's institutional development and for the integration of Chinese corporations into the global trade and investment regime.

In the following paragraphs, we briefly outline the individual contributions to the volume. We then highlight the key normative takeaways that we draw from the collective analysis of the authors.

Deng Feng begins the volume with an overview of the evolution of the Chinese state's approach to SOE regulation. He notes how China shifted from relying on a traditional Soviet model of SOE regulation in the 1980s toward a model closer to that of Singapore in the 1990s. Yet over time, and particularly since the early 2000s, China's approach to SOE regulation has evolved away from the Singapore model. This "mutation" resulted from particular characteristics of the Chinese legal and political environment and the role of bureaucrats in managing SOEs. In contrast to the Singapore model, China's approach to SOE control involved no restraints on state power and little respect for corporate governance norms. Deng highlights the multiple roles SOEs play in China, including supporting Communist Party legitimacy, and also the problems that result from the lack of constraints on SOE power. As he notes, SOEs have both become core pillars of the Chinese economy and "beds of corruption and nepotism" that have been adept at blocking market competition. He concludes that fundamental changes in China's approach to the state sector are needed to address the range of problems he identifies.

In his contribution, Donald Clarke shows how the logic of state capitalism has impacted the rules that govern the private sector. Although China's evolution of corporate law drew heavily from the West, it was primarily designed to reorganize the state sector. Key aspects of Chinese corporate law thus focus on SOEs and their interests. A keen desire to have a single corporate law to govern both SOEs and private firms resulted in a regime that took measures designed for the state sector and imposed them on private entities—a phenomenon Clarke calls "blowback." Some regulations, including extensive disclosure requirements imposed on non-public companies, appeared designed to facilitate state supervision over private entities, and are rooted in state distrust of the private sector. Other measures, such as the requirement that companies have boards of supervisors, were designed to address problems with SOEs but impose significant costs on private entities as well. Abandoning a unified legal approach might appear to offer a ready solution to these problems, but doing so is not easy. The reason lies in a crucial characteristic of Chinese state capitalism: the difficulty of precisely determining what counts as an SOE.

Nicholas Howson's contribution describes how, even after more than two decades of corporate governance reform heralding "shareholder primacy," and in the face of an increasingly flexible enabling approach to corporate law, Party-state controlling shareholders have solidified their power over listed subsidiaries seeking capital from the domestic and foreign markets. He notes a surprising phenomenon in the reality of corporate governance in China, where the China Securities Regulatory Commission (CSRC) has imposed a series of mandatory, often self-enforcing, governance mechanisms designed to offer protection to minority shareholders against the Party-state controlling shareholders. As he explains, the CSRC's role in this process is perhaps counterintuitive given the agency's weak institutional position relative to other Party-state actors (including the controlling shareholders) and common understandings that the Chinese corporate governance regime is primarily designed to advance the interests of the Party-state and its SOE groups. His analysis shows how the CSRC has intervened to protect minority shareholders, and why such steps may have been necessary, given the dysfunctions of China's legislature and judiciary. He speculates about why the CSRC has been permitted this provocative space to resist the heights of the Party-state, proposing that such steps may be necessary to ensure the continued financing of China's state capitalism model.

Much of the focus of recent scholarship on Chinese state capitalism has been on the rise of "national champions" in the form of central SOEs and prominent private firms listed on stock markets around the world. Scholars have devoted less attention to the impact and institutional underpinnings of state capitalism at the local level. In his contribution, Liao Fan begins to fill this void, examining how China's state capitalism model has given birth to local government financing vehicles (LGFVs). LGFVs serve to finance local infrastructure and public services projects by local governments faced with limited financing channels. Liao shows how the largely unrestrained growth of LGFVs has given rise to a range of problems and has strengthened the position of the state compared to the private sector. Understanding the role of LGFVs shows that conceiving of state capitalism as giving rise to a divide between the state and the private sector overlooks the fact that in practice there are multiple "states" in China pursuing their own goals, policies, and projects. As he notes, "local governments have their own wills and incentives." Unpacking state capitalism in China thus requires a more detailed examination of actors at all levels of the Party-state.

Angela Zhang's analysis of how China's Anti-Monopoly Law (AML) impacts SOEs similarly demonstrates that focusing only on large national SOEs risks overlooking important developments at the local level. As she notes, most SOEs in China are local and operate in competitive sectors. Because of the fragmentation of the Chinese market and close links between local SOEs and local authorities, cartels often develop at the sub-national level. She shows how tension has emerged between traditional infrastructure SOEs, which continue to have monopoly or quasi-monopoly power and are vertically integrated, and SOEs operating in the upstream or downstream markets, where the Chinese government has introduced limited competition. Such tension has produced demand for a particular form of anti-monopoly enforcement—demand *from* SOEs to enforce the law *against* other SOEs. Contrary to common expectations, China's antitrust agencies do act against SOEs. Yet due to the regulatory and economic structures in which they operate, such enforcement activities are often constrained and are not externally observable. Rather than enforcing through the legal system, enforcement comes through bureaucratic negotiation. Likewise, rather than focusing on enhancing public welfare, China's three agencies tasked with enforcing the AML focus on enhancing their own policy interests and authority. The nontransparency of the AML enforcement system limits the effectiveness of the AML, with the interests of SOEs and regulators coming to dominate over legal principles.

Wei Cui provides an analysis of another topic often missing from examination of the role of SOEs in the Chinese political economy: taxation. As he notes, existing literature in law and finance largely overlooks the question of how SOEs are taxed. In particular, empirical examination of how SOEs respond to taxation is scant. The issue is important because a better understanding of how SOEs respond to income taxation helps to answer theoretical questions regarding the justification for SOE taxation. Cui surveys existing empirical literature and finds that support for the view that SOEs are indifferent to taxation is limited. Instead, he argues that SOE taxation more likely serves to discipline managers and to force distributions from SOEs. Cui notes that his findings suggest that the tax system is being used for radically different purposes when it taxes private firms and when it taxes SOEs. The logic of state capitalism, and the corporate governance problems that have resulted from it, lead to a tax system that is less effective at meeting revenue generation goals. As with other areas of economic regulation addressed in this volume, the effects of this regime are seen not only in SOEs, but also in how the state taxes non-SOEs.

The next two contributions focus on human capital formation and deployment within China's political economy. Li-Wen Lin's chapter looks within SOEs, providing an empirical examination of the career paths of senior executives of the top national SOEs, those directly under the State-Owned Assets Supervision and Administration Commission. Drawing on network theory from sociology, she shows that SOE executives share similar educational, political, and career backgrounds. Although there are some benefits in terms of policy implementation that result from such cohesion, this uniformity of backgrounds threatens groupthink and continuance of out-dated practices. She suggests that the insider bias in executive recruitment in SOEs both impedes efforts to address many problems in their corporate governance and may limit the global competitiveness of these firms.

Ruoying Chen examines another limitation flowing from personnel policies in China's form of state capitalism: the restrained development of human capital. She traces the role of informality in China's economic growth, noting that in the early stages of economic development, informality in contracts and regulation likely furthered economic growth by reducing transaction costs. Informality is at the heart of how SOEs do business and how they interact with state regulators. Yet the continued reliance on informality today also challenges the ability of the Chinese state to confront a range of new problems. Most notably, the continued reliance on informality in both contracts and regulation limits the incentives for individuals to develop the human capital China needs to confront a range of new economic and legal challenges as complexity and risk increase. She argues that SOEs' influence and reliance on relationships with regulators and political officials impede the development of the human capital necessary to shift toward a rule-based system of governance.

Thus far, contributors have focused their analyses on SOEs. Curtis Milhaupt and Wentong Zheng show how the institutional inclinations of state capitalism in China affect all aspects of the Chinese economy. Much of the recent focus on economic reform in China, both in Party-state policy initiatives and academic literature, has been on ownership-based reforms. Milhaupt and Zheng demonstrate that this focus on equity ownership is often misplaced, and overlooks key aspects of state capitalism in China. Rather than focusing on state ownership of enterprise, they focus on state capture by companies with a range of ownership forms, including traditional SOEs, privately owned enterprises, and those with mixtures of private and state ownership. Recognizing that successful private enterprises and SOEs pursue similar strategies in seeking proximity to power, state largesse and privileged market access highlights a weakness in many reform proposals: reforming corporate ownership will do little to affect how firms relate to the state. Their analysis suggests that addressing the problems associated with state capitalism in China requires reforming not just SOEs, but the state itself.

In our co-authored chapter with Zheng Lei, we focus directly on the mechanisms by which state capitalism influences and stymies the development of legal institutions in China. They provide an account of how SOEs impact legal institutions, with a particular focus on the courts. Although China has long since shifted away from a pure command and control economic model, the legacy of state planning continues to give SOEs ideological and positional advantages in the political economy as compared to other actors in the legal system. At the same time, SOEs have developed new mechanisms for managing relations with the legal system. The result is not just that SOEs often get their way in litigation; it is that the legal system itself is at times focused on making sure that SOE interests are met, even at the expense of values associated with the rule of law, such as effective enforcement of legal rules. Moving legal reform forward in China requires not just reforming the courts but reforming the role of powerful economic actors in the political-legal system.

An analysis of the inner workings of China's political economy is also essential for understanding questions regarding the resilience of China's authoritarian model. As Mary Gallagher notes, literature on China's "authoritarian resilience"[7] largely omits discussion of the ways that state capitalism in China contributes to the staying power of the Party-state. At the same time, literature on state capitalism also largely ignores its institutional foundations. Gallagher links these two strands of analysis through a discussion of labor law and labor market institutions. She highlights two apparently competing goals that China has sought to balance throughout the reform period: increased market competition and state control. She describes an important and overlooked trend in China's management of the "social relations of state capitalism": as the state shifted toward greater engagement with global markets and capitalism, it felt the need to strengthen its role in managing social conflict and society more generally. In doing so China has been able to draw on an institution inextricably linked to both the state and the economy—a Leninist ruling party.

Alex Wang examines how SOEs have affected China's environmental problems. Although SOEs have been major contributors to China's environmental degradation in recent decades, this does not necessarily mean that SOEs have been rogue actors in the Chinese system. Instead, SOEs' widespread lack of compliance with environmental regulations reflects in large part the low priority that the Chinese political system has attached to environmental protection in the past. Yet this also suggests the possibility that SOEs may come to play a more constructive role in addressing China's environmental problems. The fact that SOEs are so entwined with the state and react to political incentives means that SOEs may be responsive as central authorities increase the priority of environmental goals. Moreover, SOE rent-seeking, which many have viewed as a barrier to environmental protection, may in fact provide a foundation for increased (albeit inefficient) environmental compliance by SOEs as central authorities offer a range of subsidies for greener industrial development. Regulatory sticks and the weakening of

---

[7] Andrew J. Nathan, *Authoritarian Resilience*, 14 J. DEMOCRACY 6 (2003).

vested interests through anticorruption campaigns are additional state measures that may begin to shift SOE behavior.

In Part II we turn to an examination of the global implications of Chinese state capitalism. Kart Sauvant and Michael Nolan examine an important external manifestation of China's economic rise: the emergence of China as a major capital exporter, particularly through overseas investments by SOEs. They trace the central features of Chinese outward foreign direct investment (FDI), examine how it has been received by policy-makers and other constituencies in host countries, and analyze how the rise of outbound FDI is changing China's approach to international investment treaties. They demonstrate that as China's FDI has grown, China has moved to align its positions regarding investor-state protections with those of the United States and the European Union. In particular, China has taken steps to ensure that SOEs receive protections under such treaties as investors. Thus, somewhat counterintuitively, the importance of SOEs to Chinese overseas investment has provided an incentive for China to bring its position into line with those of major Western economic powers.

Mark Wu's chapter examines the implications of state capitalism in China for the global trade regime. He demonstrates how World Trade Organization (WTO) rules are not well-suited to addressing a range of legal issues resulting from China's economic model. This is a natural consequence of the fact that the global trade regime was designed in a different era, and did not anticipate either China's economic rise or China's particular approach to state capitalism. Wu, like Gallagher, notes that the uniqueness of the Chinese economic model stems from the fact that the state and economy are deeply intertwined with the Chinese Communist Party—a fact missing in other systems that feature a heavy role for the state in the economic realm. How the WTO navigates the challenges resulting from the Chinese system is crucial to the WTO: failure to address the range of novel issues resulting from China's economic model risks undermining the multilateral trade regime. Yet Wu contends that China's political economy is in fundamental tension with the liberal global trading system. Thus the most likely result of China's rise in international trade is not convergence, but fragmentation of the trade regime into multiple subgroupings of trade partners.

In Part III, the final chapters in the volume place China's state capitalism in a comparative context. Katharina Pistor, Guo Li, and Zhou Chun examine China's financial system. They highlight the evolution of China's financial system from a socialist "mono-banking system" to a hybrid system. As they detail, China moved to reduce the dependence of financial institutions on the state at exactly the same time that Western financial institutions were enjoying the boom-and-bust cycle that led to the global financial crisis—and to extensive state intervention in the financial sector in the West. Examining China's shift from a state-controlled financial sector to a hybridized finance system suggests that historical divisions between Chinese (socialist) financial management and Western (market) management have been reduced as both China and the West have adopted hybrid systems of financial management. One result is that China faces many of the challenges and risks that Western financial systems have confronted in recent years—most significantly the "law-finance paradox" of instability deriving from rigid adherence to legal rules.

An in-depth study of a particular country's institutional structures often benefits from comparative analysis. We have thus included in this volume two contributions that place Chinese state capitalism in comparative context. Mariana Pargendler's case study of Brazilian state capitalism provides an account of the range of mechanisms through which the state influences corporate governance in Brazil, including formal law and actual practice. Brazilian state capitalism results from traditional state-controlled SOEs and through the state holding minority positions in state-controlled institutional investors. Pargendler notes both similarities with and differences from the Chinese approach, and in particular the fact that stronger legal institutions in Brazil reduce state influence on private actors. Yet her analysis of Brazil suggests that direct state involvement in the economy results in the state finding ways to set the rules of economic engagement in its own favor—even in a country with democratic political institutions and a more advanced (if imperfect) rule of law. Her chapter thus offers comparative context for understanding Chinese state capitalism and a cautionary note for the possibility of institutional reform in China.

Placing China in an even broader comparative context, Sergio Lazzarini and Aldo Mussachio find similarities between state ownership in China and state ownership elsewhere. They argue that China should not be thought of as a unique case. Instead, Chinese state capitalism shares many features with other state capitalism systems that have emerged and proved resilient in recent years. In this sense, they may disagree to some extent with Wu's claim that the "Chinese state and the Chinese economy are unlike that of any other in the world." Yet they, like Wu and many of the other contributors to the volume, note some characteristics that distinguish state capitalism in China from state capitalism elsewhere, most notably the role of the Communist Party.

Lazzarini and Mussachio end by arguing not only that state capitalism has been resilient but also that it is "here to stay." If they are correct in this assessment, and it seems a fair one from our vantage point, deeper understanding of the mechanisms of state capitalism is essential. The contributions to this volume represent a first step toward a deeper and more nuanced understanding of both the institutional underpinnings of China's state capitalism and of state capitalism's effect on governance and economic development in China and globally. In this regard, the volume offers several key takeaways.

The first is that although SOEs may be the most visible expression of state capitalism in China, they are by no means its only mechanism or manifestation. The logic of state capitalism reflects and infects the entire structure of the Chinese state and economy. As many of the chapters in this volume illustrate, developing laws primarily from the perspective of the SOE sector shapes the behavior of a wide range of Chinese actors and institutions. Milhaupt and Zheng's chapter analyzes how the porousness of the state-SOE boundary generates perverse incentives for private firms; Clarke details the ways in which a corporate law developed for SOEs is ill suited to the needs of private entrepreneurs; Wang's chapter is instructive in the ways the power of the SOE sector has affected environmental law and policy in China. Yet, as Zhang and Lin both demonstrate, the effect is not simply reflective of legal or policy choices designed to prioritize the interests of SOEs. This approach is hardwired into how the state functions, and in particular into the bureaucratic incentives facing officials in China. This is one of the reasons we refrain from taking a position on the economists' debate about state- versus private-sector contributions to the Chinese economy: framing the question in this way assumes that the impact of the statist approach can be measured in GDP and employment statistics alone.

The second takeaway, following directly from the first, is that reforming SOEs and reducing their role in the economy is not simply a question of adjusting laws in ways that balance the playing field between SOEs and private firms, or of injecting more private capital into SOEs to improve their performance. Corporate governance reforms per se will not fundamentally reshape the role of the state sector in the Chinese economy. Indeed, as Howson shows, they may actually reinforce the power of state interests. Chinese state capitalism is not the *product* of the Chinese legal system. Instead, causality typically runs in the opposite direction, with the institutional predilections of a state capitalist system indelibly affecting the development of the Chinese legal system. Uncovering the institutional underpinnings of state capitalism in China thus highlights the limitation of legal reform in effecting change in the Chinese political economy. As we discuss further in our chapter with Zheng Lei, the ambitious legal reforms announced by the Communist Party in late 2014 are likely to have only limited impact on the mechanisms of state capitalism uncovered by the contributors to this volume. Institutional reform of the state sector may actually be a prerequisite to effective legal reform.

The impact of state capitalism on legal development is all the more profound because of its self-sustaining nature. As Chen's chapter in this volume suggests, an institutional infrastructure for economic relations characterized by pervasive informality stemming from extensive state-SOE interactions affects human capital development in the Chinese legal profession and bureaucracy. Risk assessment, unbiased professional judgment, and other skills crucial to the formation of a professional class have been stunted by the outsized influence of SOEs on public governance. This problem is compounded by the incentives generated for the allocation of talent in society. In a system in which SOEs enjoy power, privilege, status, and protection, China's most talented and ambitious young people are likely to gravitate toward the state sector rather than toward more social-welfare-enhancing sectors of the economy. A vicious cycle emerges, in which the best and brightest opt for careers in rent-seeking sectors, where they will fail to nurture skills meeting global professional standards, which in turn reinforces the informality and rule-by-elite-fiat that permeates the state's interactions in the economy. These actions in turn affect the reward structure of the next generation, and the cycle repeats. Might this cycle pose an "underdevelopment trap" for Chinese law and legal institutions?

The analysis presented in this volume raises thorny questions about the sustainability of China's economic model. Although there is historical precedent, even within East Asia, for China's economic development with underdeveloped legal institutions, no country has been able to navigate the complexities of a globally connected, mature economy—let alone one of China's scale—with inchoate regulatory structures and heavy reliance on bureaucratic fiat and informal economic relationships. This point was illustrated dramatically by South Korea during the Asian financial crisis and by Japan following the collapse of its bubble economy. Indeed, late nineteenth-century U.S. history is suggestive of this point. Only time will tell whether China can maintain social stability and economic growth with a legal system that fails to address basic political-economy problems such as local protectionism, contains built-in structures for rent-seeking and corruption on a massive scale, and under-incentivizes the formation of professional human capital and private innovation.

Indeed, the challenges facing China may exceed those of other developing economies that have had to navigate the transition from middle income to developed economy against the backdrop of an unreformed political system and weak legal institutions. Pistor, Guo and Zhou correctly note that China has proved adept at managing many of the problems brought on by the global financial crisis in the past decade. Yet China now faces dual challenges. On the one hand increased international integration and the social changes accompanying economic development mean that China must confront many of the problems facing Western governments. At the same time, however, China must confront the limitations of its own Leninist political-legal system. How the leadership manages these dual challenges going forward may ultimately demonstrate that there is a successful "China model" of state capitalism. Alternatively, future developments may demonstrate that China has arrived at the worst of both worlds: no longer insulated from global crises and the problems of mature economies, but also lacking the institutional capacity to confront such challenges. Pistor, Guo, and Zhou note that China's rulers are extremely cautious. A major question going forward is whether this caution will limit their ability effectively to manage the next stage of China's economic development, which almost certainly requires more wide-ranging institutional reform and development than have been contemplated thus far.

The main conclusion of this volume could not be clearer: reducing the influence of the state sector of the economy on Chinese law and legal institutions is an essential step toward the creation of a sound institutional framework for sustainable development. Doing so, of course, poses a monumental conundrum for Chinese political leadership. But disentangling the Communist Party from business enterprise, and Party-permeated corporations from the legal system, may be the leadership's best hope for the sustained growth and stability so essential to its legitimacy.

I Domestic Institutional Implications

1 Indigenous Evolution of SOE Regulation

Deng Feng*

Introduction

Contradictory feelings about state-owned assets (SOAs) abound in contemporary China, especially among the country's political elite. President Xi Jinping is no exception. Shortly after proclaiming that state-owned enterprises (SOEs) should not be weakened but rather reinforced,[1] he remarked, "SOE (reform) should not be an opportunity for a few people to amass colossal and easy profits."[2] In 2013, the current administration released a new package of reform plans,[3] which included the concept that SOEs

* The author would like to thank Curtis Milhaupt, Ben Liebman, and participants at the Columbia Law School Workshop on State Capitalism for helpful comments on an earlier draft, Joseph Pratt for patiently correcting and polishing the text, and Yu Guangjun for helping with citations.

[1] *See* Zhu Minwu 朱珉迕 & TanYan 谈燕等 et al., 防微杜渐:针眼大的窟窿,斗大的风—夜访习近平总书记交流对话的上海代表团部分代表 (Check Erroneous Ideas at the Outset: A Tiny Hole Can Produce a Gigantic Wind: An Evening Discussion between Shanghai People's Representatives and President Xi, Jinping), 解放日报 (Jiefang Daily) (Mar. 6, 2014).

[2] *See* 习近平:不能把国有资产变成谋暴利机会 (Xi Jinping: Do Not Let State-Owned Assets Be Opportunities for Colossal Profits), 京华时报 (Beijing Times) (Mar. 10, 2014).

[3] 中共中央关于全面深化改革若干重大问题的决定 (The CCP Central Committee Resolution concerning Some Major Issues in Comprehensively Deepening Reform) (promulgated by the CCP Central Committee, Nov. 15, 2013), *available at* http://www.china.org.cn.

should be converted to a mixed ownership system. The question of how to realize mixed ownership, however, either through selling current state-held shares to private shareholders or attracting new private shareholders in secondary or public offerings, is still unclear. SOEs in China are now a leviathan, embedded in the political, economic, and social matrix, absorbing nutrients from the entire nation, and exerting tremendous influence in the political economy. Any subtle change to one part of this sector may affect the whole system. After several decades of economic reform, Xi's attitudinal swing at the annual National People's Congress (NPC) evidenced the contradictory expectations for and evaluations of the current system of SOAs, and confusion over the future direction of the current SOE system.

The current SOE system in China has a definite political meaning: it symbolizes socialism and thereby legitimates the Chinese Communist Party's (CCP) ideology in an "economically foundational" way. SOEs have social meaning—supporting government policies with needed public goods and services. They also have a general economic meaning, as a tool for controlling key natural resources and land, which lends a "red tinge" (of public or national ownership) to the otherwise market economy. Despite these two major benefits, SOEs are problematic: they are not only inefficient, but their immense bureaucracies—generally beds of corruption and nepotism—allow managers with powerful connections to siphon off state assets, a fact well known to political leaders. Supporting the CCP's legitimacy, SOEs are upheld as the foundation of socialism, but at the same time, they require substantial reforms. These contrasting attitudes toward SOEs are key considerations in regards to political ideology.

From an economic and market perspective, however, the Chinese SOE system is also a double-edged sword. Although huge capital accumulation through corporatization and securitization has made China's SOEs look like gigantic economic powers—sometimes even ranking among the world's top enterprises in the Global Fortune 500 surveys—most SOE profits actually come from their monopolistic positions, at the cost of private-sector business and the inefficient provision of public goods and services. This situation may constitute success in the eyes of SOE regulators and managers, but in the eyes of ordinary people, the enterprises represent robber barons.[4] Although the black-letter law establishes SOEs as legal actors equivalent to private firms, in reality, their close connections

---

[4] From 2004 to 2011, banking, oil, and tobacco were the most profitable industries in China, with the return on assets exceeding 20–50 percent; even the current rate of return on net assets still exceeds 20 percent. *See* Guo Tianyong 郭田勇, 中国银行业"暴利"之争 (The Arguments about Bank Industry's Colossal Profits), 《金融时报》中文网 (Fin. Times Chinese Website) (Mar. 26, 2012), http://www.ftchinese.com/story/001043808.

In 2013, the "big four" SOE banks, ICBC, CCB, BOC, and ABC, were listed as the top four most profitable corporations; ICBC alone accounted for over 12 percent of all A share corporations' net revenue. The "big five" banks, the big four plus CBA, increased from 26 percent in 2012 to 36 percent in 2013 of all Chinese Fortune 500s' net profit. *See* Xiao Yuhang 肖玉航,银行与实体企业利润差值得警惕 (Gap of Net Profit between Banking and Industry Merits Special Attention), 企业家日报 (Entrepreneur Daily) (Sept. 9, 2013).

For public opinion about SOEs, especially central SOEs, see, e.g., Zhou Xuesong 周雪松, 央企牟取垄断暴利凸显监管不力 (Central SOEs Getting Monopolistic Colossal Profits Evidences

to the central and local governments, powerful bargaining positions, and ability to hold the balance of power in specific economic communities, combined with the ineffectiveness of formalistic legal rules and enforcement, still provide them with de facto advantages over private businesses. SOEs are now a burden to the free market in China, rather than a complement to it, and do not provide necessary infrastructure for the production of public goods.[5]

Marketization is a common thread running through the last three decades of Chinese economic reform; ideologically the process is often described as "fostering and developing a socialist market."[6] With respect to SOE reform, the initial goal was to use markets, both the market mechanism and the capital markets, as an economic tool to solve problems of inefficiency and to determine social production needs. This goal was to be realized through an institutional transition based on Singapore's experience with SOE management. The Singapore model features a holding company called Temasek, established as a subsidiary of the Ministry of Finance, to manage the portfolio of SOEs under its control. Temasek emphasizes sound financial performance of SOEs and is credited with operating in a transparent and professional manner, largely free of overt political influence or considerations. Temasek's excellent performance in capital management ignited the fantasy of Chinese SOE institutional reformers that public ownership could achieve efficiency, while requiring the fewest steps of transformation without constitutional-level reforms. The process of transplanting Singapore's SOE system followed a top-down, elite-designed, and rule-driven strategy, which conflicted with Deng Xiaoping's trial-and-error strategy and the typical reform process of "gaining wisdom from practical experience." But a paradox emerged in the process of adopting the Singapore approach: even as reforms attempted to turn SOEs into private-like corporations competing with private business owners, the SOE system blocked market competition. This paradox, which reflected flaws in the initial blueprint—the Singapore model of SOE management simply was not yet suitable for China—must be resolved, especially by legal means. This chapter considers the transition of the Chinese SOE system chronologically, reviews the institutional designers' intentions and the measures they sought to introduce, and reveals the problems vexing the current system.

Many studies have already detailed the transformation of Chinese SOEs, including their operations, achievements, and pitfalls,[7] although few have reviewed the entire

---

Regulatory Failure), 中国经济时报 (CHINA ECON. TIMES) (Nov. 14, 2011). *See also* Su Peike苏培科, 反思央企垄断暴利 (Reflections about Central SOEs Colossal Profits), 中国经济时报 (CHINA ECON. TIMES) (Sept. 28, 2010).

[5] Zhang Weiying 张维迎, 歧视民营企业是对国家利益的损害 (Discriminating against Private Enterprise Damages State Interests), 2 当代经济 (CONTEMPORARY ECON.) 11 (2007). *See also* Shen Liang et al., 沈亮等, 央企凶猛: 央企的无边界扩张时代 (Ferocious Central SOEs: A Time for Unlimited Expansion of Central SOEs), 南方周末 (SOUTHERN WEEKEND) (Aug. 20, 2009).

[6] *See, e.g.*, 关于进一步促进资本市场健康发展的若干意见 (Certain Opinions about Further Promoting Capital Market Health Development) (promulgated by State Council, May 8, 2014).

[7] *See, e.g.*, STOYAN TENEV ET AL., CORPORATE GOVERNANCE AND ENTERPRISE REFORM IN CHINA: BUILDING THE INSTITUTIONS OF MODERN MARKETS (2002).

history of the current system. I will not repeat these works; instead, my aim is to provide a perspective like that of *fu pan,* a Chinese chess term where an observer replays the game and tries to explain the various tactics employed. My perspective is that SOE transformation is actually a process of decisions and choices, made in the context of a specific time and place and under both theoretical and concrete constraints, subject to path-dependence.[8] Of course, this is also my own subjective perspective as one who participated in making legal proposals and as a researcher who witnessed almost the entire process of reform.

I. Background on Introduction of the Singapore Model

China's SOE system was introduced as an exact copy of the original Soviet Union blueprint. During economic reforms in the 1980s, managerial contracts, or "contracting-out," was invented and popularized by local governments. The contracting-out mechanism, however, was merely a Band-Aid on the original planned economy and the so-called "unit system." From the time the contracting-out strategy began, strong arguments for either continuing or abolishing it were a top concern of both government officials and scholars.

Economists generally fell into two schools of thoughts on the question of how the next step of economic reform should be conducted. The majority, conservative school of thought could be labeled "market first." The core idea was that the poor performance of SOEs was due to the lack of proper market signals. Once the markets functioned properly, SOEs could obtain proper signals and operate as real enterprises. A few scholars, labeled "enterprise first" thinkers and later as the famous "property rights school," insisted that SOEs should be transformed into "real enterprises" rather than productive units, and instead prescribed a shareholding system (*gufenzhi*).[9] The core idea of the shareholding system was to use the capital market as a "survival of the fittest" mechanism, shutting down, merging, or retooling uncompetitive SOEs, and later, with the support of institutional economics, to find hard-line bosses to cure the government's "soft heart" (soft budget constraint) leading to the protection and rescue of dying SOEs.

For a few years beginning in 1992, the direction of SOE reform was unclear—a point underscored by the document "The Central Committee of the Chinese Communist Party's Resolution concerning Some Issues of Establishing a Socialist-Market Economic System" (the "Socialist-Market Document"), published on December 17, 1993. The "modern enterprise system" was introduced through the official document, but the contents

8 S.J. Liebowiz & Stephen E. Margolis, *Path Dependence, Lock-In, and History*, 11 J.L. Econ. & Org. 205 (1995); *see also* Mark J. Roe, *Chaos and Evolution in Law and Economics*, 109 Harv. L. Rev. 641 (1995–1996).

9 *See* Li Yining 厉以宁, 所有制改革和股份企业的管理 (Ownership System Reform and Share Enterprise Management), 12 中国经济体制改革 25 (China Reform of Econ. Sys.) (1986).

merely mentioned "clearly defining property rights, specifying rights and accountability, separating administrative functions from enterprise management, and scientific management." It did, however, specify several corporatization routes, including going public, sales, and reorganizations, and also directed that "corporatization should not just involve a name change, nor simply accumulate funds but instead focus on the transformation of the management mechanism." It further stated that "there can be only a few publicly held corporations," and warned, "no formalism, no herd mentality." Yet this is precisely the reality that ensued, and when the Singapore model was adopted a few years later, these doctrines were violated in the process of SOE reform.

After emphasizing the continued domination of state ownership and enforcement of the "contracting-out" mechanism, the Socialist-Market Document proposed to strengthen supervision and management of SOAs, and preserve and increase the value of SOAs. The State-owned Assets Supervision and Administration Bureau (SASAB), which was founded as a branch of the Ministry of Finance in 1988 and was later upgraded to Commission status in 2002 (SASAC), began to play a larger role in economic reform. SASAC first emerged as a response to losses in state-owned assets, but did almost nothing for SOEs actually owned by other agencies and local governments. After SOE reform became a focus of society at large, SASAC, with support from scholarly research, proposed many detailed plans for establishing the current SOA system.[10] SASAC played an important role in the process of adaptation of the Singapore model of SOE reform.

The beginning of SOE reform was a purely top-down process. The Socialist-Market Document included almost all of the ideas in currency at that time. Although comprehensive, the Document was ambiguous, in places even paradoxical. From 1992 on, many ideas and roadmaps—taking the experiences of different countries as models—were proposed and debated in all kinds of fora, including the media and scholarly journals. Many different kinds of SOE governance, familiar to any corporate scholar, such as the continental legal-style public corporation, collectively owned companies, codetermination, cooperatives, manager-oriented governance, Yugoslavia's social enterprise, British-style privatization, and the Singapore model—were examined in all of their respective stages of development. During this competition of ideas, the number of choices was limited by initial conditions, doctrines, and ideological restrictions. The final resolution was reached in the early 1990s, through great debate among scholars, local government innovations and experiments, and theoretical contributions by institutional entrepreneurs.

The first constraint, clarified by the Socialist-Market Document and contained in the Constitution and other oft-repeated ideological slogans, was that state ownership as a major feature of socialism should remain the dominant feature of the national economy. Although the ratio of SOEs to private firms might decrease, the presence of SOEs should

---

[10] *See, e.g.*, SASAB 国家国有资产管理局, 国有资产产权管理 (PROPERTY RIGHT MANAGEMENT OF STATE-OWNED-ASSETS) (1994).

qualitatively remain the same. In light of the unsuccessful rapid privatizations in Eastern Europe and the USSR at the time, the first option to be ruled out was using vouchers as a temporary substitute currency and selling shares of SOEs to every citizen. Directly distributing shares of the nationally owned SOEs to the people was also ruled out.[11] In fact, every plan that resembled direct privatization was considered a violation of socialist ideology. (Even after almost two decades, there is still a strong bias against this approach today).[12] The public-private divide of state and market—which meant copying from the civil law countries' practice, letting the SOEs exit profitable businesses and only function as public goods or service providers—was partly accepted by reformers. The view that newly founded SOEs should concentrate on public goods and key industries was widely held. After several decades, however, SOEs were spread across a whole spectrum of industries and were profit-seeking enterprises. These SOEs were at the very heart of the difficulties in the next step of reform. If these profitable SOEs adopted an exit strategy, their shares would have to be sold through a process involving partial privatization. Although most of the small and medium-sized SOEs were later sold quickly and systematically, no one at the time had figured out how to do so. The pursuit of profits by massive SOEs limited the reform options. From the beginning, the idea that the state should quit profitable areas (competitive areas or markets) was not legitimate. The public-private divide in legal doctrine separating the state and society, and the corollary that the state should not compete with the people for profits, a soft constitutional rule since ancient dynastic times, were compromised by reality on the ground.

So long as SOEs continued to pursue profits, this ad-hoc strategy gained theoretical legitimacy and had a ripple effect. Although no one liked the SOEs' bureaucratic way of doing business in market transactions, and although their inefficiency and clumsiness was subject to widespread criticism, the notion of abandoning profitable SOEs rarely appeared in public arguments and debates at the time.[13] Although most SOEs were

---

[11] Almost all research on Eastern Europe and the USSR's transformation was negative. *See, e.g.*, Kong Tianping 孔田平, 东欧经济改革: 模式选择与体制转轨 (Eastern Europe Economic Reform: Model Selection and Institutional Transition), 2 苏联东欧问题 (Issues on Soviet Union and E. Eur.) 21 (1991). *See also* Li Lin 李琳, 东欧经济形势严峻的原因 (Reasons for Economically Grim Situation in Eastern Europe), 4 世界经济与政治 (World Econ. and Pol.) 23 (1992). Only a few studies take a neutral position on shock therapy; *see* Zhu Xingqiao 朱行巧, "休克疗法的"成效辨析 (Analysis of Effect of Shock Therapy), 7 世界经济 (World Econ.) 69 (1992).

[12] *See, e.g.*, Niu Junmin 牛俊民 & Han Bingcheng 韩秉成, 经济体制改革必须坚持社会主义方向—论经济私有化在中国行不通 (Economic System Reform Must Adhere to the Orientation of Socialism: On Impracticability of Economic Privatization in China), 6 社会科学 (Soc. Sci.) 6 (1989). For group opinions against privatization, see also 坚持、改善和发展社会主义公有制—北京大学关于"国营大中型企业所有制改革理论研讨会"记实 (Persisting in, Improving, and Developing Socialism Public Ownership: Record of Conference held at Peking University for State Managed Large and Medium Enterprise Ownership Reform Theories), 12 经济科学 (Econ. Sci.) 79 (1989).

[13] *See, e.g.*, Wang Liming 王利明, 国家所有权研究 (Research on State Ownership) (1991). *See also* Shi Jichun 史际春,国有企业法论 (On State-Owned-Enterprise Law) (1998).

financially troubled and dysfunctional, most proposals still sought to rescue them.[14] This kind of paradoxical feeling is still popular even today. The SOE complex among people was not due to fear of CCP punishment; indeed it was substantiated by almost no studies or even awareness in the great debates of the 1990s.[15] Some public officials believed that having the people as a whole own assets was a call to past glory, but anxiety over unfair distribution of wealth or corruption perhaps provided a more reasonable explanation for the failure to pursue privatization. For the past three decades, the state has always been directly involved in running businesses. Corruption, tunneling, shirking, malfeasance, nepotism, and collusive or conspicuous wrongdoing—basically any type of misconduct imaginable—has occurred in the government's direct or indirect business operations. As a result, anticorruption drives have always been a major theme and a common expectation of the public.[16] The SOE complex could be viewed as an extension of the anticorruption complex; in reality, it also restricted applicable choices. This killed managerialism as a solution, though many economists strongly criticized government paternalism and micromanagement as undercutting SOE entrepreneurship. Of course, the argument also touched upon famous theories of "separation of ownership and control" proposed by Adolf Berle and Gardiner Means in the 1930s from a theoretical perspective; unfortunately, managerialism could not draw attention to this issue. In later years, some populist scholars made good use of the SOE complex and successfully prevented certain kinds of transactions that posed high risks of siphoning off state assets into private hands, for example, management buyouts (MBOs).[17]

Based on a pragmatic view that SOEs were already engaged in a comprehensive array of businesses, and privatization would induce a high social cost, most reformers accepted as unshakable doctrine the acceptability of state ownership in SOEs pursuing profits. Ownership was the keyword in discussions of SOE reform. British-style "golden shares," which meant the state owner should willingly give up its investment returns and control over assets, were also ruled out. Some pioneering scholars did propose a similar solution for the government to keep only a claim to residuals and give up control over the SOEs—whether directly through state commands or indirectly through share

---

[14] *See, e.g.*, Zhang Kunlun 张昆仑, 国有企业处境维艰原因的再认识 (Recognition for Reasons of Embattled SOEs) 1 经济理论与经济管理 (ECON. THEORY AND ECON. MGMT.) 16 (1996).

[15] Even for outside observers, see, e.g. JOSEPH. E. STIGLITZ, WHITHER SOCIALISM (1994). As far as I know, only the World Bank clearly encouraged China to adopt the strategy of real privatization. *See* WORLD BANK, CHINA: BETWEEN PLAN AND MARKET (1990). *See also* WORLD BANK, CHINA: REFORM AND THE ROLE OF THE PLAN IN THE 1990S (1992).

[16] Many have commented on this topic. *See, e.g.*, Su Xiaohe 苏小和, 中国企业家黑皮书 (Black Book of Chinese Entrepreneurs) (2010).

[17] *See* Feng Ju 冯桔 & Huo Zhongyan 霍中彦, 郎咸平: 中国在法制化未完善前一切 MBO 都该停止 (Larry Lang Says All MBOs Should Be Stopped until China Finishes the Rule of Law), 每日经济新闻 (NAT'L BUS. DAILY) (Apr. 18, 2005).

ownership, called "transforming state ownership to creditor rights"—but this option was swamped by proposals more favorable to the state.[18]

The Soviet Union, with its quick collapse, was deemed a failure in both politics and business, and thus its experience was not considered. As a result, China did not closely examine the Soviet Union, even for its negative lessons. Conservatives and pro-labor scholars proposed adoption of the Iberian model: "social enterprises"—an autonomous decision-making model in mid-twentieth century Yugoslavia[19]—however, the proposal fell victim to the same objection as the British golden share, namely the distaste for state ownership controlled by private citizens. Some empirical studies on Yugoslavia also criticized it on the ground that workers were prone to limit newcomers from entering the job market in order to maintain current workers' vested interests.[20] Facing huge unemployment in China, political leaders could not accept the potential danger of shrinking the job market.

Accordingly, most actual models operating in other ports of the world were ruled out as options for the next step of SOE reform. The Singapore model, discussed next, was essentially the only one left that could (1) meet the needs of the state as an owner having total control over the enterprise, (2) maintain the legal status of the SOE as a legal person categorized as a profit-seeking entity in the market, (3) generate revenue in the form of dividends, and (4) possibly increase the value of property held by the people as a whole.[21]

---

[18] *See* Zhang Weiying 张维迎, 从现代企业理论看国有企业改革 (SOE Reform in Perspective of Modern Industrial Organization Theory), 1 改革 (Reform) 30 (1995). *See also* Zhang Weiying 张维迎, 将国有资产变为债权—解决政企不分的有效途径 (Transforming SOA to Creditor Rights: An Effective Way of Separating Administration from Enterprises), 18 瞭望 (Outlook Weekly) 19 (1995).

[19] A translated book received numerous citations and much attention; *see* David P. Ellerman, The Democratic Worker-Owned Firm (1990), published in Chinese as: 民主的公司制 (The Democratic Corporation) (1997).

[20] *See* Lu Hongwei 陆宏明 & Hu Yongming 胡永明, 社会主义企业模式的比较和选择 (Comparison and Selection of Models for Socialist Enterprises), 2 中国工业经济研究 (China Indus. Econ.) 57 (1987). *See also* Li Xingsheng 李幸生, 南斯拉夫自治企业中消费膨胀与积累萎缩的理论剖析 (A Theoretical Analysis of Expansion of Consumption and Contraction of Accumulation in Yugoslavian Autonomous Enterprises) 5 外国经济与管理 (Foreign Econ. & Mgmt.) 10 (1988). *See also* Zhang Jun 张军, 产权结构、所有制和社会主义企业制度——关于制度创新的一个假说 (Property Right Structure, Ownership System, and Socialist Enterprise Institution: A Hypothesis of Institutional Innovation), 8 经济研究 (Econ. Res. J.) 3 (1989).

[21] For the most important report, see Investigatory Group for Visiting Singapore of Economic Development Research Center of the State Council 国务院发展研究中心赴新考察团, 新加坡的宏观经济管理和国有企业的效率 (Macro-Economic Management and Efficiency of SOA in Singapore), 4 改革 (Reform) 143 (1992). *See also* Ren Yuan 任远, 新加坡政府对国有企业的管理 (Singapore Government's Management of SOEs), 2 经济研究参考 (Rev. of Econ. Res.) 20 (1992).

II. Formation of the Singapore Model

Introducing the Singapore model—professionally managed, private-like corporations to pursue profits—as a vehicle for SOE transformation was a gradual process. Some scholars, SASAC, and economic policymakers, especially Prime Minister Zhu Rongji, played crucial roles in the design and realization of this new institution. It was politically unacceptable, however, to announce the influence of a specific country's experience; the CCP always insisted on exploring the Chinese way "scientifically," based on the whole of human society's so-called "crystallized essence of advanced experience and knowledge." The Singapore model's adoption therefore had to be explained theoretically and expressed in a Chinese way, becoming SASAC's SOA management system, instead of an exact copy of the Temasek approach. In official documents, the current SOE system was never recognized as being derivative of the Singapore model, but instead as being the result of China's own process of trial and error and bold exploration. Nevertheless, it was easy to identify the Singapore model in the Chinese approach, as it was closest in form and preexisted China's management system for SOEs. SASAC also experienced a process of learning specifically from Singapore, and the parties established mutual cooperation, with Temasek even obtaining the privilege to enter some key sectors in China. This institutional transplantation was evidenced in the outcome of the transformed system and the learning process that led to it, even if no one consciously recognized it at the time.

The first systematic expression of the Singapore model was made by scholar Wu Jinglian and some of his students and colleagues. They were essentially the first generation of believers in the new institutional economics. When Ronald Coase won the Nobel Prize in economics, his theory was introduced into China and reverberated through a new round of economic reform. Wu had been considered a market-first scholar, and he successfully combined capital market concepts with property theory to create a systematic explanation of SOE reform. After providing a roadmap to reform as a practical guide, in a book coauthored with students and colleagues, entitled *Large and Medium Enterprise Reform: To Build a Modern Enterprise System,*[22] Wu received approval from policymakers. Another economist, Li Yining, pioneered a shareholding system as a way out for the SOEs, especially from a theoretical perspective. Wu and his students also served as consultants for policymakers, sometimes directly acting as high government officers.

Combined with a series of studies, their theory mixed institutional economics and practical transformation plans for operation, described various institutional efficiencies of different arrangements of property rights regimes, and enlightened many

[22] *See* Wu Jinglian et al., 吴敬琏等, 大中型国有企业改革: 建立现代企业制度 (Large and Medium SOE Reform: To Build a Modern Enterprise System) (1993).

followers—their work could even be labeled a school of thought. After reciting the private, collective, and public ownership institutional dynamics, and incorporating famous new institutional economics doctrine, their work argued that the most efficient arrangement should be to clearly define property rights and thereby overcome information costs, collective action problems, and the tragedy of the commons, which also were principles of the SOE's transformative arrangements.

Given the conditions and doctrinal requirements, the Singapore model was almost the only acceptable solution for the rulers of China, but it still had to pass through a trial-and-error process and be aided by some pathbreaking entrepreneurship by bold reformers. Although Wu's scheme and SASAC's interpretations of the SOA system gradually gained popularity—and some experimental trials for share systems and securities exchanges already existed in the 1980s in some local governments, especially in Shanghai, Shandong, and Shenzhen[23]—existing SOEs in the form of factories, shops, and cooperatives still faced many practical obstacles or potential political risks in their transformation into private corporations.

In the early 1990s, many SOEs were close to or actually insolvent. This situation drove the need for SOE transformation.[24] A pragmatic policymaker, the CCP, as with any political party with a realistic vision, did not adopt ad-hoc strategies to change direction unless it felt the situation to be urgent. The SOEs' dire financial situation was combined with a state treasury unable to actively "cut burdens" in the planned process of shareholder reorganization. Such burdens often included discharging, instead of relocating, incompetent managers, as well as firing redundant workers and unnecessary officers. Most important, the poor financial status of SOEs normally revealed an ugly balance sheet; in fact, enterprise capital was normally zero or negative, offset by huge debts. SOEs remained safe only because of almost unlimited support from their creditor banks, which were also owned by the central government. According to official studies and reports published in newspapers and journals, SOEs were equally divided into three types of financial status: profitable, breaking-even, and insolvent. Most scholars, however, believed unpublished government reports showing that 70 percent of all SOEs were insolvent. This financial situation made the transformation difficult.

The ideological challenge was the political risk of being accused of privatization (at the time, this meant transferring publicly owned property into private hands, which was against prevailing political ideology) and loss of assets or value of national property. Since the Socialist-Market Document had already announced the selling, renting, and transferring of small or medium-sized SOEs and collective ownership enterprises,

---

[23] *See* Sun Xiaoliang 孙效良, 股份制在中国的实践 (Share System Practice in China), 5 管理世界 (MGMT. WORLD) 66 (1992).

[24] *See* Zhou Xiaochuan 周小川 & Yin Wenquan 银温泉, 经济体制改革的不同道路 (Various Paths for Economic Institutional Reform), 2 改革 (REFORM) 13 (1993).

ideological dissenters mainly focused on unfair transactions, which meant the selling of state-owned assets or shares cheaply. Considering the poor financial condition of the SOEs, attackers could easily persuade the uninformed public that a factory due to be sold for an insignificant amount of money on a per-share basis actually controlled a massive amount of tangible assets. Public opinion manipulated through the CCP's propaganda machine was used to create a glorious feeling about SOE achievements and to cover up the SOEs' poor financial condition. This kind of resistance has continued throughout the SOE transformation process, even up until today. Although there were many practical obstacles, as well as doubts in people's minds, dying SOEs needed to be changed urgently. In the later transformation process, the Singapore model was the least costly strategy for the government, if not for society as a whole.

It is commonly believed that Zhu Rongji's administration completed this breakthrough reform in a rushed manner. The process of corporatization that occurred from 1995 to 2004 has already been described by many others, including some of the contributors to this volume, and I will not repeat it here. From the mid-1990s to the mid-2000s, through the selling of assets or property, reorganizations and joint ventures, employee buy-outs, management buyouts, and public offerings, China made the transformation to a system of SOEs in the form of profit-seeking entities with a separate legal personality and full corporate capacity. The system rested on a foundation of mostly state-owned shares in a mixed ownership capital market.

These newly transformed SOE corporations were registered as common corporations, and their governance, business operations, and even distributions existed under "private" legal arrangements, mainly the corporate law. After 1993, the Chinese legal system did not have any means of distinguishing SOEs from general corporations—the concept no longer had an official expression or legal concept (see Donald Clarke's Chapter 2 in this volume). The current system should be called a state-owned equity system, according to the Enterprise State Owned Asset Act (ESOAA), or the popularized term SOA, according to SASAC's administrative rules. As mentioned above, the Singapore model of SOEs promised to satisfy the legal needs of enterprises as private for-profit corporations operating in markets and professional asset management without any actual loss of state ownership. This kind of design for the SOE system constituted what one Chinese economist has described as "drawing a black line on a white horse to have a zebra."[25] From the law's perspective, the Chinese version of the Singapore model was actually a laissez-faire-style private law model, plus a crown property public administrative law model.

---

[25] Zhang Weiying 张维迎, 从现代企业理论看中国国有企业的改革 (Chinese SOE Reform from the Perspective of Modern Firm Theory), 6 改革与战略 (Reformation & Strategy) 18 (1994).

III. Dynamics of the Singapore Model: A Further Mutation

The SOE transformation was designed prior to practice, in contrast to the successful experience of Deng's "feeling the stones to cross the river" strategy—although in reality the process involved a good deal of trial and error and still required practical experience to determine workable schemes. In the transformation process, many conflicting forces fought with one another, and the results of the reform deviated from the initial blueprint. Once the transformation was almost complete, such dynamics resulted in unexpected outcomes that magnified the design defects. Around the middle of the first decade of the twenty-first century, the Singapore model's transformation was nearly finalized and received official confirmation in promulgation of the ESOAA. Reality, however, always posed unexpected dilemmas. After the establishment of the Singapore model, the system, though well functioning in theory, met the reality of social dynamics, revealing loopholes and flaws in the system design embedded in Chinese legal institutions.

A. Managerial Rights Battles

The separation of administration from business management had been set up as one of the top priorities of reform, at least in the eyes of mainstream independent opinion. This goal required that the SOE's superior-unit-in-charge (*shangji zhuguan danwei*) give up power as an administrative agency and reallocate specific jurisdiction to SASAC. In the Singapore model, realization of state ownership did not rely directly on an administrative organ as a mechanism to promote the state's interest. In standard corporate governance practice, power is vested in the board of directors, which determines the roles of managers, and engages in monitoring, strategic decision-making, and capital management. Service on the board does not necessarily require industry-specific knowledge. In the Chinese model, however, using the state ownership concept to design corporate governance rules meant that all power should be allocated to shareholders, and therefore ultimately to the majority blockholders (the state). The board was thus deemed to be merely an executive committee of the shareholder meetings. Managers were usually appointed directly by major shareholders, and the board still played a traditional role in management,[26] which required that directors and managers have experience in and knowledge of the corporation's industry and business. SASAC did not have elite managers in a diverse range of industries, and actually was incapable of executing shareholder rights by appointing directors and managers, especially for the closely held corporations that normally hid behind publicly held corporations. The separation of administration

---

[26] *See* Deng Feng 邓峰, 中国法上董事会的角色、职能及思想渊源: 实证法的考察 (The Role, Function, and Origins of Ideas in the Chinese Corporate Board Legal Institution: From a Positive Perspective), 3 中国法学 (China Legal Sci.) 98 (2013).

from business management did not take account of the real need for shareholder voting to make major decisions inside the corporation. Therefore, even though SASAC in theory represented state ownership and had authority to exercise shareholders' rights, in reality it still needed industrial regulatory agencies to recommend high-level officers and to exercise shareholders' rights in the SOE corporations. To change this awkward situation, SASAC began many rounds of headhunting and tried to build up a pool of specialists. However, to date, it has not performed this function well. This paradox comes from the fact that: (1) corporate governance requires a shareholder meeting as the ultimate organ for corporations; (2) SASAC could not act as a full shareholder, especially for voting and making vital decisions; and (3) the goal of separating administration and regulation from business was illusory, because SASAC still used regulatory methods to manage the top-level SOEs and imposed many administrative rules on corporate actions.

The first conflict was exemplified by state-owned banks and securities corporations. In 2003, a newly founded controlling corporation in banking, Central Huijin Investment Company Limited (Huijin), announced that it would send out "share-rights directors" to the firms under its control. The concept was quite odd, as it was ostensibly designed to draw a distinction from "employee-representing directors" (a mandatory requirement for sole state-owned corporations in the Corporate Law, a concept borrowed from German corporate governance), though in reality, not a single SOE corporation had an employee-representing director. Therefore, Huijin's proposed concept of "share-rights directors" was a cover for its true intention—to supplant SASAC as the representative of state assets in the banking industry by dispatching its own directors. With its superior political bargaining power and a clever cover story, Huijin effectively took away SASAC's power over state-owned banks. The move resulted in the establishment of a clear rule under the ESOAA: banking was considered out of the sphere of SASAC's jurisdiction, and Huijin became known by its nickname, the "banking SASAC." Huijin was under the jurisdiction of the central bank (the People's Bank of China, PBC), a regulatory agency, which served as the ultimate boss of state-owned banks. This episode, in which financial SOEs came under the sway of a regulatory agency, again showed that the principle of separation of administration and regulation from business that SASAC emphasized was not sustainable.

Recently, it was reported that the Ministry of Finance (MOF) intended to set up "Huijin II," called the "State-owned Capital Management Corporation," to take over from SASAC as the state asset representative for central SOEs.[27] The MOF officially attacked the current SASAC-led SOA system, resenting its complex and comprehensive regulation "from managing people, managing matters, to managing assets," which did not conform to the basic principle of separation of administration and enterprise

[27] *See* Chen Yanpeng 陈岩鹏, "汇金二号"国资公司将设立, 国资委财政部争主导权 ("Huijin II" State Owned Capital Management Corporation Will Be Founded, SASAC and Ministry of Finance Are Fighting for Control), 华夏时报 (China Times) (Apr. 5, 2014).

management. Using Huijin as a successful example, MOF accused SASAC of blending the administration of SOEs into its own affairs, and of not doing a good job of being a representative of the state as shareholder. It argued that SASAC not only manages state-owned equity, but also personnel affairs and assets, which cover too much of SOEs' internal affairs, especially capital management. SASAC fought back against MOF, reverting to the planned economy approach, and insisted that its managerial model should not copy Temasek as the ultimate shareholder of the entire state-owned equity system. SASAC argued that this also violated the principle of separation of administration and enterprise management, because the proposed Temasek-style capital management corporations would be under the direct command and control of the government.[28] It was interesting that both sides emphasized the principle of separation of administration and enterprise management, and both sides showed a strong intention to copy the Temasek model by organizing several holding companies.[29] This dispute was essentially a struggle for agency power and, possibly, for revenue collection, as SASAC did not have any incentive to turn over the dividends collected from SOEs to the national treasury, MOF.

In reality, many SOEs are actually controlled by their former industry regulators, either through nomination of senior officers or as a result of coordination at the government level. The appointment of high-level officers of major SOEs must be approved at certain levels of the CCP's Organization Department, depending upon the SOE's administrative level, and top leaders of local governments often have the real authority to select candidates.

Thus, by indirectly appointing high-level officers in SOEs, the former "superior-unit-in-charge" retained de facto control over the SOEs. SASAC was not reconciled to the loss of power over SOEs, and was afraid the value of their equity would be diminished by managers appointed by other bureaus. In response to this concern, SASAC established a "general legal counsel" position inside the SOEs. Under SASAC's direct control, the appointees were required to be listed as high-level officers and allowed to monitor the SOEs' daily work, although they had no legitimate basis for doing so under the Corporate Law. This also evidences a battle between the industry regulators and SASAC over internal management of SOEs.

Battles over de facto control of the SOEs are ongoing. The proposition of separation of administration and regulation from business was a naive ideal arising from the map-drawer's wishful thinking. Battles over director appointments, dividend collection,

[28] *See* Feng Yuding 冯禹丁, "管资本" vs. "管人管事管资产," 200 万亿国资改革谁主沉浮 ("Managing Capital" vs. "Managing People, Managing Affairs, and Managing Assets," Who Should Lead the 20 Trillion SOA Reform), 南方周末 (SOUTHERN WEEKLY) (July 24, 2014).

[29] *See* 国资委将打造淡马锡式国企: 华润、中石油或成首批试点 (SASAC Will Organize Temasek Style SOE, CSC and CNPC May Become the First Experimental Units), 华尔街见闻 (WALL STREET CHINA) (May 27, 2014), *available at* http://www.wallstreetcn.com.

and redistribution of assets all evidence the desire to expand administrative power, against a background of lack of accountability and weak constitutional constraints. Yet continued direct government involvement in running businesses takes SOE reform back to the starting line, despite the huge social costs already incurred in seeking to follow the Singapore model.

B. FAILURE OF EFFICIENCY-ORIENTED MANAGEMENT IMPROVEMENT

Huijin won the battle over control of state-owned banks, but it still used a model of corporate governance similar to SASAC's mutated version of the Singapore model. The government worried that Chinese state-owned banks would not be able to compete with foreign banks with the opening of the financial markets following World Trade Organization (WTO) accession. In 2005, Zhou Xiaochuan, the head of the PBC, proposed a concept called "strategic investors"—introducing internationally experienced banks such as Bank of America, Goldman Sachs, Allianz, American Express, Asian Development Bank, Citigroup, Credit Suisse First Boston, Deutsche Bank, and J.P. Morgan as new participants and non-controlling shareholders in Chinese state-owned banks. Those investors made contributions to the state-owned banks' capital and, in exchange, received bank shares at a bargain price. But the real purpose of involving foreign investors as partners for the monopolized state-owned banks was to introduce "advanced management experience" into them. These experienced, professional, and international partners were supposed to transfer their internal management knowledge, strategies, and experience to the less knowledgeable state-owned banks to improve the banks' corporate governance and performance.

In the case of the China Construction Bank (CCB)–Bank of America (BOA) deal, for example, BOA obtained 30 percent of CCB's shares and thus became a strategic investor. The two parties set up a close relationship in daily business, and built up many mechanisms for attracting depositors and customers, such as Sino-American small-scale personal fund transfers. Before BOA became involved with CCB, CCB did not actually have a board with directors elected by shareholders. Instead, it followed the traditional method of appointing top leaders directly. After the two parties became partners, Huijin immediately sent directors selected from among retired former high officers of the PBC system to fill vacant positions on the board, and opened just fifty mid-level manager positions for BOA, aiming to obtain specific "advanced management experience." No doubt this move was contrary to BOA's expectation of getting into the Chinese banking services market. After years of failed investment proposals, BOA gave up. After CCB went public, BOA sold its shares at a high premium. Zhou was then attacked for the loss of SOAs on account of introducing strategic investors and for not opening the market to the domestic private sector. Meanwhile in the industrial SOE enterprises, MBOs were halted by SASAC due to public opinion against privatization.

The twin desires of maintaining control over the SOEs and SOAs, while improving SOE efficiency and competitiveness through limited relaxation of control over management, are contradictory. The bank reform episode evidences the internal conflicts of the Chinese-style Singapore model.

C. EQUALITY OF SHAREHOLDERS

As a combined and revised version of Qing Dynasty business law and Taiwanese company law, Chinese corporate law maintains its nineteenth-century theoretical foundations.[30] A corporation is deemed to enjoy independent legal personality.[31] At the same time, legal capital exemplifies an earlier regulatory type of corporate law and is still accepted as iron-clad doctrine by most legal scholars, judges, and practitioners. A shareholder has to make certain kinds of capital contributions to obtain an equivalent value of shares in every round of capital raising, while a series of regulatory rules maintain that a share's par value is the intrinsic value of the stock. Moreover, the principles "one-share-one-vote" and "equal rights for equal shares" are scrupulously followed, both in corporate law and securities law. Legal capital sets a floor for equity, and serves as a benchmark for shareholders' rights. Under these rigid restrictions, China did not need, and indeed did not develop, a complex and flexible system of equality or democracy for shareholders.

The situation was challenged by the entry of SOEs into public capital markets. The China Securities Regulatory Commission (CSRC) regulations for going public were not only intended to protect investors through information disclosure and prevention of insider transactions, similar to the regulations of its international peers, but were also tasked with promoting the development of the capital markets. The CSRC was required to control market access in consideration of industrial policy under a legal regime dominated by an overtly administrative style. Qualifying or obtaining approval from the CSRC for an initial public offering (IPO) required close scrutiny, including of the issuing firm's corporate governance, financial situation, business history, shareholder structure, legitimacy of assets, business profitability, and future dividend policy, and whether the business was consistent with industrial policy. During the Zhu Rongji administration, the public capital market played the role of the SOEs' financial savior, as heavy scrutiny ensured that most corporations going public were SOEs. The number of corporations, scale of IPOs, and even distribution of IPOs for each province were planned by the National Development and Reform Commission (NDRC), and resulted in a huge gap between supply and demand for shares, leading to massive speculation.

---

[30] *See* Deng Feng 邓峰, 中国公司治理的路径依赖 (Path Dependence of Chinese Corporate Governance), 1 中外法学 (PEKING U. L.J.) 58 (2008).

[31] *See* Deng Feng 邓峰, 董事会的起源、演进与中国的学习 (The System of Boards of Directors: Its Origins, Evolution and China's Learning Experience), 1 中国社会科学 (SOC. SCI. IN CHINA) 64 (2011).

Demand far in excess of supply raised stock prices, and no one cared about the quality of stock. Therefore stock prices had no link to the performance of SOEs, and the signaling function allocating capital to the best firms, one of the main purposes of share reform, was lost.

SOEs went public to raise capital from the mass of public investors, but control over the corporations was still retained by the state, directly or indirectly. State-owned shares were classified as promoter's shares. Many SOE promoters also included some other public agencies or corporations. Their shareholdings were referred to as state-owned-legal-person shares. To maintain the majority shareholder status and protection of SOAs, state-owned shares could not be traded, and state-owned-legal-person shares could only be exchanged with public agencies or other SOEs. After going public, individual and institutional investors bought newly issued tradable shares at a high premium compared to those held by the promoter.

Therefore, a strange situation developed: according to the black-letter law, all shares are identical and entitled to equal treatment, both in voting and dividend distributions. But in reality, shares were divided into three types, and sometimes even a fourth type: staff shares. Cracks within the institutional dynamics emerged. Fully tradable shares that investors bought at a high premium after an SOE's IPO contributed more to corporate capital, while state-owned shares or state-owned-legal-person shares were normally issued only in return for par value. Therefore, public investors holding tradable shares felt the allocation of voting rights and distributions was unfair. In a famous case in 2004 involving China Merchant Bank convertible bonds,[32] public investors, through trust fund managers, complained that the majority shareholders, which were eight SOE corporations serving as promoters, paid just one RMB per share, while public investors paid ten times that amount. The CSRC immediately issued a notorious regulation on class voting, which required that any fundamental transaction or corporate change be obtained by plurality approval of each kind or class of shares. This time the pendulum swung to the other side, as in the China Merchant Bank share structure, publicly tradable shares comprised only 30 percent of all shares; therefore, dissenters representing only 16 percent of the total share capital would be able to block a deal. The class voting rule could not be justified, for the CSRC did not provide the same treatment to foreign investors in the B share market.

In some earlier cases, the opposite outcome prevailed, as state-owned shares encountered discrimination, especially in relation to some local SOEs. Those corporations made dividend policies according to the shareholder's contribution rather than shares, as in a speculative market tradable shares made a larger contribution to the corporation. The distribution of dividends according to contribution, favoring tradable shares, was

[32] *See* Special Report: 招行百亿转债风波 (Ten-Billion China Merchant Bank Convertible Bonds Storm), 新浪财经频道 (SINO FINANCE CHANNEL) (Jan. 15, 2014), *available at* http://finance.sina.com.cn/nz/zhzz/.

much fairer in many people's minds, because in the transformation of an SOE in poor financial condition, the SOE promoters' capital contribution consisted mostly of land, equipment, and buildings, devalued by high debt prior to the IPO. Compared to the new investors' monetary capital contributions, those assets were unrealizable for cash. In response, SASAC promulgated many rules forbidding this kind of corporate distribution policy in the name of protection of state assets.[33] Those cases represented the opposite example of the so-called "equality of shareholders," and SASAC called it "discrimination against state-owned equity."

In order to solve the problem of separate share classes, the central government and CSRC from 2005 to 2006 undertook a non-tradable share reform. State-owned shares and state-owned-legal-person shares were intended to be non-tradable: the former was de jure forbidden and the latter was de facto blocked, due to complex procedures and the massive scale of shareholdings, which eliminated any potential buyers. The reform aimed at removing legal obstacles to tradable shares and creating a fully liquid stock market. After the reform, in some cases tradable blocks of shares were unloaded onto the stock market, triggering a price avalanche and causing CSRC to go back to a new kind of split market, forcing any transaction above 1 percent to be traded in a block transaction system. Through ups and downs, under constantly changing rules, a unified capital market finally was formally established to promote equality of shareholders. At present, however, this ideal exists mostly on paper.

New unequal shareholder treatment problems occurred in the cross-listings of gigantic SOEs. For example, Sino-petroleum (China National Petroleum Corporation, CNPC), cross-listed in mainland China and Hong Kong through a voting trust certificate, raising US$2.9 billion in the United States. It distributed $11.9 billion dollars to American investors in 2012.[34] By comparison, Sino-petroleum in the Chinese A stock market issued a dividend that was less than 1.5 RMB for every ten shares. This unequal dividend policy incited a great wave of public criticism, considering the company's SOE nature and the monopoly privileges it enjoys domestically.

Equality in China is a serious problem from every perspective, not only among shareholders. The issue has not generated a consensus among corporate scholars, let alone been resolved by legislative or judicial action. The problem revealed a dependence upon legal capital, which was used to maintain fairness between shareholders and to serve as a tool for measuring the SOA's value. If par value did not need to match the intrinsic value

---

[33] *See, e.g.*, 国家国有资产管理局关于在股份公司分红及送配股时维护国有股权益的紧急通知 (Urgent Notice concerning Safeguarding State Owned Equity in Publicly Held Share Corporation Distributing Dividends, Allotment or Presentation for New Shares) (promulgated by SASAB, Apr. 18, 1995). *See also* 国有资产收益收缴管理办法 (Administrative Measures for Collection of State Owned Asset Revenue) (promulgated by SASAB, Nov. 4, 1994, effective Nov. 4, 1994).

[34] *See* 中石油给美国投资者分红超 800 亿, 超融资额度四倍 (Sino-petroleum Distributed 80 billion for Outside Investors, Exceeding Four Times Their Contribution), 北京商报 (Beijing Bus. Today) (Aug. 23, 2012).

of the SOE, SASAC would not have a tool to evaluate SOAs and maintain its current managerial system. Its step-by-step approach became a vicious circle: SASAC needed to monitor both the value of the shares and the value of the corporation's assets, and therefore needed to enhance regulation of legal capital.

D. FRANCHISED INDUSTRY

High market-entry barriers provide SOEs with huge advantages in capital accumulation. Most of their businesses belong to monopolistic industry lines and facilitate a steady income stream. Those corporations had deep pockets and started to invest in the most profitable industries, beginning with the real estate market. In a real estate bubble, often leveraging their advantageous bargaining power with local governments, SOEs easily obtained land-use rights, either by raising prices in public bidding processes or engaging in private interest exchange. Some of them were labeled "land kings" (*di wang*—the highest bidder for land use rights), pushing real estate prices higher, which ordinary people already found intolerable. With monopolistic privileges in a particular sector, and providing poor services for the people, public ownership corporations competed with the private sector for profits and exacted a heavy toll on people's daily life, drawing massive objections.

Responding to public opinion, and as a precaution against a potential burst of the real estate bubble, SASAC in 2006 set up a new "main business" rule as a mandatory requirement for all central SOEs.[35] SASAC started a one-by-one confirmation process to determine the main business of every central SOE. The assets of noncore businesses were then required to be sold, restructured, or reallocated to other SOEs, with the franchise of the main business certified and approved by SASAC.[36]

The regulation, however, was simply an ad hoc measure for a systemic problem. Many paradoxical questions arose. First, based on the Singapore model, SOEs were supposed to be profit maximizing; SASAC's restrictions violated the nature of SOEs as profit-making enterprises and caused a series of chain reactions. Second, all of the SOEs were also publicly traded corporations, so an administrative order to require those corporations to give up profitable business opportunities, and even diversify existing assets, ignored the fact that those kinds of decisions should be made in corporate shareholders meetings, and might be deemed an abuse of controlling positions under the Corporate Law—although this kind of behavior happened frequently. Third, SASAC violated not only the Corporate Law, but also the ESOAA's rule that SASAC's task was to manage

---

[35] *See* 中央企业投资监督管理暂行办法 (Interim Measures' Surveillance and Regulation on the Central Enterprise Investment) (promulgated by SASAC, June 28, 2006, effective July 1, 2006).

[36] *See* 国资委为 153 家央企定主业，主业外资产将剥离 (SASAC Sets Up 153 Central SOE's Main Businesses, Non-core Assets Will Be Peeled Off), 上海证券报 (SHANGHAI SECURITIES NEWS) (June 13, 2007).

the equity of SOEs, rather than their assets. Reallocations or mandatory sales of assets, however, were actually a deep intervention into internal corporate affairs. It was an ironic solution after decades of efforts to separate administration and regulation from business, and to obtain the independent legal status of SOEs.

The central SOEs' retreat from real estate was just the beginning; a series of other problems followed closely. It was a system-design problem rather than a one-off event. The initial reason for adopting a version of the Singapore model was to remedy the poor financial situation of SOEs. Its designers did not anticipate that one day the SOEs would turn into robber barons.

E. *KONZERNS* AND FINANCIAL EMPIRE

A new SOE gold rush took place after the real estate rush, with the current version being SOE corporations investing in the finance, banking, and securities industries. With gradual deregulation in banking, finance, and private equity by the China Banking Regulatory Commission (CBRC) and PBC, and industrial production stagnating, the monopolistic banking business reaped huge profits. The potential came from SOE banks going public to raise capital for rebalancing their debt-to-equity ratio. As bank shares now had become tradable, and the industry was attractive for generating revenue, SOEs began to invest in all kinds of finance, banking, insurance, and private trust corporations. It was reported that by 2011, 87 of a total of 117 central SOEs had entered the finance industry through share holdings.[37]

Notwithstanding promulgation of SASAC's main business rule, the combination of industry and finance did not fall into the sphere of regulation. Most important, SASAC has shown itself to be of two minds—both positive and cautious concerning the combination of industry and finance.[38] Just like the main business problem, the current situation was beyond the initial design of the Chinese version of the Singapore model, and no theoretical concept offered a clear resolution of the new questions. Although the rationality and legitimacy of combining industry and finance is still in question, under the current market, by turning themselves into German-style *konzerns,* SOEs could skim off the cream of Chinese economic development and obtain the most valuable business opportunities.

---

[37] *See* 央企产融巨浪 (Central SOE Corporations' Huge Wave in the Combination of Industry and Finance), 财经国家周刊 (ECON. & NATION WEEKLY) (Apr. 20, 2011).

[38] *See* ZhouTing 周婷, 国资委支持央企产融结合, 鼓励不留存续资产整体上市 (SASAC Supported Central SOEs for Combination of Industry and Finance, Encouraged Overall Listing with Reservation for Partial Assets), 中国证券报 (CHINA SEC. J.) (Sept. 24, 2010). *See also* 央企大举进军金融领域, 产融结合加速其财团化 (Central SOEs Scaled into Finance Industry, Combination of Industry and Finance Accelerated Syndicatization), 经济参考报 (ECON. INFO.) (Feb. 23, 2011). *See also* 产融结合要有三条红线 (Three Red Lines for Combination of Industry and Finance), 中国石油石化 (CHINA PETROCHEM)(Sept. 1, 2009).

F. ASYMMETRIC COMPETITION AND ABUSE OF MONOPOLISTIC POWER

Due to inattention to general equality principles, a lack of fair competition plagues China. Despite the promulgation of the Anti-Monopoly Law, competition questions still pose a serious problem. Even without a clear definition of public goods, most Chinese SOEs were designed to operate in "key strategic industries." Because of the nature of their legitimate businesses, SOEs are effectively immune from the antitrust law, although various dissenting explanations have arisen from the ambiguous Article 7 of the Anti-Monopoly Law.[39] With their de facto bargaining power as gigantic corporations with both tremendous capital resources and high administrative influence, the competitive (or anticompetitive) behavior of SOEs is rarely challenged.

SOEs, however, are positioned as profit-making entities, and competitiveness was also a design element of the Chinese version of the Singapore model. Without actual financial constraints or current revenue requirements, competition among SOEs in China has two features. First, between SOEs, especially in industries with network effects, such as telecommunications, where competition has focused on the scale of network rather than instant investment return, cutthroat competition has taken place routinely. China Telecommunications, China Unicom, and China Mobile are set up to compete with each other, and their conduct in some areas goes far beyond fair business competition. In 2003, local subsidiaries of China Mobile and China Unicom fought each other to such an extent that they used scissors to cut their rival's communication lines. The Supreme People's Court (SPC) even organized a forum for all parties involved in public communications in Chengdu, to announce that using scissors to damage public communication lines and purposely block interconnection between networks would be punished as a felony.[40]

Second, in competition between SOEs and private corporations, SOEs often leverage their immunity from the Anti-Monopoly Law to blackmail, boycott, or economically threaten other parties to fulfill their expansion purposes. It was reported that Sino-petroleum, in an effort to expand its industrial line to natural gas and thereby realize its ambition of building up an energy empire, used the threat of cutting off the gas supply in western areas of the country to buy out local gas stations.[41] This case was just

---

[39] Article 7 provides, "With respect to the industries controlled by the State-owned economy and concerning the lifeline of national economy and national security or the industries implementing exclusive operation and sales according to law, the state protects the lawful business operations conducted by the business operators therein. The state also lawfully regulates and controls their business operations and the prices of their commodities and services so as to safeguard the interests of consumers and promote technical progresses."

[40] *See* Liu Yuqi 刘玉其 & Zhou Lu 周禄, 互联互通十大案例点评 (Comments on Ten Cases about Interconnection and Interworking), 通信信息报 (TELECOMM. NEWS) (Sept. 5, 2003).

[41] *See* Zhang Qi'an 张启安, 中石油攻略天然气下游 (Sino-petroleum Takes Strategies for Natural Gas Downstream), 《财经》杂志 (CAI JING MAG.) (Dec. 16, 2010).

the tip of the iceberg, and most similar forms of abuse have been obscured by the ability of these massive corporations to control public opinion and leverage the national information control and filtering system. The harsh competitive behaviors of SOEs, which are becoming increasingly fierce, are an unexpected result of the Chinese version of the Singapore model.

G. DUTY OF COMMON CALLING IN PUBLIC SERVICE

The paradox of the Chinese version of the Singapore model might be epitomized by a doctrine known as a public service provider's duty of common calling. Despite having adopted a continental legal system, as a reaction to heavy administrative regulations laissez-faire has become the dominant, politically correct ideology among legal scholars, lawyers, economists, and even some judges and officials. No clear concept or legal institution of a common calling duty had existed in Chinese legal culture. Unlike in Western countries, Chinese law did not require public goods providers to perform specific corporate duties, such as to care for various stakeholders' interests, to price fairly, to ensure a high standard of product quality, to cooperate with both upstream and downstream business partners, or even to open its platform as a common carrier for their rivals.[42] In the planned economy era, such duties were not specified in rules, for the SOEs were considered branches of government. In the market economy era, however, the SOEs turned into market competitors, and thus needed to be regulated like private corporations. The SOEs' dual role made an impression on the regulators; they could be both good corporate citizens and profit pursuers. The only thing that needed to be promulgated into black-letter law was a system of price regulation, and therefore, public goods providers' common calling duties were neglected by lawmakers.

When the SOEs became market participants in pursuit of profits, they inevitably faced many situations where some stakeholders' interests would be sacrificed. The SOEs competed even more fiercely than private corporations, for some of them enjoyed monopolistic privileges or real market power as a result of their gigantic assets and almost unlimited financial capability due to government paternalism.[43] The SOEs' irresponsibility caused a strong backlash from the public, and the Corporate Law in 2005 established a mandatory duty of corporate social responsibility (CSR) for all corporations, giving rise to much controversy among corporate law scholars. The dynamics in reality reflected the institutional loophole created by using price regulation as a foundation for distinguishing the public and private duties of an enterprise. It evidenced a clumsy

---

[42] *See* J.B. Whitefield, *Rights and Duties of Public Service Corporations*, 22 YALE L.J. 39 (1912–1913). *See also* Charles K. Burdick, *The Origin of the Peculiar Duties of Public Service Companies, Part 1*, 11 COLUM. L. REV. 743 (1911).

[43] *See* Zhang Weiying 张维迎 & Ma Jie 马捷, 恶性竞争的产权基础 (The Property Rights Foundation of Cut-Throat Competition), 6 经济研究 (ECON. RES. J.) 11 (1999).

public regulatory system and a poor understanding among intellectuals of markets and their proper regulation.

After SASAC placed some restrictions on the profitable businesses of SOEs and the NDRC continued to limit space for price competition, most SOEs faced a dilemma: price regulation from the NDRC on public services limited their profitability, which is the main performance metric under the Singapore model, and business regulation from SASAC, which prohibited profitable investments outside their main business lines. The result was that public service corporations set up as profitable enterprises could not meet the ESOAA's requirement of "maintenance and appreciation of values for SOA."

SASAC's attitude toward this dilemma has oscillated over time. One of SASAC's vice chairmen, Shao Ning, publicly proposed a new, dual classification for SOEs: "public-benefit SOEs" and "competitive SOEs." The idea was that SOEs with public-benefit elements concern public welfare and tend to be monopolistic, with their products and services regulated, and thus they should not be measured by the criterion of profitability. Anyone knowledgeable about basic economics would realize that this classification mirrors the classical division between public goods and private goods, but Shao did not cite any "advanced experience" on this distinction and made up a new concept in a very Chinese, bureaucratic way. SASAC immediately released an official announcement to distance itself from Shao's statement and to clarify that the concept of an "SOE with public welfare elements" differed from a "public-benefit SOE." It suggested that the latter was a journalistic misreading of Shao's remarks. SASAC wanted to state that no monopolistic SOEs exist and that all SOEs should pursue profits.[44] This about-face by SASAC evidenced an internal contradiction over the role of SOEs. After two decades of struggling to transform SOEs into private-style corporations, things have returned full circle.

After the current administration announced that SOE reform would move toward a "mixed ownership system," SASAC was provided with a chance to fix the problem and allowed to take a trial-and-error reform strategy without strictly following the existing black-letter rules. Intending to solve the dilemma of public service corporations, SASAC and its branch offices at the local level were urged to promote a so-called "categorized management" system, which mirrored Shao's proposal.[45] SOEs were divided into four types: (1) pure public-benefit SOEs, including the military, cereals, and salt industries, aimed at public service; (2) purely competitive SOEs, including automobile manufacturing and the electronics industry, in pursuit of profits; (3) mainly public-benefit and supplementary competitive SOEs, such as the petroleum and telecommunication

[44] *See* 国资委称公益型国企说法存在误读 (SASAC Announced Misreading of Public-Benefit SOEs), 京华时报 (BEIJING TIMES) (Dec. 13, 2011).

[45] *See* 国企改革大方案或明年出台，启动分类监管成重点 (Big Plan for SOE Reform Will Appear Publicly Next Year, Main Point Will Be to Start Categorized Management), 经济参考报 (ECON. INFO.) (Nov. 20, 2013).

industries; and (4) mainly competitive and supplementary public-benefit SOEs, without mentioning any specific industries. SASAC, ironically, however, seems to have lost jurisdiction over public service regulation, and is back to its original position after three decades of trial and error in search of a Chinese-style SOA system.

Conclusion

It remains to be seen what kind of institutional system will result from the recent political decision to pursue "mixed ownership" as the next step in SOE and SOA management reform. In all probability, however, it will simply be a Band-Aid on the current Singapore model in view of the following factors: (1) the concept of mixed ownership reveals an underlying understanding of corporations along property rights lines, (2) ordinary people's feelings about SOEs are still tied to the perceived "glory" of these firms, and (3) the reforms are being conducted mainly by bureaucrats themselves. Sinification of the Singapore model as an evolutionary process, and alienation from the initial blueprint in the institutional dynamics may provide a hint about the outcome, as suggested by the ancient Chinese philosophical saying, "History tells us the future." By comparing the blueprint to the result thus far from a historical perspective, we can see that some doctrines cannot be shaken. These include a doctrine against privatization through the state distributing shares into individual hands, and a doctrine against giving up profitable enterprises to roll back the state's hand.

The Singapore model was first considered by top leaders after the great debates of the early 1990s. Although SASAC still did not recognize its administrative system as a facsimile of the Temasek model, as no single controlling corporation took full responsibility for the management of state-owned capital, SASAC was set up to represent and manage the national property, both as a shareholder and as a regulatory body. Although SASAC used the doctrine of separation of administration from business management to wrest control over SOEs from other agencies, SASAC cannot justify its own position as manager of SOAs and cannot directly make business decisions as a shareholder. The very existence of an SOA regulatory agency, the SASAC, seemed to provide justification that the Chinese SOA system was not the Singapore model. If all shareholders' rights are transferred to a Huijin-style Chinese Temasek, what will SASAC's sphere of influence be?

My assertion that China's current SOE system is a distorted copy of the Singapore model is based on China's learning process and the similarity of the two system's main characteristics, including the lack of a distinction between public and corporate legal institutions, SOEs' pursuit of profits, and the absence of any specific limitations on a public corporation's capacity. From a legal perspective, the current Chinese SOE system can be clearly distinguished from the civil law concept of a "public legal person" (even though China normally claims to follow the German civil law tradition). Yet in the absence of any constitutional arrangements to constrain state power, lacking the courage to give up its desire for profits, and without any respect for corporate governance and the interests of other stakeholders, SASAC has distanced itself from the Temasek model of SOE management. Although many rules have changed in the last three decades at the corporate level, the attitude of the government has remained the same.

In order to obtain a sustainable future for the Chinese SOE system and to fulfill the SOEs' social efficiency requirements and public duties, the state must realize that it needs a well-functioning constitutional infrastructure. It must then delegate, or give up, its property rights in the shares of corporations. If the current approach to handling SOEs continues, SOEs will become Crown Property. The departure from the SOEs' public nature means a departure of the government from the people's interests; it will result in SOEs resembling Hobbes's Leviathan.

2 Blowback

HOW CHINA'S EFFORTS TO BRING PRIVATE-SECTOR STANDARDS INTO THE PUBLIC SECTOR BACKFIRED

Donald Clarke*

Introduction

All successful legal transplants are alike; each unsuccessful transplant is unsuccessful in its own way. While the borrowing of corporate law principles from advanced Western economies has encountered problems in many jurisdictions, the reasons for the problems differ. In China, an important reason is that the logic of the state-owned sector has strongly affected China's assimilation of Western corporate law principles. Although the original intention was to impose reform on the state sector by organizing it as much as possible along the lines of private corporations in the West, the state's insistence on maintaining a strong state sector combined with the reform imperative of having a single set of principles for corporate law has meant that the logic of the state sector has infected the set of rules applicable to the private sector.

This chapter will examine the history of China's reform-era adoption of Western corporate law principles and canvass specific examples of the phenomenon described above, which I call blowback. Section I examines the general phenomenon of state ownership of commercial firms and the dilemma this poses for corporate governance, as well as the

* I would like to thank participants at the June 2014 workshop on Chinese state capitalism at Columbia Law School, and especially Curtis Milhaupt, for their very helpful comments and suggestions.

range of solutions adopted in different jurisdictions. Section II discusses the history of organizational reform of state-owned enterprises (SOEs) in China. Section III, the heart of this chapter, discusses specific examples of blowback in various areas of corporate law.

I. State Ownership of Firms: General Dilemmas and International Experience

Many states have a policy of maintaining a full or controlling interest in particular firms or economic sectors. This presents policymakers with a dilemma: while they presumably want the firms to be run efficiently—that is, to achieve their goal with a minimum of waste—the goal is not necessarily profit maximization for the state. (If it were, the state would no more need a policy of being invested in *particular* firms or sectors than a private investor would.) India's Minister for Coal forthrightly declared this to Coal India's minority shareholders in 2012,[1] and a 2010 preferred stock prospectus from General Motors cautions investors that the interests of its U.S. government shareholder (approximately 37 percent) could diverge from the interests of other shareholders.[2]

The question then arises whether it makes sense for such state-controlled firms to be governed by the same set of principles that governs firms whose goal *is* profit maximization.[3] The mainstream view is that a unitary regime is best. The World Bank, for example, maintains that "[w]hen possible, SOEs should have the same legal form and be subject to the same laws as other commercial enterprises."[4] It goes further to state that "the variety of different legal forms for SOEs should be limited."[5]

---

[1] In an interview, Sriprakash Jaiswal stated:

> [A]ll shareholders knew about [Coal India (CIL)] before investing. The [prospectus] clearly tells them that CIL consults the government on pricing and mining policy has been explained. We own 90 percent of CIL. Shouldn't we be taking decisions? Whoever wants to stay invested in CIL can stay, otherwise leave. Someone's notice or threats will not bend the government. It is CIL's job to make profit and to produce coal but only making profit is not its job [while] it remains with the government.

Sindhu Battacharya, *Exclusive: 54 Coal Blocks to Be Auctioned in 1–2 Mths: Minister*, FIRSTPOST.COM (Mar. 30, 2012), http://bit.ly/1mOO68F.

[2] *See* GEN. MOTORS CO., PROSPECTUS 27 (2010), *available at* http://www.sec.gov/Archives/edgar/data/1467858/000119312510263635/d424b11.pdf.

[3] Stephen Bainbridge argues persuasively that it is the human participants in firms, not the abstract firm itself, who have intentionality and goals. *See* Stephen Bainbridge, *The Vacuity of Corporate Purpose*, PROFESSORBAINBRIDGE.COM (May 5, 2012), http://www.professorbainbridge.com/professorbainbridgecom/2012/05/the-vacuity-of-corporate-purpose.html. Nevertheless, although reification of the corporation can sometimes lead one's analysis astray, at other times it is a harmless shorthand. Here the notion of corporate goals highlights the difference in the incentives and goals of the parties participating in SOEs and privately owned firms.

[4] WORLD BANK, HELD BY THE VISIBLE HAND: THE CHALLENGE OF SOE CORPORATE GOVERNANCE FOR EMERGING MARKETS 9 (2006); *see also* ORGANIZATION FOR ECONOMIC COOPERATION AND DEVELOPMENT, OECD GUIDELINES ON CORPORATE GOVERNANCE OF STATE-OWNED ENTERPRISES 20 (2005) (similar advice).

[5] WORLD BANK, *supra* note 4, at 9.

Yet it is not entirely clear why this should be so. Certainly it is not intuitively obvious that an organization whose raison d'être is necessarily something other than making profits should operate under the same rules—particularly with respect to its internal governance—as organizations dedicated to profit-seeking. What is the point, for example, of rules designed to protect minority shareholders if a firm has a single state shareholder? Although private firms can also be held by a single shareholder, they have the potential to be held by many, and indeed, the original single shareholder may look forward to a sale of all or part of its interest to others. A state firm that is wholly owned as a matter of policy does not have this potential.

Most jurisdictions seem to follow the mainstream view. In Brazil, for example, the prominence of SOEs in the national corporate landscape led some scholars to propose that they be governed by a statute specifically designed to suit their needs and purposes, but this proposal was defeated.[6]

Recently, scholars have begun to argue that a unitary regime is not merely unsuitable for SOEs, but can also be harmful to the privately owned firms for which it was originally designed. This is so for two reasons. First, the legal regime governing SOEs will inevitably take account of their special characteristics. For example, the principle that corporate management must act to maximize profits must yield to the principle that corporate management may consider other goals as well. If state ownership and a unitary regime are both unalterable policies, then the latter principle will seep back into the private corporate governance regime.[7]

Mariana Pargendler has documented precisely this type of phenomenon in Brazil.[8] For example, the 1976 Corporations Law imposed a duty on all controlling shareholders to protect the interests not only of shareholders, but also of employees, "the community," and the national economy.[9] Thus, not only the state, but also *private controlling shareholders* have a duty to protect the public good against minority shareholders, who are presumably selfishly interested only in making money. Such a duty goes well beyond the *option* granted to corporate management in Pennsylvania to do likewise.[10]

Second, the various interests involved in SOE governance, including the state (as legislator and regulator) and SOE managers, may work to block corporate law changes that would benefit private firms but harm those interests.[11] In such a case, a separate regime

---

[6] *See* Mariana Pargendler, *State Ownership and Corporate Governance*, 80 FORDHAM L. REV. 2917, 2934 (2012).

[7] I make this argument more fully in Donald C. Clarke, *Corporate Governance in China: An Overview*, 14 CHINA ECON. REV. 494 (2003).

[8] *See* Mariana Pargendler, *The Unintended Consequences of State Ownership: The Brazilian Experience*, 13 THEORETICAL INQUIRIES IN LAW 503 (2012).

[9] *See id.* at 511.

[10] *See infra* note 44 and accompanying text.

[11] *See* Pargendler, *supra* note 6, at 2922.

for SOEs can minimize opposition to changes in the governance regime applicable to non-SOEs. This is the case Ronald J. Gilson et al. make for what they call "regulatory dualism":

> [A] single homogeneous regulatory regime for all actors would in principle be most efficient. Here, however, the preexisting system of regulation—the established regime—has been captured by a subset of the actors that it regulates and inefficiently permits those actors to pursue their private interests. A second, more efficient system of regulation—the reformist regime—is created, and is made available to all actors. Meanwhile, the established regime is maintained and is also made available to all actors, whether they have previously been governed by that regime or not. Maintaining the established regime reduces the incentive for those who benefit from that regime to oppose creation of the reformist regime.[12]

In summary, whether to have a unitary corporate governance regime that covers both SOEs and non-SOEs or a dual regime is a choice with no obvious right answer. Nevertheless, a unitary regime seems in practice to be preferred around the world, and China has gone this route as well.[13]

There are typically three justifications. First, it is argued that a unitary regime is *fair*. SOEs and privately owned firms may be in competition; a special regime for SOEs could give them an unfair competitive advantage.

Second, it is argued that the competition-promoting effects of a unitary regime are *socially beneficial* for the same reasons that competition generally is socially beneficial. Society benefits when goods and services are produced by the firm that can do so at the lowest cost without an artificial organizational advantage.

Third, it is argued that the corporate governance regime applicable to private firms should be applied to SOEs simply because it is *better* than the alternatives. This argument does not invoke the inherent virtues of a unitary regime regardless of its content. It simply says a corporate governance regime of proven value in the private sector will cause SOEs to operate more efficiently if applied to them as well.[14]

---

[12] Ronald J. Gilson et al., *Regulatory Dualism as a Development Strategy: Corporate Reform in Brazil, the United States, and the European Union*, 63 STAN. L. REV. 475, 480 (2011).

[13] In the words of Chen Qingtai, the Vice Chair and Party Secretary of the State Council's Development Research Center, "Compared with private companies, with respect to establishing a standard corporate governance structure, the great majority of state-owned enterprises can't be special [exceptions to the private model]." 陈清泰: 国企公司治理不能特殊 (Chen Qingtai: Corporate Governance in State-Owned Enterprises Cannot Be an Exception), 3 中国石油和化工 (CHINA PETROLEUM AND CHEM. INDUS.) 14 (2000).

[14] *See generally* Donald C. Clarke, *Corporate Governance in China: An Overview*, 14 CHINA ECON. REV. 494, 497–500 (2003).

II. Organizational Reform of State-Owned Enterprises in China

China's economic reforms are commonly dated from 1979, but state-owned enterprise reform did not begin in earnest until the early 1990s. Faced with growing SOE losses, falling state revenues, and rising levels of non-performing loans in the banking sector, China embarked on a series of important reforms in the SOE sector.[15] In addition to closing down large numbers of SOEs and laying off 50 million employees between 1993 and 2004,[16] the government restructured most of the remaining SOEs by converting them into a corporate form complete with stockholders and boards of directors.

Reorganization of SOEs into the corporate form was viewed as an essential part of reforming them. To understand the significance of reorganization, it is essential to understand the classic *non-corporate* organizational form of the traditional state-owned enterprise (TSOE) in China because it is unlike SOEs in other countries.

The TSOE is not simply a corporation that happens to be wholly owned by the state. It is similar to a division within a large corporation. In the pre-reform era (and for some time into it) government ministries were more like industrial conglomerates than regulators, and a chemical factory, if a state-owned enterprise, bore essentially the same relationship to the Ministry of Chemical Industry that Chevrolet bears to General Motors. No formal law governed industrial TSOEs until 1988, and none has ever governed commercial TSOEs. There was no need. Relationships among managers, suppliers of capital and raw materials, workers, and government overseers could all be handled through internal state administrative procedures.

Reformers attributed the many pathologies of TSOEs to their organizational form and sought to cure them through a change of that form. Three in particular stand out.[17]

First, the organizational form of the TSOE was said to unify control and ownership in the same hands—the state's—and thereby contribute to inefficiency in that the state owner would interfere with managers who, if left to their own devices, would run the firms more efficiently. Corporatizing SOEs would separate ownership from control by putting ownership in the hands of shareholders, while putting management powers in the hands of directors and senior management.

The diagnosis of the problem is flawed, as is the proposed cure. Whatever features of the traditional organizational form may have contributed to SOE inefficiency, the unity of ownership and control was not one of them, because it did not exist. Ownership was in the hands of an abstract entity, the state, whereas control was (and remains) necessarily in the hands of human beings. Whether those human beings are labeled state officials

---

[15] *See* Weiye Li & Louis Putterman, *Reforming China's SOEs: An Overview*, 50 COMP. ECON. STUD. 353, 356 (2008).

[16] *See* Xiao-Yuan Dong & Lixin Colin Xu, *The Impact of China's Millennium Labor Restructuring Program on Firm Performance and Employee Earnings*, 16 ECON. OF TRANSITION 223 (2008).

[17] The following discussion draws on Clarke, *supra* note 14, at 497–500, and the references cited therein.

or enterprise managers, they are not owners, and therefore pose the same principal-agent problems that arise whenever managers are not owners.

Thus, the problem with the cure is that it sees the separation of ownership and control as a benefit to be actively pursued, not as a cost—a necessary cost, to be sure, inherent in any large undertaking—to be minimized. Dispersed shareholding is viewed as valuable for its own sake precisely because it is the opposite of the single-owner model that characterized, and allegedly contributed to the inefficiency of, the TSOE.

The second pathology that corporatization was supposed to cure was that of multiple objectives. Control over different aspects of the TSOE was lodged in different agencies, sometimes at different levels of government: one might be in charge of labor, another in charge of raw material supplies, another in charge of investment, and another in charge of sales. No one agency fully internalized the costs of its own decisions, and the agencies might therefore give conflicting orders; the Chinese literature of the time called this the problem of "too many mothers-in-law" (*popo duo*). Corporatization was intended to resolve this problem by reducing the powers of all supervising agencies to a single common denominator—shareholding—and reducing their interests to the single one of maximizing profits.

The third pathology that corporatization was supposed to cure was the absence of an effective principal to monitor the manager-agents within the SOE. The ultimate human principal at the top of a system of state ownership—the citizenry—is far too distant to play a meaningful role even in a perfectly democratic polity. Government officials, themselves agents of their superiors, did not seem to be doing the job, leading to the phenomenon labeled the "absent owner" (*suoyouzhe quewei*). Corporatization was intended to replace the feckless state owner with hard-nosed, profit-seeking shareholders who would hold management's feet to the fire.

The policy imperative of state ownership, however, means that no organizational measure by itself can solve this problem. If the new post-corporatization shareholders are state bodies or ultimately owned by state bodies, then the problem has simply reappeared in a different form and is no more soluble than before. Importantly, however, it is no *less* soluble than before, either: the state is, and always has been, capable of using its ownership power to establish incentive structures for its managers, and there is no reason that such incentive structures should be inherently less capable of motivating managers than the incentive structures in place in government bureaucracies, nonprofit organizations, and large corporations with dispersed ownership in the West.

China's first Company Law, passed in 1993 and effective in 1994, was a crucial part of SOE reform because it provided the organizational vehicle that was supposed to cure the ills attendant upon the traditional organizational form.[18] Nevertheless, it embodied a

[18] For typical statements to this effect, see, e.g., Hua Wenzhai 华文斋, "公司法"十年辩出是是非非 (The Rights and Wrongs of the Company Law Are Debated for Ten Years), 5 经营管理者 (Operations Manager) 51, 51 (1994); Wang Hongyi 王红一, "公司法"修订与国有企业公司制改革 (Revision of the Company Law and the Corporatization Reform of State-Owned Enterprises), 6 学术研究 (Acad. Res.) 89, 89 (2001).

fundamental paradox. Although it was passed with the avowed intention of imposing upon SOEs a new organizational form designed for the private sector, its equally avowed purpose was to serve not the private but the public sector. Thus, although it applied equally to all companies, public and private, it strongly bore the markings of its birth.

III. Examples of Blowback in Chinese Corporate Law

This section explores several ways in which the Company Law, both at the beginning and even to this day, reflects not private-sector but public-sector imperatives, and imposes them back upon private companies.

A. PREFERENCE FOR MANDATORY RULES OVER DEFAULT RULES

A corporate law regime oriented toward the private sector is distinguished by its aspiration to be more enabling than regulatory.[19] In other words, it seeks to provide a framework that is above all *useful* to people endeavoring to organize to carry on a business. Its rules, whether default or mandatory, are typically justified (correctly or not) by the need to reduce transaction costs and correct market failures—in other words, to do what the parties themselves would have done in their own interest but for the presence of certain obstacles to reaching agreement. Rules governing corporate behavior that cannot be so justified—for example, the obligation to pay taxes or refrain from anticompetitive conduct—typically are not part of corporate organizational law, but are instead considered completely different parts of the law.

The 1993 Company Law was clearly not designed to enable; its rules were almost uniformly mandatory. Why so? One answer can be found perhaps in political culture: the notion that private parties know better than government officials what is best for them, common in the stump speeches of American politicians, simply has no strong resonance in China. As the corporate law scholar Fang Liufang observed, "[t]he whole Company Law is pervaded with the attitude of 'making decisions on behalf of the people.' The legislator shows an excessive self-confidence. It believes it is more intelligent than the parties and can make arrangements in their stead."[20]

A more important answer, however, probably lies in the SOE-centric nature of the 1993 Company Law. When lawmakers thought about companies being formed under the Company Law, they were not thinking about private parties attempting to contract among themselves for optimal governance rules. They were thinking instead of existing

---

[19] This section draws heavily on Clarke, *supra* note 14, at 500–501.

[20] Fang Liufang 方流芳, 温故知新—谈公司法修改 (Reviewing the Old to Understand the New: A Discussion of Reform of the Company Law), *in* 公司法修改纵横谈 (AN ALL-AROUND DISCUSSION OF REFORM OF THE COMPANY LAW) 35, 40 (Guo Feng 郭锋 & Wang Jian 王坚 eds., 2000).

TSOEs being reorganized into a new form. In such a situation, there *are* no contracting parties and there is no bargain; the reorganization process involves state bodies and takes place under state direction. Those involved are not strongly driven by market forces. Thus, it is understandable that lawmakers saw no particular merit in letting governance rules be the result of a "bargain" among "the parties." The rules dictated by the state might very possibly be less wasteful of state assets than whatever rules SOE managers and their supervisory officials might come up with if left to their own devices.

Even if we accept this logic, however, there is no reason the same rigidity should apply to private parties dealing with their own assets. As the sole or main shareholder in an SOE, the state may have an interest in uniform rules about dividend distributions[21] or the number of directors,[22] but it is hard to see why private parties should be subject to the same rules if they find them inconvenient.

Lawmakers have shown themselves capable of leaving a great deal to the discretion of participants in certain business enterprises when they wish to do so. The Partnership Law,[23] the Village and Township Enterprise Law,[24] and a set of regulations on stock cooperative enterprises[25] are much shorter than the Company Law and prescribe much less. It appears, therefore, that a major explanation for the mandatory orientation of the 1993 Company Law lies in its origins as a vehicle for SOE reform. As a result, instead of the intended effect—that SOEs should be governed by classical company law principles—we see the opposite effect: the entire corporate sector came under principles that make sense only in the state sector.

B. ACCESSIBILITY OF CORPORATE INFORMATION

Both the 1993 and the 2004 versions of the Company Law provide for a remarkable amount of openness of corporate information. Many jurisdictions around the world,

---

[21] *See* 中华人民共和国公司法 (The Company Law of the People's Republic of China) (adopted by the Standing Comm. Nat'l People's Cong. Dec. 29, 1993, effective July 1, 1994), Art. 177, *available at* http://www.law-lib.com/law/law_view.asp?id=96136 [hereinafter 1993 Company Law]. The 1993 Company Law was substantially amended in 2005. *See* 中华人民共和国公司法 (The Company Law of the People's Republic of China) (amended by the Standing Comm. Nat'l People's Cong. Oct. 27, 2005, effective Jan. 1, 2006), *available at* http://www.law-lib.com/law/law_view.asp?id=102906 [hereinafter 2005 Company Law]. There have been modest amendments since; the current version is available at http://www.law-lib.com/law/law_view.asp?id=445135 (last visited July 6, 2015).

[22] *See* 1993 Company Law, *supra* note 21, at Art. 112.

[23] 中华人民共和国合伙企业法 (Partnership Enterprise Law of the People's Republic China) (as amended by the Standing Comm. Nat'l People's Cong. Aug. 27, 2006, effective June 1, 2007), *available at* http://www.law-lib.com/law/law_view.asp?id=171393.

[24] 中华人民共和国乡镇企业法 (Village and Township Enterprise Law) (adopted by the Standing Comm. Nat'l People's Cong. Oct. 29, 1996, effective Jan. 1, 1997), *available at* http://www.law-lib.com/law/law_view.asp?id=313.

[25] 关于发展城市股份合作制企业的指导意见 (Guidance Opinion on the Development of Urban Stock Cooperative Enterprises) (promulgated by the State Comm'n on Reform of the Econ. Sys. Aug. 6, 1997, effective Aug. 6, 1997), *available at* http://www.law-lib.com/law/law_view.asp?id=65272.

of course, require publicly listed companies to disclose extensive amounts of information about their operations. What makes China different is the amount of disclosure required of *non*-public companies. It is as though the mere act of incorporating under the Company Law attaches a public character to a business enterprise and makes the internal operations of the firm the public's business.

Since 1985, extensive amounts of corporate information have had to be filed with the appropriate office of the State Administration for Industry and Commerce (SAIC).[26] Such information includes the amount of registered capital, the names of initial shareholders, the company's scope of business, and the company's articles of association.[27] The amount of information to be disclosed has grown over the years. Since 1994, this information has at least theoretically been available to the public; the relevant regulations stipulate that the company registration authority (the SAIC) should make company registration materials available to the public for review and copying.[28]

What is the thinking behind this policy? I believe it was intended as a measure for the regulation of privately owned companies, not SOEs. It is unlikely a coincidence that the requirement of public access entered the company registration regime in 1994, the year the first Company Law was promulgated, even though company registration had been around since 1985. Although the Company Law was indeed primarily aimed at promoting the reform of state-owned enterprises, it also opened the door much wider for the formation of private companies. In the view of officialdom, private companies need to be carefully monitored, and opening up their information to the public is one way of doing that. In short, openness of corporate information was part of the original design for privately owned firms and does not owe its existence to the logic of the state sector.

To be sure, this openness has sometimes proved to be more theoretical than real. To simply hand over information to any member of the public who asks for it runs utterly counter to the instincts of Chinese officialdom, and the SAIC seems to have developed an internal rule that those seeking corporate information must provide a justification that satisfies the SAIC office holding the information.[29] Nevertheless, David Barboza

---

[26] *See* 公司登记管理暂行规定 (Temporary Rules on the Administration of Company Registration) (promulgated by the State Admin. of Indus. and Commerce Aug. 25, 1985, effective Aug. 25, 1985), *available at* http://www.law-lib.com/law/law_view.asp?id=46832.

[27] *See* 公司登记管理条例 (Regulations on the Administration of Company Registration) (promulgated by the State Council June 24, 1994, effective July 1, 1994), Art. 9, *available at* http://www.law-lib.com/law/law_view1.asp?id=10525 [hereinafter 1994 Company Registration Regulations]; 公司登记管理条例 (Regulations on the Administration of Company Registration) (promulgated by the State Council Dec. 18, 2005, effective Jan. 1, 2006), Art. 9, *available at* http://www.law-lib.com/law/law_view.asp?id=123544 [hereinafter 2005 Company Registration Regulations].

[28] *See* 1994 Company Registration Regulations, *supra* note 27, at Art. 47; 2005 Company Registration Regulations, *supra* note 27, at Art. 57.

[29] According to a *Wall Street Journal* report,

> [t]he degree of access previously allowed to such documents is hazy. While rules issued in 2003 appeared to make data widely available, those who use it said the practice varied by region. According

of the *New York Times* reports that he was able to compile a great deal of information about the wealth of Wen Jiabao's family[30] through records publicly available at various offices of the SAIC.[31] Before the *New York Times* report, Bloomberg News had already published an equally sensational report on the wealth of the family of Chinese leader Xi Jinping, relying at least in part on publicly available documents.[32]

This openness changed abruptly in mid-2012. According to contemporary reports, while getting corporate documents from the SAIC had been simple in 2010 and 2011, it became progressively more difficult in the first half of 2012.[33] As both the Bloomberg and the *Times* reports were published after this crackdown, it is hard to attribute this change to a desire to protect information about leaders' families.[34] Instead, it seems more likely a response to a wave of unfavorable reports about Chinese companies, often generated by short sellers and based at least in part on information garnered from SAIC filings.[35] And it seems reasonable to suppose that the state was more concerned with the ability of firms in which the state held a stake to raise money and to survive a due diligence investigation by prospective business partners than with the ability of fully private firms to do likewise.

Because it is hard to understand the original policy of openness as anything other than an attempt to allow the public, on behalf of the state, to keep tabs on private corporate malefactors, it is equally hard to see the effectiveness of this policy as grounds for reversing it. Instead, it seems more likely that the unanticipated event leading to the reversal of the policy of openness was its effect on *state-associated* corporate malefactors.

> to a statement from Beijing SAIC, lawyers are allowed to access the documents if they are involved in litigation and a court grants them permission, or if a company explicitly grants a third party access to their filings.

Dinny McMahon, *Beijing Dims the Lights on Data for Investors*, WALL ST. J., June 6, 2012, http://on.wsj.com/1rectQL.

[30] The results of his investigation appeared as David Barboza, *Billions in Hidden Riches for Family of Chinese Leader*, N.Y. TIMES, Oct. 25, 2012, http://nyti.ms/10qZ45S.

[31] *See* David Barboza, *David Barboza Answers Reader Questions on Reporting in China*, N.Y. TIMES, Oct. 29, 2012, http://nyti.ms/10GSdCS:

> After having some luck with my initial requests for corporate registration documents from the State Administration for Industry and Commerce bureaus, I went on a reporting spree: requesting and paying fees for the records of dozens of investment partnerships tied to the relatives of Wen Jiabao . . . S.A.I.C. records are open to the public [and] are invaluable sources of information about private companies.

[32] *See* Michael Forsythe et al., *Xi Jinping Millionaire Relations Reveal Fortunes of Elite*, BLOOMBERG NEWS, June 29, 2012, http://bloom.bg/10roD3E.

[33] *See* McMahon, *supra* note 29.

[34] Hard but not impossible; it could of course be that the government learned through intelligence sources that the articles were forthcoming well before their publication. For various reasons, I think this is unlikely.

[35] *See* McMahon, *supra* note 29.

C. SHAREHOLDER LAWSUITS AGAINST COMPANY AND MANAGEMENT IN SECURITIES LAW

An important part of the private corporate law regime that China imported is the institution of shareholder rights, and in particular the right to sue the company and its management for various acts of malfeasance. Note that a right to sue corporate management *in one's capacity as shareholder* is not very important to a controlling shareholder; a controller can use its control to dismiss a misbehaving manager and to cause the company to sue him or her for any actionable wrongs, and so does not need standing as a shareholder. Moreover, non-controlling but substantial minority shareholders have adequate incentives to protect themselves by contract. To view a shareholder's statutory right to sue as important, then, is implicitly to contemplate a corporate ownership landscape in which passive, dispersed stock ownership is widespread and in need of protection. And passive, dispersed stockholders are not state stockholders, who typically hold majority or at least controlling positions.

Shareholder rights to sue the company and management for losses caused by misleading disclosures were provided in both the original 1998 version of the Securities Law[36] and its 2005 revision.[37] But when shareholders actually started using these provisions to sue listed companies and their management, the state, in the person of the Supreme People's Court (SPC), essentially panicked and called everything off. In a series of documents issued between 2001 and 2003,[38] the SPC first barred such lawsuits outright, then gradually opened the door, ending up with a rule that required prior government action against alleged wrongdoers before shareholders could have standing to sue over the same offense.[39]

---

[36] *See* 中华人民共和国证券法 (Securities Law of the People's Republic of China) (adopted by the Standing Comm. Nat'l People's Cong. Dec. 29, 1998, effective July 1, 1999), http://www.law-lib.com/law/law_view.asp?id=463 [hereinafter 1998 Securities Law], Art. 63.

[37] *See* 中华人民共和国证券法 (Securities Law of the People's Republic of China) (amended by the Standing Comm. Nat'l People's Cong. Oct. 27, 2005, effective Jan. 1, 2006), Art. 69, *available at* http://www.law-lib.com/law/law_view.asp?id=102905 [hereinafter 2005 Securities Law]. There have been a few modest revisions since 2005.

[38] *See* 最高人民法院关于涉证券民事赔偿案件暂不予受理的通知 (Notice on Temporarily Not Accepting Civil Compensation Cases Involving Securities) (promulgated by Sup. People's Ct. Sept. 21, 2001, effective Sept. 21, 2001), *available at* http://www.law-lib.com/law/law_view.asp?id=16373 (repealed as superseded in 2013); 最高人民法院关于受理证券市场因虚假陈述引发的民事侵权纠纷案件有关问题的通知 (Notice on Questions Relating to the Acceptance of Civil Tort Dispute Cases Arising Out of False Representations in Securities Markets) (promulgated by Sup. People's Ct. Jan. 15, 2002, effective Jan. 15, 2002), *available at* http://www.law-lib.com/law/law_view.asp?id=16956; 最高人民法院关于审理证券市场因虚假陈述引发的民事赔偿案件的若干规定 (Several Rules on the Adjudication of Civil Compensation Cases Arising Out of False Representations in Securities Markets) (promulgated by Sup. People's Ct. Jan. 9, 2003, effective Jan. 9, 2003), *available at* http://www.law-lib.com/law/law_view.asp?id=42438.

[39] For more details, see Donald C. Clarke, *Law Without Order in Chinese Corporate Governance Institutions*, 30 Nw. J. Int'l L. & Bus. 131, 183 (2010); Nicholas C. Howson, *Corporate Law in the Shanghai People's Courts, 1992–2008: Judicial Autonomy in a Contemporary Authoritarian State*, 5 E. Asia L. Rev. 303, 401–04 (2010); Hui Huang, *Private Enforcement of Securities Law in China: A Ten-Year Retrospective and Empirical Assessment*, 61 Am. J. Comp. L. 757, 760–61.

What was behind these second thoughts about shareholder rights? Zhiwu Chen, on the basis of interviews with SPC judges, suggests a reason directly linked to the logic of state capitalism: a fear that successful lawsuits could bring losses to the state in its capacity as controlling shareholder of corporate defendants.[40]

Nicholas Howson suggests two other reasons.[41] First, shareholder lawsuits against listed companies presented the Chinese state with the specter of organized mass action, even if only in the form of a group of plaintiff shareholders. Such organized mass action has always been anathema to the state. Second, shareholder lawsuits made defendants out of powerful political actors, whether SOEs themselves or their executives and controlling shareholders. Such actors are influential in the political system, and it is not surprising to see rules develop or change in order to protect their interests.

Can this development be attributed to the logic of state capitalism? Not completely, but certainly to a degree. Let me address two possible counterarguments. First, it could be argued that the Chinese state fears mass litigation by shareholders of any listed company, not just listed companies with strong connections to the state. This is certainly true. Yet there appears to be a state policy of discouraging shareholder litigation against all listed companies whether or not the litigation involves, actually or even potentially, large numbers of shareholders. The first widely known shareholder lawsuit for misleading disclosures, the Hongguang Industries case of 1998, was brought by a lone shareholder and yet was still rejected by the court.[42] And derivative lawsuits involving listed companies, while certainly affecting the shareholders of those companies, in no way involve large numbers of shareholders getting organized, and yet appear to be subject to the same informal bar.[43]

Second, it could be argued that preventing lawsuits against people and companies with good political connections is not uniquely connected with the logic of state capitalism; private companies could be driving such developments as well. We have seen precisely this phenomenon in the United States, where corporate executives descended on state legislatures in the wake of the 1980s' hostile takeover binge and persuaded some of them to enact so-called "constituency statutes" that allowed management to fend off unwanted suitors on almost any pretext.[44]

---

[40] *See* Zhiwu Chen, *Capital Markets and Legal Development: The China Case*, 14 CHINA ECON. REV. 451, 465 (2003).

[41] *See* Howson, *supra* note 39, at 405–06.

[42] The case is discussed in detail in *id.* at 403–04.

[43] Nicholas Howson and I discuss this extensively in Donald C. Clarke & Nicholas C. Howson, *Derivative Actions in the People's Republic of China, in* THE DERIVATIVE ACTION IN ASIA: A COMPARATIVE AND FUNCTIONAL APPROACH 243, 275–78 (Dan W. Puchniak et al. eds., 2012).

[44] *See, e.g.*, Henry N. Butler, *Corporation-Specific Anti-Takeover Statutes and the Market for Corporate Charters*, 1988 WISC. L. REV. 365; Roberta Romano, *The Political Economy of Takeover Statutes*, 73 VA. L. REV. 111 (1987); and other sources cited in Gilson et al., *supra* note 12, at 2011 n.160. A typical formulation is Pennsylvania's, which states:

> In discharging the duties of their respective positions, the board of directors, committees of the board and individual directors of a domestic corporation may, in considering the best interests of the

Yet the fact remains that China's listed companies and their management, the beneficiaries of this limitation on lawsuits, *are* dominated by state interests, and that the Western model of governance in privately owned corporations, *as it was imagined by those who favored importing it*, involved extensive shareholder rights to sue. Moreover, in the Western model of corporate governance *as actually practiced* (and not just in theory), there is room for significant pushback against the forces trying to restrict shareholder rights. Constituency statutes never made it past the Delaware legislature, for example; presumably the plaintiffs' bar and institutional shareholders were able to out-lobby management. In the state capitalist model of corporate governance, however, the lawmaker is not neutral; it will always favor state interests. Thus, what might be a contested battle in a private corporate governance regime becomes a rout under state capitalism.

D. THE DOCTRINE OF THE PRIMACY OF SHAREHOLDER INTERESTS

The tale of the doctrine of the primacy of shareholder interests in China is not a simple one, but its meanderings demonstrate if nothing else the sometimes counterintuitive results of heavy state involvement in corporate governance.

Although many corporate law scholars might wish it were otherwise, it is hard to make the case that as an empirical matter, American state courts hold corporate management to a duty of maximizing shareholder value. First, more than thirty states, often in response to lobbying by management of local corporations, have passed constituency statutes that allow management to consider non-shareholder interests.[45] Second, even in Delaware, which has rejected a constituency statute, management is afforded wide discretion through both the business judgment rule and an influential discourse that categorizes the maximization of share prices as a catering to short-termism, thus allowing management to pursue a wide range of goals with uncertain effect on share price. Thus, the practical import of the applicable corporate law doctrines is simply that managers must never *admit* to having a primary goal other than shareholder wealth maximization.

The norm that does and should prevail in U.S. corporate law is still hotly debated among scholars,[46] and one may reasonably doubt that those in China who advocated the

---

corporation, consider the effects of any action upon employees, upon suppliers and customers of the corporation and upon communities in which offices or other establishments of the corporation are located, and all other pertinent factors.

15 PA. CONS. STAT. ANN. § 516 (West 2014).

[45] *See* Anthony Bisconti, *The Double Bottom Line: Can Constituency Statutes Protect Socially Responsible Corporations Stuck in Revlon Land?*, 42 LOY. L.A. L. REV. 765, 768 n.13 (2009).

[46] The literature on this topic is too vast to cite in full. Among the contributions to the debate are LYNN STOUT, THE SHAREHOLDER VALUE MYTH: HOW PUTTING SHAREHOLDERS FIRST HURTS INVESTORS, CORPORATIONS AND THE PUBLIC (2012); Stephen Bainbridge, *Director Primacy: The Means and Ends of Corporate Governance*, 97 NW. U. L. REV. 547 (2003); Gordon Smith, *The Shareholder*

importing of Western (and specifically U.S.) corporate law norms were aware of this debate. Remarkably, however, the logic of state capitalism has put its weight firmly on one side of the debate: the side favoring primacy of shareholder rights.

Recall the history of corporatization in China. We begin with a view that the problem with SOEs lies with the failure to separate ownership from management. The state owns and the state manages; SOEs are inefficient; many Western corporations have passive stockholders who "own" but do not manage; those corporations are able to operate efficiently; therefore, China should separate ownership from management to achieve those same efficiencies.

I have discussed elsewhere[47] the fallacy of this diagnosis: because management is done by human beings, the state in China never could or did manage even while it owned. Therefore, the separation of ownership from management, being a necessary feature of any large business where the managers are not rich enough to own the assets, cannot possibly be the solution to the pathologies of state ownership. Nevertheless, the notion that the separation of management from ownership is an affirmatively good thing to be sought, and not a problem to be managed, persists strongly in Chinese corporate law.[48]

While "interference" by state bodies in SOE operations is decried, at the same time it appears to be widely accepted that enterprises with substantial state ownership should operate in the interests of the state shareholder. There is no Chinese Lynn Stout or Martin Lipton actively taking up the cudgel on behalf of the class of SOE managers and arguing that they should be given maximum discretion to serve the interests of multiple stakeholders instead of focusing narrowly on shareholder interests.[49] Thus, if the state shareholder wants profits, then that should be the goal of the corporation. The maximization of shareholder utility is not just legitimate; it is politically praiseworthy because it strengthens the state.

A special Chinese twist in the doctrine of shareholder primacy appears here, however: it is *not* the same thing as maximization of share value. If that is what the state shareholder wants, then there is no divergence. But if the state shareholder wants the SOE to pursue other goals, then the SOE may do so.[50]

Primacy Norm, 23 J. CORP. L. 277 (1998). *See also* Haskell Murray, *Benefit Corporations: Traditional Paradigm*, THE CONGLOMERATE, May 3, 2012, http://www.theconglomerate.org/2012/05/benefit-corporations-corporate-purpose.html (blog post and comments by several corporate law scholars discussing the shareholder wealth maximization norm).

[47] *See* Clarke, *supra* note 7.

[48] *See, e.g.*, Jiang Ping 江平,《公司法》立法前后的争论 (The Debate Before and After the Passing of the Company Law), 18 中国经济周刊 (CHINA ECON. WEEKLY) 55, 57 (2003).

[49] *See* Margaret Blair & Lynn Stout, *A Team Production Theory of Corporate Law*, 85 VA. L. REV. 247 (1999); Martin Lipton, *Takeover Bids in the Target's Boardroom*, 35 BUS. LAW. 101 (1979). Lynn Stout is a corporate law scholar well known for her vigorous defense of management prerogatives; Martin Lipton is famous as an attorney specializing in takeover defenses.

[50] *See* Tong Shenghui 同生辉 & Li Chuntao 李春涛, 上市国企与民企公司治理的异同 (Differences and Similarities in Corporate Governance in Listed State-Owned Enterprises and Privately Owned Enterprises), 4 中国金融 (CHINA FIN.) 76, 76 (2011) (viewing this phenomenon with regret but not denying its existence).

Take, for example, a report that in 2008, the China Insurance Regulatory Commission ordered China's insurance companies[51] to buy more shares of other companies in order to prop up the stock market.[52] If such purchases were a good investment, it would not be necessary to order the companies to make them. Thus, we may assume that the companies acted in a way that they knew would not maximize shareholder wealth. In other cases, SOE resources may be used in the service of social goals such as full employment, or political goals such as gatekeeping for foreign films.[53]

Are directors who cause the company to operate in non-wealth-maximizing ways in order to serve state interests in violation of any duty to other shareholders? Probably not. There is support for the idea that state-appointed directors have loyalties and responsibilities different from those of directors representing private interests. (Note that this acknowledgement of a need for separate, state-specific standards is an exception to the general theme of this chapter.) This is the position taken by corporate law scholar Dong Shi, who suggests that state-appointed directors may act to protect the interests of employees and consumers.[54] Or consider the statement of the dean of the Changjiang School of Business, who served as an independent director:

> I have never thought that the independent director is the protector of medium and small shareholders; never think that. My job is first and foremost to protect the interests of the large shareholder, because the large shareholder is the state.[55]

A subtle echo of this point can perhaps also be found in the defense offered by a corporate manager in the Nanjing Ningken Taxi Company case. Accused of wrongfully causing a subsidiary of which he was the manager and legal representative to enter into

---

[51] The companies in question included China's three largest insurers: China Life, Ping An, and China Pacific. China Life is 68.37 percent owned by China Life Insurance (Group) Company, which in turn is 100 percent owned by the Ministry of Finance. Four state-owned companies own a little more than 37 percent of China Pacific, and there is likely more indirect state ownership as well. The biggest single shareholder (direct or indirect) in Ping An is reported by the company to be Charoen Pokphand Group Company Limited, a Thai conglomerate, holding a 13.51 percent share directly and indirectly.

[52] *See* Jamil Anderlini, *Beijing Urges Insurers to Buy into Ailing Markets*, FIN. TIMES, Oct. 29, 2008, http://tinyurl.com/ljdt8ww.

[53] *See* Julia Qin, *Pushing the Limits of Global Governance: Trading Rights, Censorship and WTO Jurisprudence—A Commentary on the China-Publications Case*, 10 CHINESE J. INT'L LAW 271 (2011) (noting that for various reasons China chose to exercise import control over foreign films not through explicit governmental action, but instead by giving an SOE a monopoly over the right to import them).

[54] *See* Dong Shi 董轼, 三问国企派出董事: 国企派出董事制度是我国国有企业公司治理建设中最具特色的内容之一 (Three Questions About Dispatched Directors in SOEs: The System of Dispatched Directors in SOEs Is One of the Most Unique Elements in the Construction of Corporate Governance in China's SOEs), 4 董事会 (BOARD OF DIRECTORS) 74, 74 (2009). Dong is a scholar at the China Institute for Development and Reform at the Central University of Finance and Economics.

[55] 独立董事象花瓶？ (Are Independent Directors Just Decorative?), 港澳信息日报 (Hong Kong-Macao News Daily), Jan. 1, 2003.

a contract with the state-owned parent that had appointed him, he argued that he was essentially an administrator in charge of managing state assets.[56]

It should be noted that this twist in the doctrine of shareholder primacy is not universally accepted. A senior Chinese official recently offered a full-throated affirmation of a simple principle long rejected by Delaware courts and Chinese policymakers alike: that the goal of state-controlled listed companies was (or should be) to maximize shareholder interests, and that the specific way to do that was to maximize the share price.[57]

E. POWER OF EMPLOYEES TO SUPERVISE MANAGEMENT

In a private company, how managers are supervised and agency costs reduced is largely a matter for participants in the corporate enterprise to work out for themselves. There is no critical public interest involved if shareholders of a given company are unable to control, for example, management's paying excessive salaries to itself.[58]

Matters are different when a major shareholder is the state. In that case, the cost of waste is borne by the state to the extent of its proportionate stake in the company. One might think that if the state were a major shareholder, monitoring would be enhanced and agency costs reduced; while a 1 percent shareholder has no incentive to spend more than $1 to achieve a $100 reduction in agency costs such as excessive compensation, a 75 percent shareholder would spend up to $75 to do so. Yet it is a commonplace in Chinese corporate governance literature that the state is often an absent, or at least inattentive, owner. Management can waste vast sums of money on itself because nobody is watching.

This problem is often attributed to information asymmetry: management typically knows a lot more than a shareholder about what goes on inside the company. Of course, such asymmetry is not unique to cases in which the state is a shareholder. What is special

---

[56] *See* 南京宁垦出租汽车有限公司与王爱平赔偿纠纷上诉案 (Appeal in the Compensation Dispute between the Nanjing Ningken Taxi Company and Wang Aiping) (Nanjing Intermed. People's Ct., June 20, 2013), http://www.pkulaw.cn/fulltext_form.aspx?Db=pfnl&Gid=119473097. Regrettably (in terms of clarifying this issue), the court found for the defendant on other grounds and did not really evaluate this argument.

[57] *See* 宋志平：四举措做好国有控股上市公司市值管理 (Song Zhiping: Four Measures for Good Management of the Market Capitalization of Listed Companies Controlled by the State), 中国新闻网 (China News Net), June 10, 2014, http://finance.chinanews.com/cj/2014/06-10/6262939.shtml. For Delaware's rejection of share price as the maximand at any given time, see Paramount Communications v. Time, Inc., 571 A.2d 1140, 1150 (Del. 1990) ("[a]bsent a limited set of circumstances, a board of directors . . . is not under any per se duty to maximize shareholder value in the short term").

[58] Note that in the United States, whether this is an appropriate subject for government regulation is debated only in the public company context, and even there only in the realm of procedures governing shareholder participation in compensation decisions. State corporate law has essentially nothing to say about executive compensation provided it does not rise to the level of what can unambiguously be called waste, a case-specific standard—and even that standard can be viewed as simply an implied element of the private agreement between shareholders and management not to give away corporate assets in return for nothing of value.

about the state shareholding context is that it is impossible to have any ultimate human principal (other than in the most abstract sense of "the citizenry") at the top of a pyramid of agents. Officials in the state shareholding body generally have no personal incentive to monitor well.

Under the circumstances, one favored solution has been to enhance employee monitoring.[59] This could be especially necessary where management is not expected to maximize profits, because the lack of an easily measured goal exacerbates the problem of information asymmetry. The institution through which such monitoring would presumably take place is the Board of Supervisors, at least one-third of the members of which must be employee representatives. But because the Board of Supervisors was given a function but no real incentives or powers to exercise that function, it is universally recognized to be an institutional failure.

In a private company, this failure would make no difference. After all, the Board of Supervisors is elected by the same body that elects the Board of Directors, and whoever controls elections to the latter will also control elections to the former. If the controlling shareholder feels the need to appoint a special group of people to monitor its elected directors, it can always do so on its own and does not need authorization from the Company Law.

The problem, of course, is that the state controlling shareholder is not exercising its supervisory power diligently. Thus, the response of lawmakers has been to try to strengthen the Board of Supervisors by giving it more tools to hold management to account. The 2005 revisions to the Company Law did this—not just for state-owned companies, but for all companies. This imposes organizational complexity on companies for whom the costs are far greater than the benefits. But the ideology of a unified corporate law regime meant that a special rule applicable only to companies with a significant state stake could not be promulgated.

Indeed, so enthusiastic have state authorities become about the Board of Supervisors that even foreign-invested enterprises are required to have one, although they are formed under an entirely different set of laws and not organized under the Company Law.[60]

---

[59] *See, e.g.*, Hong Gongxiang 洪功翔 & Zhou Shijun 周世军, 经营者监督约束与国有企业公司治理 (Supervision and Constraints on Management and Corporate Governance in SOEs), 6 理论探讨 (Theoretical Investigations) 67, 70 (2010).

[60] The theory justifying this is that the Company Law can be used to fill gaps where other laws of business organization are silent, and indeed the laws on joint ventures and wholly foreign-owned enterprises say nothing about a Board of Supervisors. One might interpret this silence as meaning that the laws affirmatively reject any form of organization other than the one they specifically prescribe, and that the silence is therefore not a gap to be filled, but that interpretation apparently does not have traction in China.

F. BENIGN BLOWBACK

The general theme of this chapter has been that it is a bad thing for the logic of state capitalism to infect corporate law doctrine applying to privately owned firms. But this is not always so. Sometimes lawmakers, suspicious that some doctrine or institution of corporate law might give private actors a dangerous degree of freedom to commit fraud or other antisocial acts, have allowed it only in the state sector where it can operate under proper supervision, as it were. Having lodged in the state sector, however, such a doctrine or institution has later spread into the private corporate law regime.

Consider single-shareholder companies. The original Company Law prohibited single-shareholder companies unless the single shareholder was a state-authorized entity. The 2005 revision to the Company Law, however, allowed any natural or legal person to establish a single-shareholder company.[61] This is an example of benign blowback. The no-single-shareholder rule is a relic of nineteenth-century Western thinking about corporate law. It is easily evaded by the expedient of bringing in a second shareholder to hold a minute equity stake with essentially no economic or voting interest in the company. It is hard to see any worthy policy purpose that is furthered by allowing the second type of company but prohibiting single-shareholder companies. Apparently policymakers, having experimented with single-shareholder companies in the state sector, have come around to this view.

V. Conclusion

There is, and probably always will be, legitimate debate in the corporate law world over the proper mix of mandatory rules and default rules alterable at will by participants in the corporate enterprise. But there is probably little debate over the idea that imposing rules suitable and perhaps even necessary for SOEs upon privately owned firms creates costs—the inefficiencies of organizational rigidity—without a countervailing gain. Those costs, however, are difficult to measure.

One way of avoiding those costs is to simply abandon the self-imposed imperative of a unified corporate governance regime. Principles appropriate to SOEs can be freely applied to SOEs without worry about leakage into the non-SOE sector. This policy choice, however, has its own costs. First, of course, it gives up the hoped-for disciplining effect of subjecting SOEs to private-firm governance principles. But I believe this cost is small, because the disciplining effect has never been large in the first place: the rules always seem to get changed when the disciplining effect begins to have bite. Moreover, state policymakers retain the ability to apply private-sector governance rules when

[61] Natural persons may establish only one such company, however, and that company may not itself establish a single-shareholder company.

appropriate; the difference from a unified regime is that they must make conscious choices about which rules make sense for SOEs and which do not—not obviously a bad thing.

Second, a two-track approach requires a reliable way of determining when an enterprise should count as an SOE and thus be subject to a special set of governance rules. Establishing an ownership threshold is not a completely satisfactory solution, because the state's interest is not necessarily manifested in, or exercised through, stock ownership, particularly in a state capitalist regime.[62] Furthermore, a two-track approach that explicitly identified a large number of SOEs as such could cause difficulties for China in its foreign economic relations, because such firms would be easy targets for dumping or subsidies complaints from foreign firms or trade partners, as well as opposition when attempting foreign acquisitions.

That there is no good solution to the problem of blowback in a sense reflects some of the inherent dilemmas of state ownership of commercial firms. With its self-imposed imperative of being an owner in certain firms or sectors, the state, while seeking an economic return, has renounced economic return as the sole standard for determining where it shall invest. Moreover, it has abandoned the Wall Street Rule (i.e., complete divestiture) as a way of dealing with governance problems in most of the firms in which it has invested. This means that it must retain its ability to influence even firms in which it is a minority shareholder, and that has consequences for corporate law as it governs firms with state investment. It is simply impossible to have the state corporate sector governed by exactly the same rules that govern the private corporate sector.

[62] See Curtis J. Milhaupt and Wentong Zheng, Chapter 9 in this volume.

3 Protecting the State from Itself?

REGULATORY INTERVENTIONS IN CORPORATE GOVERNANCE AND THE FINANCING OF CHINA'S "STATE CAPITALISM"

Nicholas Calcina Howson

Introduction

Many observers assume that the "state capitalism" model of the People's Republic of China (PRC) implicates relatively unfettered control of listed subsidiary corporations by the agents of the PRC Party-state, whether direct state equity owners, state-affiliated holding companies (or groups), or the *nomenklatura*-origin individuals appointed or elected to the Chinese Communist Party committee, board, supervisory board, or senior management of such firms. This assumption may not be entirely accurate. Instead, the China Securities Regulatory Commission (CSRC) and other bureaucratic agencies have for many years imposed mandatory governance constraints on a formally shareholder-oriented and "enabling" law-based corporate governance system, with the express goal of empowering minority shareholders and constraining the power and discretion of the PRC's strongest political-economic actors under the state capitalism model.[1]

[1] *See* Nicholas Calcina Howson, *"Quack Corporate Governance" as Traditional Chinese Medicine—The Securities Regulation Cannibalization of China's Corporate Law and a State Regulator's Battle against Party State Political Economic Power*, 37 SEATTLE U. L. REV. 667 (2014).

This chapter reviews the structural reasons for this sustained intervention, and speculates as to how and why one tentacle of the Party-state—the CSRC—has been permitted to implement this constraining mechanism on other, far more powerful tentacles of the same political-economic structure: corporatized state-owned enterprises (SOEs). I conclude with thoughts on how these constraints and enhanced accountability mechanisms contribute in a significant way to the financing, and thus the continuing viability, of China's state capitalism.

I. A "Mandatory" Regulatory Intervention into the Province of "Enabling" Law

China's public company regulators have over the past two decades consistently acted to create, re-craft, or anticipate the most fundamental aspects of the PRC's formal legal corporate governance system, and to institute robust board-related and/or minority shareholder-empowering norms designed to protect against controlling shareholder oppression or malfeasance. The CSRC has historically made these incursions via two distinct methods: (1) the filling-in of substantive corporate law doctrines that still have to be enforced by a state actor, whether the judiciary or a regulator (e.g., corporate fiduciary duties); and (2) the establishment of "self-enforcing" mechanisms designed to be effective as between the parties to a firm before the state or any external actor needs to be involved in enforcement, if at all (e.g., minority shareholder "class" negative veto rights). These interventions include, inter alia:

- Corporate fiduciary duties for orthodox fiduciaries and even controlling shareholders, in both the operational and takeover contexts;
- Supermajority approval/negative veto mechanisms empowering so-called "public" shareholders;
- Supermajority approval (and/or controlling shareholder recusal) and supermajority director approval (and/or director recusal) for controlling shareholder related-party transactions and self-dealing;
- Independent directors; and
- Broad shareholder "class" negative veto rights (even when shareholder classes were prohibited).[2]

I should emphasize that the self-enforcing genus of regulatory intervention, which can be effective without recourse to enforcement by any external institution, is far more likely to be effective given the structure of China's political economy. For example, if there is concern about the political and economic power of the Party-state's controlling shareholders,

[2] *Id.* at 677–84.

or doubts about the competence, autonomy, and independence of the Chinese judiciary, the implantation of substantive corporate fiduciary duties into China's company law is not likely to have much effect, because articulation and enforcement of these norms may be frustrated by the phenomena animating the reform in the first place. Conversely, a self-enforcing mechanism such as the negative veto rights conferred on non-controlling shareholders for approval of related-party "external" guarantees forced out of listed companies constitutes a very effective constraint for the identified abuse, especially when compared to reliance on any doctrinal fill-in such as a vague and unevenly applied duty of loyalty standard applied ex post. Indeed, the real effectiveness of such self-enforcing mechanisms was seen in the run-up to the China National Offshore Oil Corporation (CNOOC) bid for Unocal (where the independent directors blocked a Unocal-invited bid), and in the bid by Singapore Airlines for a controlling stake in China Eastern Airlines (vetoed by a class vote).[3]

II. The Consequences of Corporatization without Privatization

Why has the CSRC been obligated to execute this regulatory intervention? The answer to that question lies in the PRC's two decades-old "corporatization without privatization" program and resultant state capitalism, the commitment in Chinese corporate law to what is called "shareholder primacy," and the development of China's broader political economy.

"Corporatization" as commenced in the 1980s sought to implement a "modern enterprise system," by abolishing the traditional SOE as an organizational form[4] and converting SOEs into a legal form of "company" authorized and governed by PRC company law. These organizational forums include: (1) a company limited by shares (CLS), a joint stock company form for widely held firms; (2) a limited liability company (LLC), for a smaller and closely knit group of investors; or (3) a wholly state-owned sub-form of the LLC, a company owned by a state agency with no shareholders' meeting and an optional board of directors. The modern enterprise system would thus create and empower a new class of property rights owners in the PRC, namely equity shareholders.

Critically, that process of corporatization did not implicate "privatization" of the Chinese economy generally or SOEs individually, or any real withdrawal from the economy of the state or the Communist Party. This is because a controlling equity interest in the SOE or state-owned asset groups converted into a company was maintained by state

[3] *See* Nicholas C. Howson, *China's Acquisitions Abroad—Global Ambitions, Domestic Effects*, 48 Law Quadrangle Notes 73, 78, 83–84 (2006) (regarding the CNOOC directors' vote initially blocking the proposed CNOOC bid); Barry Naughton, *SASAC and Rising Corporate Power in China*, 24 China Leadership Monitor 1 (2007) (regarding the veto rendered by China Eastern Airlines' "H" shareholders).

[4] The SOE was not given a *legal* form until 1988, which saw the promulgation of a "law" governing SOEs—concurrent, ironically, with the elimination of the SOE as an organizational form.

entities, and party committees remained important actors behind the formal governance structures required by the corporate form.[5] To the present day, the Party-state remains absolutely committed to retaining control over converted asset groups and enterprises in a very broad range of sectors—not just the usual suspects for state control (e.g., defense, natural resources, key infrastructure) but also non-national security and non-key infrastructure sectors that promise high returns to central or local state or party insiders when financed with the aid of passive public investors.

Moreover, it appears that the corporatization without privatization program was motivated by desires very similar to those which animated late nineteenth-century Qing dynasty attempts to engage in "state (court) capitalism" via establishment of *guandu shangban* ("government promoted/supervised, merchant operated") and later *guanshang heban* ("government-merchant co-operated") entities such as the China Merchant Steamships Company (*lunchuan zhaoshangju*), the Kaiping Mining Company, the Shanghai Cotton Cloth Mill, and the Jiangnan Arsenal (*jiangnan jiqi zhizao zongju*)—all attempts to reorder state-owned asset groupings into a new, "modern," and "Western" form that could attract passive capital investment from the domestic and global capital markets, without ceding any real governance power over the subject businesses.[6] At least in this regard, the PRC has been fabulously successful, as corporatized SOEs perceived as the mainstays of China's state capitalism model—still absolutely controlled by the Party-state or state holding companies—bring off some of the largest IPOs in history and are included among the world's largest firms by market capitalization.[7]

This design for corporatization without privatization, coupled with the maintenance of central or local state (and ultimately Communist Party) control, has affected both closely held LLC firms and widely held CLSs, with a pronounced effect on the ownership, control, and governance structures applicable to the PRC's listed companies and the disempowerment of those companies' public minority shareholders. First, the strong prevalence of concentrated ownership in Chinese companies, especially among listed firms, means that the key agency problem for PRC corporate governance is not *vertical* (between management insiders and a large body of disaggregated shareholders) but *horizontal* (between

---

[5] *See* Nicholas C. Howson, *China's Restructured Commercial Banks:* Nomenklatura *Accountability Serving Corporate Governance Reform?, in* China's Emerging Financial Markets: Challenges and Global Impact 123 (Zhu Min et al. eds., 2009) (detailing how party committees operate behind and exercise control over boards of directors at the PRC's largest international issuers).

[6] *See generally* Wellington K.K. Chan, Merchants, Mandarins and Modern Enterprise in Late Ch'ing China (1977); C.K. Lai, *The Qing State and Merchant Enterprise: The China Merchant's Company, 1872–1902, in* To Achieve Security and Wealth: The Qing Imperial State and the Economy, 1644–1911 139 (J.K. Leonard & J.R. Watts eds., 1991).

[7] For example, China National Petroleum (no. 4 on Fortune's 2014 Global 500), the State Grid (no. 7), Industrial and Commercial Bank of China (no. 25), China Construction Bank (no. 38), the Agricultural Bank of China (no. 47), China State Construction Engineering (no. 52), China Mobile (no. 55), etc. *See* Fortune's 2014 Global 500 (Jan. 13, 2015), http://fortune.com/global500/.

controlling shareholders and minority shareholders).[8] Second, the controlling shareholder and its insider appointees are not run-of-the-mill control parties/insiders, but instead are very often an identity of state or party organizations, representatives of central or local government institutions, or party *nomenklatura* appointments, giving them a heady mix of political and economic power, especially against disaggregated, non-politically privileged minority shareholders. Third, the combination of a strong horizontal agency problem, and the nature of the control parties, means that China's listed companies have been run as vehicles to attract passive investment from information-deprived public investors entirely in the interest of those largely unaccountable Party-state controlling shareholders. The same firms have therefore represented a ready invitation to opportunism, tunneling, minority shareholder exploitation and oppression, and outright fraud by the controlling shareholders and their appointed insiders—an invitation taken up with particular gusto at Chinese CLSs with a public float, subject to little monitoring by, or accountability to, passive, politically disempowered shareholders or thoroughly compromised judicial enforcement institutions.[9] Fourth, as addressed more than a decade ago by Donald Clarke,[10] this process of corporatization without privatization has led to a fundamental dilemma in the design and implementation of Chinese corporate governance and the legal structure supporting it: the state continues to operate enterprises in China and exercise control in furtherance of its goals, which, good or bad,[11] must be understood as distinct from the presumed narrower shareholder wealth maximization goal of other (minority) shareholders. Admittedly, the goals of the state control party and the minority shareholders may converge from time to time, in particular with respect to short-term shareholder gains. There is nothing in the corporatization program, however, or in the law, which requires the state control party to exercise its control in the service of wealth maximization for *all* shareholders in the firm. Thus, the state through its controlling shareholders in corporatized entities openly exercises an undiluted form of what (U.S.) Delaware jurisprudence has called the "right to selfish ownership," and

[8] The same problem has operated across the Taiwan Straits, in the Republic of China/Taiwan, and continues to elicit similar substantive law and institutional changes. *See* Christopher J. Guinello, *The Revision of Taiwan's Company Law: The Struggle toward a Shareholder-Oriented Model in One Corner of East Asia*, 28 Del. J. Corp. L. 75 (2003).

[9] *See* Y. Cheung, L. Jing, T. Lu, R. Rau & A. Stouraitis, *Tunneling and Propping Up: An Analysis of Related Party Transactions by Chinese Listed Companies*, 17 Pac. Basin Fin. J. 372 (2009); H. Berkman, R. Cole & L. Fu, *Expropriation through Loan Guarantees to Related Parties*, 33 J. Bank. & Fin. 141 (2009); G. Jiang, C. Lee & H. Yue, *Tunneling through Intercorporate Loans: The China Experience*, 98 J. Fin. Econ. 1 (2010); Nancy Huyghebaert & Lihong Wang, *Expropriation of Minority Investors in Chinese Listed Firms: The Role of Internal and External Corporate Governance Mechanisms*, 20 Corp. Gov. Int'l Rev. 308 (2012).

[10] *See* Donald C. Clarke, *Corporate Governance in China: An Overview*, 14 China Econ. Rev. 494, 494–95 (2003).

[11] The "goals" for which the state exercises its control rights can range from the assumed private interests of officials and cadres asked to represent "all of the people" or the state (much discussed in public governance literature) to various wider political or social imperatives (e.g., cross-subsidization of failing firms, full employment) that seem more benign, but still potentially operate to the detriment of external minority investors in a specific firm.

exploits the minority shareholders, who have no other way to benefit from their investment in the corporatized firm. As long as Chinese ideology and national industrial policy continue to sanction state shareholders controlling corporate entities where there are other shareholders, real protections for such other shareholders present either (1) a constraint on the state's ability to operate in a way that is the very reason the state has maintained control, or (2) a need for separate corporate law regimes for state-controlled corporatized firms, and nonstate controlled firms. There is no immediate prospect of a formal, separate legal regime for state-controlled firms. Indeed, the 1994 PRC Company Law, the 2006 PRC Company Law, and the "modern enterprise system" and corporatization policies were all proclaimed as major steps in the opposite direction—elimination of any distinction between state firms and nonstate controlled companies. Instead, the history of *non*-implementation/adjudication of China's company law with respect to public capital markets-financed and corporatized SOE issuers[12] indicates resistance to the idea of any constraint on, or accountability for, the Party-state's ability to operate subsidiary firms in the way it desires.[13]

III. Shareholder Primacy and Enabling Corporate Law in China: Enabling Exploitation of Minority Shareholders by the Party-State

Since 1994, China's corporate law has expressed fealty to a robust version of what scholars call a "shareholder primacy" model. Moreover, for the last decade China's company law has been made increasingly "enabling" as epitomized by the wholesale changes seen in the 2006 Company Law. Continued shareholder primacy and the increasingly enabling orientation of the corporate law and governance system, when coupled with the corporatization without privatization program, has resulted in something widely acknowledged as pernicious in China and abroad: the open and continued exploitation of minority shareholders in Chinese firms. This is the phenomenon that has made necessary the CSRC-imposed mandatory provisions discussed here.

---

[12] *See, e.g.*, Nicholas Calcina Howson, *Corporate Law in the Shanghai Courts, 1992–2008: Judicial Autonomy in a Contemporary Authoritarian State*, 5 Penn. E. Asia L. Rev. 303, 400–16 (2010); Donald C. Clarke & Nicholas Calcina Howson, *Pathway to Minority Shareholder Protection—Derivative Actions in the People's Republic of China, in* The Derivative Action in Asia: A Comparative and Functional pproach 243, 254–56, 267–69, 275–78 (Daniel Puchniak et al. eds., 2012) (noting the complete absence of widely held or listed company governance-related shareholder company law-related suits (other than securities law claims alleging fraudulent or misleading disclosure pursuant to a very limited allowance made under pressure by the PRC Supreme People's Court) in the Chinese courts, and the partially related hostility of the People's Courts to any cases involving a large number of parties, resulting in large parts of the PRC Company Law being left unimplemented).

[13] This is a nice example of the dilemma political scientist Mary Gallagher terms "authoritarian legality." *See* Mary Gallagher, Authoritarian Legality: Law, Workers, and the State (forthcoming 2016) (" . . . institutionalization brings the allure of constraints and rules on others while continued state-led control over deployment of these institutions provides opportunity for discretion and flexibility . . . This is one of the privileges (and dilemmas) of single-party regimes. It makes the rules; it doesn't necessarily bind itself to those rules.").

"Shareholder primacy" refers to a model of corporate law and governance that bestows significant formal governance power on firm shareholders, as the firm's ultimate owners, rather than the agents of those owners, the firm's directors and officers. In theory, shareholder primacy can appear justified because shareholders are the owners or stakeholders in the firm residual. Moreover, in a corporate ecology characterized by widely held firms and extensive separation of ownership and management, where there is concern about those agents acting in their own interest and not that of all the owners, any mechanism that can rein in those agents and make them accountable to the firm's owners seems advisable. Indicia of shareholder primacy include the power to elect members of the firm's centralized management body (the board of directors), to oust incumbent directors midstream with or without cause, and to vote on significant firm decisions. From this perspective, China's modern corporate law system represents a strong version of the shareholder primacy model, requiring for example that the general shareholders' meeting approve dividend distributions.

"Enabling" corporate laws are general corporation codes that provide something like a standard form contract structured around default provisions, with very few mandatory or immutable rules governing firm participants' internal rights and obligations or the firm's external activities. In most developed capitalist jurisdictions, corporate governance at specific firms is now determined by a mixed application of some default provisions left unchanged by the participants, specific arrangements crafted ex ante by the contracting out of other default rules, and extremely broad common law doctrines interpreted and enforced ex post by the judiciary when prodded by private shareholder plaintiffs (and, in the United States, their attorneys, working with the benefit of contingency fee arrangements and liberal cost-sharing/class action rules). Basic theories of the corporation have developed in parallel, from the eighteenth and nineteenth century idea that firms were a creation of the state pursuant to a specific legislative act, to the twentieth-century contractarian conception of the company as a creation of private contract. For many analysts, it is the *non*-mandatory, enabling character of corporate law that both defines and recommends it. Indeed, in the Anglo-American capitalist economies there is a bedrock confidence that private capital accumulates and will be efficiently allocated to useful projects through an infinite variety of complex and individualized arrangements regarding entity governance and investor rights, which arrangements are in turn determined by different levels of information availability, the value brought to the table by specific investors, and many other factors. Said another way, there is a strong belief in many of the developed capitalist economies that any attempt to significantly pattern or constrain those arrangements beyond what the public interest or basic accountability absolutely requires will impede realization of optimal privately negotiated arrangements and thus fatally dampen capital formation.[14]

---

[14] *See, e.g.*, Frank H. Easterbrook, *The Race for the Bottom in Corporate Governance*, 95 VA. L. REV. 685, 688 (2009) ("Corporate law came to be enabling rather than directory in the United States because that serves investors' interests, not because it serves managers' interest. States that adopt inefficient regulation propel capital out of their jurisdictions.")

In 1993–1994, the Chinese Communist Party-led government began its experiment with company lawmaking decidedly in the "mandatory" and not the "enabling" mode.[15] Indeed, that orientation was but a continuation of China's earliest conception of corporate law[16] and general approach to law (as "rule *by* law").[17] This in turn is consistent with the desire of the Chinese state (and before that, the Chinese imperial court) to control or closely monitor potentially independent capital accumulation and business activity, and benefit from it.[18] At the same time, China's first post-1949 corporate law held high the banner of shareholder primacy, putting significant formal power over directors, officers, or supervisors into the hands of shareholders. Without doubt, this was deemed permissible by PRC policymakers and legislators, and the promoters of what became state capitalism, because of the distinctive capital structure of corporatized SOEs described above—featuring a large, controlling shareholder with ties to the Party-state given full power to dominate the subsidiary firm directly as a shareholder or via a board of directors elected entirely by it.

Only with the passage of the 2006 Company Law did the PRC move away from a business regulation philosophy and toward an enabling statute—one that allows for increased contracting-out of default rules ex ante alongside continuing self-enforcing mechanisms, and that creates significant work for the judiciary applying standards ex post. This development in the direction of a formally enabling corporate law system has been celebrated widely in the PRC among academics and People's Court officials alike. For example, a 2007 commentary by the Shanghai Higher People's Court (regarding a 2003 case where the Shanghai No. 1 Intermediate People's Court had to choose between *statutory* rights of first refusal owed to existing shareholders and the rights of a good faith purchaser under a fraudulently approved securities purchase *contract*) appears to channel U.S. federal appellate judge and law and economics theorist Frank Easterbrook[19] directly:

> First and foremost, the thing we must clarify is this: the jurisprudential logic underlying the giving of priority to the [right of first refusal] over the purchase rights

[15] *See* Clarke, *supra* note 10, at 496, 500 (". . . and the [1994] Company Law is thus clearly more concerned with regulating and suppressing than with fostering and nurturing." . . . "The policy choice in the current [1994] Company Law is clear; the rules are almost uniformly mandatory.")

[16] *See* William C. Kirby, *China Unincorporated: Company Law and Business Enterprise in Twentieth-Century China*, 54 J. Asian Stud. 43 (1995).

[17] *See* Liang Zhiping, *Explicating "Law": A Comparative Perspective of Chinese and Western Legal Culture*, 3 Colum. J. Chinese L. 55, 61, 89 (1989).

[18] *See* Chan, *supra* note 6; Kirby, *supra* note 16, at 44 ("The history of this first modern Chinese [company] law is to some degree a barometer of the state's assumptions towards the economy over the course of the twentieth century . . . [T]he Chinese state would be the prime beneficiary of the adoption of the corporate form of business activity. But the first assumption of the [early-twentieth-century] Qing reformers, that the modern corporation on a Western model would be the essential vehicle for *private* Chinese economic development, would prove quite mistaken."); Madeleine Zelin, *The Firm in Early Modern China*, 71 J. Econ. Behav. & Org. 623 (2009).

[19] *See supra* note 14 and accompanying text.

> of the transferee is absolutely not because the former right is in statute and the latter is merely a contractual right. This is because statutory rights are not always superior to contractual rights—in fact, it is just the opposite. Approaching it systematically and *adhering to the orientation which protects private ordering, regulation of the market requires that application of the law fully respect the freedom to contract to encourage successful transactions* . . . There is significant meaning in this.[20]

Yet notwithstanding this rhetorical fealty to enabling corporate law, the mandatory norms imposed by the CSRC and other agencies discussed in this chapter (and the absorption of many of those regulatory mandates into the 2006 PRC Company Law)[21] have pushed the applied law of corporate governance in precisely the opposite direction.[22]

IV. Regulatory Intervention: Structural Exploitation, Legislative Competence, and the Judiciary

The pernicious implications of the corporatization without privatization program, coupled with an ever-more enabling and thus controlling shareholder-empowering corporate law, make the reasons for the CSRC's counter-strike obvious. Given lopsided capital structures and thoroughly dominated directorates and shareholders' meetings, not to mention the unconstrained political and economic power of state controlling shareholders (and their appointed insiders) and a radical information asymmetry between such controlling shareholders and diffuse public investors, an enabling company law design built on strong notions of shareholder primacy has been a broad invitation for dominant shareholders to oppress and exploit far weaker actors in the firm, especially where minority shareholders have very little power to bargain for information or effective

---

[20] Commentary regarding the case reported as "A. Investment Company v. Wang and Other Shareholders" (Shanghai No. 1 Intermediate People's Court, on appeal 2003), in 2005 年上海法院案例精选 (2005 SELECTION OF SHANGHAI COURT CASES) 106–09 (Shanghai Higher People's Court ed. 2007); with the quoted portion of the commentary *id.* at 111 (emphasis added).

[21] *See, e.g.*, 2006 PRC Company Law, art. 20 (fiduciary duties for controlling shareholders and an oppression remedy), art. 106 (cumulative voting, formally enabling but made mandatory by CSRC regulation and approval practice), art. 16 & 122 (cap on external guarantees, recusal of controlling shareholders on shareholder votes for such guarantees, and a supermajority vote for any such guaranty greater in value than 30 percent of corporate assets, or a majority of non-control shareholders; supermajority shareholder vote on disposition of significant assets), art. 123 (independent directors), art. 125 (recusal of conflicted directors), art.127 (allowance for different classes of shares and preferred shares), and art. 148 (fiduciary duties for orthodox corporate fiduciaries).

[22] Interestingly, my own research has shown how the Chinese People's Courts—contrary to some expectations and certainly the doctrinal rhetoric quoted from the *A. Investment Company v. Wang* case commentary above—have mimicked this trajectory, adjudicating some enabling provisions of the 1994 and 2006 PRC Company Laws as mandatory. *See* Howson, *supra* note 12, at 382–83.

protections, or obtain any price discount[23] to compensate for their disadvantageous position. Therefore, mandatory provisions—from whatever source—designed to protect the basic informational and governance rights of minority capital providers against such control parties were required.

Observers might respond that the remedy to this baked-in exploitation of minority property rights-holders should have been available from either the legislator or the court system. Certainly there was an effort in 2005 to create effective legal remedies for minority shareholders against politically powerful insiders and controlling shareholders via wholesale reformation of the defective 1994 PRC Company Law. This reform concretized CSRC regulatory mandates,[24] and added both substantive claims (e.g., duty of care, controlling shareholders' fiduciary duties, piercing of the corporate veil) and procedural innovations (e.g., a derivative action, the ability of shareholders to call special shareholders' meetings). However, China's developing legal system and the institutional status quo ante made clear that substantive legal change would not be enough, because of at least three additional factors. First, there have been and remain serious issues pertaining to the technical competence of legislators at the National People's Congress, especially with respect to complex fields such as corporate law and securities regulation. Moreover, it is apparent that China's national lawmaking institutions lack objectivity, at least insofar as their legislative product conflicts with the interests of the Party-state's SOE systems.[25] Second, although the situation is better than some observers surmise, there must be continuing doubts about the competence, autonomy, and political independence of judicial institutions called upon to implement corporate law standards or remedies.[26] Even if state-of-the-art substantive provisions and procedural mechanisms are introduced into

[23] This has been demonstrated empirically by the long-standing A share price premium over H shares for the same issuer listing A shares on the PRC exchanges and H shares on the Hong Kong Stock Exchange, and has been tracked by the Hang Seng "China AH Premium Index" since January 2006. *See* HANG SENG CHINA AH PREMIUM INDEX (Jan. 13, 2015), http://www.hsi.com.hk/HSI-Net/static/revamp/contents/en/dl_centre/factsheets/FS_AHPe.pdf. This A share premium has been thought to result from the limited supply of, and strong demand for, A share issues for domestic PRC purchasers who have not been permitted to invest in "overseas" (including Hong Kong) markets. No one has seriously asserted that the A share premium over H shares results from stronger investor protections or better corporate governance associated with a listing on the Shanghai or Shenzhen Exchanges. In recent years the A share premium over H shares has declined because of increased foreign investment in the A share markets via the Qualified Foreign Institutional Investor program and greater access by PRC purchasers to overseas listed equities via the Qualified Domestic Institutional Investor program, the mutual recognition of mutual funds between the PRC and Hong Kong, and the newly unveiled Shanghai-Hong Kong (Exchange) Link.

[24] *Supra* note 21.

[25] *See, e.g.*, Xi Chao, *Piercing the Corporate Veil in China—How Did We Get There?*, 5 J. BUS. L. 413, 423–27 (2011) (describing the role of the State-owned Assets Supervision and Administration Commission (SASAC) in sabotaging the CSRC's more permissive statutory veil-piercing standard originally set forth in the Company Law Amendment's Consultation Draft, due to SASAC concern that the more liberal doctrine would also be applied to the control groups of unlisted corporatized SOEs).

[26] *See, e.g.*, Howson, *supra* note 12 (corporate law adjudication in the Shanghai Higher People's Court system between 1992 and 2008); Wang Jun 王军, 公司经营者忠实和勤勉义务诉讼研究– 以 14 省, 直辖市的

PRC company law—as they assuredly were with promulgation of the final 2006 Company Law—there is a continuing concern as to whether the People's Courts will be competent and powerful enough to utilize, adjudicate, and enforce such law with respect to any kind of business enterprise, much less be permitted to accept disputes concerning the same.[27] Third, a basic dilemma in China's corporate governance revealed in my own research on the People's Courts is the almost complete *non*-implementation of China's Company Law for the benefit of minority shareholder plaintiffs in corporations financed through public capital markets. This phenomenon arises in part from the system's denial of any constraint on the state's ability to operate such firms as it sees fit, which is the reason it maintained control in the first place.

V. The CSRC: A Conflicted Actor

From an institutional standpoint, then, the above-described factors worked together to leave the CSRC as one of the only state institutions in China capable of: (1) expert drafting of substantive provisions, in particular of the self-enforcing type; (2) technical resistance against controlling state shareholders and the political-economic systems backing them; and (3) substituting for an inexpert, overly bureaucratic or politically cowed judiciary, at least with respect to publicly listed firms.[28]

---

137 件判决书为样本 (Analysis of Litigation Regarding Company Management's Duties of Loyalty and Care—Using 137 Judgment Opinions from 14 Provinces and Directly Administered Municipalities), 5 北方法学 (N. JURIS.) 24 (2011) (corporate fiduciary litigation nationwide); Clarke & Howson, *supra* note 12 (the corporate derivative action); Hui Huang, *Piercing the Corporate Veil in China: Where Is It Now and Where Is It Headed?*, 60 AM. J. COMP. L. 743 (2012) (corporate veil piercing).

[27] I should note in passing that the PRC judicial *bureaucracy*—that is, not courts issuing opinions on adjudicated cases—has played some role in implanting substantive corporate law doctrine and procedural innovations into China's corporate law and governance system. Before 2005, this was done via the creation by individual (Provincial/Directly-Administered Municipality) Higher Level People's Court systems of "opinions" on issues presented in litigation concerning the woefully deficient 1994 PRC Company Law. Notable Higher People's Court opinions on corporate law came from Jiangsu (2003), Shanghai (2003), and Beijing (2004). Importantly, none of these local court system opinions attempted to institute self-enforcing governance mechanisms such as supermajority negative veto rights in the style the CSRC has for public companies. After the effectiveness of the 2006 PRC Company Law, the Supreme People's Court has released three judicial "regulations" concerning the company statute, and has embarked on a Guiding Cases project, none of which, however, remake corporate governance norms in the same fashion as the CSRC regulation described here. To date, only one of such Guiding Cases, a corporate resolution revocation dispute, has involved corporate governance matters: "Guiding Case No. 10," 李建军诉上海佳动力环保科技有限公司公司决议撤销纠纷案 (Li Jiangjun v. Shanghai Jiapower Environmental Protection Science and Technology Co., Ltd.), 最终版本 (Final Version) Nov. 9, 2012 (Jan. 13, 2015), http://cgc.law.stanford.edu/wp-content/uploads/2013/04/CGCP-Chinese-Guiding-Case-10.pdf (shareholder challenge to a board resolution).

[28] Note that from January 1, 2013, the CSRC asserted expanded jurisdiction beyond domestically or overseas exchange-listed companies to include CLSs with more than two hundred shareholders, and CLSs that have issued securities "to the general public" or "in a public manner," an elaboration of regulatory power very likely to gain a statutory basis in the revised PRC Securities Law. *See* Howson, *supra* note 1, at 713.

I do not mean to assert in this chapter that the CSRC is entirely, or even mostly, a "good actor" under the Chinese Party-state's model of state capitalism, or that it uniformly acts to constrain the power of SOE Party-state controlling shareholder groups. Ruoying Chen's eloquent lament in this volume regarding the low quality human capital trap created by state capitalism—including specifically the CSRC with respect to IPO approvals[29] —as well as my own work on illegal and ultra vires enforcement by the CSRC against insider trading[30] and many other bodies of evidence[31] render implausible any claim that the CSRC and its human agents are the saviors of the PRC capital markets, or are immune from agency capture.

Instead, I would note that the CSRC can be a "bad actor" in its day-to-day gatekeeper, approval, and enforcement roles, while still being a "good actor" in the sense of supplying longer-term, highly sophisticated pre-enforcement or legal constraints on the power of state capitalism's control groups analyzed in this chapter.

VI. How Have the CSRC and Other Agencies Been Permitted to Push Back, and What Does It Mean for China's State Capitalism Model?

I have reviewed some of the reasons *why* the CSRC and other agencies have intervened to constrain or hold more accountable controlling shareholders with ties to the Party-state in the paradigmatic firm operating under state capitalism. A separate *why* question emerges from the dichotomy of action by the CSRC alluded to immediately above: Why is a sometimes corrupt, captured agency with increasingly degraded human capital creating sophisticated constraints on powerful actors in the economy? In answering this question there is little doubt about the significance of (1) input from foreign capital market regulators and academics (often delivered via foreign-educated officials or academics active inside the PRC), and (2) the competitiveness of highly integrated international capital markets requiring sophisticated governance mechanisms in order for Chinese issuers to attract capital.

---

29 *See* Ruoying Chen, Chapter 8 in this volume.

30 *See* Nicholas Calcina Howson, *Enforcement without Foundation?—Insider Trading and China's Administrative Law Crisis*, 60 AM. J. COMP. L. 955 (2012) (critiquing the CSRC as acting illegally with respect to the enforcement of insider trading prohibitions, a critique acknowledged as valid with issuance of a responsive joint explanation by the PRC Supreme People's Court and the PRC Supreme People's Procuratorate (SPP) drawing such illegal enforcement back within the bounds of legality, at least in criminal prosecutions by the SPP).

31 *See, e.g.*, Zhou Tianshu, *Is the CSRC Protecting a "Level Playing Field" in China's Capital Markets: Public Enforcement, Fragmented Authoritarianism and Corporatism*, (Jan. 13, 2015), http://papers.ssrn.com/sol3/papers.cfm?abstract_id=2505568. The author is a professor at the China University of Politics and Law.

The far more intriguing question is *how* the CSRC has been permitted to erect and enforce effective constraints on the power of China's Party-state-tied controlling shareholders. Although the Party-state is not the monolith many popular accounts portray, it does seem startling that there is any allowance for an agency embedded in the same Party-state (with no economic and little independent political power) to conceive and implement mechanisms that limit the power of, or seek to hold accountable, politically far better-endowed actors.

In starting to answer this question, I note at the outset that I do not address the more traditional political scientist's inquiry: the sources of the CSRC's concrete power. Thus, for example, I do not seek to answer the following questions: What rank does the CSRC have in the state bureaucracy (and its party organ in the parallel party system)? In which, or whose, patronage network does the CSRC lie? What individual or groups of leaders have empowered the CSRC at different times in its development? What resources can the CSRC attract, and conversely what resources does it control? Is the CSRC able to resist agency capture, and if so how? Although the development of the CSRC as an institution of the Party-state is a rich area for continued research, the answers to these questions will vary greatly over time, given the varied power (and power bases) of different individuals and their allies (e.g., compare recent CSRC Chairmen Zhou Xiaochuan (2000–2002), Shang Fulin (2002–2011), Guo Shuqing (2011–2013), and the present incumbent Xiao Gang (2013–present)), and the development of the PRC capital markets and their engagement with global capital markets. Variance along these dimensions may in turn obscure larger structural features that explain what the CSRC is doing. Instead, I address the CSRC's normative power in trying to explain the phenomenon identified in this chapter and its relationship with state capitalism as practiced in the PRC.

Although what I describe in this chapter may appear to be a very specific and technical aspect of the established PRC "fragmented authoritarianism" narrative,[32] it is different. The traditional fragmented authoritarianism account focuses on how vertical (from center to locality) governmental and bureaucratic systems battle across horizontal lines (within a given geographic area) with respect to governmental policy or approvals. This chapter addresses something distinct, and a phenomenon directly

---

[32] *See* KENNETH LIEBERTHAL & MICHEL OKSENBERG, POLICY MAKING IN CHINA: LEADERS, STRUCTURES AND PROCESSES 3–34 (1988); Kenneth Lieberthal, *Introduction: The "Fragmented Authoritarianism" Model and Its Limitations*, *in* BUREAUCRACY, POLITICS AND DECISION MAKING IN POST-MAO CHINA 1–32 (Kenneth Lieberthal & David M. Lampton eds., 1992); Kenneth Lieberthal, GOVERNING CHINA—FROM REVOLUTION THROUGH REFORM 186–88 (2004). Political scientist Andrew C. Mertha has also written more recently on this aspect of PRC governance. *See* Andrew C. Mertha, *"Fragmented Authoritarianism 2.0": Political Pluralization of the Chinese Policy Process*, 200 THE CHINA QUARTERLY 1 (2009); Andrew C. Mertha, *Policy Enforcement Markets—How Bureaucratic Redundancy Contributes to Effective Intellectual Property Implementation in China*, 38 COMP. POL. 295 (2006). However, all of these studies focus on horizontal competition (or, in Professor Mertha's case, redundancy in enforcement) between vertically arranged *governmental and bureaucratic* actors, usually with respect to specific policy decisions or approvals.

tied to the rise of state capitalism: a horizontal contest between a central government agency creating pre-enforcement mechanisms and ex post–applied doctrines that systemically constrain the economic and directorial power of a supremely powerful, nongovernmental, non-regulatory constituency—SOE groups and the controlling shareholders they produce. This kind of fragmentation of the Party-state is the inevitable result of the state capitalism model, where units endowed with both political and economic power are ranged against other units with governmental/administrative power alone.

My tentative answers to the *how* question focus on the CSRC's normative power against corporatized SOEs, their control groups, and the systems that support them, and the extent to which the expression of that normative power is necessary for the flourishing of state capitalism in contemporary China. In the following section, I consider the issue from four different perspectives: (1) What it is about the CSRC, as a new kind of government unit in China, that empowers it to act in this fashion?; (2) What might cause powerful controlling shareholder groups to allow the CSRC this provocative space for maneuver?; (3) Why might the human agents appointed by the Party-state to run corporatized SOEs welcome such constraints?; and (4) Why might the state capitalism model require both the expression and enforcement of the constraints identified here to finance itself in a sustained manner?

A. THE CSRC AS A NEW KIND OF PRC PARTY-STATE AGENCY

The CSRC was the first agency and subsequently ministry-level body in the PRC's history with jurisdiction over an area that is not a specific *industrial sector*, but a *market activity* in an increasingly market-oriented economy. Thus, just as the Ministry of Textile Industry, for example, once governed the PRC's entire textile industry and its productive SOEs, the CSRC can be seen—and more important, sees itself—as China's "Ministry of Capital Markets," a regulator certainly, but also a government department charged with maintaining the operation, integrity, and attractiveness of China's domestic capital markets. This sense of ownership of the capital markets, and bureaucratic investment in the success of the market it governs, contributes to the CSRC's concrete moves to resist the power of even politically well-endowed SOEs and their supporting systems. In addition, and notwithstanding the strengthening of its regional offices, the CSRC is very much an organ of the central government, and therefore an organ of the Party-state that is not tied to or reliant upon a given industrial or manufacturing sector, or any particular geographic region. Although most large SOE systems have their origin in some kind of central authority (usually a former ministry metamorphosed into a group holding company), their robust political and economic interest eventually narrows to a specific sector (e.g., telecoms, power generation, downstream oil and gas and petrochemicals), a part of that specific sector (as a member of a duopoly or tri-opoly), and then often into a region.[33] Consider how the three giant SOEs in the oil industry—CNOOC, the China National Petroleum Corporation/PetroChina, and Sinopec—have their origins at the national level, but have since each been directed into specific sectors (upstream (onshore and offshore) versus downstream and petrochemicals) and specific geographical areas in China. The same might be observed for the corporatized offspring of the former PRC Ministry of Post and Telecommunications—China Telecom, China Mobile, and China Unicom. Thus, although observers may understand the corporatized SOE systems of China's state capitalism as all-powerful, and rooted in the center, the breadth of their power is actually narrower than that of a purely central organ encompassing all industrial and service sectors such as the CSRC.

B. PARTY-STATE CONTROLLING SHAREHOLDERS

From the standpoint of the Party-state's political-economic behemoths, corporatized SOE systems and their control groups, the CSRC pushback described in this chapter may be perceived as harmlessly expressive, understood ex ante by such powerful forces to be without effect or risk of real enforcement, or to take an idiom from nineteenth-century Brazil, "*para inglês ver*" ("for English eyes").[34] This view might explain the long-standing allowance for the CSRC's mandatory constraint mechanisms, especially if they are understood as intended merely to be expressive for foreign investors and the domestic capital markets audience, or are symbolically enforced to provide comfort to public investors, in each case given the open exploitation of minority shareholders under the corporatization without privatization program. If this is true, the control groups that occupy the heights of China's state capitalism might be quite content to allow such mechanisms, secure in the knowledge that they will not generally be enforced or provide any real obstacles to the groups' power and discretion with respect to dominated subsidiaries. In my view this explanation does not possess real force, however, precisely because many of the CSRC-initiated mechanisms have nothing to do with overseas listing issuers and work purely with respect to domestically listed issuers. Moreover, although the "for English eyes" answer might fit some of the doctrinal gap-filling that the CSRC has pursued over the years—for example, fiduciary duties for, and anti-oppression remedies against, controlling shareholders that are never subject to adjudication because they involve large plaintiff groups—it does not account for the self-enforcing genus of constraints such as supermajority shareholder or board votes after recusal of related parties,

---

[33] *See generally* Li-Wen Lin & Curtis J. Milhaupt, *We Are the (National) Champions: Understanding the Mechanisms of State Capitalism in China*, 65 STAN. L. REV. 697, 704–33 (2013).

[34] Under pressure from the anti-slave trade British Parliament, in 1831 Brazil promulgated a law declaring free all slaves trafficked to Brazilian ports. As was intended, the law went largely unenforced, as slaves continued to arrive at Brazilian ports and be sold, and so the law was "for English eyes" or "for appearances only," known ahead of time as a norm for external consumption that would not be enforced.

which are respected and implemented at China's largest firms, and where there is ample evidence of concrete application of the mandatory constraints described in this chapter. And, of course, there is no guarantee that even some of the non-self-enforcing constraints introduced into the governance mix for China's state capitalism powers might not increasingly gain traction over time. A perhaps more nuanced version of this view is that these mechanisms—the self-enforcing type in particular—are understood immediately by the SOE control groups as being more than merely expressive, and known to be subject to implementation in fact, but that the prospect of implementation spurred by private claimants is nonetheless largely discounted by the most powerful controlling shareholders because of familiar collective action, information deficit, and passivity problems for the great mass of public minority shareholders.

C. PARTY *NOMENKLATURA* APPOINTEES TO STATE-CONTROLLED FIRMS

It is now well established that many of the human agents of Party-state control at the largest corporatized SOEs are officials embedded in the Chinese Communist Party's personnel appointments or *nomenklatura* system who seek advancement in reform-era China through both governmental and enterprise appointments, and rotate easily through both spheres. Thus, the nominal CEOs (but more importantly ranking party officials) at direct competitors China Mobile and China Unicom may switch jobs, the CEO of Sinopec may leave that corporate position to take up the post of governor of a major coastal province, or the head of one of the major state-owned commercial banks may become the Governor of the PRC's central bank, Chairman of the CSRC, or governor of a provincial People's Government. When such appointment rotations result in members of the *nomenklatura* being charged with direction of a large corporatized SOE that is a key instrument of the PRC's state capitalism, it may be critical for that individual's further advancement that the SOE assets or the firm the individual is tasked with operating are successful in business terms, but also that the individual does not attract public opprobrium, shareholder dissension, or negative press attention, domestically or abroad.[35] It is therefore not absurd to think that these individuals might counterintuitively welcome constraints on their power (and, indirectly, on the power of the Party-state, which brought them to the firm) to protect themselves against having to direct, for example, inefficient or unprofitable related-party transactions, or at least allow them the safety of prior supermajority, interested party-recused approvals.[36] Flat constraints may allow them to avoid risky, possibly pressurized decisions entirely;

---

[35] *See* Howson, *supra* note 5.

[36] I am grateful to my former University of Michigan colleague Professor Zhao Minyuan for this insight.

adherence to mandatory procedures for supermajority approvals and the like may provide for some measure of ex post protection for transactions that go sour.

D. THE FINANCING OF STATE CAPITALISM

Finally, and perhaps most important, the governance constraints visited on the control parties of China's state capitalism addressed in this chapter may be welcomed or at least tolerated by corporatized SOE systems and the controlling shareholders they have spawned as the small price of continued access to financing in the domestic and global capital markets. Put differently, formal constraints on controlling shareholder governance power within a listed firm may be the price that has to be paid for the appearance of functioning capital markets capable of attracting capital, something even the heights of China's state capitalist establishment desperately needs. It is difficult to prove this point to the satisfaction of law and finance scholars, as it is exceedingly unlikely that the CSRC-origin mandatory constraints presently imposed on state controlling shareholder power will be removed or weakened,[37] and thus there is no possibility of an event study tracking the pricing of PRC-listed issuers before and after such change. We do know, however, that many of the CSRC-implemented mandatory rules—such as the paradigmatic December 2004 "Regulations Regarding Strengthening Protection of the Rights and Interests of Public Shareholders," which defined public equity shareholders other than controlling shareholders as a kind of class and conferred upon that class negative veto rights regarding a broad range of important decisions[38] —were issued by the CSRC in direct response to complaints from domestic investors and the increasingly autonomous PRC financial press. This was also the dynamic at work in India more than a decade ago, where in 2001 the Indian securities regulator implemented similar reforms originating in a voluntary corporate governance code promulgated by an organization made up of, and representing the interests of, India's largest public firms.[39] Finally, this proposed rationale for acceptance of significant constraints on state controlling shareholders aligns perfectly with what I assert is the original policy rationale for the corporatization without privatization process itself—the reordering of SOE asset groupings

---

[37] Just the opposite in fact—the author has reviewed a draft of the revised PRC Securities Law distributed inside China (at the time of this writing, in January 2015), and its provisions incorporate all of the CSRC-origin mandatory rules described here, and provide for new and more robust constraints and mandatory disclosures.

[38] *See* Howson, *supra* note 1, at 680–81.

[39] *See* Bernard S. Black & Vikramaditya Khanna, *Can Corporate Governance Reforms Increase Firm Value? Event Study Evidence from India*, 4 J. EMPIRICAL LEGAL STUD. 749, 759 (2007) ("Corporate governance reform efforts in India were largely triggered by [the Confederation of Indian Industry's] promulgation of its Corporate Governance Code in 1998. CII then followed up by lobbying SEBI to implement mandatory reforms—presumably consistent with the CII Code . . . Much like the Business Roundtable in the United States, major Indian firms were the interest group most likely to oppose governance reform. Instead, however, CII *initiated* the reform effort.").

into a new legal form able to attract passive capital investment from the domestic and global capital markets.

Conclusion

In this chapter I have reviewed two distinct, and often opposing, projects of the PRC Party-state with respect to corporatized SOE groups, the undisputed engines of China's domestic and global economic activity under state capitalism. On the one hand, we can understand the Chinese Party-state as a multifaceted and overbearing economic actor spawning a parade of politically well-endowed controlling shareholders uniquely positioned to dominate subsidiary corporations established as passive vehicles to attract public capital markets financing, and to operate the firms entirely in their own interest. On the other hand, the same PRC Party-state has also established a securities markets regulator with the undisputed power to regulate the internal corporate governance arrangements for such dominated subsidiary corporations, which regulator has conceived sophisticated mechanisms of resistance against the control parties of state capitalism.

From a legal systems perspective, this understanding of two opposing prongs of the PRC Party-state should help us to comprehend better the CSRC's serial mandatory-type regulatory incursions into the province of enabling legal corporate governance norms. With the PRC's corporatization without privatization in the embrace of a shareholder primacy model, we are confronted with a notional and mostly rhetorical retreat from the economy of the Party-state "under law" (the enabling Company Law specifically). This is a retreat, however, which in fact cloaks the reassertion or maintenance of concentrated power by the Party-state metamorphosed into a politically privileged controlling shareholder. Moreover, this operates in a context of "authoritarian legality" where the control parties can reliably ensure that formally conferred "legal" protections for the exploited minority are not utilized (i.e., the absence of listed company corporate governance cases in the Chinese courts, and obstacles placed in the way of multiparty actions of any kind).

The only effective remedy for this structurally determined exploitation of minority shareholders, and the inability of the system to enforce whatever legal protections are on offer, is state intervention of another sort: the injection by a competing Party-state institution of immutable substantive doctrines and mandatory corporate governance provisions, with the best kind being self-enforcing mechanisms whereby the Party-state rule-maker cannot escape being bound by its own rules. That is precisely the path pursued by the CSRC and other bureaucratic actors over the last several decades.

From the distinct perspective of understanding how the PRC Party-state operates in the context of state capitalism, we may query how a bureaucratic agency such as the CSRC has been permitted this counter-strike against the focal point of Party-state power.

In this regard, we must remind ourselves of a central idea behind the twenty-year-old PRC corporatization program, itself a direct echo of China's nineteenth-century imperial fetish for the corporate form—repackaging SOEs and SOE asset groupings into a legal entity that can attract large-scale public investment with only minor disruption of incumbent governance arrangements. That major underlying policy driver for the corporatization program from inception aligns well with one explanation for how the CSRC and other bureaucracies have been permitted to impose constraints on the power and discretion of dominant state-tied controlling shareholders of China's listed companies. Those constraints imposed by administrative regulation, in theory and as applied, only make corporatized SOEs more competitive as they seek financing from domestic and global capital markets, and thereby help ensure continued access by the very same vehicles of China's state capitalism to abundant and relatively passive capital. Said another way, these effective governance constraints and accountability mechanisms imposed on PRC Party-state controlling shareholders in listed firms may be one of the most critical long-term elements enhancing the Party-state's ability to finance state capitalism on the domestic and global capital markets. More than merely protecting the state from itself, these mechanisms are necessary for the Chinese Party-state's continued ability to finance its involvement in capital-intensive sectors of the domestic and global economies.

4 Quenching Thirst with Poison? Local Government Financing Vehicles—Past, Present, and Future

Liao Fan*

Introduction

Mounting local governmental debts ("local debts")[1] and the associated fiscal and financial risks have become a sword of Damocles hanging over the Chinese economy. According to a recent report by the National Audit Office (NAO), by the end of June 2013 the balance of local debts nationwide had reached a record high of 17.89 trillion RMB (2.93 trillion U.S. dollars),[2]

* I am grateful to Benjamin L. Liebman, Curtis Milhaupt, and other participants at the China State Capitalism Workshop at Columbia Law School on June 13–14, 2014, for their valuable comments and suggestions. All errors and omissions are my own.

[1] According to the definition of the National Audit Office (NAO), "local governmental debts" refer to the debts of all four levels of local government (i.e., provinces, cities, counties, and townships), including debts that local governments are directly liable to repay ("government debts"), debts guaranteed by local governments ("explicitly guaranteed debts"), and debts where local governments might be obliged to render certain assistance ("implicitly guaranteed debts"). The latter two are so-called "contingent liabilities" of local governments. See NAO 审计署, 全国政府性债务审计结果 (Audit Result on Nationwide Governmental Debts), 中华人民共和国审计署网站 (NAO Official Web) (Dec. 30, 2013), http://www.audit.gov.cn/n1992130/n1992150/n1992500/3432077.html.

[2] Among the total amount, government debts, explicitly guaranteed debts, and implicitly guaranteed debts were 10.89 trillion RMB ($1.79 trillion), 2.66 trillion RMB ($0.43 trillion), and 4.34 trillion RMB ($0.71 trillion), respectively.

or about one-third of China's GDP. Compared to the figure at the end of 2010 (10.72 trillion RMB, or $1.76 trillion),[3] this was a remarkable increase. Local government financing vehicles (LGFVs) were by far the largest borrowers: borrowings by LGFVs amounted to 6.97 trillion RMB ($1.14 trillion), accounting for nearly 40 percent of the total local debts.[4] LGFVs emerged in China in the 1990s when the so-called "tax-sharing system" was introduced and the central government began to take the lion's share of tax revenue.[5] This left local governments with less money for such things as infrastructure construction and urban development.[6] Also, the excessive infrastructure investment and spending by local governments in the early 1990s with money from bank loans and the sale of bonds overseas, and the resulting rampant inflation nationwide, prompted the central government to pass a severe budget law in 1994, forbidding local governments from running a deficit or selling bonds.[7] LGFVs apparently had their roots in these restrictions imposed on local governments. Local governments used such vehicles to obtain bank loans as well as to issue so-called "Urban Construction Investment Bonds," or *chengtouzhai*, thus bypassing the prohibitions in the Budget Law. The Asian Financial Crisis in 1998 came as an opportunity for LGFVs: it required spending to stimulate the economy as China was entering its golden period of urbanization, but local governments were strapped for cash.[8] But the real fuel was the Global Financial Crisis in 2008. Heavily impacted by the crisis,

---

[3] NAO 审计署, 全国地方政府性债务审计结果 (Audit Result on Nationwide Local Governmental Debts), 中华人民共和国审计署网站 (NAO Official Web) (June 27, 2011), http://www.audit.gov.cn/n1992130/n1992150/n1992500/2752208.html.

[4] See NAO, *supra* note 1, at 6–7. Other borrowers include government departments and agencies, public institutions, state-owned enterprises, and public utilities.

[5] Before 1980, under the "unified income and expenditure" fiscal system, almost all local government revenue and profits were submitted to the central government, and were then redistributed to the provinces according to an expenditure plan. From 1980 to 1994, China used a divided budget system whereby central and local governments had their own independent financial interests. In 1994, China cancelled the contract system for taxation and began to implement the tax-sharing system. The main goal of this new policy was to strengthen the control of central government over sources of tax revenue, to raise the proportion of the central fiscal revenue in the national fiscal revenue and the proportion of fiscal revenue in GDP, and to resolve the conflict of interest between the central and local authorities. Therefore, taxes were divided into a central fixed tax, a local fixed tax, and a shared tax between the central and local authorities with a view to stabilizing the financial relationship between the two. Obviously, however, the objective of the tax-sharing system has not only been to improve the fiscal system but also to raise the proportion of the tax revenue that the central government collects. See Miguel Elosua et al., *Urbanisation in China: The Impact of the Tax-Sharing System and the Definitions of New Strategies*, UrbaChina Working Paper Series, No. 1/November 2013, http://hal.archives-ouvertes.fr/docs/00/90/32/18/PDF/UrbaChina_working_paper_no1.pdf.

[6] Central government revenues jumped in the years after 1994 as a result, while local governments saw their share of revenues fall from 78 percent in 1993 to 45 percent in 2002. *See* Henry Sanderson & Michael Forsythe, China's Superbank: Debt, Oil and Influence—How China Development Bank Is Rewriting the Rules of Finance 5 (2013).

[7] 中华人民共和国预算法 (Budget Law of the People's Republic of China) (promulgated by the Nat'l People's Cong., Mar. 22, 1994, effective Jan.1, 1995, "Budget Law"), Article 28, which provides that "local budgets at various levels shall be compiled according to the principles of keeping expenditures within the limits of revenues and maintaining a balance between revenues and expenditures, and shall not contain deficits. Except as otherwise prescribed by law or by the State Council, local governments may not issue local government bonds."

[8] *See* Sanderson & Forsythe, *supra* note 6, at 5.

China announced a 4 trillion RMB (around $570 billion at the 2008 exchange rate) stimulus package on November 5, 2008, equivalent to 12.5 percent of China's GDP. The central government, however, only committed to funding 1.18 trillion RMB of the stimulus. The rest was to be "matched" by local governments. It was only logical that local governments again turned to LGFVs and the state-owned banking system to raise these funds. Indeed, total bank lending to such companies rose from 1.7 trillion RMB of outstanding loans at the beginning of 2008 to nearly 5 trillion RMB just two years later.[9] Furthermore, in the economic downturn after the crisis, many local governments initiated their own stimulus plans with government investment at the core. A recent report shows that since June 2012, the total amount involved in the stimulus plans of over ten provinces and municipalities has exceeded 20 trillion RMB, far more than the previous "Four Trillion Plan" of the central government.[10] Given this fact, it is no surprise that LGFVs have accumulated mounting debts. Although dressed up as business corporations, LGFVs are in fact a disguised arm of local governments. Their most—and often only—reliable asset is land. Empowered by local governments as land banks, they use land as the main collateral to secure long-term loans from China Development Bank (CDB). Originally a policy bank, the CDB has gone far beyond policy-based lending over the years.[11] With the initial funding from the CDB, LGFVs are able to start operations and borrow further by seeking short-term loans from state-owned commercial banks or selling bonds on the interbank bond market. Because the proceeds from selling or developing land are the main source of repayment for such debts, local governments behind LGFVs have incentives to expropriate more land and keep property prices high, so as to continue the cycle. As a result, despite the repeated announcements and increasingly severe measures from the national government since 2009 designed to lower or at least stabilize property prices, local governments have not been interested in enforcing that policy and are always trying to find loopholes or seek exceptions. The accelerated urbanization process since the late 1990s, and the expectation of its continuation and expansion in the foreseeable future, is the main driving force behind this borrowing and investment spree.

---

[9] *Id.* at 13.

[10] *See* He Tian 禾田, "四万亿"后遗症 (The Aftermath of the "Four Trillion"), 中国经营网 (China Business Journal Web) (Mar. 24, 2014), http://www.cb.com.cn/special/show/362.html.

[11] Established in 1994, CDB was originally a policy bank. Not allowed to take deposits, it could only raise funds by selling bonds to commercial banks. Pushed by its former governor Chen Yuan, CDB underwent a reform of commercialization, and was approved by the State Council in 2008 to transform into a commercial bank. It was authorized to step into the business of commercial banking, including taking public deposits except household deposits. *See* Niu Juanjuan 牛娟娟, 国开行改制后成第五家大型国有商业银行 (CDB becomes the fifth largest state-owned commercial bank after the transformation), 金融时报 (Financial News), (Dec. 23, 2008) at 1. However, little seems to have been done to transform CDB into a real commercial bank. There are signs that it is returning to a "policy bank." For example, CDB still relies on the bond market instead of public deposits. *See* Liu Zhongsheng 刘中盛 et al., 国开行改制开倒车 (CDB reform marches backward), 每经网 (National Business Daily Web) (Dec. 25, 2013), http://www.nbd.com.cn/articles/2013-09-25/775973.html.

This reveals a crucial and often overlooked aspect of state capitalism[12] in China: state capitalism at the local level. Although constitutionally and legally China is a unitary state, in fact local governments (provincial and below) enjoy a high degree of autonomy in policy enforcement, especially with regard to economic issues. This has been the case since the beginning of the reform and opening in the late 1970s. It has been argued that the actual powers of Chinese local governments dwarf those of the local governments under a federal system. Thus China is characterized as "*de facto* federalism."[13] In this sense, there is not only a state at the central level vis-à-vis the private sector, but also numerous "states" at various local levels—provinces, cities, counties, and townships—vis-à-vis the private sector at the corresponding levels. This partly explains why "(central) government orders don't go beyond *Zhongnanhai*." In fact, local governments contributed significantly to the "state advances, private retreats" (*guojin mintui*) trend since 2002. Section I outlines LGFVs and the way they function, and provides several legal and policy explanations for their remarkable development. Section II looks into the major problems and risks associated with LGFVs. Section III offers some suggestions for reforming LGFVs and for reshaping the role of local governments.

I. LGFVs and Their Development: What, How and Why

A. DEFINITION AND FEATURES OF LGFVS

The exact number of LGFVs remains an issue of debate, partly due to the lack of a clear definition of LGFV. The NAO report of 2013 stated that 7,170 LGFVs had been audited by the NAO.[14] This sheds some light on the number of LGFVs in China. Despite their large numbers and various forms, for a long time there had been no official definition of LGFVs. Lacking clear guidance on what LGFVs should look like, how they should be organized, and what functions they may perform, local governments in practice set up all kinds of investing and financing corporations. Although the corporations shared the common label of LGFV, they differed considerably in size, functionality, and corporate structure. It was not until 2010, when LGFVs and their unregulated operations were increasingly recognized as posing substantial risks to the overall fiscal and financial system, and when the central government began to take steps to strengthen the regulation of LGFVs, that a somewhat summary definition was given. In a document promulgated

---

[12] According to Lenin, state capitalism is a form of capitalism associated with state power, and controlled and dominated by the state. Similarly, Western scholars describe state capitalism as a form of capitalism dominated by the state and government, with economic growth as the core aim, by means of supporting specific enterprises or industries. *See* Hu Leming 胡乐明 et al., 国家资本主义与"中国模式" (State Capitalism and the "China Model"), 2009 经济研究 (Economic Research Journal) no. 11, 31–32.

[13] *See* Zheng Yongnian 郑永年, 中国的"行为联邦制": 中央-地方关系的变革与动力 De Facto Federalism in China: Reforms and Dynamics of Central-Local Relations) (2013).

[14] *See* NAO, *supra* note 1, at 1.

by the State Council in June 2010,[15] the central government defined LGFVs as "economic entities with independent legal personality, which are established by local governments and their departments and agencies through fiscal appropriation or injection of assets such as land and equity, to perform the function of financing government-invested projects." According to a notice jointly issued by four major government departments to implement the LGFV Notice, such entities include all kinds of comprehensive investment corporations, such as construction and investment corporations, construction and development corporations, investment and development corporations, investment group corporations, state-owned assets management corporations, and state-owned assets management centers, as well as industry-specific investment corporations, such as communications investment corporations.[16] Based on this official definition as well as experience from practice, it has been argued that four basic features characterize LGFVs. First, LGFVs have strong government backgrounds, being established by local governments and their departments and agencies through fiscal appropriation or injection of assets such as land and equity. Second, LGFVs' objective is to tackle the problem of funding local government-invested projects. The money LGFVs borrow mainly goes to municipal infrastructure construction and public services projects of the cities. Third, LGFVs are independent economic entities with legal personality. Fourth, they essentially rely on government credit to operate, as the money they borrow might be directed to public service projects that do not generate sufficient cash flow to repay the loans. Thus, some kind of government guarantee is necessary.[17]

B. HOW LGFVS FUNCTION

Due to the lack of lawful financing channels, as will be discussed below, local governments rely heavily on LGFVs to raise funds. Capitalization of land plays a key role in the fundraising process. Typically it works like this: local governments inject the land resources they own as capital into an LGFV. The LGFV then mortgages the allocated land or pledges the future revenue from the development of the land to apply for bank loans. Banks routinely ask the local government to issue a commitment letter to the

---

15 国务院关于加强地方融资平台公司管理有关问题的通知 (Notice of the State Council on Certain Issues Related to Strengthening the Regulation of Local Government Financing Vehicle Corporations) (promulgated by the St. Council, June 10, 2010, effective upon promulgation, "LGFV Notice").

16 财政部、国家发展改革委、中国人民银行和中国银监会关于贯彻国务院关于加强地方政府融资平台公司管理有关问题的通知相关事项的通知 (Notice on the Relevant Issues in Implementing the Notice of the State Council on Certain Issues Related to Strengthening the Regulation of Local Government Financing Vehicle Corporations) (jointly promulgated by the Ministry of Finance, National Development and Reform Commission, People's Bank of China, and China Banking Regulatory Commission, July 30, 2010, effective upon promulgation, "Implementation Notice").

17 *See* Gu Gongyun 顾功耘 & Hu Gairong, 胡改蓉, 如何规制地方融资平台 (How to Regulate Local Government Financing Vehicles), 2012 上海国资 (Capital Shanghai) no. 4, 18–19.

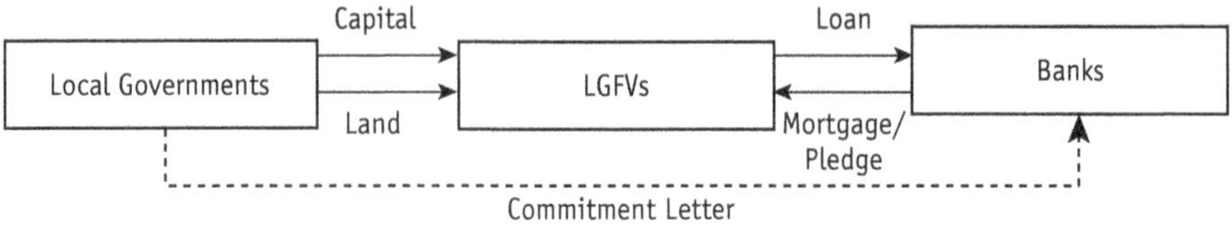

FIGURE 4.1 "Land mortgage/pledge plus government commitment" financing model.

effect that it will serve as the "deep pocket" if the LGFV is unable to repay the loan. According to a commentator, this model can be characterized as "land mortgage/pledge plus government commitment."[18] Figure 4.1 roughly shows this model.

This model largely enables local governments to bypass the prohibition imposed by relevant laws and regulations against borrowing money or serving as guarantors.[19] On the one hand, LGFVs formally are independent legal persons, and thus the prohibition that local governments themselves may not borrow from banks is circumvented. On the other hand, as land is allocated by local governments to LGFVs as the latter's capital, LGFVs can use the land as collateral to seek bank loans. Therefore the prohibition that local governments may not act as guarantors is also circumvented. The CDB is behind the whole scene. In fact, this finance model was invented by CDB. Unique among Chinese banks, the CDB is financed by bonds instead of deposits, most with maturities of ten years or more that are bought by China's commercial banks. This gives the CDB advantages in funding long-term infrastructure projects that might not generate a return on investment for many years. In this sense the CDB is the best match for LGFVs. The new urban focus of China in the late 1990s unleashed a wave of state capital boosted by growing Chinese savings. Because a policy bank, the CDB could not take peoples' deposits directly, the cycle operated as follows: the commercial banks used peoples' savings to buy bonds sold by the CDB on the nation's bond market, where the banks were the main investors. The CDB then helped local governments set up LGFVs to borrow

---

[18] *See* Hong Yuan 洪源 & Guo Ping 郭平, "土地财政"视角下的地方政府融资平台债务风险研究：以中部地区C市融资平台为例 (Debt Risk of Local Government Financing Vehicles from the Perspective of "Land Finance": Using the Financing Vehicles of City C in the Central Region as an Example), 2012 西安财经学院学报 (Journal of Xi'an University of Finance and Economics) no. 5, 74.

[19] *See* Article 28 of the Budget Law, *supra* note 7. *See also* 中华人民共和国中国人民银行法 (Law of the People's Republic of China on the People's Bank of China) (promulgated by the Nat'l People's Cong., Mar. 18, 1995, amended by the Standing Comm. Nat'l People's Cong., Dec. 27, 2003, effective Feb. 1, 2004), Art. 30, stating that "the People's Bank of China Shall not make loans to local governments or government departments at all levels"; 中国人民银行贷款通则 (General Provisions of the People's Bank of China on Lending)(promulgated by the People's Bank of China, June 28, 1996, effective Aug.1, 1996), Art. 17, stating that "the borrowers shall be . . . enterprises or public institutions as legal persons, other business organizations, individual industrial and commercial households and . . . natural persons"; and 中华人民共和国担保法 (Security Law of the People's Republic of China) (promulgated by the Standing Comm. Nat'l People's Cong., June 30, 1995, effective Oct. 1, 1995, "Security Law"), Art. 8, stating that "state organs shall not be guarantors."

and provided them with the initial long-term loans. Thus dressed up and empowered, the LGFVs were free to go on a further borrowing spree by seeking short-term loans from the commercial banks or selling bonds themselves on the bond market to banks and securities companies.[20] The "Wuhu model" serves as a classic case. In 1998, when Chen Yuan was appointed governor of the CDB, the bank created a new lending model in the city of Wuhu in Anhui, home province of the then- vice president Hu Jintao. First, the CDB cooperated with the city government to transform the Wuhu Construction & Investment Co. Ltd. into a qualified financing platform. Then all the urban construction projects were bundled into a package, with the financing platform as the single debtor. A ten-year loan agreement of 1.08 billion RMB was signed between the CDB and the platform. Finally, the city government established a "repayment reserve fund" to ensure the source of repayment. This CDB-LGFV lending model was copied and scaled up in Tianjin. In 2003, the CDB signed a loan agreement of 50 billion RMB with the Tianjin government, with the loan proceeds being mainly used for key infrastructure projects such as the construction of city expressways and subways.

One of the breakthroughs in this lending model was the association of the source of repayment of infrastructure loans with the income from land appreciation; that is, the cost of urban infrastructure construction is covered by the income from land appreciation. Infrastructure construction funds thus form a virtuous cycle. As more infrastructure is built, land values and housing prices rise. Meanwhile the land income right serves as the pledge. In case revenues from the infrastructure projects are insufficient to repay the loans, the income from land appreciation can ensure the safety of the loans.[21] Later, the Wuhu model spread nationwide and became the standard model of financing urban construction. In particular after the global financial crisis and the "Four Trillion Plan," this finance model was eagerly followed by the large commercial banks. LGFV loans became a significant part of their lending business.

C. LEGAL AND POLICY FACTORS UNDERLYING THE DEVELOPMENT OF LGFVS

LGFVs are the combined result of local governments' exuberant investment demand, limited fiscal capacity, and narrow financing channels. With the acceleration of China's industrialization and urbanization there has been a rapid increase in the demand for local construction investment. The introduction of the tax-sharing system in 1994 resulted in a mismatch between the fiscal power (*caiquan*) and administrative power (*shiquan*) of local governments, leaving them with a decreased percentage of fiscal income but an

[20] *See* SANDERSON & FORSYTHE, *supra* note 6, at 5–6.

[21] *See* Yang Naifen 杨乃芬, 国开行: 城镇化"三级跳" (CDB: "Triple Jump" in Urbanization), 新地产网 (New Real Estate Web) (May 1, 2013), http://www.xindichan.com.cn/article_18065.html.

increased percentage of fiscal expenditures.[22] Legally unable to borrow directly, local governments established numerous investment and financing entities to undertake construction tasks and receive funds from banks and trusts. The central government acquiesced in or even supported local governments' effort to tackle their financing problem.[23] After the "Four Trillion Plan," local governments had insufficient funds to "match" the investment of the central government. To solve the problem, the People's Bank of China (PBC) and the China Banking Regulatory Commission (CBRC) jointly promulgated a guiding opinion in 2009[24] stating that they "support qualified local governments to establish investment and financing platforms to issue financing instruments such as enterprise bonds and medium-term notes, so as to expand the financing channel of the matching funds for the central government invested projects." This ushered in an explosive development of LGFVs and greatly increased the potential risk. To be clear, the development of LGFVs, and more broadly, the accumulation of local debts, bore the hallmarks of the "transitional period" from the traditional planned economy to a market economy. LGFV development resulted from the incomplete adjustment of the relationship between government and market. More specifically, with the advance of the progressive reform featuring "decentralization of power and transfer of profits" from the central government, local governments gradually became administrative and economic units with their own development objectives. Local governments now had their own independent economic interests, and the relevance of such interests to local economic growth was greatly increased. The gradual decentralization of economic power provided local governments with unprecedented power and capacity to develop the local economy and seek local interests. With inertia inherited from the planned economy period, however, most local governments were keen on "substituting" instead of "supplementing" the market. They thus invested extravagantly in various areas in competition with private enterprises, resulting in excessively broad government functions. As a result, the

[22] The tax-sharing system remarkably changed the allocation of national income as well as the percentage of central government and local governments in the total income. The allocation of expenditure responsibilities, however, has not been adjusted accordingly. The result is a situation where national income mainly goes to the central government while expenditure responsibilities mostly remain with local governments. Statistics show that since 1994, the percentage of local fiscal income in the total fiscal income sharply decreased from 78 percent in 1993 to around 45 percent, while the percentage of local fiscal expenditure in the total fiscal expenditure increased from 71.3 percent in 1993 to around 80 percent in 2009. See Luo Guimei 罗桂梅, 地方政府投融资平台及相关风险研究 (A Study of LGFVs and the Related Risks), 西南财经大学硕士学位论文 (Master's Thesis, Southwestern University of Finance and Economics), 17–18 (2011).

[23] *See* Li Xiaowu 黎晓武, 地方政府举债融资制度的法律思考 (Legal Thinking on the Borrowing and Financing System of Local Governments, 2013 江西社会科学 (Jiangxi Social Sciences) no. 8, 160.

[24] 中国人民银行和中国银监会关于进一步加强信贷结构调整促进国民经济平稳较快发展的指导意见 (Guiding Opinions on Further Adjusting the Credit Structure to Promote Steady and Rapid Growth of National Economy) (jointly promulgated by the People's Bank of China and China Banking Regulatory Commission, Mar. 18, 2009, effective upon promulgation).

burden of fiscal expenditure was aggravated instead of alleviated. The expansion of fiscal expenditures pressured local governments to raise money through various channels, most remarkably the LGFVs, which in turn led to increasingly heavier debt burdens. In China, the state has an insuperable advantage over the private sector: it owns all the land. Moreover, land revenues, or the so-called "land grant fees," are extra-budgetary revenues and are not included in the central government's accounting of local budgets, meaning that there is little oversight on their use. This gives local governments much freedom to negotiate financing arrangements for projects with CDB and other banks. Local governments simply need to devise a system to leverage the future value of land into large upfront loans, as indicated above by the Wuhu model. The excessive reliance of the fiscal capacity of local governments on land has given birth to the term "land finance" (*tudi caizheng*). In fact, with the increasing significance of the land grant fees in local fiscal revenue since the 1990s, China to some extent has had the feature of a rent-state. This, combined with the increased profitability of state-owned enterprises and their contribution to the national fiscal income since the end of 1990s—which indicates that China still maintains some trace of an owner-state—means that even though China has begun to transform toward a tax-state, it remains a "hybrid" fiscal state. Apart from tax, profits and rents are also significant sources of income for the state. This in turn means that the state has more independent resources and relies less on the private sector, as compared to a standard tax-state.[25] This also helps to explain the strong interest of local governments in infrastructure financing and investment and, more broadly, the rise of state capitalism in the past decade.

II. Major Problems and Risks Associated with LGFVs

To be clear, the sustained operation of the LGFVs' "land for loans" model depends on two preconditions: unlimited supply of land and the continued increase in inland prices. Neither preconditions can be continuously met in the real world. Once land is in short supply or land prices drop, the debt-raising capacity of LGFVs will decline sharply. And considering that a large portion of the LGFV debts are paid through the "borrow new to pay the old" cycle, the sharp decrease in their capacity to borrow new money is likely to result in a break of the capital chain, thus triggering defaults.

A. THE "BARBARIAN GROWTH" OF LGFVS

As Chinese law generally prohibits local governments from borrowing, it naturally does not provide for standardizing and regulating the borrowing behavior of local

---

[25] *See* Ma Jun 马骏, 治国与理财: 公共财政与国家建设 (State Governance and Wealth Management: Public Budget and State Building) (2011), 17–18.

governments. However, due to the reasons discussed above, it is in fact widespread practice for local governments to borrow money. The result is that the motley assortment of borrowing practices of local governments are largely left unregulated. Against this backdrop, LGFVs since the very beginning have been in a state of "barbarian growth." They have two inborn defects: ambiguous relationships with local governments and chaotic internal governance.

LGFVs in name are independent corporate legal persons but in fact are controlled by the governments. Moreover, LGFVs in name are not-for-profit entities but in fact are for-profit and often monopolistic enterprises. LGFVs in name borrow in their own right but in fact rely on the guarantees of the local governments. As pointed out by one commentator, "most LGFVs have become the *de facto* second line of fiscal income and expenditure for local governments at all levels. They have very close connections with the governments in personnel and financial matters. Both the bank loans and the urban construction investment bonds are guaranteed directly or indirectly by local governments. Their debts have constituted *de facto* hidden debts of local governments."[26] Despite their true character, LGFVs often lack the internal controls and outside supervision required by China's Company Law. For example, corporate organs such as boards of directors and boards of supervisors are not established, corporate governance structures are defective, a regular information disclosure system is missing, and cases of delayed disclosure, misrepresentation, and omission are common.[27] This not only further blurs the line between LGFVs and local governments or government departments, but also adds to the risks inherent in LGFV debts.

B. LOCAL GOVERNMENTS' LIABILITY FOR LGFV DEBTS

In theory, as LGFVs are independent corporate legal persons, as shareholders local governments enjoy the protection of limited liability and are only liable to creditors to the extent of their capital contributions. In other words, local governments are not liable for debts that cannot be paid from the LGFVs' own assets. This seems to be consistent with the position of the central government. Article 4 of the LGFVs Notice provides: "Local governments bear limited liability for the LGFVs to the extent of their capital contributions, so as to internalize the risk of LGFV debts." Article 4 of the Implementation Notice further provides: "For the debts newly incurred after the date of issuance of the LGFV Notice, local governments only bear limited liability to the extent of their capital contributions. If the debtors cannot pay off all the debts, the creditors shall also bear the

---

[26] Huang Zhilong 黄志龙, 地方政府融资平台债务问题与对策建议 (Problems of and Suggestions on the Debts of LGFVs, 2011 中国物价 (China Price) no. 8, 30.

[27] *See* Yang Song 杨松 & Zhang Yongliang 张永亮, 地方政府融资平台的发展方向 (LGFVs' Direction of Development), 2012 法学 (Law Science) no. 10, 31–32.

corresponding consequences." The Implementation Notice does not specify what "the creditors shall also bear the corresponding consequences" means, but based on the context, a reasonable understanding is that creditors shall themselves bear the risk that their loans cannot be fully paid in the event of the bankruptcy of LGFVs. Judging from actual practice, however, the answer does not seem to be so straightforward. First, as pointed out above, although in name LGFVs are independent legal persons, in fact they are interwoven with local governments in terms of assets, operations, and personnel. Heads of the relevant government departments often serve as the legal representatives of LGFVs, and the whole process from establishment to finance to operation is taken care of by the governments. Quite often LGFVs are merely a different name of the relevant government departments, and their operation and development depend on the arrangement of local governments.[28] Accordingly, "banks and even local governments tend to view LGFVs as a 'tool' of local governments' investment and finance, instead of real economic entities."[29] This being the case, it is only natural to ask whether the creditors can claim to pierce the "corporate veil" of LGFVs and hold the relevant local governments—as the sole shareholder—liable for LGFVs' debts. This is at least a plausible scenario. Second, in the typical LGFV model as discussed above, the "land mortgage/pledge plus government commitment" model, local governments issue a commitment letter to the creditors (banks). Article 8 of the Security Law explicitly prohibits state organs to act as guarantors, and Article 4 of the LGFV Notice also emphasizes that "local governments at all levels and their constituent departments . . . may not use fiscal income . . . or by any other means, directly or indirectly, to provide financing guarantees for LGFVs."[30] Yet the nullification of the guarantee contract for violating legal prohibitions does not per se relieve the guarantor of his compensation liability. More specifically, Article 5 (2) of the Security Law provides: "After the nullification of the security contract, faults, if any, of the debtor, guarantor or creditor, shall be affixed with due civil responsibilities." In its judicial interpretation of the Security Law, the Supreme People's Court provides: "If the principal contract is valid and the security contract is void, the security provider and the debtor are jointly and severally liable for compensation for the financial loss of the creditor under the principal contract, provided that such creditor is not at fault. If the creditor and the security provider are at fault, the portion of civil liability borne by the security provider shall not exceed half of the portion that the debtor is unable to

---

[28] *See* Li Xiao'an 李晓安 & Zhou Xuzhong 周序中，投融资平台信用风险与地方政府信用失序：以法律为视角 (Credit Risk of LGFVs and the Disorder of Local Government Credit: From the Perspective of Law, 2012 北京行政学院学报 (Journal of Beijing Administrative College) no. 2, 89.

[29] Gu Gongyun 顾功耘 & Hu Gairong 胡改蓉, *supra* note 17, at 18.

[30] According to Article 4 of the Implementation Notice, "directly or indirectly provide financing guarantees for the LGFVs" includes without limitation the following: issuing guarantee letter for LGFVs, promising to give liquidity support by providing provisional repayment funds in case LGFVs encounter difficulty in repayment, promising to assume part of the repayment obligation in case LGFVs cannot repay the debts, and promising to incorporate the repayment funds of the LGFVs into the government budgets.

discharge."[31] According to these provisions, local governments bear liability to the lending banks at least to the extent of half of the portion of the debts that LGFVs are unable to repay. In addition, local governments, based on non-legal considerations, might take the initiative voluntarily to assume a greater share of liability. These factors all contribute to the risk of local debts.

III. Some Suggestions for Reforming LGFVs and Reshaping the Role of Local Governments

A. NORMALIZING AND COMMERCIALIZING THE OPERATION OF LGFVS

The LGFV Notice requires that LGFVs be classified and cleaned up. Only two types of LGFVs may be retained: those that are used to finance not-for-profit projects with stable business income and that mainly rely on their own income to repay debts, and those that are used to finance for-profit projects. Other LGFVs must cease undertaking financing operations.[32] Those LGFVs allowed to continue also must be substantially reformed. According to the LGFV Notice, they should bolster their capital, improve their governance structures, commercialize their operations, and promote the diversification of investors and improve the shareholder structure by introducing private investment.[33]

The key to implementing the above requirements is to reform LGFVs into corporate legal persons with independent business operations, and with decision-making and corporate management powers pursuant to the principles of modern corporate governance. This must be done in a way that ensures that LGFVs are actually separate and distinct from local governments and government departments. I refer to this as "de-governmentalization" of LGFVs. This certainly does not mean that local governments may not invest in LGFVs. On the contrary, they may invest in LGFVs and have all the rights and powers of shareholders. However, if they want to enjoy the protection of limited liability and avoid piercing of the LGFV's "corporate veil," they must not exceed the role of shareholder. In other words, local governments may enjoy the rights and exercise the powers of shareholders, but operation and management powers should be independently exercised by LGFVs themselves. In order to reduce the sense that they are merely "tools," LGFVs need to actively introduce private investment and other qualified investment, so as to diversify investors and improve the shareholder structure. Meanwhile, they should establish internal decision-making and supervisory organs

---

[31] 最高人民法院关于适用《中华人民共和国担保法》若干问题的解释 (Judicial Interpretation of the Supreme People's Court on Some Issues regarding the Application of the Security Law of the People's Republic of China) (promulgated by the Supreme People's Court, Dec. 8, 2000, effective Dec. 13, 2000), Art. 7.

[32] *See* Article 2 of the LGFV Notice.

[33] *Id.*

that meet the requirements of relevant laws and regulations. LGFVs must also enhance corporate governance and information disclosure and make efforts to operate in an independent, transparent, and market-based manner. The financing practice of LGFVs should also be normalized and regulated pursuant to the principle of market orientation. The requirements of the LGFV Notice and the Implementation Notice should be fully carried out, and local governments should be strictly prohibited from providing security for the LGFVs' financing practice. At the same time, as recently stressed by the CBRC, banks should improve their lending practice to LGFVs. For example, they should objectively evaluate the credit risk of LGFVs according to the principle of market orientation, and should base their lending and pricing decisions on such evaluation. They should also control the total amount of loans to LGFVs, set strict conditions for new LGFV loans, and strengthen the examination and approval mechanism for such loans.[34]

B. ESTABLISHING AND IMPROVING THE LOCAL GOVERNMENT BOND ISSUANCE SYSTEM

Article 28 of the Budget Law generally prohibits local governments from issuing bonds. This leads local governments to issue bonds in a disguised way through LGFVs. In the aftermath of the global financial crisis, the State Council approved the Ministry of Finance (MOF) to issue 200 billion RMB of local government bonds on behalf of provincial governments and certain municipal governments. The repayment of the principal and interest must also be made through MOF. From 2010 to 2013, the annual size of such issuance was 200 billion, 200 billion, 250 billion, and 350 billion, respectively. Meanwhile, in 2011, the State Council further approved Shanghai Municipality, Zhejiang Province, Guangdong Province, and Shenzhen Municipality to issue bonds on a pilot basis. Those governments may themselves organize the issuance of local bonds below an amount approved by the State Council, but repayment still must be made through the MOF. In 2013, the pilot was expanded to include Jiangsu Province and Shandong Province.[35] In essence, both the "issuance and repayment through the MOF" model and the "issued by local governments and repaid through the MOF" model use the credit from the central government as backing. Thus, such bonds are not local bonds in a strict sense, and might be understood as a kind of "quasi-treasury bonds." The insufficiency of those arrangements is obvious. First, the size of issuance is limited and cannot fully satisfy the financing needs of local governments. Second, local governments are restricted in many ways during the issuance and/or repayment process, with a low degree

---

[34] 中国银监会关于加强 2013 年地方政府融资平台贷款风险监管的指导意见 (Guiding Opinions on Strengthening the Risk Regulation of the LGFV Loans in 2013) (promulgated by China Banking Regulatory Commission, Apr. 9, 2013, effective upon promulgation).

[35] 2013 年地方政府自行发债试点办法 (Measures for the Pilot Scheme of Self-Issuance of Bonds by Local Governments in 2013) (promulgated by the Ministry of Finance, June 25, 2013, effective upon promulgation).

of autonomy and flexibility. Third, such "local bonds" are essentially backed by the credit of the central government, which renders it difficult for investors to make differentiated, market-based investment decisions on the basis of their evaluation of the different credit and risk conditions of different local governments.

Experiences in managing local debts from other countries show that in a tax-sharing system, it is necessary and reasonable for local governments to have moderate debt-raising power. In fact, in most market economies it is quite common for local governments to issue bonds.[36] Rather than imposing a general prohibition that is complied with only in a formal sense, it is better to allow local governments to issue bonds in their own right and subject such issuance to proper supervision and regulation. The central government now appears to be moving in this direction. In May 2014, the State Council approved on a pilot basis ten provinces and big cities to issue local bonds within an approved quota and to repay the principal and interest by themselves.[37] The real breakthrough came in August 2014 when the Standing Committee of the 12th National People's Congress (NPC) passed a decision to comprehensively revise the Budget Law.[38] Among other things, the decision allows local governments at the provincial level to raise debts by issuing local bonds. The upper limit of the total debt of local governments is to be set by the State Council and approved by the NPC or its Standing Committee. When issuing local bonds within the limit, local governments must secure the approval of the Standing Committee of the provincial People's Congress.[39] As a follow-up, the State Council issued some opinions in October 2014[40] authorizing the MOF to, within the limit approved by the NPC or its Standing Committee, specify the various regional sub-limits and submit them to the State Council for approval.[41] The opinions reiterate that only governments at the provincial level (provinces, autonomous regions, and municipalities directly under the central government) are qualified to raise debt, but add that local governments at the municipal and county level may, when necessary, raise debt through the proxy of provincial-level governments.[42] Consistent with this new development, it is imperative

---

[36] *See* Research Institute for Fiscal Science of the Ministry of Finance 财政部财政科学研究所, 我国地方政府债务风险与对策 (China's Local Governmental Debt Risk and the Countermeasures, 2010 经济研究参考 (Review of Economic Research) no. 14, 21.

[37] 2014 年地方政府债券自发自还试点办法 (Measures for the Pilot Scheme of Self-Issuance and Self-Repayment of Local Government Bonds in 2014) (promulgated by the Ministry of Finance, May 19, 2014, effective upon promulgation).

[38] 全国人民代表大会常务委员会关于修改《中华人民共和国预算法》的决定 (Decision of the NPC Standing Committee to Revise the Budget Law of the People's Republic of China) (promulgated by the Standing Comm. Nat'l People's Cong., Sept. 1, 2014, effective Jan. 1, 2015).

[39] *See* the revised Budget Law, Article 35, Paragraph 2.

[40] 国务院关于加强地方政府性债务管理的意见 (Opinions of the State Council on Strengthening the Administration of Local Governmental Debts) (promulgated by the St. Council, Oct. 2, 2014, effective upon promulgation, "Local Debts Opinions").

[41] *See* Local Debts Opinions, Article 3 (1).

[42] *See id.* Article 2 (1).

that a credit rating system for local governments be established. The credit of local governments, as the issuer, should be comprehensively evaluated and rated by professional rating agencies according to market-based principles and standards. The ratings should serve as a precondition and price basis for the issuance of debt. Foreign experiences have already proved the significance of the credit rating system to the control of risk. Statistics show that in the United States from 1970 through 2011, among rated local bonds, only 71 bonds defaulted, while among unrated local bonds 2,571 bonds defaulted.[43] This is why the State Council has called for the establishment of a credit rating system for local governments and the improvement of the local debt market.[44]

C. PROPERLY DIVIDING THE FISCAL POWER AND EXPENDITURE RESPONSIBILITY BETWEEN CENTRAL AND LOCAL GOVERNMENTS

As mentioned above, there has been a mismatch between the fiscal power and administrative power of local governments, where national income mainly goes to the central government while expenditure responsibilities mostly remain with local governments. This partly caused the spending capacity of local governments to fall short of the need to provide public services, and was one of the major reasons for the continuing expansion of local debt. In addition to establishing and improving the local bond issuance system, the division of the fiscal powers and expenditure responsibilities between the central and local governments also must be adjusted. The first step should be to adjust the division of expenditure responsibilities. Efforts should be made to define the administrative powers and expenditure/fundraising responsibilities of governments at all levels (central and local) in the area of basic public services, drawing experience from the general practice of market economies.[45] In this process, as pointed out by the Central Committee of the Communist Party of China, the administrative powers and expenditure responsibilities of the central government should be strengthened. Central and local governments should then assume and share expenditure responsibilities according to the adjusted division of administrative powers.[46] The next step should be to make necessary amendments to the Budget Law and relevant tax laws and regulations, so as to provide local governments fiscal powers matching their administrative powers and expenditure responsibilities. Local governments in China to a large extent are still playing the role of "unlimited

[43] *See* Liu Baoliang 刘宝亮, 地方债大摸底: 监管层力推信用评级 (A Thorough Survey on the Size of Local Debts: Regulators Push for Credit Rating), 中国经济导报 (China Economic Herald), Oct. 24, 2013, B01.

[44] *See* Local Debts Opinions, Article 3 (2).

[45] *See* Research Institute for Fiscal Science of the Ministry of Finance, *supra* note 36, at 24.

[46] 中共中央关于全面深化改革若干重大问题的决定 (Decision of the Central Committee of the Communist Party of China on Some Major Issues concerning Comprehensively Deepening the Reform) (adopted at the Third Plenary Session of the 18th Central Committee of the Communist Party of China, Nov. 12, 2013), V. 19.

government" or "omnipotent government." As a result, they continue to perform many functions that can and should be performed by the market. This is the real root cause of the booming LGFVs and of mounting local debt. In order to contain the impulse of local governments to borrow, government functions must be transformed to reduce direct involvement and intervention in the economy. Governments should emphasize and highlight their social management and public service functions. The goal should be to transform local governments from unlimited, omnipotent governments into limited, service-oriented governments.

Conclusion

The development of LGFVs reveals a crucial and often overlooked aspect of state capitalism in China: state capitalism at the local level. Far from being mere "bricks" making up the state, local governments have their own objectives and incentives. It was the tremendous local interests involved in the urbanization process that impelled local governments to set up and maintain numerous LGFVs. With their monopoly on land resources, local governments, under the camouflage of LGFVs, can easily obtain money from banks, in particular the CDB. This gives them an insuperable competitive advantage vis-à-vis the private sector, and increases their bargaining power against the central government. If the problem of LGFVs is really to be tackled, the relationship between the government and the market must be further clarified, and their roles properly balanced. The borrowing spree of the LGFVs based on "land finance" is simply unsustainable. It is the general rule of a market economy that the market, not the government, determines the allocation of resources. Given that recently the Party has officially recognized the decisive role of the market in allocating resources,[47] stricter regulation of LGFVs and more regularized debt-raising practices of local governments are foreseeable.[48]

---

[47] *Id.* at I. 3.

[48] The CDB's potential return to a policy bank adds a footnote in this regard. Critics have said that the transformation of the CDB into a commercial bank blurred the line between policy and business, and resulted in "the commercialization of policy banks and 'policization' of commercial banks." *See*Yang Yang 杨玚, 国开行回归政策性银行大幕拉开 (CDB Begins to Return to a Policy Bank), 腾讯财经 (Tencent Finance Web) (Aug. 8, 2014), http://finance.qq.com/a/20140808/012826.htm. Thus by pushing forward the return of the CDB to a policy bank after the retirement of Governor Chen Yuan in 2013, *id.*, the decision-makers are reconsidering the role of policy-based finance vis-à-vis that of commercial banking and more broadly, the role of government vis-à-vis that of the market. This is a move in the right direction, in my opinion.

5 Antitrust Regulation of Chinese State-Owned Enterprises

Angela Huyue Zhang*

Introduction

This chapter explores how the Anti-Monopoly Law (AML),[1] China's first modern antitrust law, is applied to a unique group of economic actors in the Chinese economy—the state-owned enterprises (SOEs). Conventional analysis predicted that the AML was unlikely to be enforced against SOEs. Although there have been perennial complaints from Chinese consumers and private businesses about the monopolistic behavior of SOEs, these actors are widely dispersed. This leads to collective action problems, and individual consumers and businesses lack the incentive to bring cases against SOEs. Even if they were to seek action, their voices would likely be suppressed by powerful interest groups

* I would like to thank the participants at the "Chinese State Capitalism and Institutional Change: Domestic and Global Implications" conference at Columbia Law School, as well as D. Daniel Sokol, for helpful comments. All errors are my own. Email: angela.zhang@kcl.ac.uk. A version of this work previously appeared in the *Stanford Journal of International Law* at 51 STAN. J. INT'L L. (2015). Where appropriate, citation may be made to that version.

[1] 中华人民共和国反垄断法 (Anti-Monopoly Law of P.R. China) (promulgated by the Standing Comm. of the Nat'l People's Cong., Aug. 30, 2007, effective Aug. 1, 2008), http://www.gov.cn/flfg/2007-08/30/content_732591.htm.

representing large SOEs. Therefore, private enforcement is unlikely to be effective in tackling the anticompetitive behavior of SOEs. Similarly, public enforcement against SOEs also seems unlikely, given the significant opposition antitrust enforcement agencies could face.

What would motivate Chinese enforcement agencies to bring actions against SOEs? And if they were to do so, would such enforcement actions be effective in addressing the anticompetitive behavior of SOEs? A recent spate of antitrust enforcement actions against SOEs set the stage for this study. On November 9, 2011, China's National Development and Reform Commission (NDRC) announced on CCTV, the primary state-owned television channel, that it had been investigating two large telecommunication firms, China Telecom and China Unicom, for allegedly conducting price discrimination against rival companies (China Telecom and China Unicom case).[2] As the first antitrust investigation of Chinese SOEs, this high-profile case marked a turning point in Chinese antitrust enforcement. Since then, the AML has frequently been applied to SOEs; the NDRC has investigated a number of high-profile cases and imposed remedies and hefty fines on a variety of state-owned actors. These include large, powerful central SOEs such as China Telecom and China Unicom as well as local SOEs, including premium liquor manufacturers Maotai and Wuliangye,[3] gold retailers in Shanghai,[4] a salt manufacturer in Wuchang,[5] large cement manufacturers,[6] and auto insurance companies.[7] The State Administration for Industry and Commerce (SAIC), another main antitrust enforcer, has also investigated a cartel involving a number of state-owned cement manufacturers in Liaoning province.[8] Within the realm of merger review, more than

---

[2] *See* CCTV, 发改委正调查中国电信和中国联通涉嫌垄断 (The NDRC Is Investigating the Alleged Monopoly Issues of China Telecom and China Unicom), 新浪财经 (SINA FIN.) (Nov. 9, 2011), http://finance.sina.com.cn/g/20111109/121510782543.shtml.

[3] Sichuan Dev. and Reform Comm'n, 四川发改委, 五粮液实施价格垄断被罚处 2.02 亿元 (Wuliangye Conducted Price-Fixing and Was Fined RMB 202 Million), SCDRC.GOV.CN (Feb. 22, 2013), http://www.scdrc.gov.cn/dir25/159074.htm; Guizhou Price Bureau 贵州物价局, 物价局关于茅台反垄断的处罚公告 (The Price Bureau's Announcement Regarding the Maotai Case Antitrust Punishment), 网易财经 (NETEASE FIN.) (Feb. 22, 2013), http://money.163.com/13/0222/16/8OB59OO800252G50.html.

[4] NDRC 发改委, 上海黄金饰品行业协会及部分金店实施价格垄断被处罚 (Shanghai Gold & Jewelry Trade Association and a Number of Gold Retailers Were Fined for Carrying Out Price-Fixing), SDPC.GOV.CN (Aug. 13, 2013), http://www.sdpc.gov.cn/fzgggz/jgjdyfld/jjszhdt/201308/t20130813_553443.html.

[5] NDRC 发改委, 湖北省物价局依法查处武昌盐业分公司强制搭售案件 (Hubei Price Bureau Investigated Wuchang Salt Company's Forced Tying Case), SDPC.GOV.CN (Nov. 15, 2010), http://www.sdpc.gov.cn/fzgggz/jggl/zhdt/201011/t20101115_380425.html.

[6] NDRC 发改委, 三家水泥企业实施价格垄断被罚处 1.14 亿元 (Three Cement Companies Were Fined RMB 114 Million for Conducting Price-Fixing), NDRC.GOV.CN (Sept. 9, 2014), http://jjs.ndrc.gov.cn/gzdt/201409/t20140909_625064.html.

[7] NDRC 发改委, 浙江保险行业违反反垄断法被处 1.1 亿元罚款 (Insurance Companies in Zhejiang Were Fined RMB 110 Million for Violation of the Anti-Monopoly Law), NDRC.GOV.CN (Sept. 2, 2014), http://jjs.ndrc.gov.cn/gzdt/201409/t20140902_624513.html.

[8] SAIC Anti-Monopoly Bureau 工商总局竞争执法局, 辽宁省建筑材料工业协会组织本行业经营者从事垄断协议案 (Liaoning Building Materials Industry Association Organized Industry Business Executives to Conduct Monopoly Agreements), 竞争执法公告 2013 年第 4 号 (2013 Competition Law Enforcement Announcement No. 4), SAIC.GOV.CN (July 26, 2013), http://www.saic.gov.cn/zwgk/gggs/jzzf/201307/t20130726_136746.html.

twenty-seven mergers involving SOEs were notified as of the end of 2013;[9] subsequently, conditions were imposed on General Electric and China Shenhua.[10] In addition, the NDRC publicly vowed to prioritize its enforcement efforts in a number of areas that are dominated by large state-owned monopolies, such as the oil, banking, and telecommunication industries.[11] Insiders working at the NDRC and SAIC indicate that they have investigated more cases involving SOEs beyond those announced in public.[12] However, due to a variety of reasons, many cases were not disclosed, and thus the exact number of SOE cases investigated by Chinese antitrust enforcement agencies cannot be verified. One reason is that some SOEs insist that their cases be kept confidential for fear that bad publicity would harm their reputation and negatively impact their stock performance (as many of them are listed on domestic or foreign stock exchanges).[13]

Although information about antitrust enforcement against SOEs is incomplete, the public enforcement record already demonstrates a far higher enforcement level than conventional analysis predicted. This disparity demands a more nuanced understanding of antitrust intervention in the state-owned sector. In his pathbreaking article "The Theory of Economic Regulation," George Stigler sought to explain the pattern of industry regulation by viewing it as a good whose output is determined by demand and supply.[14] Inspired by Stigler's article, this chapter directs attention to factors bearing on the demand and supply of antitrust regulation of SOEs in China. Section I of this chapter discusses the economic conditions necessary for SOEs to be subject to antitrust regulation. It first clarifies two common misconceptions about Chinese SOEs and analyzes how state-owned monopolies can arise in both competitive and regulated sectors. It

---

[9] Yuni Yan Sobel, *Domestic-to-Domestic Transactions—A Gap in China's Merger Control Regime*, 4 ANTITRUST SOURCE (2014). According to Yan, of the fifty-seven domestic-to-domestic merger transactions notified to the Ministry of Commerce (MOFCOM) during the period of August 1, 2008 to December 31, 2013, at least twenty-six involved SOEs. Note Yan's analysis does not include foreign-to-domestic transactions. For instance, General Electric/Shenhua was notified to MOFCOM and the deal is a foreign-to-domestic transaction.

[10] MOFCOM 商务部, 关于附条件批准通用电气中国有限公司与中国神华煤制油化工有限公司设立合营企业反垄断审查决定的公告 (Announcement Regarding the Conditional Approval of the Merger Clearance Decision of General Electric China Ltd., and China Shenhua Coal, to Liquid and Chemical Co., Ltd.), 商务部公告 2011 年 74 号 (MOFCOM 2011 Announcement No. 74), MOFCOM.GOV.CN (Nov. 10, 2011), http://fldj.mofcom.gov.cn/article/ztxx/201111/20111107855595.shtml.

[11] Kazunori Takada, *China Could Target Oil Firms, Telecoms, Banks in Price Probes*, REUTERS, Aug. 15, 2013, http://uk.reuters.com/article/2013/08/15/uk-china-antitrust-ndrc-idUKBRE97E04W20130815.

[12] Interview with officials working at the NDRC and SAIC. The interviewees wish to remain anonymous. Under the AML, with the exception of merger enforcement, enforcement agencies may disclose antitrust cases they investigate, but are not obligated to do so. *See* AML, *supra* note 1, art. 44.

[13] These SOEs' argument is dubious. A listed company has the mandatory obligation to disclose material information to its stockholders. If an antitrust investigation is likely to influence its stock price, it should be deemed material information subject to mandatory disclosure.

[14] George J. Stigler, *The Theory of Economic Regulation*, 2 BELL J. ECON. & MGMT. SCI. 3 (1971); *see also* Richard A. Posner, *Theories of Economic Regulation*, 5 BELL J. ECON. & MGMT. SCI. 335, 344 (1974).

then discusses how SOEs have achieved significant autonomy in decision-making through various rounds of reforms, in the process creating demand for the state to intervene as a regulator rather than an owner. Section II studies the supply of antitrust enforcement against SOEs by focusing on the costs and benefits antitrust enforcement agencies face in tackling such cases. My conclusion suggests the implications for the next stage of reform of SOEs.

I. The Demand for Antitrust Regulation of SOEs

For SOEs to be subject to antitrust law, at least two essential economic conditions must be satisfied. First, the individual firm or an association of firms acting collectively must enjoy significant market power: monopoly power. An SOE with no monopoly power would be unlikely to engage in anticompetitive behavior unless it joins with other firms to form a cartel. Second, there must be a market in which price plays a role, and the SOE must enjoy the autonomy to set the price. If price is tightly regulated, there is no market and therefore no room for competition.

A. HOW STATE-OWNED MONOPOLIES ARISE

In the West, Chinese SOEs tend to arouse images of large, powerful central SOEs occupying the top slots in the Fortune 500. This misconception partly stems from availability heuristics,[15] as central SOEs tend to appear in the headlines of Western media stories emphasizing the meteoric rise of the SOES or global ambitions (in particular their aggressive overseas expansion). But SOEs have a heterogeneous presence in China and are not limited to those national champions operating in strategically important industries. Indeed, despite the fact that political power is highly concentrated in the central government, the Chinese economy is highly decentralized, and its governance has mostly been delegated to regional governments.

Unlike the Soviet Union, the Chinese economy has rarely been run under a completely centrally planned model, with all business decisions strictly managed by directives from a single central planning office.[16] Rather, the Chinese economy is organized into a multilayer multi-regional form (M-form).[17] During the 1950s to the 1960s, Mao Zedong made repeated efforts to decentralize the Chinese economy and to give more authority to local governments.[18] For instance, the Great Leap Forward campaign of the 1950s

---

[15] "Availability heuristics" refers to the process through which people judge the frequency of an event by the ease with which instances can be brought to mind. *See* Daniel Kahneman & Amos Tversky, *Judgment under Uncertainty: Heuristics and Biases*, 185 SCI. 1124, 1127 (1974).

[16] RONALD COASE & NING WANG, HOW CHINA BECAME CAPITALIST 69 (2012).

[17] Yingyi Qian & Chenggang Xu, *Why China's Economic Reforms Differ: The M-Form Hierarchy and Entry/Expansion of the Non-state Sector*, 1 ECON. TRANSITION 135 (1993).

[18] COASE & WANG, *supra* note 16, at 11–21.

handed over most centrally controlled SOEs to regional governments.[19] Thus at the outset of economic reform in 1979, the central government controlled less than one-half of state-owned sector industrial output.[20] Decentralization was further accelerated in the 1980s, as China implemented a fiscal-sharing scheme between any two adjacent levels of government.[21] This provided stronger incentives to regional governments to initiate new reforms and promote economic growth. Thus, when observers and commentators fixate on those SOEs owned by the central government, they ignore the large bulk of SOEs whose control rights and income rights reside with regional governments.[22]

Over the years, the central government has gradually retreated from controlling SOEs that are solely operating in competitive sectors.[23] But to this day, many regional governments continue to control SOEs that compete head to head with other nonstate companies. These SOEs are deemed local champions and are important contributors to local Gross Domestic Product (GDP). For instance, Gree Electric Appliances, Inc., a leading manufacturer of air conditioning and electronics in China, is controlled by the Zhuhai City government in Guangdong province. Shanghai Brightfood, a multinational food and beverage manufacturing conglomerate, is controlled by the Shanghai government. Sichuan Changong Electric Co., Ltd., one of the leading television manufacturers in China, is controlled by the Sichuan provincial government. Although portions of these companies have been listed publicly, the local State-owned Assets Supervision and Administration Commissions (SASAC) continue to control the majority of their equity, and their state-owned shares are restricted from public trading.

---

[19] Chenggang Xu, *The Fundamental Institutions of China's Reforms and Development*, 49 J. Econ. Literature 1076, 1084 (2011).

[20] Gabriella Montinola et al., *Federalism, Chinese Style: The Political Basis for Economic Success in China*, 48 World Politics 50, 61 (1995).

[21] *Id.* at 63. This fiscal system was maintained until 1993. In 1994, the government introduced a new fiscal system, which established a two-tier tax administration system (national and local) that separates taxes into national, local, and shared taxes. *Id.* at 72.

[22] Andrew Szamosszegi & Cole Kyle, U.S.-China Econ. and Sec. Review Comm'n, An Analysis of State-Owned Enterprises and State Capitalism in China 26 (2011), *available at* http://origin.www.uscc.gov/sites/default/files/Research/10_26_11_CapitalTradeSOEStudy.pdf, at 26. For instance, Chinese sources indicate that in 2010, the number of SOEs exceeded 100,000. However, the number of SOEs controlled by the central government was only 120. The remainder were controlled by regional governments.

[23] When the State-owned Asset Supervision and Administration Commission (SASAC) was first established in 2003, it supervised 196 companies. The number fell to 152 in 2007, and it currently supervises only 112 companies. *See* 央企目录 (The List of Central SOEs), SASAC.gov.cn, http://www.sasac.gov.cn/n1180/n1226/n2425/index.html (last visited Mar. 6, 2015); *see also* Barry Naughton, *SASAC and Rising Corporate Power in China*, 24 China Leadership Monitor (2008).

1. SOEs in Competitive Sectors

SOEs that operate in competitive sectors are unlikely to have monopoly power. But even SOEs without monopoly power can violate antitrust law. A cartel, for instance, constitutes a form of antitrust violation committed by a group of firms with no individual monopoly power. Generally speaking, the more concentrated the market, the fewer the participants involved and the lower the cost of coordinating and maintaining the cartel. Thus, cartels tend to be more stable in concentrated markets than in highly competitive ones.

Under China's M-form economy, each region is relatively self-contained and self-sufficient, the size of the enterprise is relatively small, and industries are less concentrated than in other centrally planned economies.[24] However, as regional governments compete fiercely for economic growth within their own jurisdictions, decentralization increases the incentives as well as the range of political means for local governments to erect trade barriers and ban imports.[25] Local protectionism therefore artificially carves up a large, single Chinese market into smaller segments, reducing the size of the market as well as the quality of market demand.[26]

For instance, the cement industry has long been beset with overcapacity problems, and for decades the central government has been calling for consolidation and rationalization.[27] Local governments have an ambivalent response to such calls. On the one hand, they fiercely oppose cross-regional mergers and acquisitions, as they could harm local tax revenue and cause unemployment.[28] On the other hand, local governments enthusiastically support expansion of local SOEs through regional mergers and acquisitions as this helps to create local champions.[29] This reflects a phenomenon known as the "state advances and the private sector retreats" (*guojin mintui*), which became common

---

[24] Charles Goodhart & Chenggang Xu, Ctr. for Econ. Performance, The Rise of China as an Economic Power 15 (1996).

[25] *See* Montinola et al., *supra* note 20, at 65.

[26] *See* Yasheng Huang, Selling China 313 (2003).

[27] *See* OECD, OECD Reviews of Regulatory Reform: China—Defining the Boundary between the Market and the State 124 (2009).

[28] *See* 水泥行业遭地方保护 10 年 38 个文件难解产能过剩 (Local Protectionism in Cement Industry—38 Directives in 10 Years Cannot Solve Problems of Overcapacity), 中国网 (China Net) (Oct. 30, 2012), http://finance.china.com.cn/industry/hotnews/20121030/1102483.shtml.

[29] For instance, Jidong Cement and Yatai Cement, two of the largest cement manufacturers in China, are respectively owned by Hebei province and Jilin province. With the support of local governments, both companies have expanded within their own regions by acquiring smaller state-owned or private cement manufacturers in recent years. *See, e.g.*, 收购金圆水泥 亚泰集团区域扩张加速 (Acquiring Jinyuan Cement, Yatai Accelerates Regional Expansion), Guba.com.cn (Jan. 11, 2013), http://guba.eastmoney.com/news,600881,60833240.html; Liu Weixun 刘伟勋, 冀东水泥扩张变奏：从新建产能到区域并购 (Jidong Cement Expansion Variations: From Capacity Building to Regional Takeovers), 经济观察网 (Econ. Observer Web) (Aug. 23, 2010), http://www.eeo.com.cn/industry/weekly_firms/2010/08/23/178911.shtml.

after the recent financial crisis. This has been observed not only in the cement industry, but also in industries such as steel, iron, and coal.[30] Thus, despite the fact that national concentration is low,[31] local protectionism can give rise to market conditions conducive to cartel formation at the regional level.

When an SOE faces fierce competition from nonstate firms, it is tempting for it to form a cartel with rivals to avoid so-called "excessive competition."[32] Indeed, because SOEs are more susceptible to market risks, they are more likely to be loss-making than regulated SOEs. Local governments are often sympathetic to these so-called "crisis cartels," as bankruptcies of local SOEs can cause massive unemployment in the regional economy. In 2013, the Liaoning Administration for Industry and Commerce (AIC), a local SAIC office, investigated a cartel organized by a cement industry association.[33] According to SAIC's press release, the association organized eleven cement manufacturers in Liaoning province to fix prices and restrict output. Although the press release omitted this information, some of these manufacturers are in fact owned by regional governments. In 2014, the NDRC imposed a fine of RMB 114 million on three state-owned cement companies for forming a cartel to restrict output with the goal of preventing "excessive competition."[34]

2. SOEs in Regulated Sectors

Generally speaking, SOEs operating in regulated sectors are either legal monopolies and/or natural monopolies. These sectors occupy the "commanding heights" of the Chinese economy, including energy, aviation, telecoms, banking, railway, and shipping. These SOEs are controlled by the central government and are granted exclusive or privileged roles, thus shielding them from competition from private investors.

One unique feature of regulated sectors such as electricity and telecommunications is that they typically include segments of basic infrastructure that have the characteristics of "natural monopolies." Competition is not viable in certain segments of these sectors, and it is most efficient to have a single firm operating in the market. At the same time, many countries have come to realize that competition can be introduced in upstream or downstream sectors.[35] China has made similar reforms by unbundling the preexisting state-owned monopolies in the electricity and telecommunication industries. Although

---

[30] *See* Sheng Hong & Zhao Nong, China's State-Owned Enterprises: Nature, Performance and Reform xv (2013).

[31] World Bank & Dev. Research Ctr. of the State Council of P.R. China, China 2030: Building a Modern, Harmonious, and Creative High-Income Society 112 (2012).

[32] *See* Bruce M. Owens et al., *China's Competition Policy Reform: The Anti-Monopoly Law and Beyond*, 75 Antitrust L. J. 231, 247–52 (2008).

[33] *See* SAIC Anti-Monopoly Bureau, *supra* note 8.

[34] *See* NDRC, *supra* note 6.

[35] *See* OECD, *supra* note 27, at 22.

individual SOEs still dominate the basic infrastructure market, the government has tried to create competition in upstream and/or downstream market segments. These segments have also been opened to private investors, including foreign investors subject to ownership restrictions.[36] The problem, however, is that those SOEs that have dominance in the infrastructure markets are vertically integrated, so they also operate in the competitive segments of the markets. Vertically integrated SOEs attempt to leverage their dominance of basic infrastructure markets in competitive markets by squeezing the profit margin of other SOEs. This creates demand among those competitive SOEs for antitrust protection.

It is thus no coincidence that the first antitrust investigation involving SOEs arose in the broadband access market. According to complaints lodged by rivals, China Telecom and China Unicom charged higher fees for interconnection (fixed at RMB 1000 Mb/Month) to large Internet service providers (ISPs) that posed a serious competitive threat. China Telecom and China Unicom set lower prices (RMB 200–300 Mb/Month) for non-competitors (often small ISPs).[37] But this differential pricing scheme soon led to arbitrage opportunities, as small ISPs packaged their bandwidth and resold it to larger companies.[38] After detecting such sales, China Telecom issued a notice in July 2010 to its subsidiaries prohibiting resale by small ISPs. This action resulted in the blackout of Internet access for many large ISPs, which relied on the cheaper bandwidth sold by small ISPs. One of the companies that suffered significant loss was China Railcom, a state-owned subsidiary of China Mobile. China Railcom is a fervent supporter of the NDRC's antitrust investigation into China Telecom and closely cooperated with the NDRC during the investigation.[39] Another supporter for the NDRC's action is the State Administration for Radio, Film and Television (SARFT), whose operating business has recently entered the ISP market and become a formidable rival to China Telecom and China Unicom.[40] Despite their support for enforcement action, SOEs such as China Railcom and SARFT have called for antitrust regulation of SOEs only halfheartedly.

---

[36] *Id.* at 59–60.

[37] *See* Xiaoye Wang, *The China Telecom and China Unicom Case and the Future of Chinese Antitrust, in* China's Anti-Monopoly Law: The First Five Years 467, 470 (Adrian Emch & David Stallibrass eds., 2013).

[38] 中国电信为何遭遇反垄断调查 (Why China Telecom Was Subject to Antitrust Investigation), 经济参考报 (Econ. Info. Daily) (Nov. 11, 2011), *available at* http://finance.sina.com.cn/roll/20111111/070310796649.shtml.

[39] Some news reports suggest that China Railcom was the complainant that initiated NDRC's investigation into China Telecom and China Unicom. *See, e.g.*, 工信部望铁通取消对电信联通举报 广电总局称应彻查 (Ministry of Industry and Information Technology Hopes That China Railcom Will Withdraw Its Complaint against China Telecom but the State Administration for Radio, Film and Television Request Thorough Investigation of China Telecom), 新浪财经 (SINA Finance) (Nov. 22, 2011), http://finance.sina.com.cn/chanjing/yjsy/20111122/115310860071.shtml.

[40] *Id.*

They are well aware that they are also sheltered from competition in many of the areas in which they operate, and would rather be left in peace than disturb such arrangements.

B. INCREASED AUTONOMY FOR SOES

Antitrust law regulates market behavior, not government behavior. If the hands of the managers of Chinese SOEs were tied and the government gave detailed instructions as to how the SOEs should be run, there would be no need for antitrust regulation. But this is no longer the case in China. The evolution of SOE governance in the past three decades reveals the Chinese leadership's consistent logic in reforming SOEs: to incentivize SOEs to become profit-oriented commercial entities, they need to be granted more autonomy in running their operations. Granting more managerial autonomy to SOEs necessitates weakening the link between the state and enterprises.

For example, in the early 1980s, dual-track reform was introduced into SOE production and sales, allowing managers to sell surplus products at market prices for a profit once SOEs fulfilled their compulsory production quotas.[41] The "contract responsibility" system was implemented in the mid-1980s, whereby managers of SOEs were held responsible for profits and losses.[42] In 1992, the Chinese government conducted a massive price reform program, resulting in the price deregulation of raw materials, capital goods, and transportation services. The number of price-regulated items shrank from 737 to 89.[43] This list was further reduced to 13 in 2001.[44] The removal of price controls officially ended the history of the dual-track pricing system and was the key to the functioning of a Chinese market system. According to the Organization for Economic Co-operation and Development (OECD), more than 90 percent of the retail transactions and sales of agricultural products were determined by market prices by 2002.[45]

Concurrent with its plan for price reform, the government started to introduce modern corporate governance structures into SOEs. The first step was the passage of the Company Law in 1993, which provided a framework for converting traditional SOEs into modern corporations.[46] Beginning in the mid-1990s, the government began a comprehensive overhaul of the SOE sector. It first conducted a massive privatization program by selling off loss-making small and medium-sized SOEs. Meanwhile, the government aimed to transition the remaining SOEs from a structure involving sole state

---

[41] BARRY NAUGHTON, THE CHINESE ECONOMY: TRANSITIONS AND GROWTH 92 (2006).

[42] Gang Xiao et. al., *State-Owned Enterprises in China, Reform Dynamics and Impact, in* CHINA'S NEW PLACE IN A WORLD IN CRISIS 155, 157 (Ross Garnaut et al. eds., 2009).

[43] COASE & WANG, *supra* note 16, at 124.

[44] *Id.*

[45] OECD, *supra* note 27, at 123–24.

[46] *See* NAUGHTON, *supra* note 41, at 301.

proprietorship and control by industry-specific government agencies to a Western-style corporate governance structure.

In 2003, the Chinese government created SASAC, a special commission directly subordinate to the State Council, to manage its ownership interests in SOEs. SASAC's main responsibility is to manage and monitor the state's investments in SOEs, with the aim of maximizing value. However, SASAC is restricted to exercising arm's-length supervision, and does not intervene with the daily business decisions of SOEs.[47] Local governments—including those at provincial and municipal levels—were in turn directed to establish their own SASACs. These regional SASACs represent local governments' ownership of assets, and are not subordinate to the central SASAC.[48] Because each SASAC represents the state's ownership interests in a large number of SOEs, they have only limited ability to monitor any single firm. The central SASAC's control of the SOEs it monitors is particularly limited because multiple layers of holding companies own stakes in publicly traded SOEs. Indeed, commentators observe that it is the highest level of holding companies, rather than the central SASAC, that actually controls the SOEs.[49] According to one study, SOE executives do not regard interference by the Chinese state as their principal management challenge.[50]

II. The Supply of Antitrust Regulation of SOEs

If we view antitrust regulators as rational actors, their decision-making process is guided by the careful weighing of the costs and benefits of the consequences of their enforcement actions. Thus, in order to understand the behavior of Chinese antitrust regulators, we need to carefully examine their incentive structure—the benefits and costs they confront in tackling SOE cases. Moreover, Chinese antitrust regulators face severe capacity constraints. As with private actors, regulators are motivated to produce outputs that generate the highest profits; that is, they will optimize their resource allocation to cases that will bring them the most net benefits.

---

[47] *See* Angela Huyue Zhang, *The Single Entity Theory: An Antitrust Time-Bomb for Chinese State-Owned Enterprises?*, 8 J. Comp. L. & Econ. 805, 813 (2012).

[48] *See* Barry Naughton, *The State Asset Commission: A Powerful New Government Body*, 8 China Leadership Monitor (2003).

[49] *See* Naughton, *supra* note 41, at 317–18.

[50] *See generally* Carsten A. Holz, China's Industrial State-Owned Enterprise: Between Profitability and Bankruptcy (2003).

A. THE UTILITY FUNCTION OF ADMINISTRATIVE AGENCIES IN CHINA

In a classic paper on administrative behavior, Richard Posner modeled the utility of administrative agencies' law enforcement activity as the public benefit, if prosecuted successfully, discounted by the probability of successful prosecution.[51] To maximize expected utility, a government agency invests resources, such as its staff's time, in prosecuting violators.[52] Generally speaking, the more the defendant spends litigating against the government's action, the less likely it is that the government will succeed.[53] Posner's model has assumed a democratic setting where the judiciary provides a check on an agency's behavior and defendants fight against the government's action in court. But in a country such as China, where judicial power is often usurped by political power, judicial oversight is severely limited. Indeed, since the enactment of the AML in 2008 there has been only one appeal lodged against a local enforcement agency (in Jiangsu province), and no appeals lodged against any central enforcement agency.[54]

The near absence of judicial review does not mean, however, that Chinese agencies do not incur any costs or face any constraints in prosecuting antitrust cases. Certainly, Chinese administrative agencies must invest resources in investigating cases. But because the evidence they gather and the analysis they produce are seldom challenged in court, their cost in investigation and prosecution is low compared to the cost faced by government agencies in countries with established rule of law. Businesses in China know too well that it is not cost-effective to challenge the government's actions in court, given the low success rate of administrative litigation and the potential for retaliation from the government entity they are trying to sue.[55] As a consequence, the main recourse for defendants subject to antitrust investigation is to lobby the relevant bureaucratic departments, a practice that transforms law enforcement into a bureaucratic process of bargaining and negotiation. Indeed, in China the main battleground for administrative enforcement is not in the courts, but within the government bureaucracy. This is

---

[51] Richard A. Posner, *The Behavior of Administrative Agencies*, J. LEGAL STUD. 305, 305 (1972).

[52] *Id.* at 306.

[53] *Id.*

[54] Policy and Regulatory Report, *Trio of Chinese Concrete Players Challenged Provincial Regulator's Cartel Fine*, May 13, 2014. According to this news report, three concrete manufacturers, Nanjing Construction Group, Nanjing Jiasheng Concrete, and Nanjing Dadi Wanhong Concrete, brought an appeal against the Jiangsu Price Bureau in Nanjing Intermediate Court on April 28, 2014. The appeal challenged the Jiangsu Price Bureau's decision to fine thirty-seven concrete manufacturers for engaging in a cartel in 2013. This was the first time companies challenged an antitrust regulator in court under the AML.

[55] Angela Huyue Zhang, *Bureaucratic Politics and China's Anti-Monopoly Law*, 47 CORNELL INT'L L. J. 671, 678 (2014) (noting that because Chinese antitrust enforcement agencies are nested within central ministries that work like conglomerates, businesses fear retaliation not only from the particular department that handles their merger review or antitrust investigation, but also from other departments within the ministries that may have policy control over other aspects of their businesses).

particularly the case for SOE defendants, who have relatively easy access to the government and can spend their resources more effectively on lobbying relevant departments. As a consequence, the more politically powerful the SOE, the more resources it has for lobbying the government bureaucracy—and, thus, the higher the cost for any Chinese administrative agency that wants to challenge the SOE's actions.

Today, many of the top business leaders within SOEs continue to be appointed through the *nomenklatura* system and accordingly enjoy bureaucratic ranking (which also implicitly determines the ranking of the SOEs). This means that the leaders of SOEs have direct contact with the government—they do not need to work through business associations to convey their opinions and views and can instead lobby directly.[56] Moreover, the "revolving door" policy further strengthens the ability of SOEs to lobby the relevant bureaucratic departments.[57] In China, it is common for SOE managers to be transferred to government positions. Government officials working with SOEs can also be subsequently appointed to SOE management positions.[58] A recent survey revealed that close to 30 percent of the 183 officials above vice-ministerial level in various central ministries and organizations formerly worked for SOEs.[59] Another survey found that 115 senior executives working at forty-seven central SOEs previously served in the government.[60] For example, Zhou Yongkang, a former member of the Politburo with extensive experience working in the oil sector, maintained a large network within national oil companies through his influence on personnel appointment in these firms.[61] Crony capitalism also plays an important role in this regard. It is widely known domestically and abroad that children of senior Chinese leaders (the so-called princelings) have served as top executives at a number of large SOEs.[62] For instance, the family of Li Peng, the former premier, has tremendous power and influence in China's electric power industry.[63]

Indeed, the political pecking order of enforcement targets compared to the regulators is an important determinant of the costs Chinese antitrust agencies face in enforcing the AML. Other things being equal, the cost of bringing a case against an SOE will be higher than bringing one against a nonstate firm. Likewise, the cost of challenging the

---

[56] Kjeld Erik Brodsgaard, *Politics and Business Group Formation in China: The Party in Control*?, 211 CHINA Q. 627 (2012).

[57] *See* HONG & NONG, *supra* note 30, at 186–89; *see also* Cheng Li, *China's Midterm Jockeying: Gearing Up for 2012 (Part 4: Top Leaders of Major State-Owned Enterprises)*, 34 CHINA LEADERSHIP MONITOR 27 (2011).

[58] *See* HONG & NONG, *supra* note 30, at 188.

[59] *Id.* at xxiii.

[60] *Id.*

[61] Erica Downs & Michal Meidan, *Business and Politics in China: The Oil Executive Reshuffles of 2011*, 19 CHINA SECURITY 6 (2011). Zhou Yongkang was arrested in late 2014 for corruption. *See* Philip Wen, *Zhou Yongkang, China's Former Security Chief, Arrested and Expelled from Communist Party*, SUNDAY MORNING HERALD (Dec. 6, 2014), *available at* http://www.smh.com.au/world/zhou-yongkang-chinas-former-security-chief-arrested-and-expelled-from-communist-party-20141206-12i0qf.html.

[62] *See* Li, *supra* note 57, at 22.

[63] *Id.*

action of a central SOE will be higher than that of challenging a local SOE. The cost further varies depending on the bureaucratic rank of the antitrust agencies. The higher the agency's bureaucratic rank, the less opposition it faces from SOEs. For instance, the cost of prosecuting a local SOE will be lower for central enforcers than for local ones, as the former have a higher bureaucratic rank than the latter and thus are not subject to constraints imposed by local governments (as discussed in more detail in Section II(C) below). Meanwhile, there exists an implicit political pecking order among the three central administrative antitrust enforcement agencies—despite the fact that they officially enjoy the same ministerial rank. As elaborated in Section II(B) below, the NDRC is often deemed more powerful than the Ministry of Commerce (MOFCOM) and SAIC due to the NDRC's historical status as supra-ministerial and its pervasive policy control. SAIC appears to be the weakest of the three as it has a relatively narrow mandate and has the least policy control over SOEs.

Another limitation of Posner's model is that it can be applied only in an ideal world where no information asymmetry exists between the public and administrative agencies. In this utopian scenario, the interests of the general public and administrative agencies are perfectly aligned, and government agencies maximize their utility when they maximize the social welfare of the public. But this does not play out in reality. Unlike private enterprises, the output of government agencies is notoriously difficult to evaluate. Indeed, although regulators tout the amount of fines they impose and the number of cases they bring, these figures may have only a weak correlation with real gains in consumer welfare. This phenomenon is certainly not unique to China. In the United States, antitrust agencies have been observed to misallocate efforts on cases that they are more likely to win rather than those that could potentially prevent greater anticompetitive harm.[64]

Yet the problem in China is more severe and is not limited to the misallocation of enforcement resources. Effective judicial supervision lowers the cost of enforcement errors, particularly the cost of over-enforcement. Without an impartial judiciary supervising administrative behavior, the public is deprived of an important source of information to evaluate the performance of agencies. The fundamental question of whether an antitrust intervention is welfare-enhancing is therefore continuously left open. This absence of judicial supervision, coupled with opacity in government enforcement, has made the behavior of Chinese government agencies largely unobservable to outsiders. This information asymmetry leads to problems of moral hazard, where administrative agencies focus on collecting the benefits of regulation for themselves rather than on maximizing public welfare. Public benefit may very well be decoupled from the benefit to administrative agencies.

---

[64] *See generally* Richard A. Posner, *A Statistical Study of Antitrust Enforcement*, 13 J.L. & ECON. 365 (1970); Richard A. Posner, *The Federal Trade Commission*, 37 U. CHI. L. REV. 47 (1969).

What do Chinese administrative agencies hope to gain from prosecuting antitrust cases? Political scientists have long observed that administrative intervention in the market creates valuable resources for Chinese bureaucrats, who can then appropriate such value in the form of bribes (corruption) or political support (patronage).[65] As power tends to be fragmented within the Chinese government bureaucracy, there is an endless struggle among government agencies at all levels for policy control.[66] The more control an agency has, the more opportunities it will have for rent-seeking activities. For forward-looking government officials, policy control can also help expand resources available to agencies controlled by faction members.[67] The agencies can then capitalize on these resources to accumulate more administrative merits (*zhengji*), thus helping faction members rise in China's Communist Party (CCP) hierarchy.[68]

B. THE INCENTIVES TO REGULATE SOES

Currently, the primary responsibilities for public enforcement of the AML are split among three administrative agencies—MOFCOM, the NDRC, and SAIC. MOFCOM is primarily responsible for merger control, a preemptive form of antitrust intervention; the NDRC and SAIC are responsible for ex post antitrust enforcement. These three administrative agencies are highly resource-constrained. The NDRC and SAIC employ approximately fifteen and eight people in Beijing, respectively, responsible for antitrust enforcement.[69] MOFCOM employs approximately thirty-five people to handle merger review.[70] The total number of personnel responsible for AML enforcement at the central level is therefore no more than approximately sixty.

When demand for regulation exceeds supply, the outcome is either delay in enforcement or selective enforcement. This partly explains MOFCOM's significant delay in merger reviews, as China's merger-control procedure necessitates reviewing and responding to all notified mergers.[71] NDRC and SAIC have made little effort to identify markets in which serious problems of monopoly can arise; instead they act almost solely on complaints from disgruntled competitors, purchasers, and employees.[72] As this non-action is seldom subject

---

[65] SUSAN L. SHIRK, THE POLITICAL LOGIC OF ECONOMIC REFORM IN CHINA 142 (1993).

[66] *See* KENNETH LIEBERTHAL & MICHEL OKSENBERG, POLICY MAKING IN CHINA: LEADERS, STRUCTURES, AND PROCESSES 9–14 (1988).

[67] *See* VICTOR SHIH, FACTIONS AND FINANCE IN CHINA: ELITE CONFLICT AND INFLATION 5 (2009) (discussing the role of politics and factions in influencing China's financial policy). Note that although factions are officially prohibited within the CCP, abundant literature on Chinese politics identifies them as key to understanding political power in China. For more details on how the formation and maintenance of factions may influence the behavior of Chinese bureaucrats, *see* Zhang, *supra* note 55.

[68] *See* SHIH, *supra* note 67, at 54.

[69] Interviews with government officials at central ministries.

[70] *Id.*

[71] *See* Zhang, *supra* note 55.

[72] Interviews with government officials working at central ministries. *See also* PaRR, *Whistle Blowers Spur Vast Majority of Chinese Investigations*, May 22, 2014. At a recent conference held in Beijing, Xu Kunlin,

to challenge, NDRC and SAIC can prioritize their resources on cases that maximize their net benefit. Given this situation, what would incentivize them to bring cases against SOEs?

For sure, each of the three antitrust enforcement agencies has a clear interest in competing for antitrust policy control. But antitrust is not their only competitive arena. Each of the agencies is nested within a central ministry, and the mission of these ministries has a significant impact on shaping agency enforcement of the AML. From the perspective of leadership at the three enforcement agencies, antitrust enforcement is simply another means to fulfill their original mission—the ultimate goal being to gain more policy control within the scope of their designated responsibilities.

The NDRC in particular is an agency primarily in charge of macroeconomic management and industrial planning.[73] Its predecessor was the State Planning Commission (SPC). Also known as the "little State Council," the SPC played a crucial role during the centrally planned era.[74] Its political stature declined when China embarked on market reform and began liberalizing the prices of most commodities and services. The NDRC currently has eleven bureaus in charge of overseeing various aspects of the Chinese economy. Among its powers are the right to approve large investment projects proposed by SOEs and to oversee prices in thirteen regulated sectors—all of them dominated by SOEs. Thus long before the NDRC assumed its role as an antitrust regulator, it already had significant policy control over SOEs. It is therefore no surprise that the agency is motivated to bring antitrust actions against SOEs despite the relatively higher costs of tackling SOE cases.

Compared with the NDRC, MOFCOM is seen as a more liberal government agency. This is determined by its mission, which is tied to overseeing market development and promoting international trade and investment.[75] MOFCOM has played a key role in representing China in trade negotiations with foreign countries. One of its crowning achievements was to represent China in negotiating the trade deals necessary for accession to the World Trade Organization. In contrast to the NDRC, whose bureaucratic interest is tied to direct government intervention, MOFCOM's interest lies in endorsing the further advancement of the market economy and promotion of Chinese trade with the rest of the world.[76] Officials working at MOFCOM are trained to understand

---

the deputy director of the Price Supervision and Anti-Monopoly Bureau, publicly admitted that all of its investigations, apart from the Maotai and Wuliangye cases, were initiated upon complaints.

[73] *Main Functions of the NDRC*, NDRC.GOV.CN, http://en.the NDRC.gov.cn/mfndrc/ (last visited Mar. 6, 2015).

[74] LIEBERTHAL & OKSENBERG, *supra* note 66, at 64.

[75] *Mission of MOFCOM*, MOFCOM.GOV.CN (Dec. 7, 2010), http://english.mofcom.gov.cn/column/mission2010.shtml.

[76] For instance, Hucheng Gao, MOFCOM's incumbent minister, recently published an enthusiastic piece advocating for open markets. *See* 高虎城：中国越发展就越开放 (Hucheng Gao: China Becomes More Open as It Develops—Further Studying and Implementing Xi Jinping's Important Statements on Comprehensively Deepening Reform), 人民日报 (CHINA DAILY) (Dec. 9, 2013), *available at* http://www.mofcom.gov.cn/article/ae/ai/201312/20131200418351.shtml.

international rules of trade and investment, and many of them have experience working in government posts overseas. It is thus no coincidence that MOFCOM became the main enforcer of merger control, as most of the mergers subject to its review involve international mergers and acquisitions by multinational companies rather than domestic firms.[77] In fact, MOFCOM started to conduct merger review of foreign acquisitions of domestic assets as early as 2003.[78] MOFCOM is therefore well-positioned to play the role of gatekeeper of national interests, while ensuring that its merger review is largely consistent with international standards.

Compared to MOFCOM and the NDRC, SAIC is small in size and has a narrow mandate. It is primarily responsible for various aspects of market supervision, such as administration of enterprise registration, regulation of unfair competitive behavior, and consumer protection.[79] In terms of political power, SAIC is weaker than the other agencies. Unlike the NDRC, which used to be a supra-ministry, and MOFCOM, which has enjoyed ministerial ranking from the start, SAIC was not promoted to ministerial status until 2001. As SAIC does not assume any important regulatory role over central SOEs, it has less political influence over them and its cost of bringing cases against SOEs is higher than that of the other two agencies. The benefits to SAIC are also relatively small because regulation of SOEs is not particularly relevant to its other designated responsibilities.

It is thus no surprise that the first antitrust investigation into central SOEs was brought by the NDRC. As illustrated in the discussion of the China Telecom and China Unicom case below, the motivation for the NDRC's intervention arose not only from antitrust concerns, but perhaps more importantly from its desire to strengthen its control over telecom pricing. The main challenges the NDRC faced in investigating this case came not from gathering evidence or conducting legal analysis, but from bargaining and negotiating with the relevant SOEs and other government actors. For the NDRC, the battle was not fought in the courts, but behind the scenes within the government bureaucracy.

C. ENFORCEMENT AGAINST CENTRAL SOES

In 2011, the NDRC's investigation into two large state-owned telecommunication companies caused a stir among the Chinese public. According to the NDRC, China Telecom and China Unicom had conducted price discrimination by charging rival ISPs much

---

[77] *See* Zhang, *supra* note 55 (finding that the majority of mergers reviewed by MOFCOM in the first five years involved foreign-to-foreign transactions).

[78] *See* Interim Provisions for Foreign Investors to Merge and Acquire Domestic Enterprises (adopted at the First Meeting of the Ministry of Foreign Trade and Econ. Cooperation of P.R. China, Jan. 2, 2003, effective Apr. 12, 2003), art. 6, *available at* http://bizchina.chinadaily.com.cn/guide/law/law05.htm.

[79] *Mission of SAIC*, SAIC.GOV.CN, http://www.saic.gov.cn/english/aboutus/Mission/ (last visited Mar. 6, 2015).

higher prices than small ISPs not competing with them.[80] When the NDRC announced its investigation on national television, public sentiment was overwhelmingly positive. The case was widely applauded by Chinese intellectuals as a major breakthrough. But it soon ran into a stalemate. A few days after the NDRC's announcement on CCTV, two editorials defending the two SOEs and harshly criticizing the NDRC's investigation appeared in newspapers managed by the Ministry of Industry and Information Technology (MIIT), a telecom sector regulator.[81] A few weeks later, both SOEs proposed a number of rectifications and requested suspension of the investigation.[82] The NDRC acknowledged the receipt of the proposal and, as of early 2015, no fine had been imposed. The NDRC made no announcements regarding its decision. Well-known antitrust scholars such as Wang Xiaoye have expressed disappointment and have criticized the lack of decision.[83]

It would be difficult to understand the elusive outcome of this case without acknowledging the political dynamics among the government actors involved. When the NDRC tries to regulate large SOEs such as China Telecom and China Unicom, it faces potential opposition from a number of powerful actors. The first are the SOEs themselves. The leaders of China Telecom and China Unicom are appointed and managed by the Organization Department of the Central Committee of the CCP and enjoy a rank that equals that of the vice-minister of the NDRC. Thus, their bureaucratic rank is higher than the head of the Price Supervision and Anti-Monopoly Bureau at the NDRC. This means the director general of the Price Supervision and Anti-Monopoly Bureau cannot give direct orders to the head of these two telecom firms. The former would need to obtain support from a higher level of authority at the NDRC or an even higher level of the government—such as the State Council—in order to exert sufficient pressure to compel the SOEs to comply with orders.

---

[80] The NDRC has disclosed none of its evidence and the case has not been heard in court. This chapter thus does not comment on the merits of the NDRC's investigation. Leading Chinese scholars have different views on the case. Compare Wang, *supra* note 37 (arguing that there is solid evidence showing that the two telecom firms abused their dominant positions) with Zhang Xinzhu 张昕竹, 电信反垄断案反思: 产权改革是难以逾越鸿沟 (Reflections on the China Telecom Antitrust Case: The Reform of Property Rights Is an Insurmountable Gap), 新浪财经 (SINA FIN.) (Dec. 13, 2011), *available at* http://finance.sina.com.cn/chanjing/sdbd/20111213/073810981972.shtml (arguing that the NDRC's allegation that the two telecom firms conducted price discrimination without reasonable justification lacks legal and economic support).

[81] 工信部下属两家媒体驳电信联通涉嫌垄断报道 (MIIT Rebuts News Media Reports of the Alleged Monopoly Behavior by China Telecom and China Unicom), 新景报网 (BEIJING NEWS WEB) (Nov. 12, 2011), *available at* http://politics.people.com.cn/GB/1026/16224650.html.

[82] 电信联通申请中止垄断调查 (China Telecom and China Unicom Apply for Suspension of Antitrust Investigation), 人民网 (PEOPLE'S NET) (Dec. 2, 2011), *available at* http://tech.ifeng.com/telecom/special/fanlongduan/content-2/detail_2011_12/02/11066505_0.shtml.

[83] *See* Wang, *supra* note 37, at 478–86.

The second potential source of pressure comes from SASAC, the commission established directly under the State Council, which is responsible for overseeing the state's assets. SASAC has sought to emulate earlier efforts in Japan and Korea to develop national champions.[84] Its main bureaucratic interest lies in fostering bigger and stronger SOEs. Accordingly, SASAC has the incentive to "protect" SOEs and to grant them monopolistic resources.[85] Indeed, in recent years SASAC has emerged as the powerful and vocal protector of the telecom sector in SASAC's efforts to protect the financial interests of these two firms.[86] Thus even if these two telecom firms did abuse their monopoly power in order to maximize their profits, such behavior is consistent with SASAC's goal of maximizing asset values. From SASAC's perspective, harsh antitrust punishment of these SOEs would not only harm their reputations, but would also impact their stock performance and asset values.

Another potential source of pressure comes from the regulators overseeing certain industry sectors. Sector regulation in China is often fragmented across a number of bodies. When antitrust regulators are added to the mix, it further complicates the power dynamics among government agencies with a say in the regulation of SOEs. To compare the bureaucracy to a firm, the more actors involved in this process, the more costly the output.[87]

The rectifications proposed by China Telecom and China Unicom, if accepted and enacted, would not only address the interconnection issues brought up in the NDRC's antitrust challenge but also would "greatly enhance the penetration of fiber access and broadband access rates [and] reduce the unit bandwidth price for Internet users by 35 percent within five years . . . ."[88] In March 2012, a deputy director from the antitrust unit of the NDRC disclosed developments in the case and revealed that "China Telecom and China Unicom had completed expanding their Internet broadband width by 100G and had committed to further reduce network tariffs for consumers."[89] The official also revealed that China Unicom claimed that "the penetration rate of 4 trillion G bandwidth for public users will reach 50 percent by the end of 2012."[90] These ameliorative commitments obviously have exceeded the scope of the original antitrust complaint, thus raising the question of whether the NDRC was acting as an antitrust regulator or a sector regulator. Regardless, the MIIT's aggressive public campaign defending

[84] OECD, *supra* note 27, at 66.

[85] *See* Hong & Nong, *supra* note 30, at 278–79.

[86] *See generally* Yukyung Yeo, *Between Owner and Regulator, Governing the Business of China's Telecommunication Service Industry*, 200 China Q. 1013 (2009).

[87] Posner, *supra* note 14, at 339.

[88] *See* 电信和联通认错求和，承诺5年内单位带宽降价 35% (China Telecom and China Unicom Promise Rectification, Claim Broadband Prices Will Reduce 35% within Five Years), 广州日报 (Guangzhou Daily) (Dec. 3, 2011), *available at* http://tech.ifeng.com/telecom/special/fanlongduan/content-2/detail_2011_12/03/11076467_0.shtml.

[89] *See* Wang, *supra* note 37, at 479–80.

[90] *Id.* at 480.

China Telecom and China Unicom and denouncing the NDRC's actions is revealing. As the NDRC possesses regulatory control over telecom fees, it is likely that the MIIT interpreted the NDRC's antitrust intervention as a strategic expansionist move and an attempt to encroach upon its regulatory turf.

Based on anecdotal evidence from insiders,[91] as well as the MIIT's public denouncement of the NDRC's investigation in its newspapers, it appears that a compromise was reached among the various government actors involved. The bargaining and negotiations that happened behind the scenes, however, are shrouded in mystery. This case offers a textbook example of how antitrust enforcement against Chinese SOEs takes place not in contested legal battles, but through processes of negotiation and bargaining within a hierarchical bureaucracy. It also reveals how the utility function of an antitrust regulator such as the NDRC can influence its decision-making in tackling central SOE cases. Because regulation of telecom pricing is part of its designated responsibilities, antitrust intervention in this case could have helped to enhance its policy control in the telecom sector. The final outcome of a settlement also appears to be a rational, utility-maximizing decision for the NDRC, as the compromise reached significantly reduced its cost in handling the case. From the standpoint of the NDRC, the marginal benefits of imposing high fines on these two companies rather than settling was low. By receiving their commitments to reduce telecom fees, the NDRC largely achieved what it wanted—not only to retain existing powers, but also to expand its control of policy in telecom fee regulation.

D. ENFORCEMENT AGAINST LOCAL SOES

As discussed in Section I(A) above, the Chinese economy is highly decentralized. Law enforcement is no exception. Because the number of personnel responsible for antitrust enforcement at central ministries is extremely limited, the central government relies heavily on enforcers at the local level. This means that local governments bear most of the burden of enforcing the law. Indeed, both the NDRC and SAIC have massive networks of corresponding bureaus at various levels of regional governments.[92] In 2011, the NDRC added 150 people to various local enforcement units, but the exact number of local staff allocated to antitrust enforcement remains unclear.[93] The NDRC and SAIC may delegate their enforcement responsibilities to local authorities (hereinafter DRCs and AICs, respectively).[94] But the NDRC prefers to initiate investigations at the central level, unlike SAIC, which relies primarily on local authorities.[95]

---

[91] Interview with lawyers involved in the case.

[92] MOFCOM also has corresponding bureaus at the provincial level, but those provincial bureaus are not in charge of merger review.

[93] Interview with a government official at a central ministry.

[94] Some of the local corresponding offices of the NDRC are called price bureaus, but for simplicity I refer to all local authorities of the NDRC as DRCs.

[95] Policy and Regulatory Report, *Shortage of Manpower Is NDRC's Biggest Challenge in China*, May 23, 2014.

Based on the decisions disclosed by the NDRC and SAIC, the vast majority of cases have been initiated and enforced by local antitrust agencies. For instance, SAIC has publicly announced sixteen decisions as of August 2014, all of which were initiated and investigated by local AIC agencies, with SAIC providing professional support.[96] Considering the large nationwide network of AIC agencies, this is hardly an impressive record. The enforcement pattern of local DRC authorities sheds similar light on the predicament of local enforcement. Subsequent to announcements by local agencies of several high-profile cases (for example, the Maotai and Wuliangye case and the Shanghai gold retailer case), insiders revealed that the NDRC in Beijing in fact had taken the lead behind the scenes.[97]

Notably, the AML devotes the entirety of chapter V to addressing administrative abuse, specifically targeting local protectionist measures introduced by local administrative agencies that erect trade barriers to fend off competition from other regions.[98] The remedy for administrative abuse lacks teeth, however, as the antitrust enforcement agency can only submit a proposal to the superior department of the offending administrative agency to discipline the latter's behavior.[99] Even putting the weak remedy aside, the sad reality is that chapter V has rarely been enforced since the AML became effective and has become mere window dressing.[100] How do we explain the apparent lack of interest of local AIC and DRC authorities in prosecuting antitrust cases, whether directly against SOEs or against the local governments? To answer this question, we need to examine the incentive structure of local enforcement agencies and the constraints they face in the CCP hierarchy.

Like central enforcement agencies, local AIC and DRC authorities view antitrust enforcement as an exciting new avenue for the pursuit of greater policy control. This is particularly the case for AIC authorities, as they share overlapping responsibilities with other government agencies and have thus grown increasingly concerned that other government departments are gradually encroaching upon their powers.[101] Antitrust enforcement is perceived, therefore, as a potential new source of policy control for AIC authorities and local governments. In some jurisdictions local governments view administrative fining as a revenue-generating business.[102] To incentivize administrative

[96] SAIC's decisions have been disclosed on its website. *See* 竞争执法公告 (Competition Law Enforcement Bulletin), SAIC.GOV.CN, http://www.saic.gov.cn/zwgk/gggs/jzzf/ (last visited Mar. 6, 2015).

[97] *See* Zhang, *supra* note 55.

[98] *See* AML, *supra* note 1, arts. 32–35.

[99] *See* AML, *supra* note 1, art. 51.

[100] *See* Xu Shiying & Zhang Baisha, *supra* note 37, at 274–85 (reviewing the enforcement record for the first five years and finding only one successful case lodged by private citizens against administrative abuse under the AML; in other cases such complaints were either dismissed or withdrawn).

[101] *See* Zhang, *supra* note 55.

[102] *Id.*

agencies to generate more revenue, these local governments link salaries and bonuses to the amount of fines they receive.[103]

At the same time, local enforcers also face severe constraints in enforcing antitrust law against SOEs. Because local governments control budgets and personnel appointments, local enforcers are careful to ensure that their antitrust enforcement efforts do not run counter to the interests of local governments. Regional monopolies are often deemed local champions that substantially contribute to local GDP. As a result, they can seek protection from local governments. This explains why cases initiated by local AICs and DRCs tend to involve small rather than large, local SOEs—with the exception of those cases in which the central agencies actively intervened (such as the Maotai and Wuliangye case).

By contrast, central enforcement agencies such as the NDRC and SAIC do not face constraints from local governments in prosecuting local SOEs. As they are higher in the political pecking order, their administrative control is not subject to local government oversight. The amount of political opposition they face is thus much lower than for local AICs and DRCs. This is in particular the case for the NDRC, which prefers to initiate investigation at the central level rather than entirely relying upon local authorities. Nevertheless, the capacity of both agencies is limited, and consequently they are incapable of handling all of the regional cases on their own.[104] Barring active intervention by the central agencies, antitrust enforcement against regional monopolies is unlikely to be successful.

Conclusion

The Chinese economic system has undergone significant transformation in the past few decades. Politically, China remains a communist country controlled by a single ruling party—the CCP. But economically, it has embraced capitalism. As soon as the "market" as a controlling mechanism was introduced into economic policy, prices began to be liberalized, and greater autonomy was granted to SOEs in making operational decisions. In light of these changes, it is neither feasible nor desirable for the state to keep SOEs on a tight leash. The state no longer simply gives instructions to SOEs as to how they should behave; instead it resorts to regulation.

Meanwhile, repeated restructuring and reform of SOEs has resulted in a competitive landscape in which SOEs play a heterogeneous economic role. Contrary to the popular perception that all SOEs are monopolies, the vast majority of SOEs operate in

---

[103] *Id.*

[104] Policy and Regulatory Report, *supra* note 95. Xu Kunlin, the deputy director of the Price Supervision and the Anti-Monopoly Bureau at the NDRC, is keen to expand his bureau, noting that shortage of manpower is the biggest challenge it faces in antitrust investigation.

competitive sectors and compete head-to-head with nonstate firms. At the same time, although in many competitive sectors the national industry concentration level is very low, local protectionism fragments the Chinese market into smaller segments, thus creating market conditions conducive to the rise of cartels at the regional level. It is therefore no surprise that since the enactment of the AML many antitrust investigations into SOEs concern cartels operating at the regional level.

SOEs that operate in regulated sectors continue to be a significant source of monopolies. Over the past few decades, the Chinese government has orchestrated limited competition in these sectors by breaking up many state-owned monopolies into multiple SOEs. Although SOEs that operate in the basic infrastructure segments continue to enjoy monopoly power, competition exists in the upstream and downstream market segments. This creates competitive tension between vertically integrated SOEs and those operating solely in the competitive segments. This phenomenon has been observed in regulated sectors such as electricity and telecom. It is thus no coincidence that the first antitrust case involving central SOEs arose in the telecom sector—where two state-owned players (China Railcom and SARFT) were vocal critics of China Telecom and China Unicom and were fervent endorsers of NDRC's investigation.

On the supply side, due to the opacity of enforcement and a near absence of judicial supervision, the efforts of Chinese antitrust agencies are largely unobservable to outsiders. Yet enforcement agencies are not free from constraints. As many large SOEs are easily able to access the relevant government departments for the purpose of lobbying, the main battle Chinese administrative agencies face in tackling SOE cases is fought within the hierarchal bureaucracy. Thus, the political pecking order of enforcement targets compared to regulators is an important determinant of the costs Chinese antitrust agencies face in enforcing the AML.

At the same time, the opacity of the efforts of the enforcement agencies gives rise to agency problems, enabling the agencies to focus on seeking benefits for themselves rather than maximizing consumer welfare. From the perspective of Chinese bureaucrats, the main benefit to be achieved through antitrust enforcement is enhancement of policy control within their originally designated areas of responsibilities. As Chinese antitrust enforcement is a highly pluralistic process involving officials from various central ministries and multiple layers of government, particular organizational missions and objectives have a significant impact on how the AML is enforced with respect to SOEs.

At the Third Plenum of the 18th Congress of the CCP in 2013, the Chinese leadership decided that it will further deepen market reforms and continue price liberalization in regulated sectors.[105] In addition, the Third Plenum emphasized the importance of reducing local protectionism and improving market exit mechanisms to allow survival of the

---

[105] *See The Decision on Major Issues concerning Comprehensively Deepening Reforms*, China Daily, Nov. 18, 2013, *available at* http://www.china.org.cn/china/third_plenary_session/2013-11/16/content_30620736.htm.

fittest.[106] These reform measures, if implemented, will not only alter the distribution of resources between state-owned and nonstate enterprises, but will also affect the power and authority of various bureaucratic departments involved in overseeing state-owned sectors. Although it remains to be seen how such measures will influence the antitrust regulation of Chinese SOEs, one thing is certain: without the establishment of rule of law, China is unlikely to have an effective antitrust policy to safeguard this new round of market reforms.

---

[106] *Id.*

6 Taxation of State-Owned Enterprises

A REVIEW OF EMPIRICAL EVIDENCE FROM CHINA

Wei Cui

Introduction

The topic of taxation lies at the core of any fundamental theory of state-owned enterprises (SOEs). This is because any such theory must address the question of why there are SOEs to begin with. The likelihood of market failures resulting from purely private activities does not offer an adequate explanation for the scope of SOE activities observed around the world: in many countries, SOEs operate in sectors that may well be (and that in other countries are) efficiently served by private firms alone. The expanded scope of SOE activity must be understood in terms of governments' desire to control the resources and production decisions in the economy other than for efficiency reasons.[1] Yet taxation is an obvious alternative for governments to control resources and production decisions. Any organization of production in the form of SOEs thus reflects an implicit choice not to rely (solely) on tax instruments. Along these lines, some economists have postulated that

[1] Ian Bremmer, for instance, defines "state capitalism" as a system of state dominance that allows "governments to minimize the political risks they face by maximizing their control over activities that generate substantial amounts of wealth." IAN BREMMER, THE END OF THE FREE MARKET: WHO WINS THE WAR BETWEEN STATES AND CORPORATIONS? 157 (2010).

problems in tax policy implementation—such as the distortionary costs of high taxes and the challenges of tax administration (especially in developing countries)—partially explain the choice of public ownership of production.[2] Many non-economists may also share this intuition.

Interestingly, this conceptual connection between the topics of taxation and SOEs may have led economists to neglect the taxation *of* SOEs. The income taxation of SOEs is a very widespread phenomenon, and has been so for many decades.[3] Yet it has received relatively little attention in social scientific and legal scholarship. There are numerous possible explanations for this neglect, one of which is the strength of theoretical intuition that, if state ownership is an alternative to taxation, then the taxation of income from state-owned assets cannot be necessary, and therefore can be of only secondary importance.

But an additional, sociological explanation may be that many of the intellectual advances in public economics, corporate finance, and related areas—advances that heavily influence the research orientation of scholars today, legal scholars included—postdate the wave of privatization that swept through advanced economies in the 1970s and 1980s. Consequently, scholars in these economies have had less and less empirical material (not to mention diminished professional incentives) in their own countries to study SOEs. Theoretical views about most aspects of state ownership, including the taxation of SOEs, remain stagnant because they tend not to be empirically updated.

In this chapter, I offer a preliminary survey of recent empirical evidence regarding SOE taxation. In particular, I am concerned with the issue of how sensitive SOEs are to income taxation: whether they behave similarly to, or differently from, private firms in response to income taxation. This survey has both a theoretical and an empirical motive. From a theoretical perspective, as I explain in Section I, certain long-standing and competing perspectives on the justification for subjecting SOEs to income tax need to be adjudicated empirically. In particular, three different views of the income taxation of SOEs—that SOE taxation is superfluous, that it is necessary to ensure fair competition among state-owned and private firms, and that it is a form of forced distribution to deal with principal-agent problems in setting SOE dividend policy—are all in serious need of empirical verification. At the same time, without adopting the aim of testing theories of SOE taxation, recent empirical research conducted in different countries—and

[2] *See, e.g.*, James E. Meade, Liberty, Equality, and Efficiency (1993); Roger Gordon, *Taxes and Privatization, in* Public Finance and Public Policy in the New Century 185 (Sijbren Cnossen & Hans-Werner Sinn eds., 2003); Harry Huizinga & Soren Bo Nielsen, *Privatization, Public Investment, and Capital Income Taxation*, 82 J. Pub. Econ. 3, 399 (2001).

[3] For earlier surveys, see Robert H. Floyd, *Some Aspects of Income Taxation of Public Enterprises*, 25 IMF Staff Papers 2, 310 (1978); Glenn P. Jenkins, *Taxation of State-Owned Enterprises: Discussion Paper No. 225* (*available at* http://www.queensjdiexec.org/publications/qed_dp_69.pdf) (1986). For more recent information on this topic, see Wei Cui, *Taxing State-Owned Enterprises: Understanding a Basic Institution of State Capitalism*, forthcoming in Osgoode Hall Law Journal.

especially in China—has also uncovered interesting patterns in SOE taxation. However, the scholars who carried out this research make conflicting and largely unanalyzed assumptions about the nature of SOE taxation. It is important to hold these unreflective assumptions up against the light of a theory, so that the results can be interpreted in a more consistent manner and be made more robust in future research.

Although much of the evidence surveyed here comes from China, and its interpretation sometimes draws on an understanding of specific features of Chinese state capitalism, this evidence helps to evaluate theories that may apply to SOEs anywhere. The most remarkable feature of this evidence is that it seems to turn the theoretical intuition described at the beginning of this chapter on its head: instead of state ownership supplanting taxation as a form of state extraction and control, taxation remains fundamental to the state-owned sector.

This chapter proceeds as follows. Section I will summarize three competing views of the justification for SOE income taxation and explain how their empirical implications differ and may be tested.[4] Section II briefly outlines the history of SOE taxation in China. Section III presents original qualitative evidence of Chinese SOE tax lobbying from recent years, supporting the conclusion that SOEs are tax-sensitive. Section IV then selectively reviews some recent studies in corporate finance and accounting (in both English and Chinese) that analyze SOE tax-sensitivity, either in terms of the determinants of firm effective tax rates (ETRs) or in terms of firms' pursuit of specific tax-reduction strategies, such as borrowing and shifting income to low-tax affiliates. The Conclusion discusses the prospects for further empirical findings and their implications.

I. Competing Theoretical Perspectives on SOE Income Taxation

Why would a government subject its own SOEs to income taxation? The corporate income tax is collected from corporate profits, but if an SOE is wholly government-owned, its profit in theory already belongs to the state, and the state could access such profit by requiring dividend distributions. A tax on corporate profits merely reduces the amount of profits otherwise distributable. To many commentators, this suggests that SOE taxation merely transfers money from one pocket of the government to another. Why then do so many governments insist on this seemingly ritualistic exercise?

Past public and academic discourses have presented three conflicting perspectives on these questions. The first holds that SOE taxation is indeed superfluous, and is meaningful only in special circumstances. Generally, there is no need to tax income from publicly owned assets because that income already belongs to the government. Therefore, the taxation of SOEs is an arrangement that one should "see through" as being fundamentally different from taxing private firms. The special circumstances that justify taxation of

[4] This section is based on Cui, *supra* note 3.

SOEs include partially privatized firms (non-taxation of such firms would provide unwarranted favorable treatment of private investors in the firms), as well as revenue-sharing arrangements where government entities other than the SOEs' owners are recipients of tax revenue. But beyond these circumstances, according to this first perspective, SOE income taxation possesses neither general justification nor institutional significance.

The second perspective on SOE taxation could not be more different. It holds that SOE taxation is necessary to put SOEs on an equal footing with private firms: unless SOEs are taxed in the same way as private firms, one type of firm may suffer a competitive disadvantage relative to the other. Therefore SOE taxation is dictated by norms of market neutrality. This second view appears to have wide influence in both advanced and developing economies, and to be reflected in the policies and laws of many countries (including some constitutions and treaties). This is rather remarkable, as the view flatly contradicts the first perspective on SOE taxation, which also seems to possess considerable plausibility when first presented. The coexistence, for a long time, of these two mutually incompatible views bears witness to the weakness of existing understandings of SOE taxation.

Yet a third perspective on SOE taxation can be found in the writing of a small number of public economists who had studied publicly owned enterprises before such studies became decidedly unfashionable.[5] This view sees SOE income taxation as playing the role of forcing distributions from SOEs: collecting the income tax from SOEs secures profit distributions to the government shareholder in a way that enjoys practical advantages over dividends. The difference between this view and the first view (that taxing SOEs simply moves funds that the government is entitled to from one account ("pocket") to another) is that, even if the income tax and dividends paid by an SOE are functionally similar from the perspective of the government, taxes and retained earnings are not. A key inference in the first view is from the equivalence of tax and dividends to the equivalence of tax and retained earnings. The latter equivalence is needed for the conclusion that SOE taxation has no behavioral consequences (and therefore is ultimately superfluous). Yet if securing dividend payouts from SOE earnings is a significant institutional issue, that equivalence does not hold, and SOE taxation can have significant consequences just like the taxation of private firms.

The first two perspectives—mutually contradictory as they are—are probably much better known than the third, and one can offer some plausible speculations as to why. By the 1980s, principal-agent problems in state-owned firms in mixed economies were already recognized, just as such problems in private firms had been.[6] But the subsequent trend of privatization has meant that scholarly attempts to articulate corporate

---

[5] *See* Floyd, *supra* note 3; Jenkins, *supra* note 3; John Whalley & Li Wang, *The Unified Enterprise Tax and SOEs in China, in* China's Integration into the World Economy 179 (John Whalley ed., 2013).

[6] *See, e.g.*, John Roemer, A Future for Socialism (1994); Joseph Stiglitz, *The Economic Role of the State: Efficiency and Effectiveness, in* Efficiency and Effectiveness in the Public Domain 37 (T.P. Hardiman & Michael Mulreany eds., 1991).

governance problems in SOEs are far outnumbered by similar studies in the private firm context. Therefore, while principal-agent problems in SOEs for formulating dividend policy (and their manifestation in the continued practice of SOE taxation) may have remained a significant concern in practice in many countries,[7] they became less studied. At the same time, the spirit of privatization also gave appeal to the second perspective: insofar as the economy is not entirely privatized, measures must be taken to ensure that SOEs do not derive unjustified advantage over private firms.

However, recent scholarship on corporate governance in private firms actually gives strong support to the intuition that securing adequate dividend payouts from SOEs could be a serious challenge. In particular, it has been shown in the private firm context that shareholder monitoring and equity-based incentives for managers significantly increase firms' likelihood of making distributions. Yet these are precisely the mechanisms that SOE shareholders cannot rely on. The weakness of shareholder monitoring in SOEs has been extensively documented and was indeed an important impetus for privatization.[8] Moreover, unless an SOE is privatized, equity-based compensation for managers is also by definition impossible. Setting performance targets for dividend distributions for SOE managers could also simply aggravate the already complex incentive problems for multitasking managers.[9] Finally, SOEs (especially wholly owned ones) cannot easily go to the private capital market to seek equity financing, while obtaining public funding through the budgetary process is likely to be politically challenging. Therefore, simply for operational reasons, their managers can be expected to have greater incentives to hoard cash than private firm managers. In other words, research from the last two decades on private firms suggests that we have reasons to expect SOE managers to be more dividend-averse than private firm managers.

But this renders the first perspective on SOE taxation nonviable: if the chasm between dividends and retained earnings is great for SOEs, and if dividend and tax are equivalent for SOEs, their managers should be expected to be very averse, rather than indifferent, to paying tax. Note also that insofar as privatization alleviates monitoring and incentive problems for dividend distributions, managers of partially privatized SOEs should become less dividend-averse. In the forced-distribution view of SOE taxation, this weakens the justification for taxing the public portion of SOE profits, whereas from the first perspective on SOE taxation partial privatization is actually what creates the need for SOE taxation in the first place.

The first and third perspectives on SOE taxation have other sharply different empirical implications as well, which means that one should be able to evaluate their respective validity with real-world evidence. For example, the first perspective implies that

---

[7] *See, e.g.*, Louis Kuijs et al., SOE Dividends: How Much and to Whom? (2005).

[8] *See* Sergio G. Lazzarini and Aldo Musacchio, Chapter 17 in this volume.

[9] *See, e.g.*, Chong-En Bai & Lixin Colin Xu, *Incentives for CEOs with Multitasks: Evidence from Chinese State-Owned Enterprises*, 33 J. Comp. Econ. 3, 517 (2005).

managers of wholly owned SOEs should be indifferent to the income tax, or at least much less tax-sensitive than private firm managers. As the state owner share in a partially privatized company increases, the company should also become less sensitive. Firms paying tax to just their own shareholder government should also be less tax-sensitive than firms whose revenue goes to other government entities under revenue-sharing arrangements. By contrast, the "forced distribution" view of SOE taxation implies that SOE tax-sensitivity should be a function of the effectiveness of shareholder monitoring, SOE managers' opportunities to use funds for investment and operations as well as private gain, and incentive arrangements made with shareholders. For example, an SOE's government shareholder is in a position to reward its managers for paying taxes, which it would not normally do for private firms. This means that the degree of SOE tax-sensitivity—whether it is less than, equal to, or greater than private firm tax-sensitivity—is *intrinsically* an empirical matter.

What about the second perspective? While it advances a normative claim (that not taxing SOEs, or taxing them differently from private firms, would create "unfair" competition), it is based on factual assumptions that can also be empirically tested. Although these assumptions are rarely stated by those who advocate the second perspective, they must be that non-taxation (or different taxation) of SOE corporate profits would distort competition in the capital market, in factor markets other than the market for capital, and/or in product markets. However, it is difficult to see how such assumptions can hold, given two facts. First, the private capital market and the public budget are two entirely different sources of equity funding: private firms do not generally have access to the former, and wholly owned SOEs do not have access to the latter. Therefore private firms and SOEs do not compete for equity financing.[10] Second, it is likely that the governmental supply of equity capital to SOEs is largely inelastic with respect to the return on the capital. Therefore, any tax on such return is likely to be borne entirely by the government owner of the return, instead of being passed on to consumers or suppliers of other productive factors. Any story about distortions created by differential taxation (including exemption) of SOE profits must therefore involve unusual circumstances that differ from these two more common factual patterns.[11]

It is not difficult to see that which of the three competing theories is correct (and under what circumstances) should be of significant interest to policymakers who have to deal with SOEs.[12] For example, if the first theory is wrong and SOEs are tax-sensitive,

[10] For debt financing, because SOEs tend to have better access to loans than private firms (due either to implicit government guarantees or to policy-directed lending), they would enjoy a greater benefit from interest expense deductions if they were subject to tax, whereas there would be no tax-induced advantage from borrowing if SOEs were exempt from the income tax.

[11] In fact, given that the public discount rate is likely to differ from the private discount rate for making investment decisions, the cost of capital likely already differs between SOEs and private firms before the income tax is taken into account. There is no level playing field to start with, and it is not clear that it matters.

[12] As Ian Bremmer and many others have pointed out, these include even policymakers from countries with relatively low SOE presence. *See* BREMMER, *supra* note 1.

then behavioral distortions from SOE taxation must be taken into account, and tax policy design for SOEs could be just as complex as for private firms. If, on the other hand, the second theory is also wrong, then the normative guideline of equal taxation of SOEs and private firms may also need to be abandoned. The resolution of the conflicts among the competing theories is thus important. In the rest of this chapter, I will focus on recent empirical evidence that helps evaluate the strengths of the first and third theories (i.e., the superfluity and the forced-distribution views). Before offering contemporary evidence, however, I briefly review the historical path of SOE taxation in China.

II. A Brief History of Chinese SOE Income Taxation

China began considering taxing SOEs in the early 1980s. Prior to that time, SOEs operated in a command economy, where production decisions were administratively determined.[13] The transition out of the planned economy began with loosening control over production decisions and giving managers incentives to improve productivity. An important obstacle was that, previously, almost all profits of any enterprise had to be immediately surrendered to the government (while loss-generating firms simply received additional funds). The need for SOE managers to retain some profits became apparent. How much retention would be allowed became a central question. In 1983 and 1984, the government carried out two rounds of reform addressing this issue. Instead of requiring the surrender of all profit, SOEs were generally subject to a 55 percent income tax. After-tax profits were further divided between SOEs and their government owners according to a variety of formulae, but the 55 percent tax set a baseline. By the end of 1983, 92.7 percent of profitable SOEs "switched from surrendering profits to paying taxes." The average profits retained by SOEs as a percentage of total before-tax profits increased—though not by a lot—from 15.7 percent to 17.9 percent.[14]

The tax on SOEs, therefore, was instituted explicitly as a substitute for distributions. It allowed firms to retain *some* profits, while avoiding extensive bargaining between firms and government owners. Although this resonates with the "forced distribution" theory of SOE taxation, one needs to remember that "forced distribution" is a theoretical construct to explain SOE taxation generally, and not a description of how particular countries conceived of SOE taxation at particular times. It is easy to point out, for example, that the Chinese economy in 1983 was only beginning to be reformed, product markets were just being introduced, and urban labor, credit, and capital markets barely

[13] Turnover taxes were imposed on SOEs and generated significant revenue. *See* Christine P.W. Wong, *Fiscal Reform and Local Industrialization: The Problematic Sequencing of Reform in Post-Mao China*, 18 MOD. CHINA 197, 200–04 (1992). For a theoretical discussion of the role of turnover taxes in planned economies, see RICHARD A. MUSGRAVE, FISCAL SYSTEMS 40–62 (1969).

[14] Zuo Liu 刘佐, 国营企业"利改税"及其历史意义 (SOEs' switch from surrendering profits to paying taxes and its historical significance), 10 税务研究 (TAX'N RES.) 30 (2004).

existed. In that setting, taxing SOEs obviously was not a solution to the relatively narrow problem of corporate governance with respect to payout policy, but rather an attempt to deal with more basic problems of organizing production without markets. Moreover, SOEs dominated the Chinese economy at that time. Both because of this, and because few other tax instruments were deployed, the government relied heavily on income from SOEs for revenue.[15] This explained the very high tax rates imposed on SOEs and how little SOE managers were allowed to retain even after "switching to paying taxes."[16]

However, the forced-distribution theory can help to explain a fact about the "switching to paying taxes" system that has been somewhat obscure in China—namely that the system quickly collapsed.[17] By 1987, many SOEs switched to another regime of "contracting responsibility," where the government effectively contracted out the management of SOEs for a pre-fixed amount of tax and profits, and where the firms retained all profits in excess of that amount.[18] Why the "switching to paying taxes" system was abandoned within three years of implementation is not much discussed in China. One possibility is that because many SOEs were locally owned, other claimants to SOE funds/profits (e.g., local governments) did not like the forced-distribution mechanism represented by the tax on SOEs, and helped SOEs to hide income from the tax authorities.[19] Others postulate[20] "widespread [tax] evasion" as partially causing the demise of the system: because financial accounting was just beginning to be practiced in the 1980s, it was very difficult for the government to determine firms' taxable income. As a result, tax payment was low despite the high tax rate. Both of these explanations imply that SOEs can be sensitive at least to high taxes and would even engage in tax evasion—supporting the forced-distribution view.

In any case, because of quick economic growth and inflation, the government rapidly turned out to be the loser in the "contracting responsibility" bargain, and the country's public fisc was in danger by 1993. The crisis instigated the major tax reform in 1994,

---

[15] *See id.* for a summary of the sequence by which other taxes were introduced while the taxation of SOEs was implemented. *See also* Zuo Liu 刘佐, 中国企业所得税体制的发展 (The Development of China's Enterprise Income Tax System), 1 辽宁税务高等专科学校学报 (LIAONING TAX'N C. J.) 1 (2007). According to Kuijs et al. in 1978, revenue from enterprises was the largest source of budget revenue and accounted for more than half the total. KUIJS, *supra* note 7, at 2.

[16] This system of reliance on SOE distributions thus violates a plausible assumption, namely that SOE distributions are desirable only when the return to reinvestment is lower than the public rate of discount. *See* Cui, *supra* note 3, at 13–14.

[17] Wong, *supra* note 13.

[18] *Id.*; Youxiang Zuo 褚友祥, 改革开放以来我国国有企业所得说发展述评 (Income Taxation of State-Owned Enterprises since Reform and Opening), 3 辽宁税务高等专科学校学报 (LIAONING TAX'N C. J.) 1 (1999).

[19] *See* Christine Wong, *Central-Local Relations in an Era of Fiscal Decline: The Paradox of Fiscal Decentralization in Post-Mao China*, 128 CHINA Q. 691 (1991); Hongbin Cai & Daniel Treisman, *State Corroding Federalism*, 88 J. PUB. ECON. 819 (2004).

[20] Roger Gordon & Wei Li, *Taxation and Economic Growth in China, in* CRITICAL ISSUES IN CHINA'S GROWTH AND DEVELOPMENT 22 (Y.K. Kwan & E.S.H. Yu eds., 2005).

when all domestically owned enterprises, whether government or privately held, became subject to the same enterprise income tax. By this point, the government no longer depended as heavily on income from SOEs for revenue: the VAT and other turnover taxes were making the largest contributions to the budget. In addition, the state-owned sector was also beginning to shrink, as market liberalization proved many SOEs to be nonviable. Consequently, SOE taxation became less important from a revenue perspective. Justifications for it in terms of the need to put SOEs and private firms on an equal footing began to be circulated, notwithstanding the questionable underlying assumptions about the incidence of the income tax on SOEs.

What has become a focus of debate since then is how to design China's SOE dividend policy, as many surviving SOEs have become very profitable. SOEs' retention of profits has stood at what seems to be an obviously inefficient level. As a study by the World Bank in 2005 put it: "If 50 percent of SOE profits, estimated at 6.5 percent of GDP in 2004, were distributed to the budget and spent on education and health, this would allow an 85 percent increase in government spending on education and health."[21] The dividend averseness of Chinese SOEs can be illustrated by some more recent figures. In 2010, Chinese SOEs at the national and sub-national levels altogether earned 1.987 trillion RMB of profits, equivalent to 5 percent of GDP. If all such profits were distributed, the amount would be equivalent to 27.14 percent of total tax revenue in 2010.[22] However, SOEs owned by the central government, which accounted for 57 percent of total SOE profits, distributed only 3.8 percent of their profits to their government shareholder.[23] In fact, this was already a large improvement over the 0.86 percent rate of profit distribution in 2008. All such dividend proceeds in 2010 were used (as in prior years) to reinvest in SOEs: that is, state-owned assets made no revenue contribution to the general state budget.[24] Concrete proposals for developing institutions to achieve adequate payout from SOEs are slow to materialize. For 2011, the highest dividend payout rate,

---

[21] KUIJS, *supra* note 7, at 7.

[22] The 2008 figures are computed from Ministry of Finance, People's Republic of China, *Report on the Implementation of the 2008 Central and Local Budgetary Plans and the Draft Central and Local Budgetary Plans for 2009*, THE NATIONAL PEOPLE'S CONGRESS OF THE PEOPLE'S REPUBLIC OF CHINA (Mar. 5, 2009), http://www.npc.gov.cn/englishnpc/Special_11_2/2009-03/15/content_1493326.htm; the 2010 figures from Ministry of Finance, People's Republic of China, *Report on the Implementation of the 2010 Central and Local Budgetary Plans and the Draft Central and Local Budgetary Plans for 2011*, THE NATIONAL PEOPLE'S CONGRESS OF THE PEOPLE'S REPUBLIC OF CHINA (Mar. 5, 2011), http://www.npc.gov.cn/englishnpc/Special_11_4/2011-03/18/content_1647917.htm.

[23] *Report on the Implementation of the 2010 Central and Local Budgetary Plans and the Draft Central and Local Budgetary Plans for 2011*, *supra* note 22. For most SOEs, the ultimate shareholder is the State-owned Assets Supervision and Administration Commission (SASAC). State-owned financial institutions are held through the China Investment Corporation (CIC) and its subsidiary Huijin. Interest and dividend payments by CIC to the government also fall outside the general budget.

[24] *Id.*

applicable to fifteen centrally owned SOEs, was set at 15 percent of after-tax profits,[25] yet the distributions have not been included in the general budgets, but simply recycled into SOE investments.

By contrast, the enterprise income tax (EIT) generated 1.284 trillion RMB of tax revenue in 2010. All of China's SOEs are subject to the EIT, and in recent years SOEs contributed well over 10 percent of total EIT collected. All tax revenue is included in the general government budget. Thus both in recent history and for the foreseeable future, SOE income tax payments dominate SOE profit distributions.

Interestingly, SOEs often try to deflect criticism about their hoarding of funds and dividend-averseness by touting the amount of tax they pay. In officially organized annual rankings of firms by their tax payments[26] SOEs routinely show up as by far the largest taxpayers. The state-owned China National Petroleum Corporation, for example, boasts of having "paid" by itself 3.6 percent of the national tax revenue in 2007. The chairman of SASAC once told the press that, in 2008, SOEs under his supervision were expected to have "paid" over 1 trillion RMB in taxes[27]—close to 20 percent of the year's national tax revenue. Such announcements are patently disingenuous, as the amounts reported consist mostly of remittance of indirect taxes (such as the value added tax and the excise tax), the economic burden of which is passed on to consumers and which the SOEs do not bear. Even putting this aside, Chinese SOEs' reluctance to pay profit distributions raises the question of how willing they really are to pay taxes. As the next section will show, the image of Chinese SOEs as unhesitating taxpayers masks the fact that they also seek some of the most favorable tax treatments.

III. The Central SOE Tax Lobby

A fact little known outside the elite world of powerful SOEs and senior policymakers in China is that SOEs constitute by far the most powerful and effective tax lobby.

---

[25] 关于完善中央国有资本经营预算有关事项的通知 (Notice Regarding Issues in Improving the Operating Budget for Central State-Owned Assets) (promulgated by the Ministry of Finance, Dec. 23, 2010), http://qys.mof.gov.cn/zhengwuxinxi/zhengcefabu/201012/t20101229_393241.html. A 10 percent payout rate will apply to a second category of seventy-eight centrally owned SOEs, and a 5 percent payout rate to a third category of thirty-three centrally owned SOEs. No data is available for the practice of sub-national governments with respect to their SOEs.

[26] The central government has ceased to publish such rankings since 2009, but some provincial governments continue to do so. See, for example, a 2014 release of such rankings in Liaoning: Liaoning Provincial People's Government Network 辽宁省人民政府网, 2013 年度辽宁省纳税百强企业排行榜新闻发布会 (Press Conference on the Ranking of Top 100 Taxpaying Enterprises in Liaoning Province in 2013) (Mar. 28, 2014), http://www.scio.gov.cn/xwfbh/gssxwfbh/fbh/Document/1367528/1367528.htm.

[27] Wang Jin 王进, 李荣融透露央企今年缴税有望破万亿 (Li Rongrong Says Central SOES Expected to Pay Taxes of over a Trillion) 中国证券报 (China Security News) (Dec. 8, 2008), http://www.cs.com.cn/xwzx/03/200812/t20081208_1676309.htm.

The special benefits SOEs seek can take the form either of special rulings for particular SOEs, or of rules that have the appearance of being generally applicable but that, given other economic and regulatory circumstances, predominantly benefit SOEs. These special benefits can be interpreted in a variety of ways. Some of them, such as the exemption of accrued gains that would otherwise by taxable during corporate reorganizations, can potentially be viewed as targeted, one-time, and quantifiable subsidies. Others, such as the grant of tax consolidation treatment to corporate groups, are still explicit and targeted, but are ongoing, less quantifiable, and vulnerable to manipulation. Still others, such as the international tax rules also discussed in this section, are essentially loopholes that SOEs can exploit to their indefinite advantage and are very difficult to interpret as intentional subsidies. All of them can be seen as ways in which SOEs' tax-sensitivity is manifest. This is one reason I discuss them here. Another reason is that they also potentially explain some of the empirical patterns discovered by recent finance and accounting research—for example, that listed, centrally owned SOEs in China display ETRs that are lower than or similar to listed, privately owned firms, whereas locally owned SOEs have substantially higher ETRs. Thus, although observations of SOE tax lobbying efforts cannot reveal the exact degree of SOE tax-sensitivity—for that, quantitative studies of the kind surveyed in Section IV are needed—they comprise an important type of mechanism by which some SOEs may achieve their low ETRs. They are thus crucial to the interpretation of quantitative evidence.

A. CORPORATE CONSOLIDATION

Chinese corporate groups are generally not allowed to compute tax liability on a consolidated basis or to offset losses against profits across companies within a group.[28] Nonetheless, between 1994 and 2009,[29] the central government granted permission to more than 120 large SOE groups to consolidate their tax computation on the grounds of their "importance" to the nation. In China the benefit of consolidation treatment is conceived primarily or even exclusively in terms of the possibility of offsetting losses against profits across companies, and not (as in advanced economies that adopt corporate tax consolidation) in terms of administrative simplification or tax neutrality with respect to business organizational choices. That is, it is generally interpreted by both the government and taxpayers to be a form of tax preference.[30] The central government has

[28] This is largely because under China's central-local tax-sharing system, sub-national governments can claim only a share of the EIT revenue that is paid within their jurisdictions. Local governments are thus loath to cede revenue to the jurisdiction of the parent company of a group.

[29] The central government decided to suspend consolidated tax reporting for these enterprises beginning in 2009, in order to offset the revenue loss to local government generated by China's Value Added Tax (VAT) reform.

[30] *See* Shouwen Zhang 张守文, 企业集团汇总纳税的法律解析 (Legal Analysis of the Aggregated Taxation of Enterprise Groups), 5 法学 (Legal Sci.) 39 (2007).

zealously guarded the authority to approve this type of tax preference and has prohibited local governments from authorizing similar treatment. Although some local governments have granted consolidated tax treatment in the past to SOE groups that have local importance, the prohibition by the central government make this less common (and less well documented). SOE corporate groups also cannot self-determine their eligibility for group consolidation: each group lobbies for special treatment, and which ones receive it is a matter of political clout.[31] Fewer than 10 percent of SOE groups in China were permitted to adopt EIT consolidation prior to such practice being suspended in 2009.[32] The government estimated the magnitude of the tax savings to the selected groups from consolidation to be 40 billion RMB per year, equivalent to 4.1 percent of the total amount of EIT revenue collected in 2007 and over 25 percent of all EIT paid by SOEs.[33]

This preferential policy for SOEs has been questioned in recent years,[34] not only on the basis that it constitutes discriminatory treatment vis-à-vis privately owned corporate groups,[35] but also because the policy subsidizes favored SOE groups that keep loss-generating subsidiaries. As Chinese SOEs often operate in sectors that are occupied by private firms in other countries, losses typically reflect inefficiencies. The tax subsidy of consolidation treatment thus potentially slows the divestiture of inefficient SOEs. However, regardless of the merits of the criticisms and defenses of the policy, all seem to agree that having such preference or not *matters* to SOEs: that is, all SOEs, even the most profitable ones, care about whether the losses of some subsidiaries are taken into account in computing tax liability. This would be inexplicable if one adopts the position that SOEs cannot be tax-sensitive.

B. SPECIAL TREATMENT OF CORPORATE REORGANIZATIONS

Since the late 1990s, partly to facilitate the restructuring of the state-owned sector, China's Ministry of Finance (MOF) and State Administration of Taxation (SAT) experimented with a variety of tax-deferred corporate reorganizations.[36] Like their counterparts in the United States and elsewhere, these rules impose conditions on the

---

[31] A corporate group being state-owned is thus a necessary, but not sufficient, condition for eligibility for consolidated reporting.

[32] It is estimated that, as of 2010, there were close to 1500 SOE corporate groups in China, representing roughly half of the total number of corporate groups.

[33] Computation based on CHINA'S TAX PRESS, TAX YEARBOOK OF CHINA (2008).

[34] *See* Lei Liu 刘磊, 论现代企业组织形式与所得课税 (On the Forms and Income Taxation of Modern Enterprise Organizations), 11 扬州大学税务学院学报 (J. TAX C. YANG ZHOU U.) 19 (2006); Wenchuan Xia 夏文川, 对企业所得税汇总(合并)纳税的思考 (Study on the Aggregated (Consolidated) Income Taxation of Enterprises), 1 税务研究 (TAX'N RES.) 44 (2007).

[35] This claim of discrimination reflects the second perspective on SOE taxation discussed in Section I, *supra*. This is one example where deciding whether that perspective is correct has real-world policy implications.

[36] *See* Wei Cui & Richard Krever, *The Tax Consequences of Corporate Reorganisations in China*, 3 BRITISH TAX REV. 340 (2011).

transactional forms and types of consideration used in reorganizations, which, if satisfied, allow the reorganized companies and their shareholders to defer recognition of gain on the transfer of assets and stock. Both SOEs and private firms are permitted to use these rules. In a typical SOE reorganization, the parent company of an SOE group would rearrange its myriad subsidiaries, often with the aim of packing "good assets" into a joint-stock holding company to be listed on a domestic or foreign stock exchange. Because the reorganizations have largely been done intra-group, most of the transactions could have been carried out in forms that qualified them for tax deferral.

However, a significant number of SOE groups have chosen *not* to take advantage of these rules. Instead, these SOEs petitioned the MOF and SAT to treat the reorganizations as taxable, so that after the transfer the tax basis of the relevant stock or assets was "stepped up" to their fair market value.[37] At the same time, the SOEs asked the government permanently to *exempt* from tax the gain that should have been recognized on the transactions. Close to forty rulings for such "tax-exempt" reorganization were issued between 2000 and 2011. According to figures offered in the rulings themselves, between 2000 and 2007 the special treatment resulted in the exemption of 87.2 billion RMB of tax liability. During 2008 and 2009 the continuation of this type of special treatment resulted in 19.4 billion RMB of tax benefit to the relevant companies.[38]

In the rulings, the MOF and SAT have attempted to rationalize this type of permanent tax exemption (as opposed to tax deferral) as an investment decision: in each case, the government's share of the paid-in capital of a reorganized state-owned enterprise is required to be increased by the amount of the forgone tax revenue. Thus, conceptually, each relevant enterprise is treated as fictionally paying tax on the gain it recognizes on asset and stock transfers in a reorganization. But the fictional tax does not enter the state treasury, and is instead immediately re-contributed back into the company. However, this theory of the tax-exemption of SOE reorganizations is ad hoc and inconsistent with the details of its implementation: how much tax is saved usually depends on the SOE group itself, and not on the fictional government investor.[39] For example, even the assets and stock of lower-tier subsidiaries for which there is no direct ownership change are stepped up without taxation. In such cases, it is difficult to identify either the taxable event (because ownership has not been transferred) or the person making the investment decision (because the subsidiaries are only indirectly owned by the state).[40] A more straightforward explanation of these tax preferences is that powerful SOEs lobbied

---

[37] "Stepped-up" basis creates tax benefits through increased depreciation deductions.

[38] *See* Wei Cui 崔威, 国有企业重组的"超特殊"税务处理：法律背景及评议 ("Super-Special" Tax Treatment of State-Owned Enterprise Reorganizations: Legal Framework and Evaluation), 6 中外法学 (Peking U. Law J.) 944 (2010).

[39] Because investment decisions for China's non-financial SOEs as well as their distribution policies generally fall under the supervision of SASAC, the claim that the MOF or SAT could also decide on the making of a capital injection into these SOEs appears, from an institutional perspective, to be questionable.

[40] *See* Cui, *supra* note 38, for a detailed discussion of these issues.

for them, and in some (but by no means all) cases, the government succumbed to the lobbying.[41]

Like tax preferences granted to SOEs in the consolidated return area, special SOE treatment in corporate reorganizations suggests two things: one, SOEs are sensitive to the corporate income tax—otherwise they would not lobby for favorable tax treatment unavailable to others; and two, they are able to use their political clout to bargain with the government regarding tax matters.

C. INTERNATIONAL TAXATION

The next examples demonstrate how SOEs not only seek explicit and targeted tax preferences, but also generally attempt to influence tax policymaking to their own advantage. They thus offer even stronger evidence for SOE tax-sensitivity.

Starting in the early 1990s, so-called "round-tripping" investment structures began to be widely observed in Chinese foreign direct investment. These structures involved Chinese parties setting up a group of offshore holding companies in tax haven countries and transferring the equity interest of Chinese entities to such holding companies. Thus Chinese individuals and companies ended up owning and controlling foreign entities, the only assets of which may be Chinese companies' shares (hence the label "round-tripping"). The structures were popular because they allowed Chinese businesses to raise capital overseas and circumvent domestic regulatory requirements.[42] Among all users of such structures, SOEs stood out in that they tended to be the only Chinese companies—as opposed to individuals—that were the ultimate owners in the investment structure. This was because for all Chinese enterprises, making investments overseas (e.g., setting up offshore subsidiaries) was subject to strict capital control requirements, and generally only SOEs obtained approval for such investments.[43] In other words, if the ultimate owner in a round-tripping structure was a Chinese company, it was highly likely that it was an SOE.

In 2008, the new Enterprise Income Tax Law (EIT Law) rendered round-tripping structures highly tax-inefficient for Chinese SOEs. When a Chinese operating subsidiary distributed dividends to its offshore parent, the dividends began to be subject to Chinese withholding tax.[44] And if such amounts distributed were further repatriated

[41] Indeed, the number of SOEs that engaged in pre-listing reorganizations far exceeds the number of SOEs that obtained tax exemption rulings.

[42] Before 2008, the structure also allowed the Chinese operating subsidiaries to be treated as foreign invested enterprises (FIEs) eligible for tax preferences.

[43] For privately owned businesses, Chinese individuals tend to be the owners of the offshore holding companies, because the enforcement of capital controls against individuals used to be more lax. *See* Thomas Hall, *Controlling for Risk: An Analysis of China's System of Foreign Exchange and Exchange Rate Management*, 17 COLUM. J. ASIAN L. 433, 450 (2004).

[44] Before 2008, dividends paid by FIEs (even if ultimately owned by Chinese residents) were subject to zero withholding.

to the Chinese company that was the ultimate owner, the latter had to pay corporate income tax on the full amount.[45] By contrast, if a Chinese operating subsidiary distributed after-tax profits directly to a Chinese parent, the parent would retain the entire amount because of the inter-corporate dividend exemption under the EIT.[46]

From a tax-planning perspective, one way out of this quandary is to rely on the basic definition of resident enterprises under the EIT Law, according to which an offshore company can still be treated as being a tax resident in China if it is managed and controlled within China.[47] If offshore holding companies qualify as Chinese tax residents, distributions from Chinese operating companies to offshore entities and from such entities back to the ultimate Chinese corporate owners would all be treated as domestic inter-corporate distributions. No withholding tax would apply. However, lawmakers hesitated to specify details about the "management and control" test, both because of the novelty of the concept and because it applies beyond the context of round-tripping structures. For example, giving the "management and control" criterion broad application could impose Chinese resident status on many foreign-listed companies whose assets and management are predominantly located in China.[48] This would likely pose administrative challenges that the tax administration is unprepared to face, while not necessarily raising additional revenue.

Remarkably, in April 2009 the SAT issued a circular precisely aimed at facilitating the type of tax planning just described.[49] It prescribed the conditions under which offshore entities may qualify and elect to be treated as Chinese resident enterprises. The conditions are such that, with sufficient tax planning, tax resident status will largely be an elective matter—it can easily be chosen or avoided, depending on which is more beneficial for the taxpayer. This extremely favorable set of rules, however, applies only to offshore entities controlled by "Chinese enterprises or enterprise groups"—*that is, by SOEs*. Anecdotes among practitioners suggest that the circular was shepherded through the rule-making process by China Mobile, an SOE with Hong Kong subsidiaries that hold all of the group's operating companies in China. In other words, China Mobile was

---

[45] Thus if an operating company distributes $100 of after-tax profits to its offshore holding company, a 10 percent withholding tax may be levied. The remaining $90, if subsequently repatriated to the Chinese corporate owner of the offshore holding company, would be subject to a 25 percent enterprise income tax, leaving the ultimate owner with only $67.50.

[46] [中华人民共和国企业所得税法] (Enterprise Income Tax Law) (promulgated by the Standing Comm. Nat'l People's Cong., Mar. 16, 2006, effective Jan. 1, 2008), art. 26, § 2.

[47] *Id.* at art. 2.

[48] Many China-based companies listed on stock exchanges such as the New York Stock Exchange or NASDAQ adopt the round-tripping structure, as do all companies that make up the "red chip" section of the Hong Kong Stock Exchange.

[49] 关于境外注册中资控股企业依据实际管理机构标准认定为居民企业有关问题的通知 (Notice Regarding the Treatment of Chinese-Controlled, Foreign-Registered Enterprises as Resident Enterprises under the "Body of Substantive Management" Test) (promulgated by the State Administration of Taxation, Apr. 22, 2009), http://www.chinatax.gov.cn/n810341/n810765/n812166/n812642/c1189294/content.htm.

able to prompt regulatory action on a subject that previously had appeared too weighty and difficult for the government to tackle. It persuaded the tax authorities to craft a rule in its favor that looks general in its application but is narrow in its impact. It made an SOE tax planning idea into law.

Indeed, for specialists who closely follow Chinese tax regulations, special policy dispensations for SOEs are so routine that they require no particular effort to document. More recent manifestations of the phenomenon in the international tax policy area include the decision by the MOF and SAT substantially to relax China's foreign tax credit (FTC) rules—but only for the three SOE corporate groups that form China's oil and gas oligopoly.[50] Generally, Chinese businesses can claim indirect FTC only for three layers of foreign subsidiaries,[51] and they are subject to the "per country" limitation in computing the FTC limitation.[52] For "Chinese petroleum companies," however, the government simply waived the "per country" limitation and allowed indirect FTC for up to five tiers of foreign subsidiaries. Although there might be arguments for relaxing these limits generally, there is no reason petroleum companies especially deserve this policy treatment.[53] The sole effect of the relaxation is the reduction of the Chinese tax paid by the oil and gas SOEs—and the amount of reduction is entirely up to the SOEs themselves, and not to the government as a shareholder. Such policies would be inexplicable if SOEs did not care about paying the income tax.

The examples of SOE tax lobbying given in this section are by no means exhaustive. They provide compelling evidence of SOE tax-sensitivity. However, the evidence is also limited in its scope. First, because the evidence is all based on policies and rulings adopted by the Chinese central government, it offers insights primarily into the behavior of centrally owned SOEs. Second, it cannot really reflect varying degrees of tax-sensitivity, or the relative significance of various factors that may determine such sensitivity. The next section will examine further evidence, not of attempts by SOEs to shape the content of the law, but of their behavior once the law is fixed. Such ex post behavior has been studied for both centrally and locally owned SOEs, and potentially reveals answers to questions regarding degrees of sensitivity and causal factors.

---

[50] 关于我国石油企业在境外从事油（气）资源开采所得税收抵免有关问题的通知 (Notice Regarding Issues in Foreign Tax Credit for Chinese Petroleum Companies Engaged in Oil (Gas) Resource Exploration Overseas) (promulgated by the Ministry of Finance, State Administration of Taxation, May 26, 2011), http://www.chinatax.gov.cn/n810341/n810765/n812156/n812479/c1186648/content.html. The three SOE oil and gas groups are PetroChina, CNOOC, and Sinopec.

[51] That is, foreign taxes paid by such subsidiaries are deemed paid by the Chinese parent and therefore may be credited against the latter's Chinese tax liability.

[52] The purpose of the "per country" limitation is to reduce the ability of the taxpayer to use foreign tax paid in high-tax countries to reduce the home country tax liability on income earned in low-tax countries.

[53] Indeed, the Bank of China (a large partially state-owned bank, but not the central bank) was able to obtain the same treatment through an unpublished private ruling in 2010.

IV. Firm-Level Quantitative Evidence of SOE Tax-Sensitivity

A. DO SOEs DISPLAY HIGHER OR LOWER EFFECTIVE TAX RATES?

One basic approach to measuring SOE tax-sensitivity is to compare the ETRs among firms with different types of ownership: firms with lesser tax-sensitivity should show higher ETRs, because they would devote less effort to tax reduction.[54] As ETRs are potentially determined by a large range of factors, empirical comparisons of ETRs across firms usually incorporate control variables that represent many firm characteristics that potentially affect ETR independently of the nature of firm ownership. These include firm size, leverage ratio (greater use of loan financing produces greater interest expense deductions and therefore lower ETRs), ratios of fixed assets to total assets (fixed assets generate depreciation deductions and therefore also have a tendency to lower ETRs) and of other types of assets and inventories, measures of firm performance such as return on assets (ROA), growth prospects as measured by market to book ratios or Tobin's Q, the sectors in which the firms operate, and nominal tax rates (if they differ for different firms).[55] Thus, for example, it may be that SOEs generally have better access to loan financing and therefore claim more interest expense deductions than other firms, independent of their willingness to pursue tax-planning strategies. Any effect of firm ownership on ETRs that is detected after the leverage ratio (along with other factors) is controlled for, however, will be more likely to reflect firm propensity toward (or against) tax planning.

One of the frequently cited papers on this still-nascent research area is that of Ajay Adhikari, Chek Derashid, and Hao Zhang,[56] which examines the link between ETRs and political connections for firms in Malaysia. The paper sets a provocative baseline for comparisons with subsequent research. The authors predict that firms with stronger political connections will display lower ETRs, by being able to lobby and obtain discretionary tax deductions and tax-free subsidies.[57] They find support for this prediction using two proxies for political connections, one being percentage of government ownership, the other a measure (specifically developed in Malaysia) of the political connectedness of firm managers. Both measures are negatively connected with firm ETRs, after

---

[54] Scott Dyreng et al., *Long-Run Corporate Tax Avoidance*, 83 ACCT. REV. 1, 61 (2008).

[55] Superior data has allowed some studies to adopt an even larger set of control variables, including size of majority shareholding, manager compensation, structures of the corporate board, etc. *See, e.g.*, Xing Liu 刘行 & Xiaorong Li 李小荣，金字塔结构、税收负担与企业价值：基于地方国有企业的证据 (Pyramidal Structures, Tax Burdens and Enterprise Value: Value Based on Local SOEs), 8 管理世界 (MGMT WORLD) 91, 91–105 (2012).

[56] Ajay Adhikari et al., *Public Policy, Political Connections, and Effective Tax Rates: Longitudinal Evidence from Malaysia*, 25 J. ACCT. PUB. POL'Y 5, 574 (2006).

[57] *Id.* at 577–79. Adhikari et al. claim to be agnostic about the specific mechanisms that produce lower ETRs for Malaysian SOEs and do not offer institutional details of the kind that we offered for China. *Id.* at 579 (footnote 9), 593–94.

adjusting for firm size, sector, and other effects.[58] Between the two proxies, the extent of state ownership is a stronger predictor of ETR than personal political connections. If interpreted as bearing on firm tax-sensitivity, this Malaysian result presents a clear challenge to common intuitions: not only are SOEs not less tax-sensitive than private firms, they are more tax-sensitive!

Whether SOEs display higher or lower ETRs than private firms is a topic that received more direct attention and refinement in a number of recent studies in China. The first result to report is one that has been replicated in several papers, namely that Chinese SOEs that are owned by the central government bear similar or lower effective tax burdens when compared with non-SOEs. Shujun Cao, Xing Liu, and Wanjun Zhang conducted a study of manufacturing firms listed on the Shanghai and Shenzhen stock exchanges for the years 2002 to 2005, and divided these firms into centrally owned SOEs, locally (i.e., sub-nationally) owned SOEs, and non-SOEs.[59] They showed that for those firms that do not benefit from local tax preferences from the regions in which they operate, private firms have higher ETRs than centrally owned SOEs, and local SOEs have higher ETRs than both private firms and central SOEs.[60] Xing Li and Xiaorong Liu examined all A-share listed companies for the years 1998 to 2010.[61] In contrast to Cao, Liu, and Zhang, they found no significant difference among the ETRs of centrally owned SOEs and private firms;[62] but they confirmed the former's finding that both types of firms display significantly lower ETRs than local SOEs.[63] These careful analyses rebut some other studies, based on similar data samples but empirically less well designed (especially in failing to make the distinction between centrally and locally owned SOEs), that purported to find that Chinese SOEs in general display higher ETRs.

---

[58] The authors do not control for the nominal tax rates to which the firms are subject, presumably because nominal tax rates (including legally provided tax preferences) do not differ between firms, other than perhaps as captured by sector effects.

[59] Shujun Cao 曹书军 et al., 财政分权、地方政府竞争与上市公司实际税负 (Fiscal Decentralization, Local Government Competition and Effective Tax Rates of Listed Companies) 4 世界经济 (World Econ.) 69–83 (2009).

[60] For firms that benefit from regional tax preferences, the authors find convergence in ETRs among all three categories of firms. The study controlled for sales, leverage, and ROA at the firm level, as well as for industry.

[61] Liu & Li, *supra* note 55.

[62] This could be the result not only of differences in their samples, but also of the fact that (1) Cao et al. used fewer firm-level control variables, but (2) grouped firms into those that enjoy regional tax preferences (which generally produced convergence in ETRs) and those that do not. Cao et al., *supra* note 59. Liu and Li's finding of no differences among centrally owned SOEs and private firms may be attributable partly to not filtering out the effect of regional tax preferences, which neutralize differences among firms. Liu & Li, *supra* note 55. Cao et al. argue that not considering this factor is a crucial drawback in prior research. Cao et al., *supra* note 59, at 72.

[63] This conclusion is also supported by Danglun Luo 罗党论 & Yuping Yang 杨玉萍, 产权、政治关系与企业税负—来自中国上市公司的经验证据 (Ownership, Political Connections and Firm Tax Burden: Empirical Evidence from Chinese Listed Companies), 4 世界经济文汇 (World Econ, Papers) 1 1–19 (2013).

Thus for central SOEs, the Chinese evidence is consistent with the Malaysian study in Adhikari, Derashid, and Zhang: there is no support for any prediction of lesser SOE tax-sensitivity. What about Chinese local SOEs? Liu and Li suggest three reasons local SOEs may be expected to bear higher tax burdens. First, Chinese local governments are engaged in intense competition over capital and other mobile factors. Such competition is costly from a fiscal perspective, and local governments must rely on immobile factors, including local SOEs, to absorb the costs of fiscal competition. In other words, their expectations of and efforts at revenue extraction from local SOEs are higher than from national SOEs and private firms. By comparison, the national government has no need to squeeze national SOEs, given large central government budget surpluses. Second, there is less information asymmetry between local governments and local SOEs (compared to non-SOEs and national SOEs), with the result that hiding income to avoid tax is not an option. Third, local SOE managers' compensation may not be tied sufficiently to firm performance and value, which also makes such managers less sensitive to the impact of taxes. It should be noted that Liu and Li make these observations not by reference to any theory of SOE taxation, but only to motivate their empirical strategy. But these explanations suggest that SOE ETRs are higher only when monitoring by the government shareholder is intense and when managers do not have incentives to maximize pretax returns in the first place. The third explanation, in particular, implies managerial aversion to tax, and that aversion increases with managerial incentives. The authors' explanations for high ETRs for local SOEs thus fit best with the forced-distribution view of SOE taxation discussed in Section I, and not with the superfluity view.

Based on this reasoning, Liu and Li predict that greater enterprise autonomy and managerial incentives for local SOEs will lead to lower ETRs. As a proxy for such autonomy and increased incentives, they examine how many layers removed listed firms are from their ultimate owners—or how tall the "pyramidal structure" is above these firms.[64] Using a sample of all listed Chinese firms during the years 2004–2010, they find that locally owned SOEs' ETRs are lower the further removed they are from their ultimate government owners. By contrast, for national SOEs and non-SOEs, the pyramidal structures above listed firms have no impact on company ETR. Moreover, the effect of pyramidal structures on ETR is accentuated in regions of China where government interference is considered heavier. Finally, they find that the reduced ETRs brought about by firms' insulation from the ultimate government owners increase firm value. That is, investors in stock markets reward tax reduction that is brought about by greater autonomy and incentives of SOE managers, instead of reacting negatively to it because aggressive tax planning may in other contexts be associated with managerial misconduct. Overall, then, Liu and Li appear to discover that the more autonomous and

---

[64] The use of this proxy for autonomy and incentives is justified by independent research reviewed by Liu & Li, *supra* note 55, at 94.

profitable an SOE is, the less difference there will be between the SOE's tax-sensitivity and that of private firms.

In another recent innovative study, Danglun Luo and Yuping Yang find that firm ownership makes a difference not only directly to ETRs but also indirectly to the impact of political connections on ETRs.[65] They use an elaborate scale to measure the political connectedness of board presidents and CEOs of Chinese listed firms. They demonstrate that, as found by Adhikari, Derashid, and Zhang for Malaysian firms, political connectedness helped to reduce firm ETRs during the 2004–2009 period. However, this benefit of political connectedness is most pronounced for non-SOEs, is somewhat less pronounced for local SOEs, and is not significant for central SOEs.[66] For local SOEs, this suggests that their managers are averse to tax (somewhat like private firm managers) and make efforts to reduce it. This is consistent with Liu and Li, and complements the evidence of central SOE lobbying reviewed in Section III. For central SOEs, the evidence suggests that their presidents and CEOs do not use their political connections to reduce tax. But we know this to be false, both because, as documented by Luo and Yang themselves and by other authors, central SOEs already enjoy the lowest ETRs of all firms, and because of the strength of the central SOE tax lobby discussed above. Thus other explanations may need to be sought: for example, that the presidents and CEOs of all listed central SOEs may be already so high on the political connections scale that there is not enough variation; or that listed firms constitute a biased sample as far as central SOEs are concerned. For instance, some of the most important preferences central SOEs obtain, such as marking up tax basis to appraised value without paying tax,[67] may have been obtained before—and precisely in anticipation of—their listings on stock exchanges.

B. DO SOEs ENGAGE IN LESS TAX PLANNING?

Studying variations in ETRs while controlling for numerous firm characteristics is only one way to measure firm tax-sensitivity. One could also try to measure the intensity of specific tax reduction efforts. For example, Terry Shevlin, Tanya Tang, and Ryan Wilson studied a small sample of Chinese firms offering "B-shares" from 1999 to 2004.[68] They claim to identify a particular proxy for tax-motivated income shifting within a corporate group: firms may shift income to lower-taxed affiliates located in regions with tax preferences. They find that firms that use intangible assets more intensively engage in more

---

[65] Luo & Yang, *supra* note 63.

[66] The particular finding for central SOEs, that political connectedness has no significant impact on ETRs once state ownership is controlled for, is similar to the finding for Malaysian firms in Adhikari et al., *supra* note 56.

[67] *See* discussion *supra* Section III(B).

[68] Terry Shevlin et al., *Domestic Income Shifting by Chinese Listed Firms*, 34 J. AM. TAX'N ASS'N 1 (2012).

income shifting by this proxy, as do firms that have incentives to manage earnings before seeking new financing on equity markets. However, they find no difference between SOEs and private firms in their pursuit of income shifting. Moreover, although there was a significant change in the income tax sharing arrangement between central and sub-national governments in 2002, the degree of income shifting in SOEs did not change after 2002. These findings detract from the "superfluity" view of SOE taxation: SOEs are not found to be less tax-sensitive, nor does the significance of SOE taxation change as a result of changes in revenue-sharing arrangements.

A study by Cao, Liu, and Zhang points to similar conclusions, finding that for Chinese listed firms that operate in regions not characterized by tax preferences, ETR generally is a positive function of the strengths of tax enforcement.[69] However, this positive relation is most pronounced for private firms, slightly less pronounced for central SOEs, and least pronounced for local SOEs. This is consistent with the general finding, discussed earlier, that local SOEs bear higher tax burdens than other firms. It suggests that central SOEs respond to the intensity of tax administration, which is incompatible with the hypothesis of SOE tax insensitivity.[70]

More mixed evidence is presented in another study of A-share listed companies. Yuetang Wang, Liangliang Wang, and Yang Peng note first that, before the implementation of the new EIT Law in 2008, when two different corporate income tax systems implied very different nominal tax rates for different firms, high-tax firms displayed a significantly higher level of leverage than low-tax firms.[71] In other words, Chinese firms generally use interest expense deductions to shelter income (as do firms elsewhere). They then find that in 2008, when greater uniformity in tax rates was introduced, the level of borrowing also converged across firms: firms that saw tax rate decreases also decreased their levels of leverage, while firms that saw rate increases raised their levels of leverage. But the changes in level of borrowing (whether increases or decreases, in accordance with whether the firms were initially high-taxed or low-taxed) were more pronounced in private firms than in SOEs. SOE borrowing still changed in response to tax rate changes, but to a much less significant extent than private firms, suggesting that SOEs are less tax-sensitive.[72] The authors explicitly interpret this as evidence that SOEs are less aggressive in their tax planning.

The empirical accounting and corporate finance research reviewed in this section has emerged only in the last few years. Because of the sheer size of the Chinese state-owned sector, however, it is likely that this still nascent body of research, tracking

---

[69] Cao et al., *supra* note 59, at 79–80.

[70] Moreover, the authors find that central SOE ETRs are affected by the degree of government intervention, just as private firm ETRs are.

[71] Yuetang Wang 王跃堂 et al., 产权性质、债务税盾与资本结构 (Ownership Nature of Ultimate Controller, Debt-Related Tax Shields and Capital Structure), 9 经济研究 (ECON. RES.) 122 (2010).

[72] In this study, the authors did not distinguish between centrally and locally owned SOEs.

the relationship between state ownership and tax profiles of Chinese firms, will soon reach a critical mass: more types of evidence regarding SOE tax-sensitivity will be gathered, and the analysis of each type of evidence further refined. As it now stands, what is most striking is that there is at least as much evidence for the forced-distribution view of SOE taxation as there is for the view that SOEs are necessarily indifferent to taxation. This is remarkable because the researchers who have found quantitative evidence for tax-sensitivity have generally not made reference to the forced-distribution view in making their empirical predictions, whereas the researchers finding evidence for indifference to taxation tend explicitly to endorse the proposition that SOE taxation is inherently different from the taxation of private firms. This, I believe, is because the latter view is much more entrenched. Thus even if many have held the empirical intuition that SOEs are highly tax-sensitive, the superfluity view may have suppressed such intuition. The theoretical articulation of the forced-distribution view, therefore, is important for guiding empirical research.[73]

Conclusion

The forced-distribution view of SOE income taxation is closely intertwined with the study of corporate governance in SOEs, which forms the subject of other chapters in this book. This view suggests that as a widely adopted mechanism for forcing SOE distributions, taxation may have played an unrecognized, salutary role in disciplining SOE managers. To put it simply: if it were not for the tax system, SOEs could have been even more unproductive. However, the prominence of SOEs has also importantly shaped—and often distorted—the development of the tax system, resulting in tax preferences and tax policy initiatives that could not otherwise have been expected.[74] Using the tax system to accomplish two drastically different purposes—to raise tax revenue from private firms, and to force distributions from SOEs—risks reducing the efficiency of the system in accomplishing its normal, revenue-raising objective. This begs the question of whether better mechanisms of corporate governance for SOEs can be found: Might there be other feasible mandatory distribution mechanisms, for example?

Even if the preponderance of evidence from China turns out to support the forced-distribution view, as a general theory of SOE taxation that view should be able to command empirical support (quantitative or otherwise) in other countries as well. Indeed, the forced-distribution view may have empirical implications beyond firm-level tax-sensitivity. For example, it seems to suggest that in countries where corporate governance problems for SOEs are less severe—however measured[75]—the reliance on, or

[73] I attempt to offer such an articulation in Cui, *supra* note 3, parts III and IV.

[74] A parallel may be found in the dilemma of imposing a single body of corporate legal norms on private and state-owned firms, discussed in Chapter 2, Donald Clarke's contribution to this volume.

[75] As Musacchio and Lazzarini suggest, this is not an easy question. *See* Musacchio & Lazzarini, *supra* note 8.

effort devoted to, SOE taxation should also be more limited, again subject to the question of how that is to be measured.

Whether such empirical support is forthcoming is an open question. What must drive such empirical research, however, must be interest in the institutions of state ownership themselves. Such interest is perhaps more likely to be sustained by policy questions confronting those who have to live and work under such institutions—those who might find it difficult at least initially to abstract away from the circumstances (whether Chinese, Brazilian, Indian, Malaysian, or elsewhere) they are familiar with. Theorizing about state capitalism from within, however, precisely characterizes many of the other chapters in this book, and I am gratified that the topic of taxation has been included in the exercise.

7 Balancing Closure and Openness

THE CHALLENGE OF LEADERSHIP REFORM IN CHINA'S STATE-OWNED ENTERPRISES

Li-Wen Lin*

Introduction

The business-government relationship is at the heart of state-owned enterprise (SOE) governance. State ownership often raises the concern that the state-owner will intervene in corporate management to favor the state-owner's political interests at the expense of the individual firm's profits. International organizations such as the OECD thus regard management autonomy from government intervention as a good SOE governance standard. Politics is an important determinant in shaping corporate governance, and SOEs are immediately tied through ownership to the government. As a result, the extent to which SOEs maintain appropriate autonomy from the government largely depends on the quality of the political institutions in which the enterprises are embedded. China's SOEs are embedded in a political environment that imposes scant constraints on state intervention. The state-owner as the single ruling party faces no real threats from any opposing political coalitions. Likewise, the state-owner as the controlling shareholder

* I appreciate the comments of participants in the China State Capitalism Workshop at Columbia Law School. This is a chapter supplementary to my previous work *State Ownership and Corporate Governance in China: An Executive Career Approach*, 3 COLUM. BUS. L. REV. 734 (2013).

faces no real legal liabilities when encroaching on minority shareholders' interests.[1] The Chinese Communist Party (CCP), the real hand in the glove of state ownership in China, remains an institution that has never been truly subordinate to the rule of law. In such a case, the state-owner's intervention runs very deep.

One of the most important shareholder rights, and channels for the state-owner to intervene in corporate management, is through appointing members of the board of directors. In China, the state-owner (ultimately the CCP) appoints not only board members, but also top managers who are legally supposed to be appointed by the board of directors. How the state-owner exercises its appointment power directly shapes managerial incentives and in turn influences corporate behavior of China's SOEs. As one commentator notes, "[t]he Party's control over personnel was at the heart of its ability to overhaul state companies, without losing leverage over them at the same time."[2]

Recent studies have shown the important role of the state-owner's executive career management in corporate governance in China. Scholars have found that, in addition to monetary executive compensation, political promotion acts as another important incentive mechanism to address agency problems in China's state-owned companies.[3] Moreover, empirical evidence suggests that stock options granted to the executives of China's state-owned companies are fabricated, primarily to comfort foreign investors, because such a compensation scheme is incompatible with the Party-state's personnel management system.[4] The institutionalized personnel rotations among China's SOEs and other government units restrict the exercise of stock options that can drastically enlarge the pay gap between the SOEs and the civil service system.

Although scholarship to date has recognized that the state-owner's control over executive careers plays a significant role in shaping the governance of China's SOEs, the personnel management logic of this visible hand remains obscure.[5] A fundamental question regarding the state-owner's executive management in China is who the top managers really are. Specifically, what attributes are advantageous and sought after in the executive labor market by China's SOEs? By which career pathways have the top managers

---

[1] *See* Nicholas Howson & Donald Clarke, *Pathway to Minority Shareholder Protection: Derivative Actions in the People's Republic of China, in* The Derivative Action in Asia: A Comparative and Functional Approach 243–95 (D. Puchniak et al. eds., 2012) (showing no listed companies in China, mainly state-owned, have been subject to derivative action).

[2] Richard McGregor, The Party: The Secret World of China's Communist Rulers 69 (2010).

[3] *See* Jerry Cao et al., *Political Promotion, CEO Incentives, and the Relationship between Pay and Performance*, Wharton Financial Institutions Center Working Paper No. 11, 53 (2011).

[4] *See* Zhihong Chen et al., *Are Stock Option Grants to Directors of State-Controlled Chinese Firms Listed in Hong Kong Genuine Compensation?*, 88 Account Rev. 1547 (2013).

[5] A number of prominent sociologists have noted that business elite composition is an important but missing area of studies on Chinese corporate governance and national economy. *See* Andrew G. Walder, *From Control to Ownership: China's Managerial Revolution*, 7 Mgmt. Org. Rev. 19 (2009); Neil Fligstein & Jianjun Zhang, *A New Agenda for Research on the Trajectory of Chinese Capitalism*, 7 Mgmt. Org. Rev. 39 (2009).

of China's SOEs come to power? How cohesive are the elite at the highest echelon of China's SOEs?

Over the past decade, the Chinese government has issued a variety of rules and instructions in the name of professionalizing and marketizing executive recruitment. An analysis of these administrative guidelines sheds some light on the state-owner's logic in managing the SOE executives. A more insightful way to understand the executive personnel system, however, is to investigate empirically SOE executives' biographical backgrounds. Hence, this chapter conducts a biographic investigation of the CEOs and vice CEOs of SOEs under the State-owned Assets Supervision and Administration Commission (SASAC) of the State Council, the ownership agency of the Chinese central government. SASAC controls 113 SOEs. These SOEs are the most important players in China's state-owned sector. The focus of this chapter is on CEOs and vice CEOs rather than directors, because many central SOEs have yet to establish a board of directors.

The regulatory analysis and empirical findings in this chapter show that executive recruitment is oriented toward politically bounded, firm-specific knowledge professionalization and technical-position marketization. Executive recruitment is a system that strongly favors insiders over outsiders and presents a high degree of closure. Drawing on network theory in sociology, this chapter argues that although high elite cohesion may be conducive to national policy implementation, it poses challenges to corporate governance improvement. This is due to an increased tendency toward groupthink and the perpetuation of old practices that usually threaten governance reforms envisioned in corporate law. Striking the right balance between closure and openness in the corporate elite will be a major challenge facing China's SOE governance reform in the coming years.

This chapter proceeds as follows. Section I provides a brief description of the ownership and governance structure of central SOEs under SASAC's control. Section I also provides an organizational blueprint to contextualize executive recruitment practices and executive career pathways discussed in the following sections. Section II examines executive recruitment reform policies and their implications. Section III traces how executives come to power, by constructing six types of career pathways based on organizational structure and relational distance, and then analyzes the potential development and implications of each career pathway under institutional reforms. Section VI draws upon the specific institutional setting, social network theory, and comparative corporate governance literature to analyze the empirical findings. The Conclusion discusses the implications for China's SOE reform.

I. The Structure and Governance of Chinese SOEs

China's large state-owned non-financial enterprises are typically organized as vertically integrated business groups. Each business group has a holding company (known as a "core company") standing at the top of the ownership hierarchy. The Chinese state-owned non-financial companies on the Fortune Global 500 list, such as China National Petroleum Corporation, China Mobile Communication Corporation, and China Datang Corporation, are all core companies of a business group. Below each core company are a large number of subsidiaries, including listed companies, finance companies, research institutes, and many other related firms along the production chain.[6] Above the core company SASAC, an ownership agency of the central government. The core company acts as an intermediary between SASAC and group firms that engage in production. This chapter focuses on executive recruitment by the core companies under the supervision of SASAC.

SASAC, established in 2003, is legally tasked with consolidating shareholder control rights formerly dispersed among various government agencies.[7] In practice, SASAC's controlling shareholder status is often overshadowed by the persistent old power structure. SASAC's appointment right is eclipsed by a deep-rooted institutional practice in China: the Organization Department of the Chinese Communist Party controls the human resources management of all important organizations, including SOEs.[8] As a result, SASAC and the Party's Organization Department often jointly release executive management regulations and personnel announcements.

In cooperation with the Party's Organization Department, SASAC has introduced numerous regulatory rules seeking to improve the quality of SOE executive teams. In 2008 the Chinese government passed landmark legislation on SOE governance, the Law on State-Owned Assets of Enterprises (SOE Assets Law).[9] The SOE Assets Law formally defines how SASAC, as the agency authorized to exercise controlling shareholder rights, should manage SOE matters such as executive personnel management.

According to the SOE Assets Law and related regulations, SASAC may appoint and evaluate SOEs' directors and top managers, including chief executive officers (CEOs), vice CEOs, chief financial officers (CFOs), and other executives.[10] This appointment authority blatantly strips away the most important power of the board of directors under corporate law—selecting and evaluating top managers. Although officially advocating

---

[6] For a detailed analysis of the corporate group structure in China, see Li-Wen Lin & Curtis J. Milhaupt, *We Are the (National) Champions: Understanding the Mechanisms of State Capitalism in China*, 65 STAN. L. REV. (2013).

[7] For a brief discussion on the role of SASAC, see *id*. at 734–45.

[8] *See* John P. Burns, *Strengthening Central CCP Control of Leadership Selection: The 1990 Nomenklatura*, 138 CHINA Q. 458 (1994); Hon Chen, *Cadre Personnel Management in China: The* Nomenklatura *System 1990–1998*, 179 CHINA Q. 703 (2004).

[9] 中华人民共和国企业国有资产法 (Law of the People's Republic of China on the State-Owned Assets of Enterprises) (promulgated by the Standing Comm. Nat'l People's Cong., Oct. 28, 2008, effective May 1, 2009).

[10] SOE Assets Law § 22 (2009); 中央企业负责人经营业绩考核暂行办法 (Provisional Measures on Evaluating the Performance of Central SOEs' Leaders) (promulgated by SASAC, Dec. 28, 2009).

the establishment of boards of directors as an important reform, SASAC (and, ultimately, the Party) has been reluctant to relinquish authority to appoint the top positions in the most important SOEs.[11] Lack of the ability to use appointment authority as a monitoring device raises doubts that an SOE board of directors can play any meaningful role in improving the quality of executive management teams.

II. An Overview of SOE Executive Recruitment Rules

Since 2003, SASAC and the Party's Organization Department have introduced rules and guidelines seeking to improve the quality of SOE executive teams. These executive reform policies aim to professionalize executive teams and open the executive labor market.[12] This section discusses the implications of these professionalization and marketization reforms for SOE executive composition in three dimensions: political attributes, educational backgrounds, and career pathways.

Professionalization. State ownership often raises concerns over politics overriding professionalism. Political loyalty is an important factor in job chances and promotion opportunities in China, especially for state-affiliated organizations such as SOEs.[13] SASAC executive recruitment rules show that political allegiance to the CCP remains a paramount quality in selecting and evaluating top managers of China's SOEs.[14] The political loyalty requirement suggests that the Party has no intention of relinquishing

---

[11] In 2008, SASAC and the Organization Department of the Communist Party promulgated Guidance Opinions on Top Manager Appointments by the Board of Directors of Central Enterprises. These Opinions for the first time gave some appointment power to boards. However, the CEOs of the top fifty-three central enterprises are not covered by the Opinions. Even with respect to other enterprises, the nomination committee of the board is required to "fully consult" with the Party Committee and SASAC before nominating a CEO. The preliminary appointment must be filed with SASAC before the appointment becomes final. According to SASAC's vice commissioner Shuhe Huang, SASAC will start to experiment with allowing the board of directors to appoint top managers in a few SOEs. *See* Shuhe Huang, 国有企业改革在深化 (SOE Reform Is Deepening) (Feb. 7, 2014), http://www.sasac.gov.cn/n1180/n1566/n1881407/n1881422/15687932.html.

[12] Rather than reviewing in detail each regulatory scheme on executive recruitment, this chapter provides a summary of key points from the relevant rules. *See, e.g.*, 中央企业领导人员管理暂行规定 (Provisional Rules on Managing Corporate Leaders of Central SOEs) (promulgated by CCP Organization Department and SASAC's Party Committee, Dec. 30, 2009); 中央企业领导班子和领导人员综合考核评价办法 (试行) (Provisional Measures on Comprehensive Evaluation of Corporate Leadership Teams and Leaders of Central SOEs) (promulgated by CCP Organization Department and SASAC's Party Committee, Dec. 30, 2009); 中央企业公开招聘经营管理者工作指南 (Guidance on Public Recruitments for Senior Managers of Central SOEs) (promulgated by SASAC's Party Committee, Dec. 16, 2004).

[13] *See* Andrew G. Walder, *Career Mobility and the Communist Political Order*, 60 Am. Soc. Rev. 309, 309 (1995) (discussing the Communist Party's role in executive promotion within China's divided career path system, and noting that the path that considers political credentials leads to positions with greater authority and more material privileges than the path that considers only educational credentials).

[14] 中央企业领导人员管理暂行规定 (Provisional Rules on Managing Corporate Leaders of Central SOEs) § 4(1) (promulgated by CCP Organization Department and SASAC's Party Committee, Dec. 30, 2009); 中央企业领导班子和领导人员综合考核评价办法 (试行) (Provisional Measures on Comprehensive

control over the largest economic organizations in China. Professionalization, if at all, occurs within this political constraint; it is unlikely to touch on areas requiring or triggering sensitive political reforms. Instead SASAC's executive recruitment guidance makes clear that permissible reforms are expected to occur in less politically sensitive areas such as age, education, specialization, and work experience.

Part of the professionalization scheme is to bring young managers into, and retire old managers out of, leadership teams.[15] Young managers are desirable because they may be more active and innovative and less influenced by old traditions. The professionalization reform also sets educational requirements. As academic credentials are an approximate indicator of intellectual ability, the executive reform rules require executives to have a minimum of a bachelor's degree.[16] Moreover, although Chinese elites have traditionally been trained in engineering,[17] the number of non-engineering-trained executives is expected to grow as the division of labor becomes more complex in large business organizations.

In terms of career experience, organizations are now instructed to prefer business-related work experience over political career experience. In the past, China's SOEs were managed similarly to other government units, and thus not in line with modern business management. To address this concern, SASAC's reform rules require executives to have at least ten years of work experience in business organizations.[18]

Marketization. The SOE executive headhunting process used to take place in complete darkness. Job information and opportunities were available only to people inside the system. As a result, applicants were all system-insiders who perpetuated old habits because they lacked access to new management skills. To address this problem, the central and local SASACs, with the Party's endorsement, have openly solicited job applications for hundreds of executive positions since 2003. These positions include CEOs, vice CEOs, chief accountants (equivalent to CFOs), and chief legal officers of the core companies

---

Evaluation of Corporate Leadership Teams and Leaders of Central SOEs) (promulgated by CCP Organization Department and SASAC's Party Committee, Dec. 30, 2009).

[15] In December 2004, the central SASAC issued a regulatory order to the fifty-three most important central SOEs regarding the mandatory retirement age of top managers. According to the order, managers with ministerial rank are strictly required to retire upon reaching the age of sixty-five, and managers with vice-ministerial rank are required to retire upon reaching the age of sixty. Local SASACs have enacted stricter requirements. For example, according to the Provisional Rules on Corporate Leaders of SOEs under Heifei City SASAC, the chief-position executives, such as the board chairman and CEO, should not be older than fifty, and the vice-position executives, such as vice CEO, should not be older than forty-five. The reappointed chief-position executives should not exceed the age of fifty-five and the reappointed vice-position executives should not be older than fifty-two.

[16] 中央企业领导人员管理暂行规定 (Provisional Rules on Managing Corporate Leaders of Central SOEs) § 5 (promulgated by CCP Organization Department and SASAC's Party Committee, Dec. 30, 2009).

[17] Cheng Li, China's Leaders: The New Generation 37, 40 (2001) (noting that, of the college-educated Chinese elites who received promotions in the 1980s, most were trained in engineering and natural sciences, including 78.3 percent of ministers and vice ministers in 1988 and 74.6 percent of mayors in 1986).

[18] *See id.*

under their supervision. These who are interested in the executive openings may submit their applications and go through paper-based qualification reviews, standardized written examinations, and face-to-face interviews.[19] This executive headhunting targets not only China's domestic labor market, but also overseas talent. The political, educational, and work experience requirements discussed above are relaxed for executives recruited from overseas through this process.[20] In 2010, thirty-one senior managers of central SOEs, out of 1,410 applicants worldwide, were successfully recruited through this process.[21] This new recruitment strategy has been praised by the Chinese government as reflecting a process of "openness, fairness, competitiveness, and meritocracy."[22]

In theory, marketization of the recruitment process suggests that political affiliation with the Chinese Communist Party may become a less important factor in recruitment for executives because the value of professional experience accumulated outside the state system may compensate for a lack of political affiliation. In other words, marketization opens up opportunities for outsiders—professionals who build up their careers in private or foreign companies—to parachute directly onto the top of the SOE system. This public recruitment process also suggests a potential increase in the number of executives who have been educated abroad.

III. A Typology of Executive Career Pathways

Tracing executive career pathways is a useful method for revealing the elite training system and assessing the implementation of professionalization and marketization reforms. This chapter constructs six types of career pathways based on the prevailing organizational structures of China's SOEs and the organizational distance between the SOE of concern and the organizations that the executive (CEO or vice CEO) worked for prior to the executive appointment. Distance is defined by whether the prior organization is related to the concerned SOE in terms of supervisory authority in the government system, and whether the prior organization is an institution outside the state system (i.e., private or foreign companies). Organizations that fall outside the supervisory line or the state system are considered more distant from the SOE in question. This typology allows for evaluation of the degree of personnel integration between SOEs and other government units, as well as the degree of professionalization and openness of the executive labor market. Based on this typology, this chapter describes the features of each career

[19] 中央企业公开招聘经营管理者工作指南 (Guidance on Public Recruitments for Senior Managers of Central SOEs) (promulgated by SASAC's Party Committee, Dec. 16, 2004).

[20] *See id.*, § 6.

[21] Press Release, The First Bureau of Corporate Leader Management of SASAC of the State Council (Apr. 1, 2011) (on file with author).

[22] Press Release, Recruitment Decisions by SASAC of the State Council (May 10, 2005, Aug. 28, 2006, and May 22, 2007) (on file with author).

pathway for securing an executive position and the implications of such pathways for corporate governance.

The Single-Group Track. China's large non-financial SOEs are typically organized as business groups registered with the state. A business group is legally required to be comprised of a parent company and at least five controlled subsidiaries.[23] When an executive (CEO or vice CEO) has spent his or her whole career within one business group before being appointed an executive of that group, the executive's career follows a single-group track.

The single-group track is based on climbing the corporate ladder. If this track is the mainstream route, it suggests that a group-based seniority system operates to select the top managers of China's SOEs. Executives coming to the top through the single-group pathway possess a high volume of firm-specific knowledge and insider network resources.[24] When firm-specific knowledge is valued and insider social connections are important, managers following the single-group track have great advantages in attempting to reach the CEO position. From a corporate governance perspective, the single-group track assures some professionalism due to the executive's possession of rich, firm-specific knowledge. However, it may also present an increased risk of excessive power concentration, especially given that the board of directors is usually dysfunctional (or absent) as an internal monitoring mechanism, and that China's external governance institutions remain weak.

The Multi-Group Track. This career pathway refers to a route in which the executive has worked in other state-owned business groups prior to the executive appointment. At first blush, the SOE executives following the multi-group track look similar to those changing jobs across employers in other executive labor markets. Unlike other labor markets normally governed by the invisible hand, however, China's SOE executive market is centrally managed by the Party-state. Thus, job movements across organizations are not as free as in other labor markets. If personal reasons for job change across organizations are set aside, an important institutional reason for forming the multi-group track is the Party-state's personnel rotation management system.

Personnel rotation is a legally institutionalized system for managing civil servants in Chinese government units. Because the boundary between government units and

[23] 企业集团登记管理暂行规定 (Provisional Rules on Business Registration) (promulgated by State Administration for Industry & Commerce of the People's Republic of China, April 1998). In order to form a group, the parent company must have registered capital of at least 50 million RMB (about US$7.5 million) and at least five subsidiaries. The total registered capital of the parent and its subsidiaries must be at least 100 million RMB (US$15 million).

[24] For the early leading literature in explaining the importance of social networks to job opportunities, see generally Mark Granovetter, Getting a Job: A Study of Contacts and Careers (2d ed.1995) (arguing that the best jobs are found through personal contacts, and developing a causal model to explain the acquisition of job information through personal contacts).

SOEs is porous, the system in practice spills over into SOEs.[25] The Party-state frequently rotates top managers across business groups of the same industry. For example, in April 2011, the state-owner rotated the CEOs of the three central petroleum SOEs in China, each of which is a global Fortune 500 company. In the eyes of the Party-state, executive rotations perform two institutional functions. First, given that institutionalized corporate oversight organs such as the board of directors have yet to be fully developed, executive rotations can help reduce excessive concentration of managerial power in a business group. Second, personnel rotations facilitate management skills sharing among SOEs.[26] Personnel rotations allow executives who gained useful skills in one business group to share such experience with another group. For instance, one purported reason for Chengyu Fu's rotation from China National Offshore Oil Corporation (CNOOC) to Sinopec in the CEO rotations among China's three petroleum giants was that it was hoped his rich overseas business experience from CNOOC could alleviate Sinopec's difficulties with overseas expansion.[27]

The Supervisory-Bureau Track. An SOE executive comes to power through the supervisory-bureau pathway when the executive develops his or her career mainly in the SOE's supervisory bureau(s). China's large SOEs were carved out of industry-based government ministries or bureaus in the corporatization process, which transformed governmental organs into joint-stock companies. These corporatized SOEs are still supervised by government ministries (bureaus) related to industrial matters. The historical integration in organizational structures and the continuing supervisory relationships in business mean that personnel exchanges between the SOEs and their supervisory bureaus are quite frequent. Government officials can gain firm-specific knowledge and build social connections with employees in the supervised SOEs through supervisory relations. In addition, supervisory government officials tend to have industry-wide information and social connections. This social and informational capital can increase the usefulness of the supervisory-bureau track in securing executive positions.

Anecdotal evidence indicates that many government officials take top-echelon positions in SOEs in preparation for retirement. Transferring to an SOE is economically attractive because the large SOEs usually offer better monetary compensation than other government units. It is especially feasible for senior officials in the supervisory bureaus to adopt this transition strategy, because they have accumulated relevant social and knowledge capital. This retirement transition pattern, in fact, is not unique to China. In Japan,

---

[25] According to the Provisional Measures on Rotations of Civil Servants, enacted in 1996 and still effective today, a civil servant who has served in a leadership position for five or more years should rotate. According to the regulation, personnel rotation facilitates operational efficiency and prevents corruption.

[26] *See* Katharina Pistor, *The Governance of China's Finance*, *in* CAPITALIZING CHINA (Randall Morck & Henry Wai-Chung Yeoung eds., 2012) (making the same point for managerial rotations among the state-owned financial institutions in China).

[27] Yiming Zhang, *Sinopec and CNOOC Welcome New Heads, Top Leader Rotations Facilitate Cooperation*, CHINA ECON. TIMES, Apr. 11, 2011.

there is an institutionalized (though now waning) practice known as *amakudari*, where senior bureaucrats retire to join private companies or research institutes under the jurisdiction of, or linked with, their ministries when they reach mandatory retirement age, usually between fifty and sixty.[28] Such personnel practices in Japan have often been criticized as corrupt and as obstructing regulatory reforms.[29] The implication from the Japanese experience for China's SOEs seems to be that the supervisory-bureau pathway should be restricted in order to further executive professionalization and corporate governance reform.

The Unrelated-Government-Units Track. An executive follows the unrelated-government-units track when the executive's career mainly develops prior to CEO appointment in government-affiliated organs other than for-profit SOEs or supervisory bureaus. Such government units are largely irrelevant to the focused SOE in terms of the type of organizational identity or the nature of their business matters. For example, Yimin Lu, currently CEO of China Unicom, first worked his way up in the Party system to the position of bureau-level secretary (*zhengjuji mishu*) of the General Office of the Chinese Communist Party, and then joined China Unicom as an executive. Executives with this career pathway tend to possess more skills in political operation than firm-specific or industry-specific knowledge. If the unrelated-government-units track is the prevailing career pathway, it suggests the management logic of China's SOEs is oriented more toward political than business purposes. Under professionalization reform, the unrelated-government-units track will be limited in use.

The Multi-Sphere Track. An SOE executive comes to power through the multi-sphere track when an executive's career spans multiple types of organizations such as unaffiliated SOEs, supervisory bureaus, and other unrelated government units. For example, before being CEO of China National Travel Service Group, Shuaiting Wang initially worked his way up to the position of deputy chief secretary in the Xuzhou City government system, and then transferred to China Resources Group (a central SOE), where he was CEO of a subsidiary and then vice chairman of the core company. This type of career pathway is essentially a combination of the previous four types. Compared to the single-group executives, multi-sphere executives are more likely to have system-wide knowledge and diverse personal connections, which can be an advantage in career advancement. The prevalence of the multi-sphere track would suggest high personnel integration between SOEs and other government units. This phenomenon may be detrimental to corporate governance because the SOEs would be at a higher risk of being

---

[28] *See* Ulrike Schaede, *The "Old Boy" Network and Government-Business Relationships in Japan*, 21 J. Japanese Stud. 293, 293 (1995); *See also* Richard A. Colignon & Chikako Usui, Amakudari: The Hidden Fabric of Japan's Economy (2003).

[29] *See, e.g.*, Lonney E. Carlile & Mark C. Tilton, *Is Japan Really Changing?*, *in* Is Japan Really Changing Its Ways? Regulatory Reform and the Japanese Economy 197, 197–218 (Lonney E. Carlile & Mark C. Tilton eds., 1998); *see also* Elizabeth Norville, *The "Illiberal" Roots of Japanese Financial Regulatory Reform*, *in id.* at 111, 111–14 (Carlile & Tilton eds., 1998).

managed in a way similar to other government units. Nevertheless, the multi-sphere track may create greater elite cohesion through shared career experiences among political and business leaders, which can facilitate economic coordination and policy implementation at the national level.

The System-Outsider Track. All the career pathways discussed so far operate strictly within the boundaries of the state system. Executives traveling on these pathways are system-insiders, savvy operators within the state system. In contrast, system-outsiders accumulate their career experiences in organizations unaffiliated with the state, such as private or foreign companies.

Unlike system-insiders embedded in a closed network, system-outsiders have brokerage ties of connectivity outside the state system that provide access to new ideas and resources.[30] Executives coming from the system-outsider path are institutional brokers importing new management knowledge into the SOEs. The participation of system-outsiders in the SOE system is a good sign of improvement in corporate governance. SASAC's marketization reform of the SOE executive labor market is expected to result in the recruitment of more executives from the system-outsider path.

Although system-outsiders can use their brokerage advantages to break into the SOE system and win top management positions, it is uncertain whether these advantages can overcome the "liability of foreignness"—the competitive disadvantages of foreigners when entering a local system.[31] China's SOEs have a strict hierarchy of ranks in employee administration that parallels the government's civil service administration. This hierarchy of ranks persists despite several attempts in the past to abolish it. A system-outsider's parachuting into an executive post disrupts internal promotion expectations based on administrative ranks. It also causes a legitimacy problem when appointments diverge from institutionalized expectations. Moreover, system-outsiders often lack local personal connections (*guanxi*) necessary to gain access to job information about and opportunities in the state-affiliated organizations. As a result, system-outsiders face daunting challenges in breaking through entry barriers.

IV. Rules and Realities

Sections II and III reviewed the executive recruitment rules and discussed their possible implications. In China, however, there are usually gaps between the laws on the books and laws in action. To assess the real development of China's SOE executive recruitment, this section examines the CEO and vice CEO biographic backgrounds of the 113 central

---

[30] For the leading analysis of the idea about brokerage ties outside a closed system, see Ronald S. Burt, Brokerage and Closure: An Introduction to Social Capital (2005). In a simple sense, brokerage means connection between two or more unrelated agents or groups.

[31] The term "liability of foreignness" is commonly used in business literature. It refers to foreign firms that are less competitive compared to local firms when entering into a local market.

SOEs under SASAC's supervision as of December 2013. The dataset contains 113 CEOs and 526 vice CEOs (on average, each SOE has 4.65 vice CEOs). The biographic information was manually collected from multiple sources, including corporate prospectuses, annual reports, corporate websites, government documents and websites, industrial association websites, and news reports. Table 7.1 provides a summary of executive attributes of the 113 central SOEs.

For educational backgrounds, 76.1 percent of the CEOs and 67.6 percent of the vice CEOs hold a degree in engineering or natural science. The lower percentage of engineering/natural science-trained vice CEOs is due to the fact that some vice CEOs

TABLE 7.1
EXECUTIVE ATTRIBUTES OF CHINA'S CENTRAL SOES (DECEMBER 2013)

	CEOs	Vice CEOs
Age (as of 2013)	53.3 (N = 112)	52.7 (N = 452)
Educational Backgrounds		(N = 482)
Engineering/Natural Science	76.1%	67.6%
Graduate Degree	72.6%	66.0%
MBA/EMBA	30.1%	21.2%
PhD	18.6%	17.0%
C9 League	15.9%	13.9%
Tsinghua University	7.1%	5.2%
Foreign Education	10.6%	9.1%
Political Backgrounds		
Party Affiliation		
1. Chinese Communist Party	99.1%	89.7%
2. Others	0.9%	0.2%
3. Unknown	0%	10.1%
Total	100%	100%
Age When Joining CCP	25.1 (N = 30)	25.2 (N = 85)
Career Pathway		
1. Single-Group Track	48.7%	54.8%
2. Multi-Group Track	23.0%	17.7%
3. Supervisory Bureau Track	7.1%	5.5%
4. Unrelated-Government-Unit Track	1.8%	5.7%
5. Multi-Sphere Track	19.5%	6.8%
6. System-Outsider Track	0%	0.8%
7. Unknown	0%	8.7%
Total	100%	100%
N (unless stated otherwise)	113	526

simultaneously hold positions such as chief accountants or chief legal officers, positions that require training other than engineering. The dominance of engineering-trained executives is a result of China's industrial structure and political history. The Chinese government has been aggressively seeking technological upgrades to move up the value chain. This technological advancement cannot be achieved by financial or marketing management. Moreover, when China's education system was battered by the storms of Maoism, engineering was a politically safer field of study than most. These factors increased the tendency of students to study engineering.

Although SASAC's executive recruitment rules require only a bachelor's degree, a majority of the executives have academic achievements beyond SASAC's minimum requirement. About 72.6 percent of the CEOs and 66 percent of the vice CEOs hold at least one graduate degree. Table 7.1 shows that 18.6 percent of the CEOs and 17 percent of the vice CEOs have a doctoral degree. Among various types of graduate degrees, an MBA/EMBA was a popular choice for the executives. Because SOE executives are typically trained in engineering, an MBA/EMBA education can help enhance their business knowledge. Table 7.1 shows that 30.1 percent of the CEOs and 21.2 percent of the vice CEOs have an MBA/EMBA degree. The most popular business school among SOE executives is the China Europe International Business School (CEIBS), based in Shanghai and established in 1994 under an agreement between the Chinese government and the European Commission. Of the 136 executives holding an MBA/EMBA, twenty are from CEIBS.

A vast majority of the executives are trained in engineering, but only 7.1 percent of the CEOs and 5.2 percent of the vice CEOs are alumni of Tsinghua University, China's leading academic institute in the field of engineering. Only 15.9 percent of the CEOs and 13.9 percent of the vice CEOs are graduates of the so-called C9 League, an alliance of the nine most famous universities in China. Compared to other countries, such as France, where state ownership is common, SOE elites in China display a low degree of elite school concentration.[32] Thus, the professionalization of China's SOE leadership does not heavily rely on elite school training. It also does not rely heavily on foreign-trained executives. Only a minority of the executives, 10.6 percent of CEOs and 9.1 percent of vice CEOs, hold a foreign degree. Of the fifty-five foreign-educated executives, nineteen received their foreign degrees in the United States, eleven in Hong Kong, and the rest in twelve other countries.

The data also illuminate political backgrounds. SASAC's executive recruitment rules dictate that political loyalty to the Chinese Communist Party (CCP) is a paramount requirement. Table 7.1 demonstrates that political allegiance to the Party is beyond question: 99.1 percent of the CEOs and at least 89.7 percent of the vice CEOs are members of the CCP. While two executives are not CCP members, they are members of the China

---

[32] The elite school concentration of CEOs/directors in France was about 75 percent in 2005. *See* MAIRI MACLEAN ET AL., BUSINESS ELITE AND CORPORATE GOVERNANCE IN FRANCE AND THE UK (2006).

National Democratic Construction Association, one of the eight official other parties in China. This marginal representation of non-CCP party members in the SOE elite adds more symbolic than real political diversity to the SOE system.

The CCP-affiliated executives joined the Party at a relatively early age, approximately twenty-five years old. This suggests that an early pledge of political loyalty is helpful for later career development in the state system. Early party membership signals a higher degree of political commitment and also allows for a prolonged process of scrutiny, cultivation, and training. This process increases the likelihood of subsequent promotion into elite positions.[33]

Examination of career pathways reveals that close to half (48.7 percent) of the CEOs and a majority (54.8 percent) of vice CEOs came to power through the single-group track. The prevalence of the single-group track suggests that firm-specific knowledge is valued in China's SOE management, and that insider connections are helpful for securing executive positions. The second-most common career pathway is the multi-group track, accounting for 23 percent of CEOs and 17.7 percent of vice CEOs. The single-group and the multi-group tracks combined account for more than 70 percent of the sample observations. In other words, most of the executives developed their careers completely within the SOE system rather than moving around in different government spheres. This suggests that the Party-state maintains a certain degree of separation in human resources training between the political and business spheres within the state system.

Approximately 19.5 percent of the CEOs and 6.8 percent of the vice CEOs took the multi-sphere track. This appears to suggest that CEO positions, which have a higher status than vice CEO positions in the administrative hierarchy, are more likely to be obtained by those with more political or social connections. Although it is commonly believed that a large number of SOE executives are transferred from government bureaus, the data show that only 7.1 percent of the CEOs and 5.5 percent of the vice CEOs built their careers through the supervisory bureau track. Likewise, only 1.8 percent of the CEOs and 5.7 percent of the vice CEOs developed through the unrelated government unit track.

None of the CEOs and only four vice CEOs followed the system-outsider track. The organizations outside the Chinese state system that the four vice CEOs worked for before joining the SOEs include: KPMG (one of the world's largest accounting firms), Akzo Nobel (a global Fortune 500 company based in the Netherlands), and Defense Science Organization National Laboratories (Singapore's national defense R & D organization). A more fine-grained analysis of the system-outsiders shows that the average age of the four system-outsider vice CEOs is 45.5, much younger than the average age of the non-system-outsiders (52.9). In addition, the system-outsider executives have a higher ratio (50 percent) of foreign education experience, compared to non-system-outsiders (9.5 percent).

---

[33] Bobai Li & Andrew G. Walder, *Career Advancement as Party Patronage: Sponsored Mobility into the Chinese Administrative Elite, 1949–1996*, 106 Am. J. Soc. 1371, 1395 (2001).

To further explore the degree of openness of the SOE executive system, we now turn to the attributes of the executives recruited under SASAC's marketization reform between the years of 2003 and 2011. The data were manually collected from press releases posted on SASAC's website. The findings are reported in Table 7.2.

Between 2003 and 2011, there were 124 executives recruited through the marketization program discussed in Sectiont II. Of the 124 executives, eight are CEOs, fifty-one vice CEOs, forty-seven chief accountants, and eighteen chief legal officers. The executive labor market is more open to technical knowledge positions such as chief accountants and legal officers than to political power positions.

The average age of the executives at the time of appointment was fairly young, only 41.6 years. In terms of their education level, 24.2 percent of the executives hold a

TABLE 7.2
PUBLIC RECRUITMENT RESULTS OF CHINA'S CENTRAL SOES, 2003–2010

	Count (Percentage)
Type of Position	
CEO	8 (6.5%)
Vice CEO	51 (41.1%)
Chief Accountant	47 (37.9%)
Legal Counsel	18 (14.5%)
Total	124 (100%)
Age as of Appointment	41.6
Highest Level of Education	
Bachelor's Degree	30 (24.2%)
Master's Degree	71 (57.3%)
PhD Degree	23 (18.5%)
Total	124 (100%)
Party Affiliation	
Chinese Communist Party	110 (88.7%)
Others	4 (3.2%)
Unknown	10 (8.1%)
Total	124 (100%)
Immediate Prior Position	
Same Group (Core or Subsidiary)	58 (46.8%)
Unaffiliated SOEs (Central or Local)	51 (41.1%)
Various Government Units (City Government, Supervisory Bureau, Industrial Association, University)	9 (7.3%)
Private Enterprises	6 (4.8%)
Total	124(100%)

bachelor's degree as the highest degree, 57.3 percent a master's degree, and 18.5 percent a doctoral degree. The results are similar to the findings in Table 7.1.

As discussed in detail in Section II, SASAC's executive recruitment rules relax the CCP affiliation requirement for executives recruited through marketization channels. Nevertheless, the importance of CCP affiliation appears uncompromised. Table 7.2 shows that 88.7 percent of the executives recruited from the more transparent and competitive channels are CCP members. Although 3.2 percent of the executives are non-CCP members, they are in fact members of CCP allies, such as the China National Democratic Construction Association and the China Democratic League. The door to the SOE executive club remains largely closed to non-CCP professionals.

Career experience further shows the persistent closure of the executive recruitment system. About 47 percent of the executives held a prior position in the recruiting company or its affiliates, and about 41 percent were recruited from unaffiliated SOEs. Another 7.3 percent joined from various government or government-controlled units such as local governments, supervisory bureaus, industrial associations, and universities. Only 4.8 percent of the executives were recruited from private enterprises. Thus, although the marketization reform purports to recruit system-outsiders, the results show a big gap between the formal policy and its operation.

Conclusion

China's new leadership recently unveiled its vision of SOE reform. Chinese policymakers have sent a clear message that part of this SOE reform will be focused on professionalization and marketization of executive recruitment. This chapter, which analyzes the executive composition and recruitment of China's large non-financial SOEs, offers a timely evaluation of the reform policy.

The analysis above shows that SOE leadership teams are a very cohesive group in terms of their educational training, political affiliation, and career experience. This cohesion also characterizes those recruited from more market-oriented channels. The current executive labor market remains a system-insider's game. Elite cohesion presents some advantages but also challenges to China's corporate governance and national economy. According to sociologist Ronald Burt's analysis of "brokerage and closure" in social structure, although high cohesion can help consensus formation and policy implementation, it runs the risks of closure, groupthink, and a lack of creativity.[34] Building brokerage ties reaching outside the closed system can import new ideas and stimulate innovation. As competition in the global economy has become more dependent on innovation capacity, Chinese SOEs need inputs of new talent and new management skills in order to gain a

[34] BURT, *supra* note 30.

competitive edge. The Chinese government seems aware of the potential closure problem and has adopted some administrative measures to open the SOE executive labor market.

In the eyes of the Party, neither complete closure nor complete openness is desirable. Complete closure lacks competitiveness, and complete openness runs the risk of losing control. Chinese policymakers face an uneasy task in seeking to strike a balance between closure and openness. The openness of the executive labor market probably will start from lower-level managers before expanding to high-level managers, from the less important business groups owned by the local governments before expanding to those controlled by the central government, from companies faced with fierce competitive pressure before expanding to companies in monopolized sectors. The whole process will develop slowly because personnel management remains a highly sensitive area, and the Chinese government still uses personnel management to maintain control over large enterprises as the government reduces its ownership stake.

Moreover, although China's SOEs have a demand for professionals who are trained outside the state system, the executive reform process can be conditioned by the supply side of talent: whether system-outsiders are interested in joining SOEs. For example, in several instances, SASAC officials have extended offers to system-outsiders, only to have the candidates decline the offers because the pay was below prevailing market standards.[35] To handle this problem the Chinese government is experimenting with a dual system in executive compensation. Under the dual system the compensation of system-insiders is unilaterally set by SASAC, while system-outsiders are paid based on market prices through contract negotiation. It is unclear whether such dualism will work. Anecdotal evidence shows that it can brew resentment among system-insiders.[36] In addition, the SOE management culture, typically tainted with political complexities, may make system-outsiders shy away from joining the SOE system. As a result, the executive labor market probably will continue to be dominated by system-insiders. This insider dominance increases the risks of perpetuating old practices that deviate from international standards. The lack of substantive openness in the composition of SOE corporate leadership may be a fundamental cause of the common dysfunction of many corporate governance institutions, including the board of directors and independent directors.

---

[35] *See* Jingjing Zhong 钟晶晶, 央企全球聘高管四成来自系统内 (Forty Percent of the Central SOE Executives Recruited Worldwide Are from Inside the System), Beijing News, May 2011 (Jigang Jiang, the Director of central SASAC's Second Executive Administration Bureau, explained, "In 2005, there was a candidate who studied abroad and worked in a foreign multinational company and then transferred to the CEO position of the multinational's branch in China. The candidate applied for a vice CEO position of a central SOE. He passed the written exam and interviews with the highest scores. We really wanted to hire him, but this hiring was unsuccessful due to compensation gaps. The candidate asked for pay at least on par with his current pay (US$200,000). The candidate was very sincere and said he was motivated by patriotism and the passion to contribute to the development of the central SOEs, so he did not ask for any pay raise but hoped to stay at his current level. The deal was eventually killed because the asking pay in fact was equal to the total compensation of the other seven top managers of the hiring SOE.").

[36] *See id.*

8 Legal Informality and Human Capital Development in China

Ruoying Chen*

Introduction

China is often cited as a counterexample to the hypothesis that economic growth needs the support of certain basic legal institutions, such as strong protection of property rights and legal enforcement of contracts.[1] The widespread legal informality in contracts among SOEs and in the way government has carried out regulation supports the claim that China in fact has lacked such growth-supporting legal institutions. Indeed, legal informality may even have contributed to China's economic growth by reducing transaction costs in contracts and administrative costs in government regulation.

Correlation between legal informality and economic growth is not, however, the same as causation. Even if we could establish that informality was an effective engine of China's

* Jingyi Ge, Kai Xu, Jie Zheng, and Jiaxin Zhong, graduate students at Peking University Law School, provided excellent research assistance. I thank Ben Liebman and Curtis Milhaupt for very detailed and valuable suggestions on earlier drafts. For helpful discussions, I thank Dr. Ruijian Li, Dr. Xian Wang, and participants at the Columbia Law School Conference "Chinese State Capitalism and Institutional Change: Domestic and Global Implications," June 13–14, 2014, especially Wei Cui, Feng Deng, Mary Gallagher, Nicholas Howson, Yasheng Huang, Huyue (Angela) Zhang, Wentong Zheng, Alex Wang, and Mark Wu.

[1] Daron Acemoglu & James Robinson, Why Nations Fail 67 (2013).

economic growth over the past three decades, past success does not guarantee anything for the future. China has changed as a result of economic growth. The range of actors involved in the Chinese economy and the stakes involved have dramatically increased. The state can no longer internalize the potential losses resulting from legal informality. The nature of potential risks and consequences of decisions made by market players and regulators have become more complicated. This complexity necessitates higher-quality information and more sophisticated skills for risk assessment and management. Under these new circumstances, legal informality is increasingly likely to generate decisions that do not fully incorporate associated risks or reflect necessary risk-control measures. Continued reliance on informality fails to provide sufficient incentives to individuals to acquire the information and skills required to assess and to manage risks involved in contracts and regulation. Individuals operating in conditions of legal informality may resist reforms that would lead toward more rule-based and reason-based legal institutions because they are short of skills that are required in such a new regime. Executives of SOEs, legal professionals, and regulatory officials may be particularly likely to suffer in continued legal informality because they currently do not have enough incentives to develop the skills in dealing with complicated risks in the market. In a more developed and complicated economy, legal informality is not only ineffective and inefficient, but also detrimental to those individuals at the center of legal institutions. The rest of this chapter is organized as follows. Section I introduces the concept of "legal informality" in the context of China's legal development over the past three decades. Section II uses two examples to explain the legal informality in contracts among SOEs: (1) sales of non-performing loans (NPLs) by state-owned banks to state-owned financial asset management companies (AMCs), and (2) advances of loans by state-owned banks to the government's land-stock authorities (LSAs)[2] secured with land-stock mortgages (LSMs).[3] Section III illustrates informality in regulation, using the example of the regulatory approval process for initial public offerings (IPOs) in mainland China and Hong Kong. Section IV explains the potential cost-saving function of legal informality. Section V demonstrates the harm of legal informality in China's new stage of economic development. A brief Conclusion follows, with comparison to the evolution of administrative systems in Japan in the twentieth century.

I. Legal Development and Legal Informality in China

Over the three decades since it started comprehensive reform in the late 1970s, China has developed a rather sophisticated legal system. China has issued close to six hundred sets of national legislative rules, of which more than two hundred are currently in force,[4]

---

[2] Land stock authorities (*tudi chubei jigou*, 土地储备机构).

[3] Land stock mortgage (*tudi chubei diya*, 土地储备抵押).

[4] *See* Jingwen Zhu 朱景文, 中国法律发展报告：中国立法 60 年：体制、机构、立法者和立法数量 (China Legal Development Report: China's Legislation for the Past 60 Years: Framework, Institutions,

covering a broad range of legal subjects. The strategy of learning from international practice and extensive domestic experiments has increased the complexity and sophistication of China's legal system.[5] Although China remains a large developing country, it is famous for being a safe society with a stable social order and for having a relatively effective government.[6] Both are strong indicators of the quality of the criminal and civil justice systems and the competence of legal professionals.

Compared to other developing countries with large populations, the number and quality of legal professionals in China is also impressive. As of the end of 2013, the Chinese court system had about 196,000 judges, and the ratio of judges per million persons was about 144.[7] During roughly the same period, the ratio was 82 in Brazil[8] and 13 in India.[9] Over the past three decades, the ever-increasing level of specialized education and on-the-job training of court staff[10] has generated a modern and sophisticated judiciary.[11] The growth of a sophisticated and highly globalized group of practicing lawyers is equally prominent in China. Chinese lawyers have been playing an indispensable role in cross-border transactions, working together with top Wall Street and Magic Circle law firms from the West.[12] One of China's largest law firms "combined" with a 180-year-old Australian law firm in 2012.[13]

Legislative Entities and Legislation) (2011). The numbers are much greater if local government rules with binding force are included.

[5] A case in point is the corporate governance structure mandated under China's Corporation Law and Securities Law, which is a unique and sophisticated model that combines the features of U.S.-style independent directors and German-style supervisory boards of representatives of employees and unions.

[6] For example, China ranks 29th, 49th and 51st among 99 countries in terms of "security and order," "government absent corruption," and "criminal justice" according to the most recent World Justice Project report. The Rule of Law Index 2014, *available at* http://worldjusticeproject.org/sites/default/files/files/country_profiles.pdf (last visited Mar. 25, 2015).

[7] See announcement by the official Xinhua news agency based upon data released at a news conference held by the China Supreme People's Court, 最高法:我国法官人数已近 20 万人 将成分类管理改革重点, 责任编辑: 杨婷 (Ting Yang), July 23, 2013, *available at* http://news.xinhuanet.com/legal/2013-07/25/c_116690034.htm (last visited Mar. 25, 2015).

[8] Nat'l Council of Justice, Justice in Numbers 2009 Report—Indicators of the Judiciary Power 6–7 (2010).

[9] Supreme Court of India, National Court Management Systems Policy & Action Plan 42 (2012).

[10] *See* 《中华人民共和国法官法》 (The Judges Act of China) (effective Jan. 1, 2002) (requiring a minimum of a bachelor's degree for one to become a judge), English translation *available at* http://www.npc.gov.cn/englishnpc/Law/2007-12/12/content_1383686.htm (last visited Mar. 25, 2015).

[11] Frank Upham, *Who Will Find the Defendant If He Stays with His Sheep? Justice in Rural China*, 114 Yale L.J. 1675 (2005).

[12] In cross-border mergers and acquisition transactions, there have always been Chinese lawyers and foreign lawyers representing each side. Legal opinions issued by Chinese legal counsel are also required by foreign regulators for overseas IPOs of Chinese corporations or corporations with major assets and operations located in China.

[13] See the description of the transaction between the Chinese firm King & Wood and the Australian firm Malleson Stephen Jacques, *available at* the official website of King & Wood & Malleson, which used the term "combine": http://www.kingandwood.com/thefirm.aspx?language=en (last visited Mar. 25, 2015).

China's state-owned enterprises, the major "consumers" of law and the legal system, have engaged in complicated cross-border transactions such as IPOs,[14] mergers and acquisitions,[15] and public tender offers.[16] In negotiating and completing these transactions, SOEs hire international professional advisors from the same pool out of which their foreign competitors draw their professional advisors. In advising Chinese SOEs and other clients, these professionals use the same set of knowledge and skills, providing legal documents developed from more or less the same precedents. Given that these documents are often governed by the law of jurisdictions with a much longer history of legal and economic development, these legal documents are hence rather specific and complicated as a result of such longer period of development.

The development of formal legal institutions and trained legal professionals in China has been accompanied, however, by a substantial degree of legal informality, especially in the area of contracts and government regulation. Legal informality is not unique to China; this has been addressed in previous legal scholarship. This chapter focuses on certain aspects of informality that are different from those discussed in most existing literature, namely the impact of legal informality on the human-capital development of individual parties involved in the operation of legal institutions, such as executives of SOEs, legal professionals, and regulatory officials.

Existing legal scholarship has largely focused on two types of issues relating to informality of contract: (1) informal norms emerging from close-knit communities and informal and extralegal enforceability mechanisms for contracts, such as community networks and reputational mechanisms;[17] and (2) contracts that are informal because the underlying transactions are prohibited or otherwise restricted by law, such as informal lending and informal trading of real properties. The concept of informality in contract addressed in this chapter is slightly different from that addressed in existing literature. The contracts this chapter examines are those among substantial Chinese SOEs, some

---

[14] For example, as of December 2014, on the main board of the Hong Kong Stock Exchange, more than 42 percent of the overall market capitalization is attributable to Chinese companies (H-share companies) and foreign companies with their core assets and operations located in China (Red-chip companies). See the official website of the Hong Kong Stock Exchange: https://www.hkex.com.hk/eng/stat/smstat/chidimen/cd_mc.htm (last visited Mar. 25, 2015).

[15] Lenovo's $1.25 billion acquisition of IBM's personal computer division in 2005 and Sinopec Group's $7.16 billion acquisition of Switzerland's Addax Petroleum Corporation in 2009 are two notable examples.

[16] The first public tender offer completed by a major Chinese SOE in the global capital market was completed by a subsidiary of Sinochem for Emerald Energy PLC through a scheme of arrangement effective on October 12, 2009, and the subsequent delisting of Emerald Energy PLC from the London Stock Exchange on October 13, 2009. See statement on the official website of Emerald Energy PLC: http://www.emeraldenergy.com/ (last visited Mar. 25, 2015).

[17] *See, e.g.*, Robert Ellickson, Order without Law: How Neighbors Settle Disputes 167–83 (1997); Lisa Bernstein, *Merchant Law in a Merchant Court: Rethinking the Code's Search for Immanent Business Norms*, 144 U. Pa. L. Rev. 1765, 1770 (1996); Lisa Bernstein, *Opting Out of the Legal System: Extralegal Contractual Relations in the Diamond Industry*, 11 J. Legal Stud. 115 (1992).

of which are among the largest public corporations in the world and have shares listed and traded in global capital markets. These contracting parties can hardly be described as members of "closely knit communities." Yet contracts among SOEs are legally vulnerable. This vulnerability is not due to legal prohibitions or restrictions, but rather to the extremely high level of vagueness in contract terms and the lack of clarity and specification. Despite these weaknesses, the underlying transactions are often formally recognized and endorsed in legally binding rules issued by the government.

Another type of legal informality this chapter addresses is related to the way regulatory power is wielded by government authorities in China. When interacting with the subject of regulation, regulatory authorities often act in a rather "informal" way. Examples of such informal regulation include imposing requirements and providing guidance through verbal communication instead of written rules, delaying and even completely refraining from commencing formal approval procedures (hence keeping communications off the record), and issuing written decisions with little or no reasoning. Similar informality in regulatory activities has previously been documented by scholars in the study of government regulation by the Japanese government in the twentieth century.[18] However, the specific attributes and causes of such regulatory informality and the background of institutional settings in China are different from those in Japan, especially the role of the courts with respect to regulatory activities. Apart from the self-interest of regulators and officials, a potential reason for regulatory informality in China is that the regulatory authority is often not the true decision-maker, but is simply endorsing decisions already made by other government departments. It thus is neither possible nor appropriate to require more formal communication and reasoning.

II. Informality in Contract

Contracts are inevitably incomplete in the sense that parties cannot possibly specify all current situations or predict all future contingencies.[19] Hence, the extent of formalistic and specific provisions is always a matter of degree. A certain level of certainty and specification is necessary, however, for parties to ascertain their rights and obligations to decide their future actions. Chinese law, like other civil law and common law jurisdictions, requires a certain level of formality for a contract to be effective and enforceable.[20]

---

[18] *See* Curtis J. Milhaupt, *Managing the Market: The Ministry of Finance and Securities Regulation in Japan*, 30 STAN. J. INT'L. L. 423, 423 (1994); Peter B. Edelman, *Japanese Product Standards as Non-tariff Trade Barriers: When Regulatory Policy Becomes a Trade Issue*, 24 STAN. J. INT'L L. 389 (1988); Ken Duck, Comment, *Now That the Fog Has Lifted: The Impact of Japan's Administrative Procedures Law on the Regulation of Industry and Market Governance*, 19 FORDHAM INT'L L.J. 1686–763 (1996).

[19] Oliver Hart & John Moore, *Incomplete Contracts and Renegotiation*, 56 ECONOMETRICA 755 (1988).

[20] 《中华人民共和国合同法》 (Contract Law of China), CHAPTER 2, effective Oct. 1, 1999, English translation available at: http://www.npc.gov.cn/englishnpc/Law/2007-12/11/content_1383564.htm (last visited Mar. 25, 2015).

Among Chinese SOEs, however, very informal terms are used in certain circumstances, and contracts tend to be extremely brief. The contract terms often appear too vague to carry legal force. Substantial gaps in contract provisions are common, creating uncertainty as to rights and obligations and providing little guidance for future activities. These transactions are nonetheless officially recognized and regulated by the government, and no formal disputes have been reported resulting from such transactions.

These informal contracts are hardly marginal. Parties to these informal contracts tend to be high-profile SOEs, and the transaction values are of millions and sometimes billions of dollars. This chapter provides two examples to illustrate informality in contracts: (1) sales of NPLs by state-owned banks to AMCs, and (2) provision of LSMs by LSAs.

A. SALES OF NPLs BY BANKS TO AMCs

After the Asian financial crisis, the Chinese central government started taking measures to speed up the reform of its financial sector. One critical step taken by the government was to commercialize the five state-owned commercial banks and prepare them for IPOs in international stock markets. Each of these banks carried with it a huge portfolio of NPLs, resulting from policy-oriented lending with little or no idea of risk management. In 2003, the total value of NPLs owned by the five banks reached US$232 billion, and the ratios of NPLs to total loans owned by the banks and to China's overall GDP were 20 percent and 17 percent respectively.[21] The banks needed to dispose of these NPLs in order to become attractive in both lending markets and capital markets.

In 1999, the Chinese central government established four AMCs, and the Ministry of Finance (MOF) injected RMB10 billion (equivalent to about US$1.21 billion[22]) into each of them as an equity investment.[23] Immediately afterward, the four AMCs purchased a large chunk of NPLs from four out of the five banks at "book value," for a total price of about RMB1.4 trillion (about US$169 billion).[24]

Each AMC's capital was apparently not enough to settle the full price of the purchases. Subsequently, each AMC issued a ten-year non-transferable note to the corresponding bank, for a total principal amount of about US$98.1 billion (RMB811 billion), in addition to the right to draw down loans up to a given amount from the central bank.

---

[21] Banco de España, Alicia García-Herrero & Daniel Santabárbara, Where Is the Chinese Banking System Going with the Ongoing Reform? (2004), *available at* http://www.bde.es/f/webbde/SES/Secciones/Publicaciones/PublicacionesSeriadas/DocumentosOcasionales/04/Fic/do0406e.pdf (last visited Mar. 25, 2015).

[22] The exchange rate was about 8.27 at the time, as listed on the official website of the Federal Reserve Bank: http://www.federalreserve.gov/releases/h10/hist/dat96_ch.htm (last visited Mar. 25, 2015).

[23] See the official website of the China Oriental Asset Management Corporation, one of the four AMCs: http://www.coamc.com.cn/dfkx/jtyw/201403/t20140319_43609.html (last visited Mar. 25, 2015).

[24] *Id.*

The terms of these notes, therefore, are critical to this transaction. However, the contractual terms left a big gap as to what would happen upon expiration of the original term. Given the value involved in the transaction, such a level of vagueness was rather unusual. The vagueness looks even more striking and curious when taking into account the fact that the price was at book value on a dollar-for-dollar basis. It was very unlikely that the AMCs would be able to collect NPLs for the "book value" and therefore were not likely to be able to generate sufficient cash flow to pay off the whole amount of the notes by the due date.

In fact, a substantial discount in recovery was to be expected. A subsequent auction of its NPL portfolio by one of the four AMCs to international buyers in 2001 and the actual recovery rate by the AMCs on the NPLs provide strong evidence that the price should have reflected a deep discount of the book value. When some of the AMCs made portfolio sales of NPLs to experienced international buyers in 2001, led by Goldman Sachs and Morgan Stanley, the price was deeply discounted. It was expected that about 20 percent of the book value could be recovered.[25] As these transactions were carried out on an arm's-length basis, the price more accurately reflects the amount to be actually recovered from the NPLs. Similarly, in the first quarter of 2006, close to the original deadline for the AMCs to dispose of their NPL portfolios, it was reported that approximately 67 percent of the NPLs had been disposed of by the four AMCs, and the total cash value recovered was about 22 percent of the book value, with one AMC having disposed of more than 80 percent of its NPL portfolio.[26]

Pricing these transactions was, of course, extremely difficult. There was no precedent in the market to serve as a reference. Neither sale of loans nor legal and financial due diligence for loan portfolios had ever been heard of in the Chinese market, and the challenges raised by unclear and outdated legal rules about lending and mortgages were substantial.[27] Both the arm's-length purchase price of the NPL portfolio and the actual recovery rate pointed to a substantial discount of the book value. Both also indicated that the AMCs may have committed to pay the banks a price they could not afford given their expected cash flow from the recovery of the NPLs. The AMCs' only source of income was proceeds to be recovered from the loans. All parties should have foreseen a high possibility that the AMCs would be short of funds to repay the principal, and

[25] See the official website of Huarong AMCs on Dec. 3, 2002: http://www.chamc.com.cn/xwzx/jtxw/67719.shtml (last visited Mar. 25, 2015).

[26] *See* Report on Assets Disposal by Financial Assets Management Companies as of the year of 2006 (金融资产管理公司资产处置情况表), dated Apr. 24, 2006, published by the China Banking Regulatory Commission on its official website: http://www.cbrc.gov.cn/chinese/home/docView/2456.html (last visited Mar. 25, 2015).

[27] Some of the specific difficulties for evaluating legal title and risks associated with these NPLs are set out in Ruoying Chen, *Public Grant of Land Use Rights and Mortgage Lending Risks*, CHINA L. & PRAC., Oct. 2007, http://www.chinalawandpractice.com/Article/1690115/Issue/8508/Public-Grant-of-Land-Use-Rights-and-Mortgage-Lending-Risks.html.

a correspondingly high potential for the need to amend the terms of the notes. Such a possibility became reality: in 2010, just before the notes were to mature, the notes were extended.[28]

Such a seemingly high-probability event was not addressed in the original contracts, and the "extension" of the notes came about rather curiously.[29] The announcement made by the banks about the extension did not include terms such as "enter into a new agreement" or "agree to extend." Instead, the announcement stated that the bank "received notice from the MoF" that the note was extended for another ten years at the same annual interest rate of 2.25 percent. The MOF was then the only shareholder of the AMCs and was indirectly holding a controlling stake in the state-owned banks. However, under Chinese company law, subsidiaries enjoy a legal personality independent from their parent. Neither of these facts, however, seems sufficient to permit the MOF unilaterally to give legal effect to an extension of notes between two subsidiaries. Moreover, although the role of the MOF was not addressed in the description of the notes, the announcement stated that the MOF would "continue the support of the repayment of principal and interest by the AMCs." Apparently, the term "support" does not carry legal effect in China. The term was not defined or explained in the original prospectus for the IPOs of the banks in Hong Kong or the subsequent announcement by the banks of the extension of the notes.

The term "support" was also used in another similar transaction. In May 2005, the MOF authorized Huarong AMC to purchase, again at book value, another portfolio of NPLs from ICBC, with a total principal value of RMB 246 billion payable in five years. If this amount was not fully repaid by June 2010, the "MoF will provide special capital support to ensure that this outstanding amount be repaid in time," and a special joint account was established to earmark certain income of the MOF for repayment of the price.[30] Such additional explanation and the existence of the joint account have to some

[28] The announcement made by the Industrial and Commerce Bank of China (ICBC), one of the four banks involved, dated Aug. 13, 2010, available via the official website of the Hong Kong Stock Exchange, where the H-shares of ICBC are listed: http://www.hkexnews.hk/listedco/listconews/SEHK/2010/0813/LTN20100813451.pdf (last visited Mar. 25, 2015).

[29] *Id.*

[30] See the A-share IPO prospectus of ICBC. Such income includes: (1) tax payable by ICBC, (2) dividends payable by ICBC to MOF, (3) payment received from borrowers of loans in the portfolio, (4) sale proceeds received out of future sale of shares in ICBC, (5) other funds provided by MOF, and (6) interest accrued in the account. The relevant paragraphs in the A-share prospectus contain slightly more detail than the H-share prospectus. For the A-share IPO prospectus of ICBC, see the official website of Shanghai Stock Exchange, where the A-share of ICBC are listed: http://static.sse.com.cn/disclosure/listedinfo/announcement/c/2006-10-26/601398_20061026_2.pdf (last visited Mar. 25, 2015). For the H-share IPO prospectus of ICBC, see the official website of Hong Kong Stock Exchange, where the H-shares of ICBC are listed; for the full table of contents of IPO prospectus (links to multi-docs): http://www.hkexnews.hk/listedco/listconews/SEHK/2006/1016/LTN20061016000.htm (last visited Mar. 25, 2015). For the relevant section (page 84): http://www.hkexnews.hk/listedco/listconews/SEHK/2006/1016/01398/EWP113.pdf (last visited Mar. 25, 2015).

extent clarified the position of the MOF. Yet the statement did not identify or describe the source of funds in the joint account, rendering it almost useless as collateral.

B. LAND-STOCK MORTGAGE

In China's dual-land property system, urban land is owned by the state and rural land by rural collectives. Each rural collective consists of a number of rural households. Land use rights on state-owned land are granted only to end users.[31] During the process of urbanization, the state does not give up its monopoly over urban land. Rural land converted to urban land to facilitate urbanization requires initial capital-intensive development. Such efforts can be challenging to finance. In 1996, the Shanghai government established the first LSA to carry out such initial development of land. The Shanghai-LSA had an innovative financing arrangement: LSAs received loans from banks by creating a so-called "land-stock mortgage." This practice first emerged sporadically and later became so widespread that it was formally recognized by the central government and a large number of local governments.[32] Numerous central ministries and local governments subsequently issued rules governing various aspects of such transactions. There has been no report on the size of such loans. LSAs have become major borrowers of bank loans in China, however, and LSAs frequently rank among the top-ten borrowers of some national commercial joint stock banks.[33]

Underlying these transactions, however, remain critical legal questions. What exactly is the collateral? Is it possible for banks to foreclose on the loans? Two factors give rise to vagueness and uncertainty, one relating to the legal authority of the claimed mortgagor and the other to the subject of the mortgage interest.

On the one hand, the borrowers, LSAs, have no legal authority or capacity to dispose of rights and interests in state-owned land. Instead, they are better defined as warehousing service providers, keeping accounts of the costs of land development and revenue from land-use-right grants.[34] On the other hand, land stock cannot legally be the subject of mortgage interest and thus cannot serve as collateral. The potential candidates to

---

[31] For a general introduction to China's land property system, see Ruoying Chen, *Divided World: China's Land Tenure System and Implication for Foreign Investment in China*, DONG-A J. INT'L BUS. TRANSACTIONS L. 1 (Spring 2010).

[32] The central government issued two sets of rules governing the operation of LSM and administration of financing for LSAs. 土地储备管理办法 (Administrative Measures on Land Stock) (promulgated on and effective as of Nov,19, 2007); 土地储备资金财务管理暂行办法 (Tentative Rules on Financial Administration of Land Stock Capital) (promulgated on and effective as of Feb. 27, 2007).

[33] *See* Jinfeng Shi (史进峰), "股份行十大贷款户细剖 开发贷让位土地储备贷款" 《二十一世纪经济导报》, 第9版) (Detailed Analysis of Top 10 Borrowers of Joint Stock Commercial Banks, Loans to Land-Stock Took Over the Position of Loans to Real Estate Developers, *21 Century Business Herald*), Apr. 21, 2010, *available via Sina News at* http://finance.sina.com.cn/china/jrxw/20100421/08087794374.shtml

[34] Administrative Measures on Land Stock, *supra* note 32, at art. 22.

serve as collateral are either the land-use rights or the future cash flow generated by the land-use-rights grant fee. Rules and documents indicate the former, but the collateral cannot be the land-use right itself, because the right does not carry any monetary value until it is formally granted to market players. LSAs use the loan proceeds to carry out the initial development and then grant the use rights to market players through a bidding process. In reality, the income local governments generate by granting long-term leases is used to repay the loans, even though LSAs have no legal entitlement to such cash flow and are simply acting as agents of the local governments. Even if we recognize that the lending banks are entitled to an interest in such cash flow, it remains unclear whether their rights have any seniority over other claims, such as compensation and settlement costs paid by the government for taking the land in the first place.

There is also uncertainty over the possible foreclosure of the collateral. Although Chinese law requires official registration for mortgaged interests in real property, no registration is available for LSMs. More important, the value of the "collateral" is a moving target, because the land-use right against which the collateral is created has not started generating any cash flow.

A price would be attached to the lease only upon the grant of a long-term lease over developed land. Yet by the time such a price is set it no longer necessarily reflects the value of the relevant rights at the time the loan was made, because the time lag between initial development of the land and the actual grant of a long-term lease can be as long as a few years. The result is a very high level of uncertainty about the value of the mortgage. It is impossible to imagine that sophisticated lawyers representing commercial banks failed to notice the risks associated with such vagueness and uncertainty. In fact, various ministries and the central bank have all issued rules to alert commercial banks of such risks.[35]

III. Informality in Regulation

Entering into contracts is one important way SOEs interact with other SOEs and the state. Regulation is another way. It is no surprise that informality is also a prominent feature of regulation in China. When the state regulates market players, a large percentage of whom are SOEs, regulation is carried out in a fashion that can be described as informal.

The main body of Chinese administrative law consists of three statutes: the Administrative License Law, the Administrative Sanction Law, and the Administrative

---

[35] *See, e.g.*, 国土资源部 财政部 中国人民银行 中国银行业监督管理委员会关于加强土 地储备与融资管理的通知 (国土资发〔2012〕162号) (Notice of the Ministry of Land and Resources, the Ministry of Finance, the People's Bank of China, and the China Banking Regulatory Commission, on Enhancing Administration of Land Stock and Financing) (promulgated on and effective as of Nov. 5, 2012).

Litigation Law.[36] So far, China has not issued an administrative procedure law. None of the three existing laws imposes procedural or formalistic requirements on regulators engaged in rule-making or adjudication. In this regard, China differs substantially from the United States, where the Administrative Procedure Act imposes detailed procedural rules with respect to four different situations: formal on-the-record adjudication, formal on-the-record rule-making, informal notice and comment rule-making, and informal adjudication.[37] Another major difference lies in the fact that regulators in the United States face scrutiny from the courts. It remains extremely difficult, if not impossible, to formally challenge regulatory decisions in China. Other factors also contribute to informality in regulation in China, but the lack of legal requirements allows such informality to persist.

Regulatory rules in China tend to be broad and general, leaving regulatory officials with a great deal of discretion, including the power to issue informal policies and guidelines with general or specific application. Such policies and guidelines are not necessarily transparent to the public. Individual decisions offer little information and provide little or no reasoning or analysis. Moreover, communications between regulators and market players are often carried out in informal settings in an off-the-record fashion. Such interactions provide little basis on which parties can predict future decisions. Most of the time, it is extremely difficult even to secure a meeting with regulators. A unique feature of such informality is that many applicants never have a chance to officially start the approval procedure, as regulators often delay or refuse to formally accept an application until after they have had a chance to informally review the case and draw a positive conclusion internally.

This informality has been present in the exercise of a range of regulatory tools. For example, the National Development and Reform Commission (NDRC) recently imposed injunctions and fines on eleven Japanese firms for alleged price-fixing activities. The length of the NDRC's written analysis and reasoning was about five hundred words. This was strikingly brief in relation to the size of the fines imposed, which ranged from about US$3.3 million to US$5 million.[38]

Informality is even more prominent in entry regulation. A decision on entry regulation usually does not carry a monetary value, but the impact can be even more substantial: grant and denial of market entry goes directly to the life and death of a corporation, and even a whole industry. Entry regulation is much more widespread in China than in

[36] 行政许可法 (Administrative License Law) (promulgated Aug. 27, 2003, effective July 1, 2004); 行政处罚法 (Administrative Sanction Law) (promulgated Mar, 17, 1996, effective Oct. 1, 1996); 行政诉讼法 (Administrative Litigation Law) (last amended Nov. 1, 2014, effective Jan. 1, 2015).

[37] 5 U.S. Code § 553—Rule Making, 554—Adjudications, 556—Hearings; presiding employees; powers and duties; burden of proof; evidence; record as basis of decision, and 557—Initial decisions; conclusiveness; review by agency; submissions by parties; contents of decisions; record.

[38] These decisions are available at the official website of the NDRC: http://www.ndrc.gov.cn/gzdt/201409/t20140918_626088.html (last visited Mar. 25, 2015).

most other countries, due largely to China's history as a planned economy. Entry regulation has been used as an effective way to grant and maintain SOE monopolies that is immune from normal antitrust review.

Examining the practice of the Hong Kong stock exchange (HKSE) in approving IPOs as a baseline illustrates informality in entry regulation in Mainland China. The shares of many companies are cross-listed in both Hong Kong and mainland China, providing a unique opportunity to observe how different regulators interact in different fashions with the same companies on similar issues. Moreover, different market intermediaries serve the same clients for IPOs in mainland China and Hong Kong. We thus are able to gain insights into how different regulatory styles affect the interaction of market intermediaries with their clients and with the regulators.

A. Informal IPO Approval Process in Mainland China

The official website of the China Securities Regulatory Commission (CSRC) provides almost no guidance on how to interpret or apply the statutory provisions and numerous vague rules issued by the CSRC, other than rules on standards and documentation for IPOs. Decisions either to grant or decline approval are extremely brief, sometimes with one line of text, and provide no reasoning or analysis.[39] Meanwhile, it is difficult to arrange formal meetings with CSRC officials. It is thus difficult for market players to seek views and guidance from the CSRC before formal applications are filed. Much necessary communication is carried out off the record on informal occasions. One typical forum for such communication has been conferences and training sessions organized by entities associated with the approval authority, such as the Securities Industry Association.

"Window Guidance"[40] best exemplifies the informality of China's regulatory regime in the context of IPO approvals. "Window guidance" literally refers to the practice of officials providing verbal answers by a window in an office building. Given that such verbal and highly general answers leave no record or reference to the actual situation of individual cases, one cannot rely upon these answers or hold the regulatory authority accountable for them. Handling inquiries in this manner is ill-suited to complicated issues involving unusual facts. "Window guidance" is often carried out by low-level officials, making it a poor channel for substantial and effective communication. In addition,

---

[39] See, for example, the most recent decision of the CSRC declining approval for an IPO, dated Sept. 14, 2014, which has only one line: csrc.gov.cn/pub/zjhpublic/G00306202/201409/t20140912_260302.htm. The CSRC included more analysis in a recent enforcement decision against sponsors for a domestic IPO (中国证监会处罚决定书 [2014]103 号(平安证券有限责任公司, 韩长风, 霍永涛) (CSRC Sanction Decision (2014) No. 103, against Ping An Securities Co., Ltd., Han Changfeng, Yongtao Huo).

[40] Window guidance (*chuangkou guanli*, 窗口管理).

answers provided in this way tend to be general and broad so as to be applicable to as many cases as possible.

One famous example of "window guidance" concerns value-adjustment mechanisms adopted in pre-IPO investments in applicants for IPOs. In more than one training and professional conference, regulatory officials conveyed the message that any value-adjustment mechanism in pre-IPO investments should be terminated or eliminated before a formal application for an IPO is filed with the regulator, regardless of whether recourse was against the potential issuer or the controlling shareholders of the issuer. This rule was never formally promulgated by the CSRC, but it is well known among investment bankers and lawyers. Officials never formally explained the reasons for this rule but verbally referred to the need to protect investors' interests by maintaining certainty in shareholding and the integrity of issuers' assets. This argument was apparently unfounded, but applicants and their advisors had no choice but to comply.[41]

B. COMPARISON WITH FORMAL IPO APPROVAL PROCEDURES OF THE HKSE

In a rule-based regime, entry regulation decisions follow certain principles: they must be made only according to rules known to all parties, and they must not be the result of arbitrary or unpredictable decisions by the government. To implement these principles in a discretionary approval process, regulators must give parties sufficient access to information and opportunities to communicate with regulators. Regulators should provide reasons for their decisions. These reasons and arguments can later be relied on or challenged by market players. In such a regime, certain institutional procedures are put in place to ensure that there is a legal basis for a decision and that the reasons made known to the public are the ones actually used by the regulator in reaching the decision. For example, in reviewing the legality and rationality of regulatory decisions, courts only admit and consider evidence and reasons that the regulator cited and made known at the time the decision was made. Post-decision rationales by regulators are not accepted. The IPO approval process in Hong Kong serves as an example of rule-based regulation.

In addition to issuing formal rules governing listing matters, the HKSE also issues interpretations and guidance from time to time[42] in response to issues that emerge during the approval process. Such formal guidance often runs to twenty pages, refers to

---

[41] For details of "window guidance" of the value-adjustment mechanism, see Ruijian Li 李睿鉴 & Ruoying Chen 陈若英, 对私募投资中"对赌协议"的法经济学思考——兼评我国首例司法判决 (Law and Economics Analysis of the Value Adjustment Mechanism in Private Equity Investment), 6 广东商学院学报 (Guangdong U. Fin. & Econ. J.) 86–87 (2012).

[42] See the "Interpretation and Guidance" under the "Rules and Guidance on Listing Matters," published and updated by the Hong Kong Stock Exchange on its official website: http://www.hkex.com.hk/eng/rulesreg/listrules/rulesandguidelines.htm (last visited Mar. 25, 2015).

specific cases on an anonymous basis, and provides details of the reasoning and analysis upon which the HKSE has made decisions. When preparing their applications, future applicants and their advisors therefore can compare their own cases with the scenarios set out in such guidance.

Once a formal application is filed, officers of the HKSE provide a formal response based upon review of the application materials. Such responses include a long list of questions, to be answered by applicants within a deadline. Through a process of discussion and revision, potential issuers and their advisors answer these questions in writing. HKSE officers then follow up with more questions in writing, together with conversations on the phone or in person. Conversations may go back and forth several times until either HKSE is fully satisfied with the draft prospectus and responses from the applicant and grants an approval of listing or it formally rejects the approval application. Such a process is highly technical and reason-based.

Applicants often make formal submissions to the HKSE requesting a waiver of certain rules, or clarification of treatment under the rules. Formal correspondence then follows, and concludes with a written response to the formal submission. Even before a formal application is filed, potential applicants may consult formally with the HKSE. With respect to extremely difficult yet critical questions that influence an applicant's decision whether to go through with an IPO application, the HKSE also accepts preliminary submissions and provides written responses. Even though these submissions and responses are confidential, advisors keep track of them and produce internal memos and interpretations of them. Most important, when applicants and their advisors refer to the reasoning, analysis, and conclusions included in responses provided by the HKSE on a confidential basis, the HKSE acknowledges them and takes them into account.

IV. Cost Saving in the Early Development Stage

In the existing literature, normative assessments of informality in contract and regulation are concerned primarily with whether informal norms, informal enforcement mechanisms, and informal methods of regulation are efficient. This chapter takes a different approach. Informality may have been efficient in reducing transaction and administrative costs in China, and may thus have facilitated the rapid growth of SOEs and the overall economy. But such informality may not be efficient going forward. Legal informality takes its toll on the human-capital development of individuals involved in the legal system in China, including executives of SOEs, legal professionals, and regulatory authorities. Reliance on informality means that professionals lose the opportunity to develop the social and human capital necessary to survive and to compete globally. If informality continues, these individuals are forced to divert their attention and energy toward efforts that sustain SOE monopolies. Such diversion would fail to provide opportunities for individuals to build human capital and to encourage economic growth.

Informality in contract and regulation, as described above, deviates from the standard institutional design proposed by economists as necessary for economic growth. Given the specific circumstances in China's early stage of economic development, informality nevertheless may have played a unique role in facilitating transactions that spurred economic growth. During this early stage of development, most of the parties entering into substantial contracts were SOEs. The risks and losses of the transactions they entered into were undertaken by the state. The parties therefore acted as if they were vertically integrated. Formal contracts were replaced by hierarchical order, rendering it unnecessary to have complicated risk- and loss-sharing provisions. Informality matched these circumstances perfectly, reducing transaction costs in contracts.

The cost-saving function of informality was different in regulation: in the early stages of China's economic development, the most crucial regulatory decisions were made by entities other than the regulator. Given the limited and marginal role played by regulators in such settings, informal communication was adequate and likely saved substantial costs for regulators and corresponding parties.

A. TRANSACTION-COST SAVINGS IN CONTRACTING

Specific and complicated contractual terms are costly to formulate. To comply with and enforce these *specific* terms can also be costly. If contracting parties are vertically integrated, such transaction costs can be reduced.[43] SOEs contracting with each other can be viewed as vertically integrated in the sense that the central or local government is their commonly shared controlling shareholder, and the ultimate risks and costs are undertaken by the state.

In the case of the NPL sales discussed in this chapter, the MOF was the only shareholder of the AMCs and today remains the controlling shareholder. Meanwhile, the controlling shareholder of ICBC was Central Huijin Investment Co., Ltd., a wholly owned subsidiary of the MOF. The other three state-owned commercial banks have similar shareholding structures.[44] Even though a subsidiary enjoys its own legal identity separate and independent from its shareholder, the ultimate controlling shareholder, the MOF, implicitly guaranteed the payment obligation of the AMCs toward the banks. The MOF, the AMCs, and the commercial banks acted as fully integrated entities.

---

[43] Oliver E. Williamson, The Economic Institutions of Capitalism 86 (1985).

[44] See summary provided on the official website of 中央汇金投资有限责任公司 (Central Huijin Investment Co., Ltd.), which is fully owned by the MOF; see information on the official website of Huijin: http://www.huijin-inv.cn/wps/portal/!ut/p/a1/jZDLDoIwFES_yHQspOCygvKQ6oIQsRvSGIEmUoghLvx6ob-C1eHeTnJOZXCJJSaRRT92oUfdG3T9ZsuoIhnWQI4Xge3AfO3FyUho53gRcJiCIeOx6GQDXpojC-bRx6GwEkzOb7OZt9_DiO_3wLsLA__QKW_qmAPkQgGiIHNbYrbeqelG3f3aqrIWcirQoHugC-4zgzYXrioceiKonxldZ50_gamCr5U/dl5/d5/L2dBISEvZ0FBIS9nQSEh/ (last visited Mar. 25, 2015).

LSM transactions are less straightforward examples. The borrowers are investment platforms wholly owned by local governments. The mortgage providers are the LSAs, internal departments of the same local government. In other words, borrowers are wholly owned subsidiaries of the same entity of which the mortgage provider is an internal department. They, too, can therefore be viewed as vertically integrated. The lenders, largely consisting of state-controlled commercial banks, do not share common shareholding or control with borrowers and mortgage providers. The lender's controlling shareholder is the central government. The provincial or municipal government controls the mortgage providers. The central government does not necessarily take responsibility for the risks and losses incurred by the activities of municipal and provincial governments. However, within China's fiscal system, local governments rely heavily upon the central government for funds.[45] Meanwhile, as previously discussed, the central government has more than once bailed out commercial banks when they were running losses. The ultimate losses of these lending arrangements, if any, are thus likely to fall upon the central government. All three entities involved are therefore vertically integrated, requiring no complicated contracts at all. Informal arrangement of mortgages facilitated the flow of funds from commercial banks to various projects carried out by local governments and their wholly owned enterprises.

B. AVOIDING ADMINISTRATIVE COSTS OF REGULATION

Entry regulation usually serves the purpose of assessing the qualifications of candidates to ensure that their activities or products will be safe.[46] Regulators seek to overcome the costs of information asymmetry between them and potential candidates by collecting and processing information. Denying licenses may result in legal challenge, review, and litigation, which require regulators to mount a defense and incur substantial administrative costs. Informality can therefore yield cost savings.

In the early stages of China's economic development, information costs were not directly relevant to regulatory efforts because selection was done by entities other than the regulator. The regulator's task was to endorse decisions, thereby boosting the legitimacy of the decision. It did not matter much whether regulators were able to overcome information asymmetry. Similarly, it made little sense for regulators to spend time drafting arguments for granting or denying approvals.

---

[45] For example, during the fiscal year of 2013, the total amount of local government revenue was about RMB11,715 billion, of which RMB4,804 billion was transferred from the central government to local governments. See the annual budget implementation report for fiscal year 2013 published by the MOF on its official website: http://www.mof.gov.cn/zhuantihuigu/2014ysbg/ysbg2014/201403/t20140315_1055691.html (last visited Mar. 25, 2015).

[46] Stephen Breyer et al., Administrative Law and Regulatory Policy: Problems, Text, and Cases 14 (5th ed. 2002).

In the case of the IPO approval process, the objective of the system in the early years of China's domestic stock market was to provide quick and substantial financing to certain SOEs. These companies were selected and recommended by local governments and central ministries through a quota system.[47] Selections were not designed with investors in mind. Instead, SOEs were selected for listing based on the interests of local governments and central ministries, including factors such as maintaining employment. In other words, the securities regulator did not have final say in granting entry to the stock market. Instead, the regulator's task was to endorse the selection of other Party-state authorities and to ensure technical compliance with listing rules. Speed was of the essence: the quicker the endorsement was done, the sooner the SOEs could receive fund from the public investors. With respect to the technicalities of compliance, informal modes of communication were apparently a more cost-effective method than formal written explanations. Because it lacked the final decisional power, the securities regulator was not the proper authority to provide reasons for a positive or negative decision. As no written records were made during the decision-making process and the regulators never formally received applications from candidates that did not successfully obtain listing, regulators did not need to spend time resolving disputes with those candidates. As a result, administrative costs were avoided.

V. Informality and Incentives to Acquire Risk Assessment and Management Skills

The fact that informality may have facilitated economic growth in the past does not guarantee it will do so in the future. Much has changed over the course of economic development, and the benefits of informality are vanishing. One fundamental change has been the increasing number of private and foreign entities in the market. Their presence has increased the chances that SOEs will enter into contracts with non-SOEs and that regulators will interact with non-SOEs. As a consequence, parties to a contract or to a regulatory decision can no longer be viewed as vertically integrated. On the contrary, they are separate entities, with potentially conflicting interests that are too complicated and costly for the government to coordinate. As the number of entities participating in the market increases, the risks associated with the transactions they enter into also increase and become more complex. Similar to developed countries, Chinese society has become full of risks, and contracts and regulation have become tools to assess and manage such risks.[48] To survive and to develop in such a society, all relevant parties need to

---

[47] Zhiwu Chen, *Capital Freedom in China as Viewed from the Evolution of the Stock Market*, 33 CATO J. 587 (2013).

[48] Kui Shen, *Preface to the Chinese Translation* of RISK REGULATION: THEORY AND PRACTICE IN GERMANY 6 (Gang Liu trans., 2012) (沈岿为《风险规制:德国的理论与实践》所作"总序",第6页,刘刚编译).

acquire sophisticated skills in understanding these risks and in coming up with solutions to manage them.

Yet, informality in contract and regulation has diverted the attention and resources of the relevant parties away from such learning. Instead, attention and resources have been spent obtaining and maintaining privileges from the government. Vagueness and simplicity reduce cost only when the associated uncertainty does not carry the potential to generate substantial losses. SOEs have secured monopoly positions from the government in the product market and the factors market.[49] It is thus no surprise that SOE executives have incentives to spend time and resources on maintaining sound relationships with the government. These incentives are enhanced by the prospect that senior executives of SOEs will become senior officials in government.[50] Indeed, many independent directors of Chinese SOEs have strong ties with the government.[51]

This diversion has prevented individuals from developing the skills required to take on new challenges. In particular, continual reliance on informality has failed to provide sufficient incentives to parties to contracts and regulators to learn about and manage risks. This has hindered the human capital development of individuals involved in contract and regulation. Most repeat players are professional advisors and regulators. They are thus the most affected by the way that contracts are entered into and regulation is carried out. They also serve as the nexus of new information and experiments, making critical contributions to the overall quality of the decision-making of entities in the market. In the next section, this chapter therefore focuses on professional advisors and their clients.

A. PROFESSIONAL ADVISORS AND THEIR CLIENTS

Professional advisors include financial, accounting, and legal advisors. They are repeat players in the market for contracts and regulation, carrying out and digesting the practices of contracting parties and regulators. For example, lawyers provide value-added services to clients as transaction and production-cost engineers,[52] a function they fulfill by exercising their professional skills. When informality dominates contracts and regulation, it becomes unnecessary for professional advisors to engage in complicated and

---

[49] Angela Zhang, *The Enforcement of the Anti-Monopoly Law in China: An Institutional Design Perspective*, 56 ANTITRUST BULL. 631 (2011).

[50] For example, Liucheng Wei, the ex-CEO of CNOOC, was promoted to governor of Hainan Province, while Shuqing Guo, the ex-chairman and president of China Construction Bank, was promoted to head of the China Securities Regulatory Commission.

[51] Li-wen Lin, *State Ownership and Corporate Governance in China: An Executive Career Approach*, 2013(3) COLUM. BUS. L. REV. 743–800.

[52] Ronald J. Gilson, *Value Creation by Business Lawyers: Legal Skills and Asset Pricing*, 94 YALE L.J. 239 (1984). *See also* Manuel A. Utset, *Producing Information: Initial Public Offerings, Production Costs, and the Producing Lawyer*, 73 OR.L. REV. 275 (1995).

sophisticated analysis and reasoning. As a consequence, the quality of their analysis and reasoning may have little bearing on the result of a contract negotiation or a regulatory decision. The value of their service is therefore limited.

The ratio of one-time legal fees to overall IPO costs differs dramatically for IPOs in the U.S. market compared to similarly sized IPOs in China's domestic market. For IPOs with total proceeds below US$50 million, the ratios were 24 percent and 4.78 percent respectively; for those between US$50 million and US$100 million, the ratios were 22 percent and 3.44 percent respectively; and for those between US$100 million and US$250 million, the ratios were 18 percent and 2.58 percent respectively.[53] The comparison is rough, but it is sufficient to demonstrate the difference in perception of the value of legal services in the United States and in China.

Monetary compensation is not the only consideration in individuals' career choices, of course. Prestige, chances at influencing political and public affairs, and the power to allocate resources can be supplementary and even more important factors. In a regime dominated by informality, however, these alternative factors are also under threat: more value will be attributed to personal connections and private information channels, reducing the overall prestige and reputation of the industry.

In contrast, when professionals engage in more substantive work, their services will have higher added value. They can charge higher prices for their services and pay higher salaries to their employees. More attractive compensation packages can in turn attract and keep more talent in the industry. Similarly, an industry with higher pay and with a larger portion of pay linked to performance will attract personnel with more talent and commitment. The accumulated human capital in risk assessment, risk management, and sophisticated analysis and reasoning would, in the long run, become a natural entry barrier, further pushing up the value of services and the pay level in the industry. A virtuous circle emerges. In a rule-based regulatory world, advisory services become a more competitive industry in which it is harder for people to become successful purely by relying on their personal connections with regulators.

The difference between the two different regulatory models is not only the level of competition among services providers, but also the scope of activity in which they compete against each other. Under the off-the-record model, advisors compete on the basis

[53] For IPOs larger than US$250 million, the difference is not as great but remains substantial. These ratios are for IPOs dated between Jan. 1, 2009 and June 30, 2012. For the U.S. ratios, see PWC, CONSIDERING AN IPO? THE COSTS OF GOING AND BEING PUBLIC MAY SURPRISE YOU, figure 7 (Sept. 12, 2012), *available at* http://www.pwc.com/en_us/us/transaction-services/publications/assets/pwc-cost-of-ipo.pdf. I am not aware of a corresponding ratio for domestic IPOs in China. Conclusions in this chapter were made according to my own calculations, performed by Lei Chen (陈磊), a graduate student at Peking University Law School, based upon information disclosed in the IPO prospectuses of all domestic IPOs during the same 2009–2012 period. These IPO prospectuses are available at the official websites of Shanghai Stock Exchange and Shenzhen Stock Exchange: http://www.sse.com.cn/disclosure/listedinfo/announcement/, and http://disclosure.szse.cn/m/drgg.htm (last visited Mar. 25, 2015).

of networks. One recent example was the arrest of a senior manager of a leading global investment bank for implementing a policy of recruiting the children of senior Chinese officials.[54] Under rule-based regulation, on the other hand, competition is based on talent and experience. While the former system favors the well connected, the latter favors the hard working and skilled.

Quality records also facilitate competition among different types of professional advisors, in particular legal and accounting professionals. In China's domestic stock market, lawyers have long been regarded as not very useful. Lawyers also must undertake extensive liability. Prices have declined in an excessively competitive market.[55] As noted above, lawyers' share of the overall costs of IPOs is much smaller in China than in the United States. Contributing to this situation may be the fact that Chinese lawyers lack evidence of their value to clients. If lawyers could demonstrate the importance of their technical skills, experience, and ability—for example by designing creative legal structures—they might be accorded more respect and higher pay by issuers and investment bankers.

Similarly, more extensive documentation of the role of advisors would allow clients to observe and judge the services they receive, and therefore to distinguish more capable from less capable advisors. This would in turn make clients more confident in seeking advice from advisors and more willing to pay a higher price for their services. Such benefits are closely associated with another function of rule-based regulation: they could help reduce agency problems that clients often worry about. Quality records are powerful evidence that could protect responsible agents who are cautious but willing to take risks. Such records would also quickly expose bad or weak agents. The availability of records also makes it possible for firms to hire independent advisors to conduct internal investigations, which has proved a very effective check for multinational companies over executives, especially those working far from headquarters.

Finally, quality records can protect entities subject to regulation against unfair acts by regulators, consumers, and business partners. An off-the-record model, in contrast, makes it difficult for entities to protect themselves. High quality records are a prerequisite to effective judicial review of administrative actions. Without such evidence it is nearly impossible for companies subject to regulation to defend themselves or to seek remedies against regulators.

---

[54] Tracy Alloway & Jamil Anderlini, *JPMorgan's China Hiring under Scrutiny*, FIN. TIMES (Aug. 19, 2013), http://www.ft.com/intl/cms/s/0/799f837e-0816-11e3-badc-00144feabdc0.html.

[55] Bing Peng (彭冰), 证券律师, 何去何从 (Securities Lawyer: Where to Go), 9 金融法苑 (FIN. L.F.) 16 (2005).

B. REGULATORY OFFICIALS

As discussed above, the benefits of cost saving brought about by informality evaporate over time. Continued reliance on informality carries risks to regulators from public exposure and from lack of skill development. Reliance on informality shelters officials from competition with and challenge by enterprises and professional advisors.

Reliance on informality also means that within the regulatory bodies, more qualified and competent officials find it difficult to distinguish themselves from lower quality officials. The opaqueness created by informality increases the opportunities for rent-seeking activities, diverting regulatory officials' attention and energy away from the acquisition of information and analytical skills. A recent example is the arrest of nineteen senior officials in charge of approving energy production facilities, and senior managers of energy companies being regulated on corruption charges.[56] An opaque regulatory process encourages both individuals and enterprises to pursue rent-seeking opportunities, diverting resources away from wealth-generating production.[57] This opaqueness also makes it harder for outsiders to distinguish decisions motivated by regulators' self-interest from those that are innovative or merit based, hence reducing officials' incentives to experiment with new regulatory methods.

With the abolishment of the quota system for selecting IPO candidates, the regulatory authority (the CSRC) has undertaken the responsibility for selecting companies for public listing on the merits. Evidence suggests that such regulation has been ineffective. Investors voted with their feet, leaving the market and driving prices down,[58]and the most recent sharp rise in China's stock market has been widely regarded as a strong welcoming message to CSRC's recent deregulation of IPOs. In addition, the largest IPOs conducted by companies with all or most of their assets and operations in China, such as Tencent (QQ), Jing Dong, and Alibaba, have been overseas. There are multiple reasons that companies prefer overseas markets over the domestic regime with CSRC approving IPOs, but evidence indicates that these companies may have been deterred from a domestic listing by the inappropriate standards of risk assessment and risk management in the regulatory system in China.[59]

---

[56] *See* Fengtao Li (李凤桃), "能源系统腐败路径· 负责给项目发准生证 安置亲友分杯羹" (Path of Corruption in the Energy Sector: Regulators in Charge of Issuing Birth Certificates to Energy Project Put Relatives in Critical Position to Share the Profits), 《中国经济周刊》(CHINA ECON. WKLY.), July 22, 2014, http://finance.people.com.cn/n/2014/0722/c1004-25312350.html.

[57] Kevin Murphy et al., *Why Is Rent-Seeking So Costly to Growth?*, 83 AM. ECON. REV. 409 (1993).

[58] Robert Cookson, *Domestic Investors Lose Faith in Chinese Stocks*, FIN. TIMES (July 3, 2012), http://www.ft.com/intl/cms/s/0/188247c2-c418-11e1-850c-00144feabdc0.html.

[59] Yingmao Tang (唐应茂), 私人企业为何去海外上市：中国法律对红筹模式海外上市的监督 (Why Private Enterprises Went Overseas for IPOs: Chinese Legal Regulation of Red-Chip Overseas IPOs), 28 政法论坛 (TRIB. POL. SCI. & L.) 161 (2010).

A regulatory system dominated by informality has sheltered regulatory officials from competitive pressure to develop analytical and reasoning skills. In an informal system, the two sides of regulation are in a hierarchical relationship. Enterprises and their professional advisors supply information and make arguments, and the regulator listens and decides. Even if regulatory officials lack understanding about what is proposed by enterprises and their professional advisors, they can hide inside the black box of the decision-making process. In contrast, under a rule-based regulatory system, shortages of information and analytical skills are immediately exposed. According to the principle of publicity and transparency in administrative law, regulators must be prepared to defend their decisions in public unless national security concerns are implicated. Regulatory officials thus must formulate or develop persuasive arguments and sound reasoning.

Senior management of SOEs in China is closely controlled by the Chinese Communist Party's sophisticated and opaque personnel management system.[60] Chinese SOEs are also subject to a second layer of personnel management by their direct regulator.[61] The State-Owned Assets Supervision and Administration Commission enjoys statutory authority to appoint or nominate members of the board of wholly state-owned enterprises other than financial instiutitons, and members of the supervisory board of state-controlled enterprises.[62] It is no surprise that the criteria and procedures for selecting senior management of SOEs is dramatically different from that of non-SOEs. Empirical study of the senior management of SOEs has identified that market-oriented competition is present, but political attributes of senior management are also prominent.[63]

There is no doubt that detailed records could serve as evidence to hold individual officials liable for specific acts of malfeasance. However, such records can also serve as valuable evidence of individual officials' performance relative to that of other officials within the regulatory authority. This would make it possible for promotion decisions more accurately to reflect the performance of individual officials. The increased ability to accurately observe officials' individual performance would create internal accountability and competition. This would in turn provide stronger incentives for individual officials to acquire stronger skills. Professor Zhu Suli pointed out that the requirement of issuing published judicial opinions provides individual judges with incentives to

[60] For a general introduction to this subject, see Hon S. Chan, *Cadre Personnel Management in China: The* Nomenklatura *System, 1990–1998*, 179 China Q. 703 (2004).

[61] *See, e.g.*, 中央企业负责人经营业绩考核暂行办法 (2009) (Tentative Provisions on Management Performance Assessment of Senior Executives of Central Government-Owned State-owned Enterprises), issued by the 国有资产管理委员会 (State-owned Assets Supervision and Administration Commission of the State Council), effective as of January 1, 2010, *available at* the official website of SASAC: http://xxgk.sasac.gov.cn/gdnps/content.jsp?id=1317392.

[62] 中华人民共和国企业国有资产管理法 (Administration Act of State-Owned Assets of Enterprises of the People's Republic of China (effective May 1, 2009), art. 22.

[63] Lin, *supra* note 51, and Chapter 7 of this volume.

improve the quality of their decisions and reasoning.[64] The transparency imposed by public record-keeping would provide similar incentives to regulators.

Over time, the ineffective regulatory decisions and corruption generated by informality will threaten the legitimacy of the regulatory regime, reducing public trust and confidence in regulatory officials. The loss of public confidence will make it even more difficult to distinguish decisions motivated by the self-interest of officials from those that are law-and-reason-based. Recent antitrust sanctions imposed by the NDRC provide an example. It is settled economic theory that increasing the severity of punishment will increase deterrence,[65] and in this light the substantial fines imposed by the NDRC can be viewed as a legitimate tool to deter anti-competitive behavior. However, given that the decisions themselves are extremely brief and contain little reasoning, it is not surprising that many people suspect these decisions were in fact driven by illegitimate motives, including unjustified prejudice against foreign companies.[66]

Conclusion

Informality in the legal system and in particular in regulation is not, of course, unique to China. Japanese economic and financial regulation was similarly informal over an extended period.[67] Scholars argue, however, that Japanese voters never approved of heavy-handed state intervention, and therefore never elected politicians willing to give bureaucrats the means to intervene in business.[68] Ultimately, it was the private sector that challenged the regulatory authorities in the wake of regulatory scandals[69] and forced reforms that led to a rule-based and reason-based regulatory system. Courts provided strong support to private parties throughout, and the reform process culminated in the passage of the Japanese Administrative Procedure Law (APL).[70] The Japanese APL emphasizes the use of written requests and responses in order to increase clarity and accountability. The APL requires prior notice and the opportunity to respond so as to improve transparency, fairness, and predictability.[71] It is worth noting that the passing and enforcement of such a law was made possible by the general decline in the power

[64] Su Li (苏力), 判决书的背后 (Behind the Judicial Opinions), 3 法学研究 (Chinese J. L.) 3 (2001).

[65] Gary Becker & George Stigler, *Law Enforcement, Malfeasance, and Compensation of Enforcers*, 3 J. Legal. Stud. 1 (1974).

[66] *See, e.g.*, Tom Michelle, *China Antitrust Ruling Blunts Foreign Criticism*, Fin. Times (Aug. 21, 2014): http://www.ft.com/cms/s/0/61d3f8aa-28ff-11e4-9d5d-00144feabdc0.html#slide0.

[67] Milhaupt, *supra* note 18.

[68] Yoshiro Miwa & J. Mark Ramseyer, *Capitalist Politicians, Socialist Bureaucrats? Legends of Government Planning from Japan*, 48 Antitrust Bull. 595, 596 (2003).

[69] One of the famous scandals was the illegal compensation of clients by Japan's four largest securities houses in the 1990s. For a description of the scandal, see Duck, *supra* note 18.

[70] *Id.* at 1752.

[71] *Id.* at 1753–56.

of Japan's economic bureaucracy,[72] and the cooperation of national agencies such as the Ministry of Finance.[73]

The path of reform in Japan, however, may not set a promising precedent for China. Apart from the long-standing issues of independence from government intervention and intimidation by large SOEs, the Chinese judicial system lags far behind regulators in terms of its ability to obtain up-to-date information and knowledge stock.[74] This casts serious doubt on whether Chinese courts will be able to support challenges to regulatory authorities even if allowed to do so.[75] Moreover, the power of China's economic bureaucracy is not declining, but instead is growing quickly, consistent with the global trend of the rise of the regulatory state.[76] The unique history of a planned economy in China also means that China's economic bureaucracy is likely to be more powerful than economic regulators in other countries. The recent controversy over antitrust investigations of certain foreign companies[77] and the substantial fines imposed by the NRDC[78] provide an example of the power of economic regulators. It is difficult to imagine that regulatory authorities will enthusiastically welcome and facilitate legal reforms designed to make regulation more formal and transparent. The problems in China are exacerbated by the economic dominance of SOEs, which was not a factor in Japan. These SOEs and their managers enjoy a cozy and convenient connection with regulators and officials. Those benefiting from the old regime are likely to resist any reforms that seek to displace the informal system. Only when these individuals come to realize that they are not just beneficiaries of informality but also suffering losses from informality will they start to acquire the skills necessary to cope with a world full of complexity and uncertainty. In this sense, legal informality is much worse than an inefficient institution. Reducing legal informality is central to legal, economic, and governance reform efforts in China.

---

[72] *Id.* at 1757–58.

[73] *Id.* at 1753.

[74] Meng Hou (侯猛), 最高法院研究—以司法的影响力切入 (Supreme Court Study—From the Perspective of Impact of Judicial Opinions) 27–28 (2007).

[75] Ruoying Chen (陈若英), 超脱与应对—法院与规制部门之间的竞争 (Surpassing and Responding: Institutional Competition between Courts and Regulatory Authorities), 1 北大法律评论 (PKU L. Rev.) 51 (2013).

[76] Edward Glaeser & Andrei Shleifer, *The Rise of the Regulatory State*, 41 J. Econ. Literature 401 (2003).

[77] *See, e.g.*, Michael Martina & Matthew Miller, *"Mr. Confession" and His Boss Drive China's Antitrust Crusade*, Reuters (Sept. 15, 2014), http://www.reuters.com/article/2014/09/15/china-antitrust-ndrc-idUSL3N0RB15V20140915; *China Regulator Says Microsoft Should Not Obstruct Anti-trust Probe*, Reuters (Aug. 4, 2014), http://www.reuters.com/article/2014/08/04/us-microsoft-china-idUSKBN0G40HT20140804.

[78] *See supra* note 38.

9 Reforming China's State-Owned Enterprises

INSTITUTIONS, NOT OWNERSHIP

Curtis J. Milhaupt* and Wentong Zheng

Introduction

The Third Plenum of the Eighteenth Congress of the Chinese Communist Party ("Third Plenum"), convened in November 2013, laid out ambitious goals for reforms in a wide array of areas. Those goals include, among others, a more streamlined market economy, a more transparent and efficient government, an improved social welfare system, and a society based on rule of law.[1]

Reforming China's state-owned enterprises (SOEs) is the centerpiece of the Third Plenum's economic agenda. A top priority of China's SOE reforms, as set forth by the Third Plenum, is to promote mixed-ownership firms, or firms in which the state and private shareholders hold joint equity stakes. Subsequent to the Third Plenum, in July 2014 the State-owned Assets Supervision and Administration Commission (SASAC),

---

* We thank participants at a workshop at East China University of Political Science and Law for stimulating comments on an earlier draft. Portions of this chapter are drawn from our article, *Beyond Ownership: State Capitalism and the Chinese Firm*, 103 Geo. L.J. 665 (2015).

[1] *See Decision of the Central Committee of the Communist Party of China on Some Major Issues concerning Comprehensively Deepening the Reform*, China.org.cn (Jan. 16, 2014), http://www.china.org.cn/china/third_plenary_session/2014-01/16/content_31212602.htm.

the agency responsible for supervising the national SOEs, selected six central SOEs for a pilot mixed-ownership reform program.[2] The National Development and Reform Commission (NDRC), China's central planning agency, is reportedly developing a plan to "more or less complete" mixed-ownership reforms for all SOEs by the year 2020.[3]

Ownership-based reforms potentially have a far-reaching impact. The identity of a corporation's equity owners has enormous significance for the oversight and incentives of management, the governance challenges the corporation faces, and ultimately, the goals it pursues. The stakes are particularly high for ownership-based reforms of Chinese SOEs, considering that SOEs are widely regarded as the "primary vehicles for Chinese state capitalism."[4] We argue in this chapter, however, that ownership-based reforms of Chinese SOEs, in and of themselves, will not significantly alter a central parameter of Chinese state capitalism that heavily influences the performance, objectives, and growth patterns of firms: the relationship between firms and the state. Our central claim is that state capitalism as practiced in China today is largely synonymous with state capture, at least as that term should be understood in the Chinese context. Large firms in China—whether SOEs, privately owned enterprises (POEs), or ambiguous mixtures of state and private ownership—survive and prosper precisely *because* they have fostered connections to state power and have succeeded in obtaining state-generated rents.

We further argue that because of China's institutional environment, SOEs and large POEs share substantial similarities in areas commonly thought to distinguish state-owned firms from privately owned firms: market access, receipt of state subsidies, proximity to state power, and execution of the government's policy objectives. Merely changing the ownership structure of SOEs as contemplated by the current reform strategy, therefore, will not bring about significant changes in how Chinese firms are positioned in relation to the state.

In light of the capture dynamics in the Chinese economy, our analysis suggests that the real promise for meaningful reform of China's SOEs lies not with ownership

---

[2] *See China Names 6 SOEs for Pilot Reforms*, XINHUA NEWS NETWORK (July 15, 2014), http://news.xinhuanet.com/english/china/2014-07/15/c_133485883.htm. The six central SOEs were the State Development & Investment Corporation (SDIC), China National Cereals, Oils and Foodstuffs Corporation (COFCO), China National Building Materials Group (CNBM), China Energy Conservation and Environmental Protection Group (CECEP), Xinxing Cathay International Group (XXCIG), and China National Pharmaceutical Group (Sinopharm).

[3] *See* 发改委牵头混合所有制试点 发力国企股权多元化 (NDRC Leading Efforts on Mixed-Ownership Pilot Reforms; Aiming to Diversify Ownership of SOEs), 搜狐新闻 (SOHU NEWS) (Aug. 28, 2014), http://news.sohu.com/20140828/n403838954.shtml.

[4] USHA C.V. HALEY & GEORGE T. HALEY, SUBSIDIES TO CHINESE INDUSTRY: STATE CAPITALISM, BUSINESS STRATEGY, AND TRADE POLICY 24 (2013); *see also* Li-Wen Lin & Curtis J. Milhaupt, *We Are the (National) Champions: Understanding the Mechanisms of State Capitalism in China*, 65 STAN. L. REV. 697 (2013) (providing analysis of Chinese SOEs as a "networked hierarchy" with deep connections to the Party-state).

reforms, but with policies directed toward the establishment of market-neutral institutions. We argue that political reforms that introduce accountability to the functioning of the state itself are indispensable to the accomplishment of these institutional reforms.

This chapter proceeds in four sections. Section I briefly discusses the history of mixed-ownership firms in China. Section II explains the dynamics of capture in the Chinese economy, in which firms of all ownership types face a choice: grow and prosper by nestling up to the state and demonstrating the capacity to deliver on key Party-state objectives, or seek autonomy from the state and be marginalized. Section III argues that in China's institutional environment, corporate ownership holds relatively little explanatory power in accounting for firm-state dynamics in China. Section IV lays out the policy implications of our analysis for China's SOE reforms and makes the case for institutional, not ownership-based, reforms.

I. Mixed Ownership in China

Although mixed-ownership firms were thrust to the forefront of China's SOE reforms after the Third Plenum, they are not new. To provide the proper context for our discussion below, we begin this chapter with a brief overview of mixed-ownership firms in China.

In all economies, the boundary between public and private ownership of an enterprise is more porous than conventional analysis assumes, because the state retains control rights over firms even in the absence of ownership interests. These state control rights are typically obtained through taxation, regulation, and subsidization. The causes of and response to the 2008–2009 financial crisis in the United States illustrate that even in countries where private ownership of enterprises has strong ideological and historical roots, the boundary between government control and private control can be blurry and susceptible to change.

The boundary between public and private enterprises is even more blurred in China, a country with a long tradition of state dominance in the economy, underdeveloped legal institutions, and relatively inchoate conceptions of property rights. In practice, the ownership types of many firms in China are ambiguous. For example, one of the main drivers of China's economic miracle during the 1980s and the early 1990s was the emergence of the so-called nonstate firms, whose share of national industrial output increased from 22 percent in 1978 to 42 percent in 1993.[5] Many of the nonstate firms were "collectively" owned—that is, ostensibly owned by "all residents" in a community, yet none of the residents possessed the exclusive rights of ownership associated with traditional property rights theories. One scholar has theorized that these collectively owned firms represent

[5] Jiahua Che & Yingyi Qian, *Insecure Property Rights and Government Ownership of Firms*, 113 Q. J. ECON. 467, 467 (1998).

an arrangement in which private entrepreneurs choose to have local governments as the owner of the otherwise private firms as a response to a market environment in which business transactions are easily blocked by government regulations.[6] Another scholar has argued that these collectively owned firms were in fact privately owned and operated and were registered as collectively owned only because at the time, there was no legal framework for the registration of private firms.[7]

With the adoption of the Company Law in 1994, private entrepreneurs gained the ability to register their firms as POEs, but the state also increasingly participated in the ownership of corporate shares. It did so not only through wholly state-owned entities, but also through mixed-ownership entities where the ownership and management of the firms are shared among state and private shareholders. In 1997, China announced a massive program to privatize all but the largest SOEs under the slogan of "grasping the large, letting go of the small" (*zhuada fangxiao*). In practice, however, the newly privatized SOEs did not become private firms as that term is commonly understood; instead, they became firms with mixed ownership. It was estimated that as of 2003, mixed-ownership firms accounted for 40 percent of China's GDP.[8] Some of the best-known Chinese firms, such as Haier, TCL, and Lenovo, are mixed-ownership firms. In particular, publicly listed firms in China are typically of the mixed-ownership type. Mixed ownership has also become an important ownership form among China's central SOE groups at the subsidiary level. For example, almost all of the thirty-four subsidiaries of China National Offshore Oil Corporation (CNOOC) are mixed-ownership firms with an average state-share percentage ranging from 40 to 65 percent.[9]

When the percentage of state shares in a mixed-ownership firm is relatively large, the firm could, at least in theory, still be classified as an SOE. But the classification becomes more difficult as the percentage of state shares decreases. In some cases, the ownership structure of a mixed-ownership firm becomes so fragmented that none of its state or nonstate shareholders hold a controlling interest in the firm. An example is Ping An Insurance (Group) Co. of China Ltd. Table 9.1 shows the top ten shareholders of Ping An by type, and their respective ownership percentages:[10]

---

[6] David Li, *A Theory of Ambiguous Property Rights in Transition Economies: The Case of the Chinese Non-state Sector*, 23 J. COMP. ECON. 1, 8–15 (1996).

[7] *See* Yasheng Huang, *How Did China Take Off?*, 26 J. ECON. PERSP. 147, 154 (2012).

[8] *See* 混合所有制经济已占 40% 5–10 年后将达到 80% (Mixed-Ownership Sector Accounts for 40 Percent of Economy; To Hit 80 Percent in 5–10 Years), 新华网 (XINHUA NEWS NETWORK) (Nov. 25, 2003), http://www.southcn.com/news/china/zgkx/200311250786.htm.

[9] *See* 王润秋: 七成央企改制 大力发展混合所有制经济 (Wang Runqiu: Seventy-Percent of Central SOEs Undergoing Structural Reforms; Promoting the Development of Mixed-Ownership Economy), 人民网 (PEOPLE'S DAILY ONLINE) (Nov. 26, 2012), http://dangjian.people.com.cn/n/2012/1126/c117092-19693335.html.

[10] *See* CHINA PING AN, 2012 ANNUAL REPORT 83 (2012), *available at* http://www.irasia.com/listco/hk/pingan/annual/ar106101-e_101.pdf. We reformatted the data in the Ping An 2012 Annual Report by grouping shareholders by ownership type.

TABLE 9.1.
TOP TEN SHAREHOLDERS OF PING AN INSURANCE (GROUP) CO. OF CHINA LTD.

Type	Shareholder	
State	Shenzhen Investment Holdings Co., Ltd	6.08%
	Shum Yip Group Ltd	2.27%
Domestic Non-state	Yuan Trust Investment Co., Ltd.	4.08%
	Linzhi New Horse Inv. Development Co. Ltd	4.03%
	Linzhi Jingao Ind. Development Co. Ltd.	3.46%
	Shenzhen Wuxi Yufu Ind. Co. Ltd.	2.27%
	Gongbujiangda Jiangnan Ind. Development Co., Ltd.	1.76%
Foreign	HSBC Ltd.	7.76%
	HSBC Insurance Holdings Ltd.	4.58%
	All Gain Trading Ltd.	1.04%

Ping An's 2012 annual report notes that the "shareholding structure of the Company is relatively scattered. There is no controlling shareholder, de facto controller."[11] Because of its fragmented ownership structure, it is difficult to classify Ping An as an SOE or POE based on equity ownership alone. The inconsistent classification of Ping An by outside observers illustrates the problem. In 2012, Ping An was treated as a POE when it was included in the Fortune Global 500 ranking of the world's largest firms. Yet in the same year, Ping An did not appear on an influential ranking of China's top 500 private companies, suggesting that it was not considered a POE by the domestic organization that conducted the ranking.

For some other mixed-ownership firms, classifying their ownership type is difficult because of the way they are managed. A prominent example is ZTE Corporation (ZTE), China's second-largest telecommunication equipment manufacturer, and the subject of a U.S. House Committee investigation in 2012. ZTE's shares are listed on both the Shenzhen and Hong Kong Stock Exchanges. ZTE's largest shareholder is ZTE Holdings, which, with 30.76 percent of ZTE's shares (see Figure 9.1), might be considered ZTE's controlling shareholder.[12] The shares of ZTE Holdings, in turn, are held by

[11] *Id.* at 84.

[12] ZTE Corporation, 2012 Annual Report 98 (2012), *available at* http://wwwen.zte.com.cn/en/about/investor_relations/corporate_report/annual_report/201304/P020130414667427851218.pdf. Under both PRC and Hong Kong law, 30 percent is the point at which a shareholder is considered to have acquired a large enough stake in a publicly listed company to trigger a mandatory bid rule, a common mechanism for protecting minority shareholders against an unfair acquisition by the controlling shareholder. Under the mandatory bid rule, a shareholder intending to surpass 30-percent share ownership is required to make an offer to purchase the shares of all other shareholders. *See* 中国证券监督管理委员会上市公司收购管理办法 (China Securities Regulatory Commission Rules on Mergers & Acquisitions Involving Publicly Listed Companies) (promulgated by the Chairman of the China Securities Regulatory Commission, May 17,

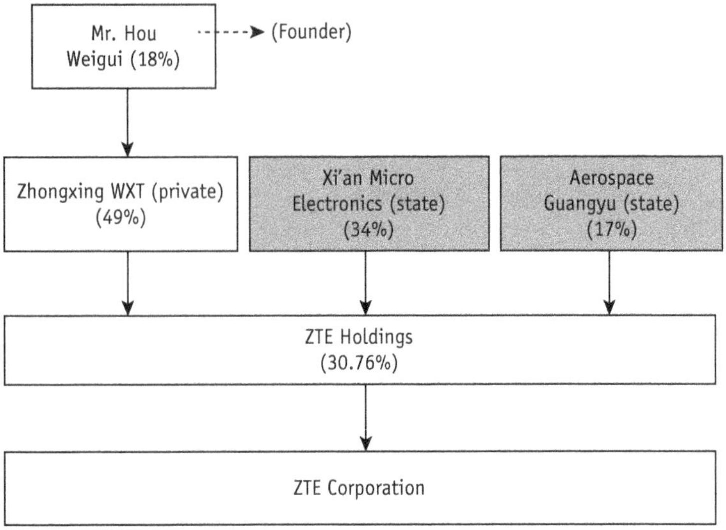

FIGURE 9.1. Ownership Structure of ZTE Corporation.

Xi'an Microelectronics (34 percent), Aerospace Guangyu (17 percent), and Zhongxing WXT (49 percent). Xi'an Micro Electronics and Aerospace Guangyu are both SOEs. State-owned entities, therefore, control 51 percent of ZTE Holdings. Perhaps for this reason, ZTE's 2012 annual report lists the ownership type of ZTE Holdings as "state-owned."[13] According to the website of ZTE Holdings, it is one of the "national key SOEs" designated by the State Council.[14] The third shareholder of ZTE Holdings, Zhongxing WXT (also known as Zhongxing Weixiantong), is a private firm owned by a group of individuals, of whom the founder, Hou Weigui, holds the largest percentage (18 percent). According to the website of ZTE Holdings, it was the first firm in China to adopt a "state owned, privately managed" model, in 1993. Under this so-called "ZTE model," the majority state shareholders contractually authorize the minority private shareholders to assume sole responsibility for managing the firm, subject only to the requirement that the state shareholders be guaranteed a minimum rate of return. Under the ZTE model, therefore, a firm is an SOE from the standpoint of ownership, but a POE from the standpoint of management.

In sum, mixed-ownership firms are not a novel phenomenon; they have been part of the Chinese economic landscape since the inception of economic reforms. The Third

2006, effective Sept. 1, 2006), art. 47, http://www.gov.cn/flfg/2006-08/02/content_352370.htm; SEC. AND FUTURES COMM'N, THE CODES ON TAKEOVERS AND MERGERS AND SHARE REPURCHASES, Rule 26.1 (1992) (H.K.), http://www.sfc.hk/web/EN/pdf/sfcRegulatoryHandbook/EN_H622.pdf.

[13] *Id.*

[14] 公司简介 (Company Overview), ZTE HOLDINGS, http://www.zteholdings.com/about-intro.htm (last visited Feb. 21, 2015).

Plenum's goal of expanding mixed-ownership reforms to include all SOEs, particularly the largest SOEs, is certainly bold. But this goal does not offer a reform path that is conceptually different from the status quo.

II. State Capitalism and State Capture

We now turn to our central claim—that ownership-based SOE reforms will not fundamentally alter Chinese state capitalism because they do not address one of its central features: the close relationship that all large Chinese firms must either inherit and maintain, or nurture, in order to survive in China's prevailing political economy and institutional environment. For lack of a more widely accepted and analytically tractable term, we use "capture" to describe the phenomenon in which firms obtain special advantages from the national or local governments by aligning themselves with the political leadership's interest, goals, and priorities. Thus, as we use the term, "capture" refers broadly to mean both corrupt access to government and a deep convergence of interests between managerial elites in the Party-state and business.

A. SUSCEPTIBILITY TO CAPTURE

Every government creates and maintains rents by virtue of its regulatory power. And in every economy where the government imposes restrictions on economic activities, firms devote resources to capturing rents generated by government restrictions. China is obviously not unique in the creation and allocation of rents through government intervention in the economy.

Among the world's major economies, however, the Chinese state is highly—and perhaps uniquely—susceptible to capture, for two reasons. First, China's huge economy and massive state interventions therein increase the opportunities for, and payoffs from, capture. The Chinese economy, at over $10 trillion as of 2014, is now the second largest in the world. Yet the economy is, in the words of the Heritage Foundation's Economic Freedom report, "mostly unfree."[15] China ranks near the bottom of the countries surveyed on measures of limited government, regulatory efficiency, and open markets.[16] Despite liberalization efforts in the past three decades that significantly reduced the formal share of the state-owned sector in the economy, the Chinese state still plays a dominant role, one far greater than its equity ownership would suggest. In addition to dispensing vast amounts of subsidies, the state intervenes in the economy in significant ways, generating rents that are crucial for firms' prosperity or even survival.

---

[15] Heritage Found., Index of Economic Freedom 165 (2013). China's world rank is 136.

[16] *Id.* at 166.

One primary example of state-generated rents is access to financing. The state imposes a ceiling on bank deposit rates, and channels credit at below market cost to firms favored by the state.[17] As a result, firms in China invest in political connections with the Party-state to obtain low-cost financing. An abundance of empirical evidence indicates that the political connections of firms in China are a strong indicator of their access to bank loans.[18] Similarly, firms with political connections are also favored in stock listings.[19] Smaller firms without political connections, by contrast, are forced to obtain financing from China's vast shadow-banking system at high interest rates.

Another example of state-generated rents is pervasive state-sanctioned monopolies. Many key industries in China, such as electricity, telecommunications, petroleum, railroads, public utilities, and banking, are dominated by firms that are de facto monopolies or oligopolies. These firms acquired their monopoly or dominant status not through market competition, but through market-entry restrictions imposed by the state. China adopted an Anti-Monopoly Law (AML) in 2007, but the AML left intact the monopoly or dominant status of firms in these industries.[20]

---

[17] *See* Tarhan Feyzioglu et al., *Interest Rate Liberalization in China*, IMF WORKING PAPER, WP/09/171, at 3 (2009).

[18] *See, e.g.*, Clement K.W. Chow et al., *Investment Opportunity Set, Political Connection and Business Policies of Private Enterprises in China*, 38 REV. QUANT. FIN. ACCT. 367, 367 (2012) (finding that firms with political connections in China are able to borrow more); Robert Cull et al., *Government Connections and Financial Constraints: Evidence from a Large Representative Sample of Chinese Firms*, WORLD BANK POLICY RESEARCH WORKING PAPER No. 6352 (2013) (finding that government connections are associated with substantially less severe financial constraints at private firms in China); Hongbin Li et al., *Political Connections, Financing and Firm Performance: Evidence from Chinese Private Firms*, 87 J. DEV. ECON. 283 (2008) (finding that Communist Party membership helps private entrepreneurs in China to obtain loans from banks or other state institutions); Wubiao Zhou, *Bank Financing in China's Private Sector: The Payoffs of Political Capital*, 37 WORLD DEV. 787 (2008) (finding that membership in China's legislative or semi-legislative organs helps private entrepreneurs obtain access to bank loans).

[19] More than half of the companies listed on the Shanghai Stock Exchange are formerly state-owned companies. *See* Shen Hong, *Weak Links Mar Investing in China*, WALL ST. J., June 26, 2013, http://online.wsj.com/article/SB10001424127887323998604578567722934644106.html. A significant percentage of the listed firms have former or current government officials as their CEOs. *See* Joseph P.H. Fan et al., *Politically Connected CEOs, Corporate Governance, and Post-IPO Performance of China's Newly Partially Privatized Firms*, 84 J. FIN. ECON. 330 (2007) (finding that almost 27 percent of the CEOs in a sample of 790 newly partially privatized firms in China are former or current government bureaucrats). Among the listed firms, firms with politically connected CEOs tend to underperform firms without politically connected CEOs, suggesting that firms with politically connected CEOs may have been unduly favored in the state's listing decisions. *See id.* Politically connected firms also reap greater benefits in the process of going public. *See* Bill B. Francis et al., *Political Connections and the Process of Going Public: Evidence from China*, 28 J. INT'L MONEY & FIN. 696 (2009) (finding that politically connected firms, irrespective of their ownership status, have relatively higher offering prices, lower underpricing, and lower fixed costs during the going-public process).

[20] The AML provides that "the state protects the lawful operations of undertakings in SOE-dominated industries concerning the health of national economy and national security, and in industries where state trading is authorized by law." 中华人民共和国反垄断法 (Anti-Monopoly Law of the People's Republic of China) (promulgated by the Standing Comm. Nat'l People's Cong., Aug. 30, 2007, effective Aug. 1, 2008), art. 7.

The second reason for the susceptibility of the Chinese state to capture is the lack of procedural checks on the process by which rents are generated and allocated. Although China has lawmaking institutions and procedures that outwardly resemble those typically found in a democracy, real lawmaking power on core issues in China resides with the Communist Party. The Party-state also enjoys broad discretion in setting administrative rules. As the Heritage Foundation's Economic Freedom report notes, the "legal and regulatory system is vulnerable to political influence and Communist Party directives. The Party's ultimate authority throughout the economic system undermines the rule of law and respect for contracts. Corruption is widespread and cronyism is institutionalized and pervasive."[21] These weaknesses are partly a reflection of China's stage of development, but are also traceable to the Communist Party's monopoly on political power. The monopoly reduces incentives to create neutral market institutions that provide a level playing field for all entrepreneurs, because the Party does not need to account for future states of the world in which it is not in power. The result is an institutional ecology that encourages all firms, whether SOE, POE, or of mixed ownership, to remain close to the Party-state as a source of protection and largesse.

B. MECHANISMS OF CAPTURE

The Chinese economy is distinctive not only in the scale of rents it presents, but also in the mechanisms used to capture those rents. To illuminate the mechanisms of capture in China, we adapt a simple model from Joel Hellman, Geraint Jones, and Daniel Kaufmann, who studied the capture of state power in transition economies in Eastern Europe and the former Soviet Union.[22] They distinguish two types of powerful firms in economies with insecure property rights: "influential firms" are incumbents, typically SOEs, that inherit their privileged position from the previous communist system; "captor firms" are de novo private firms that "choose to engage in state capture as a strategy to compete against these influential incumbents"—or, as they put it more colorfully, captor firms "purchase advantages directly from the state."[23] Because Hellman et al. focused on Eastern Europe, the currency for the purchases in their model consists solely of illicit, nontransparent payments. According to their analysis, the key distinguishing trait between these two types of powerful firms is that captor firms pay bribes to shape

[21] HERITAGE FOUND., *supra* note 15, at 165. Moreover, China receives low rankings on the World Justice Project's Rule of Law Index with respect to factors such as limited government powers, open government, and regulatory enforcement, even in regional rankings and within its income group. *See* WORLD JUSTICE PROJECT, RULE OF LAW INDEX 77 (2012–2013).

[22] *See* Joel S. Hellman, Geraint Jones & Daniel Kaufmann, *Seize the State, Seize the Day: State Capture and Influence in Transition Economies*, 31 J. COMP. ECON. 751 (2003).

[23] *Id.* at 753.

the rules of the game, while influential firms can do so simply through the power of incumbency.

Much of this model can be applied directly to China. Because property rights are weak, in order to succeed, firms must either inherit or earn privileges and protections from the state—or more precisely, from the Party in its role as the shadow monitor of state agencies and institutions. And as in their model, it is useful to distinguish between influential firms (SOE incumbents) and captor firms (large, successful POEs) in China as well. Chinese SOEs, like their counterparts everywhere, have natural advantages in capturing state power and state-generated rents. In the Chinese case, many SOEs were literally hived off from government ministries that were eliminated in the transition to a more market-oriented economy. Examples are abundant. China National Petroleum Corporation (CNPC), Sinopec, and China National Offshore Oil Corporation (CNOOC), China's three state-owned petroleum firms, were created from the operating assets of the former Ministry of Petroleum Industry. China's five state-owned power-generating firms and two state-owned power grids were all part of the State Power Corporation, which received the operating assets of the former Ministry of Electricity. China's three major SOE telecommunications firms (China Telecom, China Unicom, and China Mobile) were converted from the operating assets of the Ministry of Post and Telecommunications through many rounds of industry restructuring. When the Ministry of Railways was eliminated in March 2013, its operating assets were taken over by the newly established China Railway Corporation.

Chinese SOEs also benefit from orthodox socialist ideology, enshrined in the constitution, which emphasizes state ownership of the means of production. Article 7 of the constitution, for example, provides that "[t]he state owned economy, namely, the socialist economy under ownership of the whole people, is the leading force in the national economy."[24] Within this constitutional framework, the private sector is a "complement" to the socialist public economy.[25]

Despite these natural advantages of SOEs, it is possible for other firms in China to "purchase" the right to compete with incumbent firms—that is, to play the role of captor firms in the Hellman et al. model. Corruption certainly can buy influence in China, as seen in the widespread phenomenon of private firms bribing Party-state officials to obtain government contracts and other favors from the state. Family, personal, and professional connections also play important roles in capturing the state in China. In particular, firms connected to family members of senior government officials can gain a significant advantage over other firms in securing business deals with the state.

[24] *See* 中华人民共和国宪法 (Constitution of the Peoples Republic of China) (adopted and promulgated by the Nat'l People's Cong., Dec. 4, 1982, effective upon promulgation), art. 7. Ideology, however, may be a pretext for ulterior motives; it is difficult to disentangle influence rooted in ideology from that based on the power of incumbency or corruption.

[25] *Id.* at art. 11.

But the mechanisms of capture in China differ from those of Eastern Europe in that the key currency used by captor firms in China is not bribes, but growth potential. Because the Chinese Communist Party is averse to establishing accountability through the political process, its primary claim to legitimacy in the reform era is the ability to deliver economic development and its hoped-for counterpart, social stability. The primacy placed on sustained economic growth has enabled private firms to capture the state by demonstrating the potential to deliver that growth. For example, Huawei, China's leading telecommunications equipment company, achieved its initial success by developing a particular digital telephone switch with greater capacity than any other products available on the Chinese market at the time. After Huawei's technological breakthrough, government support flowed into the firm. Through its advanced technology and ingenious marketing strategies, Huawei was able to overtake other influential firms in the Chinese market, including Shanghai Bell, a joint venture between the business arm of the Ministry of Post and Telecommunications and the French corporation Alcatel, and Julong, which was assembled from eight SOEs supervised by key government ministries and the Chinese military.

The political imperative for growth has been institutionalized in ways that further distinguish the mechanisms of capture in China from those in other transition economies. A unique attribute of state capitalism in China is the large role played by local governments. Contrary to popular perception, China's model of economic decision-making is highly decentralized. This was true even before the commencement of economic reform, but economic decentralization accelerated under transition policies such as "fiscal federalism"—a revenue-sharing regime that grants a significant amount of autonomy to local governments in setting local budgets and expenditures.[26] In particular, a fundamental fiscal reform in 1994 assigned local governments a lower revenue share but higher expenditure responsibilities, leaving them no choice but to seek new tax bases.[27] This reform, combined with the delegation of investment approval authority to local governments, led to competition among local governments for investment projects with high potential to generate tax revenues. Oliver Blanchard and Andrei Shleifer theorized that this competition is made possible by a politically centralized Party-state that is ready to reward and punish local officials based on their economic performance.[28] This hypothesis finds support in empirical evidence indicating that the likelihood of promotion of China's provincial leaders increases with favorable economic performance.[29] Scholars

---

[26] *See* Wentong Zheng, *Transplanting Antitrust in China: Economic Transition, Market Structure, and State Control*, 32 U. PA. J. INT'L L. 643, 656–57 (2010).

[27] *See* Justin Yifu Lin et al., *Deregulation, Decentralization, and China's Growth in Transition*, *in* LAW AND ECONOMICS WITH CHINESE CHARACTERISTICS: INSTITUTIONS FOR PROMOTING DEVELOPMENT IN THE TWENTY-FIRST CENTURY 467, 485 (David Kennedy & Joseph E. Stiglitz eds., 2013).

[28] Oliver Blanchard & Andrei Shleifer, *Federalism with and without Political Centralization, China versus Russia*, NBER WORKING PAPER 7616 (2001).

[29] *See, e.g.*, Hongbin Li & Li-An Zhou, *Political Turnover and Economic Performance: The Incentive Role of Personnel Control in China*, 89 J. PUB. ECON. 1743 (2005).

have argued that competition among local governments is a main driver of China's economic growth in the reform era.[30]

This institutional setting suggests the diminishing relevance of enterprise ownership to the Party-state as the economy grows more complex. The growth imperative forces the Party to look beyond SOEs in bolstering its claim to legitimacy, and enables private firms to capture state rents by demonstrating growth potential, particularly to local government officials. As a recent report notes, "[l]ocal leaders these days are assessed based on economic growth, and are increasingly agnostic about what type of firm provides that growth."[31]

The structural dynamics of capture are enhanced by two other factors that provide special privileges to favored firms, without regard to public or private ownership. One such factor is industrial policy, which is used extensively to guide and promote economic development. Firms in preferred sectors or industries, such as renewable energy, are in a privileged position regardless of whether they are state-owned or privately owned. Another factor is nationalist sentiment, which favors Chinese firms, state-owned or private, over foreign companies.

As a result of these dynamics, successful large firms in China, irrespective of ownership, are likely to be those that have captured state power and rents, either through incumbency or by demonstrating growth potential to government officials. Industrial policies, nationalist sentiment, and outright corruption reinforce the advantages enjoyed by these firms. Firms that lack politically influential attributes tend to be marginalized in China's state-centered economy. Even SOEs that rely exclusively on incumbency, without the promise of growth, face the prospect of being absorbed by stronger SOEs.

C. STATE CAPTURE AND MARKET DOMINANCE

Patterns of market dominance in China are consistent with the claim that state capture is a main determinant of success of Chinese firms. These patterns simultaneously demonstrate how Chinese corporate development has been affected by path dependence and adaptation to the institutional environment. When the state first withdrew from direct participation in commercial activity, SOEs were the default arrangement: they inherited all of the operating assets from the supervising ministries and were the only players in the market. The subsequent path of development diverged, however, depending on whether the SOE incumbents could capture the state and secure state-generated rents, particularly state-sanctioned monopoly status. When the SOE incumbents failed to do so, they were exposed to the vagaries of market competition and often lost out to

---

[30] *See, e.g.*, Jean Oi, *Fiscal Reform and the Economic Foundations of Local State Corporatism in China*, 45 WORLD POLITICS 99 (1992); Yingyi Qian & Barry Weingast, *Federalism as a Commitment to Preserving Market Incentives*, 11 J. ECON. PERSPECTIVES 83 (1997).

[31] FATHOM CHINA LTD., PUBLIC FUNDS FOR PRIVATE FIRMS 18 (2013).

emerging firms. But if SOE incumbents captured the state and erected state-sanctioned entry barriers against emerging firms, their incumbency status became entrenched, as seen in China's monopoly industries.

Entrenchment of incumbent firms due to state capture can lock China's industries in a pattern of path dependency. When incumbent firms capture the state, they become well positioned to resist additional reforms that threaten their incumbency status. This power of incumbency can be seen from the state's repeated failures to break up SOE monopolies in key industries. With few exceptions, all such efforts have resulted in the breakup of SOEs along either geographical or product lines, ensuring minimal competition among the successor entities. In the petroleum industry, when the three giant state-owned firms—CNPC, Sinopec, and CNOOC—were initially created in the 1980s, they were assigned mutually exclusive business areas, with CNPC focusing on onshore upstream production, Sinopec on downstream refining, and CNOOC on offshore upstream production. Between 1998 and 2002, the state restructured the petroleum industry and converted CNPC and Sinopec into vertically integrated firms in preparation for China's entry into the World Trade Organization, but it did so by exchanging assets between CNPC and Sinopec along geographical lines. As a result of the restructuring, CNPC and Sinopec were assigned separate business territories, with CNPC concentrating in the north and Sinopec concentrating in the south.[32] In the telecommunications industry, since 1994 the state has engaged in a continuous process of breaking up SOEs along product or geographical lines, reshuffling industry assets, and merging state enterprises. These activities still have not resulted in nationwide competition among firms across all product lines.[33] A similar pattern of breaking up a massive SOE into smaller units along geographical lines is seen in the power-generating industry as well as in public utilities.[34]

The power of incumbency can also be seen in the marginalization of emerging firms that attempt to compete with incumbents but fail due to the lack of state support. An example is the fate of China's privately owned airlines. Following the issuance of a government guidance document aimed at encouraging private firms to enter SOE-dominated sectors, six privately owned airlines came into operation after 2005. The new airlines were unable to compete with SOE incumbents, which had been allocated the most lucrative routes. In the wake of the 2008–2009 global financial crisis, SOE incumbent airlines, but not the private carriers, received major government subsidies. Within a short period of time, most of the privately owned airlines were liquidated, acquired by SOE carriers, or in serious financial difficulty.[35]

---

[32] Bo Kong, China's International Petroleum Policy 14–15 (2010).

[33] Zheng, *supra* note 26, at 701–02.

[34] *See* OECD, China: Defining the Boundary between the Market and the State 236 (2009).

[35] Zheng, *supra* note 26, at 661–62.

Some large, successful private firms have emerged in industries with strong SOE incumbents. But they did so principally in new markets—markets not controlled from the outset by SOE incumbents. Where POEs demonstrate growth potential and technological innovation in markets valued by the state, their rise has not been blocked. Instead, it has been nurtured, particularly at the local level. SOE incumbents, inured to the rents they have captured, generally lack the acumen and incentives to anticipate or create new markets. Private firms have developed to fill the void. Once POEs have become entrenched in a new market with the backing of the state, it is difficult for SOEs to unseat them, despite the natural advantages SOEs enjoy. Examples of POEs dominating new markets in China are plentiful. Baidu, China's largest Internet search engine, spearheaded the Internet search market in China when that market was still in its infancy. AliPay, a third-party online payment platform owned by the e-commerce giant Alibaba Group, became the largest player in China's emerging online payment market despite the dominance of state-owned banks in the traditional banking market. Private firm ENN Group, China's largest downstream natural gas supplier, achieved its initial success by distributing natural gas to city residents through pipelines at a time when most city residents in China did not use natural gas at home or had it distributed in tanks. ENN Group acquired its dominant market position after it was able to secure franchise rights from over ninety cities across China. By contrast, CNPC, China's main upstream natural gas supplier, was late in entering the downstream residential market; it had to use its monopoly on upstream natural gas supply to pressure provinces and cities into granting it franchise rights for downstream distribution.[36]

Large firm development in China, therefore, illustrates a large measure of path dependence, with SOE incumbents dominating certain traditional industries and state-favored POEs controlling newer ones. It also demonstrates adaptation to the institutional environment. In a state-centered ecosystem, successful private firms are the ones that have learned to ingratiate themselves with the state. This suggests a "survivorship bias" at work in the Chinese economy—state capitalism generates considerable institutional isomorphism between SOEs and POEs in regard to their business strategies and relationship with the state. By contrast, firms that have failed to master the capture economy or that have sought autonomy from the state are disproportionately marginalized.

III. The Diminished Relevance of Ownership of Enterprise

The preceding analysis suggests that the ownership of enterprise alone reveals little information about how a given firm is positioned vis-à-vis the state in China's prevailing institutional environment. In this section, we expand upon this observation by taking

[36] *See* Sheng Hong & Zhao Nong, China's State-Owned Enterprises: Nature, Performance and Reform 152–54 (2013).

a closer look at how SOEs and POEs behave in the Chinese institutional setting. In so doing, we unsettle two parallel, faulty assumptions resulting from over-attention to corporate ownership in China. First, that the Chinese state exerts nearly unbridled control over SOEs and has free reign to use these firms as tools of government policy. Second, that large "private" firms in China are autonomous actors operating outside the mechanisms of Chinese state capitalism. We argue that neither theory nor practice suggests that the Chinese state "controls" SOEs to the degree its equity ownership would indicate. At the same time, however, it is misleading to view "private" firms in China as insulated from the state in ways that set them wholly apart from SOEs. Rather, the human agents managing Chinese SOEs and POEs respond in similar fashion to their institutional environment, fostering close ties to Party-state organs, seeking state largesse, and resisting government policies that are not in their interests.

A. STATE "OWNERSHIP"

By simple syllogism, the state "owns" an SOE. This is literally true in China: the State-owned Assets Supervision and Administration Commission (SASAC), a government agency that plays the role of both a holding company and a supervisory authority, holds 100 percent of the shares of the parent companies of each of the approximately 115 central state-owned business groups. Although the business groups may contain one or more entities whose shares are listed on a domestic or foreign stock exchange and held by minority private investors, SASAC, which reports to the State Council (China's cabinet), is the ultimate controlling shareholder atop the business groups. At least formally, this makes SASAC "the world's largest controlling shareholder."[37]

Straightforward application of agency analysis, however, highlights the problem of assuming that state "ownership" of a corporate enterprise means unbridled state control over the firm. Adolf Berle and Gardiner Means long ago identified the separation of ownership and control in large firms as a threat to "private property," because it produces a misalignment of incentives between shareholders (owners) and managers. This problem, which carries the economic label "agency costs," remains the central concern of corporate governance regimes everywhere.

Agency costs, of course, can also jeopardize *public* property. Majority or even 100 percent ownership of a firm's equity by the state does not necessarily solve the problem of misalignment of incentives between the SOE's "owners" and managers. Rather, it may multiply the agency problem. The SOE managers must be monitored by an agent of the state, which in turn must be monitored. In the case of Chinese SOEs, this chain of monitors does not lead to an ultimate principal, because the theoretical "owner" of the

---

[37] Lin & Milhaupt, *supra* note 4, at 700.

SOEs—the citizenry of China—is too dispersed and powerless to play a meaningful monitoring role.

The Chinese state does exert significant political control over senior executives of large SOEs. In particular, the Party and SASAC routinely rotate senior SOE executives among different business groups in the same sector. Top-down political control, however, does not fully eliminate agency costs. To meet its governance goals, the Chinese state must delegate a significant amount of discretion to its local agents, and accommodate special interests to ensure their participation and cooperation. The frequent rotations of senior SOE executives may be a reflection of the weakness, rather than the strength, of top-down political control, as such rotations suggest that the state has no other effective means of keeping SOE executives in check. This is all the more likely given the enormous size and complexity of China's SOEs. At the national level, SASAC is formally responsible for exercising the interests of the state as an investor in more than a hundred massive SOE business groups, some of which have over a hundred downstream subsidiaries. How likely is it that a group of bureaucrats in Beijing actually controls such a vast business empire?

Policy choices made in the transition from communism to market economies compound the agency problem in SOEs. Efforts to revitalize the state-owned sector in many formerly communist countries, including China, involved massive delegation of managerial discretion to SOE insiders. In China, the delegation of authority has been a major theme of SOE reforms since the late 1970s. As a result of such policies throughout the transition economies, "irreversible jurisdictional authority" was conferred on managers within their own SOEs.[38] These reforms, together with privatization of SOEs in the hands of entrenched managers, led to rampant "insider control."[39]

Thus, both theory and the obvious consequences of economic transition policies suggest far greater managerial autonomy from the state in the SOE sector than a focus on ownership alone would suggest. The relatively attenuated nature of the Chinese state's control over SOEs is evidenced in a variety of ways, as discussed below.

1. The State Collects Little or No Dividends from SOEs

Equity owners have a residual claim on the cash flows generated by the corporation. Residual claimant status is a key theoretical reason that equity owners, as opposed to contractual claimants such as bondholders or employees, are legally vested with the right to elect the board of directors. Although in theory the state is entitled to all of the SOEs' after-tax profits, the Chinese government has historically collected little or no dividends

[38] Masahiko Aoki, *Controlling Insider Control: Issues of Corporate Governance in Transition Economies, in* Corporate Governance in Transitional Economies: Insider Control and the Role of Banks 8 (Masahiko Aoki & Hyung-Ki Kim eds., 1995).

[39] *Id.*

from SOEs. In 2007, the State Council required central SOEs (those under SASAC supervision) to begin paying dividends ranging from 0 to 10 percent. In 2011, the SOE dividend rates were increased by 5 percent across the board, to 5 to 15 percent. The Third Plenum set a goal of increasing the SOE dividend rate to 30 percent by the year 2020. These rates, however, are still far below the average dividend rates paid by established industrial firms in the United States (50 to 60 percent) and the average dividend rate paid by SOEs in five developed economies (33 percent).[40] Moreover, the dividend rates paid by central SOEs to the government in its capacity as shareholder are lower than those paid to private shareholders by Chinese SOEs listed in Hong Kong.[41] Most important, perhaps, virtually all of the dividends paid by SOEs to the government are eventually recycled back to them: more than 92 percent of the dividends paid by central SOEs to the government in 2012 were remitted back to the SOEs in the form of subsidies.[42]

From an agency perspective, these dividend policies have a number of negative implications. First, it is difficult to justify maintaining a large SOE sector on behalf of the citizens—the ultimate principals—if profits from the enterprises are not remitted to the state. Second, low dividend payouts to the government and heavy recycling of profits back to the SOEs in the form of subsidies increase free cash flow, thus generating additional agency slack between SOE managers and the government in its role as owner-investor. By increasing the amount of cash at the SOE managers' disposal, these policies facilitate managerial misbehavior in the form of perk consumption and empire building.

2. Executive Compensation Practices at SOEs Suggest Limited State Control over Managers

Theory and cross-country experience suggest that concentrated ownership alleviates agency problems in setting managerial pay. Yet executive compensation practices at Chinese SOEs, with concentrated ownership in the hands of the state, have posed problems throughout the reform era, suggesting limited state control over SOE managers.

During the initial phase of market-oriented reforms of Chinese SOEs, individual state-owned firms were allowed to base executive compensation on firm performance. The practice led to significant disparities in pay levels across SOEs. To address this perceived problem, several ministries of the State Council in 2009 introduced a scheme that capped executive compensation at the central SOEs overseen by SASAC at twenty times

---

[40] World Bank, Effective Discipline with Adequate Autonomy: The Direction for Further Reform of China's SOE Dividend Policy 13, 23–30 (2010), http://documents.worldbank.org/curated/en/2009/11/11880532/effective-discipline-adequate-autonomy-direction-further-reform-chinas-soe-dividend-policy.

[41] *Id.*

[42] *See* 去年央企上交红利不足千亿 大部分回流内部 (Central SOEs Paid Less than 100 Billion Yuan as Dividends Last Year; Most Remitted Back), 新浪财经 (SINA Fin.) (Mar. 10, 2013), http://finance.sina.com.cn/china/20130310/142714780509.shtml.

the average employee compensation.[43] Putting aside the question of whether this is an optimal compensation formula, such a system ostensibly suggests a significant degree of state control over managerial incentives.

But beneath the surface of state control over executive pay lies a vast domain of managerial autonomy. A common form of private benefit extraction by SOE managers is the practice of "on duty consumption," a catch-all category of perquisites, expense accounts, and side payments that often significantly exceed a manager's formal compensation, which is regulated by SASAC in cooperation with senior Party organs. The scale and pervasiveness of these practices belie the notion that the Chinese government, as a controlling shareholder, is closely monitoring SOE managers and carefully tailoring incentives to maximize returns on state assets. Rather, these practices suggest a considerable degree of agency slack between SOE managers and the controlling shareholder.

3. The State Often Fails to Implement Major Operational and Policy Decisions at SOEs

It is considered good practice for the state to avoid involvement in day-to-day management of SOEs because government agents generally lack the expertise, information, and incentives necessary to run a commercial enterprise effectively. At the same time, however, a principal theoretical justification for the existence of SOEs is to accomplish objectives that, due to market failure, would otherwise be impossible. From this perspective, it would be anomalous if the state were unable to implement major operational decisions at SOEs on issues implicating key state policies. Yet at times, this is precisely the case in China.

One example can be found in the government's failure to prevent SOEs from investing in the real estate sector. One of the top priorities of the Chinese government in recent years has been to rein in skyrocketing housing prices. In furtherance of that goal, SASAC in March 2010 ordered seventy-eight central SOEs whose main business was not real estate to withdraw from the real estate sector. Yet almost three years later, as of December 2012, fewer than one-quarter of the affected SOEs had complied with the SASAC order. Many of the SOEs subject to the order actually expanded their real estate business during this period.[44]

Another example is the recent setback in the Chinese government's efforts to restructure central SOEs. Over the years, one of the government's key policies has been to consolidate the SOE sector to address market segmentation, to implement China's long-term

---

[43] *See* 国企高管薪酬上限: 20倍职工平均工资 (Pay for Senior SOE Executives Capped at 20 Times Average Employee Pay), 中国新闻网 (China News Network) (Sept. 25, 2009), http://www.chinanews.com/cj/cj-gncj/news/2009/09-25/1885412.shtml.

[44] *See* 央企三年未"退房" 78家退出不足 1/4 (Central SOEs Not Withdrawing from Real Estate Three Years Later; Less than Quarter of 78 Firms Withdrew), 新华网 (Xinhua Net) (Dec. 5, 2012), http://news.xinhuanet.com/house/2012-12/05/c_124048485.htm.

SOE strategy, and to promote China's national champions. In accordance with these objectives, the number of central SOEs overseen by SASAC was reduced through mergers to 121 in 2011, down from 196 in 2003. SASAC aims to reduce the number of central SOEs to below 100. To achieve this goal, SASAC's original plan was to package the assets of about two dozen smaller central SOEs, whose businesses were not complementary, into a holding company called Guoxin Assets Management Co. The plan reportedly met fierce resistance from the target SOEs, particularly those that had acquired monopoly status in niche industries. The holding company was eventually established in December 2010, but with no initial assets.[45] One year after its establishment, the holding company had acquired only one central SOE, as opposed to the two dozen contemplated by the government's original plan.[46] Since then it has acquired the state-held shares of Shanghai Bell, a telecommunications equipment manufacturer that has lost out in competition with other telecommunications equipment firms.[47]

4. The State Influences SOE Behavior Principally in Its Role as a Regulator, Not as a Controlling Shareholder

When the state does successfully intervene in SOE operations to achieve policy objectives, it typically does so as a regulator, not as a controlling shareholder. For example, the Chinese government has been waging an anticorruption campaign since Xi Jinping took over Party leadership in November 2012. One focus of the anticorruption campaign is to prohibit the consumption of expensive liquors by government officials. Demand for the products of two prestigious Chinese liquor firms, Maotai and Wuliangye, both SOEs, plummeted as a result of the campaign. Starting in December 2012, some distributors of Maotai and Wuliangye offered deep price discounts to win sales. Maotai and Wuliangye responded by setting minimum sales prices for their products and penalizing distributors that sold below the minimum prices. In response, the National Development and Reform Commission (NDRC), China's price regulator, conducted "interviews" with executives of the firms and warned them of their violation of China's Anti-Monopoly Law, which prohibits the fixing of resale prices. Following the NDRC interviews, Maotai and Wuliangye publicly announced that they would heed the NDRC warning and terminate their minimum resale price policies.[48]

---

[45] *See* 关于中国国新控股有限责任公司由国务院国有资产监督管理委员会代表国务院履行出资人职责的公告 (Announcement on the Assumption by SASAC of the Shareholder's Responsibility for China Guoxin Holdings Ltd), SASAC Notice No. 2010-3 (Dec. 22, 2010), http://www.sasac.gov.cn/n1180/n1566/n258252/n258629/12545689.html.

[46] *See* 中投二号成立一年业务无进展 被疑定位不清 (One Year Later, No Progress at CIC No. 2; Business Scope Unclear), 新浪财经 (SINA FIN.) (Feb. 18, 2012), http://finance.sina.com.cn/china/jrxw/20120218/073611405303.shtml.

[47] *See* 国新公司接手上海贝尔中方股份 (Guoxin Acquires Chinese-Held Shares of Shanghai Bell), 人民网 (PEOPLE'S DAILY ONLINE) (Mar. 3, 2012), http://finance.people.com.cn/GB/70846/17283754.html.

[48] *See* 五粮液继茅台后被发改委约谈 将按反垄断法整改 (Wuliangye Interviewed by NDRC after Maotai; To Correct Its Policy Pursuant to the Antimonopoly Law), 新浪财经 (SINA FIN.) (Jan. 17, 2013), http://finance.sina.com.cn/chanjing/gsnews/20130117/17341432oo12.shtml.

The important point about this incident is not that the state intervened, but the way in which it intervened. The state did not act as the liquor firms' controlling shareholder, directing management through the board of directors to change their pricing policies. It intervened as law enforcer, in the same fashion as if the firms had been privately owned. This is not in itself negative. The state should enforce laws neutrally against both SOEs and POEs, and perhaps there were public policy benefits in acting publicly in a case such as this one. But coupled with the other evidence of attenuated government control over SOEs, incidents such as this suggest that the government does not view standard mechanisms of corporate control as its most effective means of influencing SOE behavior.

B. "PRIVATE" OWNERSHIP

In the context of Chinese state capitalism, "private" ownership does not mean autonomy from the state. In fact, POEs bear a striking resemblance to SOEs along the dimensions typically thought to distinguish state-owned firms from the private sector: ready access to state power and largesse, proximity to the regulatory process, and little autonomy from discretionary state intervention in business judgment. We elaborate below.

1. Politically Connected Entrepreneurs

As one of us has written elsewhere, SOEs are deeply enmeshed in a larger system of Party-state organs, a phenomenon called "institutional bridging."[49] These bridges consist of dense, stable networks of relationships fostered through rotations of managers, personnel exchanges, and the wearing of multiple hats (on behalf of SOEs, the government, and the Party) by managerial elites in China.

Institutional bridges are also prevalent between state or party organs and senior executives of large private enterprises in China. We studied the government affiliations of the founders or de facto controllers of China's one hundred largest POEs (by revenue) as ranked by the China National Association of Industry & Commerce, as well as China's top ten Internet firms (by revenue), all POEs, as ranked by the China Internet Association.[50] Based on publicly available information, we identified ninety-five out of the top one hundred private firms and eight out of the top ten Internet firms whose founder or de facto controller is currently or formerly a member of central or local Party-state organizations such as people's congresses and people's political consultative conferences. Moreover, the fact that no such memberships could be found for founders or de facto controllers of the rest of the firms does not necessarily mean they lack

[49] Lin & Milhaupt, *supra* note 4, at 708.

[50] China National Association of Industry & Commerce publishes a ranking of China's largest five hundred POEs every year. The 2013 ranking is available at http://finance.sina.com.cn/leadership/mroll/20130829/101816602059.shtml.

high-level political connections. Information about their affiliations may simply not be publicly available, or their connections to the political establishment may have purposely been kept informal to avoid suspicion about their firm's motives, as is likely the case with the founder of Huawei.

Why do private entrepreneurs join these political organs, whose powers are largely symbolic? One potential explanation is that membership in political organs signals allegiance to and influence within the Party-state—creating and reinforcing networks with state-linked actors important to a firm's success, such as banks, SOEs, and regulators. The signal of influence sent by political participation may also help ward off potential new market entrants and local government officials eager to share in the spoils of a lucrative hometown business. At the same time, widespread membership of successful entrepreneurs in Party-state organizations is indicative of the confluence of interests and shared worldview of political and economic elites in China—the "integration of wealth and power" in the words of China scholar Bruce Dickson.[51] As the *Wall Street Journal* reported of the major Chinese Internet company Tencent Holdings, the "company is politically as well as technologically savvy . . . Tencent's chief executive, Pony Ma, joined China's nearly powerless but symbolically significant parliament, a sign the company had become part of the Chinese establishment."[52]

2. Government Support for Private Firms

The Chinese state provides extensive support to SOEs—US$310 billion in nominal terms between 1985 and 2005 according to a recent estimate.[53] But SOEs are not the only firms supported by the state. Subsidies to large, fast-growing private firms are widespread and can constitute a significant portion of a company's net profits. Privately owned Geely Automobile, for example, received subsidies totaling US$141 million in 2011, over half of its net profits for the year.[54] When Geely acquired Volvo from Ford in 2010, much of the US$1.5 billion purchase price was financed by local governments in northeast China and the Shanghai area.[55] Huawei, China's largest telecommunications equipment maker, provides another example. Huawei's shares are held by its employees under an arrangement resembling an Employee Stock Ownership Plan. Yet analysts have suggested that

---

[51] *See* Bruce J. Dickson, *Integrating Wealth and Power in China: The Communist Party's Embrace of the Private Sector*, 192 CHINA Q. 827, 827 (2007).

[52] Bob Davis, *China's Top-Down Take on Innovation*, WALL ST. J., Oct. 1, 2013, http://online.wsj.com/article/SB100014240527023479804579099640843773148.html.

[53] HALEY & HALEY, *supra* note 4, at 2–3. A recent study finds that the interest rate subsidies received by China's SOEs alone are greater than the existing profits of the SOEs. *See* Giovanni Ferri & Li-Gang Liu, *Honor Thy Creditors Beforan Thy Shareholders: Are the Profits of Chinese State-Owned Enterprises Real?*, 9 ASIAN ECON. PAPERS 50, 50 (2010).

[54] FATHOM CHINA LTD., *supra* note 31, at 10.

[55] Michael Wines, *China Fortifies State Businesses to Fuel Growth*, N.Y. TIMES, Aug. 29, 2010, http://www.nytimes.com/2010/08/30/world/asia/30china.html?pagewanted=all&_r=1&.

Huawei is viewed by the Chinese government as a "national champion," and it receives major funding from state banks.[56] As one commentator notes, "[t]he irony that the SOE [ZTE] turned to equity markets while the private company [Huawei] relied on state funds indicates the blurred lines between the public and private sectors in China's creation of industries considered to be strategic."[57]

3. Extralegal Control of Private Firms

The line between state and private ownership of enterprise in China is blurred not only due to ambiguous ownership structures of the kind discussed in Section I above, but also because the state exercises significant extralegal control rights over private firms. To be sure, corporations in every economy are subject to regulations that dilute the control rights of corporate equity owners. State encroachment into private ownership of enterprise is particularly acute, however, when the state does not scrupulously follow clearly delineated and neutrally enforced legal rules in exercising its control rights over private enterprises.

The Chinese state relies on several means to exercise extralegal control of private firms. One such means is the control of private firms through so-called industrial associations, also known in some sectors as chambers of commerce. Established in industries for which supervising ministries have been disbanded, these ostensibly private organizations are designed to coordinate activities within an industry. Yet the industrial associations are staffed by former government officials from the defunct ministries, and have the same organizational structures and functions as those ministries.[58] The industrial associations actively supervise the operations of firms in their respective industries and have retained much, if not all, of the power exercised by their state predecessors.[59] One such industrial association, China Chamber of Commerce for Import & Export of Medicine and Health Products ("Chamber"), in the early 2000s implemented an export regime for the vitamin C industry under which the export prices of all vitamin C producers were subject to review and approval by the Chamber. Some members of

---

[56] For example, in 1998, the Beijing headquarters of China Construction Bank lent Huawei RMB 3.9 billion in buyer's credit, representing 45 percent of the total credit it extended that year. *See* NATHANIEL AHRENS, CHINA'S COMPETITIVENESS: MYTH, REALITY, AND LESSONS FOR THE UNITED STATES AND JAPAN; CASE STUDY: HUAWEI 6 (2013).

[57] *Id.* at 11.

[58] *See* Zheng, *supra* note 26, at 669–70.

[59] On the official functions of such industrial associations, a U.S. court noted:

> The [industrial associations] were given both governmental functions, which had previously been performed by the [ministries], and private functions. The governmental functions included, inter alia, responding to foreign anti-dumping charges and industry "coordination." The private functions of the Chambers included organizing trade fairs, conducting market research and "mediating" trade disputes.

In re Vitamin C Antitrust Litig., 810 F. Supp. 2d 522, 526 (E.D.N.Y. 2011).

the Chamber were sued in the United States for fixing the prices of vitamin C products in violation of Section 1 of the Sherman Act. Defendants contended that the Chamber is an entity through which the Chinese government exercises its regulatory authority, and that the price-fixing agreements at issue were compelled by the Chinese government. The Chinese Ministry of Commerce took the unusual step of submitting an amicus brief in support of the defendants' motion to dismiss. The federal district court in New York, however, rejected this argument, holding that none of the laws and regulations cited by the defendants and the Ministry of Commerce actually compelled the defendants to fix the prices of vitamin C products.[60] In so doing, the court focused solely on the formal language of the relevant legal rules and directives; it did not consider the Chinese government's ability and tendency to impose its policies on private firms on an extralegal basis.

Another means by which the state exercises extralegal control over private firms is the practice of regulators conducting "interviews" with private firm managers to encourage or compel compliance with policies favored by the government. As indicated above, the NDRC, China's chief economic planning agency, engages in this practice regularly. By law, the NDRC has the authority to regulate the prices of only a small number of products and services still subject to formal price control.[61] Yet the NDRC routinely conducts interviews with firms that are not subject to these controls, to prod, and at times order, adoption of NDRC-favored pricing policies. For example, in 2010, China's main cooking oil producers increased or were planning to increase prices due to cost pressures. Concerned about the impact of these price hikes on food price inflation, the NDRC interviewed executives of the cooking oil producers three times to urge them not to increase prices. During one of the interviews, the NDRC directly ordered the producers to freeze prices for four months, and the producers complied.[62]

Yet another means by which the state exercises extralegal control over private firms is the practice of prodding or even forcing private firms to participate in state-led industry-restructuring efforts. The right of ownership implies the right to decide whether to relinquish control and be acquired by another firm. In China this right often has to yield to the state's plans for restructuring an industry. In 2009, for example, Shandong Steel Group, a major SOE steel producer in Shandong Province, acquired 67 percent of the ownership of Shandong Rizhao Steel, an emerging privately owned steel producer

---

[60] *Id.* at 550–67.

[61] In a government catalog published in 2001, the last year for which such catalogs are publicly available, only thirteen categories of products or services were subject to price control by the government, such as electricity, military products, and postal services. *See* 国家计委和国务院有关部门定价目录 (State Planning Commission and State Council Pricing Catalog) (promulgated by the State Planning Comm., July 2001, effective Aug. 1, 2001), http://www.sgpi.gov.cn/laws/wj/gjdjml.htm.

[62] *See* 食用油企业近年三次被"约谈" 下游餐饮业暂不追涨 (Cooking Oil Companies "Interviewed" Three Times in Recent Years; Downstream Restaurants Temporarily Halting Price Hikes), 新华网 (XINHUA NET) (July 30, 2012), http://news.xinhuanet.com/fortune/2012-07/30/c_123494170.htm.

in Shandong province, under the auspices of an industry-restructuring plan drawn up by the Shandong provincial government a year earlier.[63] The acquisition was completed after the owner of Shandong Rizhao Steel, Du Shuanghua, had repeatedly stated his strong opposition to the deal and had put up fierce resistance by listing 30 percent of Shandong Rizhao Steel's assets in Hong Kong through a reverse merger with a Hong Kong listed company.[64]

The point is not that the government has unbridled control over private firms, any more than it has free reign to impose its will on SOEs. Rather, the point is that where a government routinely chooses to enforce its policies by extralegal means, the added degree of autonomy from government influence that ordinarily follows from private, as compared to government, ownership of enterprise may be illusory. Of course, this is a principal reason that politically connected entrepreneurs are so prevalent in China: if private entrepreneurship does not bring added autonomy from the state, it is better to seek the benefits of affiliation with the government. Simply put, if you can't beat 'em, join 'em.

IV. The Case for Institutional, Not Ownership-Based, Reforms

The diluted impact of equity ownership on the Chinese firm provides an illustration of the by-now familiar point that "institutions matter."[65] In particular, rent-seeking, like productive innovation, is ultimately a product of institutions. Thus, as we elaborate below, reform-minded policymakers would do well to focus less on changing the ownership structure of SOEs than on changing the incentives generated by the institutions of Chinese state capitalism.

As China's investment-driven economy matures, economic growth and competitiveness will increasingly depend on the ability of Chinese firms to move up the value chain. Innovation and productivity will be central to this effort, and thus the future dynamism of the Chinese economy will depend in large measure on the country's capacity to foster entrepreneurship and to nurture enterprises that direct more efforts toward generating consumer surplus than to cozying up to the state. The late University of Chicago economist, Gary Becker, summed up the situation:

> China's new leaders have now made clear that the country needs to rely much more on the creativity and resourcefulness of the private sector if it is to move beyond

---

[63] *See* 山钢重组日钢敲定占股67% (Shandong Steel Clinches Deal to Acquire 67 Percent of Rizhao Steel), 新浪财经 (SINA FIN.) (Sept. 7, 2009), http://finance.sina.com.cn/chanjing/gsnews/20090907/04566714022.shtml.

[64] *Id.* For more background on the acquisition, *see* SHENG & ZHAO, *supra* note 36, at 145–48.

[65] According to Douglass North, institutions play an instrumental role in economic development. *See* Douglas C. North, *Economic Performance through Time*, 84 AM. ECON. REV. 359, 366 (1994) ("It is the mixture of formal rules, informal norms, and enforcement characteristics that shapes economic performance.").

> middle income status, and become a major economic power as measured . . . by per capita GDP. It remains to be seen whether even the new leaders can overcome the strong opposition of SOEs and other special interest groups to the implementation of a major shift toward the private sector.[66]

As Becker suggests, SOEs are typically seen as the major obstacle to a move toward a private-sector-driven economy. Ironically, our analysis suggests that, in China's current institutional environment, the "private sector" poses equally formidable obstacles to this transformation. Chinese state capitalist institutions do encourage private entrepreneurs to innovate and to explore new markets, and private firm innovation has undoubtedly contributed significantly to China's economic growth. But once innovative entrepreneurs become acclimated to state largesse and protection, it is to be expected that many will shift focus to maintaining the privileges of incumbency.

Does ownership matter when considering obstacles to China's institutional development? In other words, does it matter whether SOEs or POEs have captured state power and largesse? Any influential firm—whether SOE, POE, or a mixed-ownership enterprise—will resist reforms that threaten its privileged position in the economy. From this perspective, the fact that not only SOEs but also large swaths of the private sector have vested interests in the status quo bodes ill for the development of a truly entrepreneurial economy in China.

Closely related to this question is the so-called *guojin mintui* ("the state advances, the private sector retreats") debate. Critics assert that the Chinese government has failed to deliver on its commitment to the creation of a market economy, made in connection with China's accession to the WTO in 2001.[67] By some measures, and in the perception of many, over the past decade the state's role in the economy has actually expanded, to the detriment of market-oriented institutions and private enterprise.[68] Defenders of current policy assert that the *guo jin min tui* concept is "based on a one-sided perspective of the ownership of enterprise" and a "false proposition" because the state and private sectors are complementary.[69]

---

[66] Gary Becker, *China's Tilt toward the Private Sector?*, The Becker-Posner Blog (May 26, 2013), http://www.becker-posner-blog.com/2013/05/chinas-tilt-toward-the-private-sector-becker.html.

[67] *See, e.g.*, Statement of Alan H. Price, *in* Ten Years in the WTO: Has China Kept Its Promises?, Hearing Before the Congressional-Executive Commission on China 27–28 (2011) (criticizing China's continued state ownership and control over key segments of its economy as being contrary to its WTO commitments).

[68] *See, e.g.*, Sheng & Zhao, *supra* note 36, at 154–56 (discussing the dangers of the advances of SOEs in China).

[69] *Economist Defends Relationship between SOEs, Private Firms*, China Daily, May 12, 2012, http://topic.chinadaily.com.cn/index/cache?collection=cbsweb&source=Xinhua&title=Economist+defends+relationship+between+SOEs%2C+private+firms&aid=15277374 (quoting economist Hu Angang as arguing that the widening development gap between the state-owned sector and the private sector is a "false proposition").

Our analysis presents a more nuanced perspective on the *guo jin min tui* phenomenon than the views above. Conceptually, it is true that the *guo jin min tui* critique may have overemphasized the ownership of enterprise—precisely the tendency we have argued is to be avoided in analyzing Chinese firms. But our analysis does not support the view that the state and private sectors in China, as currently constituted, are complementary. They are potentially complementary only if the state sector is equated simply with the state-*owned* sector, as is common among analysts. But our analysis suggests that the *size* of the state-owned sector is not an accurate measure of the *impact* of state capitalism on the economy. Considering the incentive effects of the institutional environment, the state and private sectors are anything but complementary. Rather, a state-centered ecology creates a vacuum, siphoning oxygen out of the private sector and generating large "private" firms that are avatars of state-owned enterprises.

A shift toward the creation of a true private sector in China will thus require more than the commonly proffered prescriptions of changing the ownership structure of SOEs and shrinking the state's share of the economy. In particular, mixed-ownership reforms as proposed by the Third Plenum will likely do little to alter how the rules of the game for economic activity are shaped in contemporary China. A fundamental change in this respect will instead require the formation of robust market-neutral institutions: a corporate law that permits entrepreneurs to contract away from state-favored organizational forms, a robust and neutrally enforced anti-monopoly law, and elimination of preferential access to bank finance and the capital markets for state-favored firms, to name a few key reforms. As the World Bank's influential report, China 2030, argues, "[a]s an economy approaches the technology frontier and exhausts the potential for acquiring and applying technology from abroad, the role of government and its relationship to markets and the private sector need to change fundamentally."[70] Our analysis indicates that the way to change this relationship is through massive institutional reforms that foster the growth of firms without deep ties to the Party-state, not through changes in equity ownership, as the current reform plan contemplates.

But here the dynamics of capture again rear their ugly head. China's incremental economic reforms in the past three decades have led to the entrenchment of interest groups—perhaps an inevitable consequence of any gradualist transition model. Even if the top political leadership is serious about altering the state's relationship to the economy, a large class of powerful interests—comprised not only of SOE incumbents but of private entrepreneurs deeply connected to the Party-state as well—is positioned to undermine the impact of market-neutral policies. Worse yet, if gradualism leads to the public perception that market reforms benefit only the well-connected, the state may be prompted to backtrack on reforms in response to popular discontent. Increased state

[70] World Bank & Dev. Research Ctr. of the State Council of China, China 2030: Building a Modern, Harmonious, and Creative High-Income Society xv (2012).

intervention could prompt more rent-seeking, resulting in a political vicious circle. In light of these complexities, our analysis casts doubt on how far China can go in reducing the role of the state in its economy without significant political reforms.

Conclusion

Mixed-ownership strategies dominate the Chinese government's current thinking about reform of the state sector of the economy. But our analysis, which shifts the focus from corporate ownership to the state-centered institutional ecology in which all firms operate, whether SOE, POE, or mixed-ownership blends, exposes serious limitations in this reform program. It is the susceptibility of the Chinese economy to capture due to porous institutional structures and weak political accountability, rather than the state's ownership of enterprise per se, that is the fundamental source of the problems engendered by Chinese state capitalism. Injecting more private capital into SOEs will do relatively little to increase the market orientation of the Chinese economy. True reform of China's SOEs—and the economy as a whole—is a matter of institutions, not ownership.

10 SOEs and State Governance

HOW STATE-OWNED ENTERPRISES INFLUENCE CHINA'S LEGAL SYSTEM

Zheng Lei, Benjamin L. Liebman, and Curtis J. Milhaupt

Introduction

Literature on Chinese state-owned enterprises (SOEs) typically asks how state ownership affects their corporate governance.[1] In this chapter, we turn the question on its head, asking how SOEs influence *state* governance. A key feature of Chinese state capitalism is the integration of massive SOE business groups, under government ownership and Party oversight, with other institutions of the Party-state. As one of us put it in another work, "the mechanisms of Chinese state capitalism operate by joining the corporate groups into much larger networks of organizations affiliated with the party-state"—a process called "institutional bridging."[2] To understand how these linkages affect legal development and public governance in China, we analyze the different types of relationships between SOEs and the Party-state. Understanding the various, and at times conflicting, nature of these relationships provides insights into the forms of influence SOEs exert

[1] *See, e.g.,* Donald C. Clarke, *The Role of Non-legal Institutions in Chinese Corporate Governance, in* TRANSFORMING CORPORATE GOVERNANCE IN EAST ASIA 168, 179–80 (Hideki Kanda et al. eds., 2008).

[2] Li-Wen Lin & Curtis J. Milhaupt, *We Are the (National) Champions: Understanding the Mechanisms of State Capitalism in China*, 65 STAN. L. REV. 697 (2013).

over China's legal institutions. Emerging from the analysis is a rather dim picture of China's prospects for sound legal development: whereas SOEs may have partially compensated for weak state capacity in an earlier phase of development, today they pose a major obstacle to the creation of a legal system capable of performing the functions that theory and experience suggest are crucial to sustainable economic development and sound public governance.

Section I provides three simple conceptual frames for viewing the patterns of interaction between Chinese SOEs and the state. We refer to these patterns metaphorically as "paternalism," "prodigal son," and "partnership." Understanding how these varied interactions emerged and coexist sheds light on the different ways in which SOEs influence legal development in China. Section II explains the advantages enjoyed by SOEs in shaping the legal system simply by virtue of their status and position within the Party-state. Drawing on our analytical framework, Section III examines how SOEs influence China's legislative/regulatory processes and judicial system. Finally, Section IV explores the implications of the analysis for Chinese state governance capacity and institutional development.

I. Interaction between SOEs and the Party-State

Discussions about SOEs (Chinese or otherwise) usually involve asking how the existence of a state owner affects the governance, objectives, and profitability of the enterprise. Although in this chapter we ask the inverse question, how the existence of SOEs affects Chinese state governance, the perspectives used by scholars to answer the former question are also useful in responding to our inquiry. Typically, scholars approach the state-SOE relationship from one of two perspectives. The first assumes the existence of a command-and-control relationship and a unity of interests between the state as "owner" and the state-owned enterprise. In essence, the SOE is assumed to be an arm of the state. For corporate governance analysis, this perspective highlights a key distinguishing characteristic of SOEs as compared to private firms: the potential pursuit of social or political, as opposed to commercial, goals. The second perspective, embracing insights from agency theory, assumes that the lack of a true "principal" in the state-SOE relationship (because "the citizenry" represented by the state are too numerous and too lacking in expertise, incentives, and opportunity to monitor a commercial enterprise ostensibly operated for their benefit) leads to nearly unbridled discretion on the part of SOE managers. In this view, rather than serving as an arm of the state, the SOE is a vehicle for the pursuit of selfish interests by managers and politicians.

Although these perspectives are in tension with one another, they are not mutually exclusive ways of understanding the state-SOE relationship, particularly when the question is how the relationship may affect the development of law and legal institutions. In fact, each provides insight into SOEs' influence. The first dimension of the relationship we metaphorically label "paternalism." Paternalism reflects the view that SOEs are essentially indistinguishable from the state and, as such, are entitled to state support and are called upon to faithfully carry out state policies. But slack in the relationship between SOEs and the state gives SOE managers wide discretion to pursue objectives that are in the narrow interests of their firm or industry rather than the public interest, and at times even to disregard state policies altogether. Hence, the "prodigal son" aspect of the relationship, which corrodes public attitudes toward SOEs and undercuts their role as state servants.

Beyond these two dimensions, there is a third relationship that must be accounted for in considering SOE influence on governance in China. State institutions with important legal functions, such as the courts, often engage in a pattern of sustained cooperation with SOEs to advance mutually beneficial objectives. This relationship, which we refer to as "partnership," goes well beyond the lobbying activities common to all advanced economies and is an integral part of the lawmaking process in China. As compared to paternalism, the state-SOE relationship is turned on its head: SOEs take the lead in devising policies and shaping regulations; the state institutions effectuate legal outcomes consistent with the SOEs' preferences and interests.

A key to understanding how SOEs influence Chinese law is the recognition that all three of these relationships are manifest simultaneously, perhaps even within a single SOE. The varied nature of the relationships emerged over time, in part reflecting different stages in China's economic transition and enterprise reforms. Paternalism is a legacy of the planned economy era, in which SOEs *were* in fact arms of the state. In this era, commercial functions were carried out by operational divisions of ministries charged with industrial planning and oversight. For example, the Ministry of Metallurgical Industry produced aluminum, the Ministry of Coal directed coal extraction, and the Ministry of Electric Power Industry was in charge of electricity supply. SOEs, as an offspring of the state, carried out state plans, performed crucial roles in the economy, and were recipients of unwavering state support by virtue of their status alone.

An enduring focus of Chinese economic reforms over the past several decades has been the separation of the commercial and regulatory functions of the state. True privatization of the SOEs in the reform process, of course, would have obviated the need for the state to perform both functions. But privatization was not the objective of the reforms, as Deng Feng's contribution to this volume explores in detail. Owing to the Party's desire to maintain control over important sectors of the economy, many Chinese SOEs were "corporatized"[3] but not completely privatized. That is, commercial operations were separated from the ministries and given a separate corporate identity, but the umbilical cord to the state was only made attenuated, not cut.[4] Some SOEs listed shares

---

[3] Corporatization refers to the process of transforming SOEs from units of government into legally distinct corporate actors with ownership interests represented by shares, a board of directors, and other accoutrements of the corporate form.

[4] In some cases ministries themselves were abolished and replaced by corporate entities, with residual regulatory functions transferred to other ministries.

on national or foreign stock exchanges, but the state retained a majority ownership interest. At the national level, the newly created state-owned firms were organized over time into large business groups with a parent company whose shares are held by a state agency (the State-owned Assets Supervision and Administration Commission, or SASAC) representing the state's interests as an investor. In a parallel with other countries, such as Japan and South Korea at early stages of their development, the Chinese state compensated for weak governance capacity by managing the economy *through* business groups closely linked to the political leadership.[5] But, in contrast to those countries, the Chinese state maintained these linkages through outright ownership of the enterprises. Paternalistic attitudes toward SOEs fostered in this era persist, and are reflected in ideology (discussed in Section II) and local protectionism (discussed in Section III).

The transformation from a planned economy to a "socialist market economy" and the corporatization of state enterprises did change important aspects of the state-SOE relationship. Vertical control over the SOEs weakened as enterprises were hived off from their parent regulatory bodies. Greater operational autonomy in the hands of SOE managers created agency slack that could be exploited in dealing with their ostensible overseers in government. While SOE managers could no longer take unqualified state support for granted (indeed many of the weaker state enterprises were sold off or merged out of existence in the early years of reform), they obtained greater freedom to pursue their own interests. Thus, as Curtis J. Milhaupt and Wentong Zheng stress in their contribution to this volume, state "ownership" of an SOE today should not be conflated with effective state *control* over the enterprise. Many SOEs have effectively become powerful interest-groups, writing the rules for the state rather than the other way around. Some SOEs have sufficient political clout to fend off or even disregard policies they find objectionable. Thus, although paternalism was fostered in the era of central planning, the reform era has created opportunities for Chinese SOEs to play the role of prodigal son.

Market-oriented reforms created more space for SOEs and their managers to pursue their own interests, but they also greatly complicated the commercial environment and the governance challenges facing these firms. For example, SOEs that listed shares on a stock exchange had a new set of "principals" in the form of public shareholders. The market environment for many SOEs became more competitive with the entry of private domestic and foreign firms. China's accession to the WTO created new obligations for SOEs to play by a more transparent and neutral set of rules consistent with universal regulatory norms. The strain of these new governance complexities, for the SOEs and for those working within China's underdeveloped legal institutions, created incentives for both sets of actors to cooperate in building the legal environment in areas such as

[5] Other examples include South Korea, Taiwan, Brazil, and Chile. For in-depth discussion of this point with reference to China, South Korea, and Chile, see Ronald J. Gilson & Curtis J. Milhaupt, *Economically Benevolent Dictators: Lessons for Developing Democracies*, 59 AM. J. COMP. L. 227 (2011).

antitrust and corporate law. Thus was formed yet another relationship between SOEs and the state in the realm of governance—one of partnership.

* * *

Thirty years removed from China's central planning era, SOEs today simultaneously serve multiple masters and no masters at all. They are integral to the ideological foundations of the socialist market economy, carry out some noncommercial (including political) functions, and operate under a mandate to preserve and increase state assets. Yet they also operate in markets as profit-seeking enterprises and have become formidable, semiautonomous actors in the political economy, pursuing business and legal strategies that may or may not be consistent with the public good. The confluence of these different forces has created a class of enterprises with a unique, multifaceted influence on the development of China's formal legal system, as we explore below.

II. SOE Advantages in Shaping Law

Chinese SOEs are not alone, of course, in seeking to influence the legal environment in which they operate. Large private firms in China exploit many of the same techniques as SOEs in seeking to capture state benefits.[6] Nor is it uncommon for firms outside China to seek influence in the legal process; lobbying and "revolving door" practices are ubiquitous in market economies. But owing to their provenance, Chinese SOEs enjoy some distinct, built-in advantages in influencing the legal system. It is here that the legacy of paternalism is manifest most clearly.

One such built-in advantage is ideological. According to classical Marxist theory, the economic base (the means and relations of production) determines the superstructure (institutions, politics, and culture). Public ownership of the means of production is considered the basis of the national economy and peoples' livelihoods, safeguarding the socialist system against changes in political and social relations that would be engendered in an economy organized around private capital. From this perspective, SOEs, particularly the central SOEs at the national level, are the economic foundation of the Chinese Communist Party's rule. Indeed, the Chinese constitution can be read to support this position. It provides that "the state upholds the basic economic system with public ownership remaining dominant" and declares that "the socialist economy with ownership by the whole people is the leading force in the national economy."[7] Private

---

[6] *See* Curtis J. Milhaupt and Wentong Zheng, Chapter 9 in this volume. Scott Kennedy, The Business of Lobbying in China (2008); Kellee S. Tsai, *Capitalists without a Class: Political Diversity among Private Entrepreneurs in China*, 38 Comp. Pol. Stud. 1130 (2005); Kellee S. Tsai, Capitalism without Democracy: The Private Sector in Contemporary China (2007).

[7] Constitution of the People's Republic of China arts. 6–7 (promulgated by the Nat'l People's Cong. Dec. 4, 1982).

enterprise is constitutionally relegated to the role of "complementing" the state sector.[8] Relying upon these provisions, some argue that it is "unconstitutional" to weaken the position of SOEs in the economy.[9] Exploiting these sentiments, supporters often resort to political rhetoric in defending SOE privileges, invoking "state security," "the dominant role of public ownership," and similar incantations connoting a unity of interests between SOEs and the collective good.[10]

A second built-in advantage is structural—close proximity to the state's lawmaking institutions. The economic reform process complicated, but did not eclipse, the role of SOEs in performing state functions; nor did it sever the human ties among China's managerial elite. As mentioned previously, a distinctive feature of the environment in which Chinese SOEs operate is the extensive "institutional bridges" linking SOEs to other organs of the Party-state, such as Party Congresses and Party schools, People's Congresses, and even universities. These institutional bridges, constructed through the *nomenklatura* appointment system and personnel rotation practices of the Chinese Communist Party, bring the SOEs and their managerial elites into close contact with governmental and party organs responsible for policy formulation and enforcement. Through these personnel practices top managers in the SOE realm often simultaneously play, or have played, roles in public governance. As explored in the next section, incumbency and connections provide broad pathways for SOE influence in the legislative, regulatory, and even judicial spheres.

State largess, a principal byproduct of these built-in advantages, serves to reinforce the privileged position of SOEs in the political economy. A hallmark example is found in the aftermath of the 2008–2009 financial crisis, in which the Chinese government pumped 4 trillion RMB of stimulus into the economy in the form of loans from state-owned banks, most of which went to SOEs. SOEs also enjoy numerous other benefits, such as free or below-market use of land, subsidies, favored access to the capital markets, and other state-granted favors.[11] To be sure, subsidies and privileged market access are also enjoyed by private enterprises that have attained proximity to the state and have mastered the dynamics of China's political economy.[12] But in order to grow and prosper, private firms in China typically must find ways to replicate the advantages

---

[8] *Id.*, art. 11.

[9] There are parallels here to recent ideological debates concerning legal protections for private property. *See* Kun Lunyan 昆仑岩, 为何国企只能加强不能削弱 (Why State-Owned Enterprises Can only Be Reinforced, Not Weakened), 中国企业报 (CHINA ENTERPRISES NEWS) (Apr. 1, 2014), http://www.sasac.gov.cn/n1180/n1271/n20515/n2697206/15843868.html.

[10] For examples in the context of the drafting of China's Anti-Monopoly Law, see 发言摘登: 反垄断法草案 (Selected Discussions on the Draft of Anti-Monopoly Law), 中国人大网 (THE PEOPLE'S CONG. OF CHINA WEB) (June 30, 2006), http://www.npc.gov.cn/npc/zt/2006-06/30/content_350218.htm.

[11] *See* HONG SHENG & NONG ZHAO, CHINA'S STATE-OWNED ENTERPRISES: NATURE, PERFORMANCE AND REFORM (2012).

[12] Milhaupt & Zheng, *supra* note 6.

that come naturally to SOEs by virtue of their close identification and relationship with the state.

III. SOEs and the Legal System

Thus far we have discussed the general advantages SOEs enjoy in the legal environment. We now provide a more detailed look at how SOEs interact with and influence the development of China's legal system. We begin by briefly reviewing some well-documented forms of influence and then provide analysis of an understudied phenomenon: SOE influence on the courts.

The influence of SOEs on the process of lawmaking, including the creation of administrative rules and regulations, is well known. Such influence takes two primary forms. First, under the command and control model SOEs were often one and the same with regulators: the Ministry of Coal for example, both regulated coal extraction and was in the business of coal extraction. Despite the corporatization of SOEs and the government restructuring in the 1990s that aimed to separate out regulatory functions from operational functions in many spheres, the model continues in place with SOEs in some cases still being responsible for drafting regulations governing their own actions. This is particularly the case in the context of major state monopolies, including electric power, tobacco, salt, and railways. Administrative functions of the Party-state also sometimes continue to be outsourced to SOEs, with SOEs left in charge of drafting five- year plans for particular industries.

The second mechanism through which SOEs exert influence is direct lobbying. As noted above, close access to the Party-state means that SOE voices are often powerful ones when it comes to creating laws and regulations. Hence as China's Anti-Monopoly Law moved through the legislative process it was repeatedly altered in ways that were beneficial to SOEs.[13] SOEs' influence is made more significant by the lack of civil society: there are often few, if any, voices arguing against SOE interests within the legislative process.

SOEs also at times devote extraordinary resources to maintaining and developing relationships with government officials and other influential actors in China's political

[13] Most notably, article 7, which provides that "with respect to the industries controlled by the state-owned economy and concerning the lifeline of national economy and national security or the industries implementing exclusive operation and sales according to law, the state protects the lawful business operations conducted by the business operators therein," was not included in the original draft of the law. The provision was added in response to concerns raised by SOEs and some NPC delegates. *See* Hu Kangsheng 胡康生, 全国人大法律委员会关于《中华人民共和国反垄断法 (草案) 》修改情况的汇报 (Report from the National People's Congress Law Committee on Revisions to the Draft of the PRC Anti-Monopoly Law), 中国人大网 (The People's Cong. of China Web) (June 24, 2007), http://www.npc.gov.cn/npc/zt/2007-06/24/content_1382614.htm.

economy. More than 1700 companies listed on the Shanghai Stock Exchange reported spending a combined total of more than 10 billion RMB on "entertainment expenses" in 2012, with the top ten spenders all being SOEs. In some cases such entertainment expenses significantly exceeded annual profits. It is almost certain that a significant portion of such expenses go to maintaining relationships with government officials and entities, including those in the legal system. The practice has resulted in some high-profile prosecutions of judges who were the recipients of such largess.[14]

SOEs have also proven themselves adept at simply avoiding the law entirely. Following the enactment of the 2007 Labor Contract Law, numerous SOEs used dispatched labor to avoid new provisions that granted significant protections to workers.[15] A report from the National People's Congress on the implementation of the law found that SOEs, and in particular central SOEs, have been the primary users of labor dispatching to avoid the provisions of the new law.[16] Other cases similarly show how SOEs are adept at ignoring rules and regulations. In 2010, for example, SASAC ordered all SOEs not engaged in the property business to exit the property market. The instruction was widely ignored, and a year later the number of SOEs involved in property development had actually increased by five.[17]

A. COURTS "SERVING THE GENERAL SITUATION"

Much less attention has been paid to how SOEs interact with the courts. The relationship of SOEs to the courts must be analyzed against the backdrop of the political and power structures in which Chinese courts operate. Courts in China have taken important steps in the direction of greater competence and authority, but they nevertheless function in a political system in which the Party plays the leading role. The relationship of courts to local authorities means that courts must also serve the goals and interests of the local Party-state in the jurisdictions in which they are located.

---

[14] Wu Min 吴敏 & Yin Cong 尹聪, 10家上市国企去年招待费超29亿 (10 Listed Companies Spent More than 2.9 Billion in Entertainment Fees Last Year), 新京报 (The New Beijing News) (May 13, 2013), http://www.bjnews.com.cn/finance/2013/05/13/263318.html.

[15] Labor dispatching refers to the process of using employment agencies to provide staff in order to avoid the creation of an employment relationship between a company and a worker. Reports have noted that in some enterprises in China as many as two-thirds of all employees are hired through labor dispatching.

[16] *See* 全国人大代表陈耀中：进一步规范劳务派遣用工制度 (National People's Congress Representative Chen Yaozhong: Further Regulate the System of Hiring Workers through Labor Dispatching), 中国人大网 (China People's Congress Web) (Jan. 12, 2009), http://www.npc.gov.cn/npc/zfjc/ldbhf/2009-01/12/content_1494094.htm.

[17] Shang Xi 尚希, "退房令"出台三年收效甚微 以房地产为主业央企不减反增 (Three Years after the "Order to Exit the Property Market" the Effect Is Minimal, the Number of Central SOEs Engaged in Real Estate as Primary Business Has Not Declined but Instead Has Increased), 每日经济新闻 (Nat'l Bus. Daily) (Apr. 9, 2013), http://www.nbd.com.cn/articles/2013-04-09/730464.html.

Recent scholarship has detailed how the central Party-state policy embraced a greater role for the courts in the 1980s and 1990s before retreating from the use of the courts in the 2000s.[18] This retreat from using court adjudication to resolve disputes stemmed in significant part from increased concern with social instability and with discomfort over using law to restrain the Party-state itself. Prior literature has largely focused on Party and state interaction with the courts, and has mostly overlooked the questions of how courts interact with SOEs and how the SOEs continue to influence (and in some cases stymie) court development. Likewise, although prior literature has looked at how SOEs lobby and help shape laws and rules, no prior literature has specifically examined SOE interaction with the courts.

1. Paternalism

Our discussion of paternalism above noted the ways in which the state traditionally managed SOEs and in which SOEs become part of state structure in China. In the context of the courts, this paternalistic relationship is manifest in direct influence on the courts to resolve cases in line with SOE (and thus state) interests. Rather than being a principal in this paternalistic relationship, as an arm of the state, courts are more often the recipient of pressure resulting from the interdependence of the state and SOEs.

The effect of paternalism is evident most clearly in local protectionism. Party-state interference in the courts in China serves both political and economic goals. Courts' dependence on local authorities for appointments and finances means that courts must yield when facing powerful local economic interests. This problem is made even more acute by local governments' often close links to local SOEs.

The finances and personnel of all local courts are subordinate to local authorities.[19] In practice local party committees control the power to recommend and appoint leading cadres in the judicial system. Because of this power structure and jurisdiction, courts are unable to resist interference from the local government on behalf of locally powerful economic interests. In cases involving such powerful economic interests, the determinations of local governments become the standards by which courts decide cases. Although not all powerful local economic actors are SOEs, many are.

Two examples highlight how the merging of state and SOE interests affects the courts. According to a report by two judges on the Zhengzhou Intermediate Court, there are 387 SOEs in Gongyi County in Henan Province subject to enforcement of a court decision. More than a hundred of these enterprises have been the beneficiary of specific normative documents or instructions from the local government granting special status or

---

[18] Carl Minzner, *China's Turn against Law*, 59 AM. J. COMP. L. 935, 937 (2011); Benjamin Liebman, *China's Law Stability Paradox*, DAEDALUS (2014).

[19] Recently announced reforms may alter this dynamic, but will take many years to implement. We discuss the potential impact of court reforms on SOE-court interactions below.

protection.[20] Once SOEs have received such "protected status," it becomes extremely difficult for courts to issue or enforce decisions contrary to the interests of such SOEs.

Another example comes from Shaanxi Province. In a dispute involving a corporation under the direct supervision of the Shaanxi Provincial Land and Minerals Bureau, the Shaanxi government wrote a letter to the Supreme People's Court (SPC) after the Shaanxi High People's Court issued a decision adverse to the government party. The Bureau had entered into contracts granting mining rights to two different entities that included overlapping sites. The prior grantee sued for breach of contract and won. The Bureau's secret letter to the SPC, subsequently leaked online, argued that the court should have held the contract void, that sustaining the Shaanxi High Court's decision would result in severe loss of state-owned property and a series of dire consequences, and that the decision would harm the stability and development prospects of Shaanxi Province. The SPC eventually remanded the case for further fact-finding; no further media accounts are available.[21] The Shaanxi case received widespread attention in the Chinese media, but most instances of intervention on behalf of locally powerful enterprises fly below the radar. Courts do not need to be told when to act in the interests of powerful local SOEs; judges are well aware of the possible negative consequences of issuing a decision contrary to local interests.

The problem is not only one of local protectionism. Courts also find it difficult to resist pressure from, or on behalf of, powerful national SOEs—the "national champions." Cases involving high-profile national SOEs are sensitive due to the very fact that they include a powerful SOE. In some cases, court instructions order lower courts not to accept cases brought against specific high-profile SOEs. In 2002, for example, the Jilin Province High People's Court instructed lower courts not to accept or to resolve any civil or commercial litigation brought against China Automotive Corporation, and to lift any existing liens imposed on the company.[22] The High Court also ordered lower courts to cease enforcement of any cases that had already been decided against a number of prominent SOEs, including Guangfa Bank, Guangdong International Trust and Investment Corporation, China Venturetech Investment Corporation, and Hainan Development Bank.

---

[20] An Shiyong 安士勇 & Wang Dong 王栋, 国有企业一个两难的选择 (SOEs—A Choice of Dilemma), 郑州市中级人民法院 (Zhengzhou Intermediate Ct.) (June 16, 2006), http://zzfy.hncourt.org/public/detail.php?id=6833.

[21] 陕西省政府致函施压最高法 称判决不利社会稳定 (Shannxi Province Government Wrote Letter to Pressure SPC Stating That Ruling Had Negative Effect on Social Stability), 凤凰网 (Fenghuang Web) (Aug. 2, 2010), http://news.ifeng.com/mainland/detail_2010_08/02/1869779_0.shtml.

[22] 吉林省高级人民法院关于印发《人民法院对部分纠纷不予主管的有关规定 （试行） 》的通知 (Notice of the Jilin Province High People's Court on the Issuance of "Provisions on Some Disputes Not to Be Handled by the People's Courts (for trial implementation)") (promulgated by Jilin High People's Court, Dec. 28, 2002), *available at* http://wendang.baidu.com/view/c38f755bbe23482fb4da4c5d.html.

Not all examples of courts refusing to accept cases involve SOE restructuring. Courts are often under extreme pressure to decide more routine civil cases in favor of SOEs. Hence courts will often put a thumb on the scale of defendant SOEs in labor cases. Some SOEs have also used defamation litigation to target critics; corporate plaintiffs in such cases win the majority of cases.[23] Likewise, He Xin and Yang Su have recently shown that individuals or private companies in civil litigation against SOEs have "a next-to-zero chance of winning any case."[24] Close links between People's Congress representatives and SOEs accentuate pressure on the courts either to decline to accept cases against SOEs or to resolve cases in favor of SOEs. SOE officials often serve as representatives in local or provincial People's Congresses and may be able to use such positions to influence court decisions. Courts at all levels pay particular attention to the approval rates on their annual work reports made to same-level peoples' congresses. Part of this process involves extensive communication between courts and National People's Congress (NPC) delegates when handling cases concerning SOEs, particularly where delegates are linked to the SOE or have expressed their views on a case. Courts are concerned that mishandling disputes involving powerful SOEs could directly affect the passage rates of their annual work reports. Judges, in particular court presidents and vice presidents, may also be concerned that issuing decisions contrary to the interests of SOEs or the views of People's Congress delegates may affect their careers.[25] For example, two Henan judges wrote of how the leader of one enterprise that was facing enforcement by a court organized workers to surround the court building, holding up banners attacking the court. The enterprise leader was a local People's Congress member. Court officials had to seek out the enterprise leader to discuss the matter, and he used his status as an NPC delegate to pressure the court to alter its decision.[26]

Another manifestation of the paternalistic relationship between SOEs and the courts is the practice of "enterprises holding court." Until recently a number of SOE-dominated industries maintained their own specialized courts. Most notable were the railway courts, forestry courts, and petroleum courts. Judges and other court employees in these court systems were employees of the enterprises in which the courts were located. In 2009, China adopted reforms to the railway police, procuracy, and court management system, shifting these functions into the state judicial system. The railway courts were placed under the management of the province or directly administered municipality in which they were located. In June 2012 the reform of the railway court system was

---

[23] Benjamin L. Liebman, *Innovation through Intimidation: An Empirical Account of Defamation Litigation in China*, 47 HARV. INT'L L.J. 33 (2006). Not all such plaintiffs are SOEs, but SOEs appear particularly likely to prevail in such cases.

[24] He Xin & Yang Su, *Do the "Haves" Come Out Ahead in Shanghai Courts?*, 10 J. EMPIRICAL LEGAL STUD. 120, 132 (2013).

[25] An & Wang, *supra* note 20.

[26] *Id.*

officially completed, bringing the courts fully within the judicial system. Yet it remains to be seen whether such reformed courts will in fact operate with autonomy from the railway industry. The courts continue to exist, and almost all court personnel continued in their positions after the reorganization. Most judges still have strong ties to the railway industry, and the courts continue to hear cases involving railways.[27]

China's petroleum courts—special courts overseeing offshore petroleum fields—likewise have been brought within the state court system in recent years. Yet the courts continue to serve the interests of SOEs. In 2009, the two petroleum courts of Liaohe in Liaoning Province were renamed the Liaohe People's Court and Liaohe Intermediate People's Court and were placed under the jurisdiction of the Liaoning High People's Court. The courts thus technically no longer answer to the SOE running the oil fields. Nevertheless, the jurisdictional area of the court remains the Liaohe Oil Fields operated by China National Petroleum Corporation (CNPC). All of the cases within the court relate primarily to this one SOE, their employees, and family members of such employees. Most court personnel serving in the court have continued to serve after the reform.[28] In one case, a judge at the court received an award for being a "model employee" from the Liaohe Oil Corporation's labor union, despite the fact that the court had already been separated from the corporation.[29] The court's website states that the Liaohe Oil Corporation is a "significant economic entity in the province" and that the court's mission is "to provide caring service to the enterprise."[30]

Despite reform to the railway and petroleum courts, the practice of enterprises running their own courts continues to be common in China. These include land reclamation and cultivation courts, forestry courts, courts for mining areas, the courts of the Xinjiang Construction Corp., development zone courts, and others. For example, Jilin Province still has eighteen forestry district basic-level courts, each apparently linked to a major forestry enterprise.[31] Nationally there are still many courts affiliated with land reclamation and cultivation bureaus, mining bureaus, and other courts overseen

[27] In general, the railway courts have jurisdiction over criminal and civil cases that arise on or are related to the railways. Appeals from the trial-level railway courts go to intermediate railway courts. *See* 最高人民法院关于铁路运输法院案件管辖范围的若干规定 (Several Provisions of the Supreme People's Court on the Jurisdiction of Railway Transportation Courts over Cases) (promulgated by the Sup. People's Ct., July 7, 2012), *available at* http://www.law-lib.com/law/law_view.asp?id=391674.

[28] 法院简介 (Court Overview), 中国法院网 (China Ct. Web) (Oct. 18, 2010), http://lnlhfy.chinacourt.org/public/more.php?LocationID=0201000000.

[29] 王玉芬同志被辽河油田公司工会评为 2010 年度"先进女职工" (Comrade Wang Yufen named 2010 "Pioneer Female Employee" by Liaohe Oil Corporation), 中国法院网 (China Ct. Web) (Mar. 17, 2011), http://lnlhzy.chinacourt.org/public/detail.php?id=27.

[30] 法院概况 (Court Overview), 中国法院网 (China Ct. Web) (Mar. 17, 2011), http://lnlhzy.chinacourt.org/public/detail.php?id=32.

[31] Zhou Bin 周斌, 司法机构似企业"家丁"渐成历史 (The Practice of Judicial Institutions Serving as Enterprise "Family Servants" Gradually Becomes History), 法制日报 (Legal Daily) (Feb. 6, 2012), http://www.legaldaily.com.cn/bm/content/2012/02/06/content_3334033.htm?node=20733.

by enterprises. The personnel of these courts are effectively appointed and managed by the relevant administrative department or enterprise itself.[32] It is thus difficult to avoid the problem of departmental protectionism and enterprise protectionism. Although these courts are generally located in enterprises with paternalistic relationships to the state and are largely legacies of the planned-economy era, their persistence to the present day demonstrates the difficulty of fully separating courts from powerful SOEs, as well as the challenges courts face in attempting to serve as neutral arbiters in disputes involving SOEs.

Most examples of the paternalistic relationship between SOEs and the state involve SOEs assuming the role of Party-state and influencing court decision-making. In such situations, SOEs act like other Party-state entities that routinely exert pressure and influence on courts. Yet paternalism can also result in SOEs playing roles as arms of the state in dispute resolution. In the 2000s, China devoted enormous resources to "stability maintenance work," so as to minimize and resolve conflict and disputes before they escalated. As part of this effort, numerous SOEs established "stability maintenance offices" that still serve as extensions of the Party-state stability maintenance apparatus.[33]

Due to the significance of SOEs in China's overall economic and political structure, Party and government authorities view them as providing a form of protection for social and political stability. As a result, some degree of political influence on the courts is inevitable when dealing with SOE-related cases. SOEs exert influence on corporate litigation both through action (courts deciding cases in ways favorable to SOEs) and inaction (courts refusing to accept cases against SOEs). Official court rhetoric has made clear that courts are often ill-equipped to handle disputes concerning SOEs and other important Party-state institutions. As former SPC president Wang Shengjun stated, "Cases involving Party-state entities, the military, SOEs, reformed enterprises, enterprises facing special difficulties, hospitals, universities and other special entities are difficult to enforce because of restrictions resulting from various sources."[34]

Scholars of the Chinese courts have long observed that courts faced with cases involving core or even minor Party-state interests find it extremely difficult to play neutral roles. A key insight gained from examining developments over the last decade is that major SOEs—including both central SOEs and important local SOEs—are defined as

[32] For general criticism of enterprise courts, see Wang Doudou 王斗斗，铁路林业农垦法院体制不顺运转困难 (The Railway, Forestry, and Land Reclamation and Cultivation Court Systems Are Having a Hard Time Transitioning), 法制日报 (LEGAL DAILY) (Mar. 5, 2009), http://www.legaldaily.com.cn/bm/content/2009-03/05/content_1047439.htm?node=9.

[33] Benjamin L. Liebman, *China's Law-Stability Paradox, in* CHINA'S CHALLENGES: THE ROAD AHEAD 96 (Jacques deLisle & Avery Goldstein eds., 2014).

[34] 最高人民法院关于加强民事执行工作维护法制权威和司法公正情况的报告 (SPC Report on Strengthening Civil Enforcement Work, Maintaining Courts' Authority, and Judicial Fairness), 中国人大网 (THE PEOPLE'S CONG. OF CHINA WEB) (Oct. 28, 2009), http://www.npc.gov.cn/npc/xinwen/jdgz/bgjy/2009-10/28/content_1524149.htm.

being a part of core Party-state interests. This has occurred even as SOEs have ostensibly undergone significant reforms designed to expose them to market forces and increase their commercial orientation.

2. Prodigal Son

The prodigal son model of SOE-state interaction is also manifest in the courts, primarily through SOE disregard for court judgments. Court leaders have repeatedly commented on the difficulty of enforcing judgments against SOEs. The prodigal son relationship is interrelated with the other forms of SOE-court interactions: SOEs may seek to influence courts or to convince courts not to accept cases, at the same time as they simply disregard court actions. Yet SOE disregard for the courts continues to be a discrete form of behavior that reflects the long-protected status of SOEs and the traditionally weak status of courts in the Chinese system.

The SPC has created a database designed to track the most egregious cases of unenforceable decisions. Central SOEs made up a large portion of the companies with unenforced decisions. Of the 276 records on the list in late 2014, eighty-nine of the unenforced judgments were against China People's Property Insurance Company, and twenty-six were against subsidiaries of the China Railways Group.[35] A report by one local court in Jiangxi regarding unenforced decisions through 2009 showed that although only 17 percent of all unenforceable decisions were against SOEs, those cases constituted more than 50 percent of the total monetary value of unenforced decisions.[36]

Corruption is also a manifestation of SOEs acting as prodigal sons. Academic research has revealed that entertainment and travel costs comprise 1.65 percent of total expenditures of SOEs, much higher than the corresponding figure for private or foreign enterprises. A substantial portion of these funds is spent on maintaining relationships with government, courts, and other public institutions. Corruption is also known to be a significant factor in court decision-making. The legacy of SOEs ignoring laws—acting as a prodigal son—appears likely to accentuate the corruption problem. Understanding that corruption is a manifestation of the prodigal son model also suggests that the recent anticorruption campaign may have only limited long-term effect absent a fundamental restructuring of the relationships between SOEs and the state.

What we term the "prodigal son problem" may provide a benchmark for assessing the effectiveness of proposed reforms to China's courts. Pilot reforms in Shanghai and six other jurisdictions are designed to address the pervasive impact of local protectionism

---

[35] Calculated from 全国法院失信被执行人名单信息公布与查询平台 (National Court Database for Publishing and Searching Persons Who Have Failed to Enforce Decisions), 中华人民共和国最高人民法院 (SUP. PEOPLE'S CT.), (last visited June 6, 2015), *available at* http://shixin.court.gov.cn/index.html.

[36] He Fangyu 何方瑜, 关于解决"执行难"问题的调查报告 (Investigative Report on Resolving Difficulties in Enforcement), 九江法院网 (JIUJIANG CT. WEB) (Mar. 4, 2010), http://jjzy.chinacourt.org/public/detail.php?id=14534.

by centralizing appointments and court finances at the high-court (provincial) level. Yet centralizing appointments and finances may be far easier than actually increasing court authority over other Party-state actors. Whether courts in Shanghai and other jurisdictions that have been selected as pilot sites are able to overcome the problems resulting from both paternalism and prodigal son behavior may indicate whether courts are able to transition themselves from being targets of influence into sources of autonomous decision-making.

3. Partnership

Although paternalism continues to play a strong role in court-SOE relations, courts in the reform era have also sought to develop partnership relationships with SOEs. Court facilitation of SOE development has emerged as a key feature of court-SOE interactions over the past fifteen years. This is seen most clearly through courts' issuance of normative documents that emphasize facilitating SOE development and stability.

Courts are not mere recipients of SOE influence; courts have also been proactive in assisting SOEs. The SPC has prohibited local courts from the practice of "escorting the emperor,"[37] or treating SOEs differently from other litigants, and has emphasized that courts should determine cases based on legal principles, not the status of the litigants. Nevertheless, courts have continued to take numerous measures clearly designed to benefit SOEs. When local courts are enthusiastic in serving the interests of SOE reform, they sometimes even win praise and awards from the state.[38] Similarly, when an SOE or government-supported private business in the locality is involved in a dispute, local courts are more likely to assert jurisdiction and refuse to permit the parties to litigate in other venues.

The clearest examples of such emerging partnership relationships have been instructions issued by courts regarding how to handle cases involving SOEs, in particular those facing economic distress or undergoing restructuring. At the national level, the SPC has issued numerous documents instructing courts not to accept cases brought by SOEs concerning the reallocation of assets of SOEs undergoing reform.[39] The SPC has instructed

---

[37] *See* 最高人民法院执行工作办公室副主任葛行军在全国部分高级法院执行局局长座谈会上的总结讲话 (Concluding Remarks from the Deputy Director of the SPC Enforcement Office Ge Xingjun during Meeting of Certain Provincial High Court Enforcement Office Chiefs), 北大法律信息网 (CHINA LAW INFO) (Jan. 25, 2002), http://www.pkulaw.cn/fulltext form.aspx?gid=127244.

[38] For example, the Party Secretary of Jiangxi Province issued a notice praising the work of the Provincial High Court in "protecting SOE reform according to law and supporting SOE reform." *See* 能动司法到位服务 全省法院为国企改革助力 (Judicial Activism Provides Full Service, All of the Province's Courts Assist SOE Reforms), 江西日报 (JIANGXI DAILY) (Dec. 7, 2009), http://www.jxnews.com.cn/jxrb/system/2009/12/07/011262015.shtml.

[39] 最高人民法院关于因政府调整划转企业国有资产引起的纠纷是否受理问题的批复 (Reply of the Supreme People's Court on the Question of Whether or Not to Accept Disputes Involving the Adjustment and Transfer of State Owned Enterprises and Assets by Government) (promulgated by the Sup. People's Ct., Apr. 2, 1996), *available at* http://www.law-lib.com/law/law_view.asp?id=12288.

courts handling cases involving SOE debts to "deeply understand[] the important position of the state economy and the basic contents and rules of a socialist market economy," and thus to be "careful about protection of state assets,"[40] and has instructed courts not to accept certain cases involving SOE debts.[41] In the early 2000s, as many large SOEs underwent restructuring and were separated from their direct administrative supervisory agencies, the SPC issued instructions stating that local courts should not accept litigation challenging the distribution of assets or otherwise arising from the restructuring; such disputes were to be resolved by the relevant government departments.[42] Similar documents have been issued to courts regarding banks and the financial sector, in particular in regard to the division of assets between banks and asset management companies set up to dispose of bad debts.[43]

Other SPC directives have told courts that the allocated land-use rights of bankrupt enterprises should not constitute assets of the bankruptcy estate.[44] The SPC and provincial high courts have also instructed courts not to accept labor disputes resulting from state-directed restructuring.[45] Yet, while the SPC has told courts to be careful in

---

[40] 最高人民法院关于加强涉及国有大中型企业债权纠纷案件审判工作的通知 (Notice of the Supreme People's Court' on Strengthening Adjudication Work in Disputes Involving the Debts of Large and Medium-Sized State Owned Enterprises) (promulgated by the Sup. People's Ct., Apr. 12, 2002), *available at* http://policy.mofcom.gov.cn/blank/claw!fetch.action?id=g100000778&industrycode=S09431&secondcode=436002.

[41] 最高人民法院印发《关于审理涉及金融不良债权转让案件工作座谈会纪要》的通知 (Notice of the Supreme People's Court on Issuing the Summary of Minutes of the Meeting on Hearing Cases concerning Transfer of Distressed Debts Involving Financial Institutions) (promulgated by the Sup. People's Ct., Mar. 30, 2009), *available* at http://www.law-lib.com/law/law_view.asp?id=278487.

[42] *See* 最高人民法院关于审理与企业改制相关的民事纠纷案件若干问题的规定 (Supreme People's Court's Provisions on Some Issues Concerning the Trial of Civil Dispute Cases Relating to the Restructuring of Enterprises) (promulgated by the Sup. People's Ct., Jan. 3, 2003), *available at* http://www.law-lib.com/law/law_view.asp?id=42417; 最高人民法院关于因政府调整划转企业国有资产引起的纠纷是否受理问题的批复, *supra* note 39. Provincial courts have issued similar notices. 广西壮族自治区高级人民法院关于当前暂不受理几类案件的通知 (Notice of the High People's Court of Guangxi on the Current Temporary Non-acceptance of Certain Types of Cases) (promulgated by the High People's Ct. of Guangxi, Sept. 2003), *available at* http://www.law-lib.com/fzdt/newshtml/yjdt/20040824100627.htm.

[43] 最高人民法院关于人民法院是否受理金融资产管理公司与国有商业银行就政策性金融资产转让协议发生的纠纷问题的答复 (Reply of the Supreme People's Court on Whether or Not the People's Courts Shall Accept Disputes between Financial Asset Management Companies and State-Owned Commercial Banks over Agreements on the Assignment of Policy Financial Assets) (promulgated by the Sup. People's Ct., June 17, 2005), *available at* http://www.fdi.gov.cn/1800000121_23_66679_0_7.html.

[44] 最高人民法院关于破产企业国有划拨土地使用权应否列入破产财产等问题的批复(Approval of the Supreme People's Court on Questions Such as Whether the Right to Use Allocated State-Owned Land of a Bankrupt Enterprise Shall Be Considered to Be Insolvent Property) (promulgated by the Sup. People's Ct., Apr. 16, 2003), *available at* http://www.mlr.gov.cn/zwgk/flfg/sfjs/200601/t20060119_642187.htm.

[45] *See* section 3 of 最高人民法院关于审理与企业改制相关的民事纠纷案件若干问题的规定 (Supreme People's Court Regulations on Certain Issues Related to Hearing Civil Disputes Arising from Enterprise Restructuring)(promulgated by the Sup. People's Ct., Jan. 3, 2003), http://www.chinalawedu.com/news/1200/22598/22599/22630/2006/3/ya6003475227173600216644-0.htm; *see also* section 1 of 广东省高级人民法院关于审理劳动争议案件若干问题的指导意见 (Guiding Opinion of the Guangdong High People's Court on Certain Issues in Trying Labor Dispute Cases) (promulgated by the Guangdong High People's Ct., Sept. 15,

accepting claims against SOEs, it has also told lower courts "strictly to adhere to the law" in enforcing SOE debt claims against other parties.[46]

In 2009 the SPC issued two general documents that appeared to speak directly to the need to take account of the special status of SOEs. In the first, the SPC set forth the need for courts to uphold and preserve "the security and stability of the national economy" by "further strengthening their political ideology, their consciousness of the full situation, their consciousness regarding their responsibility and their consciousness regarding safeguarding."[47] In the second document the Court spoke more directly to the needs of SOEs and the obligation of courts to work to support SOE development:

> In situations where the enforcement of a judgment against a major SOE, financial entity, listed company or state-controlled enterprise might result in the bankruptcy of such company or might influence social stability, courts may on their own coordinate with the relevant supervisory organization of such entity in order to obtain comprehensive consideration and to assist the enterprise in resolving its debts, so as to avoid influencing the long term and steady development of the enterprise.[48]

Provincial high courts and lower courts have likewise instructed lower courts in their jurisdictions to adopt flexible approaches to handling cases involving SOEs. An intermediate court in Henan, for example, instructed local courts that "the people's courts are an important force in pushing forward the reform of SOEs," and thus that courts trying cases arising out of reform to SOEs "should take account of and approach cases from the perspective of taking account of the general situation and providing justice for the people,"[49] indicating that courts should be flexible in cases involving SOE interests. The document also stated that courts should mediate disputes so as to maintain both "social stability and enterprise stability" and should act in a manner that does not affect the functioning of enterprises. Such instructions reflect court efforts to position

---

2002), *available at* http://www.gdcourts.gov.cn/gdcourt/front/front!content.action?lmdm=LM113&gjid=20131118103912838645; 吕为民与湛江广州湾华侨宾馆有限公司劳动争议纠纷申请再审案 (Labor Dispute Application for Rehearing Case between Lu Weimin and Zhanjiang Guangzhouwan Overseas Chinese Hotel LLC), 粤高法民一申字第410号 (Guangdong High People's Court Civ. Retrial Petition) (Mar. 20, 2012) (China Law Info).

[46] 最高人民法院关于加强涉及国有大中型企业债权纠纷案件审判工作的通知, *supra* note 40.

[47] 最高人民法院印发《关于审理涉及金融不良债权转让案件工作座谈会纪要》的通知, *supra* note 41.

[48] 最高人民法院关于应对国际金融危机做好当前执行工作的若干意见 (Views of the Supreme People's Court on Responding to the International Financial Crisis by Doing a Good Job in Current Enforcement Work) (promulgated by the Sup. People's Ct., May 25, 2009), *available at* http://old.chinacourt.org/html/article/200906/08/359957.shtml.

[49] 鹰潭市中级人民法院关于为深化和完善市直国有企业改革提供法律服务的工作意见 (Yingtan Intermediate People's Court's Views on Providing Legal Services for Deepening and Perfecting Municipal State-Owned Enterprise Reform) (promulgated by Yingtan Intermediate People's Ct., Sept. 7, 2010), *available at* http://ytzy.chinacourt.org/public/detail.php?id=1384.

themselves as team players working with other Party-state entities (including SOEs) to maintain social stability and economic development. Numerous other provincial high courts have issued similar documents. The Guangdong High People's Court instructed local courts not to accept cases brought by workers laid-off due to enterprise restructuring,[50] the Jilin High Court instructed courts not to accept cases brought against certain key enterprises,[51] the Shaanxi High Court instructed courts not to accept cases relating to the debts of SOEs,[52] and the Jiangsu High Court instructed courts in Jiangsu not to take enforcement action without prior approval against certain major SOEs (or listed companies).[53]

Court efforts to facilitate SOE development are not limited to refusing to accept cases that could result in adverse outcomes for SOEs. Courts also have sought proactively to work with SOEs by entering into partnership relationships with them. These "court-enterprise joint sponsored" relationships often are formed under the guise of "SOE legal construction" or "legal education," in which courts carry out "sending law to the enterprises" campaigns.[54] For example, the NPC Standing Committee has enacted six "Five-Year Legal Education plans" since 1986. Five of these focused on enterprises, requiring courts on their own initiative to carry out legal education at SOEs. In this way, courts and SOEs create an informal social network.[55] The SPC has also recently entered into a memorandum of understanding with five of China's biggest banks, all major SOEs, regarding the creation of a direct network between the courts and the banks to facilitate the freezing or seizure of assets subject to the enforcement of court judgments.[56]

---

[50] 广东省高级人民法院审理劳动争议若干问题的指导意见, *supra* note 45.

[51] 吉林省高级人民法院关于印发《人民法院对部分纠纷不予主管的有关规定(试行)》的通知, *supra* note 22.

[52] 陕西省高级人民法院关于依法稳妥处理国有企业债务纠纷确保社会稳定的通知 (Notice of the Shaanxi High People's Court on Handling Debt Disputes Involving State Owned Enterprises in Order to Ensure Social Stability According to Law (promulgated by Shaanxi High People's Ct., July 26, 2007), *available at* http://www.sxgz.gov.cn/admin/pub_newsshow.asp?id=1000963&chid=100124.

[53] *See* section 9 of 江苏省高级人民法院关于在当前宏观经济形势下切实做好涉及企业、民生案件执行工作的指导意见 (Jiangsu High People's Court Guiding Opinion on How to Effectively Handle Cases Involving Enterprises and People's Livelihood in the Current Macroeconomic Climate) (promulgated by Jiangsu High People's Ct., Apr. 20, 2009), *available at* http://wenku.baidu.com/view/56ef50d2240c844769eaee89.

[54] Wang Haisheng 王海声, 启动"送法进国企"活动 ("Sending Law to the Enterprises" Campaigns Launched), 检查日报 (Procuratorate Daily) (Aug. 2, 2014), http://newspaper.jcrb.com/html/2014-08/02/content_165132.htm; Fan Sitan 樊斯坦 & Wu Tao 吴涛, 汉江中院送法到国企 (Hanjiang Intermediate Court Sends Law to SOEs), 湖北法院网 (Hubei Ct. Web) (May 20, 2009), http://hubeigy.chinacourt.org/public/detail.php?id=13273.

[55] The SPC's plan spoke of enterprises generally, not just SOEs. But it is clear that SOEs would be a key partner in any such efforts.

[56] Xu Juan 徐隽, 银行法院联手治"老赖" 共享失信被执行人名单信息 (Banks and Courts Work Together, Sharing Information on the Names of Defaulting Debtors), 人民日报 (People's Daily) (Aug. 31, 2013), http://finance.chinanews.com/fortune/2013/08-31/5228862.shtml.

The close working relationship between courts and SOEs is not surprising given the pervasive influence local authorities have on courts. The influence of SOEs on courts also reflects the weak institutional position of Chinese courts within the Party-state, and also perhaps a lack of expertise among court personnel. SOE-court relations may also be in part due to the fact that at least some senior court officials have work experience in the SOE system. Unlike ordinary judges, who are required to have passed China's unified bar exam, court presidents often lack legal training and are selected for their political background. A limited review of the court presidents and vice presidents of China's provincial-level high peoples' courts shows eight instances in which court websites list prior work experience in SOEs. Because biographical information on websites is often incomplete, the actual number is likely higher. Similarly, many judges who step down from their positions at courts to "jump into the sea" of the labor market wind up at SOEs, including some high-profile former senior judges.[57] With large numbers of judges leaving their court positions in recent years, the effect is potentially substantial.[58]

IV. Implications

In October 2014 the Central Committee of the Communist Party issued its most wide-ranging statement regarding legal reform since the beginning of legal reforms in 1978. The Fourth Plenum Decision ("Decision") sets forth a broad roadmap for legal reform under the continued leadership of the Communist Party.[59] Although the document does speak briefly of the need for greater emphasis on training of legal workers in enterprises, it does not specifically address the impact of SOEs on the courts. Some of the specific provisions in the Decision may be understood as having the potential to reduce SOE influence, most notably a renewed focus on limiting various forms of external interference in court decision-making. At the same time, however, the Decision reaffirms the significance of considering social effects of court decisions. Although important, the Decision will take years to implement. It also makes clear that no fundamental shift in the role the Party plays overseeing the legal system is contemplated; the focus instead is on Party self-restraint and increased legalization within the Party. Such reforms seem unlikely to grant courts significant new authority or autonomy. Indeed a key insight from our conceptual model of SOE behavior is that limited technical reforms in the

[57] General Counsels of numerous major SOEs have previously served as judges. Ma Li 马丽, 法官"变身"法务官再定位 (Judges "Changing Roles" into Legal Advisors), 法制日报 (Legal Daily) (Sept. 9, 2014), http://www.legaldaily.com.cn/xwzx/content/2014-09/09/content_5754360.htm.

[58] For discussion of the problem of judges resigning from their posts more generally, see Chen Lei 陈磊, 法官在流失 (Judges Are Leaving Their Positions), 法制周末 (Legal Wkly.) (Sept. 24, 2013), http://www.legalweekly.cn/index.php/Index/article/id/3648.

[59] 中共中央关于全面推进依法治国若干重大问题的决定 (CCP Central Committee Decision concerning Several Major Issues in Comprehensively Advancing Governance according to Law), 新华网 (Xinhua Net) (Oct. 28, 2014), http://news.xinhuanet.com/politics/2014-10/28/c_1113015330.htm.

courts are unlikely to break the interdependence of SOEs and the legal system. Solving many of the problems in the Chinese legal system requires addressing structural problems in governance and the economy.

A central question facing legal reform in China over the past thirty-seven years has been whether law and legal institutions can provide a level playing field to the full range of economic and individual actors in Chinese society. Evidence from the influence of SOEs on the legal system suggests that, despite significant progress in constructing a legal system, the playing field remains fundamentally tilted in favor of SOEs. How SOEs are treated in the current wave of reform, both economic and legal, will go a long way to informing whether legal institutions are able to play a more neutral role.

In an earlier phase of China's development, particularly in the early years of transition out of central planning, SOEs may have partially compensated for limited state governance capacity. In the absence of structures for economic regulation, and with private enterprise at a nascent stage, relying upon SOEs to serve the dual roles of economic planning and administration and production may have been a sensible default arrangement. China is not the first country to use close connections between political leaders and favored business leaders to provide a "big push" for economic development at a time when the formal institutions of state governance are weak. Thus, as with the experiences of several other twentieth-century economic miracle countries, China's recent history casts doubt on the conventional wisdom that a "rule of law" featuring transparently developed, evenly enforced regulations and courts functioning as neutral arbiters is an essential precondition to economic development.

Yet despite massive transformation of the Chinese economy in the ensuing decades, SOEs remain deeply intertwined in the structures of public governance in China. They continue to receive special treatment across a range of tax, antitrust, and other regulatory domains, and they are recipients of massive state largess, ostensibly on the ground that they are the foundation of China's socialist market economy. SOEs have a built-in seat at China's legislative and deliberative bodies, and exert extensive influence on the courts. Today, Chinese SOEs look and act not like engines of development in an institutional vacuum, but like the interest groups Mancur Olson famously analogized to barnacles on a ship's hull, accumulating over time and slowing a nation's economic progress.[60] Three decades into China's economic reforms, SOEs constitute a major obstacle to the development of robust state governance capacity.[61]

[60] Macur Olson, The Rise and Decline of Nations (1982).

[61] The seeming rejection of law as a mechanism for regulating SOEs today despite the major reforms to the state sector in the 1990s has parallels with what Carl Minzner has called China's "turn against law." This is a politically motivated "rollback against late twentieth century legal reforms" that "conceptualized law as an institution for resolving civil grievances between citizens and as a tool for limiting government power." Minzner, *supra* note 18, at 972–74.

Examining the mechanisms through which SOEs affect the legal system, and in particular dispute resolution, highlights the challenges China faces both in reinvigorating legal reform and in progressing toward a truly market-oriented economy. Reducing the influence of the state sector on Chinese law and legal institutions is an essential step toward the creation of a sound institutional framework for sustainable development. Doing so, however, is not simply a question of reforming China's courts or injecting more private capital into SOEs, the current focus of the Party's attention, but requires nothing less than a fundamental reordering of the relationship between SOEs and other Party-state organs, including the courts and legislative bodies.

11 The Social Relations of Chinese State Capitalism

Mary E. Gallagher

STATE CAPITALISM AS a concept was revived after the 2008 Global Financial Crisis when the state of free market, "neoliberal" capitalism was at its nadir. The Chinese government responded to the crisis with a massive stimulus program, averting more severe effects domestically and allowing the Chinese economy to recover. As Europe and the United States languished in prolonged recessions, China's economy expanded further into other markets, capitalizing on opportunities to invest in new markets abroad. Its state-owned "national champions" projected their growing financial power overseas and domestically. 2008 marked the resurgence of China's state sector, which was virtually insolvent only a decade earlier. It was the era of "the state advances, while the private retreats" (*guojin mintui*).[1]

Even before this critical year, however, a wide-ranging debate about the nature of the Chinese economy had raged. Is China a market economy, as its government claims, or is China's economy increasingly state-dominated, managed by technocrats in the government and the ruling Chinese Communist Party (CCP)? Is China's success due to the "bottom-up" power of its farmers, entrepreneurs, and growth-oriented local

---

[1] Michael Wines, *China Fortifies State Businesses To Fuel Growth*, N.Y. TIMES, Aug. 29, 2010, *available at* http://www.nytimes.com/2010/08/30/world/asia/30china.html?pagewanted=all.

bureaucrats?[2] Or is the Chinese model defined by top-down corporate management of a developmentalist political party now focused on ruling rather than revolution?[3] The moniker "state capitalism" is an apt shorthand way to capture the contradictions of China's current economic system. It is both state-dominated and attuned to markets. Unlike socialist regimes of the last century, state capitalist regimes do not pursue revolutionary goals to throw off the current system, nor are they aspirational in moving toward the utopian future of communism. If there is an ideology behind state capitalism, it is simply a commitment to state power and national development, the attainment of "wealth and power" at the national level. Insomuch as markets contribute to those goals, they are perfectly adequate tools, but they are not the only tools. Moreover, there exists no philosophical or ethical commitment to markets as institutions; it is a pragmatic embrace of markets. When they fail to work, or work against the interests of ruling elites, alternative modes of governance and organization are deployed.

China's economy also possesses the general characteristics emblematic of the current iteration of state capitalism.[4] According to Ian Bremmer, these "intermediary institutions" are national oil companies (NOCs), state-owned enterprises (SOEs) in other strategic industries, sovereign wealth funds (SWFs), and privately owned national champions, which are private (or privatized) firms that cultivate and benefit from strong ties with their national governments. China continues to cultivate and protect a state sector core that monopolizes strategic sectors of the economy and bank credit. As Lin and Milhaupt show, the central government has strengthened control over large SOEs, concentrated management through the creation of the State-owned Assets Supervision and Administration Commission (SASAC), and managed personnel issues in ways that contribute to the state's long-term economic goals.[5] At the same time, however, the state has allowed for greater levels of competition and oversight from other actors. Since the late 1990s, the central government has pursued fundamental changes to the system of state ownership, reducing the state's overall ownership of enterprises in a significant way, but maintaining and even strengthening ownership in key strategic sectors. In these sectors, the state has attempted to create state-owned national champions that monopolize the domestic markets through preferential policies and restrictions on entry, but that also become competitive globally through state support, technocratic management, and external competition.[6] Since 2007, China's sovereign wealth

---

[2] Victor Nee & Sonja Opper, Capitalism from Below: Markets and Institutional Change in China 32–38 (2012).

[3] *See, e.g.*, Yasheng Huang, Capitalism with Chinese Characteristics: Entrepreneurship and the State (2008).

[4] Ian Bremmer, The End of the Free Market: Who Wins the War between States and Corporations? 54 (2011).

[5] Li-Wen Lin & Curtis J. Milhaupt, *We Are the (National) Champions: Understanding the Mechanisms of State Capitalism in China*, 65 Stan. L. Rev. 697 (2013).

[6] Peter Nolan, Chinese Firms, Global Firms: Industrial Policy in the Age of Globalization 51 (2014).

fund has extended China's investment influence into developed and developing countries alike.[7] According to Bremmer's criteria, China's state capitalist credentials are indisputable.

Despite the revival of research on state capitalism, the domestic foundations of state capitalism are poorly understood, even ignored. Although Bremmer and other analysts note that state capitalism is associated with political illiberalism, there is little inquiry into how these authoritarian regimes maintain power at home. State capitalism is not integrated into research on authoritarianism, either as a descriptive ideal type or as a theoretical concept applied to the political economy of autocracy. While the study of authoritarian regimes enjoys a renaissance of sorts in political science, current research in comparative politics on authoritarian regime survival and resilience focuses on the political institutions of regime endurance, marginalizing the economic institutions that also may contribute to longevity. In other words, the policy debate on state capitalism neglects the domestic dynamics of authoritarian political survival, while the academic debate on authoritarian political survival ignores the role that state capitalism may play in shoring up illiberal regimes.

In this chapter, I explore the domestic configuration of state capitalism in China. Through a discussion of China's labor legislation and labor market institutions over the reform period, I argue that China has thus far successfully maintained a balance between two contradictory impulses: statist control and market competition. However, the state has not adopted a stable set of institutions to manage this balance; instead, the government has reacted dynamically to China's social and economic transformation during a period of extremely rapid growth. This adaptive quality of Chinese governance is thought to contribute to the staying power of the regime and its ability thus far to manage the challenges of power projection abroad and state capitalism at home.[8]

I focus on three main areas that demonstrate the state's adaptation over time: (1) market versus regulatory mechanisms to manage labor, (2) exclusionary versus inclusionary modes of social welfare, and (3) a detached versus embedded role of the state in social conflict. The state's approach to labor issues has evolved over the reform period, shifting from a detached state relying on market mechanisms to a more embedded state relying on regulation and direct intervention. The first period, from the advent of reform in 1978 to about 2003, was focused on the transition from socialism to capitalism. This period was defined by a heavy reliance on market mechanisms, exclusionary social policies, and a detached, reactive state. This period granted more power and flexibility to market mechanisms as the state withdrew its support for socialist institutions that managed labor and redistributed income and resources across the population. The state freed

---

[7] Stephen Thomas & Ji Chen, *China's Sovereign Wealth Funds: Origins, Development, and Future Roles*, 20 J. Contemp. China 467 (2011).

[8] Mao's Invisible Hand: The Political Foundations of Adaptive Governance in China 2–9 (Sebastian Heilmann & Elizabeth J. Perry eds., 2011).

up enterprises by granting them greater autonomy, and reduced the barriers to labor mobility and rural-to-urban migration.

The second wave, which parallels the increasing role of the state in the economy more generally, began around the start of the Hu-Wen administration in 2003 amid rising concerns over inequality, social stability and the long-term sustainability of China's development model. This wave was a swing back toward greater reliance on administrative and regulatory mechanisms, a more inclusionary approach to social welfare, and more embedded and involved management of labor conflict. Policies shifted as the state reacted to demographic changes, growing concerns over inequality and environmental degradation, and the related upsurge in social protests and violence. Ironically, as the state's commitment to capitalism and global markets has grown over time, the need to expand its political presence and capacity in managing society and social conflict has increased.

Although this chapter focuses on an analytical description of the social relations of state capitalism in China, this last point has important theoretical implications for our understanding of how markets work in state capitalist systems. The logic of state capitalism runs against the typical association of markets with increased freedom and autonomy. Instead we observe higher levels of state control and intervention. Although we should not ignore the consequences for political and civil freedoms, as increased state intervention involves higher levels of state coercion and repression, we should also note the welfare-enhancing possibilities of a state fearful of losing control. As is evident in the discussion below on more protective labor legislation and more inclusionary social insurance, the Chinese state has become more ambitious in its reach—both to control citizens and to co-opt them through social welfare and public goods provision.

The chapter proceeds as follows. I first situate my discussion of the domestic configuration of China's state capitalism within the study of authoritarian regimes. State capitalism as a concept has not been adequately theorized or integrated into the emerging literature on modern authoritarianism. The study of modern authoritarianism has focused on regime survival and resilience, with only glancing attention to the political economy of authoritarianism. Integrating analysis of the political economy of modern authoritarianism is needed, but the concept of state capitalism as deployed by political analysts and pundits remains mainly descriptive and superficially focused on those common institutions such as NOCs and SWFs that affect global markets and investment trends, with little research on other institutions that manage the domestic politics of state capitalism. Given that domestic political stability and regime survival are antecedents to the regime's projection of power abroad, it is critical to understand how state capitalist regimes manage domestic politics.

In order to better understand the internal components of China's state capitalism, I then turn to a discussion of its origins. China's embrace of state capitalism and its turn away from socialism go back to the lessons of the early reform period, when the rise of Japan and success of the East Asian Developmental State (EADS) in the "four tigers" (Taiwan, South Korea, Hong Kong, and Singapore) coincided with the failure of China's experiment with autarkic socialism. While China's specific mode of state capitalism has changed over the thirty-plus years of reform and has been reactive to the challenges that accompany such rapid socioeconomic change, its core characteristics remain rooted in the Chinese Communist Party's realization that it had been utterly surpassed by neighboring capitalist economies—some of them political entities long considered subordinate to or even part of imperial China.[9] China's neighboring "reference" states were absolutely critical in providing a roadmap for China's early reforms. Their geographical proximity and their own economic needs (especially rising wages at home) also facilitated China's early move toward export-oriented industrialization and labor-intensive manufacturing. Although China's current model of state capitalism is thus an amalgamation of EADS institutions and practices, it is not merely the East Asian developmental state redux. My focus here is on delineating the common principles behind the EADS and China's state capitalism.

In the third section, I turn back to the social relations of state capitalism as they pertain to China's labor market institutions and industrial relations. Although this discussion sheds light on the neglected connections between domestic social relations and China's ambitious pursuit of global economic power and influence, the domestic institutions of China's state capitalist regime are unlikely to be replicated by other late-developing countries whose leaders wish to combine market competition and political control. China's successful experiment with state capitalism does not equate to the existence of a "China model." China's experience with state socialism and the continued rule of the CCP gives it access to political and economic institutions that have fallen out of favor in other parts of the world, such as Leninist mass organizations, the integration of the Party and government, and control over personnel through the cadre evaluation system. China, unlike many state capitalist regimes that are reliant on resource wealth such as the Gulf States, is still fundamentally dependent on its global trading and investment links as well as a strong manufacturing sector that is predominantly not state owned. State capitalism regimes that enjoy large holdings of national resources and energy independence are likely to develop different institutional ties at home than those analyzed here. As Sergio Lazzarini and Also Musacchio demonstrate in Chapter 17 this volume, as with the varieties of capitalism,[10] there are also likely to be many varieties of state capitalism.

---

[9] One of the "tigers," Hong Kong, reverted to Chinese control in 1997. The PRC claims sovereignty over Taiwan as well, though this is not realized in practice.

[10] Varieties of Capitalism: The Institutional Foundations of Comparative Advantage (Peter A. Hall & David Soskice eds., 2001).

I. Liberal Economics, Illiberal Politics

The study of illiberal politics is something of a growth industry in contemporary political science. As the "low tide" of democracy's third wave exposed the failed, incomplete, and never-attempted democratic transitions of many regimes, political scientists jettisoned the "transition" lens that framed most studies of political development after the end of the Cold War.[11] The Arab Spring and various revolutions since then notwithstanding, the study of authoritarian regimes shifted to understanding how they work—and what mixture of institutions was more or less likely to lead to political survival.[12]

Much of the work done on contemporary authoritarianism focuses on political institutions that are normally associated with democracy and political liberalization. Works on electoral or competitive authoritarianism study how electoral systems are used and abused in illiberal regimes to strengthen one-party rule, co-opt elites, and channel voters into support for the status quo.[13] Works on the presence of legislatures in autocratic regimes similarly examine how institutions that foster participation and mobilization can be used effectively in illiberal regimes to structure politics, cultivate patron-client ties, and entangle potential opposition leaders in the ruling structure.[14] Finally, a smaller body of work has examined the strategic deployment of judicial institutions in authoritarian regimes not usually associated with the "rule of law."[15] Courts and the trappings of legality are used to promote foreign investment, economic growth, and the cultivation of domestic and international legitimacy.

---

[11] Jason M. Brownlee et al., *Low Tide after the Third Wave: Exploring Politics under Authoritarianism*, 34 Comp. Pol. 477 (2002).

[12] *See, e.g.*, Why Communism Did Not Collapse: Understanding Authoritarian Regime Resilience in Asia and Europe (Martin K. Dimitrov ed., 2013); Jason Brownlee, Authoritarianism in an Age of Democratization (2007); Eva Bellin, *The Robustness of Authoritarianism in the Middle East: Exceptionalism in Comparative Perspective*, 36 Comp. Pol. 139 (2004).

[13] *See, e.g.*, Steven Levitsky & Lucan Way, Competitive Authoritarianism: Hybrid Regimes after the Cold War (2010); Steven Levitsky & Lucan Way, *The Rise of Competitive Authoritarianism*, 13 J. Democracy 51 (2002); Electoral Authoritarianism: The Dynamics of Unfree Competition (Andreas Schedler ed., 2006); B. Magaloni, *Credible Power-Sharing and the Longevity of Authoritarian Rule*, 41 Comp. Pol. Stud. 715 (2008); Beatriz Magaloni, Voting for Autocracy: Hegemonic Party Survival and Its Demise in Mexico (2008).

[14] *See, e.g.*, J. Gandhi & A. Przeworski, *Authoritarian Institutions and the Survival of Autocrats*, 40 Comp. Pol. Stud. 1279 (2007); Jennifer Gandhi, Political Institutions under Dictatorship (2008); Beatriz Magaloni & Ruth Kricheli, *Political Order and One-Party Rule*, 13 Ann. Rev. Pol. Sci. 123 (2010).

[15] *See, e.g.*, Jothie Rajah, Authoritarian Rule of Law: Legislation, Discourse, and Legitimacy in Singapore (2012); Rule by Law: The Politics of Courts in Authoritarian Regimes (Tom Ginsburg & Tamir Moustafa eds., 2008); Yuhua Wang, Tying the Autocrat's Hands: The Rise of the Rule of Law in China (2015); Kathryn Hendley, *Suing the State in Russia*, 18 Post-Soviet Aff. 122 (2002); Kathryn Hendley, *"Telephone Law" and the "Rule of Law": The Russian Case*, 1 Hague J. Rule Law 241 (2009).

The adoption of institutions generally associated with democracy by autocratic regimes has been well noted. Less noted is the economic corollary of this trend: the pragmatic embrace of markets and globalization by regimes that previously trumpeted state socialism and autarkic development. What is the connection between democratic institutions in authoritarian regimes' political systems and market institutions in their economies? How do authoritarian leaders manage the risky adoption of institutions that could threaten their rule, empower new economic classes, and disrupt traditional power relations?

There are important synergies in the instrumental adoption of both capitalist and democratic institutions by autocracies, despite the risks. As I detail below in the third section, the Chinese state has used legality at the workplace to establish contractual relations between workers and firms, individualizing employees' connections to the workplace and eroding any vestiges of socialist collectivism and security. This authoritarian legality has been promoted through legislative advances that trumpet rule of law, workers' rights, and social protections. They foster a sense of political liberalization (toward a rights-based society) while also advancing the role of contracts and markets at the workplace, undermining the economic security that urban workers enjoyed under socialism. The injection of labor markets into the socialist workplace, which had relied on notions of permanent employment, was made possible via contracts and labor law.

The role of legislative institutions in mediating the social relations of state capitalism extends beyond the current literature's focus on authoritarian legislatures as arenas for elite cooptation. Although claims that these legislatures may be used as venues for bargaining and interest-sharing between the regime and its potential elite opposition have validity, the lawmaking that occurs in these legislatures has a larger role in structuring how the state engages, mobilizes, and represses ordinary citizens, whether as workers, consumers, or political actors. In state capitalist regimes that are reliant on investment, manufacturing, and global trade, the state cannot merely hope to repress citizens or co-opt small groups with side payments and private goods. Economic growth, employment promotion, and global economic competitiveness are all concerns that motivate state capitalist regimes to establish legislative and regulatory institutions to structure markets. The modus operandi of state capitalism is the calculated promotion of markets when they enhance the state's economic power. In the domestic politics of state capitalism, legislative institutions can insulate the state from social demands by using markets and regulation of markets to manage state-society relations and social cleavages in a less hands-on, interventionist way. As discussed in Section III, the early period of reform advanced pro-market labor legislation that expanded enterprise autonomy, increased flexibility, and enhanced the opportunities for workers at the higher end of the labor market (educated, skilled, urban workers). These reforms also reduced the obligations of the state and devolved much risk to individual workers, freed from the work-unit and left to fend for themselves in the marketplace.

As with many other modern authoritarian regimes, China has adopted the trappings of some democratic institutions, such as the rule of law and limited electoral competition, in order to improve its ability to govern and manage a modern economy. These are democratic institutions put to work for autocracy and to forestall pressure for deeper political change. China has, however, disavowed political competition outside of the Party, and maintains strict restrictions on social organizations that might challenge its organizing monopoly. It continues to rely on vestiges of state socialism and Leninism to enhance the stability of Party rule. In the labor realm, the CCP remains committed to the "Leninist transmission belt" model, allowing only the All-China Federation of Trade Unions (ACFTU) to exist in this space.[16] In some areas, such as legislation, the ACFTU plays a major role in shaping new laws and regulations.[17] But its representation of labor's interests on the shop floor is anemic as it is caught between divergent goals dictated by its subordinate position. The ACFTU is expected to assist the Party and government in realizing economic growth and development while serving as the representation of labor against capital.[18] The weakness of both labor and capital, organized via state-controlled bodies such as the ACFTU, China Enterprise Management Association (CEMA), and the All-China Federation of Industry and Commerce (ACFIC), is indicative of the state's reluctance to cede any political power to social actors, whether unions or business associations. Such weakness requires that the Party-state play the central role in mediating labor conflict. Embrace of labor markets on an individual level and regulation of labor market institutions via legislative interventions happen alongside the state's retrograde role as the arbiter of labor conflict. China exemplifies this new approach to autocratic rule, which mixes nominally democratic political institutions, market institutions, and older autocratic traditions of co-optation and control.

II. The East Asian Roots of China's State Capitalism

As China emerged from the Cultural Revolution, Deng Xiaoping and other reformist leaders looked abroad for models and aid in adjusting China's economy.[19] Close to

---

[16] Mary E. Gallagher, *Transformation without Transition: China's Maoist Legacies in Comparative Perspective*, *in* Working through the Past: Labor and Authoritarian Legacies in Comparative Perspective 197 (Teri L. Caraway, Maria Lorena Cook & Stephen Crowley eds, 2015).

[17] From Iron Rice Bowl to Informalization: Markets, Workers, and the State in a Changing China (Sarosh Kuruvilla, Ching Kwan Lee & Mary E. Gallagher eds., 2011).

[18] Feng Chen, *Individual Rights and Collective Rights: Labor's Predicament in China*, 40 Communist and Post-communist Stud. 59 (2007); Feng Chen, *Between the State and Labour: The Conflict of Chinese Trade Unions' Double Identity in Market Reform*, 176 China Q. 1006 (2003); Masaharu Hishida et al., China's Trade Unions: How Autonomous Are They?: A Survey of 1,811 Enterprise Union Chairpersons (2010).

[19] Ezra F. Vogel, Deng Xiaoping and the Transformation of China (2011); The China Circle: Economics and Electronics in the PRC, Taiwan, and Hong Kong (Barry Naughton ed., 1997).

home, the economies of Taiwan, Hong Kong, South Korea, and Japan were booming. Deng initiated a program that sent lower-level officials to other East Asian countries (though not Taiwan initially) to observe and study their pathways to modernization.[20] Ezra Vogel, in his study of Deng Xiaoping, found that Deng used these study tours to impress upon Chinese cadres how far China had fallen behind its neighbors. "In late 1978, Deng, summarizing the effect of the trips, happily reported, 'Recently our comrades had a look abroad. The more we see, the more we realize how backward we are.'"[21] China's opening-up program, which followed these tours, leveraged China's proximity to the East Asia boom by first opening up Special Economic Zones in provinces that faced out toward the capitalist economies of Hong Kong (Zhuhai, Shenzhen, Hainan) and Taiwan (Xiamen). In addition to attracting capital from its neighbors, PRC leaders also borrowed institutions and practices from what became known as the "East Asia Miracle" or the East Asian Developmental State (EADS) model.

Although the concept of the EADS is widely used to describe the development trajectories of these East Asian economies, there is little consensus on key issues, including whether developmental policies are the most important cause of the rapid growth experienced in post-WWII East Asia; whether a single "model" exists given the wide variation in actual policy between countries and across time; and finally, given the long-term stagnation of the Japanese economy since the 1990s and the catastrophic effects of the Asian Financial Crisis on some East Asian states, whether the EADS should be considered a successful model at all.[22] Recent considerations of the EADS have criticized previous work for descriptive "laundry lists" of attributes, failure to recognize key differences between different economies, and misspecification of the relationships between politicians and the bureaucracy, and between state and society.[23]

For my purposes here, these controversial issues can be put aside; nor is it necessary to draw up an exhaustive list of ways in which the Chinese economy has and has not borrowed from the East Asian developmental experience. The example of East Asian rapid growth and the different models that achieved this growth in Japan, Taiwan, South Korea, Singapore, and Hong Kong provided a menu of options for a growth-obsessed CCP leadership at the onset of reform. After the debacles of the Great Leap Forward

---

[20] As Vogel shows, Deng Xiaoping orchestrated a large number of foreign trips for Communist officials in the late 1970s, including two important trips to Japan and Hong Kong. VOGEL, *supra* note 19, at 218.

[21] *Id.* at 218.

[22] *See, e.g.*, Nicholas Crafts, *East Asian Growth before and after the Crisis*, 46 IMF STAFF PAPERS 139 (1999); BEYOND THE DEVELOPMENTAL STATE: EAST ASIA'S POLITICAL ECONOMIES RECONSIDERED (Steve Chan, Cal Clark & Danny Lam eds, 1998); Yongping Wu, *Rethinking the Taiwanese Developmental State*, 177 CHINA Q. 91 (2004); WORLD BANK, THE EAST ASIAN MIRACLE: ECONOMIC GROWTH AND PUBLIC POLICY (1993).

[23] *See, e.g.*, Yongping Wu, *supra* note 22; Yu-Shan Wu, *Taiwan's Developmental State: After the Economic and Political Turmoil*, 47 ASIAN SURV. 977 (2007); Lance L.P. Gore, *Labour Management as Development of the Integrated Developmental State in China*, 19 NEW POL. ECON. 302 (2014).

famine and the Cultural Revolution, the legitimacy and survival of the CCP were at stake. Given that China was entering the global economy at a different time period, with a very different relationship to the United States (which provided security protection and export markets to Japan, South Korea, and Taiwan), and a much larger and poorer population, it is not surprising that wholesale adoption of a single foreign model was not an option—assuming one existed at all. China's selective adoption of East Asian growth institutions exhibits a high level of pragmatism and instrumentalism. In order to better understand the trajectory of China's state capitalist system, it is more useful to examine the foundational concepts of the EADS rather than specific policies designed by different leaders at different times. These concepts include performance legitimacy, the primacy of political and social stability, and the use of market competition to improve quality and control moral hazard. Although all of the East Asian developmental states reflected these concepts in their policies, the actual policies adopted ranged rather widely.

Performance legitimacy—the notion that regimes should be evaluated on their ability to manage and govern the economy—has been part of the East Asian developmental model since at least the rise of the Liberal Democratic Party in post-WWII Japan.[24] The government's ability to produce and sustain growth and development are the main measures by which it should be evaluated by the people, whether this occurs in elections or in some other less-direct way, for example via protests and mobilization. Although some attribute the ubiquity of performance legitimacy in East Asia to Confucian traditions that emphasize the importance of the ruler in bringing peace and prosperity to the ruled, others have noted that the geopolitical conflict that followed the onset of the Cold War (and the hot war in Korea) was also intrinsically tied to the need to legitimate rule (especially authoritarian rule) with high levels of economic performance.[25] The political and economic systems of Taiwan and South Korea in particular were juxtaposed against those in the PRC and the DPRK (North Korea). Internal success was intended to have strong demonstration effects to the alternative communist regimes created by civil war. The United States' political, economic, and security support of the capitalist states in East Asia only further emphasized the idea of two systems in competition with one another, each needing to prove its superiority.[26]

In this sense, the performance legitimacy of the PRC goes back much further than the 1978 Decision to adopt the policy of "Reform and Opening Up." The CCP's justification for its rule and of the need for socialism goes back to the debates during the May

---

[24] States and Development in the Asian Pacific Rim (Richard P. Appelbaum & J. W. Henderson eds., 1992); The Developmental State 6–8 (Meredith Woo-Cumings ed., 1999).

[25] D. Zhao, *The Mandate of Heaven and Performance Legitimation in Historical and Contemporary China*, 53 Am. Behav. Scientist 416 (2009); The Developmental State, *supra* note 24.

[26] The Developmental State, *supra* note 24; Alice H. Amsden, Asia's Next Giant: South Korea and Late Industrialization (1992).

Fourth Movement of 1919 and the founding of the Party about which kind of political and economic system would make China strong, rich, and independent.[27] Mao Zedong's pursuit of policies such as rapid collectivization and "leap" industrialization were not only intended to pursue the shortest path to communism, but also to push China to develop as rapidly as possible, to "surpass Great Britain," and to demonstrate both to its rival socialist leader, the USSR, and its capitalist enemy in the United States that China would (again) become rich and strong. In some sense, the decision under Deng Xiaoping to abandon Maoist policies was a capitulation; Maoist policies had not made China wealthy or strong, especially when compared to its neighbors. Deng's embrace of goals such as a "well-off society" (*xiaokang shehui*) framed the reforms exactly around performance legitimacy. The justification for the change in the policies, even the embrace of capitalism, is not for the individual enrichment that occurs as society becomes well-off; it is it for the enrichment of the state. A well-off society is justification for the state's rule.[28]

The twin goals of high levels of performance and political stability are of course closely linked, with repression and state coercion justified by the need to focus on development. From Lee Kuan Yew in Singapore to Chiang Kai-Shek in Taiwan, Asian dictators have made this connection from "excessive" social and political mobilization to political instability and economic stagnation. As Adam Przeworski et al. show in relation to Korea and Taiwan, although these countries demonstrate an "ideal type" modernization story—moving through industrialization and urbanization through political and society mobilization, to elite capitulation and democratization—Korea and Taiwan were both late developers and late democratizers.[29] Taiwan, in particular, democratized with a GDP per capita far above Przeworski et al.'s "threshold" of $4,115, the level of income at which a regime's probability of democratization reaches 50 percent.[30] The state's coercive capacity, close ties to business elites, and domination of society limited and delayed political change. In the name of development, authoritarian regimes closely tied to the United States justified repression of their citizens.

The discourse of benevolent authoritarianism and the need to delay democracy until society "matures" also finds its roots in debates at the end of the Qing Dynasty about China's future.[31] While liberals and Marxists debated between communism and capitalism for the economy, even liberal modernizers such as Sun Yatsen argued that China required a period of political tutelage before its people would be ready for full

---

[27] Chow Tse-Tsung, The May Fourth Movement: Intellectual Revolution in Modern China (1960).

[28] Elizabeth J. Perry, *Chinese Conceptions of "Rights": From Mencius to Mao—and Now*, 6 Persp. Pol. 37 (2008).

[29] Adam Przeworski et al., Democracy and Development: Political Institutions and Well-Being in the World, 1950–1990, 94–98 (2000). Taiwan democratized "later" than South Korea in per capita GDP terms.

[30] *Id.*

[31] Andrew J. Nathan, Chinese Democracy (1986).

democratic citizenship and participation. In the aftermath of the Cultural Revolution, the Pro-Democracy Student Movement in 1989, and the collapse of the USSR, the CCP has consistently reiterated the message that democracy is dangerous and chaotic.[32] The connection between China's economic success and its political stability is explicit—without the Party's leadership and control over society, economic performance cannot be guaranteed.

Finally, the East Asian developmental states pursued economic development and growth through the selective and instrumental use of markets to create competition among regions, firms, and individuals. Markets were not only used as a growth mechanism, they were also closely tied to the idea of fostering internal and external competition in order to improve quality and restrain predation and inefficiency. Laura D'Andrea Tyson and John Zysman sum up "the Japanese variant of capitalism" this way:

> . . . markets are emphasized as a source of growth rather than of short-run efficiency, and a primary role of government is to supply incentives to promote growth through markets. The perspective motivating Japanese policy is explicitly dynamic and explicitly developmental.[33]

Alice H. Amsden demonstrates that the Korean government's intervention in firms and its use of heavy-handed industrial policies combined "getting the prices wrong" with a strong "disciplining" ethos.[34] The state's discipline was distinctly market-based: by setting up ambitious export targets, the government tested firms in global markets before rewarding high-performing firms with subsidies, favorable bank financing, and industrial policies. In these economies, insulated and protected sectors coexisted with sectors exposed to global competition.[35]

The decentralization of the Chinese economy in the 1980s and the use of policy experiments to expand liberal economic policies such as development zones and attraction of foreign direct investment (FDI) also fostered competition across regions, firms, and individuals. The larger policy of opening up, including attracting FDI as a substitute for domestic investment and home-grown technology, framed this domestic competition in the broader context of export-oriented industrialization and the globalization of manufacturing. Although China opened much earlier and much wider to FDI than most other East Asian economies, it too protected politically important sectors, allowing state

---

32 Anne-Marie Brady, Marketing Dictatorship: Propaganda and Thought Work in Contemporary China (2010); Yang Zhong, *Legitimacy Crisis and Legitimation in China*, 26 J. Contemp. Asia 201 (1996).

33 Laura D'Andrea Tyson & John Zysman, *Preface: The Argument Outlined*, *in* Politics and Productivity: The Real Story of Why Japan Works, xvi (Chalmers Johnson et al. eds., 1989).

34 Amsden, *supra* note 26, at 139.

35 Kent E. Calder, Crisis and Compensation: Public Policy and Political Stability in Japan, 1949–1986 (1988).

enterprises to restructure gradually over the first twenty years of reform while the private and foreign sectors developed alongside, what Barry Naughton termed "growing out of the plan."[36]

Deng's decentralization of the political and economic decision-making allowed regions to differentiate themselves in the rush toward growth and development. Although the most radical policies, such as Special Economic Zones, were initially extended to only a few places, over the 1980s and early 1990s these policies were extended to an expanding number of localities. Although there were adverse effects, such as redundant investment, overheating, and inequality, the regional competition for investment benefitted some coastal areas immensely as investment flowed in from other East Asian economies looking for cheaper labor, and eventually also from multinational corporations eager to tap the large domestic market.[37] Some have identified this quasi-federalist decentralization policy as the main mechanism by which China developed and preserved markets.[38] Others have shown how competition, learning, and diffusion facilitated the extension of the coastal development model into inland China.[39] Ang shows how the "beehive model" of investment attraction used by local governments during the early reform period compensated for the lack of an effective and professional bureaucracy of the type that existed in Japan with the Ministry of International Trade and Industry (MITI).[40] The beehive model offered economic incentives for all local cadres regardless of their particular job or sector. While local officials involved in export promotion were rewarded for bringing in investment, so were local cadres in the women's federation. As with Maoist policy, there was an "all in" quality to the early reform period, and the competition consisted of other localities doing the same thing. These policies did not mimic the Japanese experience, but as with Japan, the policy goals were "explicitly dynamic and explicitly developmental."[41]

One of the "advantages of backwardness" enjoyed by the Chinese economy in the 1980s was the large surplus pool of cheap labor in the countryside.[42] This excess labor in the part of the economy that had benefitted least from socialism, especially socialist welfare, allowed the government to promote the expansion of the private and foreign sectors while leaving the SOE sector relatively untouched for the first fifteen years of the reform period. As Naughton's metaphor of "growing out of the plan" aptly describes,

---

[36] Barry Naughton, Growing Out of the Plan: Chinese Economic Reform, 1978–1993 (1996).

[37] Mary Elizabeth Gallagher, Contagious Capitalism: Globalization and the Politics of Labor in China (2005).

[38] Gabriella Montinola, Yingyi Qian & Barry R. Weingast, *Federalism, Chinese Style: The Political Basis for Economic Success in China*, 48 World Pol. 50 (1995).

[39] Yuen Yuen Ang, How China Escaped the Poverty Trap (forthcoming 2016).

[40] *Id.*

[41] Politics and Productivity, *supra* note 33.

[42] Alexander Gerschenkron, Economic Backwardness in Historical Perspective: A Book of Essays (1962).

the economy expanded around the public sector, putting competitive pressure on the margins.[43] The major restructuring of the SOE sector that began in the mid-1990s was a radical reduction in public ownership, with tens of millions of SOE workers losing employment and large-scale closure and privatization of small-to-medium SOEs.[44] The government also expanded the degree to which foreign and private investors could invest in SOEs, and allowed for mergers and acquisitions to absorb and restructure failing firms. As I have argued elsewhere, this delayed restructuring of the state sector insulated the reforming state for a long period as the economy changed around it. The state reformulated the concept of state ownership as strategic ownership of the commanding heights of the economy in order to make China globally competitive. This formula justifies the casting-off of poorly performing firms and the rejection of ownership as a means to supply socialist welfare and security to workers. It exemplifies the Chinese state's pragmatic embrace of markets to hasten the "creative destruction" of competition under capitalism.[45]

Finally, at the individual level, the adoption of labor market institutions and legislation to regulate these markets via individual contracts embedded competition in people's daily lives. Although such competition is normal in most market economies, the shift in China was dramatic, as until the early 1990s employment assignments were administered by the state and urban workers' employment security was guaranteed. Even moving between different state firms was unusual and difficult. The labor reforms of the 1980s and 1990s significantly reduced the state's role in employment, freeing up those with high levels of education and skills to compete in tight labor markets and letting go of those with low levels of education and skills to fend for themselves.[46] According to anthropologist Yunxiang Yan, this "individualization became a developmental strategy adopted by the party-state and inevitably turned into a highly contested process since it created both losers and winners."[47]

These policies and institutional reforms (decentralization, labor flexibility, "beehive" investment incentives for local officials) cannot be found in other EADS. China's path toward state capitalism was specific to its own context as it emerged from the Cultural Revolution and Maoist experiments with the economy. Although it is indisputable that Deng reoriented the system around growth, reinforcing traditional ideas such as the "well-off society" to justify CCP rule, the decentralization and local autonomy that followed reinforced a policy style of experimentation and local variation that is not at all an

---

[43] NAUGHTON, *supra* note 36.

[44] William Hurst & Kevin J. O'Brien, *China's Contentious Pensioners*, 170 CHINA Q. 345 (2002); William Hurst, *The Chinese Worker after Socialism* (2012).

[45] JOSEPH A. SCHUMPETER, CAPITALISM, SOCIALISM, AND DEMOCRACY (2008).

[46] LU ZHANG, INSIDE CHINA'S AUTOMOBILE FACTORIES: THE POLITICS OF LABOR AND WORKER RESISTANCE (2014). Zhang describes new forms of dualism that pit workers against each other on the shop floor, divided by differences in their contracts and terms with the employer.

[47] Yunxiang Yan, *The Chinese Path to Individualization*, 61 BRIT. J. SOC. 489, 499 (2010).

apparent characteristic of the EADS model. China's initial conditions and geographical determinants also fostered policies that leveraged the "advantages of backwardness"—labor market changes were foisted upon rural migrants first, and new sectors developed as FDI flowed in from overseas Chinese communities.[48] Although some policies can clearly be linked to the EADS success—for example, reliance on export-oriented industrialization, formation of large corporate groups in the state sector, and industrial policy to foster domestic capacity in sectors such as automobiles—there were also significant differences. China and its neighbors did agree on some core principles, however, such as the primacy of growth as a metric for government legitimacy, the importance of political stability (a justification for authoritarian rule), and an instrumental (rather than philosophical) commitment to markets.

III. China's State Capitalism: Market Competition, Political Control

For the past decade, the architects of China's state capitalism have concentrated on the dilemma of shifting the development model away from dependence on government investment and exports to domestic consumption and demand. This shift intensified after the ascension of Xi Jinping to the top position in the CCP in 2013. The Third Plenum of the Eighteenth CCP Party Congress that fall heralded a new era of reform and restructuring, the likes of which had not been seen since 1978.[49] This shift in the development model has important consequences for the domestic institutions of state capitalism, particularly the management of labor markets and industrial relations. Although we speak of the Third Plenum policy changes as "reforms," for labor and social policy these are not the liberalizing, "letting go" reforms of the 1978 Plenum; they are instead a reinforcement of state power and capacity over the economy and society. Although the overall goal of the Plenum reforms is to improve the functioning of markets in China—to improve state capitalism, increase efficiency, enhance competitiveness, and create a level playing field—solving these market concerns requires domestic social and political reforms predicated on improved state capacity and control. An earlier reliance on markets and exclusive social policies that shut out many from the welfare state reflected the preferences of a detached state as it threw off the commitments of socialism. The current shift in the development model requires new attention to social protections via legislation, an inclusionary social policy that incorporates newly urbanized rural migrants, and a much more embedded and interventionist state to manage rising social expectations and related instability.

---

[48] GERSCHENKRON, *supra* note 42.

[49] Daniel H. Rosen, *Avoiding the Blind Alley: China's Economic Overhaul and Its Global Implications* (2014), *available at* http://asiasociety.org/policy-institute/china-economy.

A. LABOR REGULATION: MARKET VERSUS ADMINISTRATIVE MECHANISMS

Until the 1995 National Labor Law, regulation of labor in China occurred mostly at the workplace, which was still predominantly publicly owned, via administrative regulations.[50] There was a wide degree of fragmentation and overlapping jurisdictions within the bureaucracies, and the decentralized nature of the system reinforced unclear hierarchy between SOEs and higher-level bureaucratic units. From 1978 to 1995, labor legislation developed in different ownership sectors as the need to regulate the new and controversial foreign and private sectors became apparent. The administrative and legislative fragmentation of the early reform period became increasingly untenable, and led to the final push to pass the National Labor Law, which had been in draft form for over a decade. The National Labor Law was a foundational law that covered workers in all firms except very small individual businesses. In principle, the law also did not distinguish between urban and rural workers. Based fundamentally on the labor contract system, which required that employers sign written labor contracts with their formal employees, the Labor Law embodied strong market principles. The contract signifies the establishment of a "labor relationship," which defines the rights and responsibilities of both sides in a contractual sense. While recognizing the principle of a labor market and the commodification of work, the law was aspirational in setting out high individual standards in regards to these rights and responsibilities. The law was much less specific about implementation and enforcement issues. It also had relatively lenient or unclear punitive damages for noncompliance.[51]

As I have argued elsewhere, the Labor Law, despite its high standards and aspirational protections, was first and foremost a death knell for the "iron rice bowl" enjoyed by urban workers in the public sectors. For workers who had previously been accustomed to lifetime employment security and extensive benefits dispersed by the workplace, the Labor Law and the use of contracts to regulate employment was a reduction in workplace rights. The timing of the Labor Law is also significant as it went into effect just as the Party-state began a full-throttled assault on the state enterprise sector, with massive restructuring, firm bankruptcies, and privatization of many small and medium firms. State sector workers, especially workers hired in the latter half of the 1980s and the early 1990s, had been signing labor contracts as part of an experimental policy before the law's passage, but few believed that the contracts signified anything important. Many were shocked to find that they could be laid off or dismissed through the invocation of contract termination. The Labor Law, while promising many protections and high

---

[50] 中华人民共和国劳动法 (Labor Law of P.R. China) (promulgated by the Standing Comm. of the Nat'l People's Cong., July 5, 1994, effective Jan. 1, 1995), *available at* http://www.gov.cn/banshi/2005-05/25/content_905.htm.

[51] Mary E. Gallagher, *China's Workers Movement and the End of the Rapid-Growth Era*, 143 DAEDALUS 81 (2014).

standards, would initially at least signify the loss of socialist entitlements, not the gain of legal rights.[52]

For rural migrant workers who were beginning to flow into cities and development zones in growing numbers, the Labor Law's protections were nearly irrelevant. Although in principle the law offered universal coverage and equal treatment to rural and urban workers alike, implementation of the law was weak, and many firms continued to hire rural migrants on an informal, temporary, or seasonal basis. Most were not offered labor contracts, and without such they were unable to claim any formal protections under the law. With little employment security, marginalized both by urban society and the local state, these workers were in practice excluded from the law's protections. Rapidly integrated into China's growing labor markets, they were denied inclusion in protective regimes that could temper the severity of the market conditions, especially low wages, unsafe and unhealthy working conditions, long hours, and no employment security.

Under these conditions, the Labor Law's long-awaited passage did not immediately lead to improvements in labor conditions, either for urban public sector workers or rural migrants. A small minority of urban workers who were moving from the public sector to the rapidly growing foreign sector were the main beneficiaries, but these tended to be higher-level managerial and technical positions. Their ability to leverage the law's protections was bound up in their strong market positions in an economy with a growing need for skilled workers and managers. The law's protections accrued to those who, arguably, least needed it as they had strong market power already. Migrants and older state sector workers, the strata of workers who most needed protection, were hard-pressed to invoke the law's protections effectively. This was particularly the case for the thirty million state sector workers who were laid off during the restructuring of 1998–2001. Many localities passed regulations that treated "laid off workers" (*xiagang gongren*) as a special transitional category to be managed administratively by the state through the restructuring process, while judicial channels were shut down.[53]

Despite the high standards of the 1995 Labor Law, the labor markets and labor relations of the early-to-mid reform period were overwhelmingly determined by market forces. Institutions such as the household registration system (*hukou*) were important in segmenting the labor markets of urban and rural workers and keeping the wages of rural migrant workers artificially low. Most socialist institutions that had played a role in administrative control over labor markets—such as the work-unit, the job assignment function of lower bureaucracies, and the trade union's role in enterprise management—were all dismantled or weakened. Trade union density fell from a high

---

[52] *Id.*; Mary E. Gallagher, Authoritarian Legality: The Law, Workers, and the State in Contemporary China (forthcoming 2016).

[53] Mary E. Gallagher, *China's Older Workers: Between Law and Policy, Between Laid-Off and Unemployed, in* Laid-Off Workers in a Workers' State: Unemployment with Chinese Characteristics 135 (Thomas B. Gold et al. eds., 2009).

of 59.5 percent in 1990 to a low of 44.5 percent in 2000.[54] Work-units devolved social insurance and benefit responsibilities to local governments, and the job assignment system stopped functioning altogether. Labor relations inside of firms diversified and reflected the different backgrounds of foreign, private, and state-owned firms. Western firms initiated human resources management practices that they had employed in other venues. Private and overseas Chinese firms relied on traditional paternalistic practices of Chinese family firms around the globe. Managerial discretion was vastly increased, and conditions within firms varied considerably across regions, sectors, and types of ownership.[55]

The excessive reliance on markets to structure labor markets and the institutional discrimination of the *hukou* status had severe social consequences, including systemic wage arrears problems for migrant workers, growing inequality between the rich and poor, lack of employment security for China's aging workforce, low levels of participation in state-mandated social insurance programs, and high levels of labor disputes and conflict that threatened social stability. In 2008, the government passed the second foundational labor law, the National Labor Contract Law,[56] and a law on dispute resolution, as a response. This law targeted these problems by enacting heavy damages for failure to enter into written contracts with employees (bringing more workers into the formal sector), increasing the restrictions on short-term contracts (enhancing the security of formal workers), and reducing financial and administrative barriers to the dispute resolution system. This law was followed in 2010 with the Social Insurance Law, which targets greater inclusion in social insurance and welfare, discussed below.[57] In 2012 the Labor Contract Law was revised to further restrict the use of subcontracted labor and temporary labor in place of formal contract workers.[58] By 2013, the OECD's Employment Protection Index ranked China ahead of all OECD countries and most major developing countries in employment security and protection.[59] The 2008 National

[54] Dongtao Qi, *Progress and Dilemmas of Chinese Trade Unions*, 2 East Asian Pol'y 14 (2010).

[55] Ching Kwan Lee, *From Organized Dependence to Disorganized Despotism: Changing Labour Regimes in Chinese Factories*, 157 China Q. 44 (1999).

[56] 中华人民共和国劳动合同法 (Labor Contract Law of P.R. China) (promulgated by the Standing Comm. of the Nat'l People's Cong., June 29, 2007, effective Jan. 1, 2008), *available at* http://www.gov.cn/flfg/2007-06/29/content_669394.htm.

[57] 中华人民共和国社会保险法 (Social Insurance Law of P.R. China) (promulgated by the Standing Comm. of the Nat'l People's Cong., Oct. 28, 2010, effective July 1, 2011), *available at* http://www.gov.cn/flfg/2010-10/28/content_1732964.htm.

[58] 中华人民共和国劳动合同法 (修改) (Labor Contract Law of P.R. China, Revised) (promulgated by the Standing Comm. of the Nat'l People's Cong., Dec. 28, 2012, effective July 1, 2013), *available at* http://www.gov.cn/flfg/2012-12/28/content_2305571.htm.

[59] Danielle Venn, *Legislation, Collective Bargaining and Enforcement: Updating the OECD Employment Protection Indicators* (2009), *available at* http://www.oecd.org/employment/emp/43116624.pdf; OECD, *Protecting Jobs, Enhancing Flexibility: A New Look at Employment Protection Legislation*, *in* OECD Employment Outlook 2013, 65 (2013).

Labor Contract Law marked an important shift away from the market and toward greater protection, regulation, and administrative intervention in enterprise autonomy.

The logic of greater reliance on law and regulations and less on "laissez-faire" market mechanisms in the realm of labor is of course directly related to the state's overriding concern for political and social stability. The vast majority of the legal protections advanced in the last few years continue to emphasize individualistic labor relations and individualized dispute resolution, while minimizing any empowerment of civil society, labor activists, or even the ACFTU.[60] The state has expanded the protection and security of labor "on the books" but it has not significantly relaxed its restrictive management of social interests via state-controlled organizations such as the ACFTU and through repression and co-optation of civil society.[61]

Beyond the problem of stability, however, the state has other long-term, strategic goals that are served by these new policies. These goals include rapid urbanization of the rural population to boost domestic consumption and demand, alleviation of labor shortages and reductions in labor market segmentation through relaxation of the *hukou* policies in most cities (though not the largest and most developed cities on the coast), and inclusion of young, rural workers in social insurance schemes that will be heavily burdened by China's rapidly aging population. The legislative agenda of the early 2000s exposes this logic: expand the number of workers in the formal sector, offer these workers more security and protection, promote longer-term employment and greater participation in social insurance. The new regulatory and legal landscape is one of state intervention in labor markets, and the exchange of flexibility and mobility for other social and economic goals that reflect the concerns of a middle-income nation with its demographic and "backwardness" advantages behind it.[62]

This new model of protection and security should not be overestimated, as its impact will be gradual and selective. The "anti-market" bent of the Labor Contract Law will be mitigated by the pro-market enforcement and implementation mechanisms that grant local governments a high degree of autonomy and responsibility in implementing central laws. It will also be mitigated by labor inspection and compliance institutions that rely on "fire-alarm" complaints and lawsuits of individual workers, minimizing the role of proactive state agencies and trade unions.[63]

---

60 Gallagher, *supra* note 16; Gallagher, *supra* note 51; Feng Chen & Xin Xu, *"Active Judiciary": Judicial Dismantling of Workers' Collective Action in China*, 67 CHINA J. 87 (2012); Chen, *supra* note 18.

61 Bill Taylor, *Trade Unions and Social Capital in Transitional Communist States: The Case of China*, 33 POL'Y SCI. 341 (2000); Anthony J. Spires, *Contingent Symbiosis and Civil Society in an Authoritarian State: Understanding the Survival of China's Grassroots NGOs*, 117 AM. J. SOC. 1 (2011).

62 Rosen, *supra* note 49; Wang Feng, *The Future of a Demographic Overachiever: Long-Term Implications of the Demographic Transition in China*, 37 POPULATION & DEV. REV. 173 (2011).

63 Gallagher, *supra* note 51.

B. SOCIAL WELFARE AND SECURITY: EXCLUSIONARY VERSUS INCLUSIONARY POLICIES

The decisions adopted in the Third Plenum included ambitious goals to expand and deepen China's social welfare system. The shift toward more open and inclusionary policies is reflected in *hukou* policy, social insurance, and access to public education and health care. Decision 23 of the Plenum reads:

> We will help the eligible population to move away from agriculture and become urban residents. We will introduce new population management methods, accelerate the reform of household registration system (hukou), completely lift restrictions on new residence registration in administrative townships and small cities, relax restrictions on new residence registration in medium-sized cities in an orderly manner, lay down appropriate conditions for new resident registration in large cities, and strictly control the population size of megacities. We will steadily make basic urban public services available to all permanent residents in cities, and incorporate farmers who have registered as urban residents in to the urban housing and social security network, and make sure their previous subscription to old-age insurance and medical insurance in the countryside continues in the urban social security system.[64]

The far-off goals of the Third Plenum will have radical implications for China's economy if they are implemented. In the realm of *hukou* policy, there remains much local resistance on both sides: local officials are reluctant to absorb growing numbers of former farmers into the urban populations, while at the same time many rural residents no longer desire to give up their rural status (and land ownership) for an urban *hukou* that has become less valuable as restrictions on movement and migration have ebbed. Many migrant workers believe that it is best to hold on to both an urban job and rural land. Fundamental changes to the *hukou* status, although intended and announced by the Party-state more than once, will be politically difficult and intrinsically linked to the evolution of rural land ownership. The inclusionary impulse of the central government may be thwarted at every level as local officials stymie reforms that complicate their job responsibilities, and rural citizens decline to give up their only source of security—the land that Mao bequeathed to them through the violent land reform campaigns of the 1950s.

Social insurance and public service reforms have progressed, however, despite the delays in changes to *hukou* policy. Localities with significant labor-intensive manufacturing and large migrant populations had already opened up their social insurance programs to migrants, though there is ample variation in the type of coverage

---

[64] Rosen, *supra* note 49 at 99.

and levels of participation.[65] Public services, such as education, have also expanded to include migrants and their children, but with continued restrictions, abnormal fees, and lower-quality services compared to that received by permanent residents.[66] Compared to the 1990s, however, there are important improvements in the level of integration, and the general trend is toward more inclusion rather than less.

As with the legislative protections discussed in the previous section, the Party goals articulated in the Third Plenum and elsewhere are not only structured to address the political problems of the present, which are largely the externalities of China's development model thus far, but are also about the future of the Chinese economy and its sustainability going forward. Expansion of the urban labor force is an adjustment to China's changed demographic structure; reform of the *hukou* system is a steppingstone toward large-scale urbanization and the creation of a consumer society; expansion of the welfare state is an attempt to offer a viable social safety net to China's workers so that social risk is more evenly shared and distribution is more equitable.

C. MANAGEMENT OF SOCIAL CONFLICT: DETACHED VERSUS EMBEDDED STATE

The goals of the Chinese government to reorient its development model, improve working conditions and employment security, and reduce segmentation and mobility barriers for its rural citizens are fundamentally destabilizing because these reforms threaten those who benefit from the old model. Even though the far-off goal of reform is a more efficient, fair, and sustainable growth model, achieving that goal will require a far more effective and stronger regulatory state than currently exists.

With regard to labor, some of these reforms precede the decisions taken at the Third Plenum by several years. Thus it is possible to analyze how the state already has managed the social conflict caused by some of these changes. For example, since the passage of the 2008 Labor Contract Law, labor-capital conflict has increased exponentially; strikes and demonstrations are now a daily occurrence.[67] It is clear that the state's inclusive and protective goals for workers have emboldened them to ask for more at the workplace, and in some cases to demand it. The state's management of labor conflict has also evolved to become more interventionist at the site of labor conflict—the workplace or the street.[68]

---

[65] Mary Gallagher et al., *China's 2008 Labor Contract Law: Implementation and Implications for China's Workers*, 68 HUM. REL. 197 (2014); Zhiming Cheng et al., *The Impact of China's New Labour Contract Law on Socioeconomic Outcomes for Migrant and Urban Workers*, 68 HUM. REL. 329 (2014).

[66] Bi Ying Hu & Judit Szente, *Education of Young Chinese Migrant Children: Challenges and Prospects*, 37 EARLY CHILDHOOD EDUC. J. 477 (2010); Jessica L. Montgomery, *Inheritance of Inequality:* Hukou *and Related Barriers to Compulsory Education for China's Migrant Children*, 21 PAC. RIM L. & POL'Y J. 591 (2012).

[67] Gallagher, *supra* note 51.

[68] Yang Su & Xin He, *Street as Courtroom: State Accommodation of Labor Protest in South China*, 44 L. & SOC'Y REV. 157 (2010); Chen & Xu, *supra* note 60.

The state is no longer willing to leave labor conflict to enterprise managers or even to the legal institutions that have been constructed to handle workplace grievances. Given the state's reluctance to outsource conflict management to social actors, such as unions and NGOs, or legal professionals, such as lawyers and legal aid associations, it has had to take on a central role in conflict management.

The state's transition to a more active and interventionist role followed the explosion of disputes after the 2008 Labor Contract Law went into effect. The law's implementation coincided with the onset of the Global Financial Crisis, which had a severe though temporary effect on Chinese exports and manufacturing. The combination of new, more protective regulations, less-costly procedures, mass layoffs, and intense media coverage of the law resulted in a nationwide doubling in disputes, with some areas experiencing increases of over 300 percent. The state rapidly pushed for less formalistic resolution measures, diverting labor disputes from the formal process of arbitration and litigation to grass-roots mediation. Trade unions, neighborhood committees, and local governments all became more active in directly mediating between aggrieved workers and their employers.[69]

The state's more active intervention in labor conflict was also a consequence of the 2010 strike wave that began with a strike in a Honda auto supplier factory in southern Guangdong Province. This strike, which began as a labor dispute involving a few workers, eventually led to the nationwide shutdown of Honda plants and wage demands from many auto sector workers, as well as demands for their "own" trade union to represent and bargain for them effectively. In the same year as a rash of suicides in Foxconn plants producing high-end products for Apple, and others, these signs of collective dissatisfaction and individual alienation alerted the government to the dire need to address the rising expectations of the "new generation" of migrant workers, those born after the 1980s and 1990s.[70]

The government's approach to managing collective labor strife is a hands-on, interventionist one. The goal is social stability, which is an important indicator of local cadre performance and evaluation. In fact, large-scale social strife and violence can doom a cadre's chances of promotion.[71] Local officials deploy diverse means to achieve stability. Repression of activist leaders is combined with co-optation of followers. State-led mediation and bargaining puts pressure on both sides, labor and capital, to come to an agreement. Yang Su and Xin He describe this as "street as courtroom"—the setting for adjudication of the dispute is not the formal courtroom, but the workplace.[72] Local officials form "stability preservation committees" that collectively manage the settlement of conflict. Judges, the police, labor officials, trade union cadres, and local Party

---

[69] Gallagher, *supra* note 51.

[70] Mary Gallagher, *Changes in the World's Workshop, in* DRAGON VERSUS EAGLE: THE CHINESE ECONOMY AND U.S.-CHINA RELATIONS 119 (2012).

[71] XI CHEN, SOCIAL PROTEST AND CONTENTIOUS AUTHORITARIANISM IN CHINA (2014).

[72] Su & He, *supra* note 68.

or government leaders form the backbone of an interventionist local state. Ching Kwan Lee and Yonghong Zhang define this behavior, in labor and other realms, as "bargained authoritarianism."[73] The state no longer relies solely on coercion, but on a mix of compromise, sympathy, pressure, co-optation, and selective repression. The government of Guangdong Province during the darkest days of the financial crisis in late 2008 and early 2009 set up a fund to pay off workers who lost their jobs and their legal severance when bosses absconded overnight, leaving shuttered factories and thousands of bereft employees. The Honda strike ended with a settlement reached between the (Chinese) head of Honda China, the local government, and a Beijing labor academic who was asked to intervene on behalf of the workers. Workers received a hefty pay raise and promises of a more democratic union structure at the firm level.

The state's embedded nature, its place at the center of social conflict, is not surprising as the Party's Leninist structure gives it the necessary grass-roots links and tentacles that are critical to maintain control. The ACFTU is part of this structure, and its presence at many firms aids the state in monitoring firm-level labor relations. Party cells at many companies also serve that purpose. The ACFTU's monopoly on organization, however, has not translated into effective representation of workers' interests by the firm-level trade union. Trade union officials are still employees first and foremost; they are often appointed by top management and serve concurrently in human resources or other management positions. Trade union cadres at the local level are similarly hamstrung by their subordinate position to the local Party-state.[74] It is this very lack of effective representation that draws the local state into labor conflict. With no reform on the horizon of labor's ability to organize independently, the state's responsibility for managing labor conflict has increased as the expectations and demands of workers have grown with the economy, exacerbated by labor shortages and global economic instability.

Although state management of strikes and demonstrations is reactive and case-by-case, the Party-state has also developed legal and regulatory institutions for more systematic bargaining between labor and capital. Collective wage bargaining regulations have been passed by many localities, and the central government has encouraged "tripartite" consultation among local governments, trade unions, and employers/business associations. However, these formalized structures do not alleviate the centrality of the state in keeping labor conflict in check.[75] Neither the ACFTU nor the official business associations tasked with the work of collective consultations has the capacity to bargain

---

[73] Ching Kwan Lee & Yonghong Zhang, *The Power of Instability: Unraveling the Microfoundations of Bargained Authoritarianism in China*, 118 AM. J. SOC. 1475 (2013).

[74] Chen, *supra* note 18; Mingwei Liu, *Union Organizing in China: Still a Monolithic Labor Movement?*, 64 INDUS. & LAB. REL. REV. 30 (2010).

[75] Feng Chen, *Trade Unions and the Quadripartite Interactions in Strike Settlement in China*, 201 CHINA Q. 104 (2010); Chang Kai & William Brown, *The Transition from Individual to Collective Labour Relations in China*, 44 INDUS. REL. J. 102 (2013).

effectively. Separated from its members by its lack of legitimacy, and tied to the local Party by virtue of its organizational mandate, the ACFTU's interests are defined by the government. Similarly, associations representing capital are state-organized actors that rarely reflect the diverse interests and needs of local business. Tripartite consultation becomes a three-way conversation with one voice—that of the Party-state. Interest representation has been replaced by the state's mediation among different interests.

Conclusion

Chinese state capitalism is widely seen as the most successful model of an alternate development strategy to the neoliberal orthodoxy. It combines political illiberalism with an instrumental embrace of markets. The state's management of the economy uses markets to discipline local officials, state sector managers, and even individual workers, but it can also provide protection from markets that might damage the long-term interests of the state. The Chinese approach to development has borrowed key lessons from the East Asian developmental states that preceded it, as well as finding synergy with these economies as capitalist production networks expanded at the end of the last century to include China and its large supply of cheap labor.[76] China's earlier opening to FDI and its intense domestic competition have transformed the Chinese economy over the past few decades. Although the state sector remains politically dominant and receives protection in key sectors, many other parts of the Chinese economy have developed without excessive state control or involvement.

The political foundations of state capitalism are much less transformed—the CCP remains central to all policymaking. However, the CCP, in its bid to be a ruling party rather than a revolutionary one, has relinquished utopian goals for the technocratic developmentalism of the EADS. China's trajectory has not been determined by the past practices of its EADS neighbors as it has borrowed and experimented with a wide range of institutions from many different parts of the world. As China's development model, dependent on government investment and export-oriented industrialization, reaches its limits, the Party-state has attempted to be responsive and proactive in planning out new sources of growth through urbanization, increased domestic demand, the financing of technical upgrading, and support for development in inland China. Unlike state capitalist regimes that can rely on regular revenue from natural resources, China's economy must remain competitive and dynamic. As it loses its edge in low-cost production, and as its demographic structure becomes more growth-retarding than growth-enhancing, it must find new sources of growth and development. As Nicholas R. Lardy shows, the most dynamic sectors in the Chinese economy are not the "state capitalist" national

[76] The Market Makers: How Retailers Are Reshaping the Global Economy (Gary G. Hamilton et al. eds., 2011).

champions, but the burgeoning private sector, which now accounts for the bulk of China's growth in GDP and in new employment.[77]

Can China sustain its model of state capitalism while retooling the economy so that it is sustainable in the long term? The social reforms discussed above that enhance protection and regulation of labor markets, improve inclusion of rural migrants and newly urbanizing citizens into the urban welfare state, and mediate between the interests of labor and capital are tactical moves in a broader redesign of the "China model." Should they succeed, these reforms will decrease inequality by increasing employment security and redistributing income toward salaried and wage workers. They will reduce the institutional segmentation created by the *hukou* policy and allow rural migrants to urbanize permanently in the places where they are employed. If disputes are resolved more quickly and with less disruption, workers might be able to achieve gains in their rights and interests despite the lack of independent representation and voice.

These reforms and the other ambitious goals of the 2013 Third Plenum are much needed, but they require assaults on many vested interests of the current model. The reforms in the labor realm will not only redistribute income toward salaried and wage workers, they will also further erode the segmentation of the labor market between urban permanent residents and rural migrants. Competition in labor markets will become more fair, but also more intense, to the disadvantage of those at the bottom end of the urban labor pool. Increasing migrant access to urban public goods and services and participation in urban social insurance schemes will create more competition over scarce resources and tensions between long-time "insiders" and newly urbanizing citizens. The preferential policies of China's long-standing urban bias institution, the *hukou*, will diminish the entitlements of urban residents while enhancing the rights and social status of migrants.

The Third Plenum reforms are, then, radically redistributive. Though they may target enhanced market efficiencies, such as flatter and better-functioning labor markets, rational and fairer resource pricing, etc., they could fundamentally undermine popular urban support for the CCP. As such, implementation of these market reforms will require a more involved state, and potentially, a much more repressive one, as the state steps in to challenge the privileges and entitlements of the old model. The association between state capitalism and authoritarianism is not accidental: it is baked into a system that relies on state power to suppress the social and political instability inherent in capitalist economies. Although it is too early to predict the success of these new reforms, the experiences of China's developmentalist neighbors offer a cautionary tale. The political structures undergirding the developmental states in East Asia did not withstand the model's exhaustion, leading to democratization in South Korea and Taiwan and an interruption in the long reign of the Liberal Democratic Party in Japan. The CCP's move to reform and reorient the economy is ambitious, reflecting the dynamic nature of Chinese capitalism, but it is not without risk.

---

[77] Nicholas R. Lardy, Markets over Mao: The Rise of Private Business in China (2014).

12 Chinese State Capitalism and the Environment

Alex L. Wang*

Introduction

China's state-owned enterprises (SOEs) have contributed mightily to the country's environmental problems. Even a cursory drive around central Beijing suggests some immediate reasons that this is the case. Move along the Second Ring Road, tracing the path of the old Beijing city wall dismantled in the 1950s, and you will encounter the towering headquarters of China's industrial national champions. These central SOEs include some of China's heaviest polluters.[1] Clustered just to the west of Zhongnanhai,

* The author thanks Benjamin Liebman, Curtis Milhaupt, Ann Carlson, Edward Parson, Kal Raustiala, Maximo Langer, Stephen Gardbaum, Asli Bali, Benjamin van Rooij, Carl Minzner, Jed Purdy, and the participants in the Columbia Law School Workshop on Chinese State Capitalism; the 2014 Colorado/Duke Climate Change, Energy, and Environment Works-in-Progress Symposium; the 2014 Sabin Colloquium on Innovative Environmental Law Scholarship; the University of Chicago Symposium on China's Environmental Governance; and the 2014–2015 Climate and Law Workshop at UCLA School of Law. Tiffany Lee, Hua Jiang, and Nianruo Xu provided excellent research assistance. Any errors remain exclusively mine.

[1] In 2014, China had 112 central SOEs (央企), whose shares are held on behalf of the state by the State-owned Assets Supervision and Administration Commission (SASAC) (国有资产监督管理委员会). Most of these enterprises work in the heavy industrial sectors, including power, petroleum, iron and steel, coal,

the seat of Chinese political power, are the "Big 5" power generation SOEs.[2] The offices of the major iron and steel SOEs are arrayed along the Avenue of Eternal Peace, Beijing's central east-west axis.[3] To the northeast, the headquarters of the three major state-owned petroleum groups—CNPC, Sinopec, and CNOOC—rise above the traffic-choked thoroughfares.[4] Continue driving and you will see in the span of a few kilometers the headquarters for central SOEs involved in coal (Shenhua, ChinaCoal), nonferrous metals (Chinalco, China Minmetals Corporation), chemicals (Sinochem, Chemchina), and many others.[5] These SOEs are the "primary vehicles of Chinese state capitalism,"[6] and included among them are some of the largest companies in the world.[7]

Scholars and commentators have long treated SOEs as "vested interests" with a particular ability to thwart central Party-state environmental objectives.[8] The inability of the state to reform SOEs and stem the tide of environmental degradation is, in turn,

nonferrous metals, chemicals, coal, textiles, automobile, nuclear, and aviation industries. *See* 央企名录 (Central Enterprise Name List), 国务院国有资产监督管理委员会 (State-owned Assets Supervision and Admin. Comm'n of the St. Council), http://www.sasac.gov.cn/n86114/n86137/c1725422/content.html (Chinese, last visited Feb. 19, 2015), http://web.archive.org/web/20140420025459/http://www.sasac.gov.cn/n2963340/n2971121/n4956567/4956583.html (English, earlier cached version as of April 20, 2014, showing 117 central SOEs).

[2] Huaneng (中国华能集团公司), Guodian (中国国电集团公司), Huadian (中国华电集团公司), Datang (中国大唐集团公司), and China Power Investment Corporation (CPIC) (中国电力投资集团公司).

[3] Bao Steel (宝钢集团公司), Wuhan Iron & Steel (武汉钢铁 (集团) 公司), Anshan Iron & Steel (鞍山钢铁集团公司), and Sinosteel (中国中钢集团公司).

[4] CNPC (中国石油天然气集团公司), Sinopec (中国石油化工集团公司), CNOOC (中国海洋石油总公司).

[5] Shenhua (神华集团有限责任公司), ChinaCoal (中国中煤能源集团公司), Aluminum Corporation of China, or Chinalco (中国铝业公司), China Minmetals Corp. (中国五矿集团公司), Sinochem (中国中化集团公司), Chemchina (中国化工集团公司). Others include State Grid Corp. of China (国家电网公司) (power transmission and distribution), China Three Gorges Corporation (中国长江三峡集团公司) (power generation), China FAW (中国第一汽车集团公司) (auto), and Dongfeng (东风汽车公司) (auto).

[6] Usha C.V. Haley & George T. Haley, Subsidies to Chinese Industry: State Capitalism, Business Strategy, and Trade Policy 24 (2013).

[7] The Fortune Global 500 lists forty-six Chinese central SOEs, many of them in heavily polluting industrial sectors. In total, ninety-five Chinese companies inhabit the list. The forty-nine other Chinese companies on the Fortune ranking include state-owned banks and insurance companies (which are state-owned, but managed under a different bureaucracy), provincial-level SOEs (*see infra* note 24), and a handful of private enterprises. *See Global 500 2014*, Fortune, http://fortune.com/global500 (last visited Feb. 19, 2015).

[8] *See, e.g.*, Hua Wang et al., *Incomplete Enforcement of Pollution Regulation: Bargaining Power of Chinese Factories*, 24 Envtl. & Resource Econ. 245 (2003) (assessing data from 1993 to 1997); Peter Lorentzen et al., *Undermining Authoritarian Innovation: The Power of China's Industrial Giants*, 76 J. Pol. 182 (2014); Edward Wong, *As Pollution Worsens, Solutions Succumb to Infighting*, N.Y. Times, Mar. 21, 2013, http://www.nytimes.com/2013/03/22/world/asia/as-chinas-environmental-woes-worsen-infighting-emerges-as-biggest-obstacle.html?pagewanted=all; Brian Spegele, *Are Chinese Leaders Ready to Take on Vested Interests?*, Wall St. J., Nov. 11, 2013, http://blogs.wsj.com/chinarealtime/2013/11/11/are-chinese-leaders-ready-to-take-on-vested-interests/ ("The big state companies are seen as particularly powerful.").

seen as evidence of China's governance deficits and a threat to the ultimate legitimacy and long-term survival of the Chinese state.[9]

This chapter examines an emerging set of strategies that Chinese leaders are using to counter this dynamic. Rather than resort to the types of political, legal, and market reforms that liberal commentators typically support, Chinese authorities appear to be engaged in an effort to bring about environmental reform in significant part by accommodating elite SOE interests, bringing them along with a large helping of positive incentives and a relatively smaller dose of traditional regulatory enforcement.

This approach raises the possibility that SOEs will play a greater role in Chinese environmental reform than commonly thought. But, to the extent that SOEs cooperate with emerging Chinese environmental reforms, it is likely to be because these reforms accommodate their interests to a sufficient degree to motivate compliance.

As a theoretical matter, this argument draws from public choice concepts typically applied to democratic governance contexts. Public choice theory posits that the outcomes of policymaking and implementation are best explained, not as a reflection of public interest considerations, but as a response to the pressure of elite interest groups.[10] Related, but distinct from this, is the idea that bureaucrats act in self-interested ways, rather than in the public interest. Likewise, authoritarian policymaking and implementation are influenced by the competition among powerful elites within society, and the self-interest of regulators and policymakers.[11]

But public choice theories have very different implications for China as compared to democratic states such as the United States. In the United States, public choice explanations have critiqued "public interest" theories of regulation, and highlighted the ways in which private interest influence has led to suboptimal governance results at the

---

[9] *See, e.g.*, MINXIN PEI, CHINA'S TRAPPED TRANSITION: THE LIMITS OF DEVELOPMENTAL AUTOCRACY 175–76 (2006).

[10] Scholars have explored public choice explanations for environmental law in the U.S. context at length. *See, e.g.*, BRUCE A. ACKERMAN & WILLIAM T. HASSLER: CLEAN COAL/DIRTY AIR (1981); E. Donald Elliott et al., *Toward a Theory of Statutory Evolution: The Federalization of Environmental Law*, 1 J.L. ECON. & ORG. 313 (1985); B. Peter Pashigian, *Environmental Regulation: Whose Self-Interests Are Being Protected?*, 23 ECON. INQUIRY 551, 551–52 (1985); Michael T. Maloney & Robert E. McCormick, *A Positive Theory of Environmental Quality Regulation*, 25 J.L. ECON. 99 (1982); Daniel A. Farber, *Politics and Procedure in Environmental Law*, 8 J.L. ECON. & ORG. 59 (1992); *see also* George Stigler, *The Theory of Economic Regulation*, 2 BELL J. ECON. & MGMT. SCI. 3 (1971) ("[A]s a rule, regulation is acquired by the industry and is designed and operated primarily for its benefit.").

[11] In the Chinese context, this is often discussed within the framework of "fragmented authoritarianism." *See generally* KENNETH LIEBERTHAL & MICHEL OKSENBERG, POLICY MAKING IN CHINA: LEADERS, STRUCTURES, AND PROCESSES (1988); SUSAN SHIRK, THE POLITICAL LOGIC OF ECONOMIC REFORM IN CHINA (1993); *see also* Andrew Mertha, *"Fragmented Authoritarianism 2.0": Political Pluralization in the Chinese Policy Process*, 200 CHINA Q. 995 (2009). For a detailed review of how interest groups compete to shape Chinese air pollution legislation, see William P. Alford & Benjamin Liebman, *Clean Air, Clean Processes? The Struggle over Air Pollution Law in the People's Republic of China*, 52 HASTINGS L.J. 703 (2001).

expense of aggregate social welfare.[12] In contrast, scholars do not typically presume that authoritarian states make decisions in the public interest. Scholarly work on the logic of authoritarian governance usually assumes that authoritarian policymaking is at its core motivated both by instrumental calculations about what it takes to remain in power and rent-seeking by elite interests.[13]

This chapter argues that these aspects of authoritarian governance (i.e., instrumental concerns about legitimacy and elite rent-seeking) are not necessarily incompatible with the delivery of public goods, such as environmental quality. The logic of self-preservation offers an explanation for why Chinese leaders, in a system lacking in strong formal public accountability mechanisms, might nonetheless prioritize environmental goals (and therefore seek to provide a valuable public good).[14] Moreover, some level of elite rent-seeking can plausibly serve to enhance, rather than hinder, the delivery of such environmental performance. Although it is difficult to ascertain the intentions of central leaders, this chapter suggests that bargaining and accommodation of elite rent-seeking behavior could be as much a strategic decision by a leadership concerned with achieving environmental outcomes, as it is an organic outcome of elite political contestation and bureaucratic fragmentation. That is, the pressure of elite groups (such as SOEs) influences policymaking, but leaders are also aware that—in order to get things done—vested interest groups must be accommodated.

It is not clear whether SOEs will in fact respond to state incentives to implement Chinese environmental policies, but I argue that there are reasons to believe that SOEs may in fact be more responsive than conventional wisdom assumes. Whether this ultimately proves to be the case is an empirical question for future research.

This chapter proceeds in four parts.[15] Section I establishes the substantial contribution of SOEs to China's environmental problems. A relatively small number of large SOEs account for a disproportionate amount of China's pollution. If we are concerned with the future direction of Chinese environmental protection, a greater understanding

---

[12] *See, e.g.*, Pashigian, *supra* note 10, at 551–52 (noting that economists typically "accept[] the notion that social welfare and not private interest is the guiding principle for environmental legislation and regulation"); Farber, *supra* note 10, at 62 ("The simplest explanation for the passage of environmental laws is that they actually reflect the influence of special interests rather than the preferences of the general public.").

[13] *See, e.g.*, LIEBERTHAL & OKSENBERG, *supra* note 11; SHIRK, *supra* note 11; Lorentzen et al., *supra* note 8; Wang, *infra* note 14.

[14] As I have previously noted, increased leadership prioritization of environmental goals can be explained as a response to self-interested concerns about weakening state legitimacy stemming from China's environmental problems. *See* Alex Wang, *The Search for Sustainable Legitimacy: Environmental Law and Bureaucracy in China*, 37 HARV. ENVTL. L. REV. 365, 394–98 (2013) for a discussion of the reasons that Chinese authorities have elevated environmental priorities, particularly since 2006. These include concerns about economic development and energy security, as well as a reaction to bottom-up citizen pressures and risks to social stability.

[15] This analysis is based on a review of official government documents, media reports, eleven interviews conducted in 2014 in China and the United States, and the author's personal experience working for a U.S. environmental law advocacy organization in China between 2005 and 2011.

of the role of SOEs is absolutely essential. Section II looks at the past and examines the reasons that SOEs have been able to weaken environmental rules and persist in weaker environmental performance. These dynamics are among the reasons that commentators have viewed SOEs as vested interests able to thwart central environmental directives. I conclude this section, however, with the suggestion that past performance is no guarantee of future results. Although SOEs have in the past shown the classic signs of regulatory capture, poor environmental performance in past decades was also the result of the low priority that central leadership placed on environmental protection.

Section III turns to the present and argues that central leaders have in recent years elevated the policy priority of the environment. This section then conceptualizes three governance approaches—bargaining, regulating, and breaking—likely to affect SOE environmental performance. First of all, central policies reflect an effort to accommodate elite SOE interests through subsidies and protectionist measures that retain state control over many heavy industrial sectors ("bargaining"). Traditional regulatory approaches that would require more substantial reallocation of power to regulatory and judicial institutions or the public ("regulating") have expanded in more modest ways, likely due to opposition from other parts of the Chinese bureaucracy or Party concerns about loss of control. A wild card element in this environmental governance story is the impact of Xi Jinping's ongoing anticorruption campaign ("breaking"), which has resulted in the arrest of many current and former SOE leaders and bureaucrats within their networks. Although there is little evidence to suggest that the anticorruption campaign is intended as an environmental policy tool, in practice it may have this effect by weakening the political influence of SOEs right at a time when central policies are attempting to motivate a change in SOE environmental performance.

Section IV concludes by elaborating on how this approach to governance has the potential to deliver some level of environmental performance. Although the effort may not be efficient in an economic sense (an uncontroversial critique for an approach reliant on top-down administrative control and accommodation of rent-seeking), central leaders surely recognize that finding a solution to seemingly intractable environmental problems will generate important political legitimacy dividends, even absent broader political, legal, or market reforms.

I. The Role of State-Owned Enterprises in China's Pollution

China is the world's largest emitter of carbon dioxide (CO_2), sulfur dioxide, nitrogen oxides, mercury, and a host of other pollutants.[16] In 2012, China's CO_2 emissions were greater than those of the United States and the European Union combined, accounting for

[16] This chapter will focus in particular on the impact of SOEs on China's air pollution and climate change. The institutional dynamics with respect to pollution in other media (water, soil, etc.) may differ.

nearly 30 percent of global emissions.[17] Ninety-two percent of Chinese cities failed to meet national ambient air quality standards in 2013.[18] China ranks 118 out of 178 countries on one comparative index of country-level environmental performance.[19] On air quality, China ranks nearly last at 176.[20] The World Bank has estimated the cost of China's environmental pollution (air, water, and soil) at nearly 10 percent of GDP.[21]

At the heart of China's air pollution problem is China's economic reliance on heavy industry, powered to an overwhelming degree by coal.[22] In the parlance of the Chinese bureaucracy, the problem is an excessive commitment to the "two high, one resource" (*lianggao yizi*) industries, such as steel, chemicals, nonferrous metals (copper, aluminum, etc.), cement, coal, power, and oil. The Chinese government has, in other words, formally recognized these industries as being high in energy consumption and pollution, and resource intensive.[23]

SOEs have been central to this industrial economy. Of China's 112 central SOEs, most are engaged in heavy industry.[24] In 2010, the government designated 85 of 128 central SOEs[25] as enterprises with heavy energy use or pollution, and subjected them to special

---

[17] *See* Alex Wang, *Regulating Domestic Carbon Outsourcing: The Case of China and Climate Change*, 61 UCLA L. Rev. 2018, 2220 n.4 (2014).

[18] Greenpeace, The End of China's Coal Boom—6 Facts You Should Know 3 (Apr. 11, 2014), *available at* http://www.greenpeace.org/international/Global/international/briefings/climate/2014/The-End-of-Chinas-Coal-Boom.pdf.

[19] *See* 2014 Yale Envtl. Performance Index, Country Profile—China http://epi.yale.edu/epi/country-profile/china (last visited Feb. 10, 2015).

[20] *Id.*

[21] 6.5 percent from air pollution, 2.1 percent water pollution, and 1.1 percent soil degradation. World Bank & Dev. Res. Ctr. of the St. Council, P.R.C., China 2030: Building a Modern, Harmonious, and Creative Society 39 (2013), *available at* http://www.worldbank.org/content/dam/Worldbank/document/China-2030-complete.pdf.

[22] In 2011, 65 percent of China's total energy consumption came from coal. *See* U.S. Energy Info. Admin., China: Overview, http://www.eia.gov/countries/cab.cfm?fips=CH (last updated Feb. 19, 2015).

[23] In 2011, industry composed 47 percent of China's GDP, services 43 percent. In the United States, by contrast, industry accounted for just 20 percent of GDP, services 79 percent. *See* World Bank, Industry, Value Added, http://data.worldbank.org/indicator/NV.IND.TOTL.ZS (last visited Feb. 10, 2015); World Bank, Services, etc., Value Added, http://data.worldbank.org/indicator/NV.SRV.TETC.ZS (last visited Feb. 10, 2015).

[24] At the provincial and municipal levels, thousands of sub-national SOEs are involved in energy-intensive, high pollution industries as well. Although this chapter focuses primarily on central SOEs, many sub-national SOEs are substantial businesses in their own right. Provincial-level SOEs in the Fortune Global 500 include Hebei Iron & Steel Group (#271), Shanxi Coking (#290), Jizhong Energy Group (#304) (coal), Shandong Energy Group (#305) (coal), and Jinneng Energy Group (#309) (coal). Other Fortune Global 500 provincial-level SOEs in heavy industrial sectors include: Bohai Steel Group (#327), Henan Energy & Chemical (#328), Zhejiang Materials Industry Group (#345), Shougang Group (#348) (steel), CEFC Energy Group (#349), Datong Coal Mine Corp (#369), Shanxi Luan Mining Group (#372), Shanxi Jincheng Anthracite Coal Mining Group (#386), Yangquan Coal Industry Group (#391), Kailuan Group (#394) (coal), and Shaanxi Yanchang Petroleum (#432). *See supra* note 7.

[25] The total number of central SOEs has since declined to 112. *See supra* note 1.

monitoring procedures and incentives for environmental improvements.[26] The highest priority firms on this list include major SOEs in oil, power generation and transmission, steel, coal, construction materials, chemicals, nonferrous metals, air transport, and shipping. These are sectors in which the state-owned share remains quite high. SOEs have an overwhelming market share in the power and oil sectors. Even in sectors with significantly greater nonstate participation, SOEs still loom large. In the steel sector, for example, SOEs account for 57.5 percent of total funds.[27]

Because of their size, a relatively small number of central SOEs have a disproportionate impact on China's environment. For example, just five central SOEs in the power generation sector account for 50 percent of China's total installed power generation capacity; in all, central SOEs represent 60 percent of total capacity.[28] The power sector in turn accounts for one-half of China's CO_2 emissions.[29]

Moreover, Chinese SOEs, like state-owned businesses worldwide, are typically less profitable and more inefficient than private businesses because of competing state goals (e.g., job retention and economic stimulus) and a relative lack of market discipline.[30] One study showed that SOEs had significantly poorer environmental performance in comparison with private enterprises, collectively owned enterprises (such as township-village enterprises), or foreign companies operating in China.[31]

SOEs are not responsive to market pressures, in part because they tend to lack hard budget constraints. The state is expected to step in to support SOEs, which are often viewed as "too big to fail." SOEs receive substantial state subsidies that reduce the

---

[26] *See* 中央企业节能减排监督管理暂行办法 (Provisional Measures on Central SOE Energy Savings Emissions Reduction Supervision and Management) (promulgated by SASAC on Mar. 26, 2010, effective Mar. 26, 2010), Annex I, *available at* http://www.gov.cn/flfg/2010-04/12/content_1578699.htm.

[27] Hong Sheng & Nong Zhao, China's State-Owned Enterprises: Nature, Performance and Reform 130 (2012).

[28] The "Big Five" power generation SOEs account for 48.75 percent. Seven other central SOEs represent an additional 12.6 percent of China's installed capacity. Fifteen large sub-national SOEs are responsible for 10.05 percent. These twenty-seven firms account for 71.41 percent of China's installed capacity. 国家电力监管委员会2011年度监管报告 (China State Electricity Regulatory Commission, 2011 Annual Report on Electricity Regulation) 5 (2011).

[29] The statistic refers specifically to emissions from the "electricity and heating" sector. Int'l Energy Ass'n, CO_2 Emissions from Fuel Combustion Highlights (2013 edition) 26 (2013), *available at* http://www.iea.org/publications/freepublications/publication/CO2EmissionsFromFuelCombustionHighlights2013.pdf.

[30] Hua Wang et al., *Industrial Ownership and Environmental Performance: Evidence from China*, 36 Envtl. & Resource Econ. 255 (2006); Xuhong Liu, *Industry Environmental Performance, Economic Growth, and Environmental Regulation: Evidence from China* 76 (Dec. 2008) (unpublished PhD dissertation, University of Massachusetts), *available at* http://search.proquest.com/docview/230911291. Regarding SOEs worldwide, see Arief Budiman et al., *Improving Performance at State-Owned Enterprises*, McKinsey & Company (May 2009), http://www.mckinsey.com/insights/public_sector/improving_performance_at_state-owned_enterprises.

[31] Hua Wang et al., *supra* note 30.

incentive for efficiency and encourage greater levels of production than the market might otherwise bear. SOEs tend also to have greater access to low-interest credit,[32] fiscal subsidies,[33] and other benefits such as access to subsidized land, electricity, and raw materials.[34] And state controls on prices often limit the ability of SOEs to pass on the cost of environmental protection to consumers, a reason that SOEs use to justify not undertaking environmental measures.[35]

Official central policy is to sustain state ownership and control in many heavy industrial sectors for the foreseeable future, even though overall the SOE share of national GDP has declined in recent years.[36] Since 2006, stated policy has been to maintain absolute control (*juedui kongzhili*) over industries that relate to national security and the "lifeline of the national economy," including power and grid, oil, and coal.[37] Next in priority are the pillar industries, such as steel, nonferrous metals, chemicals, and cement, where the state is meant to retain "relatively strong control" (*jiaoqiang kongzhili*).[38] The overall proportion of state capital in these industries is to be "appropriately reduced," but the goal is to maintain absolute control over the most important enterprises—that is, those with "relatively strong influence or impact."[39] Although economic policies under

---

[32] China's banks are predominately state-owned and have traditionally offered a disproportionate amount of credit to SOEs. SOEs tend to receive preferential interest rates and easier access to unsecured loans as compared to private enterprises. SHENG & ZHAO, *supra* note 27, at 65.

[33] In 2007 and 2008, PetroChina and Sinopec received more than US$10 billion (RMB76.349 billion) in subsidies, ostensibly aimed at ensuring oil supply. *Id.* at 69.

[34] For example, Sinopec received subsidized land use rights from the state worth RMB38.5 billion (about US$6 billion). *Id.* at 53. SOEs also receive access to low-cost natural resource or energy inputs. One study estimated that, from 2000 to mid-2007, total state subsidies to the steel industry amounted to US$27.11 billion. Ninety-five percent of these subsidies related to coal and the provision of subsidized energy prices. Usha Haley & George Haley, *Subsidies and the China Price*, HARV. BUS. REV. June 1, 2008, at 25. *See also* CHINA 2030, *supra* note 21, at 105; Usha Haley & George Haley, *Zombies and Glass Houses: Chinese Industrial Subsidies*, THE GLOBALIST (Mar. 6, 2014), http://www.theglobalist.com/zombies-glass-houses-chinese-industrial-subsidies/.

[35] *See supra* Section II(A)1.

[36] SOEs accounted for 77.63 percent of industrial production in 1978, and only 30 percent in 2004. OECD WORKING GROUP ON PRIVATISATION AND CORPORATE GOVERNANCE OF STATE OWNED ASSETS, STATE OWNED ENTERPRISES IN CHINA: REVIEWING THE EVIDENCE 6 (Jan. 26, 2009), *available at* http://www.oecd.org/corporate/ca/corporategovernanceofstate-ownedenterprises/42095493.pdf.

[37] 国资委：国有经济应保持对7个行业的绝对控制力 (SASAC: The State-Owned Economy Should Maintain Absolute Control over 7 Industrial Sectors), 新华 (XINHUA) (Dec. 19, 2006), http://www.china.com.cn/policy/txt/2006-12/19/content_7527663.htm. Other key industries include defense, telecommunications, civil aviation, and shipping. The goal is to increase state capital in these enterprises and push the forty or so central SOEs to become leading global enterprises.

[38] Other pillar industries include equipment manufacturing, automobiles, information, and surveying.

[39] 国务院办公厅转发国资委关于推进国有资本调整和国有企业重组指导意见的通知 (State Council on Forwarding the Guiding Opinions of the SASAC about Promoting the Adjustment of State-Owned Capital and the Reorganization of State-Owned Enterprises) (promulgated by SASAC on Dec. 5, 2006), http://www.sasac.gov.cn/n1180/n1566/n258252/n258644/11663621.html.

Xi Jinping have emphasized a greater reliance on the market, central policy still appears to support state control or influence in these particular heavy industries.[40]

In short, SOEs are influential (or even monopolist) players in the traditional heavy industries that have served as the foundation of China's economic growth over the last four decades. These industries produce an outsized proportion of China's pollution, and evidence suggests that the state intends to maintain ownership or control over these sectors for the foreseeable future.

Given the continuing salience of SOEs in China's industrial economy, a key question is what role SOEs will play in ongoing environmental reform efforts. Section II describes the reasons SOEs have traditionally been thought to be major barriers to environmental reform, but also suggests that these reasons are less convincing as evidence of future implementation problems than commonly thought.

II. The Past: State-Owned Enterprises and Regulatory Capture

SOEs are typically characterized as vested interests able to stymie the implementation of state objectives, environmental and otherwise. Of SOEs, Premier Li Keqiang said in 2013: "Nowadays, stirring up vested interests is more difficult than stirring up one's soul."[41] Of course, Chinese enterprises—no matter the type—have generally been able to escape stringent environmental enforcement, but evidence suggests that SOEs, on average, are *even more* able to do so. SOEs have been able to distort the rule-making process, altering the rules to which they are subject, and once rules are in place they often receive more lenient treatment in enforcement compared with non-SOEs.

Whereas Section I described the environmental impact of SOEs due to their relative scale and inefficiency, this section identifies three key reasons that SOEs are commonly able to influence the regulatory process in their favor with negative consequences for the environment.[42]

First, SOEs benefit from what I term the ideology of state capitalism. For most of recent memory, this ideology has prized the role of SOEs in economic development, job provision, and other priorities often in tension with environmental compliance. This thinking continues to provide SOEs with normative support in bargaining for weaker

---

[40] Chi Hung Kwang, Res. Inst. of Econ., Trade & Indus., IAA, Post-Third Plenum Reform of State-Owned Enterprises: Can Corporate Governance Be Improved? (June 4, 2014), http://www.rieti.go.jp/en/china/14060402.html (English).

[41] *Li Urges Paring State Role to Fuel 7.5% China Growth*, Bloomberg News (Mar. 17, 2013), http://www.bloomberg.com/news/articles/2013-03-17/china-s-li-vows-to-keep-7-5-growth-and-spread-wealth-benefits.

[42] These factors are commonly thought of as indicia of regulatory capture. *See, e.g.*, Jean-Jacques Laffont & Jean Tirole, *The Politics of Government Decision-Making: A Theory of Regulatory Capture*, 106 Q.J. Econ. 1089 (1991); Michael Levine & Jennifer Forrence, *Regulatory Capture, Public Interest, and the Public Agenda: Toward a Synthesis*, 6 J.L. Econ. & Org. 167 (1990); Toni Makkai & John Braithwaite, *In and Out of the Revolving Door: Making Sense of Regulatory Capture*, 12 J. Pub. Pol'y 61 (1992).

regulations or more lenient environmental enforcement. Second, various institutional design features of the Chinese bureaucracy limit regulatory enforcement and compliance. These include problems of SOE bureaucratic rank and the "revolving door" among enterprises, regulatory bodies, and Party-state leadership positions. Third, even the *appearance* of SOE power (or proximity to power) allows SOEs to benefit (or obtain rents) in the form of lighter regulation and reduced media and public supervision.

Ultimately, however, I argue that the concept of regulatory capture is not entirely apt for describing *past* interactions between SOEs and the regulatory and lawmaking bodies with which they interact over environmental protection. Agency or capture problems—where regulators and rule-makers cannot control SOEs—no doubt exist. But in the environmental context, this framing has obscured the fact that central and local authorities alike have not traditionally prioritized environmental protection.[43] Weak SOE compliance is not, in other words, only the result of SOE defiance of state policy, but instead may reflect the fact that the state has, until very recently, not considered environmental protection a very high priority.

A. TYPES OF SOE CAPTURE

1. Rule-Making

There is little question that SOEs have in many respects been able to influence or control rule-making processes, with largely negative implications for environmental protection. An example from the state-owned petroleum and gas sector illustrates how this works in practice. In China, authority for environmental regulations involving the transportation sector is split so that environmental authorities set vehicle *emissions* standards, while a committee composed primarily of representatives from the three central oil and gas SOEs sets fuel *quality* standards (i.e., pollutant concentrations in fuel).[44] "Dirtier" vehicle fuels limit the efficacy of stringent vehicle emissions standards and result in higher vehicle emissions. The oil enterprises have long argued, however, that fuel quality standards should not be made more stringent without accompanying state funding to cover the incremental costs associated with producing higher-quality fuel. Fuel prices in China are controlled by the state, and the SOEs have no authority to pass additional costs on to consumers unilaterally through price increases.

The fuel quality standards committee is set up, in essence, as industry self-regulation, reflecting a not-so-distant planned economy past in which regulation and implementation of oil production were all handled by a single bureau. Representatives from the

---

[43] Section III(A) describes how central authorities have increased the priority of environmental protection in recent years.

[44] This fuel quality committee is known as the National Petroleum Products and Lubricant Standardization Technology Committee, or TC280 (全国石油产品和润滑剂标准化技术委员会 (石化标委会)), (n.d.) http://www.cptcstd.org/viewOrg.aspx.

Sinopec, China National Petroleum Corporation (CNPC), China National Offshore Oil Corporation (CNOOC), and other parties with interests in the oil industry make up 90 percent of the seats on the fuel quality standards committee. The committee secretariat is housed within a Sinopec-affiliated research institute. As a result, fuel quality standards set by this committee have long lagged behind environment ministry-promulgated vehicle emissions standards, with the attendant environmental consequences.[45]

SOEs have been able to affect environmental regulation by influencing rule-making processes in this way.

2. Enforcement

Evidence also suggests that SOEs are treated more leniently than other enterprise types in the enforcement of environmental regulations. Several studies have shown, for example, that SOEs pay lower discharge fees (i.e., volume-based fees for pollution discharges in excess of standards) relative to other types of enterprises, such as township village enterprises and private enterprises.[46] Scholars have posited that this is due to both the political influence of SOEs and government/regulator concerns about social stability. In one study, SOEs were on average in poorer financial health than other types of firms, and saddled with larger financial obligations to workers, such as pension benefits.[47] SOEs successfully raised concerns about financial hardship that could lead to facility closures and job losses as leverage in seeking reduced discharge fees. Another study demonstrated that large, mostly state-run, industrial firms tended to comply less with centrally mandated environmental information disclosure requirements.[48] The authors argue that this is an example of how SOEs are able to hinder central authorities' efforts to implement policy objectives.

Thus, evidence suggests that SOEs are able not only to change the rules on the books in their favor, but also to weaken the implementation of these rules in practice.

B. EXPLANATIONS FOR SOE CAPTURE

SOEs enjoy these advantages for a variety of reasons. This chapter explores three of them: ideological support for state capitalism, institutional design and practice, and the

---

[45] FREDA FUNG ET AL., INT'L COUNCIL ON CLEAN TRANSP., OVERVIEW OF CHINA'S VEHICLE EMISSION CONTROL PROGRAM: PAST SUCCESSES AND FUTURE PROSPECTS 34 (Dec. 2010), *available at* http://theicct.org/sites/default/files/publications/Retrosp_final_bilingual.pdf ("The lagged implementation of fuel standards . . . has become a major roadblock to ratcheting down vehicle emission standards.").

[46] XIAOYING MA & LEONARD ORTOLANO, ENVIRONMENTAL REGULATION IN CHINA: INSTITUTIONS, ENFORCEMENT, AND COMPLIANCE 143–49 (2000); Wang, *supra* note 8; Zhi Tang & Delmonize A. Smith, *How Does State Ownership Affect Pollution Control? Evidence from the Chinese Iron and Steel Industry*, 7 INT'L J. BUS. GOVERNANCE & ETHICS 173, 173–88 (2012).

[47] MA AND ORTOLANO, *supra* note 46.

[48] Lorentzen et al., *supra* note 8, at 182–94.

informal benefits or rents that accrue to SOEs simply because regulators and civil society actors *believe* them to have ready access to levers of state power.

1. The Ideology of State Capitalism

Chinese SOEs, like SOEs in other countries, justify state subsidies as the price the state must pay for the various public goods that SOEs ostensibly offer to society.[49] SOEs are job providers. Subsidies make up for economic losses that result from state-controlled prices. Major Chinese SOEs are vehicles for pursuing national economic and political objectives of various sorts, at home and abroad. Critics have sought to puncture this narrative by arguing that SOEs are inefficient, unprofitable, and even corrupt, and in practice do not achieve these goals.[50]

Regardless of the empirical truth of the matter, among bureaucrats, civilians, and even advocates alike, the belief that SOEs serve as important vessels for achieving positive state objectives continues to influence policy debates. This ideology of SOEs and state capitalism is a useful tool for SOEs seeking to affect rule-making and implementation of environmental regulations, and can serve as a barrier to efforts to limit SOE pollution.

2. Bureaucratic Design and Practice

SOEs can also influence enforcement processes both because of formal institutional structures and de facto bureaucratic practices. The dynamics that limit enforcement include problems of bureaucratic rank, mobility within the bureaucracy, and revolving-door issues that create conflicts of interest or otherwise weaken the authority of regulators.

First of all, SOEs are unresponsive to regulation in part because of conflicts created by the relative administrative rank (*jibie*) of SOEs and regulators. Within China's bureaucratic hierarchy, SOEs often hold administrative rank superior or equal to the environmental protection bureaus tasked with regulating them. For example, central SOEs commonly hold ministerial or vice-ministerial rank. Many will therefore be of equal administrative rank to the Ministry of Environmental Protection (MEP). Prior to its elevation to full ministry status in 2007, MEP, then known as the State Environmental Protection Administration (SEPA), was only at vice-ministerial rank, and thus outranked by many central SOEs. This problem is replicated at lower levels

---

[49] *See, e.g.*, Richard McGregor, The Party: The Secret World of China's Communist Rulers 34–69 (2012) (describing the various political and economic roles of SOEs); Hans Christensen, OECD Corporate Governance Working Papers No. 6, Balancing Commercial and Non-Commercial Priorities of State-Owned Enterprises 6–8 (2013), http://www.oecd.org/daf/ca/OECDCorporateGovernanceWorkingPaper6.pdf (comparing SOEs in Hungary, Israel, the Netherlands, New Zealand, and Norway).

[50] Sheng & Zhao, *supra* note 27.

of the system. Provincial environmental bureaus, which are division-level entities (just below vice-ministerial rank), are often tasked with regulating facilities of central or provincial-level SOEs, which will almost always be of higher administrative rank. These dynamics create a tension between the laws and regulations that authorize regulatory supervision, and the rules and norms of the bureaucratic system, which establish a strict hierarchy of authority that carries a great deal of weight in China.

Second, SOEs are embedded within a broader bureaucratic system characterized by significant personnel cross-pollination among SOEs, regulatory bureaus, and other Party-state institutions. Successful SOE leaders can expect to move into a variety of positions in the Party or government at different points in their careers, granting them formal powers and the ability to retaliate against regulators who might have proven too aggressive in the past. The Party's ability to direct the career trajectories of bureaucrats (including SOE leaders) is a critical mechanism for maintaining control over the bureaucracy.[51] But the embeddedness of SOE leaders within the bureaucracy also gives them significant political leverage within the system as well.[52]

These issues of revolving doors and challenges to regulatory authority certainly exist in other systems. But weak rule of law, insufficient norms governing conflicts of interests and retaliation, and the critical importance of personal networks (*renmai guanxi*) in the Chinese system render these dynamics a particular challenge. And given that Chinese SOEs are now among some of the largest companies in the world, the role of money is greater than ever, increasing the opportunities for graft, influence peddling, and the prospect that regulators will treat SOEs leniently in order to preserve the possibility of lucrative relationships with the targets of their regulatory supervision.

Examples of the revolving door are legion. SOE leaders, like government leaders, are appointed by the Party's Organization Department one level above them in the bureaucratic hierarchy. It is typical to find SOE leaders who have also held government or Party posts. For example, Zhou Yongkang, the former Politburo Standing Committee member charged with corruption in 2014, previously served as Party Secretary and General Manager of China National Petroleum Corporation (Petrochina is its publicly traded subsidiary) in the 1990s. But Zhou also held numerous government and Party positions in Sichuan Province, the Ministry of Land and Resources, the Ministry of Public Security, the powerful Politics and Law Commission, and the Politburo Standing Committee.

---

[51] *See* Wang, *supra* note 14, at 378–81; *see also* McGregor, *supra* note 49, at 84 (relating the story of the Party Organization Department shuffling the heads of China's three state-owned telecom companies: "[i]t was the equivalent of the CEO of AT&T being moved without notice to head its domestic US competitor, Verizon, with the Verizon chief being appointed to run Sprint, at a time when the three companies were locked in a bruising battle on pricing and industry standards.").

[52] Lorentzen et al., *supra* note 8, at 185.

Although Zhou is probably the most prominent example of a revolving door politician-businessman, there are countless other examples.

- Liu Qi worked in the iron and steel industry for thirty years, rising to become manager of central SOE Wuhan Iron & Steel in the early 1990s.[53] He was then appointed Party Secretary and Minister of the Ministry of Metallurgical Industry, Secretary and Mayor of Beijing, and a member of the Politburo.
- Pu Haiqing worked in the iron and steel industry, becoming manager of Chongqing Iron and Steel, and later served as Mayor of Chongqing and Director of the National Metallurgical Industry Bureau, among other positions.[54]
- Wei Liucheng was a member of the 17th Party Central Committee, governor of Hainan Province, and former head of CNOOC, the central petroleum SOE.[55]

As these examples show, officials can move both horizontally and vertically within the system. With little warning, local bureaucrats and enterprise leaders may be elevated to senior posts at higher levels of the state. A target of regulation one day could very well be in a more senior position in the bureaucracy the next, and in a position to exact retribution. Strict environmental enforcement can suffer as a result.

3. The Appearance of Power

SOEs and their leaders may have access to levers of power in a variety of formal and informal ways, but they can also derive benefits (in the form of weaker enforcement and limited citizen complaints) simply from conveying the *appearance* of power. Regulators and advocates in China, as elsewhere, seek to minimize risks associated with environmental enforcement or advocacy. Bureaucrats tasked with regulating SOEs, and citizens who might wish to bring complaints against SOEs, must consider the potential risk of taking action against actors thought to be powerful and well connected. The specter of state power—or the "anaconda in the chandelier"—can lead subjects to self-censor or construct the informal rules of the game in ways that enhance state control.[56]

For example, in Shandong Province, state-owned coal-fired power plants often violate emissions standards. The director of the provincial EPB reportedly has been reluctant

---

[53] Liu Qi Biography, CHINA VITAE, http://www.chinavitae.com/biography/Liu_Qi|31/bio (last visited Feb. 10, 2015).

[54] Pu Haiqing Biography, CHINA VITAE, http://www.chinavitae.com/biography/Pu_Haiqing/bio (last visited Feb. 10, 2015).

[55] Wei Liucheng Biography, CHINA VITAE, http://www.chinavitae.com/biography/Wei_Liucheng (last visited Feb. 10, 2015).

[56] Perry Link, *China: The Anaconda in the Chandelier*, N.Y. REV. BOOKS (Apr. 11, 2002), http://www.nybooks.com/articles/archives/2002/apr/11/china-the-anaconda-in-the-chandelier; *see also* Rachel Stern & Jonathan Hassid, *Amplifying Silence: Uncertainty and Control Parables in Contemporary China*, 45 COMP. POL. STUD. 1230 (2012).

to bring enforcement actions against these facilities because of their perceived political backing (e.g., affiliation with the Big 5 central power SOEs).[57] Private enterprises may very well project the impression of close connections with powerful supporters who can obstruct or retaliate against regulators.[58] But the presumption that SOEs have such connections is long-standing and well established.

Civil society groups carefully consider the risks of confronting SOEs as well. For example, in 2013, Greenpeace's China office launched a campaign against Shenhua, the central state-owned coal group and the world's largest coal producer by volume, to protest Shenhua's alleged dumping of toxic industrial wastewater at a coal-to-liquids plant in Ordos, Inner Mongolia. Although Greenpeace had worked in China since 1997, this was the first time the group had ever campaigned against a Chinese SOE.[59] Greenpeace's unwillingness to act against SOEs in nearly two decades of work in China likely reflected concerns about political repercussions, and a belief that campaigns would not likely change the behavior of well-connected SOEs.[60]

None of this is to deny that SOEs can in many cases *actually* retaliate against regulators or citizen advocates. In the Greenpeace campaign, the Communist Party's Propaganda Department reportedly banned all domestic reporting about the Greenpeace report and campaign, suggesting that the SOE had ready access to and support from senior levels of the Party-state.[61] But SOEs enjoy the additional benefit of projecting the impression of power. Those who wish to confront SOEs must reckon with the possible repercussions of challenging power, making SOEs a riskier target perhaps best left alone. In a situation where many enterprises (state-owned or not) are violating environmental rules, regulators and civil society actors may rationally conclude that SOEs are likely to be riskier targets on average than other types of enterprises.

C. ROGUE ACTORS OR AGENTS OF THE STATE?

Though these dynamics suggest that SOEs are vested interests with the ability to flout environmental regulation, I argue that these dynamics may not in fact be *pathologies* at all. For most of the last three decades or so, the Chinese state has made environmental protection a relatively low priority objective. Local actors were rewarded primarily based on economic performance, maintenance of social stability, and development of

[57] Interview with Chinese NGO representative, Beijing, July 2014.

[58] Email exchange with Chinese environmental lawyer (noting that lawyers do not view the distinction between private entities and SOEs as determinative in evaluating whether an enterprise has influence or not; private enterprises with significant investment in a jurisdiction may be viewed as having more influence on local officials than a relatively smaller SOE) (Aug. 2014) (on file with author).

[59] Press Release, Greenpeace, World's Biggest Coal Company Shenhua to Stop Exploiting Groundwater in China (Apr. 8, 2014), http://www.greenpeace.org/international/en/press/releases/Worlds-biggest-coal-company-Shenhua-to-stop-exploiting-groundwater-in-China/.

[60] Interview with environmental consulting firm representative, Beijing, July 2014.

[61] *Id.*

important personal relationships within the bureaucracy.[62] Given this ordering of priorities, weak environmental compliance is not necessarily evidence of goal displacement or the inability of higher levels of the state to influence the behavior of local-level actors. Central authorities might prefer that economic, stability, *and* environmental objectives are all met, but weak implementation of environmental objectives has also been tolerated so long as other more important goals are achieved.

The Chinese leadership has only recently elevated environmental protection to a higher priority. The evidence that SOEs have undermined environmental protection in the past leaves open the question of how they will respond to a changed context in which environmental objectives are more important than before. Section III examines changed environmental strategies for SOEs in just such a context.

III. The Present: Building SOE Support for Green Development

In recent years, central authorities have elevated environmental priorities. I have previously argued that this reflects the rational self-interest of leaders concerned with maintaining state legitimacy and control.[63]

This shift in environmental priorities has begun to disrupt the institutional context within which SOEs operate, and has led to an evolving set of Party-state strategies for obtaining SOE cooperation. Although central leaders still appear to place primary value on economic growth and stability, environmental issues have come to take on a higher priority, and officials have positioned environmental priorities as a way to achieve growth and stability goals at the same time.[64] This has particularly been the case since 2006 and the start of the 11th five-year plan.[65] This new state of affairs offers an opportunity to examine how central authorities attempt to alter the behavior of elite SOE actors in a fragmented governance system.

---

[62] *See* Hongbin Li & Li-An Zhou, *Political Turnover and Economic Performance: The Incentive Role of Personnel Control in China*, 89 J. Pub. Econ. 1743 (2005); Victor Shih et al., *Getting Ahead in the Communist Party: Explaining the Advancement of Central Committee Members in China*, 106 Am. Pol. Sci. Rev. 166 (2012); Ruixue Jia et al., *Political Selection in China: The Complementary Roles of Connections and Performance*, IFN Working Paper No. 1003, *available at* http://papers.ssrn.com/sol3/papers.cfm?abstract_id=2468801.

[63] *See* Wang, *supra* note 14.

[64] Chinese officials have announced that they will no longer weight economic growth targets as heavily in evaluating the performance of government officials. According to President Xi Jinping, China "can no longer simply use GDP growth rates to decide who the [party] heroes are." Gabriel Wildau, *Shanghai First Major Chinese Region to Ditch GDP Growth Target*, Fin. Times (Jan. 26, 2015), http://www.ft.com/cms/s/0/2c822efc-a51d-11e4-bf11-00144feab7de.html#axzz3RO8BMkez; Gabriel Wildau, *Small Chinese Cities Steer Away from GDP as Measure of Success*, Fin. Times (Aug. 13, 2014), http://www.ft.com/intl/cms/s/0/a0288bd4-22b0-11e4-8dae-00144feabdc0.html#axzz3RO8BMkez.

[65] *See* Wang, *supra* note 14, at 399.

I label these new strategies (perhaps with some irony) a "no regrets" approach to environmental protection in both a traditional and nontraditional sense.[66] On the one hand, it suggests an effort to promote environmental protection that does not limit economic growth (e.g., through new renewable energy industries or energy efficiency measures that lower the cost of energy use). This is the standard definition of *green development*.[67] On the other hand, "no regrets" also refers to environmental reform without the requirement of substantial market, legal, and political reforms. This approach to environmental protection would not fundamentally alter the power dynamic between the Party-state and society, or among powerful actors, such as SOEs, within the system. It is also an approach that willingly borrows useful components from more liberal political, legal, and economic systems, but in a way that allows the Party-state to remain in command.

A. THE RISE OF ENVIRONMENTAL GOALS

Chinese authorities have signaled the elevation of environmental goals in leadership speeches, government plans, bureaucratic targets, policy pronouncements, and legislative enactments. This is seen most clearly in the increased priority of environmental objectives in China's five-year plan targets and the incorporation of these environmental targets into the formal evaluation criteria for bureaucrats. The elevation first appeared in the 11th five-year plan (2006–2010), which designated energy efficiency and pollution reduction targets as "binding."[68] In the 12th five-year plan (2011–2015), the leadership added binding targets for carbon intensity reduction and mitigation of additional air and water pollutants.[69] These targets have served as the basis for a range of state policies and programs to support energy efficiency, pollution reduction, and the growth of less-polluting economic sectors.

With the worsening of air pollution in China's major cities, Chinese authorities have also issued an unprecedented number of environmental policy documents, such

---

[66] *See, e.g.*, CHINA 2030, *supra* note 21, at 224–25 (describing no-regrets options for reducing CO_2 emissions that produce environmental benefits that pay for themselves through energy and resource savings); KEITH BURNARD ET AL., INT'L ENERGY AGENCY, EMISSIONS REDUCTION THROUGH UPGRADE OF COAL-FIRED POWER PLANTS: LEARNING FROM CHINESE EXPERIENCE 11 (2014), *available at* http://www.iea.org/publications/freepublications/publication/PartnerCountrySeriesEmissionsReductionthroughUpgradeofCoalFiredPowerPlants.pdf.

[67] CHINA 2030, *supra* note 21, at 39 (defining green development as "a pattern of development that decouples growth from heavy dependence on resource use, carbon emissions, and environmental damage, and that promotes growth through the creation of new green product markets, technologies, investments, and changes in consumption and conservation behavior").

[68] *See* Wang, *supra* note 14, at 399.

[69] 第六篇: 绿色发展, 建设资源节约型, 环境友好型社会 (Chapter Six: Green Development, Constructing a Resource-Saving, Environmental Friendly Society), 中华人民共和国国民经济和社会发展第十二个五年规划纲要 (People's Republic of China National Economic and Social Development 12th Five-Year Plan Outline) (2011), *available at* http://www.gov.cn/2011lh/content_1825838_7.htm.

as the September 2013 Air Pollution Prevention Action Plan.[70] The core components of the plan include reducing reliance on heavy industry, installation of pollution control equipment, coal management, other technological upgrades, and transportation-related measures. These elements of the plan are to be incorporated into the assessments of government officials in the major pollution "airsheds" of China.[71]

The comprehensive revision of the Environmental Protection Law (EPL) in 2014 also demonstrates the elevation of environmental priorities. The revised EPL includes, among other things, stronger enforcement and penalty provisions, greater opportunity for public supervision of polluters, and explicit measures to deal with prevalent compliance problems, such as falsification of data and illegal dumping of pollution.[72]

One characteristic of all of these policies is their compatibility with overall economic transformation objectives. China is attempting to move away from heavy industry and reliance on exports, and to develop an economy based on high value added industries and domestic consumption. At the tactical level, this involves consolidation in heavy industry (which is now quite fragmented), elimination of inefficient older facilities, expansion of clean energy resources, investment in environmental protection infrastructure, and state support for less energy- and pollution-intensive industries.[73]

Chinese policy does not reflect a naturalist's view of environmental protection, or a moral or rights-based view. Rather, Chinese leaders appear to have taken an instrumental approach that uses environmental protection as a means to achieve economic and social stability, *as well as* environmental aims.

B. BIG CARROTS, MODEST STICKS—THE TOOLS OF THE STATE

In order to implement green development policies, Chinese authorities are using a number of approaches to induce SOE cooperation. First and foremost, these include accommodation of SOE interests, offering SOEs incentives to move in the direction of green development (i.e., bargaining). Other strategies include a range of tools of bureaucratic

---

[70] 大气污染防治行动计划 (Air Pollution Prevention and Control Action Plan) (issued by the State Council on Sept. 10, 2013), *available at* http://www.gov.cn/zwgk/2013-09/12/content_2486773.htm.

[71] The Jing-Jin-Ji region (i.e., Beijing, Tianjin, and Hebei); the Yangtze River Delta region (i.e., Shanghai, Jiangsu, and Zhejiang); the Pearl River Delta region; and Chongqing (in China's western interior). *See* 大气污染防治行动计划实施情况考核办法（试行）(Performance Assessment Measures for Air Pollution Prevention and Control Action Plan (Trial)), art. 3, (promulgated on Apr. 30, 2014).

[72] 中华人民共和国环境保护法 (Environmental Protection Law of the People's Republic of China) (Apr. 24, 2014), *available at* http://www.npc.gov.cn/npc/xinwen/2014-04/25/content_1861279.htm (Chinese), https://www.chinadialogue.net/Environmental-Protection-Law-2014-eversion.pdf (unofficial English translation) [hereinafter EPL].

[73] Industrial consolidation tends to improve the overall efficiency of these sectors by eliminating the worst facilities and generating economies of scale for investment in pollution control. Fewer facilities also reduce enforcement costs for regulators who can concentrate their efforts on a smaller number of larger facilities.

control, traditional command and control regulation (*xingzheng shouduan*), and market measures (i.e., regulating). The methods that would require expansion of traditionally weak institutions, such as the environmental regulators or the courts, show only modest signs of expansion. The wild card factor is the role that President Xi Jinping's anticorruption campaign (i.e., breaking) will play. Although not likely driven by environmental considerations, the campaign has led to the incarceration of many SOE leaders and staff, weakening these vested interests just as central leaders are trying to implement relatively extensive reform. I discuss each of these three approaches (bargaining, regulating, and breaking) in turn.

1. Bargaining

State efforts at goal achievement in China typically require a greater degree of bargaining and negotiation among institutional actors than casual observers—who assume more top-down power and control—commonly recognize. Scholars have long recognized this as an aspect of China's fragmented authoritarian state. Susan Shirk has, for example, offered a detailed account of the bargaining between central authorities and the provinces in enacting the shift to a "socialist market economy" in the 1980s.[74] Central authorities offered a variety of economic incentives to the provinces to enhance local buy-in for greater marketization, which faced opposition from conservatives within the leadership.

Likewise, bargaining and negotiation have characterized the relationship between central authorities and SOEs, which have gained greater autonomy from the state in the last two decades due to greater corporatization (structural separation from the state) and the significant increase in fiscal resources earned in the course of business (reducing state fiscal leverage).[75] These trends have led to a relationship between SOEs and the authorities more akin to regulation and lobbying than to traditional administrative delegation.[76]

China's current environmental reform strategy reflects accommodation of SOEs in two ways: strengthening state market power in traditional heavy industries, and green industrial policies that primarily subsidize SOE investment in renewable and "new" energy resources, environmental technologies, and other less environmentally intensive industries.

(a) Industrial Consolidation

State support for industrial consolidation in favor of SOEs is one manifestation of state bargaining and accommodation of SOE interests. Chinese heavy industry is on the whole much less consolidated than industry in other countries, meaning that firms are

---

[74] *See* Shirk, *supra* note 11.

[75] Scott Kennedy, The Business of Lobbying in China (2005).

[76] *Id.*

more numerous and produce less on average per facility or firm.[77] Policymakers have long argued that low levels of consolidation are inefficient and result in detrimental price competition that hinders the development of larger firms capable of becoming global competitors.

Central authorities have attempted to use SOEs as vehicles for effecting industrial consolidation.[78] SOEs receive various forms of state support for increased market share. These include state subsidies, favorable treatment toward SOEs in the shutdown of outdated industrial capacity, and policies that encourage SOE expansion through organic growth and purchase of private enterprises.[79] These approaches constrain private market competition and allow SOEs to absorb the most productive private assets, sometimes at below-market prices.

Chinese authorities justify these policies not only on economic but also on environmental grounds. As stated above, central policy is to maintain absolute or strong influence in a range of heavy industry sectors. Subsequent official documents have argued for greater consolidation in these industries as a way to improve "energy savings and pollution reduction" (*jieneng jianpai*), a key thrust of the 11th and 12th five-year plans. This strategy of shutting down "backward production capacity" (*luohou channeng*) and supporting the consolidation of production capacity in SOEs can be seen in numerous sectors. Highlighting the confluence of economic and environmental goals, officials have justified shutdown orders as needed to reduce industrial overcapacity (the excess of production capacity over market demand for product). In 2013, China's Ministry of Industry and Information Technology ordered shutdowns of thousands of facilities considered to be backward capacity in nineteen industrial sectors, including steel, aluminum, copper smelting, cement, and paper.[80] In the power sector, the 11th five-year plan set forth a policy of "up with the large, down with the small" (*shangda yaxiao*). From 2006 to 2011, the policy resulted in the shutdown of 77 gigawatts (GW) of small, inefficient power plants.[81]

Overall, rapid construction of new capacity (with larger, high-efficiency units) combined with the shutdown of older capacity has resulted in significant increases in average fleet efficiency.[82] Iron and steel is another industry that central leaders have attempted

[77] CHINA 2030, *supra* note 21, at 106.

[78] *Id.* at 104–09, 141–42; Burnard, *supra* note 66, at 22, 25; SHENG & ZHAO, *supra* note 27, at 129–34.

[79] CHINA 2030, *supra* note 21, at 109; SHENG & ZHAO, *supra* note 27, at 141–48; interviews.

[80] 工业和信息化部公告今年首批工业行业淘汰落后产能企业名单 (MIIT Announcement: This Year's First Batch Enterprise Name List of Industrial Sector Outdated Industrial Capacity), 中华人民共和国工业和信息化部 (MINISTRY OF INDUS. & INFO. TECH. OF P.R. CHINA) (July 18, 2013), http://www.miit.gov.cn/n11293472/n11293832/n11293907/n11368223/15535781.html; *China Cuts Capacity in Some Industries to Reshape Economy*, BLOOMBERG NEWS (July 25, 2014), http://www.bloomberg.com/news/2013-07-25/china-cuts-capacity-in-some-industries-to-reshape-economy.html.

[81] Burnard, *supra* note 68, at 22.

[82] *Id.* at 23 (noting that during the 11th five-year plan, average thermal efficiency of China's coal fleet improved from 370 gce/kWh to 335 gce/kWh); *see also* Keith Bradsher, *China Outpaces U.S. in Cleaner Coal-Fired Plants*, N.Y. TIMES (May 10, 2009), http://www.nytimes.com/2009/05/11/world/asia/11coal.html.

to consolidate.[83] Private small and medium enterprises in this sector contribute significantly to environmental pollution.[84] As with the power sector, central authorities ordered shutdowns of outdated production capacity in the steel sector.[85] Although the policy was initially motivated by economic considerations, beginning with the 11th five-year plan the State Council framed consolidation and industry upgrade explicitly as environmental policy.[86]

Despite the potential environmental benefits of consolidation and shutdown of outdated facilities, critics have raised concerns about discrimination against private enterprises in shutdowns without adequate compensation and through forced, below-market sales. In 2009, for example, Shandong Iron & Steel Group, a loss-making SOE formed in 2008,[87] completed a hostile takeover of Rizhao Steel Holding Group, a profitable private enterprise. Critics have suggested that consolidation of the coal industry in Shanxi Province was tainted by government involvement in forced sales and below-market compensation to the private actors forced to sell their assets to SOEs.[88] In my conversations with regulators and enterprises in recent years, a number of sources suggested that government shutdowns of older facilities disproportionately target private enterprises, and,

---

[83] OECD, Developments in Steelmaking Capacity of Non-OECD Economies 2010 27–36 (2011), *available at* http://browse.oecdbookshop.org/oecd/pdfs/product/5811013e.pdf.

[84] *Id.* at 27 ("[M]any small and medium-sized steelmakers have not met environmental standards effectively.").

[85] "During 2010, the government plan[ned] to close 25 million tonnes of obsolete iron-making capacity and 6 million tonnes of steel production capacity." *Id.* at 28.

[86] 国务院办公厅关于进一步加大节能减排力度加快钢铁工业结构调整的若干意见 (State Council Several Opinions Regarding Further Strengthening the Impact of Energy Savings, Emissions Reduction by Accelerating Adjustment of Industrial Structure in the Iron & Steel Sector), 中华人民共和国中央人民政府 (Cent. People's Gov't of P.R. China) (June 4, 2010), *available at* http://www.gov.cn/zwgk/2010-06/17/content_1629386.htm.

[87] Shandong Iron & Steel was formed through the combination of enterprises affiliated with Jigang Group, Laigang Group, and Shandong Metallurgical Industry General Company. At its formation, the enterprise was the largest state-owned enterprise in Shandong Province, the sixth largest steel enterprise in China, and the ninth largest steel producer in the world. Sheng & Zhao, *supra* note 27, at 145–48; Barry Naughton, *Loans, Firms and Steel: Is the State Advancing at the Expense of the Private Sector?*, 30 China Leadership Monitor (2009), *available at* http://media.hoover.org/sites/default/files/documents/CLM30BN.pdf; *Shandong Iron Acquires Rizhao Steel through Venture (Update 1)*, Bloomberg News (Sept. 7, 2009), http://www.bloomberg.com/apps/news?pid=newsarchive&sid=a_ZaNgSyZNv8; Jamil Anderlini, *Shandong Steel Closes in on Rizhao*, Fin. Times (Aug. 26, 2009), http://www.ft.com/intl/cms/s/0/cb36d29a-91d8-11de-879d-00144feabdc0.html#axzz3IVtTHVnf.

钢铁产业调整和振兴规划 (Iron & Steel Sector Adjustment and Revitalization Plan), 中华人民共和国中央人民政府 (Cent. People's Gov't of P.R. China) (2009), *available at* http://www.gov.cn/zwgk/2009-03/20/content_1264318.htm.

山东省钢铁工业调整振兴规划的通知 (Shandong Province Iron & Steel Sector Adjustment and Revitalization Plan) 山东省人民政府 (Shandong Prov. People's Gov't) (Apr. 21, 2009), cached version *available at* http://web.archive.org/web/20120516043319/http://www2.shandong.gov.cn/art/2009/4/25/art_3883_1532.html.

[88] Sheng & Zhao, *supra* note 27, at 142–43.

in cases of SOE shutdowns, may be accompanied by various benefits, such as administrative permissions for SOE industrial expansion and loans.[89]

These "benefits" granted to SOEs may be the product of effective SOE lobbying or the triumph of local agents against a principal not in full control, but they can also be viewed as part of an implicit bargain through which central authorities have sought to gain the cooperation of the state-owned sector in exchange for a grant of stronger monopolies, use of the regulatory apparatus to limit competition, and provision of state subsidies. And, inasmuch as consolidation results in more efficient plants, SOE pursuit of economic self-interest (and leadership accommodation thereof) produces environmental benefits.

(b) Green Industrial Policy

In addition to strategies to consolidate and improve the efficiency of traditional heavy industry, China has also instituted a range of policies to support the development of green industries. These include sector-targeted subsidies, local-content policies, and export restrictions.[90] SOEs have benefitted substantially from these policies. These subsidies can be viewed as a tool for shifting SOEs toward investment in more environmental strategic emerging industries—another aspect of the state strategy of bargaining with SOEs. But, green development subsidies support private companies as well. They are an example of how Chinese policy is relatively more agnostic as to ownership type outside of traditional heavy industrial sectors long dominated by traditional incumbent SOEs.[91] State support for SOEs *and* private enterprises can be viewed as a way to motivate SOEs through a modest level of market competition, while maintaining party control over the most significant assets in these sectors.

Chinese authorities, according to one source, offered more than US$216 billion in green technology subsidies in recent years.[92] These include subsidies for research and development, manufacturing subsidies (such as low-interest loans, under-market provision of land, subsidized energy prices, and direct credits and grants), and feed-in tariffs to subsidize the higher cost of renewable energy.[93] Of the seven strategic emerging industries identified in China's 12th five-year plan, all of which receive significant state policy

---

[89] Interviews.

[90] Mark Wu & James Salzman, *The Next Generation of Trade and Environmental Conflicts: The Rise of Green Industrial Policy*, 108 Nw. U. L. Rev. 401 (2014).

[91] Curtis Milhaupt & Wentong Zheng, *Beyond Ownership: State Capitalism and the Chinese Firm*, 103 Geo. L.J. 665 (2015).

[92] This figure is drawn from the United Steelworkers' Section 301 Petition at the WTO, however, and so is likely a generous estimate; *see* United Steelworkers, United Steelworkers' Section 301 Petition Demonstrates China's Green Technology Practices Violate WTO Rules (n.d.), http://assets.usw.org/releases/misc/section-301.pdf. According to the petition, this is "more than twice as much as the U.S. spent in the sector and nearly half of the total 'green' stimulus spent worldwide." *Id.*

[93] *See, e.g.*, Keith Bradsher, *On Clean Energy, China Skirts Rules*, N.Y. Times (Sept. 8, 2010), http://www.nytimes.com/2010/09/09/business/global/09trade.html?pagewanted=all.

and fiscal support, three are environmental industries.[94] The other four are high value added industries with lower energy- and pollution-intensity (per unit of GDP).[95]

These and other policies have been the target of trade disputes with the United States and European Union, suggesting that the subsidies are significant. Other policies include subsidy programs, such as a 2008 Ministry of Finance special fund that offered grants to wind turbine producers so long as critical components were manufactured in China.[96] Begun in 2009, the Golden Sun program subsidizes the expansion of photovoltaic power generation. In 2012, the program announced support for 2.83 GW of solar power capacity.[97] Export restrictions on rare earth metals, which are essential to renewable energy technologies, are another policy designed in part to promote the domestic development of green technologies.[98]

SOEs benefit disproportionately from these subsidies, as they are the main developers of wind and solar technology.[99] Large SOEs accounted for 80 percent of total installed wind capacity as of June 2012.[100] Government mandates require that a certain percentage of SOEs' new installed generating capacity come from wind power. Solar developers are more diverse in corporate structure, but are still dominated by SOEs. SOEs accounted for 60 percent of aggregate installed photovoltaic capacity as of June 2012.[101] In August 2010, China put up for bid thirteen photovoltaic projects with a generating capacity of 280 megawatts (MW) under the Golden Sun solar subsidy program. More

---

[94] These are energy-efficient and environmental technologies, new energy, and new energy vehicles.

[95] These are next-generation information technology, biotechnology, advanced equipment manufacture, and new materials.

[96] *See* UNITED STEELWORKERS, *supra* note 92.

[97] Becky Beetz & Wenjing Feng, *China: 2.83 GW of Solar to Be Installed under Golden Sun Program*, PV MAG. (Dec. 11, 2012), http://www.pv-magazine.com/news/details/beitrag/china--283-gw-of-solar-to-be-installed-under-golden-sun-program_100009542/#axzz3LFlPIZpR; 2012 年金太阳示范工程项目目录(第二批)(2012 Golden Sun Pilot Program Project List), 中华人民共和国科学技术部 (MINISTRY OF SCI. & TECH. OF P.R. CHINA) (2012), http://www.most.gov.cn/tztg/201212/t20121211_98422.htm; *China's National Solar Subsidy Programs*, CHINA POLICY IN FOCUS, https://sites.google.com/site/chinapolicyinfocus/china-s-solar-subsidy-programs/china-s-solar-industry/china-s-national-solar-subsidy-programs (last visited Feb. 10, 2015).

[98] WAYNE MORRISON & RACHEL TANG, CONG. RES. SERVICE, CHINA'S RARE EARTH INDUSTRY AND EXPORT REGIME: ECONOMIC AND TRADE IMPLICATIONS FOR THE UNITED STATES 17–18 (Apr. 30, 2012), https://www.fas.org/sgp/crs/row/R42510.pdf.

[99] CHINESE RESEARCH PERSPECTIVES ON THE ENVIRONMENT, SPECIAL VOLUME: ANNUAL REVIEW OF LOW-CARBON DEVELOPMENT IN CHINA (2011–12) 210 (Ye Qi ed., 2013).

[100] The "Big 5" central power SOEs accounted for 53.7 percent; central SOEs in total, 71.6 percent. These include (in descending order of installed capacity): Guodian (20.9 percent); Datang (12.8 percent); Huaneng (12.6 percent); China General Nuclear Power Group (4.2 percent); Shenhua (3.7 percent); China Huadian (3.7 percent); CPIC (3.6 percent); Power Construction Corp. of China (2.8 percent); Huarun (2.3 percent); and Beijing Energy Investment (1.8 percent). *Id.* at 212, 215.

[101] The "Big 5" power SOEs comprised 31.6 percent; central SOEs in total, 57.2 percent. These include (in descending order of installed capacity): CPIC (15.25 percent); China Guodian (8.3 percent); China Energy Conservation Environmental Protection Group (7.98 percent); China General Nuclear Power Group

than 70 percent of the bids were awarded to major state-owned enterprises, with the vast majority going to the central SOE, China Power Investment Corp.[102]

2. Regulating

With the ascension of environmental priorities, central authorities have initiated or allowed the development of a range of regulatory innovations heralded as mechanisms for strengthening the hand of party institutions, regulators, courts, and citizens in environmental regulation. These include using bureaucratic evaluations to promote environmental actions by local bureaucrats and SOE leaders, stronger environmental penalty and injunctive provisions, authority for environmental public interest litigation, and the development of environmental courts, expanded public supervision channels, and transparency measures.[103]

Recent evidence suggests some level of enhanced environmental enforcement through each of these channels. However, the Party's use of bureaucratic targets as a tool of control is still limited by agency problems. And the role of environmental agencies, courts, and the public continues to be constrained by bureaucratic competition and party concerns about loss of control.

Party and state regulatory entities (including SASAC) are attempting to use bureaucratic targets to motivate and control SOEs.[104] The core metrics of evaluation are related to financial performance, but in 2010 SASAC promulgated energy- and environment-based targets for SOE officials.[105] Poor environmental performance

(5.71 percent); China Huaneng (4.75 percent); Power Construction Corp. of China (2.75 percent); Ningxia Electric Power Group Ltd. (2.71 percent); China Huadian (2.18 percent). *Id.* at 213.

[102] Zhongxiang Zhang, Energy and Environmental Policy in China: Towards a Low-Carbon Economy 133–34 (2011).

[103] On bureaucratic evaluations, see Wang, *supra* note 14; on penalty and injunctive provisions, see EPL, *supra* note 72, at arts. 25, 44, 59; on environmental public interest litigation, see *id.* at art. 58; Alex Wang & Jie Gao, *Environmental Courts and Public Interest Litigation in China*, 43 Chinese L. & Gov't 4 (2010); Alex Wang, *The Role of Law in Environmental Protection in China: Recent Developments*, 8 Vt. J. Envtl. L. 195 (2006–2007); on environmental courts, see Rachel Stern, *The Political Logic of China's New Environmental Courts*, 72 China J. 53 (2014); Alex Wang & Jie Gao, *Environmental Courts and the Development of Environmental Public Interest Litigation in China*, 3 J. Ct. Innovation 37 (2010); on public supervision channels and transparency, see Benjamin Van Rooij, *The People vs. Pollution: Understanding Citizen Action against Pollution in China*, 19 J. Contemp. China 55 (2010) [hereinafter Van Rooij, *People vs. Pollution*]; Lorentzen et al., *supra* note 8. On regulatory pluralism in general, see Benjamin van Rooij et al., *The Authoritarian Logic of Regulatory Pluralism: Understanding China's New Environmental Actors*, Reg. & Gov. 1 (2014).

[104] *See* 中央企业负责人经营业绩考核暂行办法 (Interim Measures for Assessment of the Operational Performance of Persons in Charge of Central State-Owned Enterprises No. 378) (2003). SASAC has subsequently amended these measures three times—in 2006, 2009, and 2012.

[105] *Id.* at arts. 7–9. SOE leaders are delegated the tasks of establishing internal departments and staffing, monitoring and reporting systems, and incentives for staff at all levels to implement energy savings and pollution reduction.

can, in theory, result in penalties.[106] These targets attempt to systematize earlier pilot efforts to encourage industrial polluters to improve their environmental performance. The Top 1,000 Enterprises Energy-Saving Program, which required the top (largely state-owned) industrial energy consumers in China to sign agreements pledging energy efficiency improvements, was considered a success, with enterprises meeting efficiency targets well ahead of deadlines.[107] In the 12th five-year plan, the program was expanded to include targets for approximately seventeen thousand industrial enterprises, transportation companies, and public buildings, which account for two-thirds of China's total national energy consumption.[108]

Evidence regarding use of environmental targets for managing bureaucrats suggests, however, a mixed picture: hierarchical management methods have increased bureaucratic commitment to environmental enforcement, but have also in some cases driven a range of local efforts designed only to create the appearance of such commitment, without actual performance.[109] Anecdotal evidence suggests that SOEs will react in a similar fashion to these targets—appearing to comply, while surreptitiously shirking where possible. For example, commentators report that industrial facilities install pollution control equipment, which is costly to operate, only to leave it unused.[110] As another example, large SOEs are now required to release annual corporate social responsibility reports, which uniformly tout the positive environmental performance of SOEs. But commentators have noted that SOEs with glowing corporate social responsibility reports have simultaneously been found to have serious environmental performance problems.[111]

---

[106] Falsification of data, major accidents with significant social impacts, and major violations of ESER rules and regulations with very bad consequences require leadership grade demotions. Missed targets and accidents or violations with relatively large impacts result in point deductions on leadership evaluations. *Id.* at art. 7.

[107] Jing Ke et al., *China's Industrial Energy Consumption Trends and Impacts of the Top-1000 Enterprises Energy-Saving Program and the Ten Key Energy-Saving Projects*, 50 Energy Pol'y 562, 565 (2012).

[108] China, CN-3b: Top-10,000 Energy-Consuming Enterprises Program, *Industrial Efficiency Policy Database*, http://iepd.iipnetwork.org/policy/top-10000-energy-consuming-enterprises-program. (last visited June 1, 2015).

[109] Wang, *supra* note 14, at 416–30.

[110] *Id.*; comments of Hu Tao, China Program Director, World Wildlife Fund—U.S., *Capping China's Coal*, China Env't Forum (Nov. 24, 2014), *available at* http://www.wilsoncenter.org/event/capping-china%E2%80%99s-coal. An earlier study by MIT researchers found more systematic misuse of pollution control equipment. The study was based on a survey conducted in 2007, early in what I consider the process of Party-state elevation of environmental priorities (e.g., elevated environmental targets were instituted in 2006, and campaigns to emphasize their newfound importance were commenced only in 2007). *See* Edward Steinfeld et al., MIT Indus. Performance Ctr., Greener Plants, Grayer Skies? A Report from the Front Lines of China's Energy Sector (Aug. 2008).

[111] Christina Larson, *"Corporate Social Responsibility" Reports in China: Progress or Greenwashing?*, Bloomberg Businessweek (Dec. 12, 2013), http://www.businessweek.com/articles/2013-12-12/corporate-social-responsibility-reports-in-china-progress-or-greenwashing; Li-Wen Lin, *Corporate Social Responsibility in China: Window Dressing or Structural Change?*, 28 Berkeley J. Int'l L. 64 (2010).

In some cases, environmental regulators appear to have gained strength and authority from the rising priority of environmental protection and the alignment of political incentives (i.e., targets) with these priorities. For example, environmental impact assessment (EIA), which requires the approval of environmental regulators, has traditionally been viewed as ineffectual, as regulators seldom failed to approve EIAs. Since the 11th five-year plan, however, environmental officials have rejected projects in disfavored high-energy, high-pollution, or resource-intensive categories.[112] Moreover, the Total Emissions Department of MEP (and counterpart departments at lower levels of the system) was formed to implement the pollution reduction targets under the 11th and 12th five-year plans. These departments have generally been considered the most prestigious within the environmental bureaus and have gained significant staffing and resources in recent years. Their work has primarily revolved around monitoring shutdowns of backward capacity and installation of pollution controls.[113] Yet traditional monitoring, focused on the levying of penalties for emissions violations, misuse of pollution control, and falsification of data, has not obviously improved.

Judicial reforms ostensibly designed to support environmental protection present a similarly mixed picture. China now boasts some 130 environmental courts, established between 2007 and 2013.[114] However, these courts have not to date served as a forum for prosecuting China's worst polluters, let alone politically connected SOEs.[115] Quasi-governmental groups (known as GONGOs) have brought a few successful public interest suits, typically against small private enterprises or weak local agencies, but these cases appear to be one-off interventions rather than the initial volleys in long-term campaigns.[116] Rules authorizing environmental public interest litigation have only recently come into force, and so it is too early to tell what role the mechanism will play in China's regulatory landscape.

Central authorities have signaled that public participation and transparency of environmental information will play a more significant role in environmental regulation. One of the seven chapters of the newly amended Environmental Protection Law, effective as of January 2015, is devoted entirely to information disclosure and public participation.[117] Citizens and advocacy groups have been increasingly active in environmental

---

112 四川数十个"两高一资"项目因环评不达标被拒 (Dozens of Sichuan "Two High, One Resource" Projects Rejected for EIA Not Meeting Standards), SINA (Feb. 10, 2014), http://sc.sina.com.cn/news/m/2014-02-10/0641177323.html; 环保部紧急发文 严控"两高一资"项目环评审批 (MEP Urgently Issues Documents, Strictly Controlling EIA Approvals for "Two High, One Resource" Projects), SOHU (Dec. 9, 2008), http://news.sohu.com/20081209/n261090035.shtml.

113 Wang, *supra* note 14, at 404.

114 *See* Stern, *supra* note 103.

115 *Id.* at 54 ("What emerges is a reminder that China's new environmental courts are not a step toward judicial empowerment . . .").

116 *See* Wang & Gao, *supra* note 103; Edward Wong, *Fines Total $26 Million for Polluters in China*, N.Y. TIMES (Dec. 31, 2014), http://news.cntv.cn/2013/09/26/VIDE1380140758843768.shtml.

117 第五章: 信息公开和公众参与 (Chapter Five: Open Information and Public Participation), EPL Chpt. 5; *see supra* note 72.

regulation in recent years, but state-instituted constraints on such advocacy are apparent as well.[118] Security officials monitor and visit advocacy groups. Various levels of government have instituted or are discussing rules that tighten regulation over foreign-funded or affiliated advocacy groups.[119] Officials deal in a punitive way with citizens whose advocacy leads to social unrest.[120]

Perhaps unsurprisingly, bureaucratic targets have played the more important role in signaling and implementing the elevation of environmental priorities. Although there is little evidence of officials being formally punished for poor performance, local officials have clearly gotten the signal that environmental priorities are more important than before. In contrast, the reforms to environmental law meant to strengthen the role of environmental regulators, the courts, and the public have to date had only modest effect in practice. More powerful development-oriented bureaus, such as the National Development and Reform Commission (NDRC), regularly oppose any enlargement of power for environmental regulators.[121] Enlargement of judicial power is constrained by, among other things, opposition to judicial independence in the Western liberal sense and a general view of courts as members of the broader bureaucracy tasked with a role in furthering Party-state objectives.[122]

Central reliance on bargaining to a greater degree than regulation can be explained as the result of pressure from powerful vested interests, leadership reluctance to alter existing elite power dynamics within China, or a reflection of what central authorities believe is necessary to garner SOE compliance. It is also arguably a part of the governance culture in China. The relative ineffectiveness of various mechanisms of regulation—bureaucratic targets, stronger regulatory bureaus and courts, and greater public involvement—suggest another reason that central leaders might rely on bargaining with SOEs to bring about environmental improvements in practice. In other words, a heavy dose of positive incentives is necessary because alternative regulatory methods simply do not work sufficiently well, or carry high sociopolitical costs.

---

[118] Observation based on author's personal experience as an environmental advocate in China. *See also* Andrew Mertha, China's Water Warriors: Citizen Action and Policy Change (2010); Van Rooij, *People vs. Pollution, supra* note 103.

[119] Ben Blanchard, *China to "Regulate" Foreign NGOs with New Law*, Reuters (Dec. 22, 2014), http://www.reuters.com/article/2014/12/22/us-china-politics-ngos-idUSKBN0K00NX20141222.

[120] Jonathan Ansfield, *Alchemy of a Protest: The Case of Xiamen PX, in* China and the Environment: The Green Revolution 136 (Sam Geall ed., 2013).

[121] Observation based on author's personal experience participating in Chinese legislative reform projects.

[122] *See* Jun Xia, *China's Courts Fail the Environment*, China Dialogue (Jan. 16, 2012), https://www.chinadialogue.net/article/show/single/en/4727--China-s-courts-fail-the-environment-; *see also* Adam Taylor, *A Secret Document Reportedly Reveals the 7 Things That Keep China's Political Elite Up at Night*, Bus. Insider (Aug. 19, 2013), http://www.businessinsider.com/secret-memo-from-chinese-leaders-2013-8.

3. Breaking

Finally, anticorruption campaigns commenced under President Xi Jinping have the potential to break or weaken the political networks that have supported SOEs. There is no evidence that anticorruption campaigns are indirect environmental measures. Rather, most commentary assumes that the campaigns are intimately connected with elite factional power struggles, if not a genuine commitment to eliminating the worst excesses of Chinese official graft. However, it is possible that these campaigns are at least in part driven by a desire to break the vested interest groups that are barriers to President Xi's economic and energy sector reforms.[123] Regardless of motivation, such campaigns may in practice weaken the ability of vested SOE interest groups to hinder environmental reforms.

Recent campaigns have targeted numerous individuals affiliated with the oil, power, coal, and other sectors.[124] The most prominent anticorruption campaign has been against Zhou Yongkang, a former member of the Politburo Standing Committee and head of the Communist Party Political-Legal Committee.[125] Zhou has long been associated with the oil and gas sector.[126] His positions included heading China National Petroleum Corporation (CNPC) from 1996 to 1998 and serving in various government positions with authority over the oil industry. CNPC is a central SOE, the largest energy company in China, and the fourth largest company in the world by revenue.[127] Numerous former

---

[123] Christina Larson, *China's Corruption Crackdown Takes Down Former Security Czar*, BLOOMBERG BUSINESSWEEK (July 30, 2014), http://www.businessweek.com/articles/2014-07-30/chinas-xi-jinping-steps-up-his-anti-corruption-drive; Kerry Brown, *Why Zhou Yongkang Had to Go*, CHINA POWER (Aug. 4, 2014), http://thediplomat.com/2014/08/why-zhou-yongkang-had-to-go/.

[124] Although Jiang Zemin and Hu Jintao also made extensive use of anticorruption campaigns, Xi is different in that "many of the senior officials probed in the course of the anti-corruption campaign have either direct or indirect ties to retired Party leaders." Samson Yuen, *Disciplining the Party: Xi Jinping's Anti-Corruption Campaign and Its Limits*, 3 CHINA PERSPECTIVES 41 (2014).

[125] *See* Chris Buckley, *China Arrests Ex-Chief of Domestic Security in Graft Case*, N.Y. TIMES (Dec. 5, 2014), http://www.nytimes.com/2014/12/06/world/asia/zhou-yongkang-china-arrests-former-security-chief.html?_r=0; 中国中央决定对周永康严重违纪问题立案审查 (Party Central Committee Decides to Bring a Case concerning Zhou Yongkang's Serious Violations of Discipline), XINHUA (July 29, 2014), http://news.xinhuanet.com/politics/2014-07/29/c_1111853756.htm (official public announcement of disciplinary action against Zhou Yongkang). Authorities reportedly seized more than US$14 billion in assets from Zhou's family members and associates in the course of an anticorruption campaign that continues as of this writing. Benjamin Kang Lim & Ben Blanchard, *Exclusive: China Seizes $14.5 Billion Assets from Family, Associates of Ex-security Chief: Sources*, REUTERS (Mar. 30, 2014), http://www.reuters.com/article/2014/03/30/us-china-corruption-zhou-idUSBREA2T02S20140330. *See also*, *Zhou Family Ties*, N.Y. TIMES (Apr. 19, 2014), http://www.nytimes.com/interactive/2014/04/20/world/asia/Zhou-Family-Ties.html?_r=0.

[126] Zhou graduated from the Beijing Petroleum Institute (now known as the China University of Petroleum) and worked in the oil and gas industry for more than three decades.

[127] CNPC's publicly listed subsidiary is known as Petrochina. *Interactive Graphic: Zhou's Power Base*, CAIXIN ONLINE, http://english.caixin.com/2014-07-29/100710458.html (last visited Feb. 11, 2015).

senior executives at CNPC and other oil enterprises have been detained, including Jiang Jiemin, former Chairman of CNPC and head of SASAC.[128]

In the steel sector, the resignation of Wang Yifang, chairman of the state-owned Hebei Iron & Steel Group, offers another example of the possible confluence of anticorruption efforts, economic transformation, and environmental protection. Hebei Province surrounds Beijing and is home to seven of the ten most polluted cities in China, in large part due to overcapacity in steel and other heavy industry sectors. Central authorities instituted a plan to shut down almost one quarter of Hebei Province's steel capacity.[129] Under Wang's leadership, Hebei Iron & Steel's output capacity had increased from 31 to 71 million tons within five years, and evidence suggested that Wang did not intend to comply with central policy to reduce capacity.[130] In September 2013, President Xi required Hebei provincial party officials to engage in publicly broadcast Mao-era-style self-criticism sessions.[131] Wang resigned in December 2013 under a cloud of suspicion of corruption concerning "stolen mine assets."[132]

The anticorruption probe has also extended to officials and enterprise executives from SOEs involved in the electricity grid, construction, coal, cement, gas, and nonferrous metals industries, as well as dozens of government officials based in the coal-producing

---

[128] Isaac Stone Fish et al., *Tiger, Tiger, Burning Bright*, CHINAFILE (Mar. 20, 2014), http://www.chinafile.com/Tiger-Tiger-Burning-Bright. Other CNPC officials detained in the campaign include CNPC vice president Wang Yongchun; Petrochina vice presidents Bo Qiliang, Li Hualin, and Ran Xinquang; and Petrochina chief geologist Wang Daofu. By one estimate, more than three hundred people have been arrested, detained, or questioned in the course of the campaign. Of these, 120 from CNPC and its subsidiaries have been investigated, with 45 people detained for CNPC-related reasons. David Lague et al., *Special Report: Inside Xi Jinping's Purge of China's Oil Mandarins*, REUTERS (July 25, 2014), http://reut.rs/1GNDlua; Jeffrey Young, *China's "Corruption Crackdown" Nabs State Oil Chief*, VOICE OF AM. (June 2, 2014), http://www.voanews.com/content/chinas-corruption-crackdown-continues/1926102.html.

[129] Chuin-Wei Yap, *China's Leaders Move to Rein in Steel Mecca*, WALL ST. J. (Jan. 5, 2014), http://online.wsj.com/news/articles/SB10001424052702304773104579267930186015534.

[130] See *id.* (noting Wang's comment to a reporter in March 2013 that "[w]e don't have such a plan [to reduce capacity] and will act according to market demands"; and quoting China Iron & Steel Association report: "Under Wang's leadership, Hebei Iron and Steel 'missed an opportunity by simply adding capacity at a time when others like Baosteel [a central SOE] were developing product quality'").

[131] Zhang Qinwei, the Governor of Hebei, said of Zhang Benshun, the Party Secretary of the province: "Comrade Benshun has talked about reforming evaluation criteria, increasing the proportion focused on development quality and ecosystems. But I felt that [he] was relatively focused on the speed of development." 《焦点访谈》批评和自我批评是一剂良药 (*Focus Interview:* Criticism and Self-Criticism Is a Dose of Good Medicine), CCTV, http://news.cntv.cn/2013/09/26/VIDE1380140758843768.shtml (at 7:00). Zhang Hong, *Sweating and on the Verge of Tears: Chinese Officials Carry Out Self-Criticism on TV*, S. CHINA MORNING POST (Sept. 28, 2013), http://www.scmp.com/news/china/article/1319552/senior-chinese-officials-face-mao-style-self-criticism-sessions.

[132] Toh Han Shih, *Hebei Steelmaker's Chairman Leaves under a Cloud*, S. CHINA MORNING POST (Dec. 13, 2013), http://www.scmp.com/business/china-business/article/1379317/hebei-steelmakers-chairman-leaves-under-cloud.

province of Shanxi.[133] Several senior bureaucrats in the National Energy Administration (NEA) in charge of coal, renewable energy, nuclear, and other areas have also been investigated for corruption.[134]

These anticorruption efforts are seen broadly as not only an effort to prosecute corruption, but also a means for central leaders to amass political power and eliminate rivals. These efforts allow President Xi the opportunity to place loyalists in positions of power, and also have the effect of cowing those who might oppose proposed reforms.[135] In June 2014, he called for a "revolution in energy" at a meeting of top economic advisors.[136] To the extent that central leaders continue to focus on economic transformation and to view energy efficiency and environmental protection as important state goals, these

---

[133] State Grid Corp. of China, China Resources, Aluminum Corp. of China (Chinalco), Power Construction Corp. of China. James T. Areddy, *Chinese Ex-official Admits Bribery in High-Profile Trial*, WALL ST. J. (Sept. 24, 2014), http://online.wsj.com/articles/chinese-ex-official-admits-bribery-in-high-profile-trial-1411562471 [hereinafter Areddy, *Ex-official Admits Bribery*]; *Hao Weiping Probe May Signal Future Purge of China's Power Sector*, WANT CHINA TIMES (Apr. 24, 2014), http://www.wantchinatimes.com/news-subclass-cnt.aspx?id=20140424000005&cid=1103; James T. Areddy, *China Alleges $1 Billion in Misappropriated Spending on Electricity Grid System*, WALL ST. J. (June 16, 2014), http://online.wsj.com/articles/china-alleges-1-billion-in-misappropriated-spending-on-electricity-grid-system-1402921910; Keira Lu Huang, *State Grid Shanghai Chief Feng Jun Detained in Corruption Sweep*, S. CHINA MORNING POST (Oct. 30, 2014), http://www.scmp.com/news/china/article/1627808/state-grid-shanghai-chief-feng-jun-detained-corruption-sweep; Chen Heying, *Shanxi "Tigers" Snared in Graft Probe*, GLOBAL TIMES (Aug. 25, 2014), http://www.globaltimes.cn/content/877936.shtml; Chuin-Wei Yap, *Aluminum Corp. of China President Placed under Investigation*, WALL ST. J. (Sept. 16, 2014), http://online.wsj.com/articles/aluminum-corp-of-china-president-placed-under-investigation-1410845162?cb=logged0.39797142217867076; Adrian Wan, *Shanxi Governor Li Xiaopeng Vows to Fight Corruption amid Rash of Probes*, S. CHINA MORNING POST (Sept. 17, 2014), http://www.scmp.com/news/china/article/1537991/shanxi-governor-li-xiaopeng-vows-fight-corruption-amid-rash-probes.

[134] Liu Tienan (former head of the NEA and senior director of the National Development and Reform Commission), Xu Yongsheng (NEA deputy director), Wang Jun (head of NEA renewable energy department), Hao Weiping (head of NEA nuclear department), and Wei Pengyuan (NEA deputy director of coal). *See* Areddy, *Ex-official Admits Bribery*, *supra* note 133. The chairman (Cao Guangjing) and general manager (Chen Fei) of China Three Gorges Corp. were replaced in March 2014 after an anti-graft investigation revealed "extravagant spending, a lack of transparent decision-making, and unspecified personnel problems," although the Central Commission for Disciplinary Inspection did not accuse either of individual wrongdoing. Wayne Ma, *China Three Gorges Replaces Chairman following Corruption Probe*, WALL ST. J. (Mar. 26, 2014), http://online.wsj.com/articles/SB10001424052702304688104579462742738913028.

[135] Shannon Tiezzi, *What's Behind Xi's Anti-Corruption Campaign?*, THE DIPLOMAT (Apr. 17, 2014), http://thediplomat.com/2014/04/whats-behind-xis-anti-corruption-campaign/. Benjamin Kang Lim & Megha Rajagopalan, *China's Xi Purging Corrupt Officials to Put Own Men in Place: Sources*, REUTERS (Apr. 16, 2014), http://www.reuters.com/article/2014/04/16/us-china-corruption-xi-insight-idUSBREA3F1UT20140416.

[136] Maria Gallucci, *China "Energy Revolution" Needed to Meet Soaring Energy Demand and Cut Pollution Problems, President Xi Says*, INT'L BUS. TIMES (June 16, 2014), http://www.ibtimes.com/china-energy-revolution-needed-meet-soaring-energy-demand-cut-pollution-problems-president-1602352; *Xi Stresses Efforts to Revolutionize Energy Sector*, XINHUANET (June 13, 2014), http://news.xinhuanet.com/english/china/2014-06/13/c_133405882.htm.

anticorruption efforts may weaken the ability of SOEs and powerful informal political networks to thwart policy implementation.

IV. The Future: Implications

SOEs and Chinese state capitalism are at the center of debates about the appropriate direction of politico-legal and economic reform in China. As environmental and green development priorities have grown in importance, observers have worried that SOEs, as influential vested interests, will thwart these central ambitions. This chapter has argued that the characterization of SOEs as rogue actors in China's environmental protection is not as strongly supported by the evidence as commonly supposed, and that a plausible future outcome is that SOEs will respond to state incentives in an environmentally favorable manner. In fact, state policy reflects an effort to grant SOEs positive incentives to comply with newly elevated environmental priorities.

The political feasibility of this state approach is enhanced by the fact that it requires limited trade-offs with respect to the current Party-state-led approach to state capitalism, authoritarian legality, and political determination. And it imposes minimal disruption on the power of elite interest groups, such as SOEs. This "no regrets" approach with Chinese characteristics is likely part express strategy—a reflection of what it takes to change behavior in a system with high levels of fragmentation, low levels of administrative capacity, and too many things to do. But it likely also reflects the influence of SOEs, whose current and former leaders are often in senior positions in the Party or government, on the development of central policy priorities.

The analysis in this chapter has viewed Chinese environmental governance through the lens of public choice theory. The notion, in short, is that policymaking and implementation can be explained in terms of the competing interests of state leaders, bureaucrats, and elite pressure groups. But the different framings of the Chinese and U.S contexts tell us a great deal about a priori expectations regarding authoritarian and democratic systems.

Public choice studies of U.S. environmental law have served to critique the idea that policymaking and implementation is fundamentally motivated by public interest considerations, and demonstrate how elite interest groups can force results that fail to maximize aggregate social welfare. For example, *Clean Coal, Dirty Air*, Bruce A. Ackerman and William T. Hassler's classic work on the passage of the U.S. Clean Air Act, argued that the Clean Air Act was not the triumph of democracy that some supposed, but rather a "multibillion-dollar bail-out for high sulfur coal producers."[137] On the other hand, scholars conventionally argue that China's political system is in a trapped transition, unable to deliver performance without substantial market, political,

[137] *See* Ackerman & Hassler, *supra* note 10.

and rule-of-law reforms.[138] SOEs are among the sources of China's systemic barriers to capable governance.

This chapter argues that public choice rent-seeking by SOEs is in fact a reason to believe that the Chinese system will actually deliver *some level of* performance. It is plausible that China will succeed to some degree in green development precisely because potential opponents of reform have been accommodated. And performance is possible, even if, as critics suggest, state capitalism is extraordinarily inefficient. Just as China's railway bureau delivered a high-speed rail system despite billions of yuan in graft and waste,[139] China's "no regrets" approach to green development may generate environmental improvements, however imperfect. This is the bet that the state is apparently placing. Whether SOEs will in fact respond to the incentives of the state remains unknown, and whether any improvements will be commensurate to the severity of the problem remains to be seen.

Thus, this is not a story about the possible triumph of the authoritarian, state-led model of development. Rather, it is the suggestion of a plausible path forward for environmental reform in China. This assessment is meant as a counterpoint to those who believe that China's form of governance is fundamentally unable to resolve the country's environmental problems. Here is a path by which the Chinese state could muddle through and even enhance its legitimacy through improved environmental performance without significant liberalizing market or politico-legal reforms.

Although this is not a clarion call for greater acceptance of China's particular approach, it is a suggestion that some productive environmental outcomes can emerge even from—and indeed maybe because of—policymaking that caters to the powerful, the self-interested, and China's fragmented authoritarian, state capitalist status quo.

---

[138] *See* Pei, *supra* note 9.

[139] Evan Osnos, *Boss Rail*, The New Yorker (Oct. 22, 2012), http://www.newyorker.com/magazine/2012/10/22/boss-rail.

II Global Institutional Implications

13 China's Rising Outward FDI, Its Reception in Host Countries and Implications for International Investment Law and Policy

Karl P. Sauvant and Michael D. Nolan*

AS CHINA'S OUTWARD foreign direct investment (FDI) has grown, its approach to international investment agreements (IIAs) has changed. China is now one of the world's most important outward investors, with state-owned enterprises (SOEs) playing the dominant role, and Chinese FDI facing widespread criticism. The challenge for China is to adapt to this new configuration of interests stemming from these developments, both in terms of its national policies and the contents of its IIAs. This chapter deals briefly with the salient features of China's outward FDI and the policies that support it (Section I); the perception and reception of China's outward FDI in key host countries (Section II); and the changing nature of the country's approach to international investment treaties (Section III). The chapter concludes with a brief review and outlook.

* The authors would like to thank Louis Brennan, Filip De Beule, Christoph Doerrenbaecher, Noha Rubins, Anthea Roberts, Stephan Schill, and Wenhua Shan for their helpful peer reviews, as well as Camilla Gambarini, Schahram Ghalebegi, Thomas Jost, Nancy Lee, Andrei Panibratov, and Adrian Torres, who prepared the host country analyses on which Section II of this chapter is based, and Kamel Aït-El-Hadj, Victor Z. Chen, Monica R. DiFonzo, Ksenia Gal, Premila Nazareth Satyanand, Zhang Sheng, Yina Yang, and You Zhou, for their very helpful assistance in the preparation of this chapter. Special thanks goes to Camilla Gambarini for helping to finalize this manuscript.

I. Salient Features of China's Outward FDI and Policy Issues Related to Them

China has become a major player in the world FDI market. The country's outward FDI flows grew from US$7 billion in 2001 to US$101 billion in 2013,[1] for a cumulative stock of US$614 billion. In terms of outflow, this made China the single most important home country among all emerging markets[2] in 2013, and the third (behind the United States and Japan) largest among all home countries. In fact, China's outward FDI flows have almost caught up with China's inward FDI flows. In 2001, outward FDI flows as a percentage of inward FDI flows were 15 percent; in 2013, they were 81 percent. China may soon be a net outward-FDI-flows country.

China's 16,000 multinational enterprises (MNEs) had established some 22,000 foreign affiliates in 179 countries and territories by the end of 2012.[3] Mergers and acquisitions (M&As) have become an important entry mode into foreign markets for Chinese enterprises. It is, however, difficult to ascertain how the country's FDI is distributed across sectors and geographic regions, as more than two-thirds of China's non-financial sector outflows are channelled via financial centers and tax havens (especially Hong Kong, the Cayman Islands, the British Virgin Islands, Luxembourg, and Panama).[4] Consequently, it is not known which countries and sectors the outflows are ultimately invested in, but it seems likely that services and natural resources are considered the most important sectors. Chinese firms have invested substantially in both developed and developing countries.

These figures should not disguise, however, that globally China's share in world FDI outflows averaged only 5 percent during 2010–2012, while its share in the world's outward FDI stock was 2 percent in 2012.

Apart from its rapid and speedy rise and the salient features already mentioned, there are three other features that characterize China's outward FDI. The first is that, in distinction to virtually all other major outward investors, SOEs account for a substantial share of the country's outward FDI flows and stock. In addition, many non-SOEs (especially the bigger ones) are linked to China's government in one way or another. Often, many top executives and board members are members of the Chinese Communist Party,

---

[1] Unless otherwise indicated, all data are from *Report Folders,* UNCTAD Stat, http://unctadstat.unctad.org/ReportFolders/reportFolders.aspx (last visited Mar. 6, 2015).

[2] *See* UNCTAD, World Investment Report 2014: Investing in the SDGs: An action plan (2014), *available at* http://unctad.org/en/pages/PublicationWebflyer.aspx?publicationid=937.

[3] MOFCOM 商务部, 2012 年度中国对外直接投资统计公报 (2012 Statistical Bulletin of China's Outward Foreign Direct Investment) (2013), *available at* http://images.mofcom.gov.cn/hzs/201409/20140918133802073.pdf.

[4] MOFCOM 商务部, 2011 年度中国对外直接投资统计公报 (2011 Statistical Bulletin of China's Outward Foreign Direct Investment) (2012), *available at* http://images.mofcom.gov.cn/hzs/201309/20130923082710756.pdf.

sometimes occupying high positions.[5] Although, as of the end of 2011, some 13,500 Chinese financial and non-financial enterprises had established around 18,000 foreign affiliates in 177 host economies,[6] the 113 central SOEs controlled by the State-owned Assets Supervision and Administration Commission (SASAC)[7] alone accounted for 66 percent of China's non-financial FDI outflows and 76 percent of the country's non-financial outward FDI stock in 2011. This raises the question of whether China's outward FDI (or at least a good part of it) might be made for purposes other than commercial ones and, more specifically, whether Chinese FDI may be detrimental to the national security of host countries.[8] The extent to which this might be the case systematically is difficult to ascertain, as it is for the outward FDI of SOEs headquartered in other countries. Still, as will be discussed below, these concerns have led to the creation or strengthening of regulatory review processes of incoming M&As in a number of countries, in particular for certain sensitive industries. The September 2012 veto by the president of the United States of a Chinese windmill project near a military base in Oregon—the first such veto in twenty-two years, and only the second one in the history of the Committee on Foreign Investment in the United States—is emblematic of these concerns.[9]

The second feature that distinguishes Chinese outward investment is the fact that China has a relatively sophisticated regulatory framework dealing with such investment. It is a framework that has moved within two decades from restricting to encouraging.[10] Embedded in an overall development strategy, China's "going out" strategy has two principal purposes. The first is that the regulatory framework facilitates and supports outward FDI to create globally competitive Chinese firms. The second is that China's outward FDI framework encourages the type of outward FDI that contributes directly to China's development, especially by obtaining natural resources, promoting exports, or strengthening the country's technological base. The government has put in place an institutional structure and various instruments ("home country measures") for this purpose.

Although a number of government institutions have, in one way or another, a say on outward FDI, the principal ones are the National Development and Reform Commission (NDRC) and the Ministry of Commerce (MOFCOM). Together with a

---

[5] *See* Curtis J. Milhaupt & Wentong Zheng, *Beyond Ownership: State Capitalism and the Chinese Firm*, 103 Geo. L.J. 665 (2015). It is of course difficult to determine how much influence this has on the day-to-day operations of a firm, as many of the founders and chief executives of that generation were members of the Party and/or government.

[6] MOFCOM, *supra* note 4.

[7] *See* 央企目录 (The List of Central SOEs), SASAC.gov.cn, http://www.sasac.gov.cn/n1180/n1226/n2425/index.html (last visited Mar. 6, 2015).

[8] For a discussion of these concerns, see Sovereign Investment: Concerns and Policy Reactions (Karl P. Sauvant et al. eds., 2012).

[9] *In Rare Move, Obama Unwinds Chinese Acquisition of U.S. Wind Farms*, 12(39) Inside U.S.-China Trade 1, 16–17 (2012).

[10] For a detailed discussion, *see* Karl P. Sauvant & Victor Zitian Chen, *China's Regulatory Framework for Outward Foreign Direct Investment*, 7 China Econ. J. 141, 141–63 (2013).

number of other institutions, the NDRC in 2006 established a "sector direction policy" that provides guidance for specific promotional measures on the basis of investment that is encouraged, allowed, and prohibited.[11] The specific instruments used to encourage outward FDI include various subsidies (including financial and fiscal support); priority access to loans; expedited approval; priority access to foreign exchange; tax rebates on (or waivers for) the export of goods (for example, equipment); priority regarding overseas financing, investment consulting, risk assessment, risk control, and investment insurance; and priority treatment regarding information questions, consular protection, customs exit and entry of personnel, expatriate personnel approval, registration and the domestic coordination of import-export operation rights, and international communication. These home country measures seem to be equally available to SOEs and private enterprises, at least as far as the formal regulatory framework is concerned.[12]

The third distinguishing feature is that 130 bilateral investment treaties (BITs),[13] as well as a number of other international investment agreements, provide protection to China's outward investors. Although these treaties were originally concluded with inward FDI in mind, they have evolved considerably over time to reflect the rise of China as an outward investor, an evolution discussed below.

Against this background, three observations are in order. First, although China's regulatory framework for outward FDI appears to be very sophisticated, the approval process is complex and cumbersome and can be slow. With the further growth of outward FDI, the approval process will have to be simplified considerably, if not replaced by mere notifications, in order to avoid the possibility of collapsing under its own weight (given the growing number of Chinese MNEs and their foreign affiliates). Reform may indeed be in the offing as part of Xi Jinping's broader reform efforts. Indicative of this is the change, beginning in May 2014, of requiring only deals valued at more than US$1 billion to be approved by the NDRC, as compared to the previous requirement of deals valued at more than US$100 million.[14] It would also be more efficient to create a one-stop shop for the various measures available to qualifying outward investors. The combination of both approaches, if pursued, would imply that control measures regarding outward FDI would increasingly be replaced by incentives in order to support

---

[11] *Id.*

[12] In practice, however, SOEs may benefit more from the home country measures that are available. For example, the approval process may be faster for (especially large) SOEs.

[13] *See International Investment Agreements Navigator*, UNCTAD Div. on Inv. and Enter., http://investmentpolicyhub.unctad.org/IIA/IiasByCountry#iiaInnerMenu (last visited Mar. 6, 2015).

[14] *See* 境外投资项目核准和备案管理办法 (The Approval of Overseas Investment Projects and Record Management Procedures) (promulgated by the Nat'l Dev. and Reform Comm'n, May 8, 2014, effective upon promulgation) *available at* http://www.sdpc.gov.cn/fzgggz/wzly/zcfg/wzzcjwtz/201404/t20140410_606603.html. MOFCOM still uses the same review documents as before, but is proposing a new document in which only sensitive areas/industries will require full reviews. *See* 境外投资管理办法（修订）（征求意见稿）(Administrative Measures on Overseas Investment Management (Amendment) (draft for public comment)), MOFCOM Dept. of Treaty and L., http://tfs.mofcom.gov.cn/article/as/201404/20140400551680.shtml (last visited Mar. 7 2015).

the government's broader economic development goals. Such reforms would make home country measures all the more important for encouraging outward FDI that contributes as much as possible to the country's development.

The second observation is that, as already noted, China is in the process of becoming a net outward investor. One likely implication of this trend is that the government's interest in protecting its outward investments and facilitating access to markets for its firms would be further enhanced, perhaps eventually trumping its interest in protecting its own firms from inward FDI in certain sectors. This, in turn, would most likely have implications for the country's policy stance on international investment agreements. The watershed accord reached in July 2013 between the governments of China and the United States (in the context of the United States-China Strategic and Economic Dialogue) to continue their negotiations of a BIT on the basis of pre-establishment national treatment (granting foreign investors market access), and the negative list approach to exceptions from such treatment (listing sectors that are restricted to foreign investors, as opposed to sectors that are open to them)[15] highlights the shift in emphasis in the country's perspective from a host country to a home country. At the same time, it is of course entirely possible that this shift in approach was also motivated—perhaps greatly so—by the expectation that it could help in internal economic reform processes, including capital market and SOE reforms. For this reason, the BIT negotiations ("century negotiations") between China and the United States have at times been compared to the negotiations that led to China's entry into the World Trade Organization in terms of the internal reform consequences the entry brought with them.[16]

Third, China is not the only country that pursues its own national objectives with regard to the outward FDI of its firms, and that has put home country measures into place to promote these objectives. Virtually all developed countries (but only a few developing ones) pursue—to a larger or lesser extent—similar policies, and support them through appropriate instruments.[17] Hence, if home country measures become an object of international negotiations, a number of countries would be directly affected.

Nevertheless, in the view of a number of developed countries, helping firms to invest abroad has become undesirable, at least when it involves SOEs. The principal reason

---

[15] Li Jiabao, *China, US "Pragmatic about Pact,"* China Daily, Jan. 16, 2014, http://www.chinadailyasia.com/business/2014-01/16/content_15112679.html.

[16] This is according to a representative of the MOFCOM delegation negotiating the BIT,

> [T]he significance of the China-US BIT negotiation is comparable to that of the WTO accession. While the WTO access negotiation is related to opening up of trade, the BIT negotiation is related to the reform of the administrative system of foreign investment and the opening up of foreign investment. Hence the BIT negotiation will have more challenges but more profound implications.

See Jiang Wei 江纬, 中美双边投资协定进入文本谈判阶段 (China-US BIT Negotiations Advance to Negotiations on Text), 21 世纪经济报道 (21st Century Bus. Herald)(Jan. 16, 2014), http://jingji.21cbh.com/2014/1-16/yMMDA2NTFfMTA0NTIyMA.html.

[17] For an extensive analysis, *see* Karl P. Sauvant et al., *Trends in FDI, Home Country Measures and Competitive Neutrality, in* Yearbook on International Investment Law and Policy 2012–2013 (Andrea Bjorklund ed., 2014).

might well be that MNEs from emerging markets, and especially SOEs from China, have become significant outward investors. Such help, in the form of home country measures, is seen as giving special advantages to SOEs,[18] distorting the competitive outward FDI landscape in favor of these enterprises in the markets in which they invest. The relevant concept is "competitive neutrality."[19] In the international context, this concept means that no entity in an international market should have undue competitive advantages vis-à-vis its competitors. Thus, measures to help firms in their outward FDI, even when available equally to both public and private entities, may in the future be evaluated in terms of their impact on competitive neutrality.

The international discussions so far have, however, focused only on advantages that are enjoyed by SOEs. This is so in spite of the fact that, in the case of countries that make such incentives available, home country measures are accessible to both public and private firms. There also is no systematic evidence that home country measures regularly provide SOEs with competitive advantages over their private or mixed ownership counterparts when engaging in FDI, regardless of whether SOEs are based in developed economies or emerging markets.[20] A recent OECD study came to the same conclusion when it noted, regarding the types of advantages granted to SOEs by governments with respect to cross-border activities, that "[e]xisting information on such advantages is often either anecdotal or limited to individual cases."[21]

The competitive neutrality discussions are being carried out in the OECD, but this issue has also entered the negotiations of the Trans-Pacific Partnership Agreement. The competitive neutrality issues will most likely also be on the agenda of other negotiations in the future toward imposing disciplines on the availability of measures supporting outward FDI by SOEs. Depending on the outcome of these negotiations and, in particular, future negotiations in which China might participate, the support that China's SOEs obtain when investing abroad may eventually become a difficult policy issue.

II. The Perception and Reception of China's Outward FDI in Host Countries

China's outward FDI is facing rising scepticism. Numerous factors contribute to this scepticism: the speed with which Chinese investment has grown; the leading role of SOEs in the country's outward FDI (and the associated concern that FDI serves

---

[18] SOEs and also other enterprises may be able to draw on other advantages, for example, when they have a monopoly position in their domestic market. The discussion here focuses narrowly on specific measures meant to help firms invest abroad.

[19] *See* OECD, Guidelines on Corporate Governance of State-Owned Enterprises 18 (2005), *available at* http://www.oecd.org/corporate/ca/corporategovernanceofstate-ownedenterprises/34803211.pdf.

[20] *See* Sauvant et al., *supra* note 17.

[21] Przemyslaw Kowalski et al., *State-Owned Enterprises: Trade Effects and Policy Implications*, OECD Trade Policy Paper No. 147, at 10, TAD/TC/WP(2012)10/FINAL (2013).

noncommercial purposes); the negative effects sometimes associated with FDI, such as the transfer of research-and-development facilities from newly acquired firms to parent firms; the fear, in particular regarding natural resource projects, that host countries do not get a fair deal in the distribution of benefits from such projects, including when these projects employ primarily Chinese workers; perceived unfair competition, especially in the case of SOEs (for example, the suspicion of subsidized financing); the negative image of the home country in some host countries, related also to the fact that members of the Chinese Communist Party are often in leading positions in Chinese MNEs; and the fear that China's outward FDI might compromise national security, through investment in critical industries and infrastructure, while supporting the country's emergence as a global strategic competitor. A look at the most important host countries among developed countries and emerging markets for China's outward FDI helps to shed more light on these concerns.[22]

Overall, FDI from China receives considerable attention in most of the countries researched, even though in most countries Chinese FDI remains relatively small both in absolute amounts and relative to the sums invested by firms from other countries. Such investment is regarded with some trepidation in most countries researched. In contrast, Chinese greenfield investment is generally welcome, although there are concerns in the case of FDI in natural resources and telecommunications.

Perceptions of incoming Chinese FDI are not uniform across constituencies within countries or across countries. In most of the host countries researched, *newspapers* tend to represent a more critical constituency—albeit, unevenly so. Headlines in newspapers

[22] Extensive research was conducted between early September 2013 and the end of March 2014 on the following countries, primarily using Google to locate local newspapers, institutions, and government websites, as well as the Factiva database, with a focus on the years 2012 and 2013. We consulted roughly seven hundred items in the following countries (in a number of cases, the Google Chrome translation service was utilized): Australia, Belgium, Brazil, Cambodia, Canada, Chile, China, France, Germany, India, Indonesia, Iran, Ireland, Italy, Kazakhstan, Laos, Mexico, Mongolia, the Netherlands, Russia, Saudi Arabia, Singapore, Spain, Sudan, the United Kingdom, the United States, and Zambia. In addition, research was undertaken for the European Union (EU) as a whole, reflecting the fact that, after the entry into force of the Lisbon Treaty on December 1, 2009, the EU has exclusive authority in the FDI area. The listed countries, plus other members of the EU, accounted for some two-thirds of China's outward FDI stock in 2011, and a somewhat higher share of China's average outward FDI flows during 2009–2011 (as reported by MOFCOM), not counting Chinese FDI in the tax havens and financial centers mentioned earlier in the text. *See* MOFCOM, *supra* note 4. Note, however, the observation made earlier that the MOFCOM data do not provide an accurate picture about the ultimate destination of China's outward FDI, precisely because most of it is channeled via financial centers and tax havens. Research for Germany was conducted by Schahram Ghalebegi, "The Perception and Reception of China's FDI in Germany" (Berlin School of Economics and Law, April 2014) (on file with the authors); research for Kazakhstan and Russia was conducted by Andrei Panibratov, "Perceptions of Chinese FDI in Neighboring Emerging Economies: Different Groups' Opinions in Russia and Kazakhstan" (St. Petersburg State University, May 2014) (on file with the authors); and research for all other countries was conducted by Camilla Gambarini, Nancy Lee, and Adrian Torres, "The Perception and Reception of China's Outward FDI in Key Host Countries" (New York: Columbia Center on Sustainable Investment, April 2014) (on file with the authors).

read, for example: "Latin America Playing a Risky Game by Welcoming in the Chinese Dragon,"[23] "Kazakh Opposition Calls for Halt to Chinese Expansion,"[24] and "Chinese Investment and Aid in Cambodia a Controversial Affair."[25] National security concerns are particularly salient in the United States, France, and the United Kingdom. Chinese FDI in natural resources sectors receives attention in natural resource-rich countries, such as Australia, Canada, Kazakhstan, and Zambia. The fear in such countries is that, when critical resources are controlled from abroad, the benefits associated with such projects may not be equitably distributed between foreign investors and host countries, in part because labor is often imported from China, and working conditions are often poor. Other media criticism involves broader negative effects such investment can bring. For example, in Cambodia, the activities of Chinese firms have been criticized for severely damaging the environment.[26] In Mongolia, the influx of foreign laborers, particularly Chinese, has been noted negatively, in particular as many Mongolians remain unemployed.[27]

On the other hand, other newspapers—often the business press[28]—are neutral in tone. Examples of such neutral headlines include: "New Study Shows No Evidence of German 'Industrial Crown Jewels' Sell Off to China,"[29] "Chinese Firms to Invest 700m in Holland,"[30] and "China Keen on Investing in Brazil Infrastructure, Manufacturing."[31]

Other media focus on positive aspects, reflected in such articles as: "*Le développement de la Chine n'est pas une menace mais une opportunité*,"[32] "India Invites Foreign Direct

---

[23] Kevin Gallagher, *Latin America Playing a Risky Game by Welcoming in the Chinese Dragon*, The Guardian, May 30, 2013, http://www.theguardian.com/global-development/poverty-matters/2013/may/30/latin-america-risky-chinese-dragon.

[24] Robin Paxton, *Kazakh Opposition Calls for Halt to China Expansion*, Reuters, May 28, 2011, http://uk.reuters.com/article/2011/05/28/kazakhstan-china-protest-idUKLDE74R02M20110528.

[25] Heng Pheakdey, *Chinese Investment and Aid in Cambodia a Controversial Affair*, East Asia Forum (July 16, 2013), http://www.eastasiaforum.org/2013/07/16/chinese-investment-and-aid-in-cambodia-a-controversial-affair/.

[26] *Id.*

[27] M. Zoljarga, *Contractors Bring Illegal Workers while Mongolians Remain Unemployed*, The UB Post, Dec. 17, 2013, http://ubpost.mongolnews.mn/?p=7031.

[28] For example, the *Frankfurter Allgemeine Zeitung* and the *Manager Magazine* in Germany and *Il Sole 24 Ore* in Italy.

[29] *See* Press Release, BGM Associates, New Study Shows No Evidence of German "Industrial Crown Jewels" Sell Off to China (Jan. 23, 2013), *available at* http://www.bgmassociates.com/fileadmin/downloads/publications/press_releases/Weltmarktfuehrerkongress%20-%20Press%20release%20-%20Chinese%20acquisitions%202013-01-23.pdf.

[30] *Chinese Firms to Invest €700m in Holland*, Dutch News, Oct. 30, 2009, http://www.dutchnews.nl/news/archives/2009/10/chinese_firms_to_invest_700m_i.php.

[31] Gerald Jeffris, *China Keen on Investing in Brazil Infrastructure, Manufacturing*, Wall St. J. May 10, 2013, http://online.wsj.com/article/BT-CO-20130510-715152.html.

[32] *Le développement de la Chine n'est pas une menace mais une opportunité*, People's Daily Online, Sept. 25, 2013, http://french.peopledaily.com.cn/International/8410014.html.

Investment from China,"[33] and "Fear of Chinese Investment Misses the Economic Point."[34] In the United States, for example, Chinese investments in depressed areas, such as Detroit, have received positive press.[35] In the Netherlands and Luxembourg, there was little negative public opinion, perhaps because Chinese investments there typically require relatively higher-skilled labor.

The *business community* itself does not appear to be deeply engaged in the public debate on this subject. Big business—out of self-interest—typically supports an open international investment regime that provides strong protections for investors and investments and access to markets. Moreover, China is an important export market and host country for many firms, making the enterprises involved reluctant to advocate restrictive policies, for fear of retaliation. It may well be that firms and business associations lobby their governments to take action against perceived competitive threats. The arrival of new competitors is not always welcome. In the case of FDI by SOEs, concerns about possible competitive advantages of these enterprises come into play. In fact, the Business Coalition for Transatlantic Trade (BCTT—the most important United States' business coalition for the Transatlantic Trade and Investment Partnership negotiations) is a driving force behind efforts to to impose disciplines on SOEs, in the context of outward FDI and competitive neutrality.[36] BCTT's position is very similar to that of the U.S. Business Coalition for TPP (the Trans-Pacific Partnership).[37]

Trade unions, likewise, do not appear to be that engaged. This is somewhat surprising as many acquisitions by Chinese firms involve firms that are in difficulty or insolvent, and such transactions typically involve layoffs. On the other hand, if such firms are taken over and continue as going concerns, this is a positive development. In the end, trade unions welcome any investment, whether domestic or foreign, that creates or maintains jobs, as long as working conditions do not deteriorate. At the same time, the AFL-CIO has voiced concerns about FDI by SOEs in the United States, fearing that such investment results in asset stripping or consists only of toehold investments.[38]

---

[33] *India invites Chinese Foreign Direct Investment*, THE ECON. TIMES, Feb. 28, 2013, http://articles.economictimes.indiatimes.com/2013-02-27/news/37331014_1_chinese-companies-china-s-jaishankar-mutual-investment.

[34] Jiang Wenran, *Fear of Chinese Investment Misses the Economic Point*, EDMONTON J., Feb. 15, 2012, http://www2.canada.com/edmontonjournal/news/ideas/story.html?id=763d030e-f0d3-4f45-8fe9-7e64d2221a1f.

[35] Kathy Chen, *U.S. Cities Seek to Woo Chinese Investment*, WALL ST. J., Apr. 6, 2010, http://online.wsj.com/news/articles/SB10001424052702303410404575151593460208482.

[36] *See Competition Policy*, BUS. COAL. FOR TRANSATLANTIC TRADE, http://www.transatlantictrade.org/issues/competition-policy/ (last visited Mar. 6, 2015).

[37] *See Principles*, U.S. BUS. COAL. FOR TPP, http://tppcoalition.org/about/ (last visited Mar. 6, 2015).

[38] *See* Cong. Exec. Comm'n on China, *China's Compliance with the WTO and International Trade Rules, Jan. 15, 2014*, at 7 (Testimony of Thea Mei Lee, Deputy Chief of Staff, Am. Fed'n of Labor and Cong. of Indus. Org.), *available at* http://www.cecc.gov/sites/chinacommission.house.gov/files/CECC%20Hearing%20-%20WTO%20-%20Thea%20Lee%20Written%20Statement.pdf.

Finally, *governments*, including both executive and legislative bodies, reflect the conflicted attitude of other stakeholders. On balance, however, the *executives* of the countries we researched maintain a welcoming attitude regarding incoming FDI in general and investment from China. For instance, in May 2007, the president of the United States, George W. Bush, issued a statement on "open economies,"[39] reaffirming the country's openness to FDI. Governments from all parts of the world have supported missions to China to attract investment. Competition for such investment often also takes place at the sub-national level. Chinese FDI was especially welcome in the European countries most affected by the Eurozone crisis, both as a means to forestall the bankruptcy of domestic firms and to relaunch economic growth. Some countries even introduced regulations to facilitate such investment, for example, by simplifying visa processes.[40] In Russia, the highest authorities welcome Chinese FDI, although there are also fears that China's role might become too strong.[41] The same approach appears to prevail in Kazakhstan,[42] where Chinese FDI is also viewed as a counterbalance to Russia. Southeast Asian countries, for their part, are tightly linked with China through regional value chains, and governments therefore regard Chinese FDI as benefitting development.

Yet the executives of a number of countries also have voiced concerns about Chinese FDI. They are also subject to pressure from their *legislatures* or the individual members of such bodies. Concerns relate to the various issues mentioned at the beginning of this section, especially in the areas of national security and the role of SOEs in China's outward FDI. Security concerns are particularly pronounced in the United States, where the issue of cybersecurity (particularly in the area of telecommunications) adds an additional dimension.[43] In Australia and Canada, governmental concerns focus more on the control of natural resources and the net benefits associated with their exploitation (mirroring the discussions in media), although other tests (including national security) are employed as well. In the Latin American countries researched, it does not appear that Chinese FDI issues have figured noticeably in parliamentary discussions. But in India, nineteen questions relating to FDI from China were asked in the Lower

[39] Press Release, Office of the Press Secretary, President Bush's Statement on Open Economies (May 10, 2007), *available at* http://georgewbush-whitehouse.archives.gov/news/releases/2007/05/20070510-3.html.

[40] Ireland reportedly introduced new visa regulations specifically with Chinese investors in mind. Ireland introduced the Immigration Scheme for Investors and Entrepreneurs in 2012. *See* 213 No. 6, Seanad Deb., Immigrant Investor Programme and Start-up Entrepreneur Scheme: Statements (Feb. 9, 2012), http://debates.oireachtas.ie/seanad/2012/02/09/00006.asp.

[41] Panibratov, *supra* note 22.

[42] *Id.*

[43] *See* Chairman Mike Rogers and Ranking Member C.A. Dutch Ruppersberger of the Permanent Select Comm. on Intelligence, 112th Cong., Investigative Rep. on the U.S. Nat'l Sec. Issues Posed by Chinese Telecomm. Cos. Huawei and ZTE, H. R. Rep. (2012), *available at* http://intelligence.house.gov/sites/intelligence.house.gov/files/documents/Huawei-ZTE%20Investigative%20Report%20%28FINAL%29.pdf. Most of the concerns surrounding Huawei relate to its perceived links to the Chinese government.

House of Parliament and nineteen in the Upper House during the period from July 7, 2009 to February 22, 2014, with ten of these questions involving national security.[44] The best-known parliamentary reaction was probably a 2005 resolution adopted by the United States House of Representatives condemning, in a vote of 138 to 15, the attempted takeover of the United States firm Unocal by CNOOC of China.[45]

These various cross-cutting pressures are reflected in the fact that a number of countries have strengthened or established review mechanisms for incoming FDI, focussed on M&As by SOEs (and also, before the Western financial crisis, by sovereign wealth funds). Such steps require walking a fine line of balancing the mitigation of concerns with maintaining an investment climate that remains attractive to (in this case) Chinese MNEs. The focus of these mechanisms is on national security and net benefits for the host country, but they also reflect concerns about SOEs benefitting from various subsidies that give them a competitive advantage vis-à-vis domestic firms.

The competitive advantage concern has been taken up in international negotiations that are likely to be of particular interest to China. A number of countries have strengthened their review mechanisms for incoming M&As in order to make sure that such transactions are in their national interest. The actions taken by the United States, Canada, and Australia exemplify this approach.

In the United States, the Foreign Investment and National Security Act,[46] adopted by Congress in 2007, strengthens the role of the Committee on Foreign Investment in the United States (itself established in 1988 as a reaction to the rapid growth of Japanese FDI in the United States) in reviewing incoming M&As. Among other things, the law requires that incoming M&As by state-controlled entities not only must be notified but also in principle are subject to investigations.

In December 2007, the government of Canada issued guidelines for investment by SOEs in order[47] to clarify the investment process applicable to acquisitions of a certain size by SOEs. The continued growth of M&As by such firms led the government to issue further clarifications in December 2012, noting among other things: "Each case will be examined on its own merits; however, given the inherent risks posed by foreign SOE acquisitions in the Canadian oil sands the Minister of Industry will find the acquisition

---

[44] This is, however, a small percentage of all 1,185 questions asked during this period. Still, they show the saliency of Chinese FDI in India. *See* Premila Nazareth Satyanand, *Policy Brief: What Do India's MPs Want to Know about FDI?*, New Dehli Nat'l Council of Applied Econ. Research, *available at* http://www.ncaer.org/

[45] H.R. Res. 344, 109th Cong. (2005), *available at* https://www.govtrack.us/congress/bills/109/hres344/text.

[46] Foreign Investment and National Security Act of 2007, Pub. L. 110–49, 121 Stat. 246 (codified as amended at 50 U.S.C. App. § 2170 (2007)), *available at* http://www.gpo.gov/fdsys/pkg/BILLS-110hr556enr/pdf/BILLS-110hr556enr.pdf.

[47] *See* News Release, Government of Canada, Policy Statement and Revised Guidelines for Investments by State-Owned Enterprises (Dec. 7, 2012), *available at* http://news.gc.ca/web/article-en.do?nid=711489.

of control of a Canadian oil sands business by a foreign SOE to be net benefit to Canada on an exceptional basis only."[48]

The government of Australia announced in February 2008 a new policy that requires the Treasurer to examine a number of specific issues when considering applications for investments by foreign governments and their agencies. These issues include whether an investor's operations are independent from the relevant foreign government and whether the investment may have an impact on the country's national security.[49] The influx of Chinese investment reportedly triggered this action.[50]

The principal purpose of the measures taken by these three countries was to create the tools to block, if need be, undesirable M&As—not only from China, but also from firms headquartered in other countries. However, it is noteworthy that these actions took place—in fact, were probably triggered—when China's outward FDI began to rise rapidly. The screening mechanisms in all three countries are particularly strong for M&As undertaken by SOEs.

From China's perspective, government activities that impact Chinese (SOE-dominated) outward FDI through host country review mechanisms are, not surprisingly, of concern. This creates an interest in addressing this subject in international investment agreements. In fact, all countries that have some kind of review mechanism would want to protect such mechanisms in their international investment agreements.

In sum, the perception and reception of China's growing outward FDI in the country's principal host countries has been decidedly mixed, both regarding the entry strategies of Chinese MNEs into host countries (M&As versus greenfield investments), and the perceptions of and reactions to such investment by and within various host country constituencies. This was recently recognized publicly in China. The Governor of China's Central Bank, Zhou Xiaochuan, commented that "Different entities have behaved differently. There may have been some phenomena of Chinese investors [that were] not so good, not so satisfactory."[51] As China's outward FDI grows, scepticism toward such investment may grow in some circles as well. The obvious question is: What could be done to deal with reactions to China's outward FDI in order to avoid a backlash and build trust? Host countries, and especially developed ones, also face the challenge of accommodating the rise of China's outward FDI and respecting China's interests.

---

[48] *See id.*

[49] *See* AUSTRALIAN GOV'T, FOREIGN INV. REVIEW BD., 2008–2009 ANNUAL REPORT 7 (2010), *available at* http://www.firb.gov.au/content/Publications/AnnualReports/2008-2009/_downloads/2008-09_FIRB_AR.pdf.

[50] Peter Cai, *Delicate Balancing Act for the Foreign Investment Board*, SYDNEY MORNING HERALD, Oct. 26, 2013, *available at* http://newsstore.smh.com.au/apps/viewDocument.ac;jsessionid=BD5FEACDC3FE58239A711B03BC59962A?sy=afr&pb=all_ffx&dt=selectRange&dr=1month&so=relevance&sf=text&sf=headline&rc=10&rm=200&sp=brs&cls=1435&clsPage=1&docID=SMH131026 29BJ57M4T2E.

[51] Javier Blas, *China's Central Bank Chief Admits Difficulties with Africa*, FIN. TIMES, May 22, 2014, *available at* http://www.ft.com/intl/cms/s/0/5b212302-e1c9-11e3-b7c4-00144feabdc0.html#axzz3EolVbxrE (quoting the governor).

At the national level, SOEs have a special responsibility to make sure that their investments abroad are well planned, prepared, and received. This is particularly important when investments take the form of M&As and are in industries that are sensitive for national security, for cultural reasons or for those involving iconic targets. Even M&As in other areas may elicit concerns as they are frequently associated with restructuring and the shedding of jobs. Hence, governments at all levels need to be carefully prepared, and the benefits of a particular acquisition need to be spelled out. Moreover, SOEs need to make an extra effort to become "insiders," good corporate citizens that are recognized as such. This can be achieved through sourcing from local suppliers, employing nationals in high corporate positions, becoming members of local associations, and engaging in various corporate social responsibility (CSR) activities. In fact, SOE affiliates in host countries should commit themselves to dedicating a small percentage of their earnings to CSR activities in their host countries,[52] and to supporting the initiative of the Group of 7[53] to establish a global facility that helps developing countries (and especially the least developed among them) negotiate large-scale contracts with MNEs to ensure that both host countries and investors benefit equitably from the investments made, especially in natural resources.

But China's government also has a role to play. For example, it could pay more attention to enforcing the various instruments that it already has in place to guide the behavior of its foreign investors abroad. More ambitiously, China could complement its "going-out" strategy with a "going-in" strategy.[54] Such a strategy would seek to maximize not only the benefits of the country's outward FDI for China and its firms, but also for the economic, social, and environmental development of the host countries in which Chinese firms invest, and would take place in fair governance mechanisms—in short, a strategy for sustainable FDI. Key elements of such a "going-in" strategy could be to reinforce China's current regulatory framework dealing with the behavior of Chinese MNEs abroad, to expand it, for example, in line with the OECD Guidelines for Multinational Enterprises to which China could adhere, and improve monitoring and enforcement of the framework. Such a strategy could be underpinned by requiring, through law, that Chinese SOEs (and, for that matter, other outward investors) dedicate a small percentage of their

---

[52] A variation of what India's Companies Act 2013 mandates for corporate responsibility spending by its own firms in India. *See* The Companies Act, No. 18 of 2013, India Code (2013), *available at* http://indiacode.nic.in/acts-in-pdf/182013.pdf.

[53] The Group of 7, in its June 2014 Summit, announced "a new initiative on Strengthening Assistance for Complex Contract Negotiations (CONNEX) to provide developing country partners with extended and concrete expertise for negotiating complex commercial contracts, focusing initially on the extractives sector . . . ." *See* Press Release, European Commission, The Brussels G7 Summit Declaration (June 5, 2004), *available at* http://europa.eu/rapid/press-release_MEMO-14-402_en.htm.

[54] For a brief elaboration of such a strategy, see Karl P. Sauvant & Victor Z. Chen, *China Needs to Complement Its "Going-Out" Policy with a "Going-In" Strategy*, Colum. FDI Perspectives, No. 121 (2014), *available at* http://ccsi.columbia.edu/publications/columbia-fdi-perspectives/.

earnings to CSR activities in host countries, elevating such action from a voluntary to a mandatory one. The government itself could furthermore support the earlier mentioned initiative of the Group of 7 to establish a negotiations support facility.

A "going-in" strategy by China along these lines could become a model for other home countries, whether they are developed or developing. Conceivably, it could also influence the content of international investment agreements and give home country governments a role in ensuring that the outward investment by firms headquartered in their territories has as much as possible the characteristics of sustainable FDI.

The mixed perception and reception of China's outward FDI in important host countries strengthens China's interest in international investment agreements that protect the country's outward FDI (especially against discriminatory treatment of its investors, including SOEs) and that help secure access to markets. Such considerations may well be one of the principal driving forces behind China's interest in concluding BITs with the United States and the European Union, the world's biggest markets, as well as with other important host countries.

China's interests thus have changed profoundly since it entered the world FDI market in a substantial manner more than a decade ago. Accordingly, the country's approach to international investment agreements has changed, and can be expected to evolve further—a topic considered below.

III. China's Changing Approach to International Investment Agreements

As mentioned above, China has signed more BITs than any other country except Germany.[55] China also has in place other IIAs, including nine free trade agreements (FTAs) including investment chapters, and a trilateral agreement with Japan and the Republic of Korea.[56] China's IIA program, which was initiated in 1982, has had a major shift in focus since the 2000s.

A. China's Investment Treaty Program: Three Generations

After decades of isolation, China opened up to foreign investment beginning in 1980.[57] China's focus for the major part of the 1980s was on inward investment. During this period, most of China's BITs were concluded with European countries. It was only in

---

55 As of December 2014, Germany had concluded 134 BITs and China 130. *See International Investment Agreements Navigator, supra* note 13.

56 *See China FTA Network*, MOFCOM, http://fta.mofcom.gov.cn/english/index.shtml (last visited Mar. 6, 2015).

57 *See* Stephan W. Schill, *Tearing Down the Great Wall*, 15 Cardozo J. Int'l & Comp. L. 73, 77–80 (2007).

the 1990s that China's investment treaty endeavors gained significance.[58] Between 1988 and 1998, China signed more than sixty BITs, the majority with developing countries.

This first generation of China's BITs, concluded between 1982 and 1998, was marked by the restrictive approach taken with respect to both substantive protections and investor-state dispute resolution. China was then a predominantly capital-importing country, and it had little incentive to place its trust in a dispute resolution mechanism through which its sovereignty could be impinged. The dispute resolution clauses in these first BITs exhibited language to the effect that only "disputes involving the amount of compensation for expropriation" could be arbitrated.[59] As a result, disputes arising out of a first generation treaty arguably were limited to the very narrow question of whether a foreign investor was dispossessed of its investment.[60]

In keeping with such limited consent to arbitrate disputes with foreign investors, China qualified its ratification of the International Centre for Settlement of Investment Disputes (ICSID) Convention by stating that it would consider submitting to the jurisdiction of ICSID only "for disputes over compensation resulting from expropriation and nationalization."[61]

In its second generation of BITs, starting in 1998, China broadened its consent to arbitration for investment disputes. The majority of treaties concluded between 1998 and 2008 vested arbitral tribunals with the competence to hear "any disputes concerning an investment."[62] The broadening of China's consent to arbitration at the turn of the century coincided with an impending announcement of the country's "going out" strategy and the subsequent fiftyfold rise in outward investment.[63]

---

[58] *See* Congyan Cai, *Outward Foreign Direct Investment Protection and the Effectiveness of Chinese BIT Practice*, 7 J. WORLD INV. & TRADE 621–22, 626 (Oct. 2006).

[59] *See, e.g.*, Agreement between the Government of the People's Republic of China and the Government of the Mongolian People's Republic concerning the Encouragement and Reciprocal Protection of Investments, art. 8(3), Aug. 25, 1991, *available at* http://investmentpolicyhub.unctad.org/Download/TreatyFile/760.

[60] *See, e.g.*, Peter J. Turner & Mark Mangan, *China's Investment Treaties: Substantive and Procedural Rights*, 5 ASIAN COUNSEL 43–44 (May 2007); *see also* Schill, *supra* note 57, at 89–91. Some tribunals have taken the opposite view. *See infra* Section III(C).

[61] *See* ICSID, Notifications concerning Classes of Disputes Considered Suitable or Unsuitable for Submission to the Centre, *available at* https://icsid.worldbank.org/apps/ICSIDWEB/icsiddocs/Documents/ICSID%208%20-%20latest%20-%20Nov%2010%202014.pdf (last visited May 24, 2015). This notification was never repealed, but it does not prevent arbitrating disputes that would be subjected to IIAs of second or third generation. *See* CHRISTOPH H. SCHREUER, THE ICSID CONVENTION: A COMMENTARY 930 (2009).

[62] *See, e.g.*, Agreement between the Government of Barbados and the Government of the People's Republic of China, July 20, 1998, *available at* http://www.investbarbados.org/docs/BIT%20-%20Republic%20of%20China.PDF; Agreement between the People's Republic of China and the Federal Republic of Germany on the Encouragement and Reciprocal Protection of Investments, Jan. 12, 2003, *available at* http://investmentpolicyhub.unctad.org/Download/TreatyFile/736.

[63] *See Report Folders, supra* note 1.

The third generation of China IIAs embody distinctive features showing a seemingly more careful approach to treaty protection with, on the one hand, a tightening of the admissibility of investors' claims and, on the other hand, an increased level of substantive protections afforded to investors.

1. Restrictions in China IIAs to Admissibility of Investor Claims

(a) "Investors"

The IIAs that China has entered into in recent years use language requiring that a foreign investor have "real economic activities"[64] or be "engaged in substantive business operations"[65] in the territory of the contracting state. Several treaties refer to the requirement that the foreign investor, if a corporate entity, must be controlled by nationals of the contracting state to be entitled to treaty protection.[66]

Importantly, Chinese SOEs are now directly included as falling within the ambit of bilateral treaty protections. Indeed, in recent Chinese IIAs, "public institutions"[67] or "governmentally owned or controlled"[68] investors are protected. This language presumably follows the example of NAFTA or the 2004 U.S. Model BIT.[69] Other countries have expressly referred to their government in the definition of "investor," including

[64] Agreement between the Government of the People's Republic of China and the Government of Romania concerning the Encouragement and Reciprocal Protection of Investments, art. 2(b), July 12, 1994, *available at* http://investmentpolicyhub.unctad.org/Download/TreatyFile/773.

[65] Agreement between the Government of the United Mexican States and the Government of the People's Republic of China on the Promotion and Reciprocal Protection of Investments, art. 1(b), July 7, 2008, *available at* http://investmentpolicyhub.unctad.org/Download/TreatyFile/759 [hereinafter "China-Mexico BIT"].

[66] *See, e.g.*, Free Trade Agreement between the Government of the People's Republic of China and the Government of the Republic of Peru, art. 126, Apr. 28, 2009, *available at* http://fta.mofcom.gov.cn/bilu/annex/bilu_xdwb_en.pdf [hereinafter "China-Peru FTA"].

[67] *See, e.g.*, China-Korea BIT, art 1(2)(b), July 7, 2007, *available at* http://investmentpolicyhub.unctad.org/Download/TreatyFile/751.

[68] Free Trade Agreement between the Government of New Zealand and the Government of the People's Republic of China, art. 11, Apr. 7, 2008, *available at* http://investmentpolicyhub.unctad.org/Download/TreatyFile/2564 [hereinafter "China-New Zealand FTA"]; China-Mexico BIT, art. 1; Agreement on Investment of the Framework Agreement on Comprehensive Economic Cooperation between the People's Republic of China and the Association of Southeast Asian Nations, art. 1(f), Aug. 15, 2009, *available at* http://investmentpolicyhub.unctad.org/Download/TreatyFile/2596; Agreement among the Government of Japan, the Government of the Republic of Korea, and the Government of the People's Republic of China for the Promotion, Facilitation, and Protection of Investment, art. 1(4), May 13, 2012, *available at* http://investmentpolicyhub.unctad.org/Download/TreatyFile/2633 [hereinafter "China-Japan-Republic of Korea TIT"].

[69] The 2004 U.S. Model BIT defines "investor of a Party" as "a Party or state enterprise thereof, ... that attempts to make, is making, or has made an investment in the territory of the other Party." 2004 U.S. Model BIT, *available at* http://www.state.gov/documents/organization/117601.pdf. This language is almost identical to that of the North American Free Trade Agreement, U.S.-Can.-Mex., art. 1139, Dec. 17, 1992, 32 I.L.M. 289 (1993) [hereinafter "NAFTA"].

Saudi Arabia,[70] Qatar,[71] and the United Arab Emirates.[72] As seen above, SOEs are crucial to China's outward FDI as they account for between two-thirds and three-quarters of total FDI.[73] As with the vast majority of IIAs,[74] China did not expressly include state entities in the scope of protected investors in previous iterations of IIAs. Despite the lack of express provisions, one may wonder whether an investment treaty's protections should be extended or denied to an SOE. This question is important, as China has historically operated heavily through SOEs.[75] One author emphasized that "if an [SOE] is established as required under the law of a contracting party, it [therefore] qualifies as an 'investor'" such that it is not excluded from the scope of investment protections.[76] Another commentator advanced the view that "exclusion of State entities from coverage would leave the investment treaty with no meaningful application" for BITs concluded with communist states.[77] Yet SOEs, as state-owned entities, presumably have greater

---

[70] *See, e.g.*, Tra il Governo Della Repubblica Italiana ed il Regno dell'Arabia Saudita Sulla Reciproca Promozione e Protezione degli Investimenti, art. 1(3)(a)(iii), Sept. 10, 1996, *available at* http://investmentpolicyhub.unctad.org/Download/TreatyFile/1710; Accord Entre Le Gouvernement de la Republique Francaise et le Gouvernment du Royaume D'Arabie Saoudite Sur L'Encouragement et la Protection Reciproques des Investissements, art. 1(2), June 26, 2002, *available at* http://investmentpolicyhub.unctad.org/Download/TreatyFile/1275.

[71] *See, e.g.*, Agreement between the Federal Republic of Germany and the State of Qatar concerning the Encouragement and Reciprocal Protection of Investments, art. 1(3)(b)(3), Jan. 19, 1999, *available at* http://investmentpolicyhub.unctad.org/Download/TreatyFile/1395; Accord Entre le Conseil federal Suisse et le Gouvernement de l'Etat du Qatar concernant la promotion et la protection réciproque des investissements, art. 1(1)(c), Nov. 12, 2001, *available at* http://investmentpolicyhub.unctad.org/Download/TreatyFile/2205.

[72] Agreement between the Republic of Austria and the United Arab Emirates for the Promotion and Protection of Investments, art. 1(1)(c), June 17, 2001, *available at* http://investmentpolicyhub.unctad.org/Download/TreatyFile/224; Agreement between the Government of Finland and the Government of the United Arab Emirates on the Promotion and Reciprocal Protection of Investments, art. 1(4)(a), Mar. 12, 1996, *available at* http://investmentpolicyhub.unctad.org/Download/TreatyFile/1221; L'accord entre la République française et l'Etat des Emirats arabes unis sur l'encouragement et la protection réciproques des investissements, art. 1(2), Sept. 9, 1991, *available at* http://investmentpolicyhub.unctad.org/Download/TreatyFile/1291; Agreement between the Government of the United Arab Emirates and the Swiss Federal Council on the Promotion and Reciprocal Protection of Investments, art. 1(1)(b)(iii), Nov. 3, 1998, *available at* http://investmentpolicyhub.unctad.org/Download/TreatyFile/2325.

[73] *See supra* Section I.

[74] *See* Jo En Low, *The Status of State-Controlled Entities under International Investment Agreements, in* Yearbook on International Investment Law and Policy 2012–2013 543 (Andrea Bjorklund ed., 2014).

[75] It was reported that, by 2010, there were 26,319 "centrally controlled non-financial SOEs" in China, accounting for 10 percent of China's GDP. Sixty-six of these SOEs made the 2012 Fortune Global 500 list. *See* Duanjie Chen, *China's State-Owned Enterprises: How Much Do We Know? From CNOOC to Its Siblings*, Univ. of Calgary SPP Research Paper No. 6–19, June 2013, *available at* http://papers.ssrn.com/sol3/papers.cfm?abstract_id=2277938.

[76] Low, *supra* note 74, at 547.

[77] Claudia Annacker, *Protection and Admission of Sovereign Investment under Investment Treaties*, 10(3) Chinese J. Int'l L. 531–64 (2011), *available at* http://chinesejil.oxfordjournals.org/content/10/3/531.short.

access to state support when investments are distressed than "private" BIT claimants. Therefore, their access to investor-state arbitration seems less justifiable per se, especially if one considers the concept of competitive neutrality that mandates maintaining a level playing field between SOEs and private businesses.[78]

In a landmark investor-state arbitration case, the arbitral tribunal took the position that protections should be extended where the SOE is not "performing State functions."[79] This view corresponds with the traditional dichotomy between "*acta jure gestionis*"—where the country acts in a commercial capacity—and "*acta jure imperii*"—where the state acts as a sovereign.[80]

The drafting history of the ICSID Convention is enlightening on this point. The *travaux préparatoires* reflect that the drafters debated, and ultimately rejected, the possibility that investor-states could appear in ICSID proceedings.[81] Yet the drafters also considered that an SOE "should not be disqualified as a 'national of another Contracting State' unless it is acting as an agent for the government or is discharging an essentially governmental function.'"[82] Indeed, the purpose of the ICSID Convention was to "stimulat[e] a larger flow of private international investment,"[83] which arguably bars access to arbitration for "nationals" whose investment reflects only governmental concerns.[84]

An UNCTAD report stated that "[u]sually, State enterprises are covered even if not explicitly stated while States themselves tend not to be unless this is expressly provided."[85] Yet it bears noting that China's SOEs, in contrast to some other SOEs and privately owned companies, have often been said not to have financial performance as their core motivator—as evidenced by their profitability ratios[86]—but instead are animated by strategic state-related considerations. Indeed, China is said to be "going out" through some of its SOEs in an effort to have access to foreign resources to further China's industrial policy "aimed at leapfrogging global economic powers."[87] In the context of access to investor-state arbitration, it is legitimate to wonder whether SOEs should qualify under

---

[78] *See supra* Sections I and II.

[79] CSOB v. Slovak Republic, Case No. ARB/97/4, ICSID, Decision on Jurisdiction, ¶¶ 23–27 (May 24, 1999).

[80] Also known as the "Broches test," a reference to ICSID's founder Aron Broches. *See infra* note 82. *See also* Rumeli Telekom AS and Telsim Mobil Telekomikasyon Hizmetleri AS v. Republic of Kazakhstan, Case No. ARB/05/16, ICSID, Award, ¶ 211 (July 29, 2008).

[81] *See* History of the ICSID Convention: Vol. II-1, 401, 976–79, 1018 (2006).

[82] Aron Broches, ICSID, The Convention on the Settlement of Investment Disputes between States and Nationals of Other States 331, 355 (1972).

[83] Barton Legum & William Kirtley, *The Status of the Report of the Executive Directors on the ICSID Convention*, 27(1) ICSID Review 4–5 (2012).

[84] Caution should be exercised, however, as the distinction between private and public capital is often artificial. *See* Low, *supra* note 74, at 558–59.

[85] UNCTAD, *International Investment Agreements: Key Issues*, UNCTAD/ITE/IIT/2004/10 (Vol. I) (2004). For a recent discussion, *see* Low, *supra* note 74.

[86] Chen, *supra* note 75, at table 6.

[87] *Id.* at 12.

IIA regimes absent an express agreement to that effect in the applicable IIA. Further clarification is required on a case-by-case basis as to whether Chinese SOEs constitute instrumentalities of the Chinese state.

(b) "Investments"

For most of its BIT history, China has operated under the assumption that "every kind of asset" qualifies as an investment.[88] In its most recent treaties, following the example of countries such as the United States, China specifically excludes certain business transactions from the definition of qualified investments.[89] Furthermore, in order to qualify as an "investment" under China's BITs, an economic investment must be made "in accordance with the laws" of the host state.[90] Depending upon the formulation used in a particular treaty, failure to abide by the domestic law of the host country may be interpreted as excluding protection under a treaty.[91]

(c) Umbrella clause

So-called "umbrella clauses" may allow investors to claim that a breach of a contractual undertaking arising out of an associated contract between the foreign investor and the state constitutes a treaty violation.[92] Umbrella clauses were a hallmark of the second generation of China's BITs, with some of these treaties imposing on a contracting state the observance of "any contractual obligation it may have entered into towards an investor."[93]

---

[88] *See, e.g.*, L'accord entre le Gouvernement de la République française et le Gouvernement de la République populaire de China sur l'encouragement et la protection réciproques des investissements, art. 1(1), Nov. 26, 1984, *available at* http://investmentpolicyhub.unctad.org/Download/TreatyFile/734.

[89] These include loans, *see* China-Mexico BIT, art. 1(c-d); China-New Zealand FTA, art. 135; China-Peru FTA, art. 126, and claims to money arising out of commercial contracts, *see* China-Mexico BIT, art. 1(h).

[90] *See, e.g.*, Agreement on the Mutual Protection of Investments, China-Swed., art. 1, Mar. 29, 1982, *available at* http://investmentpolicyhub.unctad.org/Download/TreatyFile/782 [hereinafter "China-Sweden BIT"].

[91] "In accordance with the law" provisions may deny jurisdiction should the investment contravene the domestic laws of the host state. *See, e.g.*, Fakes v. Republic of Turkey, Case No. ARB/07/20, ICSID, Award, ¶ 115 (July 14, 2010); Inceysa Vallisoletana v. Republic of El Salvador, Case No. ARB/03/26, ICSID, Award, ¶ 195 (Aug. 2, 2006); Saluka Investments BV v. Czech Republic, UNCITRAL, Partial Award, ¶ 204 (Mar. 17, 2006). *See generally* Rahim Moloo & Alex Khachaturian, *The Compliance with the Law Requirement in International Investment Law*, 34(6) Fordham Int'l L.J. (2011). *See also* Stephan W. Schill, *Illegal Investments in International Arbitration*, SSRN (Jan. 4, 2012), *available at* http://ssrn.com/abstract=1979734.

[92] *See, e.g.*, SGS Société Générale de Surveillance S.A. v. Republic of the Philippines, Case No. ARB/02/6, ICSID, Decision of the Tribunal on Objections to Jurisdiction (Jan. 29, 2004); Salini Construtorri S.p.A. and Italstrade S.p.A. v. Morocco, Jurisdiction, Case No. ARB/00/4, ICSID, Award (July 23, 2001). Some tribunals, however, denied such an effect to umbrella clauses. *See, e.g.*, SGS Société Générale de Surveillance S.A. v. Islamic Republic of Pakistan, Case No. ARB/01/13, ICSID, Award on Jurisdiction (Aug. 6, 2003); *see generally* Laura Hanonen, *Containing the Scope of the Umbrella Clause*, 1 Investment Treaty Arb. & Int'l L. 27–38 (2008).

[93] *See, e.g.*, Agreement between the Government of the Hashemite Kingdom of Jordan and the Government of the People's Republic of China on the Reciprocal Promotion and Protection of Investments, art. 9(2), Nov. 15, 2001, *available at* http://investmentpolicyhub.unctad.org/Download/TreatyFile/748.

This prior dispute settlement clause has been revised in the current generation of Chinese IIAs. China again followed the example of the United States and other countries and abandoned umbrella protections by restricting arbitration to breaches of treaty obligations only.[94]

(d) Non-precluded Measures

Recent IIAs concluded by China contain so-called "non-precluded measures" (NPM) clauses excusing derogation from a party's treaty duties. The most common derogation pertains to measures taken in the interest of security under specific circumstances.[95] Other possible NPMs are prudential measures[96] or taxation measures.[97] Such measures, however, should not permit unfettered indirect expropriation. Recent treaties executed by China state that "deprivation of property [through] measures taken in the exercise of a state's regulatory powers as may be *reasonably justified* in the protection of the public welfare . . . shall not constitute an indirect expropriation."[98]

2. Enhanced Substantive Protections in Recent Chinese BITs

(a) Fair and Equitable Treatment

With a few exceptions,[99] all Chinese BITs contain a fair and equitable treatment (FET) clause. Like BITs from many other nations, the language adopted in second-generation BITs generally referred to FET "in accordance with International Law."[100] This language, coupled with broad arbitration clauses ("any investment dispute"), arguably exposed China to extensive liability. This is because the vague reference to international law presumably gives wide latitude to an arbitral tribunal to interpret the applicable FET standard without necessarily resorting to *opinio juris sive necessitates* (general practice accepted as law).[101] This may have been one reason behind change in China's recent investment treaties, in which FET is due "in accordance with customary international law."[102] This provision presumably leaves less room for interpretation as the concept of customary international law commonly refers to "established state

---

[94] *See, e.g.*, China-Mexico BIT, art. 11.

[95] *See, e.g.*, China-New Zealand FTA, art. 201.

[96] *See, e.g.*, China-Peru FTA, art. 197.

[97] *See, e.g.*, China–New Zealand FTA, art. 204.

[98] *See, e.g.*, China-New Zealand FTA, Annex 13 (emphasis added).

[99] Agreement between Japan and the People's Republic of China concerning the Encouragement and Reciprocal Protection of Investment, Aug. 27, 1988, *available at* http://investmentpolicyhub.unctad.org/Download/TreatyFile/747; Agreement between the People's Republic of China and the Republic of Turkey concerning the Reciprocal Promotion and Protection of Investments, Nov. 13, 1990, *available at* http://investmentpolicyhub.unctad.org/Download/TreatyFile/789.

[100] 2007 China-Costa Rica BIT, Oct. 24, 2007.

[101] *See generally* James Crawford, Browlie's Principles of Public International Law 25 (2013).

[102] China-Peru FTA, art. 132. *See generally* Rudolph Dolzer & Christoph Schreuer, Principles of International Investment Law 134–39 (2012).

practice."[103] This has been cited as an example of NAFTA's influence on China's drafting of its third generation IIAs.[104]

(b) Most Favored Nation

China's BITs, even from the early days, include a most favored-nation (MFN) clause granting investments subject to a BIT containing such a clause the same prerogatives offered to investors under other BITs concluded by China.[105] MFN clauses foster equality in the competitive environment among foreign investors.[106] Although the content of the MFN clause itself has not varied substantially, its import does, as new BITs now grant broader protection.[107] Thus, an investor with an investment subject to the protections of a first-generation BIT may attempt to invoke enhanced protections of a second- or third- generation BIT.[108]

(c) National Treatment

In the first generation of its BITs, China refused to grant national treatment (NT) to foreign investors equal to that afforded to its own citizens, or did so only on a best-effort basis.[109] China's reluctance was said to be caused by the lack of strength of its nascent economy compared to international actors,[110] or by a desire to uphold "structures of a socialist planning economy."[111] Yet NT is a "core guarantee" of investment treaty practice for instilling a sense of fairness in competition between foreign and local actors.[112] With China's accession to market economy prominence, and accession to the stringent World Trade Organization regime,[113] NT clauses are now routinely inserted.

---

[103] *See Definition of Customary International Law*, Legal Information Institute, Cornell University Law School, http://www.law.cornell.edu/wex/customary_international_law (last visited Mar. 7, 2015); *see also* Case concerning the Continental Shelf (Libyan Arab Jamahiriya v. Malta), 1985 I.C.J. 13, ¶ 27 (June 3) ("It is of course axiomatic that the material of customary international law is to be looked for primarily in the actual practice and *opinio juris* of States").

[104] *See* Axel Berger, *Investment Rules in Chinese PTIAs—Partial "NAFTA-ization," in* PREFERENTIAL TRADE AND INVESTMENT AGREEMENTS: FROM RECALIBRATION TO REINTEGRATION (R. Hofmann et al. eds., 2013).

[105] *See, e.g.*, China-Sweden BIT, art. 2(2).

[106] Schill, *supra* note 57, at 100.

[107] *Id.*

[108] *See infra* Section III(B)2 for a summary analysis of MFN treatment.

[109] *See, e.g.*, Agreement between the Government of the United Kingdom of Great Britain and Northern Ireland and the Government of the People's Republic of China concerning the Promotion and Reciprocal Protection of Investments, art. 3(3), May 15, 1986, *available at* http://investmentpolicyhub.unctad.org/Download/TreatyFile/793.

[110] ARMAND DE MESTRAL & CÉLINE LÉVESQUE, IMPROVING INTERNATIONAL INVESTMENT AGREEMENTS 65 (Routledge ed., 2013).

[111] WENHUA SHAN, THE LEGAL FRAMEWORK OF EU-CHINA INVESTMENT RELATIONS—A CRITICAL APPRAISAL 163 (2005).

[112] Schill, *supra* note 57, at 94.

[113] *Id.* at 99.

During negotiations with the United States in 2013, China conceded to granting NT at the pre-establishment stage of an investment.[114] China has also agreed to switch from a positive list system (where allowed investments are exhaustively enumerated) to a negative list system (where only the sectors where foreign investment is prohibited are listed). China had used a positive list for decades, delineating the sectors in which foreign investment was encouraged, allowed, and prohibited.[115] This positive list system was coupled with post-establishment—meaning only after approval by Chinese authorities—NT protection.

The major change from a positive to negative list approach is meant to "help establish a level playing ground for market players . . . as two-way trade and investment have continued to expand."[116] China's remarks underline a potentially greater adherence to international standards of protection for investors and a possible move toward a fourth generation of IIAs. But even if China decides to adopt pre-establishment national treatment in a more systematic way,[117] the contours of such protections are unclear. Depending on the content of the negative list, they could very well be hampered in practice. Indeed, one could imagine a list so extensive as to defeat its purpose.[118]

(d) Full Protection and Security

Chinese BITs initially flatly affirmed that foreign investment "shall enjoy protection."[119] China has used more expansive language in recent treaties, such as "constant protection and security,"[120] "full protection,"[121] or "full protection and security."[122] There is

[114] *See* Paxton, *supra* note 24; Pheakdey, *supra* note 25.

[115] *See* Nie Pingxiang, *Negative List in Need of Some Positive Tweaks*, China Daily Asia, May 19, 2014, http://www.chinadailyasia.com/business/2014-05/19/content_15135843.html.

[116] *MOC: China Using Global Approach in Investment Talks with U.S.*, Xinhua News, July 12, 2013, http://english.peopledaily.com.cn/90778/8323785.html.

[117] China has been experimenting with the system in its Shanghai Free Trade Zone since September 2013, and in Pingtan Island since June 2014. *See* Luo Liexin, *China's Second Negative List a Move Forward*, China Daily, June 4, 2014, http://www.chinadaily.com.cn/china/2014-06/04/content_17563011.htm.

[118] It seems that the approach is to make a mirror image of the former positive lists. *See* Pingxiang, *supra* note 113. The Shanghai Free Trade Zone's pilot program implements a negative list system that reportedly has resulted in a mere 27 percent reduction in its foreign investment restrictions. *See* Matthew Zito, Camille Chen & Rainy Yao, *Shanghai FTZ Revised Negative List Introduces Targeted FDI Reforms*, China Briefing (July 3, 2014), http://www.china-briefing.com/news/2014/07/03/shanghai-ftz-revised-negative-list-introduces-targeted-fdi-reforms.html.

[119] *See, e.g.*, Agreement between the People's Republic of China and the Government of the Republic of Croatia concerning the Encouragement and Reciprocal Protection of Investments, art. 3(1), June 7, 1993, *available at* http://investmentpolicyhub.unctad.org/Download/TreatyFile/723.

[120] *See, e.g.*, Accord Entre L'Union Economique Belgo-Luxembourgeoise et le Gouvernement de la Republique Populaire de Chine Concernant L'Encouragement et la Protection Reciproques des Investissements, art. 2(3), June 6, 2005, *available at* http://investmentpolicyhub.unctad.org/Download/TreatyFile/338.

[121] *See, e.g.*, Agreement between the Government of the Russian Federation and the Government of the People's Republic of China concerning the Promotion and Reciprocal Protection of Investments, art. 2(2), Nov. 9, 2006, *available at* http://investmentpolicyhub.unctad.org/Download/TreatyFile/774.

[122] *See, e.g.*, Agreement between the Czech Republic and the People's Republic of China on the Promotion and Protection of Investments, art. 2(2), Dec. 8, 2005, *available at* http://investmentpolicyhub.unctad.org/Download/TreatyFile/725.

no consensus as to whether full protection and security (FPS) clauses should be understood as being limited to physical protection of the investment by the host state,[123] or also extend to circumstances not involving physical violence or damage.[124] In its recent treaties, China circumscribes the FPS clause with "commonly accepted rules of international law,"[125] "international law minimum standard of treatment of aliens,"[126] or "customary international law."[127]

B. THE IMPLICATIONS OF THE CHINA INVESTMENT TREATY PROGRAM FOR INVESTMENT ARBITRATION

Only seven cases are reported to have been brought pursuant to a Chinese BIT: five by Chinese investors against foreign states, and two by a foreign investor against China.[128] As mentioned above, investment arbitration under a Chinese BIT very much depends upon the generation of the BIT. For example, although second- and third-generation treaties do provide for investment arbitration for "any dispute concerning an investment" or disputes arising out of a violation of the treaty, respectively, first-generation BITs allow only those arbitrations "involving the amount of compensation for expropriation." According to the dominant view, the only disputes that China agreed to arbitrate in its early BIT were those over the quantum due for expropriation. Proponents of an expansionist stance on the scope of China's consent to arbitration have, however, gained some traction recently.

One such example is the *Tza Yap* case, which involved an alleged expropriation by Peru of the investment in a fish flour company by a Chinese investor, Tza Yap, under the China-Peru BIT. Tza Yap argued that the language of the BIT did not limit arbitration to the question of the determination of the quantum for expropriation, but also covered the predetermination of the existence of an expropriation. The tribunal agreed, basing its decision on the fact that the word "involving" is not restrictive as

---

[123] *See, e.g., Rumeli v. Kazhakstan, supra* note 80, ¶ 668; *Saluka Investments v. Czech Republic, supra* note 91, ¶¶ 483–484; BG Group PLC v. Republic of Argentina, UNCITRAL Final Award, ¶ 324 (Dec. 24 2007); Wena Hotels v. Egypt, Case No. ARB/98/4, ICSID, Annulment Proceeding Decision, ¶ 84 (Feb 5, 2002).

[124] CME v. Czech Republic, UNCITRAL Partial Award, ¶ 613 (Sept. 13, 2001); Azurix v. Argentina, Case No. ARB/01/12, ICSID, ¶ 406 (July 14, 2006); Vivendi v. Argentina, Case No. ARB/97/3, ICSID, Award, ¶ 7.4.12 (2007); *Biwater Gauff v. Tanzania*, Case No. ARB/05/22, ICSID, Award, ¶ 729 (July 24, 2008).

[125] China-New Zealand FTA, art. 143.

[126] China-Mexico BIT, art. 5.

[127] China-Peru FTA, art. 132.

[128] Señor Tza Yap Shum v. Republic of Peru (ICSID Case No. ARB/07/6); Sanum Investments Limited and The Government of the Lao Democratic People's Republic (PCA Case No. 2013-13); China Heilongjiang International Economic & Technical Cooperative Corp., Beijing Shougang Mining Investment Company Ltd., Qinhuangdaoshi Qinlong International Industrial Co. Ltd. v. Mongolia (PCA Case No. 2010-20); Ping An Life Insurance Company of China, Ltd and Ping An Insurance (Group) Company of China, Ltd v. Kingdom of Belgium (ICSID Case No. ARB/12/29); Beijing Urban Construction Group Co Ltd v Republic of Yemen (ICSID Case No. ARB/14/30).

opposed to the words "limited to" or "exclusively."[129] In the *Sanum v. Laos* arbitration, the tribunal adopted a similar approach. Such an expansionist analysis has been criticized.[130] Certain elements seem to mitigate against the adequacy of the *Tza Yap* and *Sanum* tribunal rulings, including a line of precedents under similar BITs from other countries that limits the amount of compensation for expropriation only.[131] Yet at least one other precedent lends support to the findings of the *Tza Yap* and *Sanum* tribunals.[132]

It has also been reported that the China-based company Sanum Investments attempted to bypass the narrow arbitration clause of the China-Laos BIT through its MFN clause. In doing so, Sanum was hoping to benefit from other Lao BITs granting access to international arbitration for disputes beyond issues of quantum. Some tribunals have held that all treaty provisions, including dispute resolution clauses, are subject to the MFN clause.[133] Other commentators have posited that the drafters of the BITs intended to reserve MFN benefits for substantive protections only.[134] Some arbitral tribunals have adopted this approach.[135] Confirming such an understanding, China's recent treaties expressly state that the MFN clause does not apply to dispute resolution.[136] The tribunal in the *Sanum* case eventually denied Sanum's argument.[137]

Despite the gradual broadening of China's consent to arbitration in its IIAs, few disputes arising under China's IIAs have been reported.[138] The relative scarcity of cases

---

[129] Señor Tza Yap Shum v. Republic of Peru, Case No. ARB/07/6, ICSID, Decision on Jurisdiction and Competence ¶¶ 149–153 (2009).

[130] Wei Shen, *The Good, the Bad or the Ugly? A Critique of the Decision on Jurisdiction and Competence in* Tza Yap Shum v. The Republic of Peru, 10 CHINESE J. INT'L L. 55, 71 (2011), *available at* http://chinesejil.oxfordjournals.org/content/10/1/55.short.

[131] *See, e.g.*, Vladimir Berschader and Moïse Berschader v. The Russian Federation, Case No. 080/2004, SCC, Award, ¶ 153 (Apr. 21, 2006); RosInvestCo UK Ltd. v. The Russian Federation, Case No. Arb. V079/2005, SCC, Award on Jurisdiction, ¶¶ 112–114 (Oct. 2007); ST-AD GmbH (Germany) v. The Republic of Bulgaria, Case No. 2011-06 (ST-BG), PCA, Award on Jurisdiction, ¶¶ 368–374 (July 18, 2013).

[132] *See, e.g.*, Renta 4 S.V.S.A et al. v. Russian Federation, No. 24/2007, SCC, Award on Preliminary Objections, ¶¶ 19, 30–45 (Mar. 20, 2009).

[133] *See, e.g.*, Emilio Augustìn Maffezini v. The Kingdom of Spain, Case No. ARB/97/7, ICSID, Decision on Jurisdiction, ¶ 64 (Jan. 25, 2000); Austrian Airlines v. Slovak Republic, UNCITRAL, Final Award, ¶ 124 (Oct. 20, 2009).

[134] *See* CAMPBELL MCLACHLAN QC, LAURENCE SHORE & MATTHEW WEINIGER, INTERNATIONAL INVESTMENT ARBITRATION: SUBSTANTIVE PRINCIPLES ¶ 7.168 (2007); *see also* Zachary Douglas, *The MFN Clause in Investment Arbitration: Treaty Interpretation off the Rails*, 2(1) J. INT'L DISP. SETTLEMENT 97–113 (2011). *But see* Stephan W. Schill, *Allocating Adjudicatory Authority: Most-Favoured-Nation Clauses as a Basis of Jurisdiction—A Reply to Zachary Douglas*, 2(2) J. INT'L DISP. SETTLEMENT 353–71 (2011).

[135] Plama Consortium Ltd v. Bulgaria, Case No. ARB/03/24, ICSID, Decision on Jurisdiction, ¶ 223 (Feb. 8, 2005); *see also Berschader v. Russia, supra* note 129, ¶ 206; Wintershall Aktiengesellschaft v. Argentine Republic, Case No. ARB/04/14, ICSID, Award, ¶¶ 173–176 (Dec. 8, 2008).

[136] *See, e.g.*, China-New Zealand FTA, art. 139(2).

[137] Sanum Invs. Ltd. v. Lao People's Democratic Republic, UNCITRAL, Case No. 2013-13, PCA, Award on Jurisdiction, ¶ 358 (Dec. 13, 2013).

[138] *See* op. cit., *Beijing Urban Construction v Yemen*; and *Ansung Housing v China*.

involving China BITs is perplexing considering the number of treaties it has concluded and its volume of inward and outward investment.

Some authors advance that the reasons are cultural: "praise of harmony usually comes first," making it preferable not to resort to litigation.[139] The reasons may actually be pragmatic. Foreign investors in China may be discouraged from risking time, money, and effort in cases in which the chances of enforcing the award in China are slim. Indeed, China's legal landscape has been said to currently disallow enforcement of foreign investor-state arbitral awards. China expressly excluded enforceability of investor-state awards when it acceded to the New York Convention,[140] which leaves only ICSID awards directly enforceable. But the self-executing nature of ICSID awards is subject to the laws of the state "in whose territories such execution is sought,"[141] and China does not have any law allowing enforcement of arbitral awards against state-owned property.[142]

The reasons for lack of disputes appear similar for outbound investment. The massive underwriting by the China Export & Credit Insurance Corporation ("Sinosure") of export credit insurance to extend credit enhancement to Chinese investors[143] makes resorting to legal protections unappealing. For a Chinese investor, it is presumably more efficient to attempt to collect under its export credit insurance than it is to initiate a protracted and expensive arbitration against a respondent government.

The Way Forward

China's transition into a major contributor of outward FDI has led to a profound reformation of its investment treaty regime. The data establish the extent to which China has departed from being a purely capital-importing country and has become a capital-exporting country, catching up with Europe and the United States.[144] At the same time, a closer analysis of the data reveals that the picture is more complicated than what is commonly presented.[145] The size of China's outward FDI stock was only US$614 billion in 2013, significantly smaller than that of the United States, where the figure was

139 *See* Wang Guiguo, *Investor-State Dispute Settlement in China*, 5 Transnat'l Disp. Mgmt. 7 -8 (2011), *available* at http://www.transnational-dispute-management.com/article.asp?key=1764 at 19.

140 Notice on the Implementation of China's Accession to the Convention on the Recognition and Enforcement of Foreign Arbitral Awards, issued by the Supreme People's Court on Apr. 10, 1987, *available at* http://www.cietac.org/index/references/Laws/47607b5429f8c27f001.cms.

141 Washington (ICSID) Convention, art. 54(3).

142 *See* Wang, *op. cit.*, at 24–25.

143 As of late 2013, Sinosure had "supported export, domestic trade and investment with a total value of USD 1484.65 billion" and had "facilitated the lending of CNY 1.8 trillion by 190 banks" (about US$290 billion). *See Company Profile*, SINOSURE, http://www.sinosure.com.cn/sinosure/english/Company%20Profile.html (last visited Mar. 7, 2015).

144 *See supra* Section I.

145 *Id.*

US$5 trillion. Although much has been made of China's takeover of Africa,[146] China is in third place among developing country investors.[147] In the view of one commentator, China is largely limited to financing infrastructure in "remote locations often with poor quality."[148]

By juxtaposing the economic raw data with the actual investment treaty practice of China, one cannot help but notice the correlation between the language adopted in its IIAs and its transformation into a major source of FDI. China has had an active BIT program since the early 1980s, but it was originally of limited applicability. Without China's consent to arbitration of investor-state disputes, BITs were "toothless."

Under the second generation of IIAs, investors finally obtained a dispute resolution mechanism to ensure that the treaty protections were upheld. It remains unclear, however, whether such investors can recoup any potential losses incurred as a result of a treaty violation. China's position on unenforceability of non-ICSID investor-state arbitral awards and its lack of domestic legal mechanisms allowing enforcement of awards against state assets could discourage even the boldest investor.

In its third generation of IIAs, China appears to align its views on the fundamental tenets of investor-state protection with and adopt the key provisions of E.U. or U.S. IIAs. In keeping with U.S. practice observed through the 2004 U.S. Model BIT, China now largely accepts ICSID arbitration of disputes against investors,[149] has abandoned umbrella clauses, subjects FET and FPS protections to customary norms of international law, and even agrees to the concept of pre-establishment NT on the basis of a negative list.[150] China also ensures that its SOEs, through which most of its foreign resources-oriented investments are channeled, are expressly covered by the investment protections that are owed to "investors."

It remains to be seen, however, whether the position of China in its interaction with other mature home countries will result in the further adoption of recent investment protection standards and its engaging in a fourth generation of IIAs. For example, the 2012 U.S. Model BIT anticipates resorting to a future multilateral appellate mechanism,[151] provides for transparency of arbitral proceedings,[152] recognizes the obligations of states under domestic labor laws,[153] and establishes that environmental concerns may justify

---

[146] Huiping Chen, *Sino-African BITs Practice: A New Legal Paradigm?*, Taipei Conference on Int'l and Comparative L. (2013).

[147] *See* UNCTAD, *supra* note 8, at 40.

[148] Chen, *supra* note 144, at 4.

[149] *See, e.g.*, China-Japan-Republic of Korea TIT, art. 15.

[150] *See supra* Section III(A)2.

[151] U.S. Model BIT, art. 28, *available at* http://www.state.gov/documents/organization/188371.pdf.

[152] U.S. Model BIT, art. 29.

[153] U.S. Model BIT, art. 13.

non-precluded measures.[154] In light of global efforts spearheaded by the OECD[155] and UNCTAD[156] toward encouraging "sustainable" foreign direct investment, it is possible that China will follow the lead of other capital-exporting nations. There is some indication that China may decide to do so upon review of recent treaties in which, for example, environmental measures enjoy a basic level of observance.[157] If this is the future trajectory of China's IIAs, then there is hope for a largely uniform international investment law and policy regime.

---

[154] U.S. Model BIT, art. 12.

[155] *See* OECD, OECD Guidelines for Multinational Enterprises (2011), *available at* http://www.oecd.org/daf/inv/mne/48004323.pdf.

[156] *See* UNCTAD, World Investment Report 2012: Towards a New Generation of Investment Policies 97–160 (2012).

[157] *See, e.g.*, China-Japan-Republic of Korea TIT, art. 23.

14 The WTO and China's Unique Economic Structure

Mark Wu*

Introduction

In 1994, after eight long years, the Uruguay Round of trade negotiations concluded. The Uruguay Round Agreements amounted to a major expansion and revision of global trading rules, including the establishment of the World Trade Organization (WTO). China did not partake in these negotiations. It had sought to rejoin the WTO's predecessor, the General Agreement on Tariffs and Trade (GATT) in 1986, but its accession process had stalled following the Tiananmen Square crackdown in June 1989. Although the country had begun embarking on economic reforms in 1978, the process was uneven. State-owned enterprises (SOEs) dominated the economy, with the private sector playing a nascent role.[1] China was still a socialist economy experimenting with market elements, and not yet a major player in the global economy.

* This chapter is based on a larger project examining the impact of the Chinese economic system on the WTO regime. I wish to thank all those who have contributed comments and suggestions to that project. Mark Jia provided outstanding research assistance, for which I am immensely grateful.

[1] National Bureau of Statistics of the People's Republic of China, China Statistical Yearbook 377 (1995).

Consequently, when revising the global trading rules, China was not at the forefront of the treaty drafters' minds. This was logical. After all, the dominant economy in East Asia at the time was Japan. Throughout the course of the Uruguay Round negotiations, Americans and Europeans remained obsessed with Japan's anomalous economic structure.[2] If there was one Asian economy whose unique features should have been considered when revising the legal rules, it was Japan. China remained outside of the system altogether.

Fast forward two decades, and the world is vastly different. In 2001, the WTO welcomed China into its fold. Today, China is the world's largest or second-largest economy, depending on what metrics one employs.[3] It is the world's largest exporter, having surpassed Germany in 2009.[4] And it plays an active role in WTO negotiations and dispute settlement. Trade undoubtedly has played a critical role in transforming China. The world economic order has benefited, with hundreds of millions of individuals lifted out of poverty, and rising Chinese demand fueling economic growth in several countries.

Although the economic welfare gains from China's WTO accession are clear, its impact on global trade governance remains much murkier. This chapter seeks to illuminate the consequences of China's rise—and in particular, the rise of its unique economic system—on the global trading order. My argument is that WTO rules, as currently defined, are not well-equipped to handle a series of legal problems facing the WTO concerning China's economic structure. This chapter explains why this is the case and illustrates a series of emergent issues. I contend that China's unique economic structure gives rise to several critical choices ahead, with important implications for the future of the legal order governing the world trading system. Handled incorrectly, it may well lead to a weakening of the strong multilateral trade regime that has governed the economic order since World War II and pose a threat to the vibrancy of the WTO.

Even though China has experienced a tremendous metamorphosis, it has not evolved into simply yet another country operating within the global community. In many ways, China remains exceptional. Rising living standards have not led to overt demands for political reforms by an emerging middle class. The Chinese Communist Party remains firmly in command of a one-party state. Despite a decade of deepened market-oriented

---

[2] *See, e.g.*, CHALMERS JOHNSON, MITI AND THE JAPANESE MIRACLE: THE GROWTH OF INDUSTRIAL POLICY, 1925–1975 (1982); WILLIAM G. OUCHI, THEORY Z: HOW AMERICAN BUSINESS CAN MEET THE JAPANESE CHALLENGE (1981); EZRA VOGEL, JAPAN AS NUMBER ONE: LESSONS FOR AMERICA (1979).

[3] *China Set to Overtake U.S. as Biggest Economy in PPP Measure*, BLOOMBERG NEWS, Apr. 30, 2014, http://www.bloomberg.com/news/2014-04-30/china-set-to-overtake-u-s-as-biggest-economy-using-ppp-measure.html; *Crowning the Dragon*, ECONOMIST, Apr. 30, 2014, http://www.economist.com/blogs/graphicdetail/2014/04/daily-chart-19; Hugo Duncan & David Martosko, *America Usurped: China Becomes World's Largest Economy—Putting USA in Second Place for the First Time in 142 Years*, DAILY MAIL, Oct. 8, 2014, http://www.dailymail.co.uk/news/article-2785905/China-overtakes-U-S-world-s-largest-economy-IMF-says-economy-worth-17-6trillion-America-falls-second-place-time-1872.html.

[4] Steven Mufson, *China Surpasses Germany as World's Top Exporter*, WASH. POST, Jan. 11, 2010, http://www.washingtonpost.com/wp-dyn/content/article/2010/01/10/AR2010011002647.html.

reforms, the state and Party have not retreated from the economy. SOEs continue to dominate certain facets of the economy.[5] The wording of its Five-Year Plans and the communiques of Plenums of the Communist Party Congress are still carefully analyzed for signs of where the economy is headed.[6] In short, the Chinese state and the Chinese economy are unlike that of any other in the world.

Although Deng Xiaoping christened this phenomenon as "socialism with Chinese characteristics," most commentators today have taken to describing the Chinese economic model as Chinese state capitalism.[7] The concept of state capitalism is one in which the state plays an important role in the economic activity of a country, through direct ownership stakes or by playing a major role in supporting or directing enterprises, but in which enterprises are subject to market forces typically associated with capitalist societies.

The Chinese version of state capitalism differs from that found elsewhere (e.g., Brazil, discussed by Marianna Pargendler in Chapter 16 in this volume) because the state is closely intertwined with a single political party whose central role is preordained and whose machinations are regularly deployed to support the state in its endeavors. The entity asserting control and providing support extends beyond the formal governmental apparatus to include the Chinese Communist Party.

Nevertheless, the Party-state is not necessarily the only engine driving the country's extraordinary recent growth. Nicholas Lardy's recent study offers convincing evidence that China's growth is due in large part to its nonstate sector, which has consistently outperformed the state sector along most metrics.[8] Nor does the Chinese economy conform to the archetype of state capitalism in which the state monopolizes control of all of the economy's "commanding heights." Market forces and competition play an increasingly

---

[5] For example, the state's share of industrial output is 99 percent for extraction of petroleum and natural gas and 78 percent for automobiles. NAT'L BUREAU OF STATISTICS OF P.R. CHINA, CHINA STATISTICAL YEARBOOK 2013, Tables 14-5 & 14-6 (2013).

[6] *See, e.g.*, JOSEPH CASEY & KATHERINE KOLESKI, U.S.-CHINA ECON. & SEC. REVIEW COMM'N, BACKGROUNDER: CHINA'S 12TH FIVE-YEAR PLAN (2011); NARGIZA SALIDJANOVA & IACOB KOCH-WESER, U.S.-CHINA ECON. & SEC. REVIEW COMM'N, THIRD PLENUM ECONOMIC REFORM PROPOSALS: A SCORECARD (2013); Guangyu Li & Jonathan Woetzel, *What China's Five-Year Plan Means for Business*, MCKINSEY Q. (July 2011), http://www.mckinsey.com/insights/economic_studies/what_chinas_five-year_plan_means_for_business; Chris Buckley, *Chinese Leader Gets More Sway on the Economy and Security*, N.Y. TIMES, Nov. 12, 2013, http://www.nytimes.com/2013/11/13/world/asia/chinese-leader-gets-more-sway-on-the-economy-and-security.html; Joshua Rosenfield, *What Does China's Third Plenum Suggest about Prospects for Reform?*, ASIA SOCIETY (Nov. 15, 2013), http://asiasociety.org/blog/asia/what-does-chinas-third-plenum-suggest-about-prospects-reform.

[7] *See, e.g.*, IAN BREMMER, THE END OF THE FREE MARKET: WHO WINS THE WAR BETWEEN STATES AND CORPORATIONS? 128–45 (2010); ANDREW SZAMOSSZEGI & COLE KYLE, AN ANALYSIS OF STATE-OWNED ENTERPRISES AND STATE CAPITALISM IN CHINA (2012); USHA C.V. HALEY & GEORGE T. HALEY, SUBSIDIES TO CHINESE INDUSTRY: STATE CAPITALISM, BUSINESS STRATEGY, AND TRADE POLICY (2013).

[8] *See* NICHOLAS R. LARDY, MARKETS OVER MAO: THE RISE OF PRIVATE BUSINESS IN CHINA (2014).

important role. Indeed, the state is neither as fearsome nor as ubiquitous in economic management as others have asserted.[9] But nevertheless, the playing field may be tilted in some sectors on account of state interference.

Although the editors of and many contributors to this volume adopt the term "state capitalism," I assert that China's economic structure is unique and not exactly akin to the state capitalist systems of other countries. What makes China difficult for outsiders to understand is that its complexity defies labels. Strict categorical delineations that apply elsewhere do not always hold in contemporary China. As the other chapters in this volume suggest, the lines are often blurred between Party and state, state and market, public and private. In some sectors, the Party and state continue to play active roles, but not in others. When the Party and/or state interferes, its methods of engagement may vary. At their disposal are a wide range of tools, some of which differ significantly from those utilized by governments and political parties elsewhere. The Party-state retains control over not only the traditional organs of the state itself, but also the instruments necessary to control and deploy the world's largest political party, with a membership exceeding 80 million. Moreover, it has woven these elements together in parts of the economy. This modality of intervention—selective in scope and with great variance in depth—has resulted in an economic structure that is uniquely Chinese.

The current Chinese economic model is one that has evolved dynamically over the past two decades. I argue that it is one that would have been unfathomable in the early 1990s, when the Uruguay Round negotiations were completed. After June 1989, the extent to which China was committed to further capitalist-oriented economic reforms was unclear. Only following Deng Xiaoping's Southern Tour in 1992 did the leadership signal its willingness to embrace market reforms once more. Even so, reforms in the early 1990s proceeded cautiously.

By the late 1990s, when China's WTO accession negotiations swung into high gear, the contours of the present model were only beginning to take shape. Following Zhu Rongji's assumption of the premiership in 1998, the state embarked on reforms designed to tackle structural weaknesses in the Chinese economy. The concept of state-backed "national champions" started to emerge, with the notion that the state would maintain control or influence over "pillar" industries but relinquish its direct role in other nonessential sectors. Even so, the present form of the Chinese economy had yet to fully emerge in 2001, when China's WTO accession was finally completed. For example, the State-owned Assets Supervision and Administration Commission (SASAC) of the State Council, which plays an outsized role today, had yet to be established.

This leads to the question of just how well-equipped WTO rules are to deal with the trade-related challenges posed by Chinese state capitalism. Because the form of

---

[9] Note that Lardy's study was undertaken in response to these earlier studies that emphasized the state's dominant role. *Compare id. with* BREMMER, *supra* note 7.

economic organization that is the Chinese economy today was not fully contemplated at either the time of the formation of the general legal rules or the formation of additional specific legal rules applied to China's accession, I suggest that important questions remain unresolved. This chapter seeks to highlight several of these questions. My hope is to spark a conversation over how such issues should be treated in advance, before any escalate to a politically charged trade conflagration.

Why have these issues not flared earlier? And what makes them more likely to do so in coming years? Special provisions of China's Protocol of Accession have allowed the WTO to sidestep several of these questions during the years immediately following China's WTO accession. Until 2011, China's trading partners were allowed to apply a special safeguard mechanism to limit Chinese imports when they caused unexpected injury to domestic producers.[10] Through 2016, China is to be considered a non-market economy unless it can demonstrate otherwise, making it relatively easy for its trading partners to apply anti-dumping duties against imports from China.[11] But as these special provisions expire, China's trading partners will need to turn increasingly to the general legal rules of the WTO Agreements and the provisions of the China Protocol of Accession itself to seek recourse against Chinese trade practices. In the past five years alone, we have seen a dramatic uptick in such cases.[12] In other words, the questions over how to treat China's economic structure under its legal rules will be a much more vexing challenge for the WTO in the coming decade than it has been in the past.

This challenge might not be that significant were China any other normal member of the WTO. But it is not. China is already the world's largest exporter, and depending on how one measures, already or soon to be the world's largest economy. Commentators increasingly realize that greater leadership from China is necessary if the WTO is to maintain its vitality and not slip into a slow decline toward gradual irrelevance.[13] Keeping China engaged is vital for the multilateral trading system.

At the same time, China is also not simply any other country politically. Questions related to the Chinese economic system cut to the very heart of the structure that the Communist Party has chosen to put in place to sustain the economic growth necessary to achieve the so-called "Chinese dream" while maintaining its hold on absolute power. Opining on this structure is a tricky task for an international organization that will

---

[10] WTO, Accession of the People's Republic of China, Decision of Nov. 10, 2001, ¶ 16, WT/L/432 (2001) [hereinafter PRC Protocol of Accession].

[11] *Id.* ¶ 15.

[12] Between 2010 and 2014, fifteen complaints were filed against China at the WTO. In comparison, only four complaints were filed against China between 2002 and 2006. *See* WTO, *Disputes by Country/Territory*, http://www.wto.org/english/tratop_e/dispu_e/dispu_by_country_e.htm (last visited May 29, 2015).

[13] *See* James Bacchus, *The WTO Needs China to Lead*, WALL ST. J., May 29, 2014, http://www.wsj.com/articles/bacchus-the-wto-needs-china-to-lead-1401381136; Jean-Pierre Lehmann, *The Global Trade Impasse: The Chinese Leadership Conundrum*, THE GLOBALIST, July 7, 2014, http://www.theglobalist.com/the-global-trade-impasse-the-chinese-leadership-conundrum/.

increasingly rely on China to play an active role. Getting this challenge right is critical for the WTO and for the future of the multilateral trading regime.

This chapter proceeds as follows: Section I discusses the alternative forms of economic systems besides market capitalism contemplated under WTO rules. Section II presents a short overview of China's economic structure as it exists today, with the aim of highlighting how it deviates from the alternative forms discussed in Section II. Section III then highlights several points of emerging tension. Section IV discusses the larger systemic issues that arise from such tensions and evaluates potential options for handling these issues.

I. The WTO and Alternative Economic Structures

The Uruguay Round began in 1986 at a time when the world was a vastly different place. The Cold War still raged, trade tensions with Japan necessitated the Plaza Accord, and Latin America was in the midst of its "lost decade." The Round would take eight years to complete. From it emerged the institution of the WTO and the multilateral trading rules that apply today. In this section, I examine briefly the alternative economic structures that negotiators bore in mind as they revised existing rules and drafted new treaties. As we shall see, none is in line with the present form of Chinese state capitalism. Nevertheless, this corpus of alternative economic structures informs the WTO treaties that govern global trade today.

A. ALTERNATIVE ECONOMIC STRUCTURES AND THE URUGUAY ROUND

Although most of the founding members of the GATT had market-oriented economies, from its inception, the global trading system has contemplated the possibility that a member's economy may adopt another economic structure instead. This section suggests that four forms of economic structures were likely to have been on the minds of the Uruguay Round negotiators when the global trading rules underwent major revision. It explores briefly how GATT/WTO members intended for each to be dealt with under global trading rules. Overall, negotiators sought to balance the heterogeneity of economic structures with the need to establish a common set of global trading rules applicable to all.

1. Command Economies

After joining the GATT as original signatories, communist governments came to power in two countries: Czechoslovakia and Cuba. Each developed centrally planned, command economies. Nevertheless, the GATT continued to embrace each as full-fledged members. In the 1960s, several other Warsaw Pact countries (Poland, Romania, and Hungary) also acceded to the GATT.

Even at its inception in 1947, the GATT explicitly recognized that the state might play an active role in the economy. Article XVII specifically addresses the concept of a "State enterprise" that is established or maintained by a GATT contracting party. The GATT is agnostic about this organizational form, so long as it continues to "act in a manner consistent with the general principles of non-discriminatory treatment prescribed in [the GATT] for governmental measures affecting imports or exports by private traders."[14] In addition, GATT members must apply the principle of "fair and equitable treatment" for "imports of products for immediate or ultimate consumption in government use and not otherwise for resale or use in the production of goods for sale."[15]

So long as these conditions were met, the GATT was accepting of command economies. Czechoslovakia nevertheless worried that its trading partners might take advantage of its different economic structure to discriminate against its exports by applying anti-dumping duties against a broad array of its products. GATT Article VI:1 allows a member to impose additional duties against imports if a member is found to be "dumping" the good into the markets of its trading partner and such dumping causes injury. One basis for determining dumping is to compare the export price with the domestic price. However, in a centrally planned, command economy, the Czechoslovakians noted that the domestic price is set by the state and not the market. Worried that this might lead its exports to be unfairly considered in dumping determinations, Czechoslovakia proposed an amendment to Article VI:1(b) that explicitly discusses the scenario of centrally planned economies.[16]

The GATT Working Party recommended that Czechoslovakia's proposal be incorporated into the GATT text not as an amendment, but instead as an Ad Note through Annex I.[17] This gave rise to the concept of a "non-market economy" (NME) in trade law and an explicit acknowledgment that members of the trade regime may have different, but equally legitimate, economic structures.

An NME, by name, stands in contrast to a market economy. For anti-dumping purposes, this is a country "which has a complete or substantially complete monopoly of its trade and where all domestic prices are fixed by the State."[18] This definition does not rule out the possibility that other less extreme forms of an NME may also exist. But because the typology of the NME that was relevant at the time was that of a centrally planned, command economy, this is the form that is explicitly recognized in the text of the GATT itself.

---

[14] General Agreement on Tariffs and Trade, Oct. 30, 1947, 61 Sat. A-11, 55 U.N.T.S. 194, art. XVIII:1 [hereinafter GATT].

[15] *Id.* art. XVIII:2.

[16] GATT Secretariat, *Article VI—Proposals by the Czechoslovakia Delegation*, W.9/86/Rev. 1 (Dec. 21, 1954).

[17] GATT Secretariat, *Report of Working Party III on Barriers to Trade Other than Restrictions or Tariffs*, L/334 (Mar. 1, 1955); *see also* Vera Thorstensen et al., *WTO—Market and Non-market Economies: The Hybrid Case of China*, 1 Latin Am. J. Int'l Trade L. 765, 780 (2013).

[18] GATT, *supra* note 14, ad art. VI, ¶ 1.2.

2. Transition Economies

During the course of the Uruguay Round itself, several GATT members experienced momentous political change. The fall of communist regimes in the Warsaw Pact in the early 1990s formed an important backdrop for the Round. The economies that developed during this period were deemed hybrid economies—partially market-oriented but with elements of the centrally planned regime still intact. This hybrid structure was considered to be a temporary transitional form. Such countries were moving toward a market economy, but had not fully reached such a status.

Consequently, in the text of numerous treaties that emerged out of the Uruguay Round, one sees how the rigid description of the command economy of old gave way to more flexible language used to encompass a broader array of alternative economic structures. Let us consider two examples that will prove highly relevant to our later discussion.

The Uruguay Round resulted in a new comprehensive agreement on subsidies, the Agreement on Subsidies and Countervailing Measures (SCM Agreement). Unlike the GATT and the Tokyo Round Subsidies Code, which it replaced, the SCM Agreement includes a definition of a subsidy.[19] That definition notes that a subsidy is a "financial contribution by a government *or any public body* within the territory of the [WTO] Member."[20] This expansive definition captures an understanding that certain entities existing outside of the formal bounds of government may nevertheless facilitate government objectives.

Another place where acknowledgment is made of alternative economic structures is in the law governing the application of anti-dumping duties. As discussed above, the notion of an NME had already taken root in GATT law. But when drafting the Tokyo Round Anti-dumping Code in 1979, the framers deliberately employed broad language of a "particular market situation" to describe instances where comparison should not be made with home-market prices.[21] This broad term captures a wide range of scenarios in which the level of state control may not rise to the level of an NME (i.e., one where the state has a substantial monopoly on trade and fixes most prices), but where nevertheless, market forces do not play a sufficient role for domestic prices to be a reliable indicator. This aptly describes the state of many transition economies, where market forces were

---

[19] Alan Sykes, *The Economics of WTO Rules on Subsidies and Countervailing Measures*, *in* THE WORLD TRADE ORGANIZATION: LEGAL, ECONOMIC AND POLITICAL ANALYSIS 83 (Barry Appelton et al. eds., 2005).

[20] Agreement on Subsidies and Countervailing Measures, Apr. 15, 1994, Marrakesh Agreement Establishing the World Trade Organization, Annex 1A, THE LEGAL TEXTS: THE RESULTS OF THE URUGUAY ROUND OF MULTILATERAL TRADE NEGOTIATIONS 231 (1999), 1869 U.N.T.S . 14, art. 1.1(a)(1) (emphasis added) [hereinafter SCM Agreement].

[21] *See* Agreement on Implementation of Article VI of the General Agreement on Tariffs and Trade, Apr. 15, 1994, Marrakesh Agreement Establishing the World Trade Organization, Annex 1A, THE LEGAL TEXTS: THE RESULTS OF THE URUGUAY ROUND OF MULTILATERAL TRADE NEGOTIATIONS 147 (1999), 1869 U.N.T.S . 201, art. 2.4 [hereinafter ADA Agreement].

only introduced gradually as the economy shifted away from a centrally planned model. The "particular market situation" terminology was then carried over to the WTO Anti-dumping Agreement as well.[22]

These two examples highlight the strategy that Uruguay Round negotiators took toward hybrid transitional economies. By incorporating broad and somewhat vague terminology, such as "public body" and "particularly market situation," they sought to create the flexibility within the law to address any potential trade-related issues arising from this alternative economic structure.

3. Corporatism

A third economic structure that featured prominently in the global economy from the 1960s onward is corporatism. Corporatism refers to "a system of social and political organization in which major societal and interest groups are integrated into the governmental system, often on a monopolistic basis or under state guidance, tutelage and control, to achieve coordinated national development."[23] This system is achieved through organizing the constituent elements of interest representation "into a limited number of singular, compulsory, noncompetitive, hierarchically ordered and functionally differentiated categories."[24] Each is then "granted a deliberate representational monopoly within their respective categories in exchange for observing certain controls on the selection of leaders and articulation of demands and supports."[25] Examples of a state-controlled constituent group would be organized labor or agricultural producers, which in a corporatist economy, would each have its operations integrated with those of the state itself.

Corporatism is often contrasted with the pluralist nature of market capitalism, in which interest groups act independently and compete in the political economy but are not integrated with the state itself. The most ardent practitioners of corporatism were governments in Latin America and parts of Europe. Some have also tried to apply the term to newly industrialized economies in Asia.[26] However, I resist making such a move and insist on treating these economies as their own distinct category, as elaborated below.

One prominent scholar has separated corporatism into two strands: societal corporatism and state corporatism.[27] Societal corporatism refers to an economic structure in which labor, management, and other constituent groups are integrated with one another and come to shape the state's policies in an attempt to advance wider public interests. State policy results from collective bargaining and not from an authoritarian dictate. Examples of

[22] *See id.* art. 2.2.

[23] Howard J. Wirada, Corporatism and Comparative Politics ix (1997).

[24] Philippe C. Schmitter, *Still the Century of Corporatism?*, 36 Rev. of Pol. 85, 93 (1974).

[25] *Id.* at 93–94.

[26] *See, e.g.*, Jonathan Unger & Anita Chan, *China, Corporatism, and the East Asian Model*, 33 Austl. J. of Chinese Affairs, 29, 31 (1995).

[27] Schmitter, *supra* note 24, at 103–04.

economies that have practiced this form of corporatism include the Netherlands and several Scandinavian countries. State corporatism, on the other hand, refers to a situation in which an anti-liberal state creates organs of interest group representation in an effort to co-opt and subordinate these groups to advance the objectives of the state itself. Examples include the dictatorship-era economies of Brazil, Chile, Greece, Mexico, Portugal, and Spain.

GATT, and later WTO, law are accepting of corporatist economic arrangements. But they are cognizant of the fact that a closely entwined relationship of the type found in a corporatist economy may lead to protectionist regulation. To guard against this possibility, the Uruguay Round agreements impose several requirements for regulations affecting trade. For example, WTO law requires that sanitary and phytosanitary regulations must be based on "scientific evidence" or employed temporarily on account of the "precautionary principle." It also stipulates that technical regulations should be based on international standards when available, unless they prove to be ineffective or inappropriate for fulfilling a legitimate objective.[28] Such provisions ensure that a corporatist state cannot simply enact a regulation tailored specifically to support domestic interest groups as a quid pro quo for supporting the state's agenda.

Note that unlike the NME language found in WTO anti-dumping law, the provisions described above were not drafted to be targeted specifically against corporatism per se. Instead, they target protectionist regulatory tendencies generally, regardless of whether they are found in corporatist, pluralist, or otherwise configured economies. Nevertheless, they do serve to counteract potential negative collusive effects of close interactions between state and domestic producer groups of the form found in corporatist economies. Although the popularity of corporatism had started to wane by the 1990s, this economic structure still helped inform the design of WTO law.

4. Integrated Conglomerate-Led Economies

Finally, one other economic form that faced heavy scrutiny during the Uruguay Round was the integrated conglomerate-led structure found in East Asia. The best known of these was Japan's *keiretsu* structure. During the 1980s, Western academics, impressed by Japan's rising economic might, developed a fascination with this structure and the government bureaucracy necessary to sustain it.[29]

This economic structure is characterized by the dominant presence of several large industrial conglomerates. Each conglomerate has several companies within it that span across a variety of sectors. In addition, a "main bank" serves as the financing vehicle for

[28] Agreement on Technical Barriers to Trade, Apr. 15, 1994, Marrakesh Agreement Establishing the World Trade Organization, Annex 1A, THE LEGAL TEXTS: THE RESULTS OF THE URUGUAY ROUND OF MULTILATERAL TRADE NEGOTIATIONS 121 (1999), 1869 U.N.T.S. 120, art. 2.4.

[29] *See, e.g.*, JOHNSON, *supra* note 2; MICHAEL GERLACH, ALLIANCE CAPITALISM: THE SOCIAL ORGANIZATION OF JAPANESE BUSINESS (1997); KENICHI MIYASHITA & DAVID RUSSELL, KEIRETSU: INSIDE THE HIDDEN JAPANESE CONGLOMERATES (1995).

the conglomerate. Companies within each conglomerate are linked through a pattern of cross-shareholding. A series of nimble, smaller firms serve the various conglomerate companies. Overall economic development is coordinated by the government in conjunction with the conglomerates.

Japan was not alone in embracing this economic structure. The South Korean economy was also dominated by large industrial conglomerates, known as *chaebols*.[30] The rapid growth of these Asian economies led some in the early 1990s to believe that the Asian-style conglomerate-led economic structure offered important generalizable lessons for other economies.[31] GATT law, and later WTO law, deemed this economic structure to be permissible so long as it did not lead to collusion that negatively impacted foreign competitors. This stance was firmly established by the GATT ruling in the *Japan—Semiconductors* case.[32] Drafters sought to ensure that law provided sufficient flexibility for countries to implement such a structure, so long as close integration did not lead to protectionist policies.

B. CONCEPTUALIZING CHINA AT THE TIME OF ITS WTO ACCESSION

Despite having implemented a first round of dramatic economic reforms, at the start of the Uruguay Round, China appeared to fall squarely within the category of a command economy, albeit one experimenting with some market mechanisms. In the late 1980s, China embarked on a second stage of economic reforms; they would eventually trigger the growth of private enterprises.[33] However, the state was still the dominant player in the economy. Through direct top-down planning or bottom-up, local-level control by townships and village enterprises, the state was still firmly in control of the overall economy.

Logically then, the Uruguay Round drafters had no need to develop rules specific to China. After all, China did not even have a seat at the negotiating table. But even if the drafters could foresee a day when China would rejoin the GATT/WTO, the legal rules appeared more than sufficient to address the Chinese economy. After all, they covered command economies. And were China to venture away from this structure, many envisioned that the path of Chinese reforms would mimic that of predecessors in East Asia or Eastern Europe. Those alternative structures were also already covered.

---

[30] *See* Richard Steers et al., The Chaebol: Korea's New Industrial Might (1991); *see generally* Barry Eichengreen et al., eds., From Miracle to Maturity: The Growth of the Korean Economy (2012).

[31] *See, e.g.*, DAVID BURT, AMERICAN KEIRETSU: A STRATEGIC WEAPON FOR GLOBAL COMPETITIVENESS (1993); Jeffrey H. Dyer, *How Chrysler Created an American* Keiretsu, HARV. BUS. REV., July 1996 (describing the results of borrowing from Japanese business practices as "astounding"); Kevin Kelly et al., *Learning from Japan*, BUS. WEEK, Jan. 26, 1992 ("In short, there's a pressing need for U.S. manufacturers to develop something similar to the keiretsu.").

[32] Report of the Panel, *Japan—Trade in Semi-conductors*, L/6309 (May 4, 1988).

[33] For a concise discussion of these two sets of economic reforms, see BARRY NAUGHTON, THE CHINESE ECONOMY: TRANSITIONS AND GROWTH 85–98 (2007).

The opportunity to craft WTO rules specific to China emerged during the course of China's WTO accession. As many commentators have duly noted, China's negotiating partners drafted a series of China-specific provisions.[34] These provisions, captured in the Protocol of Accession, require China to conform to additional rules beyond those that apply to other WTO members. However, one wonders whether the drafters of the Protocol of Accession could have anticipated fully the exceptional nature of the Chinese economy as it stands today. Or was it the case that they believed that WTO rules applicable to alternative economic structures were more than sufficient to cover the transforming Chinese economy? With the historical record still sealed, it is difficult to discern the answers to these questions. Nevertheless, their choices concerning scope and specificity of the provisions give rise to some of the current difficulties confronting the WTO system.

Due to a bold course of economic reforms in the 1990s, China's economic structure did alter dramatically between 1994 (when the Uruguay Round was completed) and 2001 (when China acceded to the WTO). By 2001, China was clearly no longer a pure-form command economy.[35] Although the market played a more important role, it was also clear that China was not yet a market economy. Nor did its trading partners expect it to develop into one overnight.

The prevailing view of China's trading partners was that the Chinese economy was of a "transitional nature."[36] During the Working Party discussions, China's representative noted that China was in the midst of embarking on a series of economic reforms. The state of the economy was described as follows:

> Since 1979, China had been progressively reforming its economic system, with the objective of establishing and improving the socialist market economy. The reform package introduced in 1994, covering the banking, finance, taxation, investment, foreign exchange ("forex") and foreign trade sectors, had brought about major breakthroughs in China's socialist market economy. State-owned enterprises had been reformed by a clear definition of property rights and responsibilities, a separation of government from enterprise, and scientific management . . . A nationwide unified and open market system had been developed . . . Further liberalization of

[34] *See, e.g.*, Ka Zeng & Wei Liang, China and Global Trade Governance: China's First Decade in the World Trade Organization 77 (2013); Julia Ya Qin, *"WTO-Plus" Obligations and Their Implications for the World Trade Organization Legal System*, 37 J. World Trade 483 (2003); Xiaohui Wu, *No Longer Outside, Not Yet Equal: Rethinking China's Membership in the World Trade Organization*, 10 Chinese J. Int'l L. 227 (2011).

[35] By 2001, SOEs were contributing only 18 percent of gross industrial output value. *See* National Bureau of Statistics of the People's Republic of China, China Statistical Yearbook 2002, 423 (2002).

[36] World Trade Organization, Report of the Working Party on the Accession of China, WT/MIN(01)/3, ¶ 9 (Nov. 10, 2001).

> the pricing policy had resulted in the majority of consumer and producer products being subject to market prices. The market now played a much more significant role in boosting supply and meeting demand.[37]

Five points should be noted about the views prevalent at the time of China's WTO accession. First, of the WTO members that had shifted away from command economies beginning in the 1980s, most had evolved in the direction of genuine market economies. In retrospect, this trend may have been due to geographic reasons rather than any form of historical determinacy. At least in instances in Central and Eastern Europe, a strong factor in this push was the desire of states to integrate with the European Union. However, for most of the 1990s, the view of the market economy as superior was ascendant, with the corresponding belief that transitional economies were inclined toward this direction.[38] Although criticism of the Washington Consensus was already rampant, a credible alternative had yet to emerge.

As a result, the main impetus of China's trading partners was to use the WTO accession obligations to steer China in this direction. They did not take for granted that this evolution would happen naturally. Rather, they created a series of requirements to try to lock China in to this path. For example, the Protocol of Accession required that, apart from declared exceptions, "China shall . . . allow prices for traded goods and services in every sector to be determined by market forces, and multi-tier pricing practices for such goods and services shall be eliminated."[39]

Second, to the extent that China's reforms might not lead to a genuine market economy, one prevalent view at the time was that China might emulate the economic form of its East Asian neighbors. *The Economist* noted that the leaders of China's largest conglomerates "are borrowing some things from Japan, especially the *keiretsu* system which individual Japanese companies, often with their own stockmarket [*sic*] listings, are linked together through cross-shareholdings."[40] But the magazine famously predicted that "the real role models are South Korea's conglomerates, the mighty *chaebol*, which are far less focused in their range of businesses than big Japanese companies and (at least in the past) much more closely linked to the state."[41]

Note that the issue of whether conglomerate-style arrangements such as the *keiretsu* or *chaebol* should be permitted under international trade law had already been considered through GATT jurisprudence and during the Uruguay Round negotiations. To the extent that the Chinese economy might wind up with a form of capitalism different

---

[37] *Id.* ¶ 9.

[38] *See, e.g.*, Robert Heilbroner, *The Triumph of Capitalism*, NEW YORKER, Jan. 23,1989 ("[T]he great question now seems how rapid will be the transformation of socialism into capitalism.").

[39] World Trade Organization, Accession of the People's Republic of China, ¶ 9.1, WT/L/432 (Nov. 23, 2001) [hereinafter PRC Protocol of Accession].

[40] *China Adopts the Chaebol*, THE ECONOMIST, June 5, 1997, http://www.economist.com/node/90635.

[41] *Id.*

from the pure market economy, the belief was that WTO law had already contemplated the likely resulting scenario and was equipped to address issues that would arise. Furthermore, in the wake of the Asian financial crisis of 1997–1998 and Japan's economic malaise, the appeal of large-scale conglomerate-style growth had declined. Even if China still chose to venture in this direction, the view was that the law was sufficient to cover any potential problems that might arise.

Third, some scholars had the foresight to anticipate that the state might not readily retreat into the background. Unlike Eastern Europe, China's economic transformation was not accompanied by a political transformation. But to the extent that the state was to remain involved, a prevailing view of the 1990s and early 2000s was that the Chinese economy would evolve in a direction akin to that of other corporatist regimes.[42] Drafters did attempt to guard against this possibility in a few provisions. For example, the Protocol of Accession included provisions concerning state trading, import and export licensing, and price controls.[43] Overall, though, general WTO rules were viewed capable of dealing with corporatist economic arrangements. Consequently, drafters did not feel a need to develop a wide array of detailed provisions for the Chinese economy.[44]

Not all scholars, however, shared the view that China's path would mimic that of others. Some prominent sinologists emphasized the importance of historical and political factors, stressing that these factors may lead China to strike its own exceptional path forward.[45] Nevertheless, possibly on account of political reasons and ideological pre-dispositions, the warnings of this group of experienced scholars was not widely heeded by negotiators. Instead, some clung to an expectation, or hope, that China's path after WTO accession would likely converge onto that of a market economy or one of the existing alternatives.

Fourth, WTO members attempted to forestall any controversies over China's economic structure by explicitly declaring that regardless of whatever direction China's economic reforms took the country, its trading partners were free to consider China to be a non-market economy for the purposes of trade remedies investigations. For

---

[42] *See, e.g.*, Jean C. Oi, The Evolution of Local State Corporatism, *in* ZOUPING IN TRANSITION: THE PROCESS OF REFORM IN RURAL NORTH CHINA 35 (Andrew G. Walder ed., 1998); Bruce J. Dickson, *Cooptation and Corporatism in China: The Logic of Party Adaptation*, 115 POL. SCI. Q. 517, 532–38 (2001); Jonathan Unger & Anita Chan, *China, Corporatism, and the East Asian Model*, 33 AUSTL. J. OF CHINESE AFFAIRS 29 (1995). Not all adopted this view necessarily. *See, e.g.*, Thomas Rawski, *China Reform Watch: Turning Point Looming*, 38 CHINA PERSPECTIVES 28 (2001).

[43] PRC Protocol of Accession, *supra* note 39, ¶¶ 6, 8–9.

[44] Note that the general provisions section of the Protocol of Accession consisted of only eighteen paragraphs. *See id.*

[45] *See, e.g.*, WILLIAM ALFORD, TO STEAL A BOOK IS AN ELEGANT OFFENSE (1995); William Alford, *Making the World Safe for What*, 29 N.Y.U. J. INT'L L. & POL. 135, 140, 145 (1996); Dwight Perkins, *Industrial and Financial Policy in China and Vietnam: A New Model or a Replay of the East Asian Experience, in* RETHINKING THE EAST ASIAN MIRACLE 247, 249 (Joseph Stiglitz & Shahid Yusuf eds., 2001); Rawski, *supra* note 42.

anti-dumping duties, this concession was to apply for only the first fifteen years following China's WTO accession.[46]

Finally, WTO members added one additional check, the China-specific safeguard. Through the WTO's safeguard mechanism, a WTO member may restrict imports of a particular product temporarily in order to protect a domestic industry, if increased imports are causing or threatening to cause serious injury to the domestic industry. Normally, WTO rules require that a WTO member, when enacting a safeguard, must apply the restrictions to imports across the board.[47] However, China agreed to allow WTO members to apply a safeguard against Chinese imports only, without necessarily applying them to imports from other trading partners.[48] In short, even if China managed to use its economic heft to boost exports after gaining WTO entry, its trading partners retained the option to withdraw the beneficial concessions temporarily to protect their domestic industry during the first ten years.

Overall, China's WTO accession contributed to a sense of optimism about the future of the Chinese economy. Some believed China to be headed in the direction of a market economy.[49] But even if this were not the case, negotiators for China's trading partners likely believed that they had put in place sufficient legal provisions to deal with problems that might emerge in the most likely scenarios over the ties between the state and enterprises.[50] They had bought themselves over a decade to cope and adjust while the Chinese economy transformed.

II. The Rise of an Unforeseen Chinese Economic Model

Following China's WTO accession, the role and influence of market forces in the Chinese economy did grow. As noted above, several provisions in China's Protocol of Accession created an impetus for this, but more important was the genuine desire of Premier Zhu and other reformers to embark on large-scale market-oriented reforms.[51]

---

[46] *See* PRC Protocol of Accession, *supra* note 39, ¶ 15(d).

[47] *See* GATT, *supra* note 14, art. XIX; Agreement on Safeguards, Apr. 15, 1994, Marrakesh Agreement Establishing the World Trade Organization, Annex 1A, THE LEGAL TEXTS: THE RESULTS OF THE URUGUAY ROUND OF MULTILATERAL TRADE NEGOTIATIONS 275 (1999), 1869 U.N.T.S. 154.

[48] PRC Protocol of Accession, *supra* note 39, ¶ 16.

[49] *See, e.g.*, Jeffrey E. Garten, *The Wrong Way to Punish Beijing*, N.Y. TIMES, Mar. 23, 1999, http://www.nytimes.com/1999/03/23/opinion/the-wrong-way-to-punish-beijing.html ("Whatever else you want to say about China, the sheer scale and scope of the move toward capitalism—from a Communist system—make it potentially one of history's most remarkable turnarounds."); Arthur Levitt, *China's Free Market Must Stress Cooperation*, N.Y. TIMES, Jan. 17, 1997, http://www.nytimes.com/1997/01/17/opinion/l-china-s-free-market-must-stress-cooperation-201944.html ("A market revolution is underway in China.").

[50] *See Hearing on the Accession of China to the WTO Before the H. Comm. on Ways and Means*, 106th Cong. (2000) (statement of Charlene Barshefsky, United States Trade Representative) ("Finally, our bilateral agreement deals, appropriately, with the special and unusual circumstances of the Chinese economy.").

[51] *See generally* LAURENCE J. BRAHM, ZHU RONGJI AND THE TRANSFORMATION OF MODERN CHINA (2002).

China, however, has defied traditional patterns of economic transformation. Its economy today does not resemble that of former Communist countries. Nor does it resemble that of the other East Asian economies with large-scale industrial conglomerates and an investment- and export-oriented growth model. Instead, due to distinct policy choices made following its WTO accession, China has developed a unique economic structure of its own—one that was not anticipated during either the Uruguay Round or at the time of China's WTO accession negotiations.

Because this entire volume is dedicated to examining Chinese state capitalism, I shall not devote much space in this chapter to describing the system's salient features. I leave it to readers to examine the rich analyses provided by my fellow contributors in the other chapters. Instead, I focus primarily on explaining why China's contemporary economic structure differs from the four dominant alternative economic models contemplated in the WTO rules.

A. THE MARKET EMERGES, BUT UNDER THE SHADOW OF STATE OVERSIGHT

The economic reforms of the late 1990s resulted in the sale of state assets in numerous sectors of the Chinese economy. Following Premier Zhu's directive to "capture the large, and let go of the small" (*zhua da fang xiao*), the state deliberately exited out of certain sectors that it deemed not vital. However, in sectors that the state considered to be important, it maintained strict control and sought to improve the competitiveness of SOEs.

Among the means by which the state sought to do so was through subjecting SOEs to greater pressure from the market. SOEs were encouraged to seek capital through equity markets, not only in Shanghai or Shenzhen, but also in Hong Kong and/or New York.[52] This provided a market mechanism for monitoring the performance of SOEs. SOEs also formed joint venture partnerships with foreign firms and/or allowed foreign investors to buy stakes in their ventures.

Some mistook these moves as an indication that China was moving toward quasi-privatization of its socialist economy, as other transition economies had done in Eastern Europe. For example, former U.S. President George H.W. Bush is said to have asked Premier Zhu in 1998 how China's privatization plan was going. When Premier Zhu, taken aback, responded that China was not undergoing privatization but simply corporatizing its state assets, President Bush is reported to have responded with a nudge and a wink, saying that no matter how Zhu described the process, "we know what's going on."[53]

---

[52] *See generally* Lixian Liu, International Cross-Listing of Chinese Firms (2014); *see also* Li Jia, *The Firstborns*, NewsChina, Mar. 2014, http://www.newschinamag.com/magazine/the-firstborns (discussing how central SOEs were encouraged to list their best assets overseas).

[53] Richard McGregor, The Party: The Secret World of China's Communist Leaders 43 (2010).

Premier Zhu's characterization of China's economic reforms was nevertheless correct. Although China may have opened up shareholding of SOEs to outsiders, the shares offered were minority stakes. The state effectively remained in control of key state-owned assets.[54] Although an SOE may list in Hong Kong and issue company reports similar to those of private enterprises, it nevertheless remains in the firm hands of the state.

Moreover, following China's WTO accession, the state moved to centralize its control over state assets. When state assets were first spun off from various state organs into corporations, they were overseen by the various ministries from which they had originated. In 2003, state assets were consolidated into a single government agency, SASAC. The central level of SASAC today is the controlling shareholder of 117 SOEs, including more than half of the Chinese companies on the Global Fortune 500. Examples of SASAC-controlled firms include China Telecom, Sinopec, and Chinalco. SOEs of lesser importance are overseen by provincial or local SASACs. This degree of centralized control, done through a single government agency, is one unique feature of Chinese state capitalism.

Although SASAC acts as the controlling shareholder for a sizeable portion of the Chinese economy, it should not be thought of as the overarching master of Chinese state capitalism. As Curtis J. Milhaupt and Wentong Zheng note in Chapter 9 in this volume, SASAC does not always take a hands-on role in corporate governance matters. Moreover, power is dissipated across various other entities. The largest state-run banks do not fall under SASAC's control, but instead are controlled by Central Huijin, which was also established in 2003 and today falls under the sovereign wealth fund, the China Investment Corporation. Economic planning and macroeconomic coordination falls to the National Development and Reform Commission (NDRC).

Prices for key inputs affecting industries remain firmly in the hands of the state. For example, NDRC continues to regulate the price of electricity, oil, natural gas, and water.[55] Through 2014, banks were not able to compete for depositors on the basis of interest rates, which have not yet been liberalized by the state. Although the market may function, the state remains its overseer. In addition, before investments or projects can begin in various sectors, firms, regardless of ownership type, must first gain approval from state officials.

State oversight of China's economic structure, therefore, follows a model unlike that found anywhere else in the world. As in other state capitalist countries, the state oversees only certain key sectors of the economy, and leaves the rest to private enterprises.[56]

---

[54] The level through which the state exerts control differs depending on the enterprise. *See* U.S.-China Econ. and Sec. Review Comm'n, *Chinese State-Owned and State-Controlled Enterprises, Feb. 15, 2012* (Testimony of Adam Hersh, Economist, Ctr. for Am. Progress Action Fund), *available at* http://cdn.americanprogress.org/wp-content/uploads/issues/2012/02/pdf/hersh_testimony.pdf.

[55] *China to Reform Prices in Energy Sector*, Xinhua News, Feb. 29, 2012, http://news.xinhuanet.com/english/china/2012-02/29/c_122767792.htm.

[56] Note that in comparison to other state capitalist countries, the Chinese state has been willing to relinquish control of certain industries. For example, in 2011, the state's share of industrial input for the raw chemical materials and chemical products sector was only 18.7 percent, and for the textiles sector was only 2.4 percent. *See* Lardy, *supra* note 8, at 77.

However, its oversight structure is highly centralized, with a single agency overseeing the state's major industrial assets and another overseeing the state's financial assets. A third directs overall economic planning.

This structure of state oversight was not one that was anticipated during the drafting of the Uruguay Round agreements or China's Protocol of Accession. As noted, SASAC and Central Huijin were only created in 2003. Although NDRC existed beforehand, its role was also transformed in 2003. All of these policy initiatives were undertaken by the Hu-Wen administration (2003–2013), and not the Jiang-Zhu administration (1998–2003), which oversaw China's WTO accession. Importantly, then, the series of reforms that shifted how the state governs the Chinese economy occurred after China's accession was already complete.

Moreover, the end result was not what experts had anticipated. The state did not devolve control to private entities through de facto privatization, as in other transition economies. Nor did it set up several large-scale conglomerates to compete against one another, along the lines of a *chaebol* or *keiretsu* structure. Instead, the economy is a mixed bag. Some sectors (e.g., mining and processing of nonmetal ores, manufacturing of electrical machinery) are dominated largely by nonstate actors.[57] However, others (e.g., petroleum, aviation) remain firmly in the hands of one large economic behemoth, the Chinese state, run by a handful of all-powerful agencies.

B. THE COMMUNIST PARTY AS A DOMINANT ACTOR, SEPARATE BUT ENTWINED WITH THE STATE

Complicating the equation even further is the fact the state's role is shared with the Communist Party. Commentators will sometimes make reference to China as a Party-state, but it is important to note that the Party and state are not fused, but remain two distinct entities. Nor does the Party simply operate as a political conduit to fill positions in the state, leaving the latter to handle the day-to-day management of the economy. Instead, the Party itself remains an active participant, alongside the state, in managing the Chinese economy.

Several mechanisms allow the Party to inject itself regularly into economic and corporate affairs. Most Chinese enterprises include a party committee. This is not simply a relic from China's command economy past; the party committee provides a means for the Party to monitor an enterprise's activities. The Party also plays an important role in personnel evaluations and promotions, not just within the state but also within business.[58] Moreover, success in one realm may lead to a higher position in the other. Although individuals move between government and the private sector in other

---

[57] *See id.* at 59–89 (discussing the rise of the private sector across industries).

[58] *See* McGregor, *supra* note 53, at 72.

countries, the "revolving door" is usually an individual's choice; personnel flow is not dictated by apparatchiks in a specialized organ of a political party akin to the Party's Organization Department.[59]

Li-Wen Lin and Curtis J. Milhaupt have suggested that two uniquely Chinese characteristics of industrial organization and corporate governance arise from this type of close-knit arrangement among the Party, state, and business. First, the relationship between the Chinese Party-state and firms is organized along the lines of a networked hierarchy.[60] Networks extend beyond firms themselves to reach the state and Party organs. Second, the various formal and informal pathways that connect these networks constitute a form of institutional bridging.[61] Again, these extend beyond shareholding and corporate governance practices to encompass those of state entities, such as SASAC, as well as the Party itself.

Two points are worth noting about how the Party's activist role in the economy results in Chinese exceptionalism. First, unlike Japan or South Korea, the most powerful figures in some of China's largest industrial entities are not simply industrialists with close ties to the dominant political party. In the fifty-three top SASAC-owned firms, the Party appoints top management, judges their performance, and determines their future career prospects.[62] The Party also vets appointments to the board of directors. Thus, corporate leaders in SASAC-owned firms have much stronger direct agency ties with the dominant political party than their counterparts in other state capitalist countries.

Second, the Party's continued dominance precludes the emergence of any alternative rival center of power to challenge the state or the Party itself. Even in state corporatist regimes where various interest group constituencies are organized by the state, these groups have actual bargaining power to enact trade-offs with other interest groups. China, however, is lacking in any such group. Labor or industry associations all continue to operate under the Party's instruction.[63]

China's economic structure, therefore, is not only unique because of its ownership structure. It is also unique to the extent that the dominant political party continues to exercise direct oversight and control over economic organs, both in conjunction with the state and also independent of the state.

---

[59] *See* LARDY, *supra* note 8, at 51.

[60] Li-Wen Lin & Curtis Milhaupt, *We Are the (National) Champions: Understanding the Mechanisms of State Capitalism in China*, 65 STAN. L. REV. 697, 707 (2013).

[61] *Id.* at 708.

[62] *See* JAMES MCGREGOR, NO ANCIENT WISDOM, NO FOLLOWERS: THE CHALLENGES OF CHINESE AUTHORITARIAN CAPITALISM 72 (2012).

[63] *See Membership Required*, ECONOMIST, July 31, 2008, http://www.economist.com/node/11848496; RUDOLF TRAUB-MERZ, GLOBAL LABOUR UNIV., INT'L LABOUR OFFICE, ALL CHINA FEDERATION OF TRADE UNIONS: STRUCTURE, FUNCTIONS AND THE CHALLENGE OF COLLECTIVE BARGAINING (2011), *available at* http://www.global-labour-university.org/fileadmin/GLU_Working_Papers/GLU_WP_No.13.pdf.

C. THE BLURRING OF THE PUBLIC AND PRIVATE DISTINCTION

So far, the discussion above has focused on how developments in China's state ownership structure and Party oversight have evolved differently than expected since the 1990s. Events in another dimension have also transpired differently than expected—the relationship between the Party-state and private entrepreneurs.

Although the Party, since the start of economic reforms, has acted to co-opt private entrepreneurs,[64] during the 1990s, the distinction between state-owned and private enterprises remained relatively intact. But this began to change once the state started to spin off enterprises, and the People's Liberation Army (PLA) was ordered to divest its commercial operations.[65] Gradually, a large series of private enterprises emerged with strong historical ties to the Party-state. A quintessential example is Huawei, the telecommunications equipment company considered to be one of China's most successful private enterprises but with historical ties to the PLA.[66]

Although many anticipated that the Party would continue to co-opt private entrepreneurs, few accurately foresaw just how much more blurred the lines dividing the state and private sectors would become. Hints of the radical turn in the Party's approach toward private enterprises started to emerge only in July 2001. At the Party's eightieth anniversary celebration, China's leader Jiang Zemin formally declared that private businessmen were welcome to join the Party, and then quickly acted to amend the Party's Constitution to welcome capitalists.[67] These events took place just months before China's WTO accession, when the drafting of China's Protocol of Accession was already largely complete.

Curtis J. Milhaupt and Wentong Zheng's Chapter 9 in this volume explains in detail why ownership cannot serve as the basis for framing our understanding of the state's role in the Chinese economy. Instead, they suggest that the state, through a variety of mechanisms, is also able to capture nominally private enterprises in which it has no direct ownership stake. This blurring of the lines between state and private further contributes to the uniqueness of the Chinese economic structure. Rather than build upon those arguments here, I suggest that readers interested in further understanding this element of Chinese economic exceptionalism turn to Milhaupt and Zheng's chapter for more details.

---

[64] *See generally* Dickson, *supra* note 42, at 522–27.

[65] For more about the impact of the 1998 order for the PLA to divest from commercial ventures, see James Mulvenon, *PLA Divesture and Civil Military Relations: Implications for the Sixteenth Party Congress Leadership*, 1 CHINA LEADERSHIP MONITOR, Dec. 2001.

[66] *See* NATHANIEL AHERNS, CHINA'S COMPETITIVENESS: MYTH, REALITY, AND LESSONS FOR THE UNITED STATES AND JAPAN, CASE STUDY: HUAWEI (2013).

[67] Charles Wolf, Jr., *China's Capitalists Join the Party*, N.Y. TIMES, Aug. 13, 2001, http://www.nytimes.com/2001/08/13/opinion/13WOLF.html.

When it comes to the ties between the Chinese state and its private enterprises, the relationship is again unlike that found in any of the alternative economic structures contemplated by WTO law. In contrast to a transition economy, the state did not simply divest itself of these assets and let them operate as purely private enterprises. Instead, the state and the Party remain actively tied to these organizations. The continued existence of Party committees inside private enterprises serves as but one example. Furthermore, unlike a corporatist or Asian conglomerate structure, private entrepreneurs are not organized into distinct groups. Finally, unlike other authoritarian state-capitalist regimes, the ties between private enterprises and the state do not revolve around a specific leader or ruling family. Instead, these are links between individual entrepreneurs and a full-functioning Party-state regime bigger than any other in the world.

D. SUMMARY

Overall, the structural transformation of the Chinese economy from the late 1990s to the present has followed a path different than that anticipated at the time of the Uruguay Round or China's WTO accession. China's trading partners saw the economic reforms of the late 1990s as a move toward either quasi-privatization or a structure along the lines of other newly industrialized Asian economies. Even if one understood the reforms differently, few expected the Party-state to succeed in delivering rapid economic growth without relinquishing political control.[68] Yet, the Party-state has proven to be much more adaptive and resilient than anticipated.[69] The economic structure implemented soon after China's WTO accession has delivered a decade of impressive growth.

China today has more Fortune Global 500 firms than any other country besides the United States.[70] Four of the eight largest banks in the world today are Chinese.[71] Not surprisingly, then, the Chinese are increasingly confident in the long-term sustainability of their economic model.[72] Although policymakers readily recognize that additional

---

[68] *See, e.g.*, Rawski, *supra* note 42, at 9. Several predicted the regime's imminent demise. *See, e.g.*, GORDON CHANG, THE COMING COLLAPSE OF CHINA (2001); George Gilboy & Eric Heginbotham, *China's Coming Transformation*, FOR. AFFAIRS, July/Aug. 2001, *available at* http://www.foreignaffairs.com/articles/57050/george-j-gilboy-and-eric-heginbotham/chinas-coming-transformation.

[69] *See* BRUCE DICKSON, WEALTH INTO POWER (2008); DAVID SHAMBAUGH, CHINA'S COMMUNIST PARTY: ATROPHY AND ADAPTATION; Andrew J. Nathan, *Authoritarian Resilience*, 16 J. DEMOCRACY 6 (2003).

[70] Ivana Kottasova, *Is China about to Take Over Global Business?*, CNN.COM (Sept. 16, 2014), http://www.cnn.com/2014/07/08/business/fortune-500/index.html (noting that China has 95 companies in the Fortune Global 500, second only to the United States, which has 128 companies).

[71] Halah Touryalai, *World's 100 Biggest Banks: China's ICBC #1, No U.S. Banks in Top 5*, FORBES, Feb. 12, 2014, http://www.forbes.com/sites/halahtouryalai/2014/02/12/worlds-100-biggest-banks-chinas-icbc-1-no-u-s-banks-in-top-5/.

[72] *See* Joshua Kurlantzick, *Why the "China Model" Isn't Going Away*, THE ATLANTIC, Mar. 21, 2013, http://www.theatlantic.com/china/archive/2013/03/why-the-china-model-isnt-going-away/274237/; Eric X. Li, *The Life of the Party*, FOR. AFFAIRS, Jan./Feb. 2013, *available at* http://www.foreignaffairs.com/articles/138476/eric-x-li/the-life-of-the-party.

reforms are necessary, including the injection of additional market competition and a shift toward consumption-led growth, such changes will be implemented with the Party-state firmly in control.[73] No serious proposals are being floated to dismantle the structure that has taken root over the past decade. Therefore, barring any unforeseen economic calamity or political upheaval, the general contours of China's economic structure are likely to remain in place for the foreseeable future.

III. Emerging Points of Tension

What then are the consequences of the rise of an alternative economic structure whose form is unlike that envisioned by the drafters of the WTO rules? For much of the past decade, policymakers were largely able to avoid confronting this question. China's Protocol of Accession included a number of temporary provisions, thereby equipping its trading partners with instruments to handle China-related trade disputes.[74] But as these temporary provisions gradually expire, China's trading partners will increasingly need to turn to the standard provisions of the Uruguay Round agreements and China's Protocol of Accession to address their concerns.

This raises the possibility of interpretative challenges for the WTO, as legal provisions drafted with other alternative economic structures in mind will now need to be applied to a new form unforeseen at the time. Below, I highlight two emergent issues as examples of the challenges that the WTO faces as it confronts trade issues concerning China's economy.

A. SUBSIDIES AND THE "PUBLIC BODY" DEBATE

One key issue that has already surfaced to date is the extent to which selective state interventions by various actors in the Chinese economy constitute illegal subsidies. WTO law does not bar subsidies altogether. However, certain types of subsidies are prohibited.[75] Other subsidies, under certain circumstances, are deemed to have adverse effects on trade; trading partners adversely affected can seek remedies through the WTO.[76] Still others are deemed to cause or threaten material injury to domestic producers of the like

---

[73] *See* 中共中央关于全面深化改革若干重大问题的决定 (Decision of the Chinese Communist Party Central Committee on Several Major Questions about Deepening Reform) (promulgated by the Third Plenum of the 18th CPC Cent. Comm., Nov. 12, 2013, effective upon promulgation), *available at* http://news.xinhuanet.com/politics/2013-11/15/c_118164235.htm.

[74] *See supra* notes 46, 48.

[75] These are export subsidies and subsidies with local-content requirements. *See* SCM Agreement, *supra* note 20, art. 3.

[76] *Id.* arts. 5–6.

product, allowing their trading partners to impose unilateral trade remedies in the form of a countervailing duty (CVD) against the good.[77]

The SCM Agreement clarifies that a subsidy must involve: (1) the provision of a "financial contribution"; (2) "by a government or any public body"; (3) in which "a benefit is thereby conferred."[78] In addition, the subsidy must be "specific," meaning that it is conferred in a limited manner rather than being generally available.[79] With respect to this last requirement, China's Protocol of Accession included a specific provision concerning Chinese SOEs. Paragraph 10.2 states that, for purposes of the SCM Agreement, "subsidies provided to state-owned enterprises will be viewed as specific if, *inter alia*, state-owned enterprises are the predominant recipients of such subsidies or state-owned enterprises receive a disproportionately large amount of such subsidies."[80]

Because of the negotiators' experience with command economies and transition economies, they readily anticipated that they might need greater clarity on situations where the Chinese state is providing financial contributions to SOEs—whether in the form of direct financial grants, special tax privileges, land use rights, etc. Paragraph 10.2 addresses and helps to clarify such situations.[81] But the Protocol of Accession fails to address another situation—that in which a Chinese SOE acts as a potential *provider*, rather than recipient, of a subsidy to another Chinese enterprise.

Consider two such examples: First, what are we to make of situations in which a Chinese state-owned bank, such as the Bank of China, provides a loan on preferential terms to another enterprise? Is this loan in fact a subsidy? Should the Bank of China be considered an extension of the state itself? After all, certain of its attributes differ from commercial banks elsewhere. For example, its main shareholder is the state. It falls under the authority of Central Huijin, which, as noted earlier, is a state entity without parallel in most market-oriented banking systems. Or should the Bank of China be considered just another commercial bank, separate from the state? After all, the Bank of China also has attributes similar to other large global commercial banks. It is listed on the Hong Kong Stock Exchange; therefore, foreigners can readily buy an ownership stake in the bank, and it must comply with Hong Kong's securities regulations. It also has branches around the world, allowing foreigners to readily deposit and withdraw funds from it, just as they would with any other global bank. On what basis are we to determine whether preferential loans from a Chinese state-owned bank amount to a "subsidy"?

---

[77] *See* GATT, *supra* note 14, art. VI; *see also* SCM Agreement, *supra* note 20, arts. 10–23.

[78] *Id.* art. 1.

[79] *Id.* art. 2.

[80] PRC Protocol of Accession, *supra* note 39, ¶ 10.2.

[81] *See* Julia Ya Qin, *WTO Regulation of Subsidies to State-Owned Enterprises*, 7 J. INT'L ECON. L. 863 (2004) (suggesting that this represents a "curious departure" "from the ownership-neutral philosophy of the world trading system").

Second, consider another scenario in which an SOE supplies a good at preferential terms to a downstream customer, which relies on the good as an input. For example, what are we to make of a situation in which Baosteel, a state-owned steel producer, provides steel to another Chinese enterprise on terms that are better than those provided to most other customers? Does this transaction amount to a subsidy? Should Baosteel be considered an extension of the state because it is owned primarily by the state? Or should its behavior be considered akin to those of other commercial enterprises, even if the state is its primary shareholder? After all, firms regularly engage in price discrimination. Should Baosteel's transactions receive greater scrutiny because it is owned by the state through SASAC, and its top-level executives are appointed through the Party Organization Department? On what basis are we to determine whether transactions with preferential terms involving a Chinese SOE amount to a "subsidy"?

In other words, where are we to draw the boundaries of the Chinese state when considering what a subsidy is in the Chinese context? This question has already surfaced on multiple occasions because the SCM Agreement does not solely cover financial contributions made by the government itself, but also extends to those made by a "public body." Under what circumstances is an SOE to be considered a "public body," and therefore, its preferential actions to be considered as subsidies?

In 2008, China filed a complaint before the WTO challenging several determinations made by the United States Department of Commerce (DOC) in several instances where the DOC deemed the provision of a loan by a state-owned commercial bank or an input from an SOE to amount to a subsidy.[82] These findings then led the United States to levy CVDs against Chinese goods benefiting from the subsidy. China argued that the DOC had decided that an SOE or bank was a "public body" on the basis of a per se majority ownership test, whereas it should have instead employed a multi-factor test to assess whether the entity was in fact government controlled.[83]

The Panel rejected China's arguments, declaring that "on its own, majority government ownership is clear and highly indicative evidence of government control, and thus whether an entity is a public body for purposes of the SCM Agreement."[84] It then declared that the United States did not err by giving primacy to evidence of majority government ownership in assessing whether an entity is a public body.[85]

The Appellate Body, however, overturned the Panel's ruling in the *US—AD/CVD* dispute. It declared that a public body "must be an entity that possesses, exercises or is

---

[82] *See* Request for Consultations by China, *United States—Definitive Anti-dumping and Countervailing Duties on Certain Products from China*, WT/DS379/1, (last visited Sept. 22, 2008).

[83] Panel Report, *United States—Definitive Anti-dumping and Countervailing Duties on Certain Products from China*, ¶ 8.124, WT/DS379/R (Oct. 22, 2010).

[84] *Id.* ¶ 8.135.

[85] *Id.* ¶ 8.136.

vested with government authority."[86] A case-by-case analysis is required, as "the precise contours and characteristics of a public body are bound to differ from entity to entity, State to State, and case to case."[87] Consequently, the analysis requires "a proper evaluation of the core features of the entity concerned, and its relationship with government in the narrow sense."[88]

Where an express statutory delegation of authority to the entity itself exists, the Appellate Body noted that the inquiry is straightforward.[89] However, in the absence of an express delegation, the Appellate Body noted that government authority may be found through evidence that "the entity is, in fact, exercising governmental functions, . . . particularly where such evidence points to a sustained and systematic practice."[90] Furthermore, the Appellate Body declared that "the mere fact that a government is the majority shareholder of an entity does not demonstrate that the government exercises meaningful control over the conduct of that entity, much less that the government has bestowed it with government authority."[91] Before an inference that government ownership is tantamount to an exercise of government authority by the SOE, there ought to be evidence showing that "the formal indicia of government control are manifold" and "such control has been exercised in a meaningful way."[92]

How, then, are we to apply the Appellate Body's "public body" test to the various economic entities that exist in the Chinese economic structure? In select instances, application of the Appellate Body's test is straightforward, at least for now. For example, with state-owned banks, Article 34 of China's Commercial Banking Law expressly states that banks are required to "carry out their loan business upon the needs of [the] national economy and the social development and under the guidance of State industrial policies."[93] The Bank of China's Global Offering also contained an excerpt advising investors that the "Chinese Commercial Banking Law requires commercial banks to take into account government macroeconomic policies in making lending decisions."[94] Where express acknowledgment of this form exists and other indicia of control are also considered, then it is clear that such entities can be considered to be a "public body" for a WTO subsidy analysis.[95]

---

[86] Appellate Body Report, *United States—Definitive Anti-dumping and Countervailing Duties on Certain Products from China*, ¶ 317, WT/DS379/AB/R (Mar. 11, 2011).

[87] Id.

[88] *Id.*

[89] *Id.* ¶ 318.

[90] *Id.*

[91] *Id.*

[92] *Id.*

[93] *Id.* ¶ 349.

[94] *Id.* ¶ 350.

[95] Among the other factors considered by the DOC were: (1) an OECD report stating that the CEOs of the head offices of state-owned banks are government appointed and the Party retains significant influence in their choice, (2) the lack of adequate risk management and analytical skills, and (3) the unresponsiveness to inquiries made over the loan evaluation process for select industries. *See id.* ¶¶ 349–350.

But what about the various instances where formal statutory or regulatory command is lacking? Such cases are more difficult, as the delegation of government authority is much more opaque and may even be informal. The Appellate Body's ruling, moreover, does not provide sufficient guidance as to what steps must be taken to apply its test properly. It simply states that an examination of formal ownership levels is insufficient, without stipulating exactly what other criteria must be examined to determine government control and exercise of government authority.

One possibility is to conduct a multi-factor inquiry to gauge the extent to which the entity possesses government authority. The DOC, for example, has conducted a five-factor analysis in previous inquiries. Besides examining government ownership and whether the entity was created by statute, it also considered three other factors: (1) government presence on the board of directors, (2) government control over activities, and (3) pursuit of government policies or interests. Thomas J. Prusa and Edwin Vermulst have suggested that application of this type of multi-factor analysis would be sufficient to meet the Appellate Body's command.[96]

Ming Du has emphasized the importance of the mode of Party supervision, suggesting potential differences between firms supervised by central SASAC and other firms.[97] Ru Ding has suggested three other factors that may be useful for providing evidence of government authority. These include formal classification according to Chinese statistical sources, the set of applicable laws governing the enterprise, and its role in facilitating the government's economic reform agenda.[98]

Time will tell whether the Appellate Body's formulation in the *US—AD/CVD* ruling will prove workable or not when applied to the Chinese context. Some have noted surprise that the Appellate Body made no mention of the China-specific provisions in the Protocol of Accession and Working Party Report.[99] Joost Pauwelyn, for example, sees the Appellate Body's sharp reversal of the Panel ruling as indicative of the Appellate Body's increasing willingness to engage in judicial lawmaking.[100] Three high-profile authorities have sharply criticized the Appellate Body's turn in this direction. They describe the ruling as activist, divorced from the letter and spirit of the SCM Agreement, and disputable in its logic and coherence.[101] They argue that the Appellate Body has created

---

[96] Thomas J. Prusa & Edwin Vermulst, *United States—Definitive Anti-dumping and Countervailing Duties on Certain Products from China: Passing the Buck on Pass-Through*, 12 World Trade Rev. 197, 227 (2013).

[97] Ming Du, *China's State Capitalism and World Trade Law*, 63 Int'l & Comp. L.Q. 409, 439 (2014).

[98] Ru Ding, *"Public Body" or Not: Chinese State-Owned Enterprise*, 48 J. World Trade 167, 184–87 (2014).

[99] *See, e.g.*, Joost Pauwelyn, *Treaty Interpretation or Activism: Comment on the AB Report on United States—ADs and CVDs on Certain Products from China*, 12 World Trade Rev. 235, 240 (2013).

[100] *Id.*

[101] Michael Cartland, Gérard Depayre & Jan Woznowski, *Is Something Going Wrong in the WTO Dispute Settlement?*, 46 J. World Trade 979 (2012). The three authors are the former chair of the negotiating group on subsidies and countervailing duties during the Uruguay Round, the former chief negotiator for the EC on subsidies, and the former director of the WTO Rules division.

an excessively onerous test, with the perverse incentive of encouraging greater opacity.[102] The implication is that the Appellate Body's ruling may have hurt not only its credibility as an impartial and effective adjudicator but also the system's capacity to address trade distortions arising from the Chinese economic structure.

Are they correct? Or will countries be able to apply the Appellate Body test to address subsidies provided under China's unique economic structure? What is certain is that the recent *US—AD/CVD* dispute represents only the first of looming disputes over how transactions undertaken by Chinese state-owned or state-affiliated enterprises are to be considered under WTO subsidies law. By not providing definitive guidance on this issue, the Appellate Body has indicated its preference to leave questions unresolved for decisions in future cases. However, the recent *US—Carbon Steel (India)* ruling provides an indication of the Appellate Body's willingness to stick to the general contours of the earlier public body jurisprudence, while again affirming the need to examine issues in light of their particular contexts.[103]

What this means is that as the size and reach of Chinese enterprises owned or affiliated with the state expands, the possibility for more disputes of this sort lingers on the horizon. Furthermore, as the *US—Carbon Steel (India)* dispute suggests, the stakes will be high for the WTO even when China is not a direct litigant, because whatever rule the Appellate Body declares will need to be applied to the Chinese context.

B. HOW TO TREAT CHINA IN POST-2016 ANTI-DUMPING CASES

Another lingering question concerns anti-dumping duties, the most popular form of trade remedies taken against Chinese products.[104] For the first fifteen years following China's WTO accession, application of such trade remedies has been relatively straightforward. The fact that China's economy differs dramatically from that of other WTO members has not mattered much to date.

This is because WTO rules governing anti-dumping duties permit the importing country to apply an alternate methodology when investigating a petition for anti-dumping duties if the exporting country is considered a "non-market economy."[105] For NMEs, authorities may use the price found in a surrogate third country instead of the NME when investigating the dumping petition. Allowing authorities to search for an appropriate third-country surrogate with a high price makes it easier for the authorities to

---

[102] *Id.* at 1010–14.

[103] Appellate Body Report, *United States—Countervailing Measures on Certain Hot-Rolled Carbon Steel Flat Products from India*, ¶ 4.29, WT/DS436/AB/R (Dec. 8, 2014).

[104] China is the leading target of anti-dumping duties worldwide. *See* World Trade Organization, *Anti-dumping Measures: By Exporters*, https://www.wto.org/english/tratop_e/adp_e/AD_MeasuresByExpCty.pdf (last visited May 29, 2015).

[105] *See supra* Section I(A)1 for a discussion of the treatment of non-market economies under WTO law.

make a positive dumping determination in favor of the domestic producer.[106] It also allows authorities to charge a higher anti-dumping duty. The NME approach, therefore, benefits domestic interests seeking temporary protection against foreign imports.

Prior to China's WTO accession, most major economies, including the United States and the European Union, treated China as an NME.[107] Sensing that China's economy was in transition, but not wanting to lose the advantage of being able to apply the alternate methodology, China's trading partners negotiated special rules on anti-dumping investigations for Chinese goods. Paragraph 15(a)(ii) of China's Protocol of Accession requires the Chinese producer of the allegedly dumped good to "clearly show that market economy conditions prevail in the industry producing the like product with regard to the manufacture, production and sale of that product."[108] If it cannot, then the importing WTO member may use "a methodology that is not based on strict comparison with domestic prices or costs in China" (e.g., the surrogate third-country approach used for NMEs).[109] Consequently, this has made it easier, at least from a technical perspective, to take anti-dumping actions against Chinese imports.

However, the ease of applying anti-dumping duties against Chinese goods may soon change. Paragraph 15(d) stipulates that Paragraph 15(a)(ii) is to expire fifteen years after China's date of accession (i.e., December 11, 2016).[110] The WTO will soon need to face the question of how China's trading partners are to treat its economy in anti-dumping cases in the post-2016 era.

As the deadline looms, a small, but relatively fierce, debate has raged on this question. Some commentators have suggested that the expiration of Paragraph 15(a)(ii) automatically bestows upon China market-economy status.[111] After 2016, this camp believes that WTO law requires China to be treated in line with other market economies, so far as application of anti-dumping laws is concerned. However, others have suggested that this interpretation is incorrect.[112] Instead, they suggest that WTO members will continue to have the option to apply an alternate methodology to Chinese producers under certain conditions.

---

[106] One of the requirements for the imposition of an anti-dumping duty is a showing that the price of the allegedly dumped import is lower than that of the normal value of the product. The price in the surrogate third country can substitute for the domestic price when determining the normal value.

[107] Rao Wenjia, *China's Market Economy Status under WTO Antidumping Law after 2016*, 5 Tsinghua China L. Rev. 151, 156 (2013).

[108] PRC Protocol of Accession, *supra* note 39, ¶ 15(a)(ii).

[109] *Id.*

[110] *Id.* ¶ 15(d)

[111] *See* Rao, *supra* note 107; Matthew Nicely, *Time to Eliminate Outdated Non-market Economy Methodologies*, 9 Global Trade & Customs J. 160 (2014).

[112] *See* Brian Gatta, *Between "Automatic Market Economy Status" and "Status Quo": A Commentary on "Interpreting Paragraph 15 of China's Protocol of Accession,"* 9 Global Trade & Customs J. 165 (2014); Bernard O'Connor, *Market Economy Status for China is Not Automatic*, VoxEU.org (Nov. 27, 2011), http://www.voxeu.org/article/china-market-economy.

Most likely, the latter camp will prove to be correct, at least technically. In *EC—Fasteners*, the WTO Appellate Body confirmed that Paragraph 15(a) amounts to a temporary burden-shifting requirement, allowing WTO members to deviate in their treatment of China with respect to the determination of price comparability.[113] After 2016, the burden simply shifts back to the investigating authority, rather than the Chinese producer, to demonstrate that NME conditions prevail.[114] This reading of the Protocol of Accession suggests that other WTO members are not required to automatically grant China market-economy status.

With the burden shifted back to the state, the question still remains whether any WTO member will be able to demonstrate that China indeed remains an NME. The evidentiary bar is quite high. GATT Ad Article VI describes an NME as "a country which has a complete or substantially complete monopoly of its trade and where all domestic prices are fixed by the State."[115] An open question remains as to whether one is to consider the condition of the Chinese economy as a whole or the condition of the particular sector(s)/segment(s) of the Chinese economy.

The wording of the Ad Note would seem to suggest that the condition ought to be assessed broadly. The use of the term "country" suggests that authorities must either find China as a whole to be an NME or not. However, the wording of Paragraph 15(a) of the Protocol of Accession suggested that the analysis is to be done on an industry-specific level. Under Paragraph 15(a), Chinese producers, in order to obtain market-economy status, must demonstrate that their particular industry, and not the country as a whole, operates under market economy conditions. Therefore, some countries may argue that if the expiration is simply a burden-shifting exercise, they too can make NME determinations on an industry-specific level.

If the industry-specific view prevails, then it is possible that certain sectors of the Chinese economy will be deemed to operate under NME conditions. The state continues to dominate industries such as certain raw materials. These might qualify as a sector where the state has a near-monopoly on trade and where prices are fixed by the state. Under this scenario, the particular attributes of China's economic structure become important.

More likely than not, however, the NME analysis will be done on a country-specific level. In that case, given the reforms of the Chinese economy, it is unlikely that an authority would find that China meets the Ad Note's requirements for an NME. After all, China today is no longer the state-dominated command economy that it once was. Nevertheless, even under this scenario, it does not mean that price comparisons will necessarily be done using Chinese prices, as would be the case were China a true market economy.

---

[113] Appellate Body Report, *European Communities—Definitive Anti-dumping Measures on Certain Iron or Steel Fasteners from China* ¶¶ 286–289, WT/DS397/AB/R (July 15, 2011).

[114] *Accord* Jorge Miranda, *Interpreting Paragraph 15 of China's Protocol of Accession*, 9 Global Trade & Customs J. 94, 103 (2014).

[115] GATT, *supra* note 14, ad art. VI, ¶ 1.2.

Even if the NME issue disappears, the unique conditions of China's economic structure remain highly relevant for anti-dumping determinations. This is because WTO members can also apply an alternate methodology for price comparisons in other circumstances besides those of an NME. Article 2.2 of the WTO Anti-dumping Agreement stipulates that an alternate methodology may be deployed when proper price comparisons cannot be made because of the "particular market situation" in the domestic market of the exporting country.[116]

The meaning of this term, "particular market situation," has not been extensively interpreted in WTO law. Therefore, the relevant questions for anti-dumping disputes post-2016 are the following: If China's trading partners find it difficult to declare it to be an outright NME, will they instead resort to Article 2.2 to continue applying an alternate methodology for price comparisons in anti-dumping cases against Chinese goods? If so, on what grounds will they establish that the Chinese economy for that good reflects a "particular market situation" that requires them to abandon the use of Chinese prices? And on what basis, then, will WTO jurists decide whether to accept such explanations?

As discussed in Section II, there are multiple reasons the Chinese economic structure today is unique and not reflective of those found in other market-oriented capitalist systems. But are these differences sufficient to allow China's trading partners to continue to treat Chinese goods differently under anti-dumping rules, even after Paragraph 15(a)(ii) expires in December 2016?

In the years following the 2016 expiration, it appears highly likely that the WTO will be called upon to evaluate this question. China's trading partners may well choose to test whether they can employ the alternate methodologies permitted under Article 2.2. If that turns out to be the case, a trade dispute will surface between China and whichever of her trading partners undertake such an approach. Once more, questions over the Chinese economic structure—and the particular modes of analysis used by foreign authorities to evaluate it—will likely surface in future WTO litigation.

IV. Questions and Implications for the Future

Over time, future jurists will be asked to resolve incrementally the emergent legal issues identified above. These, however, are not the only challenges associated with China's economic structure. Looming on the horizon is a series of broader questions about how the rise of China will influence global trade governance, and vice versa.

---

[116] The alternate methodologies that may be used for price comparisons include the use of "a comparable price of the like product when exported to an appropriate third country, provided that this price is representative," or a constructed normal value approach. *See* ADA Agreement, *supra* note 21, art. 2.2.

A. TO WHAT EXTENT SHOULD WTO LAW TREAT CHINA'S ECONOMIC STRUCTURE AS EXCEPTIONAL?

One overarching question is the extent to which jurists will wish to regard the Chinese economy as "exceptional" versus simply yet another form of state capitalism. As discussed earlier, there are ways in which the Chinese economic structure is similar to other economies in which the state intervenes, but there are also elements that are distinctly Chinese. The question is which of these criteria jurists will choose to emphasize when crafting legal rules.

A wide range of criteria can apply to economies generally, without any indication that they are necessarily targeted at China specifically. For example, on the "public body" issue, considerations over the extent of government ownership, whether the government appoints board seats, and whether the government includes the entity in policy planning are general criteria that can be applied to all economies. These are not China-targeted or China-specific in any way. Similarly, on interpreting whether a "particular market situation" applies, one can also adopt a set of general criteria. For example, one might consider the extent to which the state sets input prices, or the extent of state ownership in any given sector.

The advantage of employing a set of general criteria that do not treat the Chinese economy as exceptional is that it has the potential to keep the law relatively clear and consistent across all WTO members. Moreover, it avoids the appearance of using legal rules to discriminate against particular WTO members. Given China's relative size and status, from the WTO's institutional perspective, this is important. Finally, it allows the WTO to maintain a semblance of neutrality with respect to controversial questions of state ownership and state capitalism. This also furthers its institutional interests to serve as a forum to negotiate and adjudicate trade disputes that arise across these different systems.

Employing general criteria, however, does come with accompanying risks. Other WTO members may balk at applying general criteria that may capture practices that they themselves employ or that are widely used by strategic allies. For example, if price setting and involvement in economic policy planning are among the criteria employed, not only Chinese practices, but also those of many Gulf countries, will be implicated.

In order to avoid such resistance, it is possible that WTO jurists will resort to a set of criteria that embrace a fairly restrictive interpretation of a term. For example, future jurists may establish additional criteria for "public body" that allow most SOEs to escape its grasp. If this is the case, then WTO members may come to view the WTO as a relatively ineffective forum for adjudicating disputes concerning the impact of Chinese practices related to state capitalism on trade.

Given these risks, it is possible that the WTO may decide instead to rely on criteria that does implicitly treat the Chinese economy as exceptional. One such criterion is the embedded nature of the Party within Chinese enterprises, including, but not limited to, SOEs. Authorities may take the presence of Party committees—and the unwillingness of such committees to release minutes of their proceedings or other relevant records—as indicative of signs of enduring government control and authority. Because this feature is unique to the Chinese structure, use of this criterion would not capture other WTO members, but rather serve as a means to address China-specific concerns.

Another is to consider the powers associated with the state itself. This would involve foreign authorities asking various Chinese entities such as central SASAC, local SASACs, Central Huijin, and various government agencies to divulge in greater detail their actions and relationships pertaining to the companies that they oversee. Such an inquiry will likely yield information highlighting how certain practices, such as the appointment of executives through vetting by the Party's Organization Department outside of standard board- or management-driven procedures, diverge from those of other regimes and are indicative of continued government authority. Were authorities to use such practices as the criteria for interpreting open-ended terms, this again could serve as a means for distinguishing China from other WTO members.

However, the WTO must engage in a careful balancing act. It will need to maintain the confidence of China's trading partners that the system will continue to serve as an effective forum for addressing trade disputes arising from China's economic system. Yet, it will not want to appear to discriminate against China, out of fear of antagonizing a country whose continued support will be vital for its long-term institutional interests.

To date, the Appellate Body may have "passed the buck" on some of these difficult legal issues.[117] But they are likely to resurface in the future. How the WTO chooses to further clarify legal rules affecting Chinese state capitalism may well decide whether it can continue to maintain this balance successfully.

B. TO WHAT EXTENT WILL THE WTO INFLUENCE THE FUTURE COURSE OF DEVELOPMENT OF CHINA'S ECONOMIC STRUCTURE?

China's economic structure is not static, but adaptive. Thus, a second question is whether WTO rulings concerning Chinese state capitalism, or the possibility of such rulings, will influence the direction of its future evolution.

The notion that WTO rules might affect the course of China's economic development is not without precedent. To meet its WTO accession requirements, China amended a significant number of its laws and regulations to conform to its treaty obligations.[118] Economic reformers, led by Premier Zhu, utilized the WTO accession process to push

---

[117] This phrasing is borrowed directly from Prusa & Vermulst, *supra* note 96.

[118] *See* Cong. Exec. Comm'n on China, *Is China Playing by the Rules? Free Trade, Fair Trade, and WTO Compliance, Sept. 24, 2003* (Statement of Charles W. Freeman III, Deputy Assistant U.S. Trade Rep.) (noting that in the twenty-one months since China joined the WTO, it "has completed much of the nuts-and-bolts work of WTO implementation [including] amending and promulgating thousands of laws and regulations to effect its WTO commitments").

their agendas. WTO commitments served as a means to lock in desired reforms of China's economic structure.[119]

With Chinese leaders once again touting the need to transform the country's economy, could WTO law again serve to steer the direction of economic reforms? Is it possible that Chinese policymakers will once again shape their economy along certain lines in order to reap certain advantages afforded by WTO law?

For three reasons, the answer is likely to be no. First, a major difference is that whereas the applicable WTO law was relatively clear and straightforward in the 1990s, this is not the case today. During the accession process, much of the law was already fixed in the form of the WTO agreements negotiated during the Uruguay Round. Those elements that were not fixed could be negotiated by China directly, through discussions of the Working Party Report and the Protocol of Accession. This stands in stark contrast with the present situation in which, as noted earlier, elements of applicable law remain unclear, and will be shaped by WTO jurists in the years to come. In this process, China does not have a direct say, but can only seek to influence legal development through arguments made during the course of litigation.

This difference is significant because it adds uncertainty to the equation. Thus, a Chinese leader today is not able to anticipate with the same high degree of confidence that Premier Zhu could in the late 1990s that WTO law will strongly align with his own reform agenda.[120] Without this certainty, at best, a leader might turn to WTO judicial rulings as an ex post justification for pushing forward on a particular issue. However, China's compliance strategy for WTO rulings is often one of what Timothy Webster has termed "paper compliance"—that is to say, compliance in form, but not necessarily in line with the broad spirit of the ruling.[121] Given this tendency, one cannot expect that the Chinese leadership today will turn to WTO law as a means to push forward on a reform agenda.

Second, unlike the earlier episode of the 1990s, the stakes are not large enough to matter for most domestic constituencies. With WTO accession, export producers stood to gain from the reduced tariffs and certainty of receiving MFN status overseas. Hence, they constituted a sizeable natural constituency in favor of pushing forward with reforms in line with WTO law.[122] In contrast, it is not obvious that most producers today have something at stake. Targeting of exporters in anti-dumping and CVD investigations is selective at best. Reforms of Chinese economic structure to advantage China in such

---

[119] *See* BRAHM, *supra* note 51, at 275–76 (highlighting specific elements of the reform agenda that would be facilitated by WTO entry).

[120] *Id.* at 279–80.

[121] Timothy Webster, *Paper Compliance: How China Implements WTO Decisions*, 35 MICH. J. INT'L L. 525 (2014).

[122] *See* BRAHM, *supra* note 51, at 272 (emphasizing the lobbying done to push forward on WTO entry, even following political setbacks in Spring 1999).

trade proceedings do not lead to immediate tangible gain, as they did in the 1990s with WTO accession. Without a natural constituency to support a move to align economic reforms with WTO law, it becomes even more unlikely that WTO law could hope to shape the broad direction of China's economic development. Again, at best, one might expect periodic constituencies to emerge within the context of a particular ongoing WTO or foreign trade remedy litigation proceeding to support reforms of a particular issue area only.

Finally, although the stakes may not be very large for any particular exporter, that is not the case for the Communist Party itself. The economic structure to date has been instrumental in allowing the Party to preserve its hold on power, by delivering on the economic growth agenda while maintaining control over certain key segments of the economy.[123] How Party leaders decide to tweak and reform this structure is critical to the Party's short- and long-term interests.[124] Leaders will be better served justifying any reforms on their own terms, rather than turning to international law as a cover for unpopular moves, especially when the existing state of that law is not yet fully formed.

For these reasons, it is unrealistic to expect that WTO law will be a heavy influence in shaping the overall direction of the future of Chinese state capitalism. At best, it may do so with respect to a particular facet that emerges within the context of a WTO case. But one cannot hope that WTO law will once again serve as the impetus for yet another round of broad-based economic reforms akin to those of the 1990s.

C. HOW WILL CHINA'S ECONOMIC STRUCTURE AFFECT GLOBAL TRADE GOVERNANCE?

Although WTO law may not play a strong role in directly affecting the future of China's economic structure, what about the reverse relationship? To what extent will the rise of Chinese state capitalism impact the future of global trade governance?

For much of the postwar era, the trend has been to absorb greater numbers of states and trade-related issues into the multilateral regime. The Uruguay Round and China's subsequent WTO accession fell squarely within this trend. But with the rise of China's alternative economic structure, this trend is coming to a halt, and may be reversed. In other words, the need to tackle trade-related issues concerning the Chinese economy

---

[123] *See* MINXIN PEI, CHINA'S TRAPPED TRANSITION: THE LIMITS OF DEVELOPMENTAL AUTOCRACY (2008); CARL WALTER & FRASIER HOWIE, RED CAPITALISM: THE FRAGILE FOUNDATION OF CHINA'S EXTRAORDINARY RISE (2011); Panos Mourdoukoutas, *How the Chinese Communist Party Holds Its Grip on the Economy*, FORBES, Nov. 4, 2012, http://www.forbes.com/sites/panosmourdoukoutas/2012/11/04/how-the-chinese-communist-party-holds-its-grip-on-the-economy/.

[124] MICHAEL PETTIS, AVOIDING THE FALL: CHINA'S ECONOMIC RESTRUCTURING (2013); Michael Schuman, *The Chinese Communist Party's Biggest Obstacle Is the Chinese Communist Party*, TIME, Nov. 25, 2013, http://world.time.com/2013/11/25/the-chinese-communist-partys-biggest-obstacle-is-the-chinese-communist-party/.

may contribute to a slow unraveling of the strong multilateral framework governing global trade and its increasing fragmentation.

Although the WTO treaties provide a common body of international law governing cross-border trade, the earlier discussion in Section III highlighted some of the difficulties in applying this body of law to an economic structure not envisioned by its framers. In addition, there are a set of issues that affect trade, but for which the WTO regime does not offer an extensive set of rules. Some examples that have surfaced in recent years concerning China include currency issues,[125] enforcement of its Anti-Monopoly Law,[126] and indigenous innovation policies.[127] Many of these link back to China's economic structure and the unique relationship found among the state, Party, SOEs, and private enterprises.

If the WTO regime is unable to craft new law—through negotiations and/or judicial decisions—to address these issues, then one possibility is for a subset of WTO members to develop these rules separately, outside of the WTO. The regime itself allows for the creation of plurilateral trade agreements that apply to a subset of its members. So long as the countries adhere to the requirements set forth in GATT Article XXIV and/or the Enabling Clause, they are free to develop additional legal rules that apply to members of the subgroup.

One high profile example of such an initiative is the Trans-Pacific Partnership (TPP) being negotiated by twelve WTO members in the Pacific Rim. The United States has openly acknowledged that the TPP is an initiative designed to "reshape the rules for international trade" for the twenty-first century by working with a set of like-minded partners.[128] Left unsaid, however, is the view held by some, including growing numbers

---

[125] *See* Robin Harding & Josh Noble, *US Treasury Slams China on Currency*, FIN. TIMES, Apr. 16, 2014, http://www.ft.com/intl/cms/s/0/fbf79048-c4e8-11e3-9aeb-00144feabdc0.html#axzz3Tkr4paYs. For additional commentary, see, e.g., Bryan Mercurio, *Is China a "Currency Manipulator"? The Legitimacy of China's Exchange Regime under the Current International Legal Framework*, 43 INT'L LAWYER 1257 (2009); Elizabeth Pettis, *Is China's Manipulation of Its Currency an Actionable Violation of the IMF and/or the WTO Agreements?*, 10 J. INT'L BUS. L. 281 (2011); Dukgeun Ahn, *Is the Contemporary Chinese Exchange-Rate Regime "WTO Legal"?*, VOXEU.ORG (Apr. 16, 2010), http://www.voxeu.org/article/chinese-exchange-rate-regime-wto-legal.

[126] *See* U.S. CHAMBER OF COMMERCE, COMPETING INTERESTS IN CHINA'S COMPETITION LAW ENFORCEMENT: CHINA'S ANTI-MONOPOLY LAW APPLICATION AND THE ROLE OF INDUSTRIAL POLICY (2014); Laurie Burkitt, *China's Use of Antimonopoly Law May Violate WTO Pact, U.S. Group Says*, WALL ST. J., Sept. 8, 2014, http://www.wsj.com/articles/chinas-use-of-antimonopoly-law-may-violate-its-wto-commitments-1410166981.

[127] *See* ROBERT ATKINSON, ENOUGH IS ENOUGH: CONFRONTING CHINESE INNOVATION MERCANTILISM (2012); Daniel C.K. Chow, *China's Indigenous Innovation Policies and the World Trade Organization*, 34 NW J. INT'L L. & BUS. 81 (2013).

[128] Press Release, Office of the U.S. Trade Rep., In Pacific Pact, Obama Aims to Shape 21st Century Trade (Mar. 11, 2010), *available at* http://www.ustr.gov/about-us/press-office/blog/2010/march/-pacific-pact-obama-aims-shape-21st-century-trade.

of Chinese academics, that the TPP is a tool employed by the United States and its allies to contain China economically.[129]

Although, as of this writing, the exact details of the TPP agreement are still being negotiated, what is clear is that the twelve parties are seeking to create additional legal rules, some of which are designed to address issues related to China. One example is the inclusion of a chapter on SOEs. Another is a call to include provisions addressing currency manipulation. Whether negotiators will be able to reach agreement on these issues, or decide to omit them from a final TPP agreement, remains to be seen.

Why would trading partners develop rules in a trade agreement designed to address issues involving a country that is not a party to the agreement? One reason is that some partners hope that the TPP and other comprehensive free trade agreements will serve as a basis for a new multilateral agreement.[130] Another is the desire to avoid being blindsided by similar issues in Vietnam, which is a party to the TPP.[131] Finally, some hold out a remote hope that China might one day seek to join the TPP in order to avoid being placed at a competitive disadvantage as compared to its Asian neighbors that stand to benefit from the increased market access afforded by the TPP.[132]

Assuming that the TPP and/or other comprehensive free trade agreements (FTAs) can be successfully concluded, how will it impact the existing WTO regime? The growing proliferation of FTAs is leading to increasing fragmentation of the regime, what some commentators have termed the rise of "mini-lateralism."[133] Rather than

---

[129] *See, e.g.*, Wei Jin Yuan, The Trans-Pacific Partnership and China's Corresponding Strategies (Center for Strategic & Int'l Studies Freeman Briefing, June 2012) at 1–2; Christine Ahn, *Why the Corporate Friendly Trans-Pacific Partnership Is Really about Containing China's Rise*, Foreign Policy in Focus, ALTERNET.ORG, Mar. 14, 2014, http://www.alternet.org/world/trans-pacific-partnership-really-about-containing-chinas-rise?paging=off&current_page=1#bookmark.

[130] *See, e.g.*, Lucian Cernat, *TPP, TTIP and Multilateralism: Stepping Stones or Oceans Apart*, VOXEU.ORG, (Nov. 8, 2013), http://www.voxeu.org/article/bilateral-renaissance-or-multilateralism ("TPP and TTIP may act as powerful stepping stones for further MFN liberalisation under the aegis of the WTO"); Meredith Kolsky-Lewis, *Plurilateral Trade Negotiations: Supplanting or Supplementing the Multilateral Trading System*, ASIL INSIGHTS (July 12. 2013), http://www.asil.org/insights/volume/17/issue/17/plurilateral-trade-negotiations-supplanting-or-supplementing (positing that plurilateral agreements "may also be planting the seeds for future changes and additions to the WTO agreements.").

[131] *See State Capitalism in Vietnam: Blowing in the Trade Winds*, ECONOMIST, Oct. 19, 2013, http://www.economist.com/news/asia/21588143-will-american-led-trade-deal-aid-vietnamese-reformers-blowing-trade-winds; *Vietnam Rejects US Push on State Firms in Trade Talks*, REUTERS, Oct. 28, 2011, http://www.reuters.com/article/2011/10/28/trade-asiapacific-idUSN1E79R1AL20111028 (noting that U.S. proposals are made with an "eye toward future trade talks with China").

[132] *See, e.g.*, Shannon Tiezzi, *Will China Join the Trans-Pacific Partnership?*, THE DIPLOMAT, Oct. 10, 2014, http://thediplomat.com/2014/10/will-china-join-the-trans-pacific-partnership/; *PBOC's Ma Urges Joining TPP to Boost Growth, Report Shows*, BLOOMBERG, June 25, 2014, http://www.bloomberg.com/news/articles/2014-06-24/pboc-s-ma-urges-joining-tpp-to-boost-growth-report-shows.

[133] *See* CHRIS BRIMMER, MINILATERALISM: HOW TRADE ALLIANCES, SOFT LAW, AND FINANCIAL ENGINEERING ARE REDEFINING FINANCIAL STATECRAFT (2014); Moises Naim, *Minilateralism*, FOR. POLICY (June 21, 2009), http://foreignpolicy.com/2009/06/21/minilateralism/.

confronting issues as a group in a multilateral setting, they are tackled in subgroups on an ad hoc basis.

In short, the need to deal with China-specific issues, and the inability to do so via the WTO negotiating process, is causing China's trading partners to look outside of the WTO to reshape rules governing global trade.[134] Having worked so hard to integrate itself into the core of the global trading system, China may find its trading partners attempting to shift the relative terms of the bargain once more.

Unlike the 1980s, however, the Chinese economy is large enough and competitive enough for China to rely solely on WTO commitments and not seek to accept any additional rules. Instead, China will likely turn to its own regional initiatives, such as the Regional Comprehensive Economic Partnership and the "One Belt, One Road" initiative, to push forward a competing regional agreement that addresses its interests.

Thus, although the first decade of China's WTO accession may have been about the global trading system transforming China, the long-term impact may be the opposite. A transformed China with a unique economic structure is now, in turn, transforming the global trading system. With the Doha Round in deadlock, the strong commitment of the advanced economies to a multilateral legal framework since 1945 is now coming to an end. In its place will be a more fragmented global trade regime, anchored by WTO rules, but with additional layers of FTAs that supplement those rules, and additional dispute settlement frameworks outside of the WTO's Dispute Settlement Body.

Conclusion

As China's economy has reformed since the 1990s, its structure has evolved into a form unlike that of any other economy in the world. Although some speak of Chinese state capitalism as a form in which the Communist Party maintains firm control over the "commanding heights" of the economy, I have argued in this chapter that the economy is much more nimble and dynamic, and that therefore, this descriptor is too simplistic. Overall, elements of China's economic structure resemble those found in other countries, but much of it remains distinctly Chinese. In particular, the institutional structures created in the 2003 reforms have allowed China to become a global export

[134] Some believe that the rise of emerging economies such as China threatens the traditional liberal order, anchored by the United States and European Union, that has guided international institutions such as the WTO. They assert that it is futile to engage directly with the rising powers in such fora as a venue to negotiate new rules concerning emergent issues. Instead, they advocate having the United States and European Union utilize plurilateral arrangements to shape the next-generation of trade issues outside of the WTO. *See, e.g.*, Daniel Hamilton, *TTIP's Geostrategic Implications, in* THE GEOPOLITICS OF TTIP vii, xvii (D. Hamilton ed., 2014) (asserting that such a strategy is "less about containing China than about the terms and principles guiding China's integration and participation in the global economy" and that "TTIP, TPP, and related initiatives are important instruments to help frame Beijing's choices").

powerhouse, while at the same time, allowing the Party-state to maintain its grip over the process of economic transformation.

The root of China's trade tensions lies in the fact that this economic structure was not one that was adequately addressed by China's trading partners during the process of negotiating its WTO accession. Thus, WTO rules are not necessarily well-equipped to deal with certain behaviors of Chinese firms and/or government entities vis-à-vis its trading partners. For much of the first decade following China's accession, these problems could be circumvented because of special transition mechanisms that allowed China's trading partners to impose safeguards and other trade remedies against Chinese exports. But as these special transition mechanisms expire, these problems are more likely to come to the fore.

This chapter has attempted to highlight a few of these emerging issues. Others beyond those mentioned here will certainly surface, especially as China's economic structure evolves. What is clear, however, is the fact that the negotiating arm of the WTO is not equipped to deal with these issues.[135] This, in turn, will mean that the judicial branch will be left to react to the China-specific problems brought before it. Lacking full confidence that the WTO Dispute Settlement Body will be up to the task, China's trading partners will likely take advantage of their flexibility under WTO rules to craft new legal rules through FTAs. The end result is likely to be that the multilateral trading system gradually will become more fragmented.

In the end, therefore, it will likely be China that transforms the global trading system, rather than the reverse. The Party-state's desire to preserve its unique political economy is threatening to shatter the liberal postwar project of building a strong multilateral trading regime. In the end, both cannot stand. It may well be trade multilateralism that will be forced to yield to its mini-lateral successor, rather than China's political economy converging on a liberal model. But only time will tell which of these two projects, both crafted in the aftermath of World War II, will prove more enduring.

---

[135] The Doha Round remains stalled, as of this writing. Even if it were not, many of these issues are not within the scope of the Round's negotiating mandate. *See* World Trade Organization, Ministerial Declaration of November 14, 2001, WT/MIN(01)/DEC/1, 41 I.L.M. 746 (2002). To the extent that the negotiating mandate may change, it will be in the direction of further limiting, rather than broadening, negotiating scope. *See* Shawn Donnan, *WTO Chief Attempts to Breathe Life Into Doha Talks*, FIN. TIMES, June 26, 2014, http://www.ft.com/intl/cms/s/0/194c8440-fd2a-11e3-8ca9-00144feab7de.html#axzz3Tkr4paYs.

III Chinese State Capitalism in Comparative Perspective

15 The Hybridization of China's Financial System

Katharina Pistor, Guo Li, and Zhou Chun

Introduction

The most glaring difference between socialism and capitalism is the absence or presence of a credit-based financial system that is intermediated by entities with binding survival constraints.[1] Pooling assets and investing them in projects that will produce returns only in an uncertain future is both capitalism's strength and weakness. It requires risk-taking, but those who dare take risk may profit from a rate of return on their capital investments that will make them richer than the rest.[2] Credit is a critical element in capitalism, because few own sufficient resources to make large bets without resorting to external

[1] Hyman P. Minsky, *The Transition to a Market Economy*, 6 Jerome Levy Economic Institute Working Paper Series No. 66 (1990). In contrast, most observers of the transformation process in the former socialist world emphasized private property as the most critical variable for market-based or capitalist economies. *See, e.g.*, Andrzej Rapaczynski, *The Role of the State and the Market in Establishing Property Rights*, 10 J. of Econ. Persp. 87 (1996); Andrei Shleifer, *Establishing Property Rights, in* World Bank: Proceedings of the Annual Conference of Development Economics 93, 116 (1994); Robert D. Cooter, *Organization as Property: Economic Analysis of Property Law Applied to Privatization, in* The Emergence of Market Economies in Eastern Europe 77, 102 (Christopher Clague & Gordon C. Rausser eds., 1992).

[2] Thomas Picketty, Capital in the 21st Century (2014).

finance. Using credit rather than equity allows investors to make even larger bets, as they are no longer constrained by owning the assets they wish to invest. The downside of this system is that the future may turn out to be different from ex ante expectations. Upon closer scrutiny, these expectations, often based on assumptions, turn out to be closer to hopes than predictions. Investments can turn sour. This is particularly painful when they were financed with debt, because these liabilities are not eliminated when the investment fails.[3] Critical to the capitalist system is the concept that most market participants face their own "survival" or "hard budget constraint," that is that they are private rather than public entities.[4] This implies that when bets go wrong, the participants are, in principle, forced to exit the market. Without the threat of liquidation, firms are much more likely to engage in massive misallocation of resources. The softer the budget constraint, the greater this danger tends to be.

In contrast, socialist systems were historically characterized by a centralized system of resource allocation. The overall objective is plan fulfillment, not the survival of individual entities in a competitive market-based system. Socialist entities thus operate under a soft budget constraint: they benefit from additional resource allocation to ensure plan fulfillment even as this undermines their operational efficiency. Janos Kornai has asserted that the soft budget constraint is the Achilles heel of the socialist system.[5]

A soft budget constraint is, however, not unique to socialism. Not all survival constraints are enforced equally in a capitalist system—whether for political reasons or for fear of contamination and systemic instability. The financial system in particular is frequently protected from the full enforcement of survival constraints, that is, the liquidation of every entity that is unable to balance its assets and liabilities when refinancing opportunities vanish in the middle of a crisis.[6] Protection is accomplished by safety valves of different kinds, such as deposit insurance, reorganization options in bankruptcy, and liquidity provisioning in the form of the central bank discount window, emergency lending, or acquisitions of toxic assets that no longer find private buyers. In the context of the global crisis, these facilities have been greatly expanded by way of ad hoc bank bailouts and the establishment of lending facilities designed to offer liquidity to financial intermediaries throughout the system without the stigma of the discount window—in

---

[3] Exceptions inlude non-recourse loans for houses or, more recently, SPVs whose assets form the only base for satisfying creditor claims.

[4] HYMAN P. MINSKY, STABILIZING AN UNSTABLE ECONOMY (1986); Jonos Kornai et al., *Understanding the Soft Budget Constraint*, 41 J. OF ECON. LITERATURE 1095 (2003); Eric Maskin, *Recent Theoretical Work on the Soft Budget Constraint*, 89 AM. ECON. REV. 421 (1999).

[5] JANOS KORNAI, THE ROAD TO A FREE ECONOMY—SHIFTING FROM A SOCIALIST SYSTEM (1990).

[6] Erik Berglöf & Patrick Bolton, *The Great Divide and Beyond: Financial Market Architecture in Transition*, 16 JOURNAL OF ECON. PERSPECTIVES 77 (2002); Mathias Dewatripont & Gerard Roland, *Soft Budget Constraint, Transition, and Financial Systems*, 156 JOURNAL OF INSTITUTIONAL AND THEORETICAL ECONOMICS 245 (2000).

some cases even irrespective of whether they had access to the discount window at all.[7] A look at the balance sheets of central banks reveals the extent to which entire markets have effectively been socialized as a result of these interventions.[8] Moreover, the difficulties central banks face in tapering "quantitative easing" strategies demonstrate how far the system has departed from the notion of binding survival constraints.

That finance in capitalist systems is vulnerable to the soft budget constraint was noticed long before the global crisis.[9] The fear of contagion and the specter of financial meltdown, accompanied by economic or even political unrest, put ample pressure on any government in a crisis to relax hard budget constraints and suspend the full force of legal devices designed to maintain them. The question therefore is not whether budget constraints are always hard, but whether states can credibly commit to hard budget constraints in principle, even as they stand ready to rescue the financial system from self-destruction in exceptional times. Hyman P. Minsky, who asserted that financial systems are *inherently* unstable, suggested that states should lend freely during a crisis, but should invalidate the practices that led to it post-crisis.[10] A related question is who benefits from the largess of state rescue operations. In principle, it would make sense to target entities that are most likely to pose a serious threat to the survival of the system. This, however, raises the specter that firms will position themselves at the core of the system by becoming too big or too interdependent to fail; in short, it would exacerbate the problem of moral hazard. Balancing moral hazard, that is, the strategic gaming of the system to avoid market discipline, with the need to periodically stabilize an inherently unstable financial system, is the key governance challenge of credit-based finance. The transition from socialism to capitalism has forced countries to learn how to deal with this challenge. The global crisis demonstrated, however, that even mature capitalist systems still have considerable learning to do.

We use the Legal Theory of Finance (LTF)[11] as the analytical framework for analyzing the transformation of China's state-controlled mono-bank system into a hybridized system existing somewhere on the continuum between state and market, public and private. LTF has four key elements. First, financial systems are characterized as rule-bound systems where the scale of financial markets is positively correlated with legally enforceable commitments. Second, in a world beset by uncertainty and liquidity

---

[7] Thomas Cooley et al., *The Power of Central Banks and the Future of the Federal Reserve System, in* REGULATING WALL STREET: THE DODD-FRANK ACT AND THE NEW ARCHITECTURE of GLOBAL FINANCE 51, 71 (Viral V. Acharya et al. eds., 2011).

[8] PERRY MEHRLING, THE NEW LOMBARD STREET: HOW THE FED BECAME THE DEALER OF LAST RESORT (2011).

[9] *See* Cooley et al., *supra* note 7.

[10] *See* MINSKY, *supra* note 4.

[11] Katharina Pistor, *A Legal Theory of Finance*, 41 J. OF COMP. ECON. 315 (2013), tracing the history of LTF since 1978. For an account of China's bank privatization, see also KATHARINA PISTOR, BANKING REFORMS AND BANK BAIL OUTS IN THE CHINESE MIRROR (2010).

volatility, making claims credible by backing them with the full force of law can lead to the self-destruction of the system. The system can be rescued from this outcome only by relaxing the full force of the law, even as this undermines the credibility of legal systems necessary for scaling finance. This is the Law-Finance Paradox. It emphasizes the tension between credible, binding commitment on the one hand, and the manifestation of fundamental uncertainty on the other. The self-destructive effects of this combination can be exacerbated by fraud, herd effects, and the like, but the critical point is that even in the absence of such aberrations, and precisely when the system operates by the rules of the game, it can self-destruct. Third, the relative elasticity of law in the financial system is not random; elasticity tends to be greater at the core of the system than on its periphery. Fourth, because fundamental uncertainty paired with competition and the rigidity of legal systems renders financial systems inherently unstable, their survival depends ultimately on a backstop that can suspend the survival constraint. This backstop must have unlimited recourse to high-powered money, the ultimate soft budget constraint. By definition, it must therefore be a public entity. In what follows, we discuss each of these elements in relation to China's financial development since the mid-1990s.[12]

I. Legal Construction of Finance in China

In a highly simplified fashion the development of finance can be described as evolving from relational to entity-based, and then to market-based finance. Relational finance is based on trust rooted in social norms and relations. Credit is extended to credit-worthy members of society, whose standing and reputation compel them to live up to their commitments. Monitoring by other members and enforcement mechanisms based on shaming and exclusion lends credibility to promises made outside the shadow of coercive law enforcement. In a second stage, entities emerge that specialize in financial intermediation. They accept debt against cash and use deposits and other liabilities to finance lending operations, often long-term lending, even as they face short-term liabilities themselves. This allows them to expand their balance sheets and thus broaden their lending beyond their immediate social network. However, they also face the specter of a bank run in the event that their own liquidity is in doubt. Jointly, these factors make financial intermediaries more dependent on formal law. In a third stage, intermediaries seek to diversify the risk of holding long-term debt while facing short-term claims by adopting pass-through models of financing. They generate loans, repackage them, and sell them to dispersed investors. This model is even more dependent on credible legal commitments than entity-based finance, as investors who buy (fractional) loans from banks have little

[12] *See also* Dan Awrey, *Law and Finance in the Chinese Shadow Banking System*, 48 CORNELL INT'L L.J. (forthcoming 2015), *available at* http://papers.ssrn.com/sol3/papers.cfm?abstract_id=2381171.

incentive to investigate the creditworthiness of the ultimate borrowers. Instead, they rely on the commitments these borrowers made in law and/or the value of the collateral, that is, assets that are legally recognized as property, put up by the borrower.

Along this trajectory from relational, to entity, to market-based finance, China's financial system is best described as entity-based. The development of China's financial system does not neatly fit into the evolutionary model advanced above, as the entities were originally state creatures meant to channel resources to state-owned enterprises. Nonetheless, as a description of the current state of China's finances this statement is largely accurate. In recent years, marketable credit products have made important inroads into the financial system in the form of wealth products. Still, most credits continue to be intermediated by entities. According to statistics published by the Chinese central bank, among the aggregate financing to the real economy of 2013, loans from the banking sector accounted for nearly 60 percent.[13] From another perspective, the total market value of the Chinese stock market is roughly RMB24 trillion, which equals 40 percent of the country's 2013 gross domestic product (GDP).[14] By contrast, the total assets of the banking sector have reached approximately RMB160 trillion, twice the country's 2013 GDP.[15] The shadow banking system has arisen, but its scale is still relatively small compared to the formal banking system, at approximately 40 percent of GDP.[16] A large proportion of total residential savings is kept in the banking sector, which reached RMB46 trillion at the end of 2013, while GDP was RMB57 trillion.[17]China's financial system has been dominated by a large banking system,[18] indeed by relatively few, large financial intermediaries (see Table 15.1 below). The top sixteen banks control over 64 percent of all bank assets. China's "big five"—Industrial and Commercial Bank of China (ICBC), China Construction Bank (CCB), Agricultural Bank of China (ABC), Bank of China (BOC), and Bank of Communications (BoCom)—make up about 47 percent of the total, and the "big four" (the first four) 43 percent (see Table 15.1 below).

---

[13] *See* the PBOC published data of aggregate financing to the real economy. 社会融资规模统计 (Aggregate Financing to the Real Economy), 中国人民银行 (The People's Bank of China), *available at* http://www.pbc.gov.cn/publish/html/kuangjia.htm?id=2013s18.htm.

[14] *Statistics of Stock Market*, The People's Bank of China (Sept. 24, 2014), *available at* http://www.pbc.gov.cn/publish/html/kuangjia.htm?id=2014s10.htm.

[15] 中国银行业监督管理委员会 2013 年报 (2013 Annual Report of China's Banking Regulatory Commission), 中国银行业监督管理委员会 (China Banking Regulatory Commission) (Sept. 25, 2014), http://www.cbrc.gov.cn/chinese/home/docView/3C28C92AC84242D188E2064D9098CFD2.html.

[16] *See* Institute of Finance of Chinese Academy of Social Science, Annual Report on Financial Regulation of 2014 (Hu Bin ed., 2014).

[17] *2013 Statistics of Financial Sector*, People's Bank of China (Sept. 25, 2014), http://www.pbc.gov.cn/publish/diaochatongjisi/3172/2014/20140115094127727196947/20140115094127727196947_.htm.

[18] Franklin Allen et al., *China's Financial System: Opportunities and Challenges* (Nat'l Bureau of Econ. Research, Working Paper No. 17828, 2012).

TABLE 15.1
SIZE AND INDUSTRY SHARES OF MAJOR BANKS IN THE DOMESTIC MARKET [2012-12-31]

Banks	Total Assets (RMB Millions)	Industry Share (Percent)
ICBC	17,542,217	13.1
CCB	13,972,828	10.5
ABC	13,244,342	9.9
BOC	12,680,615	9.5
BoCom	5,201,943	3.9
Merchants Bank	3,408,219	2.6
Industrial Bank	3,250,975	2.4
Min Sheng Bank	3,212,001	2.4
Pudong Development Bank	3,145,707	2.4
CITIC Bank	2,959,939	2.2
Everbright Bank	2,279,295	1.7
Ping An Bank	1,606,537	1.2
Hua Xia Bank	1,488,860	1.1
Bank of Beijing	1,117,644	0.8
Bank of Ningbo	373,536	0.3
Bank of Nanjing	339,608	0.3
Total	133,624,400	64.2

Source: Data from the 2013 annual reports of the sixteen banks listed in the Hong Kong, Shanghai, and Shenzhen stock exchanges.

The legal construction of finance—LTF's first building blocks—refers to the fact that all financial instruments are IOUs: they are contractual commitments for payment at a future date that can be backed by collateral, that is, property rights, pooled in entities to secure other claims, and traded on secondary markets. In short, contracts, property rights, and organizational law, including bankruptcy, are the foundations of a legally constructed financial system. In addition, most countries have introduced regulation to address problems that arose in the evolution of financial systems. We refer to this as the "regulatory scaffolding." Here again, China poses an interesting example, as contract, property, and organizational law coevolved with, rather than preceded the development of, regulatory law. Indeed, ownership stakes served important regulatory functions, as they gave key agencies at the center of state administration direct control over the financial sector. Importantly, control through ownership was complemented with human resource control.

The Chinese banking system is regulated jointly by the central bank, namely the People's Bank of China (PBOC), and the Banking Regulatory Commission (CBRC). Most banks continue to be majority owned by the state. State ownership, however, no longer means monolithic control at the center of the system or necessarily centralized resource allocation (at least not outside crises). In contrast to the non-financial sector, where ownership interests in different entities have been consolidated in the hands of the State-owned Assets Supervision and Administration Commission (SASAC),[19] in finance state control is relatively more decentralized. Figure 15.1 illustrates the hybrid ownership structure of sixteen listed banks in China. As can be seen, more than one state entity typically holds shares in the major banks. The Ministry of Finance (MOF) was once one of the major banking regulators, and still holds stakes in two of the largest banks (ICBC and ABC) alongside Huijin. Huijin is an investment company specially established for holding state-owned financial enterprises, now wholly owned by China Investment Corporation (CIC), the sovereign wealth fund founded in 2007. In other banks Huijin shares ownership with other state-controlled entities. For instance, Aluminum Corporation of China, China Shenhua Group, and China Southern Power Grid Company each owns less than 0.05 percent of the shares of BOC. State Grid Corporation of China and Shanghai Baosteel Group own 1.14 percent and 0.93 percent shares of CCB respectively. All firms mentioned are state-owned enterprises (SOEs). Moreover, some banks have attracted foreign investors, among them primarily major international banks and foreign sovereign wealth funds. A few of these foreign investors, however, chose to divest after receiving a high premium for their shares since the global financial crisis.[20]

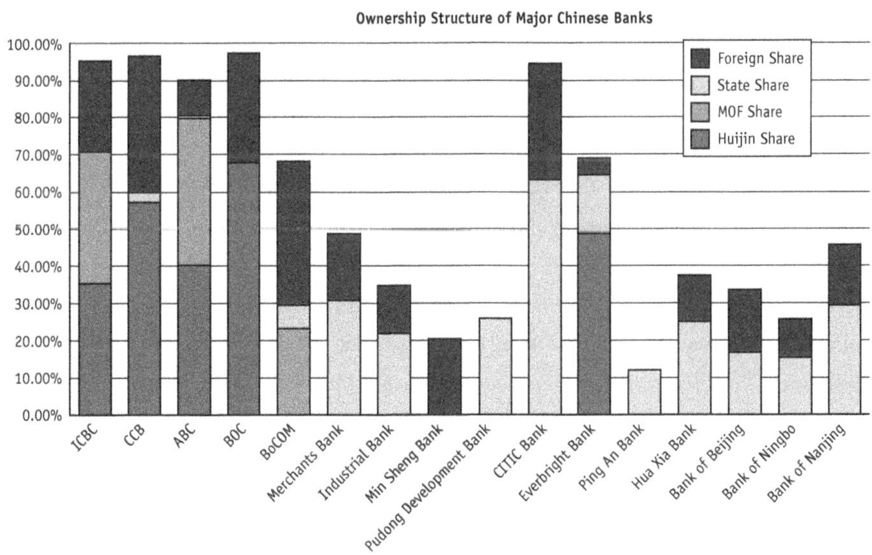

FIGURE 15.1 Ownership Structure of Major Chinese Banks [2012-12-31].

Source: Data from the 2013 annual reports of the sixteen banks listed in Hong Kong, Shanghai, and Shenzhen stock exchanges.

---

[19] For a detailed account of patterns of state ownership in the non-financial sector, see Li-Wen Lin & Curtis J. Milhaupt, *We Are the (National) Champions: Understanding the Mechanisms of State Capitalism in China*, 5 STAN. L. REV. 697, 704–21 (2013).

[20] For example, Goldman Sachs exited from ICBC, China's largest bank, in May 2013. Goldman Sachs bought a 4.9 percent stake in ICBC for US$2.58 billion in April 2006 before the bank's initial public offering in

TABLE 15.2
SEPARATION OF OWNERSHIP AND CONTROL OF BOCOM (2012-12-31)

Five Largest Shareholders		
Name of the Shareholder	Stake	Nature of the Shareholders
MOF	26.37%	State
HK SCC Nominees Limited (Investors in Hong Kong Market)	20.06%	Private
HSBC	18.07%	Private
National Council of Social Security Fund	4.42%	State
Capital Airports Holding Company	1.68%	State

Data collected from the annual report of BoCOM of 2013, available at http://www.bankcomm.com/BankCommSite/cn/invest_relation_index.jsp.

Looking at China from a Western perspective, one would assume that share ownership is correlated with control. The reason is that corporate law in China and elsewhere ascribes to shareholders the right to vote on key issues and to elect top management directly or indirectly. In China's financial system, however, share ownership is sometimes secondary to human resource management, that is, the centralized process of promoting and nominating candidates to key financial positions at regulatory agencies, the top banks, and other intermediaries, by the Communist Party Organizational Committee.[21] The Committee also controls the career paths of individuals in the Party, the administration, and government-controlled sectors.[22] Although the ownership of some banks is shared by the state, foreign investors, and the private-sector control over personnel remains in the hands of the state. Taking BoCom, the country's fifth largest bank as an illustration, the hybrid ownership structure of BoCom is shown below in Table 15.2, but only the Communist Party Organizational Committee has the power to appoint its top executives, including chairman, vice-chairmen, president, and vice presidents.

A typical career pattern takes an official from service at the PBOC, China's central bank, the MOF, or CBRC, to state-controlled intermediaries that control financial entities, such as Huijin or CIC, and finally to the boards of these entities. Many individuals have been posted sequentially at different entities; they have moved between commercial banks and other financial institutions, back to SOEs, and even back to regulators that are part of government. To illustrate, consider the career path of Wang Qishan,

---

Hong Kong. The share sales were said to be made in order to satisfy the new capital rules after the 2007–2009 financial crisis, and Goldman Sachs earned about US$10 billion from the sale.

[21] Katharina Pistor, *Governing China's Finance, in* CAPITALIZING CHINA 35, 60 (Randall K. Morck & Henry Wai-chung Yeung eds., 2011).

[22] *Id.*

the Chairman of one of the top four banks (CCB) from 1994 to 1997. Wang is a current member of the Standing Committee of the Political Bureau—which is part of the CPC Central Committee, the body that continues to hold the reins over the country. Indeed, the chief executives of the "big four" have a well-established history of serving as top government officials, and vice versa. Another example is Shang Fulin, the current Chairman of CBRC, who was president of ABC from 2000 to 2002, and was with PBOC from 1994 to 2000. Likewise, Guo Shuqing, the current governor of Shandong Province and the former Chairman of CSRC, also once served as the deputy governor of the PBOC and subsequently headed the CCB from 2005 to 2011.

The fact that human resource management is widely used as a governance mechanism in China, and at times trumps formal ownership relations, does not mean that China's financial system is not rule-bound. China has been governed for most of its history by closely monitoring and controlling officials through its vast empire.[23] Indeed, the described career and promotion patterns in finance suggest that the path through the system is well laid out and, as such, capable of creating a "self-sustaining system of shared beliefs."[24] This, of course, is just another way of defining institutions as the "rules of the game."[25] In short, China's financial system today is a rule-bound system, even though formal legal rules promulgated by the state apparatus do not always prevail. They must be seen in the context of the parallel system of the Chinese Communist Party apparatus, which manages largely via human resource management.

Formal law, including ownership stakes and human resource management, can contribute to regularized patterns of behavior. We are primarily interested in the ability of this governance regime to impose financial discipline—that is, to move from a system characterized by a soft-budget constraint to one that adheres largely to a hard-budget constraint. We use the relative firmness of banks' budget constraints as a proxy for overall rule compliance in the system—whether through rules governing property rights or through human resources. The harder the budget constraint, that is, the greater the probability that firms will be forced to exit from the system if they fail to balance their assets and liabilities, the more rule-bound the system, and vice versa.

China's state-owned banks have a long history of non-performing loans, an indicator of their inability to lend on economic terms and/or enforce their loans.[26] Still, compared to the 1990s, budget constraints have been hardened substantially—at least until the global financial crisis. In the 1990s most banks were saddled with non-performing loans that rendered them technically insolvent. Liquidating the major financial intermediaries

---

[23] *See* YASHENG HUANG, INFLATION AND INVESTMENT CONTROLS IN CHINA (1996).

[24] MASAHIKO AOKI, TOWARD a COMPARATIVE INSTITUTIONAL ANALYSIS 10 (2001).

[25] DOUGLASS C. NORTH, INSTITUTIONS, INSTITUTIONAL CHANGE, AND ECONOMIC PERFORMANCE 4 (1990).

[26] NICHOLAS LARDY, INTEGRATING CHINA INTO THE GLOBAL ECONOMY (2002); DICK NANTO & RADHA SINHA, *China's Banking Reform*, 14 POST-COMMUNIST ECONOMIES 469 (2002).

in a highly concentrated financial system was not a viable policy option. This left two alternatives: opening the system to competitors and allowing them to compete with the state-owned banks—a policy China pursued quite effectively in sectors outside finance—or, restructuring existing state-owned banks and hardening their budget constraints over time. For the most part, China has opted for the second strategy. "Growing out of the plan"[27] may have been deemed too risky in the financial sector—an assessment that was confirmed by the experience of the 1997–1998 East Asian financial crisis that wrought havoc in neighboring countries that had pursued a strategy of privatizing and rapidly liberalizing their financial sectors in the preceding decade.

Meanwhile, Chinese banks have followed the lead of Western banks and greatly expanded credit through financial innovation. This rise of China's shadow banking system—estimated to have reached between US$2.2 and 4.8 trillion[28] in 2013—would not have been feasible without constructing new financial instruments while arbitraging around existing regulatory constraints. In short, the banks have created their own shadow banking system.[29] As Dan Awrey suggests:

> . . . , one would be hard pressed to make sense of the legal structure of Wealth Management Products (WMPs) without reference to the regulatory regime governing Chinese banks. The use of legally separate fund pools, for example, appears principally motivated by the desire to ensure both that: (1) the relevant liabilities are not characterized as deposits subject to the PBOC's ceiling on deposit rates and (2) the assets in which WMPs invest are not consolidated on bank balance sheets or subject to the PBOC's credit quotas.[30]

In sum, China's financial system does not operate outside rules, but neither does it strictly follow formal legal rules. Financial stability is the overarching goal, with formal rules and human resource management deployed in its pursuit. This inevitably leads to compromises with regards to the binding nature of legal rules and, not coincidentally, the hardness of financial intermediaries' budget constraints.

II. Banking Reforms and the Hard Budget Constraint

China implemented bank restructuring in several stages. First, the big banks that had been carved out from the mono-banking system were relieved of their policy functions—lending to companies and sectors that were deemed weak and in need of

---

[27] Barry Naughton, Growing Out of the Plan (1996).

[28] *See* Awrey, *supra* note 12.

[29] *Id.*

[30] *Id.* at 36.

continuous state support. These tasks were shifted to designated policy banks, including China Development Bank, Export-Import Bank of China, and the Agricultural Development Bank of China. Meanwhile, the newly formed commercial banks were informed that they could no longer rely on constant backstopping by the state; instead, they were to become financially responsible and lend only to borrowers they deemed creditworthy. In short, the government sought to signal the hardening of the budget constraint without privatizing the institutions or otherwise severing the umbilical cord to the state. These measures turned out to be insufficient. By 2003, the big four banks still had 35 percent non-performing loans (NPLs) on their books. This can be attributed largely to a relapse after an initial tightening when NPLs dropped to 10 percent. Many observers suspect that new bad loans were accumulated between 1999 and 2003, although precise numbers are difficult to come by—not the least because the classification and calculation method was changed around 2004. This created substantial uncertainties as to what percentage of the bad loans was a legacy of the past or was newly accrued. Nonetheless, this episode demonstrates that weaning banks off state subsidies proved challenging. Even when bank managers tried to improve internal risk management they may well have responded to overriding policy concerns about financial stability. A system that responds to the first signs of stress by relaxing the banks' budget constraint can hardly be described as one that embraces a hard budget constraint in principle. In that sense, China's reform path has not been unidirectional, but has run in circles at times.

As the second step in the restructuring process, the major banks' NPLs were removed from their balance sheets and transferred to specially created Asset Management Companies (AMCs), which were tasked with disposing of the NPLs over time. All four AMCs, Cinda, Huarong, Great Wall, and Oriental, were established in 1999 to assume NPLs from the "big four," respectively totaling RMB1.4 trillion. In return, the "big four" received AMC bonds, supported by MOF's explicit guarantees as consideration, which dramatically improved their balance sheets.[31] At the time of their establishment, the four AMCs were owned by the MOF. They were tasked with managing the NPLs that had been transferred to them from the major state-owned banks. Significantly, their mandate did not include a fixed expiration date, suggesting that they too operated under a flexible regime. Nonetheless, the first AMCs have recently been publicly listed—as demonstrated by Cinda's successful public offering in Hong Kong at the end of 2013, which raised US$2.5 billion. Whether this can be attributed to their improved performance, or, as in the case of the government-sponsored entities in the United States, to the implicit government guarantee, is not entirely clear.

[31] 建行所持信达资产管理公司债券延期 (Extension on Cinda AMC's Bonds Held by CCB), 财经 (Caijing) (Sept. 21, 2011), http://www.caijing.com.cn/2009-09-21/110257022.html (last visited June 9, 2014).

As with other transition economies,[32] China has gone through several waves of recapitalizing banks. This first took the form of swapping bank reserves with the central bank into capital injected onto the banks' balance sheet. The PBOC lent a helping hand by lowering the reserve ratio of the big four from 13 to 8 percent, returning the difference to the banks, which then used the amount (RMB270 billion) to purchase treasury bonds issued by MOF. MOF in turn used the cash receipts from the bond offering as new capital on the balance sheet of the banks. This example illustrates how modern techniques of capitalizing firms developed in a capitalist system were employed to remake China's financial system. In contrast to old-fashioned state control, these techniques are rooted in legal devices that are highly malleable in the hands of private or public actors.

Nonetheless, the described capital infusion covered only a small fraction of the non-performing loans, which amounted to US$3.3 trillion. A larger-scale recapitalization, the second wave of banking reform, was implemented in 2003–2004, when US$45 billion capital was injected through the newly established Central Huijin Investment Ltd. (Huijin), to improve the balance sheets of the "big four." The State Council established Huijin in 2003 to "conduct equity investments in major state-owned financial enterprises, and ... exercise the rights and perform the obligations as an investor on behalf of the State in accordance with applicable laws."[33] This recapitalization took the form of MOF issuing new government bonds and using the proceeds to acquire U.S. dollars from the state's foreign-exchange reserve, which were then placed on the banks' balance sheets. This capital injection was meant to put the largest banks in China on a sound footing and enable them to take on new, reasonable risks without endangering their survival.

The third wave was to incorporate the banks and diversify their investor base. The Chinese government sold significant, though not controlling, stakes in the major financial intermediaries in 2005 and 2006 to new investors, including foreign investors.[34] This not only attracted additional capital, it also provided these intermediaries with expertise in banking and financial intermediation. For instance, the dual initial public offerings (IPO) of ICBC on the Hong Kong Stock Exchange and Shanghai Stock Exchange raised US$22 billion and were the world's largest IPO to that point by market capitalization. Before the IPO, ICBC sold a 10 percent stake to a group of investors, including Goldman Sachs, American Express, and Allianz. Partial privatization went hand in hand with listing banks on major stock exchanges in mainland China and Hong Kong.

---

[32] Jacek Rostowski, Banking Reform in Central Europe and the Former Soviet Union (1995).

[33] See the introduction of the company on the official website of Huijin, 中央汇金投资有限责任公司 (Central Huijin Investment Ltd.), http://www.huijin-inv.cn/ (last visited July 20, 2014).

[34] Lamin Leigh & Richard Podpiera, *The Rise of Foreign Investment in China's Banks— ... Taking Stock*, 2006 IMF Working Paper (2006); *see also* Katharina Pistor, Banking Reforms and Bank Bail Outs in the Chinese Mirror (2010), *available at* http://papers.ssrn.com/sol3/papers.cfm?abstract_id=1446930.

The ultimate success of restructuring hinges on the effective hardening of the banks' budget constraints—vis-à-vis the state and vis-à-vis their own borrowers. With regards to bank-state relations, it may still be too early to declare victory. New structures have been put in place and funds are not simply reallocated at will; rather, complex processes of recapitalization and restructuring give the appearance of a system that operates within a set of predetermined rules that allow for some flexibility, but not unbound fiat. Yet, by using banks to stabilize the economy, the government may have inadvertently contributed to another potential source of instability—"too big to fail" dynamics. Moreover, the central government has never explicitly confirmed that the above-mentioned restructurings were one-time measures. State-owned banks and their creditors may therefore be under the impression that the government will again come to their rescue in the future. In fact, data shows that the average NPL ratio of the "big five" is once more on the rise in 2014, having increased to 1.30 percent, which was deemed a warning sign.[35] Given the size of non-performing assets on Western central bank balance sheets, this fact should not be blamed on a system that has not been able to free itself entirely from its socialist legacy. However, it does suggest that high levels of financial volatility are not conducive to weaning banks off state support and implementing policies that set them on the path to a hardening of the budget constraint.

China's banking reforms continue in the global context. In 2007, at a time when the major banks were just beginning to operate as publicly listed entities with fairly substantial foreign ownership, the global financial system began to unravel. In July 2007, the small German bank IKB was the first financial intermediary in the West to require a bailout, followed by BNP Parisbas in France, and then the "run on the rock," Northern Rock in the UK. At the time, China's financial system was still fairly isolated from the global financial system, as capital and currency controls remained firmly in place. The expectation that foreign investors would instill discipline in Chinese banks certainly proved to be mistaken, as these very banks went hat in hand first to foreign sovereign wealth funds—including, but not limited to China's CIC—and ultimately to their home governments to recapitalize themselves. Indeed, as the crisis continued, Western banks sold their stakes in Chinese banks as soon as lock-in periods expired, thereby contributing to the latter's instability.[36] The Chinese system proved fairly resilient during the crisis; only its secondary effects threatened China's overall performance as capital and trade flows declined. China's policymakers and regulators did not stand by passively as the crisis unfolded. But they did not re-nationalize the banks or revert to direct state control. Instead, they pursued a mixture of strategies meant to release pressure from the system while appearing to operate within the rules they had only just begun to enforce.

---

[35] *See the* 2014 annual reports of ICBC, CCB, BOC, ABC, and BoCom.

[36] Katharina Pistor, *Global Network Finance*, 37 J. OF COMP. ECON. 552 (2009).

III. China's Escape from the Law-Finance Paradox

The Law-Finance Paradox (LFP) states that if all legal commitments and rules are enforced ex post as written ex ante, irrespective of fundamental change, a financial system can find itself on autopilot to self-destruction. This outcome results from the potentially toxic mix of rigid legal commitments with fundamental uncertainty. To avoid this outcome, legal rules are often suspended or relaxed in times of crisis and liquidity, or fresh capital injections are provided even where none are required by law. As demonstrated by the series of recapitalizations and bailouts during the period of 1998–2006, the strong presence of state-controlled entities that can negotiate for new top-down-provided capital, and the premium placed on stability, have so far mitigated the risk of endogenous self-destruction. Yet, as the LFP predicts, the willingness to relax or suspend the full force of the law undermines the credibility of legal commitments, and thus the very foundation of large-scale, market-based financial systems. Where the credibility of law and effective law enforcement is in doubt, the scale of markets will be limited.

The post-crisis experience, both in China and in the West, reveals that trust in the prowess of central banks has replaced confidence in legal commitments. For instance, the total assets on the balance sheet of PBOC has ballooned, reaching approximately RMB30 trillion at the end of 2012.[37] A good indication of the "socialization of markets" in the wake of the global crisis—not only in China but also in the West—is the market reaction to any signal that central bank or state support will be withdrawn. Witness the calming effect the European Central Bank's announcement of "outright monetary transactions" had on European sovereign debt markets, or, conversely, the hiccup in global financial markets when the U.S. Federal Reserve chairman, Ben Bernanke, in May 2013 announced that the Fed would taper quantitative easing. In China the backstopping mechanisms have been more diverse and as such less reliant on the central bank alone. This can be explained by the strong presence of state intermediation within the system. This allowed China's central bank to extend emergency lending throughout the economy and advise the largest banks to expand credits in the midst of the global crisis. In the credit crunch of 2013, the PBOC changed its approach from using open market instruments to providing liquidity to a few major state-owned banks. These banks then released liquidity through the interbank market to smaller banks, including joint-stock banks, city banks, and other financial institutions. The ICBC, CCB, and ABC were reported to have lent nearly RMB2 trillion to other banks as a "market stabilizer" in late June of 2013.[38]

---

[37] 货币当局资产负债表 (Balance Sheet of Monetary Authority), 中国人民银行 (People's Bank of China), http://www.pbc.gov.cn/publish/html/kuangjia.htm?id=2012s04.htm.

[38] *See* 工行农行建行借6月钱荒获利 120 亿元 (ICBC, CCB and ABC Earned 12 Billion during the Credit Crunch), 北京青年报 (Beijing Youth) (Aug. 30, 2013), *available at* http://finance.qq.com/a/20130830/004530.htm, (last visited May. 25, 2015). Supporting evidence can be found from 2013 semiannual reports of ICBC, CCB, and ABC.

The system's strong presence of state intermediation also offered expedient recapitalization strategies for smaller banks that found themselves on the brink of collapse, such as Everbright, CITIC (which incidentally had entered into a joint venture with Bear Stearns before that bank's demise) and Guangfa. Both Everbright Bank and CITIC Bank are controlled by central SOEs, while Guangfa is one of the earliest provincial banks, and controlled by the government of Guangdong. None of these banks posed a serious threat to the survival of the system, but they were rescued nonetheless. Everbright Bank was bailed out directly by Huijin, along with the "big five" and the DBC. CITIC survived through subordinated bonds issuance and recapitalization by its parent company, the central SOE CITIC Group. Guangfa Bank sold its NPLs to a local government-owned investment company, and a group of investors led by Citigroup acquired its newly issued shares. These transactions confirm that entity-based finance offers a range of buffers or safety valves in times of crisis. The flip side is that intermediaries face few incentives to manage their own risks effectively. Of course, China's system of human resource management offers, at least in theory, another sanctioning mechanism: criminal punishment or demotion of cadres who lead their banks into trouble. However, there is little evidence that this mechanism was employed in the recent crisis.

Indeed, human resource management as a means of maintaining financial stability is likely to be less effective as the system evolves from an entity-based to a market-driven one. When liquidity in asset markets dries up or markets collapse, identifying culprits is more difficult than when entities fail. In recent times, China has experienced several episodes of liquidity contraction in interbank loan markets. On June 5, 2013, for example, Everbright, which had benefited from an earlier state-engineered bailout in 2007, defaulted on a RMB6.5 billion interbank loan. The default unsurprisingly dampened confidence in the liquidity of the interbank market. PBOC first tried to hold its ground and refused to intervene, presumably in an attempt to reassert rule-bound finance; reportedly it even withdrew its previous plan of releasing liquidity through short-term liquidity operations.[39] Continuing market uncertainty, however, prompted Huijin, the state entity controlled by CIC and a major shareholder in Everbright, to intervene and acquire 24.11 million shares (in addition to the stake it already held) in the company on June 13. Huijin also increased its holdings in the "big four" on the same day. These actions still did not calm markets. Interbank lending rates shot up to 28 percent at one point on June 20, and ended at 13.4 percent, with the one-week lending rate at 11 percent. By contrast, the overnight lending rate was 3.28 percent, with the one-week lending rate at 3.42 percent on June 20, 2012. After the Shanghai Stock Market Index dropped by 5.3 percent, indicating that uncertainties in lending markets were drying up liquidity,

---

[39] Shi Jinfeng 史进峰,银行间债市再现违约黑天鹅央行勒紧缰绳打击套利 (Breach of Interbanking Contract in Bond Market Causes a Black Swan Event, PBOC Tighten Regulation to Combat Arbitrage), 21 新浪网 (Sina.com) (June 8, 2013), *available at* http://finance.sina.com.cn/money/bank/bank_hydt/20130608/100415746995.shtml (last visited May 26, 2015).

the PBOC finally announced additional cash injections. This intervention took place on June 25; it resulted in the appreciation of the overnight lending rate to 5.73 percent and the weekly rate to 7.64 percent. In a subsequent episode, in December 2013, the PBOC did not wait for the credit crunch to affect stock markets, but used short-term liquidity operations to inject RMB300 billion into the markets.

These episodes suggest that with the turn to more decentralized, market-based finance, China is increasingly exposed to the Law-Finance Paradox, that is, to legally induced financial instability. So far, it appears that it is ready to add liquidity and relax the rules of the game whenever there are the slightest signs of greater market disturbances. In fact, central bank policies in China are not only reactive but proactive, seeking to directly influence economic structure and development processes. Recently the PBOC has used monetary tools to release liquidity into specific economic areas, for instance lowering the interest rate for loans to small and rural businesses as well as reducing the statutory reserve rate for institutions that hold a significant share of such loans. Still, in broader comparative perspective, China's reactions do not appear to be out of the ordinary. In the aftermath of the bankruptcy of Lehman Brothers in the United States, the Federal Reserve created six major liquidity facilities, known by their acronyms: TSLF (Term Securities Lending Facility), PDCF (Primary Dealer Credit Facility), AMLF (Asset-Backed Commercial Paper Money Market Mutual Fund Liquidity Facility), CPFF (Commercial Paper Funding Facility), MMIFF (Money Market Investor Funding Facility), and TALF (Term Asset-Backed Securities Loan Facility).[40] None of the facilities had been explicitly anticipated in law; nor had the Fed ever pursued such targeted policy intervention sector by sector. This interventionist stand can be explained only by the fact that few governments (at least, among those that could afford it) were willing to risk another failure by a major bank, and few central banks had the nerve to stand idle when markets tumbled, if they had means at their disposal to mitigate if not prevent such an outcome. The joint effect of these interventions is that central banks—in China, the United States, and elsewhere—are insuring market participants against excessive volatility and losses. By softening budget constraints in de-centralized market relations central banks are endorsing soft-budget constraints, if not effectively socializing markets.

IV. Elasticity of Law and the Hierarchy of Finance

Whenever financial systems are in crisis and intervention becomes necessary, the question is who should benefit from stabilization measures. LTF predicts that the full force of the law is more likely to be suspended where the system's very survival is at

[40] Office of Inspector General, The Federal Reserve's Section 13(3) Lending Facilities to Support Overall Market Liquidity: Function, Status, and Risk Management, Nov. 16, 2010; *see supra* note 11, at 319.

stake—that is at the apex of the system, not on its periphery. Testing this prediction is difficult, though, because concerns other than stabilizing the system may motivate decision-makers. Identifying the entities that were bailed out is therefore not a reliable indicator of their position within the hierarchy of finance prior to the crisis. Further, in the midst of a crisis assessments are clouded by the urgency of action and perceptions; intuitions rather than objective analysis tend to guide policymakers. Finally, the decision-makers themselves are often self-appointed rescuers who lack specific designation or authorization to take extraordinary actions. As such, their actions may not be representative of true social-welfare concerns.

To take two examples from the West: the U.S. Fed's extraordinary lending authorities allowed it to lend in an emergency against "adequate collateral."[41] How this provision should be interpreted was ultimately left in the hands of the Fed itself. As noted above, the Fed used it not only to lend to specific entities, but also to create a whole series of liquidity facilities for different market segments. This was unprecedented, and though not necessarily in direct contravention of the law, based on a rather expansive interpretation. Similarly, the European Central Bank's outright monetary transaction program, announced in July 2012, has no firm legal basis in treaty law or the statute of the bank. Indeed, the legality of these actions has been challenged in the German constitutional court, as the Maastricht treaty explicitly prohibits the monetization of fiscal debt. Although it prohibits the ECB only from purchasing sovereign debt on primary markets, unlimited purchases on secondary markets can arguably have similar effects. Indeed, the German court indicated that a treaty violation had likely occurred, but ultimately referred the matter to the European Court of Justice.[42]

Even without specific designation of a rescuer of last resort, in most developed market economies it is highly predictable who will act in the midst of a crisis—the legislature. The legislature acts in order to back emergency intervention proposed by the government or the central bank as the de facto, if not de jure, lender of last resort. This is not surprising, because in a system based on commitments to formal legal rules, extralegal measures will be left to the entities that have the power to renegotiate the rules of the game: governments, as the head of the executive with the de facto or de jure power to propose legislation, and central banks, as the entities with unlimited recourse to high-powered money.

In China's financial system, where direct state or party participation in firms—in the form of equity and control over top management or board membership—is the norm rather than the exception, and state control is pervasive throughout the system, it is more likely that interventions occur farther down in the hierarchy. Theoretically this should have two effects: first, it should help stabilize the system before a full-blown crisis

---

[41] Federal Reserve Act Sec. 13(3).

[42] Carsten Gerner-Beuerle et al., *Law Meets Economics in the German Federal Constitutional Court: Outright Monetary Transactions on Trial*, 15 German Law J. 281 (2014).

evolves; second, and simultaneously it raises moral hazard concerns throughout the system. To illustrate, consider the case of Hailong, a firm based in Shandong province, whose credit rating nosedived from A (Sept. 2011) to CCC (Feb. 2012) on the corporate bond market, as news spread that it had engaged in fraudulent activities and was under investigation—particularly after it announced a RMB1.02 billon loss and possible default on its bonds.[43] Eventually the company received short-term funding provided by local banks and a guarantee from the local government, so that the corporate bonds were fully repaid two months after the company's credit rating was lowered to CCC.[44] If market participants expect state aid to be forthcoming—the discipline that comes with a (relatively) hard-budget constraint will never be achieved. If state-owned entities that own shares in financial intermediaries are known for taking responsibility for them, this will cast an even longer shadow of state insurance throughout the system. Huijin is the most prominent example of indirect state insurance provided by corporate entities that mediate between state control and financial intermediaries that supposedly act in accordance with market principles. As discussed previously, Huijin was originally controlled by MOF but was transferred into CIC ownership in 2009. Table 15.3 below reports Huijin's interventions between 2003 and 2012 by financial intermediary. All told, Huijin has invested RMB894.08 billion—or US$139.65 billion at current exchange rates—over the course of nine years.

There are both pros and cons to this early intervention scheme to stabilize the financial system. On the positive side, early intervention may lower the overall cost of rescue actions. Typically, entities on the periphery of the system are the first ones to feel stress when liquidity dries up and default spreads. They quickly lose access to refinancing options, as they are perceived to be of higher risk due to information asymmetries; they also tend to be more vulnerable to collapse than larger entities with bigger balance sheets and a higher number of built-in buffers. The more entities fail, even if they are small, the greater the pressure that builds at the apex of the system, where larger intermediaries have to deal with the fallout from greater demands for refinancing, which dries up as defaults (or the mere specter of defaults) spread. The normal pattern of financial crisis is that stress spreads from the periphery to the apex. Only if it reaches alarming levels at the apex will governments or central banks intervene. At that stage, however, huge sums are necessary to rescue a system that appears to be too-big- or too-interconnected-to-fail.

Early interventions can stop this cascade midway. However, they also undermine financial discipline as more and more entities come to rely on the helping hand of the

[43] The relevant data can be found on the website of China Lianhe Credit Rating Co., which is a state-owned rating agency in China. *See* 联合资信评估有限公司 (Lianhe Credit Rating Co.), http://www.lianheratings.com.cn/ (last visited Jan. 15, 2015).

[44] 神秘之手兜底山东海龙短融躲过违约 (Unnamed Backstop Saved Shandong Hailong from Short-term Bonds Defaults) (Apr 10, 2012), http://finance.ifeng.com/stock/ssgs/20120410/5895778.shtml (last visited May 26, 2015).

TABLE 15.3
HUIJIN AS BACKSTOP TO FINANCIAL INTERMEDIARIES [2012-12-31]

Date	Company	Nature of Business	Amount/billion (RMB, converted at the exchange rate as of May 28, 2014)	Amount/ billion (U.S. Dollars)
Commercial or Policy Banks[1]				
2003.12	BOC	state-owned commercial bank	140.86	22.5
2003.12	CCB	state-owned commercial bank	140.86	22.5
2004.6	BoCom	state-owned commercial bank	3	0.48
2005.4	ICBC	state-owned commercial bank	93.81	15
2005.7	Export-Import Bank of China	state-owned policy bank	31.27	5
2007.11	Everbright Bank	state-controlled commercial bank	135.30	20
2007.12	CDB	state-owned policy bank	135.30	20
2008.11	ABC	state-owned commercial bank	130	20.79
Investment Banks and Securities Firms				
2003.12	China Jianyin Investment Co.	state-owned investment company	15.63	2.5
2005.6	China Galaxy Securities Co.	state-owned securities firm	10	1.6
2005.8	Shenyinwanguo Securities Co.	state-controlled securities firm	2.5	0.4
2005.8	Guotai Junan Securities Co.	state-controlled securities firm	1	0.16
2005.8	China Galaxy Financial Holding Co.	state-owned financial holding co.	5.5	0.88
Insurance companies				
2006.12	China Reinsurance Co.	state-owned reinsurance co.	25.05	4
2009.11	New China Life Insurance Co.	state-controlled insurance co.	4	0.64

(continued)

TABLE 15.3
(*CONTINUED*)

Date	Company	Nature of Business	Amount/billion (RMB, converted at the exchange rate as of May 28, 2014)	Amount/ billion (U.S. Dollars)
2012.11	China Export & Credit Insurance Co.	state-owned insurance co.	20	3.20
Total Amount			894.08	139.65

[1] Huijin also transacts in shares on the secondary market. For example, on Sept 23, 2008, Huijin bought two million shares each of ICBC, BBC, and BOC on the Shanghai Stock Exchange.

Source: Data from Almanacs of China's Finance and Banking, 2003–2012

state and succumb to inefficiencies. This outcome can be avoided if rescue goes hand in hand with punishment. As Minsky suggested, in the midst of a crisis, the government should lend freely, but once the crisis has been controlled, it should invalidate all practices that led to the crisis in the first place.[45] This rarely happens in developed market economies, because the rescue actions undermine the political will for structural reforms. So far, it does not seem that China is better at rectifying developments that tend to destabilize the system. The country may have a more draconian criminal law regime and a highly centralized human resource management system that could be employed to this end. We lack systematic data to document the actual use of these mechanisms, but evidence from selected rescue efforts suggests that they are not used very frequently. In the case of Everbright, for example, the bank was insolvent in 2005, with RMB29 billion in non-performing assets and core capital of negative RMB3 billion after years of mismanagement. In 2007, Huijin injected 20 billion into the bank and became its controlling shareholder, but the management survived the rescue efforts unscathed. Wang Mingquan, the president of Everbright Group and Everbright Bank since 2000, retired at the normal retirement age of sixty, and was replaced by Tang Shuangning, the former Deputy Chairman of CBRC, China's banking regulator, in 2007. In short, at least in this case, bailouts were not followed by sanctions or significant institutional reforms.

Finally, as we have seen, concerns with financial stability have prompted the PBOC to intervene preemptively in short-term lending markets even before further stress built up in the system. These actions help undermine financial discipline in decentralized credit markets. China, of course, is not alone in struggling with the proper balance of financial discipline and financial stability. Given its peculiar political structure, China tends to err on the side of stability.

---

[45] *See* MINSKY, *supra* note 4.

V. China's Financial System: State, Market, or Hybrid

As stated at the outset, *all* credit-based financial systems are essentially hybrid.[46] Even when most intermediaries are private rather than public entities, they ultimately rely on a public lender or dealer of last resort to avoid the system's self-destruction. Those who do not have an effective domestic backstop have to rely on outside help in the form of foreign governments, the IMF, or the Troika.[47] The reason is that private intermediaries face a binding survival constraint. If and when ex ante commitments are enforced relentlessly in the context of a crisis, this can push too many entities into default and thereby destabilize the entire system. At this stage, only entities with unlimited resources to high-powered money can come to their rescue; these entities are by definition public, not private. In contrast, when the majority of intermediaries are themselves public rather than private, few would assert the system's private nature. The critical question then is whether there is room for the claim that the system is hybrid.

Given the dominance of state ownership in most Chinese financial intermediaries and the extensive control the Communist Party of China exerts over human resource management in the financial sector, it is tempting to classify the system as purely public. That, however, would disregard the considerable reforms that have been implemented over the past twenty years to harden the budget constraint of financial intermediaries and impose greater discipline in the system. As outlined in this chapter, both the relation between financial intermediaries and the state and between financial intermediaries and their customers have changed considerably. Banks and other financial intermediaries no longer regularly operate under direct orders from above. They are fairly autonomous in good times; in bad times they may respond to orders, such as to lend, but they still do this largely at their own peril. Only when they face serious liquidity if not insolvency threats do state agencies step in. Further, the delay in interventions suggests that presently this requires a substantial amount of coordination. The relationship between banks and their customers has arguably changed even more considerably. Chinese banks, just like their Western counterparts, have made extensive use of contractual devices and collateral when dealing with one another and with third parties. They also seek to enforce such commitments to ensure that they are able balance their own assets and liabilities.

Recent years have also witnessed the entry of new private banks into China. In 2014, the CBRC approved the establishment of three banks completely funded by private investors to operate in designated areas. So far this is a trial program meant to ease restrictions of the state-controlled financial system. Allowing competition from

---

[46] The term was originally coined by Mehrling. *See* Perry Mehrling, *Essential Hybridity: A Money View of Law and Finance for Foreign Exchange*, 41 J. of Comp. Econ. 355 (2013).

[47] In the context of the European debt crisis, the IMF joined forces with the European Commission and the European Central Bank.

the private sector into the banking industry also should be counted as a step toward greater hybridization of the financial system. In fact, China is mimicking Western reform efforts and has imposed obligations on these new banks to develop a living will (meant to enhance transparency of daily operations and facilitate bankruptcy procedures should their demise become inevitable) as well as shareholder bail-ins in case of distress. China is also following some examples in the West by regulating executive pay more explicitly. In August 2014, the central government targeted the executive pay at SOEs, including state-owned banks, by establishing an upper limit for top executives' salaries at RMB600,000[48] per year. The top managers of the "big five" were reported to have agreed to this plan, which effectively reduces their salaries. This is in and of itself noteworthy, because in a pure state-controlled system such agreement would not be necessary. Clearly, such agreement would also have no part in a purely private system, in which salary control by the central government remains the exception rather than the rule.[49] As a result of this peculiar arrangement, whereby top executives of supposedly autonomous banks agree to a salary cut from above, the salary of the chief of ICBC is estimated to have decreased by two-thirds from RMB1,990,000 to RMB600,000. In contrast, the chief of Ping An Bank, a privately owned bank, continues to receive RMB8,332,600 per year.

The fact that China is experiencing financial instability may well be the best proof that China has moved from a state-controlled system to a hybrid one. Mono-banking systems do not collapse, because they are fully backed by the central government. In fact, a strong case could be made that mono-banking systems are not financial systems in the true sense, because there are no risk-taking intermediaries, only top-down orders. Massive misallocations of resources in such a system can bring it to its knees—as the collapse of the USSR socialist system has amply demonstrated. Capitalism, however, is also prone to crisis, albeit for different reasons.

Viewed in this light it is perhaps not surprising that China's foray into legally constituted credit-based finance has made the system more, not less, prone to crises. This inherent instability, not only of credit-based financial systems as Minsky argued long ago,[50] but of legally constructed credit-based systems, is largely overlooked when legal reforms are advocated as a means of developing financial systems. Credible legal commitments, so the standard argument goes, entice investors to part with their money and thus deepen financial markets.[51] This argument assumes a static world, in which most investments are self-funded rather than debt-financed. In a dynamic world that

[48] This is approximately US$97,560 at the current exchange rate of 0.1612 USD per RMB.

[49] One such exception is, of course, Switzerland, where salary cuts were introduced by way of referendum. Another is the regulation of executive salaries by the pay tsar the U.S. government installed during the period when it held significant stakes in U.S. banks from late 2008 to early 2010. *See* Pistor, *supra* note 36.

[50] *See* MINSKY, *supra* note 4.

[51] *See* Andrei Shleifer & Robert W. Vishny, *A Survey of Corporate Governance*, 52 THE J. OF FIN. 737 (1997).

can change in unforeseeable ways, these very commitments may, however, exert negative system-wide effects. They may protect individual institutions from the immediate effects of financial distress—primarily those smart enough to shift the costs of dealing with future uncertainties to their counterparties. Uncertainty and a shortage of liquidity, however, cannot be purged from the system, and uncompromising adherence to ex ante commitments is likely to exacerbate a crisis.

China meanwhile is pursuing a mixed reform strategy—one that encourages a greater role for markets, but still under state tutelage. In November 2013, the CPC held its third Plenum of the 18th Central Committee. It declared that "the focus of the restructuring of the economic system is to allow the market to play a decisive role in the allocation of resources."[52] More diverse ownership structures, including public/private partnerships as well as purely private ownership structures, were encouraged. Hybridization, though, is, as we have seen, a double-edged sword. It can help stabilize markets earlier in times of crises, but it can also exacerbate moral hazard, thereby promoting actions that may lead to crises. Policymakers seem to be aware of this challenge. The continuing state support for the financial sector is increasingly paired with calls for more marketization and greater market discipline. The Governor of the PBOC, Zhou Xiaochuan, recently expressed that China should place stronger emphasis on the role of market-based exchange rates, and that the central bank will "basically end normal intervention in the currency market." Moreover, financial institutions will establish a formal deposit insurance system and a proper market exit mechanism. These measures are supposed to enhance the business competitiveness of banks and offer greater protection to depositors in case of default.

Conclusion

This chapter has sought to shed a new light on the evolution of China's financial system. Rather than asking whether China has completed a transition from a state-controlled to a market-based financial system, we have asserted that all contemporary financial systems are hybrids between states and markets, public and private, and "essentially" so. Two interrelated factors account for this: first, financial systems are constructed in law; and second, they are inherently unstable and as such require effective backstopping in times of crises. The challenge China faced was therefore not a unidirectional transition from a state to a private system, but how to redefine the role of the state vis-à-vis the financial sector, given that a complete separation is impossible.

[52] 中共中央关于全面深化改革若干重大问题的决定 (The CPC's Decision on Key Issues of Comprehensively Deepening Reform), 新华网 (XINHUA NET) (Nov. 15, 2013), *available at* http://news.xinhuanet.com/politics/2013-11/15/c_118164235.htm.

We found that China's financial system has been substantially transformed over the past decades. Today there are a variety of financial intermediaries, many of which autonomously allocate resources most of the time. The state continues to play a substantial role in this system, but it is no longer the sole or even primary actor in finance. The state has, however, not relinquished its role as guardian of the financial system. The specter of financial instability, and its possible repercussions for social and political stability, has led state agents in China to err on the side of caution. A Lehman Brothers event did not happen in China, and is unlikely to happen as long as state agents command sufficient resources to intervene effectively. Neither, however, have the leading market economies in the West witnessed another Lehman. The fear of financial collapse was simply too great to let this happen. Instead, governments have been busily bailing out financial entities, and central banks have been buying assets for which no private buyers could be found, at least at prices that would not destabilize the market. It would be an overstatement to assert that financial systems East and West have therefore converged. Still, a strong aversion against extreme events with unpredictable outcomes is not unique to China. Nonetheless, the evidence presented in this chapter suggests that China's rulers are extremely cautious. Even where central banks hesitate and seek to signal that agents need to face up to market discipline, other agents—such as Huijin—step in to alleviate pressure.

It remains to be seen how the hybrid financial system of the Middle Kingdom will evolve in comparison to other financial systems. The major contribution of this chapter is to assert that what is at stake is hybridization rather than privatization. A deeper understanding of the nature of finance in China and the West requires an investigation into the specific institutional mechanisms that link the allocation of resources to leverage, and leverage to public backstopping. It is here that the systems diverge—not on the fundamental question of public versus private.

16 Governing State Capitalism

THE CASE OF BRAZIL

Mariana Pargendler*

Introduction

China is not the only major economy to embrace a system of state capitalism. In order to better appreciate the distinctive traits of the Chinese model, examination of the operation of state capitalism elsewhere can be particularly useful. In this context, Brazil emerges as a main exemplar of the contemporary pursuit of state capitalism by a Western economy.[1]

Major state-owned enterprises (SOEs) have survived the wave of privatizations in the 1990s, but they are by no means the only avenue for state influence over corporate governance in Brazil. As scholars have recently highlighted, the state increasingly acts as a minority, rather than majority, investor in Brazil as elsewhere.[2] The particular variety of state capitalism prevailing in Brazil today reflects a combination of governmental

---

* I thank Mario Engler, Curtis J. Milhaupt, Bruno Salama, Mario Schapiro, and participants at workshops at FGV Direito SP and Columbia Law School for helpful comments on an earlier version of this chapter. All errors are my own.

[1] *See, e.g.*, IAN BREMMER, THE END OF THE FREE MARKET (2011).

[2] ALDO MUSACCHIO & SÉRGIO G. LAZZARINI, REINVENTING STATE CAPITALISM (2014).

control of traditional SOEs with the conspicuous exercise of shareholder activism by state-controlled institutional investors (SCIIs).

This chapter provides a picture of the various instruments for state influence in Brazilian corporate governance, and examines the role of law in enabling and constraining this evolving variety of state capitalism. Despite its economic significance, the role of legal institutions in the governance of state capitalism has only recently begun to receive scholarly attention. With a few notable exceptions, case studies have focused primarily on transitional and Asian economies.[3] The influential OECD Guidelines on Corporate Governance of State-Owned Enterprises are, as their name suggests, prescriptive rather than descriptive in nature.[4]

This chapter's analytical framework posits that state capitalism entails a significant degree of governmental discretion in guiding economic activity. Consequently, the governance of state capitalism calls for a particularly intricate balance. On the one hand, the very choice of government ownership is premised on the benefits of *discretionary* state action; otherwise, arm's-length regulation and subsidies could arguably achieve similar results in curing market failures or promoting developmental objectives.[5] On the other hand, excessive state discretion raises the specter of abuse and cronyism, and, if taken to an extreme, may undermine performance and also pose a threat to the rule of law.

The analysis that follows examines how the legal infrastructure of state capitalism in Brazil strikes this balance. It begins by outlining the basic legal framework for state involvement in corporate governance. It then shifts to examine the relationship between law and state capitalism in action by scrutinizing two high-profile transactions involving state actors.

The *Petroquisa* case shows the rich legal and governance developments following the privatization of the chemical subsidiary of oil giant Petrobras in the 1990s. Such developments included the outcome of a shareholder derivative suit claiming billions of dollars in damages for controlling shareholder abuse and Petrobras's subsequent 49 percent reinvestment in the private conglomerate to which it had sold most of Petroquisa's assets. The *CBD* dispute, in turn, revealed how Brazil's development bank came to play a key, though ultimately unsuccessful, role in a control contest between a well-connected local businessman and a foreign investor.

This chapter's analysis sheds light on the legal underpinnings of the observed partial transition from majority to minority state ownership of enterprise and the corresponding shift in the mechanisms for the exercise of state discretion in Brazil. First,

---

[3] For excellent case studies on China, Russia, and South Korea, see CURTIS J. MILHAUPT & KATHARINA PISTOR, LAW & CAPITALISM (2008); Li-Wen Lin & Curtis J. Milhaupt, *We Are the (National) Champions: Understanding the Mechanisms of State Capitalism in China*, 65 STAN. L. REV. 697 (2013). A notable exception is provided by David M. Trubek, Diogo R. Coutinho & Mario G. Schapiro, *New State Activism in Brazil and the Challenges for Legal Institutions, in* LAW AND THE NEW DEVELOPMENTAL STATE 28 (David M. Trubek et al. eds., 2013) (focusing on the new functionalities of the legal system in Brazil).

[4] OECD GUIDELINES ON CORPORATE GOVERNANCE OF STATE-OWNED ENTERPRISES (2005).

[5] Mariana Pargendler, Aldo Musacchio & Sérgio G. Lazzarini, *In Strange Company: The Puzzle of Private Investment in State-Controlled Firms*, 46 CORNELL INT'L L. J. 569, 574–75 (2013).

state capitalism in Brazil is embedded in a particular legal infrastructure that makes it viable. Brazil's corporate law is particularly amenable to the interests of the state, both as controlling and as minority shareholder. In particular, both the strength of shareholder agreements and the board representation rights afforded to minority shareholders under the Corporations Law support the exercise of corporate influence by SCIIs.

Second, the choice between majority and minority government ownership implies a legal and economic trade-off in shaping state discretion. Uncontested and explicit government control of enterprise under majority ownership leads to a public law regime that limits the state's discretionary power. When the state is a minority investor, however, full corporate control over the firm is sacrificed in favor of a private law regime that is less rigid and, therefore, more amenable to discretionary action. The more governmental control of enterprise is uncontested and explicit, the more it is subject to countervailing legal controls—and vice versa.

Finally, as the *CBD* episode made clear, law is not the only available check on the exercise of state discretion. In a democratic regime media coverage and popular pressure can serve as antidotes to at least the most egregious instances of governmental abuse.[6] Nevertheless, the promise of democratic accountability hinges critically on the availability of information on state action. An unfortunate byproduct of the shift to governmental influence through minority positions has been a corresponding reduction in the amount of information available to the public.

The remainder of this chapter is structured as follows. Section I defines state capitalism in terms of the scope of the government's discretionary power over the economy and the role of legal institutions in ensuring the optimal level of discretion. Section II outlines the current legal framework for the state's direct involvement in corporate governance in Brazil. Section III then turns to the relationship between law and state capitalism in action by examining two major transactions involving government actors. The Conclusion draws policy lessons from Brazil's recent experience.

I. Governing State Capitalism: The Analytical Framework

State capitalism is a concept that is often used but ill-defined. Understood as a system in which the government plays a key role in promoting economic activity, the term encompasses too much: all capitalist economics would qualify. There is no such thing as "state-free" capitalism. On the contrary, if there is one chief lesson from the burgeoning literature on neo-institutional economics, it is precisely that state-provided legal institutions are essential for the proper functioning of capitalist systems.[7]

---

[6] *See id.* at 589–90.

[7] For a review of this literature, see Kevin E. Davis & Michael J. Trebilcock, *The Relationship between Law and Development: Optimists versus Skeptics*, 56 Am. J. Comp. L. 895, 945 (2008) (concluding that the empirical evidence generally supports the strong consensus that law matters for economic development, but precisely what types of legal institutions matter remains an open question).

Attempts to circumscribe the concept in view of its effects—as in Ian Bremmer's definition of state capitalism as "the manipulation of market outcomes for political purposes"[8]—have been equally unsatisfying. Every capitalist economy today is subject to laws aimed at altering market outcomes in view of politically determined ends, from minimum wage and other standard labor regulations to the bail-outs of financial institutions and the award of agricultural subsidies.[9] The pursuit of political objectives characterizes democratic and autocratic regimes alike; it can hardly serve as the distinguishing trait of state capitalism.[10]

At the other end of the spectrum, state capitalism is conflated with substantial government ownership of enterprise. Such a view has a long historical pedigree, dating back to the origins of the term.[11] This conception may at times prove to be deceptively narrow, however, for the state can exercise discretionary influence over economic activity and corporate governance through mechanisms other than outright ownership of a controlling stake in the firm.[12]

A more illuminating criterion to distinguish state capitalism from other "varieties of capitalism"[13] is the relative scope of state discretion in shaping economic activity. Although the degree and contours of market interventions vary, in both liberal and coordinated market economies the state's actions are generally explicitly grounded in and constrained by law.[14] For instance, the state might outlaw insider trading and cartels (as it does in the United States, but historically not in Germany), or impose employee board representation and tenure requirements (as it does in Germany, but not in the United States). The government may also extensively promote industrial policy and other public objectives through the tax system, as is the case in the United States.[15] These interventions, however, are clearly enunciated ex ante and justiciable ex post. Instances of state

---

[8] Ian Bremmer, *State Capitalism and the Crisis*, MCKINSEY & COMPANY INSIGHTS & PUBLICATIONS (July 2009), http://www.mckinsey.com/insights/public_sector/state_capitalism_and_the_crisis.

[9] HA-JOON CHANG, 23 THINGS THEY DON'T TELL YOU ABOUT CAPITALISM (2010) (for a forceful articulation of this point).

[10] Quantitative measures of state size map poorly onto conventional characterizations of state capitalism. Both government spending and consumption as a percentage of GDP are higher in Europe and the United States than in China. *See* Niall Ferguson, *We're All State Capitalists Now*, FOREIGN AFFAIRS, Feb. 9, 2012, http://foreignpolicy.com/2012/02/09/were-all-state-capitalists-now/.

[11] Friedrich Pollack employed the expression in the 1940s to downplay the differences between the capitalist regimes of the West and the state-owned and directed economy of the Soviet Union. *State Capitalism, in* CRAIG CALHOUN, DICTIONARY OF THE SOCIAL SCIENCES (2002).

[12] MUSACCHIO & LAZZARINI, *supra* note 2; Curtis J. Milhaupt & Wentong Zheng, *Beyond Ownership: State Capitalism and the Chinese Firm*, 103 GEO. L.J. 665 (2015).

[13] For the classical formulation of the concept, see PETER HALL & DAVID SOSKICE, VARIETIES OF CAPITALISM: THE INSTITUTIONAL FOUNDATIONS OF COMPARATIVE ADVANTAGE (2001).

[14] *See id.* (on the definition of liberal and coordinated market economies).

[15] *See* Anne Alstott, *Gender Quotas for Corporate Boards: Options for Legal Design in the United States*, 26 PACE INT'L L. REV. 38, 46 (2014) ("the tax system spends trillions of dollars of government money to shape business decisions and craft what amounts to an industrial policy for the United States").

ownership and the related exercise of state discretion exist in all capitalist systems,[16] but, viewed as a continuum, are circumscribed by law.

By contrast, this chapter argues that the distinctive trait of state capitalism is the relatively unfettered exercise of discretion in the pursuit of political objectives. From a legal perspective, such expanded discretion is at least partially achieved through substantial (and appropriately structured[17]) levels of state ownership. Ownership is the ultimate legal and economic institution for the exercise of discretion.[18] Thus, at face value at least, state ownership of enterprise achieves a formidable feat: it reconciles the ample scope for state discretion with the central tenet of the rule of law—according to which state power is necessarily based on and limited by law. If this legal loophole is used too broadly, however, the standard conception of the rule of law risks becoming illusory.[19] Conversely, in the absence of the rule of law, the distinction between formal private and public ownership is blurred, as the state can effectively exercise discretionary power over the entire economy of firms.[20]

We have known at least since Ronald Coase that the degree of discretion afforded by ownership (or, in Oliver E. Williamson's terms, "hierarchy") can offer distinct advantages. By using its voice or fiat power within the firm's hierarchy, the state can economize on the transaction costs of writing and enforcing formal contracts or laws.[21] Now-canonical lessons from organizational economics suggest that state ownership is particularly appropriate when there is a market failure that cannot be cured by laws and regulations alone, be it because contract institutions are weak (hampering regulatory

[16] Mariana Pargendler, *State Ownership and Corporate Governance*, 80 FORDHAM L. REV. 2917, 2925 (2012) (describing historical and contemporary instances of government ownership in the United States).

[17] Not all state-owned enterprises are alike. The legal regime can go a long way toward reducing the scope for political influence in SOE governance. For instance, the legal framework affords the Norwegian government far less say over state-owned oil firm Statoil compared to the Brazilian state's influence over Petrobras. Pargendler et al., *supra* note 5, at 593, 600 (describing the ban on SOE board service by politicians and the stronger role of the industry regulator in Norway as mechanisms that ensure greater SOE independence compared to their Brazilian counterparts).

[18] In Roman law parlance, the owner enjoys broad rights (*ius utendi, ius fruendi, ius abutendi*) to employ her property as she sees fit. In economic terms, ownership reflects the "residual rights of control" over an asset that have not been contracted out. *See* Sanford J. Grossman & Oliver D. Hart, *The Costs and Benefits of Ownership: A Theory of Vertical and Lateral Integration*, 94 J. POL. ECON. 691 (1986).

[19] For an excellent discussion of the tension between pervasive state ownership and the rule of law in transition economies, see Katharina Pistor & Joel Turkewitz, *Coping with Hydra—State Ownership after Privatization, in* CORPORATE GOVERNANCE IN CENTRAL EUROPE AND RUSSIA,192 (Roman Frydman, Cheryl W. Gray & Andrzej Rapaczynski eds., 1996).

[20] Milhaupt & Zheng, *supra* note 12.

[21] Pargendler et al., *supra* note 5, at 574–75. Brazil's swift government response to the financial crisis of 2008 brings home this point. The government resorted to its existing SOEs (in particular, state-owned banks BNDES and CEF) significantly to increase its credit to the private sector and to lower market interest rates, therefore circumventing the need for cumbersome and potentially contentious legislative action.

enforcement) or because non-contractible national security or sovereignty considerations are involved.[22]

The allotment of ample discretionary power to the state is not free from inconveniences. The overly broad exercise of discretion by the state as enterprise owner is in tension with the rule of law. Discretion can unsettle both predictability and equality—two fundamental attributes of the rule of law that have profound economic implications.[23] The potential instability of governmental action, coupled with the specter of unequal treatment dispensed to different parties, discourages long-term investment and undermines a level playing field in which individuals and firms can compete. In other words, discretion holds perils of its own, ranging from excessive uncertainty to cronyism.

II. The Instruments of State Influence in Brazilian Corporate Governance

State involvement in Brazilian corporate governance takes place through ownership of a majority or a minority of a firm's voting capital as well as through the extension of long-term loans subject to conditions. The prototypical SOEs are majority investments, with the government exercising uncontested corporate control over the firm by holding more than 50 percent of its voting stock. Minority state investments, in turn, can be channeled through a constellation of SCIIs, such as the development bank, SOE pension funds, and other public investment vehicles.

A. THE STATE AS MAJORITY SHAREHOLDER

SOEs are a key instrument of state capitalism in Brazil. Created by law, they are technically termed mixed enterprises (*sociedades de economia mista*), when the state holds the majority of the voting stock, or public enterprises (*empresas públicas*), when the state is the sole shareholder. Although the absolute number of SOEs declined sharply following the wave of privatizations in the 1990s, their economic clout remains significant.

Listed SOEs currently include large firms such as Petrobras, one of the world's chief oil companies, and Banco do Brasil, Latin America's largest bank by assets. Taken together, listed SOEs accounted for nearly 17 percent of Brazil's market capitalization in 2013, down from a staggering 70 percent in the 1970s and more than 30 percent in 2007.[24]

---

[22] Oliver E. Williamson, *Public and Private Bureaucracies: A Transaction Cost Economics Perspective*, 15 J.L. ECON. & ORG. 306, 321–24 (1999); Andrei Shleifer, *State versus Private Ownership*, 12 J. ECON. PERSP. 133, 133 (1998).

[23] On these two features of the rule of law, see Stephen Holmes, *Lineages of the Rule of Law*, *in* DEMOCRACY AND THE RULE OF LAW 19(Adam Przeworski & José María Maravall eds., 2003).

[24] Sérgio G. Lazzarini, Aldo Musacchio & Mariana Pargendler, *O Governo Como Acionista: Desafios para a Governança Corporativa no Brasil*, *in* O FUTURO DA GOVERNANÇA CORPORATIVA 77, 80–81 (Joaquim Fontes Filho & Ricardo Leal eds., 2013).

Wholly owned public enterprises—which include the likes of Brazil's Development Bank (*Banco Nacional de Desenvolvimento Econômico e Social*—BNDES) and CEF (*Caixa Econômica Federal*), a state-owned commercial bank—are also major economic players. At 6 percent of GDP, BNDES's outstanding loan volume in 2013 was two times larger than that of the World Bank.[25]

In Brazil as elsewhere, a main driving force behind the establishment of government-controlled corporations was the greater degree of discretion afforded by a private law regime, and the corresponding increase in much-needed flexibility and expediency in government action. In 1933, President Franklin Delano Roosevelt exalted the newly created Tennessee Valley Authority as "a corporation clothed with the power of government but possessed of the flexibility and initiative of a private enterprise."[26] The same goal of using the corporate form to achieve "zero bureaucracy, as if it were a private company," was also an explicit rationale behind the rise of government corporations in Brazil.[27] Nonetheless, discretion invariably creates the potential for abuse, which in turn triggers countervailing legal responses.

Brazil's evolving legal treatment of contracting practices and employee recruitment at SOEs illustrates this evolution. Under a largely discretionary regime for the better part of the twentieth century, Brazilian SOEs experienced excessive politicization of employment practices, with job positions often filled based on favoritism and political connections, rather than on firm needs and labor capabilities.[28] This outcome led to a strong reaction: Brazil's 1988 Constitution subjects SOEs' hiring to public examinations, the same mode of recruitment applicable to public servants. Public examination procedures are hardly the best method to select prime talent in employee hires (as suggested by their virtual absence from competitive private sector recruitment), but have the merit of ensuring equal opportunity and reducing favoritism.

For similar reasons, government contracting in Brazil is subject to strict and formalistic public procurement requirements that in theory reduce the opportunities for corruption but at the cost of expediency. State-controlled corporations created by law are only partially subject to such restrictions, which apply (if at all) only to ancillary agreements that are not central to their business. For contracts that are inextricably linked to their economic purpose—for example, the extension of loans by a public bank—the state as owner operates with a degree of discretion akin to that of a private actor. Although

---

[25] Anthony Boadle, *Brazil's BNDES Crowding Out Private Banks from Loans, OECD Says*, REUTERS, Oct. 22, 2013, http://www.reuters.com/article/2013/10/22/bndes-brazil-oecd-idUSL1N0I81RP20131022.

[26] Pargendler, *supra* note 16, at 2926.

[27] The expression comes from Miranda Valverde, in his Exposition of Motives of the bill that led to Brazil's 1940 Corporations Law.

Trajano de Miranda Valverde, *Exposição de Motivos ao Anteprojeto convertido em Decreto-Lei n. 2.627 de 1940* [Exposition of Purpose to the Draft Bill Converted in the Decree-Law n. 2.627 of 1940] (1940).

[28] CELSO ANTÔNIO BANDEIRA DE MELLO, CURSO DE DIREITO ADMINISTRATIVO 197–98 (25th ed. 2007).

generally subject to public procedures for recruitment and contracting at large, BNDES thus operates like a private bank in its ability to choose when, under what terms, and to whom it offers its (highly subsidized[29]) lines of credit—making it arguably the paradigmatic instrument of Brazilian-style state capitalism.[30]

In order to appropriately circumscribe the state's discretionary power as a controlling shareholder, the legal regime currently applicable to SOEs is partially enshrined in at least three respects in Brazil's constitution. First, in view of Brazil's embrace of a market economy based on "free enterprise,"[31] SOEs face limitations as to scope. Article 173 of the Brazilian Constitution specifically restricts the direct undertaking of economic activity by the state to contexts in which it is "necessary" for "national security" or for "relevant collective interest"—even if the latter concept is arguably too vague to effectively restrain government expansion.[32]

Second, the Constitution outlines the key features of SOE governance. Each SOE must be created by a statute that specifically defines its corporate purpose.[33] As previously mentioned, SOEs are generally subject to public procurement requirements for contracting, and to formal public contests for employee recruiting.[34] SOE operations are also exposed to the external oversight of *Tribunais de Contas,* administrative bodies constitutionally in charge of external control of government activities and expenditures.[35] Finally, in order to level the playing field vis-à-vis their private competitors, SOEs cannot enjoy fiscal privileges that are not extended to private sector firms, and must be governed by the same legal regime applicable to private companies with respect to civil, commercial, labor, and tax obligations.[36]

As a general rule, the same body of corporate law applies to SOEs and private firms. Only a handful of special rules and exceptions apply—some of which are designed to protect minority shareholders, others to ensure state prerogatives. An instance of the former is the rule granting appraisal rights to minority shareholders whenever the government takes full control of an existing private firm. The assumption behind the rule is that private shareholders have not consented to participate in a company that may pursue public objectives.[37] Conversely, the distinctive feature of the legal regime

---

[29] *See* Sérgio G. Lazzarini et al., *What Do Development Banks Do? Evidence from Brazil, 2002–2009* (working paper, 2012), http://ssrn.com/abstract=1969843.

[30] To be sure, the optimal degree of discretion to be conferred on BNDES is the subject of debate. *See, e.g.,* Mario G. Schapiro, *Making the Developmental State Work: How Does a Mandate Matter for the Brazilian Development Bank?* (working paper, 2012), http://ssrn.com/abstract=1986850 (arguing that the adoption of a narrower mandate for BNDES is necessary in order to increase the Bank's accountability).

[31] Constituição Federal [C.F.] [Constitution] art. 10, IV, and 170 (Braz.).

[32] Constituição Federal [C.F.] [Constitution] art. 173 (Braz.).

[33] Constituição Federal [C.F.] [Constitution] art. 37, XIX (Braz.).

[34] Constituição Federal [C.F.] [Constitution], art. 173, § 1º, III and art. 37, II. (Braz.).

[35] Constituição Federal [C.F.] [Constitution] art. 71, III (Braz.).

[36] Constituição Federal [C.F.] [Constitution] art. 173, § 1º. II (Braz.).

[37] Lei No. 6.404, de 15 de Dezembro de 1976, Diário Oficial da União [D.O.U.] de 17.12.1976, art. 236 (Braz.).

governing mixed enterprises is provided by Article 238 of the Corporations Law. The article imposes on the government the same duties and responsibilities applicable to a private controlling shareholder, but explicitly authorizes the state to "direct the activities of the company so as to attend to the public interest that justified its creation."[38]

Yet corporate law as a whole has imposed only feeble constraints on the behavior of SOEs.[39] First, corporate law typically grants managers substantial discretion in decisions that are untainted by conflicts of interest, by force of the "business judgment rule" doctrine of U.S. corporate law and its functional equivalent in Brazil.[40] Second, as I have argued elsewhere, the state's dual role as corporate governance player and referee means that the government is uniquely positioned to shape the applicable legal regime with its interests as shareholder in mind.[41]

As vividly demonstrated by the narrative of Petroquisa's privatization below, this can happen in at least three ways: (1) the original corporate law regime is made particularly amenable to the interests of the state as shareholder; (2) the state sponsors legal reforms to change the applicable rules when the latter prove to be inconvenient; and (3) courts and regulatory agencies are reluctant to enforce legal restrictions against state actors. All of this, in turn, increases the discretion enjoyed by the state as controlling shareholder above that is afforded by ownership to private actors.

B. THE STATE AS MINORITY SHAREHOLDER

1. SOEs

SOEs—be they public or mixed enterprises—can and do serve as minority shareholders in a number of corporations in Brazil. As described in Section III(A) below, Petrobras is a large shareholder in major chemical firm Braskem. Particularly significant are the equity stakes of BNDESPAR, a wholly-owned subsidiary of BNDES that operates as its equity arm. With equity stakes in seventy-four closely held firms and seventy-one publicly traded corporations (which account for nearly 60 percent of Brazil's total market capitalization),[42] BNDESPAR plays a central role in supporting Brazil's national

---

[38] Lei No. 6.404, de 15 de Dezembro de 1976, Diário Oficial da União [D.O.U.] de 17.12.1976, art. 238 (Braz.).

[39] Brazilian law is not unique in this regard. *See* Marcel Kahan & Edward Rock, *When the Government Is the Controlling Shareholder*, 89 Tex. L. Rev. 1293 (2011) (arguing that U.S. law fails to provide adequate protection to minority shareholders of government-controlled firms).

[40] For the application of the "business judgment rule" in Brazil, see Mariana Pargendler, *Responsabilidade Civil dos Administradores e Business Judgment Rule no Direito Brasileiro* (July 17, 2014) (unpublished manuscript) (on file with author).

[41] *See* Pargendler, *supra* note 16; Mariana Pargendler, *The Unintended Consequences of State Ownership: The Brazilian Experience*, 13 Theoretical Inq. L. 503, 505–06 (2012).

[42] Author's calculation based on Relatório de Informações Trimestrais—BNDES (Sept. 2013), http://www.bndes.gov.br/SiteBNDES/export/sites/default/bndes_pt/Galerias/Arquivos/empresa/download/ITR_bpar0913.pdf.

champions. Because these investments involve formally minority positions—narrowly defined as representing less than 50 percent of a firm's voting capital—the recipient firms continue to be de facto classified as wholly private companies.

2. Public Pension Funds

Any thorough account of the instruments of state influence over Brazilian corporate governance must encompass the role of public pension funds. In this respect, one caveat is necessary: unlike the other actors discussed here, public pension funds are not legally owned by the government. Consistent with international practice, public pension funds in Brazil are organized as separate legal entities managed for the benefit of SOE retirees.[43]

The governance structure of SOE pension funds is particularly conducive to political interference. By law, the SOEs appoint half of board members, as well as the board president, of SOE pension funds. The remaining directors are elected by the fund's beneficiaries.[44] As a result, the CEOs of SOE pension funds are typically appointed by the CEOs of the respective SOEs, who, in turn, are directly or indirectly appointed by the country's president.[45] The upshot is that political interference in pension fund investment and governance decisions is not only theoretically feasible but also common.[46]

The well-known role of Previ (together with BNDES) in ousting the chief executive of mining giant Vale do Rio Doce, a privatized firm, illustrates the use of pension funds to further the government's economic agenda. Despite Vale's stellar financial performance, its CEO Roger Agnelli attracted the ire of President Lula for what the president viewed as unnecessary employee firings and underinvestment in the country. Through the use of minority holdings by state actors (and especially Previ's holding of nearly 15 percent of Vale's equity), Agnelli was replaced by an executive more sympathetic to the government's policy priorities.[47]

Indeed, pension funds of SOEs play a particularly dominant role in Brazil's equity markets. Previ, the pension fund of Banco do Brasil's employees, is the largest such

---

[43] Lei Complementar No. 208, de 29 de Maio de 2001, Diário Oficial da União [D.O.U] de 30.05.2001, art. 8 (Braz.) (requiring SOE pension funds to be organized as the equivalent of a foundation or nonprofit corporation).

[44] *See id.* art. 11.

[45] Media coverage habitually attributes the choice of a pension fund's chief to Brazil's President. *See Dilma muda comando de fundo de pensão*, O Estado de S. Paulo, May 25, 2012.

[46] The use of public pension funds to further governmental objectives is by no means a novel phenomenon. In order to contribute to the government's goal of promoting Brazil's stock market development, SOE pension funds were required to invest a portion of their portfolio in local equity markets. Ary Oswaldo Mattos Filho, *Prefácio*, *in* Roberta Nioac Prado, Oferta Pública de Ações nas S.A.—Tag Along [Mandatory Bid Rule in Business Corporations—Tag Along] 21 (2005) (referring to pension funds' "unusual character of mandatory shareholder"). Brazil is not unique in boasting pension funds that promote a political agenda. *See, e.g.*, Roberta Romano, *Public Pension Fund Activism in Corporate Governance Reconsidered*, 93 Colum. L. Rev. 795 (1993) (describing instances of political pressure over public pension funds in the United States).

[47] For a more detailed description of this episode, see Lazzarini et al., *supra* note 24, at 84–87.

fund in Brazil and holds equity stakes in forty-three publicly traded companies, which together account for over one-half of Bovespa's market capitalization. In 2006, Previ alone held the equivalent of 5 percent of Brazil's market capitalization.[48] Taken together, public pension funds in Brazil accounted for 64.6 percent of the country's pension fund industry in 2013.[49]

The corporate governance clout of public pension funds is significantly magnified by their peculiar investment strategy. Private pension funds in Brazil have typically allocated less than 30 percent of their investment portfolio to corporate stocks,[50] due to the historically high interest rates paid on sovereign debt.[51] Previ, by contrast, apportions over 60 percent of its portfolio to equity investments "in the main Brazilian corporate groups."[52] Counter to international practice,[53] its equity positions are made of very large stakes in only forty-five firms in strategic sectors, such as energy, banking, tourism, and telecom—with a median of 6.79 percent and an average of 15.87 percent of the equity capital.[54]

These sizable stakes translate into significant governance clout. Every year, Previ elects more than a hundred members of boards of directors and supervisory boards (*Conselho Fiscal*).[55] Previ is also known for promoting an activist agenda. The fund's latest priority has been to defend the position that Brazilian firms, whenever possible, adopt a "global" strategy so as to improve Brazil's balance of payments.[56] Obviously such an agenda has more to do with the current government's goal of fostering national champions than with the pursuit of shareholder value.

---

[48] Catherine Vieira, *Fundação Previ tem cerca de 60% dos investimentos no mercado de ações*, VALOR ECONÔMICO, Jan. 18, 2006.

[49] Author's calculation based on the consolidated statistics as of September 2013 by Superintendência Nacional de Previdência Complementar. Relatório de Estatística Trimestral da Superintendência Nacional de Previdência Complementar (PREVIC), http://www.previdencia.gov.br/wp-content/uploads/2013/05/Relatorio-Previc-3%C2%BA-Trim2013_FINAL.pdf.

[50] Consolidado Estatístico, ABRAPP (Feb. 2015), Table 1, http://www.abrapp.org.br/Consolidados/Forms/AllItems.aspx.

[51] In the last ten years, Brazil's real interest rate (adjusted for inflation) averaged 3.7 percent, by far the highest among the BRICS. Russia, India, China, and South Africa offered real interest rates of -0.25 percent, 0.4 percent, -0.7 percent, and 0.4 percent, respectively.

[52] PREVI CODE OF BEST CORPORATE GOVERNANCE PRACTICES (2d ed. 2012).

[53] *See* Bernard Black, *Shareholder Passivity Revisited*, 89 MICH. L. REV. 520, 553 (1990) (attributing the preference of U.S. pension funds for "broad diversification and passivity" to the regulatory environment).

[54] PREVI, Relatório de Empresas Participadas (2012), http://www.previ.com.br/quemsomos/relatorio2012/pt/o-valor-dos-investimentos/relacao-de-empreendimentos.html.

[55] Graziella Valenti, *Previ quer ampliar ativismo nas companhias*, VALOR ECONÔMICO, Aug. 30, 2013, http://www.valor.com.br/empresas/3252820/previ-quer-ampliar-ativismo-nas-companhias.

[56] *See id.*

3. New Investment Vehicles

In recent years, Brazil has established two new SCIIs that have reinforced the government's participation in corporate governance. The FI-FGTS, an investment fund of *Fundo de Garantia por Tempo de Serviço* (FGTS), was created in 2007 to finance investments in energy and infrastructure. It is funded by the preexisting FGTS, a fund instituted in 1966 to compensate for the elimination of stability in employment contracts. Financed by employers' mandatory monthly contributions of 8 percent of wages, FGTS provides workers with individual accounts from which amounts can be withdrawn only in specific circumstances dictated by law, such as involuntary termination of employment, major illness, retirement, or housing acquisition. By law, FGTS's resources are to be channeled to housing and urban infrastructure; workers' accounts, in turn, grow according to a predetermined rate—which, in recent years, has been significantly lower than actual inflation.

With net assets at approximately US$13 billion in 2013, FI-FGTS employs FGTS's excess resources in debt and equity investments in a variety of infrastructure and energy companies. Such investments include bond holdings in the former port-operations subsidiary of LLX, a publicly traded company controlled by (recently disgraced) Brazilian magnate Eike Batista, and a 30 percent equity stake in Odebrecht TransPort S.A., a transportation firm of the powerful Odebrecht group. Odebrecht TransPort S.A.—a chief player in the recent privatization of Brazilian airports during the Dilma administration—alone accounts for 7.6 percent of the FI-FGTS's assets, and also boasts BNDESPAR in its ranks of shareholders.[57]

In 2008, following the lead of other resource-rich countries, Brazil created its sovereign wealth fund (*Fundo Soberano do Brasil—FSB*). The purpose of the fund is to "promote . . . investment in assets in Brazil and abroad, constitute public savings, mitigate the effects of economic cycles, and further strategic projects located abroad." The fund has since invested in Brazilian government debt and in SOE stocks, such as Petrobras and Banco do Brasil. The state's minority investments in SOEs might at first appear puzzling. It would seem as though the government has little to gain in terms of additional influence by accumulating stakes through SCIIs in firms that are already under state control. But this is not always the case. Until loud protests by minority shareholders eventually led the government to reverse course, SCIIs had a decisive voice in electing the representatives of minority shareholders to the board of directors of Petrobras, thereby ensuring an even greater degree of dominance by the state in the company's governance.[58]

---

[57] Clarisse Spitz, *Governo aumenta sua participação em Galeão já privatizado*, O Globo, Dec. 24, 2013, http://oglobo.globo.com/economia/governo-aumenta-sua-participacao-em-galeao-ja-privatizado-11149933 (noting that, through FI-FGTS and BNDESPAR combined, the government's total stake in Odebrecht Transport exceeded 40 percent),

[58] This change in position took place after minority investors complained to CVM about the practices. Although CVM has not punished Petrobras, it issued a staff letter outlining its position on this issue, which ultimately led Petrobras to reverse course. Maria Helena Santana, *Brazil: The Corporate Governance*

4. The Legal Regime of Minority State Investments

As indicated by the discussion above, the fact that state actors hold minority (rather than majority) positions in the firm does not mean that their governance influence is muted. The reverse is true. Brazilian corporate law confers significant rights on minority shareholders holding a large stake in the firm. For instance, the Corporations Law allows holders of at least 15 percent of the company's voting stock or 10 percent of the company's nonvoting preferred stock to appoint one board member each.[59] Board representation of minority shareholders can be even greater, however, as the statute also contains a mandatory rule providing for cumulative voting upon request.[60] In addition, a closely held corporation's charter may grant special board appointment rights to holders of certain classes of preferred stock—a provision that, according to the official "Exposition of Motives" of the corporate statute, was included in the statute to endorse a practice then habitually used by BNDES.[61]

Focusing on the mandatory provisions of the corporate statute alone, however, would greatly understate the clout of SOEs as minority shareholders. The main reason for this is the widespread use of shareholder agreements, a mechanism that has become a staple of modern Brazilian corporate governance. A 2001 legal reform gave the enforcement of shareholder agreements a boost: it explicitly recognizes the availability of specific performance as a remedy for their breach, and prevents votes cast in violation of duly filed agreements from being counted in shareholders meetings and board meetings (despite criticism from corporate governance advocates, who claim that this compromises the exercise of directors' independent business judgment).[62]

SCIIs have also made ample use of shareholder agreements to influence corporate strategy and governance. BNDESPAR alone is party to twenty shareholder agreements with publicly traded companies,[63] and SOE pension funds are party to several others. Although their clauses vary from case to case, it is common for shareholder agreements to have a voting component, according to which the parties (including government-controlled actors) have director appointment rights as well as veto rights over major corporate decisions.

Framework and Practices relating to Supervision and Enforcement, in OECD, Supervision and Enforcement in Corporate Governance 58 (2013).

[59] Lei No. 6.404, de 15 de Dezembro de 1976, Diário Oficial da União [D.O.U.] de 17.12.1976, art. 141, § 4o., I and II (Braz.).

[60] Lei No. 6.404, de 15 de Dezembro de 1976, Diário Oficial da União [D.O.U.] de 17.12.1976, art. 141 (Braz.).

[61] Exposição de Motivos n. 196, de 24 de Junho de 1976, pelo Ministro da Fazenda, http://www.cvm.gov.br/export/sites/cvm/legislacao/anexos/leis/EM196-Lei6404.pdf.

[62] Érica Gorga, *Corporate Control & Governance after a Decade from "Novo Mercado": Changes in Ownership Structures and Shareholder Power in Brazil* (July 29, 2014) (unpublished manuscript), http://ssrn.com/abstract=2473832.

[63] BNDESPAR. Relatório de Administração 2012, http://www.bndes.gov.br/SiteBNDES/export/sites/default/bndes_pt/Galerias/Arquivos/empresa/download/RelatAdm1212.pdf.

Yet even though the state can have substantial influence over corporate governance through what are formally "minority" holdings, outside investors enjoy little formal protection from political interference, for two reasons. First, although appraisal rights apply in view of a government taking of corporate control, this remedy is unavailable if state actors become shareholders through market purchases. Second, the fiduciary duties of controlling shareholders and managers under Brazilian law are sufficiently broad as to encompass non-shareholder constituencies. Controlling shareholders may breach their fiduciary duties when they direct the company to pursue a goal that is foreign to its purpose, to the detriment of minority shareholders or even the "national economy."[64] According to the Corporations Law, managers shall discharge their duties in view of the company's purpose, but with due regard to the "requirements of public good and of the social function of enterprise."[65] Consequently, the government may be able to exercise nontrivial influence through its minority stakes—and, with respect to closely held corporations, with very little transparency to the public.[66]

The main constraint on governmental interference through minority shareholdings is of an economic rather than legal nature. Because the government is unable to control the firm on its own, it must necessarily garner support from private investors. Some private shareholders specifically negotiate for contractual protection against value-destroying political interference. Their shareholder agreements with SCIIs overtly specify the firm's purpose of maximizing the financial returns to investors and mandate that shareholders exercise their voting rights accordingly.[67] But even in the majority of cases where such a provision is absent, the lack of voting control requires the state-controlled institutional

---

[64] Lei No. 6.404, de 15 de Dezembro de 1976, Diário Oficial da União [D.O.U.] de 17.12.1976, art. 117, § 1°, a (Braz.) (qualifying as abuse of control power the action of a controlling shareholder that "guides the company towards an objective that is foreign to its corporate purpose or damaging to national interest, or that leads it to favor another company, domestic or foreign, to the detriment of minority shareholder's participation in the profits or assets of the company, or the national economy").

[65] Lei No. 6.404, 15 de Dezembro de 1976, Diário Oficial da União [D.O.U.] de 17.12.1976, art. 1540 (Braz.).

[66] As part of this project, the author has formally requested the shareholder agreements entered into between BNDESPAR and closely held corporations under Brazil's Access to Information Law (Law 12,527 of 2011), which specifically covers SOEs (art. 1, II). Despite the constitutionally and legally guaranteed access, the request was systematically denied following four rounds of administrative appeals, based, inter alia, on the allegation that the agreements in question constituted "business secrets," the disclosure of which would "weaken the State's operation in stock markets, putting the financial performance of public resources at a disadvantage vis-à-vis private resources." As this chapter went to press, a number of ongoing lawsuits sought to compel disclosure of financing documents and practices of BNDES, with some initial success.

[67] For instance, the Shareholders Agreement of América Latina Logística S.A.—ALL, dated Feb. 1, 2011, which has BNDESPAR and SOE pension funds Previ and Funcef as parties, among others, provides that "the Company and its subsidiaries shall be managed with the primary purpose of generating profit and maximizing the return on the investment made by the parties in the shortest term possible, in view of the best interests of the Company and its subsidiaries" (Section 2.1(a)).

investors to broker deals with private investors, who are presumably more interested in maximizing their financial returns than in furthering the government's agenda.

III. State Capitalism in Action

Any overview of ownership structures and the "law on the books" applicable to both SOEs and SCIIs would mean little if it did not reflect the operation of state capitalism in action. The discussion that follows offers a glimpse into the relationship among state ownership, legal infrastructure, and corporate governance through the analysis of two cases: one involving Petroquisa, once a subsidiary of Petrobras, and another featuring CBD, a private firm in the supermarket and retail industry.

A. PETROQUISA: THE SHIFTING MODES OF GOVERNMENTAL INFLUENCE

Perhaps the most prominent lawsuit involving a state-controlled enterprise in Brazil concerned alleged abuse in asset sales by Petrobras Química S.A.—Petroquisa, during the country's large-scale privatization program. The controversy drew significant attention, both because derivative actions are rare in Brazil, and due to the sums involved. When the Superior Court of Justice (*Superior Tribunal de Justiça*—STJ) issued a final decision on the case in 2012, the plaintiff's damages claim amounted to roughly US$12 billion after adjustment for compound interest and inflation. The case achieved even greater notoriety for the content of the decision—and the insights it offered into the relationship between law and state capitalism in Brazil.

Petroquisa was established in 1967 as the first subsidiary of Petrobras, Brazil's state-owned giant. Petroquisa was in charge of Petrobras's major chemical business, holding substantial stakes in thirty-four companies and accounting for roughly one-third of Brazil's chemical industry.[68] In 1989, Petroquisa went public, raising a total of US$40 million from private minority investors. Following the IPO Petroquisa remained a subsidiary of Petrobras, part of a pyramidal structure that is frequently used by Brazilian SOEs.[69]

Only two years after the offering, however, the government decided to privatize Petroquisa's subsidiaries. Law 8,031 of 1990 (the "Privatizations Law") authorized the

---

[68] SabrinaValle&MarianaDurão,*Petroquisatinhaumterçodosetorquímico*,OESTADODES.PAULO,25Aug.2012, http://economia.estadao.com.br/noticias/geral,petroquisa-tinha-um-terco-do-setor-quimico-imp-,921416.

[69] *See, e.g.*, Pargendler, *supra* note 16, at 2939 (describing the pyramidal structure of SOE telecom Telebras prior to privatization). The resort to pyramidal structures by Brazilian SOEs remains alive and well. BB Seguridade, a subsidiary of SOE Banco do Brasil, accounted for the world's largest IPO in 2013. Cristiane Lucchesi & Francisco Marcelino, *BB Seguridade Raises $4.25 Billion in World's Biggest 2013 IPO*, BLOOMBERG NEWS, Apr. 25, 2013.

government to receive junk government bonds (*moedas podres*) in consideration for the sale of privatized assets—a provision that allegedly served the government's interest in reducing Brazil's mounting public debt. *Moedas podres* were so dubbed because they traded at a substantial discount due to illiquidity. Under the new law, however, the government accepted them as payment at face value. Petrobras, as the controlling shareholder of Petroquisa, approved the sale of almost all of Petroquisa's holdings in exchange for only US$1,000 in cash and more than US$940 million in *moedas podres*.[70] This resulted in the "virtual liquidation" of the company.

Anticipating complaints by minority shareholders, Petroquisa initially contemplated the possibility of repurchasing its minority shares and delisting before implementing its asset sales. The plan was abandoned, however, based on the conclusion that such a move would only increase the legal risks by transferring the controversy to Petrobras and *its* minority shareholders.[71] Minority shareholders complained of expropriation following the asset sales, but Petroquisa was unwilling to settle the dispute by agreeing to pay back the amounts it raised during its IPO.[72]

Porto Seguro Imóveis Ltda., a minority shareholder in Petroquisa, filed suit. It claimed that Petrobras, as the controlling shareholder of Petroquisa, acted in an abusive fashion in approving the sale, which privileged the interests of the federal government over those of the company and its minority shareholders.[73] Both the lower court and the state court of appeals agreed with plaintiff's argument, holding Petrobras liable to Petroquisa for damages of US$2.37 billion.[74] Throughout the lawsuit Petroquisa's lawyers emphasized the importance of the case for the credibility of Brazil's institutional environment.[75]

In 2012, however, twenty years after the claim was filed, the dispute took a surprising turn. The Superior Court of Justice in Brasilia, Brazil's court of last resort for the interpretation of federal legislation, reversed the prior decisions and dismissed the lawsuit for lack of standing.[76] The Court's decision rested primarily on the argument that a subsequent merger between Petroquisa and Petrobras in 2011 led to the merging of the identity—or, in technical terms, the "confusion" (*confusão*)—between debtor (Petroquisa) and creditor (Petrobras), which, under the Brazilian Civil Code, extinguished outstanding obligations between the parties.

---

[70] André Rocha, *Os riscos de investir em ações de estatais*, Valor Econômico, 3 June 2013, http://www.valor.com.br/valor-investe/o-estrategista/3147780/os-riscos-de-investir-em-acoes-de-estatais.

[71] *See id.*

[72] *See id.*

[73] *See supra* note 62 for the relevant statutory provision.

[74] T.J.R.J-Fourth Civil Chamber, EAC 2003.005.00333, Relator: Desembargador Jair Pontes de Almeida, 18/05/2004.

[75] *See infra* note 77 and accompanying text.

[76] STJ, Special Appeal 745.739–RJ, Third Chamber, Reporting Justice Massami Uyeda, decided on 28 Aug. 2013.

Although based on an apparent technicality, such a legal conclusion carries profound implications for Brazilian corporate law applicable to both private and public firms.[77] If broadly applied, it permits a corporate controlling shareholder to erect an absolute shield from liability for abuse of minority shareholders of a controlled company by later promoting a merger between the two entities. The outcome of the Petroquisa lawsuit thus offers a textbook illustration of a case driven by the interests of the state as controlling shareholder imposing negative externalities on the legal regime applicable to private firms. The result is decreased protection for minority shareholders as a whole.[78]

The procedural argument alone was sufficient to dismiss the suit. Nevertheless, and of particular interest, the Court's sympathies toward the interests of the state as shareholder led it further to elaborate on the merits of the case. Confirming its general unwillingness to use corporate law to constrain state action, it affirmed the absence of abuse, based on the Court's view of the state's right to change the rules of the game through subsequent statutes. The Court argued that the state's representatives in Petrobras were under a legal duty to comply with the Privatization Law's provisions even if they conflicted with the Corporations Law. The Court concluded that, in light of SOEs' "strategic role for the state," the government is entitled "for strategic reasons and with legal basis to adopt decisions that are quite different from those that would be made by a private shareholder."[79]

Following the Petroquisa decision, minority shareholders of both private firms and SOEs had reasons to worry. For minority shareholders of private firms the risk is of the use of a subsequent merger as an absolute defense against a derivative suit for abuse by a controlling shareholder. For minority shareholders of SOEs the concern is that the court made clear that special statutory changes could eliminate the protections apparently afforded to SOE shareholders by the corporate statute.

Separate from the lawsuit, the developments following Petroquisa's privatization are also emblematic of the changing contours of state capitalism in Brazil. In the privatization auctions, Odebrecht, a large diversified conglomerate that is one of Brazil's major business groups, emerged as the acquirer of the lion's share of Petroquisa's subsidiaries. Yet such a change in ownership structure did not entail a retreat of state support to the chemical industry. As one member of the House of Representatives (*Câmara dos Deputados*) put it in 2001, Brazil had transitioned from a "state monopoly to a private firm oligopoly," generously funded by BNDES.[80]

---

[77] Memorial da Recorrida [Additional Brief of Appellee], Special Appeal 745,739-RJ, at 49 (arguing that the Petroquisa lawsuit amounted to a "*leading case* about Brazilian capital markets and abuse of control power" and that "saying to a minority shareholder that has litigated for over twenty years that its lawsuit will not have its merit appreciated due to a unilateral corporate maneuver by the defendant . . . represents not only a gross injustice, but also sends a catastrophic message to the market as to the dignity and reliability of the country").

[78] On the impact of state ownership on the corporate governance environment, see *supra* note 38.

[79] STJ, *supra* note 76.

[80] Speech of Pedro Valadares, Câmara dos Deputados [Chamber of Deputies], May 28, 2001, http://goo.gl/5q0FiH.

Both state involvement and sector concentration intensified in subsequent years. Ironically, after having sold most of its chemical business to Odebrecht in exchange for arguably too low a price paid in junk government bonds in the 1990s, Petroquisa held 11 percent of Braskem (the vehicle of Odebrecht's chemical business) when the company went public in 2002. At the time, a shareholders agreement was in place granting Petroquisa significant veto rights.[81] Following Petroquisa's merger with Petrobras in 2011, the latter became a direct shareholder with a substantial stake in Braskem.[82]

Braskem's current ownership and governance structure is illustrative of the new modes of government involvement in business corporations in Brazil. Braskem is a publicly traded firm whose shares are listed on the São Paulo Stock Exchange (BM&F Bovespa) and whose ADRs are traded on the New York Stock Exchange. By the end of 2013, Odebrecht and Petrobras held 50.1 percent and 47 percent of Braskem's voting capital and 38.3 percent and 36.1 percent of its total capital, respectively. BNDESPAR held an additional 11.6 percent of its preferred nonvoting stock. Finally, BNDES is a major creditor of the firm, which in 2013 had more than US$1.5 billion of debt outstanding at the usual subsidized rates.[83]

Petrobras, a key supplier of Braskem, and Odebrecht are parties to a shareholders agreement that gives Odebrecht the upper hand: it appoints the majority of the board and the CEO, and is solely responsible for approving the business plan. Petrobras's rights under the agreements are far from negligible, however. It appoints four (out of eleven) members of Braskem's board of directors and its vice-chairman, as well as two members and the chairman of the supervisory board. The agreement also grants Petrobras veto rights with respect to mergers, spin-offs, and large investment and asset sales.

Even more illuminating of the current style of state capitalism in Brazil are the "guidelines for the exercise of voting rights" in Braskem by Odebrecht and Petrobras, which strive to reconcile the private shareholders' emphasis on profitability with the government's promotion of national champions. Under the agreement, Odebrecht and Petrobras "undertake to exercise their voting rights in the Companies so that Braskem and Braskem's Controlled Companies have a professional, efficient and productive management, preserving and increasing their profitability, in order to maximize their shareholders' compensation."[84] The parties also agree to adopt a dividend policy that "seeks to maximize the distribution of profits" (subject to the firm's financial health), and to pursue only new projects that are "explicitly profitable" in view of the weighted average cost of Braskem capital. Yet the voting guidelines also expose Braskem's status as a

[81] Braskem's Annual Report on Form 20-F for the year ended Dec. 31, 2012, at 108–09, http://www.sec.gov/Archives/edgar/data/1071438/000129281413000719/bakform20f_2012.htm.

[82] Petrobras's Form 6-K, for the month of December 2011, http://www.sec.gov/Archives/edgar/data/1119639/000129281411003316/pbra20111229_6k1.htm.

[83] Braskem's Annual Report on Form 20-F for the year ended Dec. 31, 2013, at 111, F-65, http://www.sec.gov/Archives/edgar/data/1071438/000129281414000902/bakform20f_2013.htm.

[84] Shareholders' Agreement of BRK Investimentos Petroquímicos S.A. and Braskem S.A., dated 5 April 2010, § 2.1, http://www.braskem-ri.com.br/show.aspx?idCanal=OxIsNDdQ/sz37EhqiG8SFA==.

national champion by mandating the "permanent pursuit of Braskem's growth in Brazil and abroad."[85]

Nor is Petrobras the only state actor involved in Braskem's governance. According to its securities filings, the company has two other corporate agreements in place that are relevant to its relationship with the state: one with BNDESPAR and another with SOE pension funds Previ and Petros.[86] Although BNDESPAR holds only nonvoting preferred shares, its shareholders agreement with Odebrecht grants it the right to appoint a board member so long as it holds at least 5 percent of Braskem's total capital. Under a memorandum of understanding, Previ and Petros enjoy special tag-along rights in control sales.

Even though government involvement in the chemical industry persists, the applicable legal framework has changed dramatically due to the different choice of ownership and governance structures. Prior to privatization, Petroquisa was a mixed enterprise under the uncontested direct voting control of Petrobras and, indirectly, of the federal government. Such control rights were accompanied by important legal checks and mechanisms of accountability aimed at mitigating the abuse of state discretion. As a mixed enterprise, Petroquisa was legally required to hire employees through public examinations and to choose suppliers through formal public procurement procedures. Its operations also fell under the purview of *Tribunais de Contas*, the body with the constitutional power of oversight of government accounts and spending.

Because the government's substantial support and influence takes the form of "minority" stakes, Braskem remains formally a private venture subject to a wholly private legal regime. Even if the government relinquishes discretion by sharing control with private business groups, it increases the scope for discretionary action by evading the restrictions imposed by public law. Functional discretion thus persists, with the public-private alliance arguably leading not only to potentially greater efficiency, but also to cronyism and opacity. For instance, escaping supervision by *Tribunal de Contas* was a key argument in the proposal for Braskem to take over a major government project for the construction of an integrated refinery and petrochemical complex.[87]

B. CONTROL CONTEST FOR CBD: THE STATE AS SUPPORTING ACTOR

State influence over corporate governance in Brazil extends far beyond SOEs and firms in which SCIIs hold significant equity stakes. The control contest over *Companhia*

---

[85] *See id.* §§ 2.1.1, 2.1.2.

[86] Braskem's Annual Report on Form 20-F for the year ended Dec. 31, 2012, at 135, http://www.sec.gov/Archives/edgar/data/1071438/000129281413000719/bakform20f_2012.htm.

[87] Ricardo Rego Monteiro, *Com a Braskem, Comperj sai da mira do Tribunal de Contas*, BRASIL ECONÔMICO, Mar. 16, 2010, http://brasileconomico.ig.com.br/ultimas-noticias/com-a-braskem-comperj-sai-da-mira-do-tribunal_78703.html.

Brasileira de Distribuição (CBD) between businessman Abílio Diniz and French group Casino Guichard-Perrachon shows that the state can exert influence in unexpected contexts. The episode also reveals that, under special conditions, appropriately targeted media campaigns can operate as a potent extralegal check on state discretion.

CBD is a large Brazilian consumer retail company that, among other things, operates the popular supermarket chain *Pão de Açucar.* Founded as a local bakery in 1948 by a Portuguese immigrant, *Pão de Açucar* grew into a large business through a combination of organic expansion and multiple acquisitions. In the mid-1990s, its founder's eldest son, Abilio Diniz, assumed control of the business and took the company public in both São Paulo and New York, raising hundreds of millions of dollars.[88]

By the late 1990s, however, CBD faced high levels of indebtedness and was on the lookout for new investors. It eventually agreed to join forces with a leading French retailer, Casino Guichard-Perrachon SA, which became a large minority shareholder in CBD in 1999. In 2005, Casino increased its voting stake in CBD to 50 percent and executed a shareholders agreement with Diniz family members to regulate their joint control over the firm. The agreement granted Casino an option to take over control of CBD in 2012. Brazil's Securities Commission (*Comissão de Valores Mobiliários*—CVM) understood that Casino had effectively paid for control of the company as early as 2005, and mandated a public bid for minority shares, as provided under Brazilian corporate law.

As the 2012 deadline approached, Abilio Diniz grew increasingly uneasy about relinquishing control of CBD. After several attempts to negotiate an extension of his tenure as CBD board chair failed, he orchestrated a bold plan: a merger between CBD and the Brazilian division of Carrefour, a French supermarket chain with a significant presence in Brazil and Casino's chief rival at home. Under the proposed transaction structure, Diniz would retain control of the combined entity. Controversially, though, Diniz's strategy was facilitated by significant state support: the transaction proposal advanced by BTG Pactual, an investment bank, was premised on an equity investment of more than US$2 billion by BNDESPAR.[89]

BNDESPAR's conspicuous role in the planned merger between CBD and Carrefour drew substantial scrutiny. The prospect of consolidation of two of Brazil's largest supermarket chains enraged consumers and set off red flags from a competition law standpoint. Observers soon began to raise questions about the rationale for BNDESPAR's support of the transaction, whose contribution to economic development in Brazil was far from evident.

---

[88] *Pão de Açucar completa 65 anos sem Diniz no comando*, UOL Economia, Sept. 7, 2013, http://economia.uol.com.br/noticias/redacao/2013/09/07/pao-de-acucar-completa-65-anos-sem-diniz-no-comando-veja-historia-do-grupo.htm.

[89] Guillermo Parra-Bernal, *Brazil's Pao de Acucar Agrees to Investor Buyout*, Reuters, June 28, 2011, http://www.reuters.com/article/2011/06/28/us-paodeacucar-merger-idUSTRE75R2UP20110628.

Unsurprisingly, Diniz praised BNDES's effort to prevent the sector from being "totally denationalized," which he characterized as a "service to society."[90] Development Minister Fernando Pimentel underscored the transaction's "strategic importance" for Brazil, noting that it would "for the first time, through a large international retail chain, place Brazil's industrialized products abroad."[91] Nonetheless, it was the statement by Civil Cabinet Chief Gleisi Hoffman that most irked commentators. Even though BNDESPAR is a wholly owned subsidiary of BNDES—which is, in turn, wholly owned by the federal government—she claimed that BNDESPAR's equity investment "was a market action" that "had nothing to do with the government's decision," as "there were no public funds involved."[92]

In response to these developments, Casino launched an aggressive communications campaign accusing Diniz of devising a value-destroying subterfuge in order to "frustrate the provisions of the shareholder agreements that regulate CBD and, indirectly, expropriate Casino of its control rights acquired and paid for in the year 2005."[93] Casino described Diniz's plan as disrespectful of "the rule of law and of the respect for private property that characterize Brazil."[94] Casino's attorney (the former Minister of Justice in a previous administration) characterized the developments as a "corporate coup," for "they made a secret agreement and they are using BNDES to pressure the French."[95] Jean-Charles Naori, Casino's chief and controlling shareholder, then flew to Brazil and met with BNDES managers to discuss the matter. As subsequently reported in an interview with a major local magazine, he asked BNDES not to "compromise its credibility by tolerating a fraud and an expropriation."[96] His not-so-implicit message was that a government-owned bank was assisting a Brazilian oligarch in repudiating a valid agreement with a foreign investor.

In the face of the ensuing public backlash—and despite several prior statements denying political interference in BNDES's operational decisions—President Dilma's response was explicitly to condition support by BNDES on Casino's consent to the

---

[90] Márcio Falcão & Ana Carolina Oliveira, *Fusão não terá dinheiro público, diz Gleisi*, FOLHA DE S. PAULO, June 30, 2011, www1.folha.uol.com.br/fsp/mercado/me3006201106.htm.

[91] *See id.*

[92] *See id.*

[93] Rafael Manzoni Jr. & Eliana Sobral, *A batalha mais difícil de Abilio*, ISTOÉ DINHEIRO, July 1, 2011, http://www.istoedinheiro.com.br/noticias/negocios/20110701/batalha-mais-dificil-abilio/77803.shtml.

[94] CBD Notice to the Market, dated June 28, 2011, http://www.gpari.com.br/grupopaodeacucar/web/arquivos/GPA_CM_Carta_Cassino_20110628_ENG.pdf (quoting Casino's letter to CBD).

[95] Mario Cesar Carvalho, *Casino Lawyer Accuses Abilio of "Corporate Coup,"* FOLHA DE S. PAULO, June 30, 2011, http://www1.folha.uol.com.br/internacional/en/business/2011/06/913820-casino-lawyer-accuses-abilio-of-corporate-coup.shtml.

[96] Beatriz Ferrari, *BNDES não deve compactuar com uma fraude, diz Naori* (interview to Veja website), VEJA, July 6, 2011, http://veja.abril.com.br/noticia/economia/bndes-nao-pode-compactuar-com-uma-frade-e-uma-expropriacao-diz-naouri.

transaction. Such a decision is best understood from a political rather than a legal or technical standpoint. If the deal were indeed beneficial to the company and the national economy, as its proponents claimed, any existing contractual arrangements between the controlling shareholders would have to give way. Brazilian corporate law explicitly subordinates the effects of shareholder agreements to the fiduciary duties of controlling shareholders.[97]

Casino never agreed to the proposed merger with Carrefour, which it regarded as flawed for multiple strategic and financial reasons.[98] The deal thus fell apart, culminating in various arbitral claims and counterclaims before the International Chamber of Commerce under the shareholder agreement. Casino alleged that Diniz breached the shareholders agreement by procuring Carrefour's bid without its prior consent, while Diniz argued that Casino thwarted a transaction that was beneficial for the company due to its conflict of interest as a competitor of Carrefour and future controlling shareholder of CBD.

The incident illustrates the mechanics of government intervention in corporate governance in Brazil. First, the state through BNDESPAR played a pivotal role in a control contest of an entirely private firm by offering to finance a transaction that could not be exclusively funded by private lenders—as evidenced by the deal's instant demise after the withdrawal of BNDESPAR's support. Second, although the existing legal framework confers ample discretion to BNDESPAR in its operational decisions, its choices are not immune from political and democratic controls. Given the suspicion with which the public received the proposal's announcement, a direct message from Brazil's president rapidly derailed the merger.

Casino had won the battle but not the war. It remained unclear if further obstacles would emerge to the control transfer scheduled for June 2012. The agreement was eventually performed as planned, and Casino took over the group. The partners-turned-foes continued to share the company's management despite their ongoing legal disputes. According to the terms of the same shareholders agreement, Diniz would continue to chair CBD's board of directors for as long as his physical and mental condition permitted and the company maintained good performance.[99]

---

[97] Lei No. 6.404, 15 de Dezembro de 1976, Diário Oficial da União [D.O.U.] de 17.12.1976, art. 118, § 2° (Braz.) ("These [shareholder] agreements cannot be invoked to exempt the shareholder from the responsibility in the exercise of voting rights [art. 115] or power of control [arts. 116, 117]").

[98] These reasons ranged from an allegedly flawed strategic vision based on a declining model of hypermarkets to the overestimation of potential synergies and the dilution of CBD shareholders. CBD Notice to the Market, July 12, 2011, http://www.gpari.com.br/grupopaodeacucar/web/arquivos/GPA_CM_PRCasino_20110712_ENG.pdf (quoting Casino's press release).

[99] Wilkes Shareholders' Agreement, dated Nov. 27, 2006, § 5.1.3.4.3(b), http://www.sec.gov/Archives/edgar/data/1038572/000129281407001889/exhibit4_12.htm.

An additional ground for disagreement—also influenced by state actors—appeared in early 2013 when news surfaced that Diniz had been appointed board chair at processed meat firm Brasil Foods (BRF), another national champion backed by government support. The company resulted from a 2009 merger between processed meat competitors Perdigão and Sadia after the latter experienced outsized financial losses when its exchange rate derivative bets turned sour during the 2008 financial crisis. BRF was widely identified as a national champion following the merger. It enjoyed the support of various pension funds that had significant stakes in Perdigão, as well as generous funding from BNDES.[100] Public pension funds Previ and Petros each account for more than 12 percent of BRF's capital.

Previ, the public pension giant, and Tarpon, a private investment fund, took credit for Diniz's nomination, which failed to receive unanimous approval. SOE pension fund Petros was among the dissidents, arguing that the speed of the appointment prevented consensual deliberation. This new development led Casino to initiate still another arbitral proceeding against Diniz, claiming that his dual role as board chair of both CBD and BRF posed a conflict of interest, as BRF was one of CBD's principal suppliers. It was not until September 2013 that Casino and Diniz settled all legal proceedings, with Diniz agreeing to resign from CBD's board and to exchange his voting shares in the company for preferred nonvoting shares at a one-to-one ratio.

The dispute between Diniz and Casino for control of CBD demonstrates that the influence of state actors in Brazilian corporate governance looms large. The episode also reveals the different ways in which law can constrain the behavior of SOEs. Although controversial from a social welfare standpoint, there was nothing illegal in BNDESPAR's proposed financing of the transaction: the absence of a detailed mandate gives the bank substantial leeway in reaching its investment decisions.[101] The role of law in constraining state action was mostly rhetorical. Casino's loud protests claiming that the transaction defied the "the rule of law" and the "respect for private property" in Brazil were likely a factor in its delegitimization in the eyes of the public and, ultimately, its loss of political support.[102]

Nonetheless, it would be premature to conclude that extralegal mechanisms are sufficient to restrain the harmful excesses of state capitalism in Brazil. In the CBD controversy,

[100] In 2011, BRF obtained a USD1.2 billion line of credit from BNDES. Sérgio Spagnuolo & Fabíola Gomes, *BRF autoriza contratação de R$2,5 bi junto ao BNDES*, BR REUTERS, Jan. 30, 2012, http://br.reuters.com/article/businessNews/idBRSPE80T06Y20120130.

[101] For a proposal of a more meticulous mandate for BNDES, see Schapiro, *supra* note 30.

[102] As reported by the international press, "Brasilia cannot be seen to have sided with a party in a dispute whose outcome risks undermining the rule of law—a commodity critical to a country's ability to attract private investment." Agnes T. Crane, *Brazil Steps In It by Siding with Carrefour deal*, REUTERS, July 5, 2011, http://uk.reuters.com/article/2011/07/05/idUKN1E76414U20110705.

Casino had every incentive to launch a campaign against the merger. Whenever the harm of misguided policies is more diffuse—as is often the case—collective action problems serve as an obstacle to democratic accountability.[103]

Conclusion

State capitalism is fundamentally about the degree of state discretion in economic affairs. In its present form, state involvement in Brazilian corporate governance relies on a combination of traditional government-controlled SOEs and the formally minority positions of SCIIs. From a legal standpoint, these different instruments reflect a trade-off between corporate control and countervailing legal controls. Majority ownership confers greater corporate control, but at the cost of a stricter legal regime molded by public law. Minority stakes free state actors from legal constraints, but require them to broker deals with private actors.

This emerging structure contrasts with the precise contours of state capitalism in China, as depicted in this volume. As described by Sérgio G. Lazzarini and Aldo Musacchio, China continues to display a bias toward state ownership of large equity stakes in listed firms, enabling state discretion through the exercise of corporate control.[104] As in Brazil, the prevalence of state-controlled firms in China also affects the legal regime applicable to private firms—a phenomenon, generally associated with SOEs,[105] which Donald Clarke here dubs "blowback."[106] Yet, as Curtis J. Milhaupt and Wentong Zheng have argued, the relentless emphasis on state ownership might lead one to miss the significant exercise of state discretionary influence over private firms in China.[107] Such an influence is relatively reduced, but by no means eliminated, by the presence of a stronger rule of law in Brazil.

Another distinction between the Chinese and Brazilian systems concerns the greater potential for democratic control of state discretion in Brazil. It is for this reason that the association between the growing use of a private legal regime and the reduction in the amount of information available to the public is particularly worrisome. Requests by journalists and academics for material agreements entered into by BNDES have been systematically denied based on dubious legal arguments. By sharing control with private actors, state power has plunged into obscurity. This is particularly challenging because extralegal constraints on state power depend crucially on the availability of information.

---

[103] Mancur Olson, The Logic of Collective Action (1965) (for a classical articulation of this problem).

[104] Sérgio G. Lazzarini & Aldo Musacchio, Chapter 17 in this volume.

[105] *See supra* note 40 and accompanying text.

[106] Donald Clarke, Chapter 2 in this volume.

[107] Curtis J. Milhaupt & Wentong Zheng, Chapter 9 in this volume.

Reversing this trend through stricter enforcement of existing laws or the enactment of new regulations is therefore imperative for both efficiency and legitimacy reasons.

Addressing the shortcomings of state capitalism requires a better and more nuanced understanding of its nuts and bolts. The precise relationship between majority and minority state investment, for instance, remains unclear. Scholars have posited that these two modes of ownership operate as substitutes, but they might also work as complements. It may be that the discretion afforded by fully controlled SOEs enhances the government's leverage over companies under shared public and private control. I leave this and other questions for future research.

17 Chinese Exceptionalism or New Global Varieties of State Capitalism

Aldo Musacchio and Sergio G. Lazzarini

Introduction

The number of papers studying Chinese state capitalism and its state-owned enterprises has exploded in the last two decades. Most of these works tend to see China as having a unique form of state capitalism in which the government has complicated pyramidal ownership structures to hold majority and minority equity positions in about a hundred firms or so. Other works also study the misallocation of capital by state-owned banks when they lend to "national champions" (large private and state-owned firms with government support in the form of subsidized loans, trade protection, and state-funded research facilities). Thus, outsiders of this growing literature on Chinese state capitalism and Chinese overseas foreign direct investment tend to assume that the findings of these works are specific to China.

In this chapter we argue that Chinese state capitalism has a lot in common with state capitalism in other parts of the world, both in developing and developed countries. The industrial organization and the ownership schemes used across countries, we maintain, bear much resemblance to the industrial organization in China, and raise important questions for the existing literature on state-owned enterprises (SOEs). Our main argument is that the varieties of state capitalism we find today (mostly within countries, but also across countries) are significantly different from the way state capitalism worked in the Soviet days (or in the pre-management responsibility system days in China). More specifically, we argue that we need new frameworks to think about the implications of new forms of state ownership. Understanding the new forms of state ownership, control, and support of firms may actually shed some light on why state capitalism in China, and around the world, has been so resilient.

Chinese SOEs, and those of other countries, have become more central to the world economy. One way to gauge the resilience and importance of these SOEs is to look at how they have populated the lists of the largest companies in the world. For example, in 2005 the Fortune Global 100 list, which ranks companies by revenues, had no SOEs among the top ten firms and included only about a dozen in the top 100. By 2012, in contrast, there were four SOEs among the top ten and twenty-five among the top 100. Furthermore, in the twenty-five largest SOEs the government was a majority investor in seventeen and a minority investor in eight.[1]

Moreover, large SOEs at the beginning of the twenty-first century seem to be more focused on profitability and internationalization than their predecessors. For instance, in 2012, the largest twenty-five state-owned firms had a return on assets of 3.44 percent and an operating margin of 14 percent, while the largest seventy-five private firms had a return on assets of 3.19 percent and an operating margin of 5.7 percent.

The rise of large SOEs, with new ownership and governance structures, to the center stage of global capitalism has raised interesting questions for academics and policymakers. Of interest to academics are, for instance, the various institutional mechanisms by which states exercise control, why state capitalism re-emerged and in which form, and state capitalism's effects on both firm performance and state governance. Most of the literature on the inefficiency of SOEs examined firms in which the government was the sole owner, and in which politicians or bureaucrats were appointed as managers. In our view these studies of SOEs are problematic because these firms operated in systems that relied heavily on state planning to determine prices and the allocation of raw materials. Hence, this large theoretical and empirical literature has characterized SOEs as less efficient than their private counterparts because they usually have a variety of agency problems. Additionally, according to this literature, these state-owned firms have a hard time remaining profitable because they have a variety of social and political objectives to meet.

---

[1] We define state capitalism as the widespread influence of the government in the economy, either by owning majority or minority equity positions in companies or through the provision of subsidized credit and/or other privileges to private companies. Such majority and minority equity positions can be held directly by ministries and other government departments, or indirectly through holding companies, development banks, pension funds, sovereign wealth funds, and the government itself. We label these two alternative ownership forms *Leviathan as a majority investor* and *Leviathan as a minority investor* respectively. See, for instance, the discussion in *The Economist*, special issue on state capitalism: Adrian Wooldridge, *The Visible Hand*, THE ECONOMIST, Jan. 21, 2012, *available at* http://www.economist.com/node/21542931.

Yet the evidence on the rise of large global SOEs, and the resilience of medium-sized SOEs in a variety of countries, creates an interesting puzzle. How could these SOEs, which in theory are supposed to be plagued with agency problems and political interference, climb to the top of the global ranking of firms by profitability?[2]

The puzzle arises because the dominant academic view on SOEs characterizes them as having two corporate governance problems. On the one hand they suffer from what we call the Type I corporate governance problem. That is, SOEs suffer from a traditional agency problem because their managers lack pay-for-performance contracts; they have no pressure to perform because they know they will be bailed out if they fail; and they are not well monitored by bureaucrats, boards of directors, or investors. On the other hand, SOEs suffer from a Type II corporate governance problem because there are "public" benefits of control when governments are the controlling shareholders. In other words, in SOEs controlling shareholders have disproportionate pecuniary and non-pecuniary benefits from running the firm. In private firms it is easier to understand what "private benefits of control" entail; such is the case when controlling shareholders steer the firm to tunnel resources to a related firm by, for example, selling assets or products at below-market price. In SOEs, tunneling by the controlling shareholder can entail selling output (e.g., gasoline, electricity, or gas) at below-market prices to "related" firms that the government wants to support (i.e., national champions) or to the public (to gain political support). The literature on SOEs has traditionally called this second problem the problem of "multiple objectives" inside SOEs, because managers are expected to achieve financial, political, and social objectives simultaneously.[3]

In this chapter we argue that governments around the world have started to find new corporate governance arrangements to solve the first problem. Governments have partially privatized a large fraction of their SOEs and ended up with new forms of hybrid state ownership, in which the government is a majority shareholder in many SOEs, sharing ownership with large institutional investors, or a minority shareholder in privately run firms.[4] This has allowed the government to shift monitoring responsibilities

---

[2] All lists taken from the Fortune Global 500 list web page. *Global 500*, FORTUNE, http://money.cnn.com/magazines/fortune/global500/ (last visited Mar. 3, 2012).

[3] Obviously one could argue that the main reason SOEs exist is precisely because governments want to use such firms for political and social objectives. Yet, we counter with two arguments. First, not all SOEs are in industries with social and political objectives and, historically, systematic deviations from their main objectives have created financial difficulties for such firms. Second, even in the case of SOEs with social objectives, such as the provision of public services, having more distance between the government and the firm and minimizing the "public benefits of control" can lead to better quality in the provision of public goods. This is the case, for instance, of Sabesp, a publicly traded water company in Sao Paulo, Brazil, which has improved corporate governance in a way that minimizes agency problems but also government intervention (e.g., to maximize employment). It is the most profitable and efficient SOE in Brazil.

[4] We do not argue that governments having minority ownership in corporations is new; this has existed since the corporate form was created. What we think is distinctive about having governments as a minority investor is that they rely to a large extent on minority investments to influence companies and to extract returns from economic activity, something that represents a shift from the predominantly majority-owned model of state capitalism of the second half of the twentieth century. Relying on minority investments is

to private investors, rating agencies, and equity analysts, and has forced publicly traded SOEs to be more transparent and to improve their corporate governance by adopting new checks and balances, both for the power of managers and for the possible intervention by the state to extract public benefits of control. Yet, we also acknowledge that it is precisely in regard to this last point that governments have had more trouble. That is, despite the ways in which governments have reinvented the governance of SOEs, they have had a hard time isolating SOEs from the temptation governments have to steer them toward social or political goals that directly affect the welfare of the other shareholders of these firms.

Hence, in this chapter we not only explain how governments have reduced agency problems using these new corporate governance forms, but also discuss some of the most common forms of industrial organization around the world. Studying the industrial organizations of SOEs is important because, other than a couple of case studies, we know very little about how governments run and control their SOEs. Li-Wen Lin and Curtis J. Milhaupt provide a detailed account of the pyramidal ownership structures adopted by Chinese SOEs, under the control of the government's largest holding company, SASAC, and explain the promotions criteria inside these group structures and some of their governance traits.[5] In their account of Chinese SOEs the main governance concern is the second type of agency problem present in SOEs: namely the excessive control rights of the Chinese government and SASAC, and how the steering of these SOEs to maximize national welfare, rather than shareholder value, may entail a possible abuse of minority shareholders.

Below we explain how the industrial organization observed in China is very similar to that of other countries. Yet very few countries have structures similar to the Communist Party to align incentives, manage careers and promotions, and punish deviations from the party line. We suggest that perhaps the ways in which some of the Gulf countries manage SOEs and align the incentives of their managers may be the closest to the Chinese model.

I. The Resilience of State Capitalism

In China, every time there is a new group of Party members in power, journalists and observers in the West speculate about how much reform and privatization will take place. In particular, there is always a debate about whether the privatization process will

---

perhaps closer to the form of state capitalism that prevailed in Europe and Latin America before the Great Depression. For Europe, see for instance ROBERT MILLWARD, PRIVATE AND PUBLIC ENTERPRISE IN EUROPE: ENERGY TELECOMMUNICATIONS AND TRANSPORT, 1830–1990 (2005). For Brazil, see ALDO MUSACCHIO, EXPERIMENTS IN FINANCIAL DEMOCRACY: CORPORATE GOVERNANCE AND FINANCIAL DEVELOPMENT IN BRAZIL, 1882–1950 (2009).

[5] Li-Wen Lin & Curtis J. Milhaupt, *We Are the (National) Champions: Understanding the Mechanisms of State Capitalism in China*, 65 STAN. L. REV. 697 (2013).

be deepened, and how much the state will retreat. Yet, the outcome is always disappointing from the point of view of these observers. There is always more state intervention and more state ownership than was expected.

Part of the problem is that state capitalism is more resilient than most observers think. For instance, after almost three decades of privatization in developed and developing countries, the outcome was not a general strip-down of the state's productive assets. On the contrary, privatizations faced intense political opposition, and in many sectors governments decided that it was better to keep certain companies under state control. Bernardo Bortolotti and Mara Faccio's survey of SOEs in OECD countries reveals that, despite strenuous efforts to privatize, governments still control a large share of the privatized firms.[6] Except for the capital goods sector, transportation, and utilities, the share of firms under government control did not go down between 1996 and 2000 in that set of rich countries. The OECD surveys of 2005 and 2011 also show that in developed countries (including Chile, Mexico, and South Korea) governments kept control in tens, if not hundreds, of firms; they kept minority equity positions in a large number of firms; and they also kept stakes in some of the largest publicly traded firms, representing between 10 and 20 percent of the total value of the stock market in their home countries.

In emerging markets governments also hold equity positions in tens or hundreds of firms. In Table 17.1 we show the emerging markets for which we found ownership data, and we describe the extent of state ownership, the relative importance of SOE output to GDP, and the way in which governments hold their equity positions in SOEs. It is impressive to see that SOE output is still a large share of GDP in these countries. In most countries SOEs produce between 20 and 30 percent of total output. This share, in fact, has not decreased much since 1980. That is, despite the massive privatization wave of the 1990s and 2000s, in many of these countries the large SOEs remain in government hands and their output represents a large fraction of GDP. Moreover, from Table 17.1 it is also evident that governments in emerging markets have kept controlling positions in a significant number of SOEs, as well as keeping minority equity positions in hundreds, if not thousands, of firms.

In both developed and developing countries, governments that kept minority equity positions in the privatized firms also often kept shares with special veto rights. These shares, called "golden shares," grant them special power to veto decisions such as mergers or changes to the objectives of the firm. These shares usually also carry veto rights for any major change in the firm's corporate governance, such as changes in voting rights attached to different shares.[7]

Brazil, Russia, India, and China (BRIC), the largest emerging markets, display the same pattern of ownership we find in other parts of the emerging and developed

[6] Bernardo Bortolotti & Mara Faccio, *Government Control of Privatized Firms*, 22 THE REV. OF FIN. STUD. 2907 (2009).

[7] For a more thorough discussion of golden shares and their widespread use in OECD countries, see *id*. at 2918.

TABLE 17.1

STATE OWNERSHIP IN EMERGING MARKETS C. 2010

	SOE output (revenues) to (non-financial) GDP	Number of SOEs in which the central government is a			Ownership vehicle			
		majority shareholder	minority shareholder	Direct ownership (Ministry or Treasury)	Holding co's	Insurance & Pension funds	SWF	Dev. banks
Brazil	30.0%	247	397	X	X	X		X
China	29.7%	120+	n.a.	X	X		X	
UAE (Dubai)	n.a.	n.a.	n.a.		X		X	
Egypt	n.a.	57	59	X	X			
India	13.1%	217	404	X		X		
Indonesia	18.0%	142	21	X				
Malaysia	n.a.	52	28		X		X	
Mexico	3.0%	205	0	X				
Poland	28.0%	498	691	X				
Qatar	>80%	n.a.	n.a.	X	X		X	
Rep. of Korea	10.0%	n.a.	n.a.	X	X			X
Russia	20.0%	7964	1418	X	X			
Singapore	12.0%	20	n.a.		X		X	
South Africa	n.a.	270	n.a.	X				
Thailand	26.0%	60	n.a.	X				
Turkey	14.0%	74	67	X				
Vietnam	33.9%	1805	1740	X	X			

Source: Created with data FROM ALDO MUSACCHIO & SERGIO G. LAZZARINI, REINVENTING STATE CAPITALISM: LEVIATHAN IN BUSINESS, BRAZIL AND BEYOND (2014).

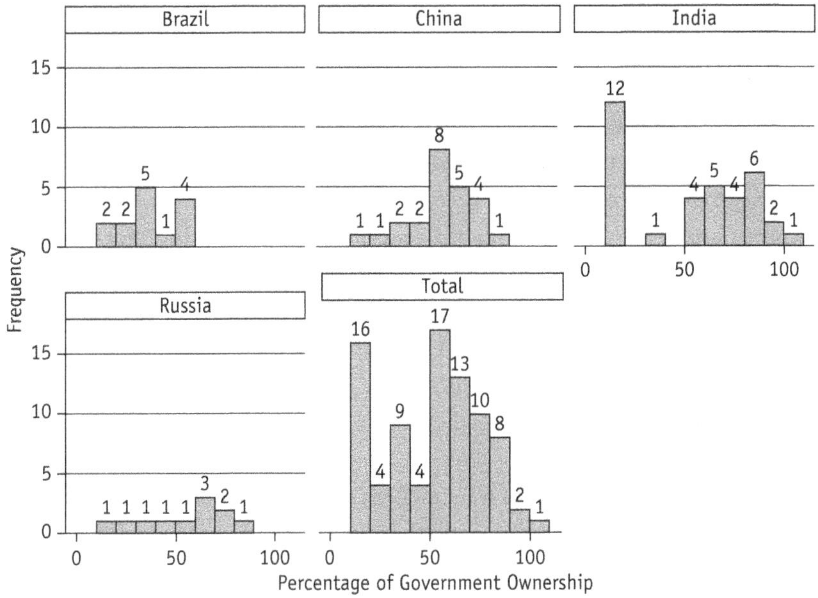

FIGURE 17.1 Distribution of the Number of Government Equity Holdings in Publicly Traded Companies in BRIC Countries, 2007.

Source: Created by the authors from Capital IQ and company web pages using a sample of the largest 150 publicly traded companies in these markets.

world—that is, a mix of majority and minority ownership. In Figure 17.1 we show the distribution of ownership using a database of the largest 150 publicly traded companies (by market capitalization) in 2007. Leviathan acts most often as a minority shareholder in Brazil and Russia, followed by India, where the government, or one of its holding companies (e.g., The Life Insurance Corp. of India), holds minority positions in a variety of firms. In China we see a greater bias toward large ownership stakes in publicly traded companies, but we still find some minority shareholdings. These minority stakes mostly occur through holding companies that are fully controlled by the government and that then invest in a variety of firms. Furthermore, as we discuss below, governments not only act as shareholders but also provide credit to firms through development banks and state-owned banks.

How can we make sense of this varied configuration of state ownership? Next we propose stylized models of state capitalism and then discuss alternative theoretical explanations for their emergence.

II. Models of State Capitalism

Economists have usually juxtaposed state capitalism and either liberal market economies or free markets in general. Ludwig von Mises, one of the most influential Austrian economists, equated state capitalism with socialism or "planned economy." Murray

N. Rothbard, a central figure in the American libertarian movement, went even further by defining state capitalism as "violent expropriation."[8] Moreover, for Rothbard, the cozying up of big business with the government was also a manifestation of state capitalism. Therefore, these two libertarian scholars equated state capitalism with government intervention in markets, central planning, governments favoring big business, and even the outright expropriation of private property.

Ian Bremmer provides the beginnings of a conceptual framework for understanding various degrees of state involvement in the economy. He distinguishes state capitalism from "command economies," involving planning and state-led resource allocation, and "free-market economies," featuring minimal governmental intervention (e.g., along the lines of securing property rights and establishing stable rules for private investment). He defines state capitalism as a system in which:

> ... governments use various kinds of state-owned enterprises to manage the exploitation of resources they consider the state's crown jewels and to create and maintain large numbers of jobs. They select privately owned companies to dominate certain economic sectors. They use so-called sovereign wealth funds to invest their extra cash in ways that maximize the state's profits. In all three cases, the state is using markets to create wealth that can be directed as political officials see fit. And in all three cases the ultimate motive is not economic (maximizing growth) but political (maximizing the state's power and the leadership's chances of survival).[9]

All those definitions, however, lack nuance. Hence, consistent with Bremmer we conceptualize state capitalism as a system where the government has a marked influence on the business sector. We, however, advance the discussion by separating state capitalism into three broader classes (see Figure 17.2).[10]

Closer to the more familiar view of state capitalism as a process involving outright state management, the state can act as a majority shareholder *and manager* of SOEs—a mode we refer to as *Leviathan as an entrepreneur.* According to Yair Ahroni,[11] such SOEs are conceptualized as *enterprises*—that is, they should effectively produce and sell goods and services. These companies should be distinguished from government entities in charge of providing public services (such as courts, the police, social security, or

---

[8] Murray N. Rothbard, A Future of Peace and Capitalism (1973).

[9] Ian Bremmer, The End of the Free Market: Who Wins the War between States and Corporations? 4–5 (2010).

[10] Our work thus contributes to the evolving literature on the varieties of capitalism. *See, e.g.*, Peter A. Hall & David Soskice, *An Introduction to Varieties of Capitalism*, *in* Varieties of Capitalism: The Institutional Foundations of Comparative Advantage 1 (2001); Ben Ross Schneider & David Soskice, *Inequality in Developed Countries and Latin America: Coordinated, Liberal and Hierarchical Systems*, 38 Econ. and Soc'y 17 (2009). We, however, focus on state capitalism and its varied forms, which has not been studied in detail by that literature.

[11] Yair Ahroni, The Evolution and Management of State Owned Enterprises (1986).

national health services), which often do not have a corporate form and depend directly on orders from government officials.

As we explained in the introduction, SOEs face two types of corporate governance problems. The Type I problem is a typical principal-agent one that stems from the fact that managers in SOEs are poorly monitored, lack high-powered incentives, and face a soft-budget constraint. Therefore, managers can end up running inefficient firms, shirking their responsibilities, etc. The Type II problem is related to the public benefits of control or the capacity that managers or governments, as controlling shareholders, have to steer the firm for their own personal or political benefit. For instance, politicians may ask SOEs to build a plant in a location that is not strategically convenient, or to invest in a business line outside the core competency of the firm, simply because that will bring them votes. That is, SOEs sometimes undertake projects that have positive political net present value, but that would not be undertaken on the grounds of social or financial net present value.

The Type I problem, of delegating decisions to agents whose objectives may not be aligned with those of principals, has been long discussed by agency theorists. Part of the reason the Type I governance problem exists is that monitoring in public bureaucracies is challenging. The remedies for principal-agent misalignment normally involve performance-contingent incentive contracts for managers, direct monitoring by principals, or a combination of both. Those remedies are far more difficult to implement in SOEs than in privately owned firms. Hence, incentive contracts usually work best when there are objective, readily observable performance metrics such as profits or share prices. However, SOEs may also have to consider social objectives, beyond pure financial objectives, which may lead to confusing goals and more complex performance metrics. The kind of scorecards managers need to use to track their progress in both social and financial objectives are hard to design and to evaluate. The Republic of Korea has been the exception in that regard, because since the 1980s managers of SOEs have been evaluated on a combination of performance metrics and social goals.

State organizations also lack a well-defined group of monitors, such as shareholders actively participating in corporate boards. In fact, governments may appoint politicians or politically connected actors to "monitor" SOEs, thereby leading to the fundamental question of "who monitors the monitors" or "who guards the guardians." Unlike shareholders of private firms, those appointed board members do not have their wealth at stake when executing their monitoring duties. In addition, managers in wholly owned SOEs do not have the threat of a hostile takeover when they underperform relative to their peers, and do not face risk of bankruptcy because they know the government will recapitalize or bail out the company if it becomes insolvent.

Below we explain how the new forms of state ownership can help governments reduce the Type I and II corporate governance problems. For a summary of these arguments, see Table 17.2, where we explain how the Leviathan as a majority and minority investor models can mitigate these corporate governance problems.

TABLE 17.2

CORPORATE GOVERNANCE PROBLEMS IN SOES AND HOW THEY ARE ADDRESSED BY THE NEW VARIETIES OF STATE CAPITALISM

	Traditional wholly owned SOEs (Leviathan as an entrepreneur)	SOEs with Leviathan as a majority investor	Firms with Leviathan as a minority investor
Type I corporate governance problem in SOEs (principal-agent)	Managers: – lack high-powered incentives – Poor monitoring by ministries, departments, and boards – Soft-budget constraint	Managers – can have high-powered incentives (e.g., stock or stock options) – are monitored by private investors, analysts, and rating agencies – have to meet targets (easy to measure performance metrics such as stock price) – have to report financials regularly following international accounting standards – may not face soft-budget constraint if governments let them fail or make them go through painful renegotiations – managers can be fired if they underperform	Managers – are professionals selected by boards of directors – have close monitoring from private controlling investors, institutional investors, rating agencies, and analysts. – have to meet targets (easy to measure performance metrics such as stock price) – have to report financials regularly following international accounting standards – have no soft-budget constraint unless firm is too big to fail – are fired if they underperform
Type II corporate governance problem in SOEs (public benefits of control or political intervention)	– Managers get pecuniary and non-pecuniary benefits – Politicians use firms for political goals unrelated to the main objective of the firm	Firm can be isolated from political intervention by having financial autonomy, being publicly traded, and having a majority of independent directors on the board	– Firm isolated from political intervention by having financial autonomy – Firm can meet social objectives through corporate social responsibility programs

		– Firm can meet social objectives either through corporate social responsibility programs or by following balanced scorecards with social dimensions – Yet, managers and controlling shareholders *can* obtain pecuniary and non-pecuniary benefits of control (e.g., selling assets below market price), using firm's assets for personal or political objectives, etc. – Abuses of minority shareholder rights will depend on the corporate governance institutions of the country (e.g., stock markets, securities regulators, corporate laws, and court system)	– Firm can meet social objectives through corporate social responsibility programs

A. LEVIATHAN AS A MAJORITY INVESTOR

Governments around the world only partially privatized their strategic companies. This is why we commonly find them as controlling shareholders of large SOEs. When governments act as majority shareholders in publicly traded firms, those SOEs tend to have corporate governance regimes that reduce the Type I problem found in wholly owned SOEs. On the one hand they can align the incentives of managers by incentivizing them with pay-for-performance compensation schemes and by having external investors and credit rating agencies monitoring their actions. These firms also have boards of directors, sometimes with external members, monitoring the actions of managers. On the other hand, rather than having politicians running these firms, in large SOEs boards of directors, consulting with ministries, are starting to select their chief executive officers (CEOs) on the basis of experience or merit. Furthermore, these SOEs now commonly follow international accounting standards and report financials frequently (usually quarterly).

It is obviously extremely hard to generalize, partly because there is too much variation in ownership and corporate governance arrangements within each of the modes of government ownership we have in Figure 17.1. Yet, it should be clear that in the model in which the government is a majority shareholder, many of the Type I corporate governance problems could be reduced if the monitoring of managers improves. Empirically, academics have shown that after partial privatization there are significant improvements in firm performance. These partially privatized firms (SOEs with majority government ownership) fare better than state-owned firms, but not necessarily better than private companies.[12]

Now, let us turn to the ways in which the Leviathan as a majority investor model can reduce political intervention. In our analysis of SOEs we have found that reducing political intervention is one of the hardest problems for governments that have reformed their public enterprises. This is particularly the case in large firms in strategic sectors (electricity and other network infrastructure) or firms in sectors that generate large rents (e.g., oil, gas, and mining). The problem, particularly in democratic countries with weak rule of law or with weak checks and balances on the executive power, is that governments have the temptation to intervene in these firms to channel rents to politically connected sectors or populations, or to control prices to benefit national champions or domestic consumers.

In countries in which SOEs seem to have been better isolated from politics; the corporate governance regime of such enterprises usually involves clauses providing firms with financial autonomy (e.g., independence from the government budget to fund its operations). Independent SOEs also tend to have boards of directors that include a large number of independent (e.g., nonpolitical) directors that can provide checks and balances to

[12] Nandini Gupta, *Partial Privatization and Firm Performance*, 60 J. OF FIN. 987 (2005).

the actions of the controlling shareholder. Finally, for SOEs to operate autonomously from politics, it is necessary to have a system of checks and balances at the national level that allows minority shareholders to sue the controlling shareholder, the government, and win.

To illustrate this point, we created two separate governance indices for national oil companies that measure how many moderators there are on basic agency problems—that is, checks and balances limiting the power of managers to avoid the Type I problem, and how many checks and balances there are to avoid the Type II problem, the power of government to extract public benefits of control. In Table 17.3 we present the index of Type I moderators. The index is the sum of six different governance indicators. First we add one point if the company is publicly traded, as this would imply there are private investors monitoring managers. The literature would argue private investors are better than the government at monitoring managers. Second, we add another point if the government is actually a minority shareholder, as this would imply there are private monitors taking the main role as monitors. Third, we add another point if the chairman of the board is not the CEO; this usually means that there are more counterbalances to the power of the CEO. Fourth, we add a point if there are independent board members on the board of directors. This is now very common among private firms, but some SOEs have been slow to adopt this practice. Obviously we do not know if these independent directors are actually a counterweight to the power of CEOs, but in general they are selected by the government or legislature to act precisely as a check on CEO power and to also serve as a balance against government influence. Sixth, we add another point if the independent directors constitute a majority of the board. Finally, we add one point if the financials of the firms are audited by a private auditing firm with a global reputation.

Table 17.3 shows how much variation there is in corporate arrangements in thirty large National Oil Companies (NOCs), most of which have full or majority control by the government. NOCs are energy companies in which governments usually have either full ownership (e.g., Aramco in Saudi Arabia or Pemex in Mexico) or at least control (e.g., ENI in Italy, Statoil in Norway, Sinopec in China, Petrobras in Brazil, or Gazprom in Russia). Those firms in which governments have control but not full ownership are usually publicly traded. Some current SOEs also resulted from previously privatized companies that were subsequently "re-nationalized"—as is the case of Russia's state-owned gas company Gazprom (re-nationalized through the purchase of control from private parties) and the former private oil company Yukos (which after being charged with tax evasion went into bankruptcy and sold its assets to state-owned companies in a series of auctions).

The table shows that a large majority of the NOCs have adopted provisions to mitigate the Type I agency problem by listing the firm on a stock exchange, by adding independent directors to the board, or by improving their financial transparency. There is still wide variation in the type of governance measures firms use against the power of managers, but the majority have three or more of the measures we track. Even firms that

TABLE 17.3.

INDEX OF TYPE I CORPORATE GOVERNANCE MODERATORS IN 30 NATIONAL OIL

NOC	Country	Publicly traded	Total gov't share of voting stock	Has some of the equity been privatized? (Yes = 1, No = 0)	Is the gov't a minority shareholder? (Yes = 1, No = 0)
		(A)	(B)	(C)	(D)
ENI	Italy	Y	30.3	1	1
Statoil	Norway	Y	70.8	1	0
Ecopetrol	Colombia	Y	89.9	1	0
OGDCL	Pakistan	Y	85.2	1	0
GDF Suez	France	Y	36.4	1	1
Sinopec	China	Y	75.8	1	0
Rosneft	Russia	Y	83.0	1	0
Saudi Aramco	Saudi Arabia	N	100	0	0
Gazprom	Russia	Y	50.0	1	0
CNOOC Ltd	China	Y	66.0	1	0
ONGC	India	Y	84.2	1	0
Petro China	China	Y	86.7	1	0
Petrobras	Brazil	Y	55.7	1	0
KazMunayGas	Kazakhstan	Y	62.0	1	0
PTT	Thailand	Y	67.1	1	0
PDO	Oman	N	60.0	1	0
OOC	Oman	N	100	0	0
PEMEX	Mexico	N	100	0	0
Petronas	Malaysia	Y	100	0	0
KPC	Kuwait	N	100	0	0
Pertamina	Indonesia	N	100	0	0
QP	Qatar	N	100	0	0
Libya NOC	Libya	N	100	0	0
NIOC	Iran	N	100	0	0
Petro SA	South Africa	N	100	0	0
Sonatrach	Algeria	N	100	0	0
Adnoc	UAE	N	100	0	0
EGPC	Egypt	N	100	0	0
INOC	Iraq	N	100	0	0
NNPC	Nigeria	N	100	0	0
PDVSA	Venezuela	N	100	0	0

Source: Created with data from MUSACCHIO & LAZZARINI, *supra* Table 17.1.

COMPANIES

Chairman of the board of directors is not the CEO? (Not CEO = 1, otherwise 0)	Are there independent or external board members? (Yes = 1, No = 0)	Are the external board members a majority? (Yes = 1, No = 0)	Are financials audited by a global auditing firm? (Yes = 1, No = 0)	Type I moderator index
(E)	(F)	(G)	(H)	(Sum C to H)
1	1	0	1	5
1	1	1	1	5
1	1	1	1	5
1	1	1	1	5
0	1	0	1	4
1	1	0	1	4
1	1	0	1	4
1	1	1	1	4
1	1	0	1	4
1	1	0	1	4
1	1	0	1	4
1	1	0	1	4
1	1	0	1	4
1	1	0	1	4
1	1	0	0	3
1	1	0	0	3
1	1	0	1	3
1	1	0	1	3
0	1	0	1	2
0	1	1	0	2
0	1	0	1	2
1	0	0	1	2
1	0	0	0	1
1	0	0	0	1
0	0	0	0	0
0	0	0	0	0
0	0	0	0	0
0	0	0	0	0
0	0	0	0	0
0	0	0	0	0
0	0	0	0	0

are not privately traded, such as ARAMCO in Saudi Arabia, have independent directors on their boards.

In Table 17.4 we include a similar index of provisions to limit the public benefits of control, that is, the capacity that the government has to influence the national oil companies and steer them toward projects that are more beneficial to politicians than to the firm itself. In this index of Type II problem moderators we also add points in the index if the firm is partially privatized (the government has majority ownership), if the government is a minority shareholder, if the firm has independent directors, and if the independent directors constitute a majority of the board of directors. We go further, however, and add points if the chairman of the board is not a politician or a firm insider, and if the firm has financial autonomy from the government. This variable is crucial because in some SOEs the government audits the investment plans and has to fund them, while others have complete autonomy to make investments. When the latter is the case it usually means that the SOE has some discretion over how much it will pay in dividends to the government.

In contrast with Table 17.3, in Table 17.4 we can see that very few NOCs have actually adopted corporate governance schemes that limit the power of the government. In fact, most of the checks and balances NOCs have introduced to limit the power of the government have been partial privatizations of capital, as if having private shareholders would credibly commit the government to keep from extracting from private firms. Very few firms have introduced checks and balances on the boards, such as having a majority of independent directors, independent chairmen, or financial autonomy.

Having SOEs listing shares on stock exchanges as a shortcut to solve both Type I and Type II problems assumes there is credible commitment on the part of the government to refrain from using SOEs to obtain public benefits of control, simply because the government does not want to offend the private investors in these firms. This, in turn, assumes that the legal system in the home country of each of these SOEs and their corporate governance institutions are powerful and sophisticated enough to act as a constraint on the power and influence of the government. But there are many examples of how this assumption has been violated when it is convenient to the government.[13]

B. LEVIATHAN AS A MINORITY SHAREHOLDER

Governments privatized control of many of their SOEs in the last two or three decades, but kept minority equity positions in them. Furthermore, not only have they privatized majority control, governments have also bought new minority equity positions in private

[13] See examples of abuses of minority shareholders in Petrobras, the Brazilian national oil company in Mariana Pargendler et al., *In Strange Company: The Puzzle of Private Investment in State-Controlled Firms*, 46 CORNELL INT'L L.J. 569 (2013).

TABLE 17.4

INDEX OF TYPE II CORPORATE GOVERNANCE MODERATORS IN 30 NATIONAL OIL COMPANIES

NOC	Country	Has some of the equity been privatized? (Yes = 1, No = 0)	Is the gov't a minority shareholder? (Yes = 1, No = 0)	Are there independent or external board members? (Yes = 1, No = 0)	Are the external board members a majority? (Yes = 1, No = 0)	Are there no government officials on the board? (Yes = 1, No = 0)	Chairman of the BOD is external, not a gov't official (Yes = 1, No = 0)	Firm has financial autonomy from gov't (Yes = 1, No = 0)	Type II moderator index
		(A)	(B)	(C)	(D)	(E)	(F)	(G)	(Sum A to G)
ENI	Italy	1	1	1	0	1	1	1	6
Statoil	Norway	1	0	1	1	1	1	1	6
Ecopetrol	Colombia	1	0	1	1	0	1	1	5
GDF Suez	France	1	1	1	0	0	0	1	4
Sinopec	China	1	0	1	0	1	0	1	4
Rosneft	Russia	1	0	1	0	0	1	1	4
OGDCL	Pakistan	1	0	1	1	0	0	1	4
Saudi Aramco	Saudi Arabia	0	0	1	1	0	1	1	4
PTT	Thailand	1	0	1	1	0	0	1	4
Gazprom	Russia	1	0	1	0	0	0	1	3
CNOOC Ltd	China	1	0	1	0	1	0	0	3
ONGC	India	1	0	1	0	0	0	1	3
Petro China	China	1	0	1	0	1	0	0	3
Petrobras	Brazil	1	0	1	0	0	0	0	2
KazMunayGas	Kazakhstan	1	0	1	0	0	0	0	2

(continued)

TABLE 17.4
(*CONTINUED*)

NOC	Country	Has some of the equity been privatized? (Yes = 1, No = 0)	Is the gov't a minority shareholder? (Yes = 1, No = 0)	Are there independent or external board members? (Yes = 1, No = 0)	Are the external board members a majority? (Yes = 1, No = 0)	Are there no government officials on the board? (Yes = 1, No = 0)	Chairman of the BOD is external, not a gov't official (Yes = 1, No = 0)	Firm has financial autonomy from gov't (Yes = 1, No = 0)	Type II moderator index
		(A)	(B)	(C)	(D)	(E)	(F)	(G)	(Sum A to G)
Petronas	Malaysia	0	0	1	0	0	0	1	2
PDO	Oman	1	0	1	0	0	0	0	2
KPC	Kuwait	0	0	1	1	0	0	0	2
OOC	Oman	0	0	1	0	0	0	0	1
PEMEX	Mexico	0	0	1	0	0	0	0	1
Pertamina	Indonesia	0	0	1	0	0	0	0	1
QP	Qatar	0	0	0	0	1	0	0	1
Petro SA	South Africa	0	0	0	0	0	1	0	1
Sonatrach	Algeria	0	0	0	0	0	0	1	1
Adnoc	UAE	0	0	0	0	0	0	0	0
EGPC	Egypt	0	0	0	0	0	0	0	0
INOC	Iraq	0	0	0	0	0	0	0	0
Libya NOC	Libya	0	0	0	0	0	0	0	0
NIOC	Iran	0	0	0	0	0	0	0	0
NNPC	Nigeria	0	0	0	0	0	0	0	0
PDVSA	Venezuela	0	0	0	0	0	0	0	0

Source: Created with data from ALDO MUSACCHIO & SERGIO G. LAZZARINI, REINVENTING STATE CAPITALISM: LEVIATHAN IN BUSINESS, BRAZIL AND BEYOND (2014).

firms through their investment arms, sovereign wealth funds, and development banks. Yet, we know very little about these new hybrid forms of state ownership. How should we expect these new forms of ownership, in which the government gives the private sector control of the firm and keeps cash flow rights and some veto power, to work?

The extent to which the Type I governance problem is eliminated depends on how well the shareholders of the company can monitor managers, and what kind of checks and balances the firm has against managerial abuse. Thus, the extent to which the Type I problem is mitigated depends on the institutions of corporate governance in a country, the configuration of corporate governance of the specific firms, and the kind of shareholders it has and the incentives they have to monitor managers closely. For instance, in some institutional environments, dispersed ownership is linked to less monitoring of managers and thus to more Type I problems.

In a stylized way we could think that in these firms the selection of managers will be based on merit, rather than political connections. We would expect the board of directors to select and monitor managers, rather than having a government entity performing those tasks.

The Type I governance problem should be mitigated if private shareholders (e.g., the controlling shareholder), institutional investors, rating agencies, and equity analysts perform the monitoring of management and have levers to penalize abuses by management. Moreover, when the government is a minority shareholder, we would expect these firms to have less convoluted social objectives; thus managers could have easier-to-follow performance metrics, something that facilitates the monitoring. In fact, social objectives could be rolled into corporate social responsibility programs and could be achieved following the standard criteria and metrics private firms use.

Most of these firms with minority state ownership are publicly traded; therefore the stock market itself can help to align manager incentives. The stock price can serve as an indicator of management actions, and if managers have pay-for-performance contracts, their incentives can be aligned with those of shareholders in terms of maximization of value. Additionally, most stock exchanges require that firms report financials regularly, following international financial standards somewhat closely. Thus, we would expect that the transparency afforded by the fact that these firms with minority state ownership are listed would also help mitigate the Type I problem.

Finally, whether managers take on too much risk because they expect to be bailed out if they fail will depend on the type of firm they are running. Only in firms that are too big or to strategic to fail should we expect the moral hazard of having a "soft-budget constraint." For most other firms, managers should not expect to be bailed out simply because the government is a minority shareholder.

The extent to which the Type II governance problem is mitigated in firms where the government is a minority shareholder will depend on how much *residual interference* there is from the government. Beyond the power governments have to exercise veto rights for major decisions, for instance using their golden shares, governments may participate in coalitions with other shareholders to exercise more influence on the management decisions of the firm based on considerations other than efficiency.

The way in which governments may exercise residual influence and steer firms to financially unprofitable, but politically attractive business is illustrated with the case of Vale. Formerly known as Vale do Rio Doce, Vale is one of the five largest mining firms in the world, among the top three exporters of iron ore in the world, and Brazil's largest mining firm. Brazil's development bank (BNDES), through its investment arm, BNDESPAR, is a minority shareholder in the holding company that controls Vale. In 2009 President Luis Inácio da Silva—Lula—publicly pressured Vale to invest in local steel mills and to buy Brazilian ships. The CEO of Vale argued against those investments on the ground that there was overcapacity in the steel industry worldwide, thus making steel mills an unattractive investment. Moreover, he claimed that the shipbuilding industry in Brazil was not developed enough to build the large carriers the company needed. Vale was supposed to be a private company, and yet the Brazilian government, exerting pressure through the board of directors, acted as if the company were an SOE under its control. In reality, Vale was partly privatized in 1997 when a consortium headed by private owners, BNDESPAR, and pension funds bought Vale's controlling shares and created a controlling entity, Valepar. Although BNDESPAR and the pension funds individually had minority stakes, if they voted as a block they had more than 50 percent of the shares. After much public debate and after taking a lot of criticism and pressure from the Brazilian government, Vale's private shareholders eventually acquiesced, and, in April 2011, the board of directors dismissed its CEO, Roger Agnelli. Vale ended up investing in new steel mills, together with Thysen, Posco, and others, and caved in and purchased some Brazilian-made ships to complement its fleet of Korean- and Chinese-made carriers.

III. The Organization of SOEs around the World

A. State-Owned Holding Companies (SOHCs)

One of the main reasons SOEs around the world suffered from the Type I corporate governance problem in the 1970s and 1980s was because the ministries and departments in charge of monitoring and controlling them did not have the tools, information, or capacity to monitor the actions of managers. Alternatively, there were many ministries or departments in charge of monitoring each SOE, and that led to free-riding on the part of each government entity and weak monitoring overall. Therefore, managers in most countries in the 1970s and 1980s enjoyed autonomy from the government, with perverse consequences for their governments and their home country economies as a whole.

In the early 1980s the IMF conducted a study in which it surveyed the size, profitability, and debt levels of SOEs around the world and found that governments did not know how many firms they owned, governments were bailing out these firms regularly, and governments were systematically allowing (or pushing) SOEs to obtain debt in foreign currency to help them finance the country's current account deficit. The findings raised several red flags at the time, but the study came out too late to prevent the debt and macroeconomic crisis that affected most developing countries and Western Europe during the early 1980s.

Between the 1970s and 1990s, governments experimented with state-owned holding companies (SOHCs) as a way to improve monitoring and control over their SOEs. These SOHCs were introduced to control all SOEs (e.g., in Khazanah Nasional Berhad in Malaysia or Temasek in Singapore), or to create conglomerates in specific sectors (e.g., initially in Spain or Brazil and more recently in China). In Spain, in the late 1970s and early 1980s, the government created three holding companies, the INI Group (manufacturing), INH Group (oil and gas), and the Patrimonio Group (with firms in telecommunications, banking, and other services) to manage firms and privatize inefficient firms. These holding companies were also in charge of fully privatizing inefficient firms or partially privatizing strategic ones.

SOHCs that control a variety of subsidiaries (sometimes with majority or minority equity ownership by the government) can provide governments with a series of advantages. Among the most important advantages of this form of organization is the capacity governments have to monitor, coordinate, and facilitate collaboration among firms. The literature that has studied private business groups, especially in emerging markets, sees their development as a response to failures in capital, labor, and product markets.[14] State-owned business groups also can have internal markets for products (e.g., having an oil company selling crude oil to a refinery), and can have an internal talent market. Typically, the SOHC can train managers, test them in some firms, and then rotate the most capable ones to run underperforming firms or new companies. Further, state-owned business groups can help group members to overcome important institutional voids in capital markets (one firm could bail out, subsidize, or co-invest with other member firms). Having such internal capital markets can also help state-owned business groups to protect affiliated firms from industry or firm-specific shocks. Additionally, the large scale of some of these groups allowed governments to achieve economies of scale, to rationalize production and capital investments, and to have more bargaining power in procurement.

When one thinks about state capitalism in China in the twenty-first century, one has to imagine a giant holding company, SASAC, or holding companies by province, that then have a variety of holding companies for each specific sector. Those holding companies are usually wholly owned and, in turn, hold majority and minority positions in a variety of subsidiaries. In China, SASAC has created business groups (sub-groups)

---

[14] *See* Tarun Khanna & Krishna Palepu, *The Future of Business Groups in Emerging Markets: Long-Run Evidence from Chile*, 43 ACAD. OF MGMT. J. (2000). In Brazil, a notable exception is THOMAS J. TREBAT, BRAZIL'S STATE-OWNED ENTERPRISES: A CASE STUDY OF THE STATE AS ENTREPRENEUR (1983).

by industry to oversee and coordinate more than a hundred SOEs. That is, state-owned business groups in China operate like private business groups in emerging markets, with pyramidal ownership structures and oftentimes with a financing arm affiliated to the group and a research institute that coordinates the group's innovative efforts. Vietnamese officials have also created holding companies by industry, following the logic of the advantages of such organizations. In Thailand and Indonesia, in contrast, such groups do not yet exist, but holding companies or state-owned business groups are being planned because they are perceived to be better for the monitoring of SOEs.

In Russia, Gazprom acts as a holding company. Not only does it control its own gas distribution network, but it also has a pyramidal ownership structure that gives it majority equity shares in other gas distribution companies such as Gazprom Neft (73.02 percent), JSC "TGC-1" (51.79 percent), and JSC Latvijas Gaze (53.56 percent), among others.

The government of Dubai also organizes all of the companies it controls under the umbrella of two large SOHCs: Dubai World and Investment Corporation of Dubai (ICD). In addition, the ruler of Dubai, Mohammed bin Rashid, has under his command Dubai Holding, another SOHC. These holding companies, in turn, control a series of wholly-owned subsidiaries, several companies in which they have minority ownership (e.g., Emaar), and two sovereign wealth funds—Istithmar World and Dubai International Capital, controlled by Dubai World and Dubai Holding, respectively (see Figure 17.2).

In other cases, governments use SOHCs to handle minority stakes in various sectors; these are holding companies that operate as portfolio managers for the government. Examples in emerging markets range from Khazanah Nasional Berhad in Malaysia to Temasek in Singapore. Malaysia is an extreme case in terms of consolidating the management of state equity under the umbrella of one big holding company. In 2010, Khazanah Nasional Berhad owned stock in fifty-two companies, with minority positions in about twenty-six of them, in sectors including financials, transportation, and utilities.[15]

B. DEVELOPMENT BANKS AS FINANCIAL INSTITUTIONS AND HOLDING COMPANIES

Development banks have been used extensively as sources of long-term capital for private firms, so it is natural to expect them to play a role in the governance of national champions. Although the liberalization and privatization reforms of the 1990s reduced the scope of development banks in some countries, in several cases those banks were preserved and even strengthened. We identify 286 development banks throughout the world as of 2011, chiefly concentrated in South and East Asia (29.7 percent), Africa (24.5 percent), and Latin America and the Caribbean (17.8 percent).

[15] All of the data for Khazanah come from its 2010 annual report, available on its website, KAZANAH NATIONAL, http://www.khazanah.com.my/ (last visited Jan. 10, 2012).

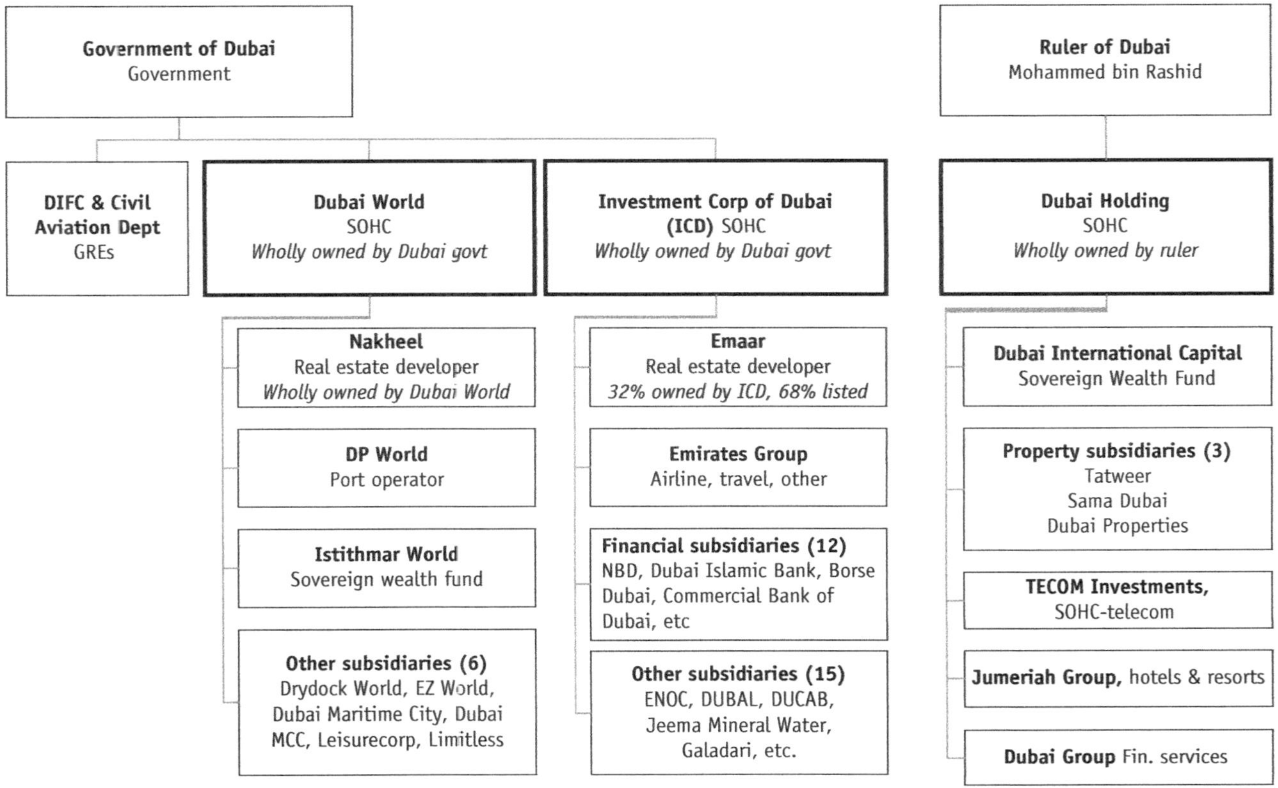

FIGURE 17.2 The Organization of SOHCs in Dubai, 2009.

Source: Adapted from Morgan Stanley Report, Deutsche Bank Report, ThompsonOne, and SWF Institute. We thank Andrew Goodman for putting together this figure.

Despite their prevalence, development banks have not been studied thoroughly as a part of state capitalism. Their roles in economic systems with heavy state presence are little understood. For instance, Brazil's development bank, Brazilian Bank for National Economic and Social Development (BNDES), acts not only as a lender, but also as a minority shareholder. Over two thousand firms receive subsidized loans from BNDES (about a third of the publicly traded firms report having loans from BNDES), and a few hundred also get investments in minority equity positions through its specialized private investment arm, BNDESPAR. As of the end of 2012, BNDESPAR held equity in 142 publicly traded companies.

In Korea, the Ministry of Strategy and Finance owns 100 percent of the Korean Finance Corporation, a company that, in turn, controls the Korean Financial Group. This financial group is a holding company that controls the Korean Development Bank (KDB) and the Korean Capital Group. Through the KDB, then, the government has majority stakes in a variety of firms. According to S&P's Capital IQ database, KDB controls Daehan Shipbuilding, Dsme Shandong in China, an asset management company, and a variety of subsidiaries of KDB around the world. Through its majority stake in Daehan Shipbuilding, KDB also controls Taejeon Heavy Industries Co., Ltd.

C. SOVEREIGN WEALTH FUNDS (SWFS)

With the rapid dissemination of SWFs as an alternative way to channel country savings into investments with higher risk and return, minority shareholding positions in publicly listed companies have increasingly become targets for those funds. For the most part, however, SWFs are invested outside the home country because the whole idea is to keep a pool of savings in foreign-currency-denominated assets. In particular, many SWFs are designed to diversify the investment of national foreign exchange reserves into assets other than U.S. or European government bonds.

According to Edwin M. Truman, there are at least three investment strategies that SWFs follow. First, they use foreign exchange reserves for domestic "development" purposes.[16] This is common in developing countries. China Investment Corporation (CIC) buys shares (minority positions) in Chinese companies and banks. Temasek, Singapore's SWF, invests 32 percent of its portfolio locally, in companies such as Singapore Technologies Telemedia, Singapore Communications, Singapore Power, and Singapore Airlines.[17] Mubadala, an SWF in Abu Dhabi, invests heavily in large domestic development projects in energy, telecommunications, healthcare, and other sectors.[18] In contrast, the Abu Dhabi Investment Authority, one of the world's largest SWFs, does not invest in its home country, the United Arab Emirates.

---

[16] EDWIN M. TRUMAN, SOVEREIGN WEALTH FUNDS: THREAT OR SALVATION? (2010).

[17] TEMASEK, http://temasekreview.com.sg/en/major-investments.html (last visited Mar. 18, 2015).

[18] MUBADALA, http://mubadala.com (last visited May 17, 2012).

Second, SWFs use foreign exchange reserves to meet international objectives such a making loans or investing in other countries for political or diplomatic reasons. A third approach—the one Truman recommends—is for SWFs to invest their assets following strict financial criteria and maximizing returns. We believe his approach is now widespread among the world's largest SWFs, most of which already have professional management and a team of professional analyst and portfolio managers. Still, Truman and other observers believe that SWFs are not as transparent as they could be with their investments in other countries, and that this sometimes provokes nationalist responses against their investments. For instance, when the CIC invested in a minority stake in the U.S. investment bank Morgan Stanley in 2007, it raised some concerns among the public and the U.S. investment community regarding the ultimate objectives of such investments.[19]

D. OTHER STATE-CONTROLLED FUNDS

In India, the Life Insurance Corporation (LIC) plays the role of large holding company for the government. LIC is the largest active stock market investor in India, with total assets of $270 billion at the end of 2013. The government controls LIC and selects its board and management teams. It often directs LIC to invest in the shares of SOEs, especially when demand for a firm's IPO is low. However, LIC and the government have sometimes disagreed publicly. Our computations indicate that, as of 2012, the government of India invested in about four hundred companies through LIC, mostly in minority stakes, which make up about 4 percent of India's total stock market capitalization. The median investment of LIC was 4 percent and the mean was 7.4 percent. LIC is usually a passive investor. Yet, when the government directs it to buy shares in partial privatizations, those investments significantly underperform the market.[20] Thus, LIC is an example of Leviathan as a minority shareholder.

In Brazil, pension funds of SOEs, whose managements are influenced by the government, have minority shareholding positions in several publicly traded firms and often behave as active investors, influencing the strategy of firms and even fostering mergers of

---

[19] For a look at the popular reaction against CIC in the United States, see the CBS report on China's sovereign wealth funds in its program *60 Minutes. China Investment an Open Book? 60 Minutes: Sovereign-Wealth Fund's President Promises Transparency*, CBS (April 4, 2008), *available at* http://www.cbsnews.com/2100-18560_162-3993933.html.

[20] This is based on an analysis of LIC's investments in the privatization (divestments) of NPC, NMDC, SJVN, Engineers India, Power Grid Corporation, the Shipping Corporation of India, PTC India Financial Services, and ONGC. LIC had a cumulative loss of 24 percent on these investments by April 2012. For data on the government of India and LIC's ownership, as well as on the performance of LIC's investments, see SANJEEV VAIDYANATHAN & ALDO MUSACCHIO, STATE CAPITALISM IN INDIA AND ITS IMPLICATIONS FOR INVESTORS (2012).

firms in which they have common stakes. In mid-2012, the largest pension fund in Brazil, Previ (controlled by state-owned bank Banco do Brasil), had a total equity of around 80 billion U.S. dollars, more than five times the equity of the wealthiest Brazilian private capitalist at that time (Eike Batista).

IV. Aligning Incentives in State-Owned Holding Companies

States that use networks of firm ownership, either inside SOHCs or SWFs, to manage firms need to align the incentives of the managers of such firms with the objectives of the controlling shareholders (i.e., the state) and the interests of minority shareholders. In places with relatively sophisticated financial markets, governments use pay-for-performance compensation schemes to incentivize managers (e.g., this is the case of Statoil in Norway). In Europe, the managers of firms in which the government is a majority investor rely on such contracts. In Brazil the majority of SOEs that are publicly traded have some form of pay-for-performance incentive scheme.

In China, even if publicly traded SOEs formally provide bonuses for their managers tied to performance, there is controversy as to whether managers actually collect such bonuses. This is because the real incentive mechanism in China is run by the Communist Party and its Central Organization Department. This is where promotions are decided and where managers and directors of SOEs are selected. Incentives are supposed to be aligned when they are running SOEs because these managers care about their career within the Party, and their pay is determined by the promotion system of the Party.

There is really no other place where such a system exists. In India, Brazil, and France, the civil service is supposed to serve that purpose, and middle and upper managers of SOEs (with the exception of France) are public officials who have their pay determined by tenure, rather than by merit or by recent achievements. In China, rapid progress in the ranks of the Party can be made by, for instance, making an SOE more efficient, privatizing one piece of its capital at a high price, or managing a series of companies. Officials who do so can be promoted within the Party, within an industrial conglomerate (e.g., the manager of one state-owned oil company can be promoted and moved to a different oil company), or to a Ministry. For instance, some of the Chinese officers who have participated in the reform of the banking system in the last twenty years have been promoted within banks and then to the People's Bank of China (the central bank).

In our view, in some Gulf countries the royal family plays the role of the Chinese Communist Party, selecting managers within the family, promoting them based on the results they obtain in managerial posts, and aligning their incentives in multiple ways. For instance, in Gulf countries the survival of the regime is tied to the efficiency of major SOEs, especially oil and gas firms, and the quality of the public services these firms provide. Thus, family members should be incentivized to run these firms profitably, because the future stream of rents of the family is at stake. Additionally, members of the royal

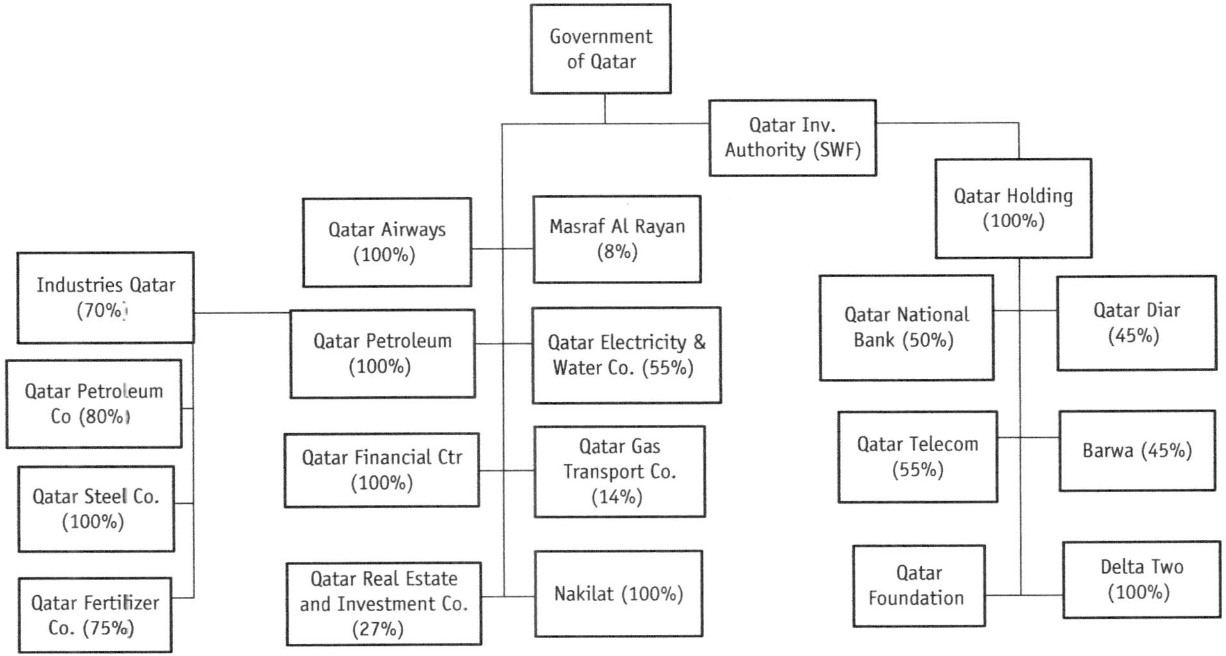

FIGURE 17.3 Pyramidal Government Ownership in Qatar, 2012.

Source: Created with data from www.swfinstitute.org and Thompson One.

family have incentives to run SOEs profitably and efficiently because they have their own fortunes at stake. This is because members of the royal family have their money invested in SOEs (if they are publicly traded) or managed directly by SWFs. Some of these members may also participate in private equity deals in which SWFs are involved. Finally, there is a system of promotions inside these countries in which able managers get top positions within the hierarchy of firms, and rulers promote those managers whom they trust to accomplish developmental and financial goals.

Take for instance the case of Qatar, where the Al Thani family, the royal family, runs a vast network of SOEs and SWFs, and their close relatives participate in the management of firms. The government of Qatar also operates as a giant holding company that has direct ownership of large SOEs or ownership in SWFs and SOHCs that in turn control a variety of firms. For a representation of this ownership scheme see Figure 17.3. How the Al Thani family appoints and incentivizes managers in all of these firms has some similarities with China and exemplifies how many Gulf countries manage their SOEs. In Qatar, the Al Thani family appoints either close or distant relatives to top executive positions. For instance, relatives of the former Emir, Sheikh Hamad Al Thani, were represented on the boards of forty-three firms listed on the Qatar Stock Exchange, including SOEs. These are firms in which these family members and the royal family as a whole keep some of their investments. Successful managers can be promoted to better positions over time or as Emirs rotate. And there are reports arguing that the fortune of the royal family is not only invested in SOEs, but managed directly by Qatar Investment Authority, the sovereign wealth fund (see Figure 17.3).

How much incentives are aligned in these countries is still not a testable hypothesis because most of the firms in question do not publish detailed financials, and these members of the royal family are sometimes rotated to positions in which it is hard to measure their performance (e.g., government positions). Still, the fact that many of the SOEs from Gulf countries operate profitably and are some of the largest multinationals in the world (e.g., Qatar Telecommunications) implies SOEs in these nations operate very differently from what existing theories would predict.

Conclusion

This chapter makes three general arguments. First, we argue that state capitalism has been more resilient and persistent than previous accounts of privatization and theoretical work on the inefficiencies of SOEs would lead us to believe. Second, we argue that governments have adopted new ownership schemes that seem to mitigate the Type I corporate governance problem associated with SOEs, namely principal-agent problems, but are still struggling to mitigate the Type II corporate governance problem of public benefits of control. Finally, we defend the idea that the way Chinese state capitalism is organized at the turn of the twenty-first century is not that different from the organizational structures prevalent in many developing countries around the world. In the Middle East, Latin America, and South Asia it is common to find governments using pyramidal ownership schemes or creating holding companies to own and manage a variety of firms with majority and minority state ownership.

In sum, state capitalism is here to stay. We need to better understand how governments own and manage firms in order to understand the implications of this system for global capitalism.

Index